Sports Collectors Digest

Complete Guide To

Baseball Memorabilia

Second Edition
By Mark K. Larson

Published by

**krause
publications**

700 E. State Street • Iola, WI 54990-0001

Library of Congress Catalog Number: 92-71451
ISBN: 0-87341-317-2
Printed in the United States of America

Preface

In what would be the most important game in his short-lived major league career, the 29-year-old Red Sox rookie left the Fenway Park mound to a standing ovation.

The matchup pitted the lanky right-hander against a 27-game winner and soon-to-be-named 1990 Cy Young Award winner, Oakland's Bob Welch. But the off-season United Parcel Service driver delivered a gutsy performance, allowing just six hits and one run over 5 2/3 innings pitched.

Dana Kiecker departed that day with a no decision, the score tied at 1-1. The Red Sox would eventually lose the game - Game 2 of the 1990 American League Championship Series - 4-1, and be swept by the A's in the series. But Kiecker had given the team its last bright individual performance of the season.

Kiecker had played a key role in the team's success in the down-to-the-wire pennant race against the Toronto Blue Jays, too. In his last three starts, the Sleepy Eye, Minn., native went 2-0 with a 0.90 ERA, including a seven-inning no-decision effort against Chicago when the Red Sox clinched a tie for the Eastern Division crown.

After compiling an 8-9 record and a 3.97 ERA over 152 innings pitched during the regular season, Kiecker was named the 1990 Red Sox Rookie of the Year by the Boston Baseball Writers Association. His performance in the stretch run and in the ALCS game offered Red Sox fans something to hope for in 1991.

But an elbow injury kept Kiecker on the disabled list most of the 1991 season; he pitched just 40 1/3 innings, going 2-3 with a 7.69 ERA. By March of 1992 his career was over. After toiling in the minors eight years, his dream had ended in a 10-12 lifetime major league record with a 4.68 ERA.

I don't recall ever seeing Kiecker pitch. But I did get to meet him once, after I'd met his parents during Twinsfest '91, a sports collectibles show held at the Metrodome in Minneapolis in February.

Dana's father, Kermit, owns a Walnut and Frame-it Shop near Minneapolis and makes a variety of ball and bat holders. He and his wife were at the show selling their crafts and distributing information regarding the scholarship fund their son Dana had established to raise money to help young people further their educations. Dana was asking for a $1 donation for every item he signed.

My short visit with the Kieckers was the highlight of the show. The two were down-to-earth, good-natured, genuine and very personable - good old-fashioned Midwestern folk. In fact, Mrs. Kiecker snapped a picture of me with her husband, Kermit, and later sent it to me. It's in my photo collage on my wall at home, mixed in with pictures of my friends and family.

I later met Dana in Cleveland in April 1991 when the Red Sox were in town to play the Indians. After finishing an interview with Wade Boggs for *Sports Collectors Digest*, I asked if Dana by chance was pitching that day and warming up, or if he was still around somewhere in the locker room. We tracked him down, and Dana and I talked in the dugout for a few minutes.

I explained who I was and that I'd met his terrific parents at Twinsfest, then complimented him on his attempts to give something back to the fans through his fundraising efforts. We talked a little bit about the importance and value of a good education. And we threw in a few fishing stories, too. It wasn't an interview setting, so we didn't talk much at all about baseball. It almost seemed as if we were old friends just catching up on things...

I did contribute to Dana's scholarship fund; I bought the autographed baseball pictured in the Red Sox collage shown on this book's cover. When I returned to Twinsfest in 1992, the Kieckers had come from Fairfax, Minn., to sell their wares again. I told them I was thrilled to meet Dana in Cleveland and that I was real impressed with him - as a person...

Later, when the show was winding down, Mrs. Kiecker came over to our booth with the autographed picture and bat which are also shown on the cover. She wanted me to have them for recognizing her son's efforts in a *Sports Collectors Digest* column. They don't have a whole lot of monetary value, but then again I don't put price tags on things. Or memories. And that is what this book is all about...

— Mark K. Larson

3

Introduction

This second-edition book is meant to serve collectors who want checklists and fair, accurate prices for baseball collectibles, other than baseball cards, from the 1900s to 1990s. It's a compilation of material taken from the Krause Publications archives - which includes back issues of *Sports Collectors Digest*, *Baseball Card News* and *Baseball Cards* magazine - and is an outgrowth of the company's line of baseball card price guides. These prices reflect those which were current advertised market prices since the beginning of 1994 until May 1994, taken in general from those advertisers who have specialized in the particular areas. At least two comparable sources have been used to determine the prices and ranges of the items, some of which are being cataloged for the first time ever. The condition of the items being priced is, unless noted, Excellent or Mint. Remember, the buyer and seller ultimately determine an item's price.

Each chapter has been repriced and reedited; the typos and errors in the first edition have been corrected. The author's desk copy, which is almost missing its front and back covers because it is so dogeared, has chicken scratches throughout it, indicating where mistakes were made, and what new values should be. Although the number of pages remains the same as the first edition, the second edition has fewer photos, and no ads, thus making room for expanded and/or additional checklists which were omitted from the first edition.

Dave Miedema's information on uniforms has been condensed in Chapter 2, making room for Dave Bushing's overviews on bat and glove collecting in Chapter 3. Chapter 7 has included prices for playoff and All-Star game programs. Chapter 8, which provides checklists of who has been featured on all the major sport magazines' covers, has been increased to include additions to *The Sporting News* checklist. Chapter 9, which lists the top 25 books which every collector should have in his sports library, has been expanded to include a general price list for hardcover and paperback books. Chapter 12, on pins, includes some additional pin sets, such as PM10 Stadium Photo pins. Chapter 13 adds a general overview on values for full tickets and ticket stubs. Chapter 17 offers the most thorough coverage and prices realized from some of the biggest sports memorabilia auctions in 1991-93, plus many unique photos from auctions held by Leland's Inc. and Richard Wolffers Auctions Inc. Chapter 18 offers a variety of items, which, if you can't find them listed in the rest of the book, may very well be mentioned in this section.

With its first edition of The Complete Guide to Baseball Memorabilia, Krause Publications set the standard by issuing the first major comprehensive memorabilia book out there; others followed. KP's book did quite well; it sold out. But the added competition has been beneficial; the publishers hope to make each successive edition bigger and better than the last one, and a few notches above the competitions' efforts.

The author and publisher would be interested in your thoughts regarding this book - what's good, what you disliked, what needs to be added or deleted, or explained in more detail or made less confusing. Also, there are items which invariably will turn up in someone's attic which haven't been mentioned in this book. So, send descriptions, pictures and checklists along, too. Thanks.

Contents

Autographs

Brooks Robinson, signing at a basball card show, poses with a youngster.

The most common memorabilia which is autographed includes baseballs, index cards, photographs and postcards, Hall of Fame plaques and postcards, Perez-Steele postcards, equipment (shoes, bats, hats, jerseys), programs and books, letters and documents, bank checks, and cut signatures, which have been taken from another piece of writing, such as a manuscript, letter or check.

Autographs can be obtained by several ways. The most personable, and perhaps memorable, experience would be acquiring the autograph from the player at the ballpark. This is the best place to catch a player, and the best time to get his signature. But get there early, before practice; once a player is into his game routine he doesn't want to be distracted. Give yourself an edge over fans who are rude and obnoxious with their requests by being polite and courteous. Having a pen ready and keeping your request simple and fast also helps.

Another alternative is at a baseball card show. Show promoters often impose time/or quota limitations, so if you know a player is going to be signing at a show it's wise to get tickets in advance and get there early.

Dealers and card show promoters also often hold private signings with the players, during which the player fills the mail-order requests sent to the dealer. Non-flat items which are signed sometimes require an extra fee. These private signings are usually advertised in hobby publications. Authenticity is generally guaranteed, and most dealers also have a return policy.

Direct requests can be sent to the player via the mail in care of his team's address, which is the best way, or his home, but the results can be unpredictable, due to the amount of mail the players receive. Some players also believe mail sent to their homes is an invasion of their privacy, so your request might go unheeded.

When dealing through the mail, send less valuable items; you don't want the post office to lose or damage them. Always include a self-addressed, stamped envelope or package with the required postage for its return. A courteous, creative, brief request, which distinguishes and sets off your letter from the others, will yield better results.

Specify if the item is to be personalized or dated, and don't ask the player to sign more than two items. Perhaps you can include an extra for the player to keep, but players are becoming wary of those who request several autographs, perhaps to be sold at a later date. Thus, sometimes the player, in return for his autograph, might ask for a donation to his favorite charity.

Auctions are another source for autographed material. These events, whether by telephone or live, often offer quality material. Items may also turn up at antique shops and flea markets, but questions regarding authenticity, value, condition and scarcity may occur if the seller has limited knowledge of the item.

Trading is always another easy means in acquiring material. A trading network can be established if you take out a classified advertisement in a hobby publication such as *Sports Collectors Digest*.

Prices for autographed materials are set by the principles of supply and demand, based on regional interest, scarcity, condition (not faded, dirty, shellacked, smudged, scuffed, ripped), player popularity, and significance of the event commemorated. Factors for autographed baseballs also include the signature form (style, placement, nickname), type of ball and writing medium used.

Individually-signed baseballs usually have the autograph on the sweet spot, the shortest distance between two seams. Team balls, those which should include the signatures of all the key players, starters and bench players, generally reserve the sweet spot for the manager's signature.

The more complete the ball is with key players, the more valuable it is. It's also easier to pinpoint the year being represented. But having other signatures, such as those of umpires and broadcasters, detracts from the value.

Some baseballs have just select players who have signed it. These group-signed balls commemorate a particular accomplishment or event, such as the Shot Heard 'Round the World (Bobby Thomson and Ralph Branca), or the living members of the 500 Home Run Club.

When examining an item for authenticity, consider the writing medium used. Was the player alive when the ink, such as in a felt-tip pen or ballpoint pens, was available? Quilled pens were prominent in the mid-1800s until fountain pens were developed in 1884. Ballpoints became prominent in the 1940s, felt tips in the 1960s and Sharpies in the 1970s. However, whatever medium is used, don't retrace the signature.

Another subtle hint in detecting a faked signature is to check the manufacturer of the ball and the president's signature on it. This may help distinguish deceased players who could not possibly have signed the ball.

Official manufacturers have been - 1) American League baseballs: Reach (1901 to 1974), Spalding(1975-1976), and Rawlings (1977 to present); 2) National League baseballs: Spalding (1876 to 1977), Rawlings (1978 to present); 3) American Association baseballs: Mahn (1882), Reach (1833 to 1891) and 4) Federal League: Victor. Rawlings has produced commemorative balls for use in World Series and All-Star games.

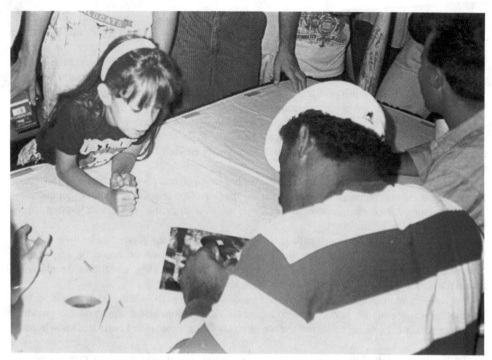

This youngster anxiously waits for Detroit's Cecil Fielder to finish signing.

American League presidents whose signatures should be on baseballs used during their tenures have been: Byron B. Johnson (1901 to 1927), Ernest S. Barnard (1927 to 1931), William Harridge (1931 to 1959), Joseph E. Cronin (1959 to 1973), Leland S. MacPhail Jr. (1974 to 1983) and Robert W. Brown (1984 to present). National League presidents have been: John A. Heydler (1918 to 1934), Ford C. Frick (1934 to 1951), Warren C. Giles (1951 to 1969), Charles S. Feeny (1970 to 1986), A. Bartlett Giamatti (1986 to 1989), and William D. White (1989 to present).

Realize, however, that signatures can vary, based on the writing tool, item being signed, person's age, popularity, health and mood, time spent during a signing session, and circumstances when it was signed. Learn the player's signature evolution. Slant, size, characters, flamboyancy, legibility and capitalization may all change during a player's career and after.

Forgeries can sometimes be detected by uncommon breaks, peculiarities in pressure and movement in strokes, and changes in thickness in the letters. Facsimile signatures also exist; they are exact reproductions which are printed or screened on the item, often through computer-based technology. Rubber stamps and ghost writers have also been used by players to sign their mail.

When collecting autographed material, become familiar with collector terminology in your area of interest. Utilize the knowledge of skilled, reputable, experienced dealers and maintain good rapport with them. They can be future sources in helping you build a collection.

Also, the **Baseball Autograph Handbook**, second edition, and **Team Baseballs**, both by Mark Allen Baker, or hobby publications, such as *Sports Collectors Digest*, are also good sources. But in the end, before buying, use your own best judgment. Don't buy an item if it's questionable.

Collections can be stored in a file cabinet or display case, with background information on the event and purchase also included. The best conditions for display cases are when effective, indirect lighting is used, so as to not damage or fade the item. The ideal temperature and humidity conditions are 65 to 70 degrees and 50 percent humidity. More valuable items can be kept in safe-deposit boxes.

It's wise to periodically check your collection for signs of deterioration, but avoid excessive handling. Restoration is best left to a professional conservator who's done that type of work before.

Hall of Fame Autograph Gallery

Hank Aaron (1934-) 1982

Availability: *Plentiful*
Demand: *Average*

Cut signature	$7-$8
Single-signature ball	$35-$40
3x5" index card	$10
Photograph/baseball card	$25-$30
HOF plaque postcard	$20-$30
Perez-Steele postcards	$30-$40

Grover Cleveland Alexander (1887-1950) 1938

Availability: *Limited*
Demand: *Average*

Cut signature	$300
Single-signature baseball	$5,000-$5,500
3x5" index card	$400
Photograph/baseball card	$850-$950
HOF plaque postcard	$800-$1,000
Perez-Steele postcards	Impossible

Walt Alston (1911-1984) 1983

Availability: *Above average*
Demand: *Average*

Cut signature	$7-$10
Single-signature baseball	$150
3x5" index card	$20-$25
Photograph/baseball card	$150
HOF plaque postcard	$85-$100
Perez-Steele postcards	$1,000-$1,200

Cap Anson (1852-1922) 1939

Availability: *Limited*
Demand: *Strong*

Cut signature	$1,100-$1,275
Single-signature baseball	$18,000
3x5" index card	$1,000-$1,250
Photograph/baseball card	$3,500
HOF plaque postcard	Impossible
Perez-Steele postcards	Impossible

Luis Aparicio (1934-) 1984

Availability: *Plentiful*
Demand: *Little*

Cut signature	$3
Single-signature baseball	$25
3x5" index card	$5-$8
Photograph/baseball card	$15
HOF plaque postcard	$12-$15
Perez-Steele postcards	$20-$30

Luke Appling (1907-1991) 1964

Availability: *Plentiful*
Demand: *Little*

Cut signature	$5
Single-signature baseball	$50
3x5" index card	$8
Photograph/baseball card	$20
HOF plaque postcard	$10-$15
Perez-Steele postcards	$40-$65

Earl Averill (1902-1983) 1975

Availability: *Plentiful*
Demand: *Little*

Cut signature	$8
Single-signature baseball	$400-$500
3x5" index card	$15
Photograph/baseball card	$75
HOF plaque postcard	$20-$30
Perez-Steele postcards	$800-$900

Frank Baker (1886-1963) 1955

Availability: *Average*
Demand: *Average*

Cut signature	$75
Single-signature baseball	$3,000-$4,000
3x5" index card	$200-$250
Photograph/baseball card	$800
HOF plaque postcard	$700
Perez-Steele postcards	Impossible

Dave Bancroft (1891-1972) 1971

Availability: *Average*
Denmand: *Average*

Cut signature	$50
Single-signature baseball	$2,800-$3,200
3x5" index card	$50-$100
Photograph/baseball card	$175-$250
HOF plaque postcard	$600
Perez-Steele postcards	Impossible

Ernie Banks (1931-) 1977

Availability: *Plentiful*
Demand: *Little*

Cut signature	$3
Single-signature baseball	$30-$35
3x5" index card	$5
Photograph/baseball card	$20-$25
HOF plaque postcard	$15-$22
Perez-Steele postcards	$25-$40

Al Barlick (1915-) 1989

Availability: *Plentiful*
Demand: *Little*

Cut signature	$2
Single-signature baseball	$20
3x5" index card	$4
Photograph/baseball card	$10
HOF plaque postcard	$8-$10
Perez-Steele postcards	$20

Edward Barrow (1868-1953) 1953

Availability: *Average*
Demand: *Average*

Cut signature	$60
Single-signature baseball	$4,000
3x5" index card	$80-$150
Photograph/baseball card	$400
HOF plaque postcard	Impossible
Perez-Steele postcards	Impossible

Jake Beckley (1867-1918) 1971

Availability: *Scarce*
Demand: *Strong*

Cut signature	$1,200-$1,300
Single-signature baseball	$5,000-$5,500
3x5" index card	$1,700-$1,800
Photograph/baseball card	$3,500
HOF plaque postcard	Impossible
Perez-Steele postcards	Impossible

Cool Papa Bell (1903-1991) 1974

Availability: *Above Average*
Demand: *Average*

Cut signature	$5
Single-signature baseball	$75-$100
3x5" index card	$7-$13
Photograph/baseball card	$50
HOF plaque postcard	$20-$30
Perez-Steele postcards	$65-$100

Johnny Bench (1947-) 1989

Availability: *Plentiful*
Demand: *Average*

Cut signature	$5
Single-signature baseball	$35-$40
3x5" index card	$8
Photograph/baseball card	$25-$30
HOF plaque postcard	$25-$30
Perez-Steele postcards	$30-$40

Chief Bender (1883-1954) 1953

Availability: *Average*
Demand: *Average*

Cut signature	$100-$115
Single-signature baseball	$3,200-$3,500
3x5" index card	$200
Photograph/baseball card	$400-$500
HOF plaque postcard	$1,200
Perez-Steele postcards	Impossible

Yogi Berra (1925-) 1971

Availability: *Plentiful*
Demand: *Little*

Cut signature	$3
Single-signature baseball	$25-$30
3x5" index card	$5-$7
Photograph/baseball card	$15-$20
HOF plaque postcard	$15-$20
Perez-Steele postcards	$20-$35

Jim Bottomley (1900-1959) 1974

Availability: *Limited*
Demand: *Average*

Cut signature	$100-$150
Single-signature baseball	$3,500
3x5" index card	$225-$275
Photograph/baseball card	$400
HOF plaque postcard	Impossible
Perez-Steele postcards	Impossible

Lou Boudreau (1917-) 1970

Availability: *Plentiful*
Demand: *Little*

Cut signature	$2
Single-signature baseball	$15-$20
3x5" index card	$5
Photograph/baseball card	$10
HOF plaque postcard	$10
Perez-Steele postcards	$15-$25

Roger Bresnahan (1879-1944) 1945

Availability: *Average*
Demand: *Average*

Cut signature	$500
Single-signature baseball	$6,000
3x5" index card	$700
Photograph/baseball card	$1,200
HOF plaque postcard	Impossible
Perez-Steele postcards	Impossible

Lou Brock (1939-) 1985

Availability: *Plentiful*
Demand: *Little*

Cut signature	$3
Single-signature baseball	$20-$25
3x5" index card	$4
Photograph/baseball card	$12
HOF plaque postcard	$5-$15
Perez-Steele postcards	$20-$25

Dan Brouthers (1858-1932) 1945

Availability: *Scarce*
Demand: *Strong*

Cut signature	$1,250-$1,750
Single-signature baseball	$7,250-$8,000
3x5" index card	$1,500-$2,700
Photograph/baseball card	$3,500-$5,000
HOF plaque postcard	Impossible
Perez-Steele postcards	Impossible

Mordecai Brown (1876-1948) 1949

Availability: *Limited*
Demand: *Average*

Cut signature	$275-$300
Single-signature baseball	$5,000
3x5" index card	$400-$500
Photograph/baseball card	$900
HOF plaque postcard	Impossible
Perez-Steele postcards	Impossible

Morgan Bulkeley (1837-1922) 1937

Availability: *Average*
Demand: *Average*

Cut signature	$800
Single-signature baseball	$6,000
3x5" index card	$1,200-$1,500
Photograph/baseball card	$3,750-$4,000
HOF plaque postcard	Impossible
Perez-Steele postcards	Impossible

Jesse Burkett (1868-1953) 1946

Availability: *Average*
Demand: *Average*

Cut signature	$450
Single-signature baseball	$4,500-$5,500
3x5" index card	$750
Photograph/baseball card	$700-$1,000
HOF plaque postcard	$1,500
Perez-Steele postcards	Impossible

Roy Campanella (1921-1993) 1969

Availability: *Limited*
Demand: *Strong*

Cut signature	$100-$250
Single-signature baseball	$400-$3,500
3x5" index card	$150-$400
Photograph/baseball card	$250-$700
HOF plaque postcard	$300-$400
Perez-Steele postcards	$225-$350

Rod Carew (1945-) 1991

Availability: *Plentiful*
Demand: *Little*

Cut signature	$3-$5
Single-signature baseball	$30-$35
3x5" index card	$7-$9
Photograph/baseball card	$20
HOF plaque postcard	$20
Perez-Steele postcards	$30

Max Carey (1890-1976) 1961

Availability: *Plentiful*
Demand: *Average*

Cut signature	$10
Single-signature baseball	$750
3x5" index card	$15
Photograph/baseball card	$75
HOF plaque postcard	$65-$75
Perez-Steele postcards	Impossible

Steve Carlton (1944-) 1994

Cut signature	$3
Single-signature baseball	$25-$30
3x5" index card	$7
Photograph/baseball card	$15-$20

Alexander Cartwright (1820-1892) 1938

Availability: *Limited*
Demand: *Strong*

Cut signature	$600-$700
Single-signature baseball	Unknown
3x5" index card	$750-$850
Photograph/baseball card	$3,000
HOF plaque postcard	Impossible
Perez-Steele postcards	Impossible

Henry Chadwick (1824-1908) 1938

Availability: *Scarce*
Demand: *Strong*

Cut signature	$1,000-$1,500
Single-signature baseball	Unknown
3x5" index card	$1,200-$1,600
Photograph/baseball card	$3,200-$4,000
HOF plaque postcard	Impossible
Perez-Steele postcards	Impossible

Frank Chance (1877-1924) 1946

Availability: *Average*
Demand: *Average*

Cut signature	$600-$750
Single-signature baseball	$6,500-$7,000
3x5" index card	$750
Photograph/baseball card	$1,700-$2,000
HOF plaque postcard	Impossible
Perez-Steele postcards	Impossible

Happy Chandler (1898-1991) 1982

Availability: *Plentiful*
Demand: *Little*

Cut signature	$4
Single-signature baseball	$75
3x5" index card	$7-$10
Photograph/baseball card	$20-$25
HOF plaque postcard	$12-$15
Perez-Steele postcards	$40-$55

Oscar Charleston (1896-1954) 1976

Availability: *Scarce*
Demand: *Above average*

Cut signature	$600-$1,000
Single-signature baseball	$5,000-$7,000
3x5" index card	$1,000-$1,750
Photograph/baseball card	$2,200-$3,000
HOF plaque postcard	Impossible
Perez-Steele postcards	Impossible

Jack Chesbro (1874-1931) 1946

Availability: *Limited*
Demand: *Above average*

Cut signature	$600-$1,000
Single-signature baseball	$6,500-$8,000
3x5" index card	$750
Photograph/baseball card	$2,000-$2,750
HOF plaque postcard	Impossible
Perez-Steele postcards	Impossible

Fred Clarke (1872-1960) 1945

Availability: *Average*
Demand: *Average*

Cut signature	$75-$100
Single-signature baseball	$2,500-$3,000
3x5" index card	$150-$200
Photograph/baseball card	$350-$400
HOF plaque postcard	$325-$400
Perez-Steele postcards	Impossible

John Clarkson (1861-1909) 1963

Availability: *Scarce*
Demand: *Strong*

Cut signature	$1,200-$2,000
Single-signature baseball	Unknown
3x5" index card	$2,000-$3,000
Photograph/baseball card	$2,500-$4,000
HOF plaque postcard	Impossible
Perez-Steele postcards	Impossible

Roberto Clemente (1934-1972) 1973

Availability: *Average*
Demand: *Strong*

Cut signature	$100-$125
Single-signature baseball	$2,000-$2,500
3x5" index card	$150-$200
Photograph/baseball card	$275-$400
HOF plaque postcard	Impossible
Perez-Steele postcards	Impossible

Ty Cobb (1886-1961) 1936

Availability: *Average*
Demand: *Strong*

Cut signature	$175-$250
Single-signature baseball	$2,500-$3,000
3x5" index card	$275-$325
Photograph/baseball card	$1,200
HOF plaque postcard	$875-$1,000
Perez-Steele postcards	Impossible

Mickey Cochrane (1903-1962) 1947

Availability: *Average*
Demand: *Average*

Cut signature	$60-$75
Single-signature baseball	$1,800-$2,000
3x5" index card	$125-$150
Photograph/baseball card	$250-$350
HOF plaque postcard	$375-$450
Perez-Steele postcards	Impossible

Eddie Collins (1887-1951) 1939

Availability: *Average*
Demand: *Above average*

Cut signature	$85-$100
Single-signature baseball	$4,000-$5,000
3x5" index card	$175-$200
Photograph/baseball card	$400
HOF plaque postcard	$550
Perez-Steele postcards	Impossible

Jimmy Collins (1870-1943) 1945

Availability: *Scarce*
Demand: *Strong*

Cut signature	$500-$750
Single-signature baseball	$6,000
3x5" index card	$950
Photograph/baseball card	$1,500-$1,800
HOF plaque postcard	Impossible
Perez-Steele postcards	Impossible

Earle Combs (1899-1976) 1970

Availability: *Plentiful*
Demand: *Average*

Cut signature	$15
Single-signature baseball	$1,800-$2,000
3x5" index card	$20-$30
Photograph/baseball card	$350
HOF plaque postcard	$100
Perez-Steele postcards	Impossible

Charles Comiskey (1859-1931) 1939

Availability: *Average*
Demand: *Average*

Cut signature	$350-$375
Single-signature baseball	$3,000-$7,500
3x5" index card	$450-$500
Photograph/baseball card	$1,200
HOF plaque postcard	Impossible
Perez-Steele postcards	Impossible

Jocko Conlan (1899-1989) 1974

Availability: *Plentiful*
Demand: *Little*

Cut signature	$5
Single-signature baseball	$50-$100
3x5" index card	$5-$10
Photograph/baseball card	$15-$25
HOF plaque postcard	$15-$20
Perez-Steele postcards	$70-$700

Thomas Connolly (1870-1963) 1953

Availability: *Average*
Demand: *Average*

Cut signature	$250-$275
Single-signature baseball	$7,000
3x5" index card	$250-$350
Photograph/baseball card	$900
HOF plaque postcard	$1,000-$1,200
Perez-Steele postcards	Impossible

Roger Connor (1857-1931) 1976

Availability: *Limited*
Demand: *Above average*

Cut signature	$1,000
Single-signature baseball	$7,000-$8,000
3x5" index card	$1,700-$2,250
Photograph/baseball card	$2,500
HOF plaque postcard	Impossible
Perez-Steele postcards	Impossible

Stan Coveleski (1889-1984) 1969

Availability: *Plentiful*
Demand: *Little*

Cut signature	$3
Single-signature baseball	$325
3x5" index card	$6-$15
Photograph/baseball card	$60
HOF plaque postcard	$20-$30
Perez-Steele postcards	$650-$700

Sam Crawford (1880-1968) 1957

Availability: *Average*
Demand: *Average*

Cut signature	$45-$65
Single-signature baseball	$2,200-$2,500
3x5" index card	$75-$125
Photograph/baseball card	$250
HOF plaque postcard	$200-$300
Perez-Steele postcards	Impossible

Joe Cronin (1906-1984) 1956

Availability: *Above average*
Demand: *Little*

Cut signature	$10
Single-signature baseball	$275-$350
3x5" index card	$15
Photograph/baseball card	$80-$100
HOF plaque postcard	$35-$45
Perez-Steele postcards	$900-$1,100

Candy Cummings (1848-1924) 1939

Availability: *Scarce*
Demand: *Strong*

Cut signature	$1,500
Single-signature baseball	Unknown
3x5" index card	$1,600
Photograph/baseball card	$4,500
HOF plaque postcard	Impossible
Perez-Steele postcards	Impossible

Ki Ki Cuyler (1899-1950) 1968

Availability: *Average*
Demand: *Average*

Cut signature	$150
Single-signature baseball	$2,000-$3,000
3x5" index card	$175
Photograph/baseball card	$375-$425
HOF plaque postcard	Impossible
Perez-Steele postcards	Impossible

Ray Dandridge (1913-) 1987

Availability: *Plentiful*
Demand: *Little*

Cut signature	$2-$6
Single-signature baseball	$25-$35
3x5" index card	$3-$7
Photograph/baseball card	$10
HOF plaque postcard	$9-$15
Perez-Steele postcards	$15-$20

Dizzy Dean (1911-1974) 1953

Availability: *Average*
Demand: *Average*

Cut signature	$35-$50
Single-signature baseball	$600
3x5" index card	$45-$60
Photograph/baseball card	$125-$200
HOF plaque postcard	$100-$150
Perez-Steele postcards	Impossible

Ed Delahanty (1867-1903) 1945

Availability: *Scarce*
Demand: *Strong*

Cut signature	$1,200-$1,800
Single-signature baseball	Unknown
3x5" index card	$1,800-$2,300
Photograph/baseball card	$4,000-$4,700
HOF plaque postcard	Impossible
Perez-Steele postcards	Impossible

Bill Dickey (1907-1993) 1954

Availability: *Plentiful*
Demand: *Little*

Cut signature	$6
Single-signature baseball	$100-$125
3x5" index card	$12
Photograph/baseball card	$30-$35
HOF plaque postcard	$18
Perez-Steele postcards	$30-$40

Martin Dihigo (1905-1971) 1977

Availability: *Limited*
Demand: *Strong*

Cut signature	$650-$750
Single-signature baseball	$4,000
3x5" index card	$900-$1,200
Photograph/baseball card	$1,500-$2,000
HOF plaque postcard	Impossible
Perez-Steele postcards	Impossible

Joe DiMaggio (1914-) 1955

Availability: *Plentiful*
Demand: *Strong*

Cut signature	$15-$25
Single-signature baseball	$250-$350
3x5" index card	$40-$50
Photograph/baseball card	$130-$150
HOF plaque postcard	$75-$125
Perez-Steele postcards	$250-$300

Bobby Doerr (1918-) 1986

Availability: *Plentiful*
Demand: *Little*

Cut signature	$5
Single-signature baseball	$21
3x5" index card	$5
Photograph/baseball card	$11
HOF plaque postcard	$6-$10
Perez-Steele postcards	$15-$20

Don Drysdale (1936-1993) 1984

Availability: *Plentiful*
Demand: *Little*

Cut signature	$5
Single-signature baseball	$45-$75
3x5" index card	$8
Photograph/baseball card	$20-$35
HOF plaque postcard	$15-$20
Perez-Steele postcards	$50

Hugh Duffy (1866-1954) 1945

Availability: *Average*
Demand: *Average*

Cut signature	$300
Single-signature baseball	$3,500
3x5" index card	$350-$400
Photograph/baseball card	$750
HOF plaque postcard	$750-$900
Perez-Steele postcards	Impossible

Leo Durocher (1905-1991) 1994

Availability: *Above average*
Demand: *Above average*

Cut signature	$6
Single-signature baseball	$65-$90
3x5" index card	$10
Photograph/baseball card	$40

Billy Evans (1864-1956) 1973

Availability: *Limited*
Demand: *Above average*

Cut signature	$150-$200
Single-signature baseball	$3,500-$4,000
3x5" index card	$300-$350
Photograph/baseball card	$400-$550
HOF plaque postcard	Impossible
Perez-Steele postcards	Impossible

Johnny Evers (1881-1947) 1946

Availability: *Limited*
Demand: *Average*

Cut signature	$250-$300
Single-signature baseball	$6,000
3x5" index card	$325-$400
Photograph/baseball card	$1,200
HOF plaque postcard	$1,100
Perez-Steele postcards	Impossible

Buck Ewing (1859-1906) 1939

Availability: *Scarce*
Demand: *Strong*

Cut signature	$1,200-$1,700
Single-signature baseball	Unknown
3x5" index card	$2,700-$3,200
Photograph/baseball card	$4,000-$4,500
HOF plaque postcard	Impossible
Perez-Steele postcards	Impossible

Red Faber (1888-1976) 1964

Availability: *Above average*
Demand: *Average*

Cut signature	$15
Single-signature baseball	$1,500-$2,000
3x5" index card	$35
Photograph/baseball card	$100
HOF plaque postcard	$65-$90
Perez-Steele postcards	Impossible

Bob Feller (1918-) 1962

Availability: *Plentiful*
Demand: *Little*

Cut signature	$2
Single-signature baseball	$18
3x5" index card	$5
Photograph/baseball card	$10-$15
HOF plaque postcard	$7-$12
Perez-Steele postcards	$25-$35

Rick Ferrell (1905-) 1984

Availability: Plentiful
Demand: Little

Cut signature	$3
Single-signature baseball	$20-$25
3x5" index card	$5
Photograph/baseball card	$12
HOF plaque postcard	$10-$15
Perez-Steele postcards	$18-$25

Rollie Fingers (1946-) 1992

Availability: *Average*
Demand: *Average*

Cut signature	$3
Single-signature baseball	$20-$30
3x5" index card	$7
Photograph/baseball card	$20
HOF plaque postcard	$10

Elmer Flick (1876-1971) 1963

Availability: *Above average*
Demand: *Average*

Cut signature	$15-$20
Single-signature baseball	$2,200-$2,500
3x5" index card	$40-$50
Photograph baseball card	$250
HOF plaque postcard	$300-$450
Perez-Steele postcards	Impossible

Whitey Ford (1926-) 1974

Availability: *Plentiful*
Demand: *Little*

Cut signature	$3
Single-signature baseball	$25-$35
3x5" index card	$5
Photograph/baseball card	$15
HOF plaque postcard	$12-$15
Perez-Steele postcards	$25-$30

Rube Foster (1878-1930) 1981

Availability: *Limited*
Demand: *Above average*

Cut signature	$2,000-$3,000
Single-signature baseball	$10,000
3x5" index card	$3,800
Photograph/baseball card	$5,500-$6,500
HOF plaque postcard	Impossible
Perez-Steele postcards	Impossible

Jimmie Foxx (1907-1967) 1951

Availability: *Average*
Demand: *Average*

Cut signature	$75-$125
Single-signature baseball	$2,000-$2,500
3x5" index card	$250
Photograph/baseball card	$500
HOF plaque postcard	$525-$575
Perez-Steele postcards	Impossible

Ford Frick (1894-1978) 1970

Availability: *Average*
Demand: *Average*

Cut signature	$20
Single-signature baseball	$800
3x5" index card	$40-$50
Photograph/baseball card	$100
HOF plaque postcard	$125
Perez-Steele postcards	Impossible

Frankie Frisch (1898-1973) 1947

Availability: *Above average*
Demand: *Average*

Cut signature	$15
Single-signature baseball	$1,500-$2,000
3x5" index card	$40-$60
Photograph/baseball card	$150-$200
HOF plaque postcard	$100-$150
Perez-Steele postcards	Impossible

Pud Galvin (1855-1902) 1965

Availability: *Scarce*
Demand: *Strong*

Cut signature	$1,300-$1,875
Single-signature baseball	$10,000
3x5" index card	$2,500-$3,200
Photograph/baseball card	$3,000
HOF plaque postcard	Impossible
Perez-Steele postcards	Impossible

Lou Gehrig (1903-1941) 1939

Availability: *Average*
Demand: *Strong*

Cut signature	$650-$750
Single-signature baseball	$5,500
3x5" index card	$800-$850
Photograph/baseball card	$2,000-$2,200
HOF plaque postcard	Unknown
Perez-Steele postcards	Impossible

Charlie Gehringer (1903-1993) 1949

Availability: *Plentiful*
Demand: *Little*

Cut signature	$4
Single-signature baseball	$43
3x5" index card	$5
Photograph/baseball card	$15
HOF plaque postcard	$30-$40
Perez-Steele postcards	$50-$85

Bob Gibson (1935-) 1972

Availability: *Plentiful*
Demand: *Little*

Cut signature	$4
Single-signature baseball	$25
3x5" index card	$5
Photograph/baseball card	$15
HOF plaque postcard	$10-$15
Perez-Steele postcards	$25

Josh Gibson (1911-1947) 1972

Availability: *Limited*
Demand: *Strong*

Cut signature	$700-$1,100
Single-signature baseball	$5,500
3x5" index card	$2,150
Photograph/baseball card	$1,200
HOF plaque postcard	Impossible
Perez-Steele postcards	Impossible

Warren Giles (1896-1979) 1979

Availability: *Above average*
Demand: *Average*

Cut signature	$20
Single-signature baseball	$800
3x5" index card	$35-$45
Photograph/baseball card	$100-$125
HOF plaque postcard	Impossible
Perez-Steele postcards	Impossible

Lefty Gomez (1908-1989) 1972

Availability: *Plentiful*
Demand: *Little*

Cut signature	$7
Single-signature baseball	$100
3x5" index card	$5-$10
Photograph/baseball card	$35
HOF plaque postcard	$20-$25
Perez-Steele postcards	$50-$100

Goose Goslin (1900-1971) 1968

Availability: *Average*
Demand: *Average*

Cut signature	$45-$65
Single-signature baseball	$3,000
3x5" index card	$55-$75
Photograph/baseball card	$300
HOF plaque postcard	$475-$3,500
Perez-Steele postcards	Impossible

Hank Greenberg (1911-1986) 1956

Availability: *Above average*
Demand: *Average*

Cut signature	$20
Single-signature baseball	$400-$600
3x5" index card	$35
Photograph/baseball card	$75
HOF plaque postcard	$50-$75
Perez-Steele postcards	$400-$450

Clark Griffith (1869-1955) 1946

Availability: *Average*
Demand: *Average*

Cut signature	$100-$135
Single-signature baseball	$1,500-$2,200
3x5" index card	$150
Photograph/baseball card	$350
HOF plaque postcard	$600
Perez-Steele postcards	Impossible

Burleigh Grimes (1893-1985) 1964

Availability: *Plentiful*
Demand: *Little*

Cut signature	$7
Single-signature baseball	$200-$250
3x5" index card	$10-$25
Photograph/baseball card	$55
HOF plaque postcard	$20-$25
Perez-Steele postcards	$275-$350

Lefty Grove (1900-1975) 1947

Availability: *Above average*
Demand: *Average*

Cut signature	$20-$25
Single-signature baseball	$900-$1,200
3x5" index card	$35-$45
Photograph/baseball card	$200
HOF plaque postcard	$100-$125
Perez-Steele postcards	Impossible

Chick Hafey (1903-1973) 1971

Availability: *Above average*
Demand: *Average*

Cut signature	$35
Single-signature baseball	$1,500
3x5" index card	$50
Photograph/baseball card	$150
HOF plaque postcard	$500-$625
Perez-Steele postcards	Impossible

Jesse Haines (1893-1978) 1970

Availability: *Above average*
Demand: *Average*

Cut signature	$35
Single-signature baseball	$950
3x5" index card	$40
Photograph/baseball card	$125
HOF plaque postcard	$70-$90
Perez-Steele postcards	Impossible

Billy Hamilton (1866-1940) 1961

Availability: *Limited*
Demand: *Strong*

Cut signature	$500-$1,275
Single-signature baseball	$5,000
3x5" index card	$750
Photograph/baseball card	$2,500-$3,000
HOF plaque postcard	Impossible
Perez-Steele postcards	Impossible

Will Harridge (1883-1971) 1972

Availability: *Above average*
Demand: *Average*

Cut signature	$85
Single-signature baseball	$2,500
3x5" index card	$125
Photograph/baseball card	$300
HOF plaque postcard	Impossible
Perez-Steele postcards	Impossible

Bucky Harris (1896-1977) 1975

Availability: *Above average*
Demand: *Average*

Cut signature	$15-$25
Single-signature baseball	$800-$1,000
3x5" index card	$25
Photograph/baseball card	$200
HOF plaque postcard	$135-$175
Perez-Steele postcards	Impossible

Gabby Hartnett (1900-1972) 1955

Availability: *Above average*
Demand: *Average*

Cut signature	$33
Single-signature baseball	$1,025
3x5" index card	$55
Photograph/baseball card	$250
HOF plaque postcard	$200-$325
Perez-Steele postcards	Impossible

Harry Heilmann (1894-1951) 1952

Availability: *Average*
Demand: *Above average*

Cut signature	$200
Single-signature baseball	$2,000-$2,500
3x5" index card	$325
Photograph/baseball card	$400-$500
HOF plaque postcard	Impossible
Perez-Steele postcards	Impossible

Billy Herman (1909-1992) 1975

Availability: *Plentiful*
Demand: *Little*

Cut signature	$3
Single-signature baseball	$40
3x5" index card	$5
Photograph/baseball card	$15-$18
HOF plaque postcard	$10-$12
Perez-Steele postcards	$30-$50

Harry Hooper (1887-1974) 1971

Availability: *Above average*
Demand: *Average*

Cut signature	$15
Single-signature baseball	$1,000
3x5" index card	$20-$30
Photograph/baseball card	$150
HOF plaque postcard	$65-$125
Perez-Steele postcards	Impossible

Rogers Hornsby (1896-1963) 1942

Availability: *Average*
Demand: *Above average*

Cut signature	$150
Single-signature baseball	$1,800-$2,500
3x5" index card	$250
Photograph/baseball card	$500
HOF plaque postcard	$500-$625
Perez-Steele postcards	Impossible

Waite Hoyt (1899-1984) 1969

Availability: *Plentiful*
Demand: *Little*

Cut signature	$7
Single-signature baseball	$275
3x5" index card	$12-$18
Photograph/baseball card	$50-$60
HOF plaque postcard	$25-$35
Perez-Steele postcards	$550-$650

Cal Hubbard (1900-1977) 1976

Availability: *Above average*
Demand: *Average*

Cut signature	$30
Single-signature baseball	$750-$1,000
3x5" index card	$60
Photograph/baseball card	$250
HOF plaque postcard	$500
Perez-Steele postcards	Impossible

Carl Hubbell (1903-1988) 1947

Availability: *Plentiful*
Demand: *Little*

Cut signature	$8
Single-signature baseball	$100-$125
3x5" index card	$12
Photograph/baseball card	$25-$30
HOF plaque postcard	$20-$30
Perez-Steele postcards	$50-$125

Miller Huggins (1879-1929) 1964

Availability: *Limited*
Demand: *Above average*

Cut signature	$600
Single-signature baseball	$6,000
3x5" index card	$1,000
Photograph/baseball card	$1,500
HOF plaque postcard	Impossible
Perez-Steele postcards	Impossible

Catfish Hunter (1946-) 1987

Availability: *Plentiful*
Demand: *Little*

Cut signature	$3
Single-signature baseball	$20
3x5" index card	$4
Photograph/baseball card	$12
HOF plaque postcard	$7-$12
Perez-Steele postcards	$15-$20

Monte Irvin (1911-) 1973

Availability: *Plentiful*
Demand: *Little*

Cut signature	$3
Single-signature baseball	$20
3x5" index card	$3
Photograph/baseball card	$13
HOF plaque postcard	$7-$10
Perez-Steele postcards	$18-$25

Reggie Jackson (1946-) 1993

Availability: *Above average*
Demand: *Above average*

Cut signature	$8
Single-signature baseball	$45-$65
3x5" index card	$12
Photograph/baseball card	$25-$35

Travis Jackson (1903-1987) 1982

Availability: *Plentiful*
Demand: *Little*

Cut signature	$7
Single-signature baseball	$180
3x5" index card	$17
Photograph/baseball card	$50
HOF plaque postcard	$30-$40
Perez-Steele postcards	$80-$125

Fergie Jenkins (1943-) 1991

Availability: *Plentiful*
Demand: *Little*

Cut signature	$2
Single-signature baseball	$20-$25
3x5" index card	$4
Photograph/baseball card	$12
HOF plaque postcard	$10-$20
Perez-Steele postcards	$20

Hugh Jennings (1869-1928) 1945

Availability: *Limited*
Demand: *Strong*

Cut signature	$350-$500
Single-signature baseball	$6,000-$7,500
3x5" index card	$900
Photograph/baseball card	$1,000
HOF plaque postcard	Impossible
Perez-Steele postcards	Impossible

Ban Johnson (1864-1931) 1937

Availability: *Average*
Demand: *Average*

Cut signature	$200
Single-signature baseball	$3,500
3x5" index card	$250
Photograph/baseball card	$500
HOF plaque postcard	Impossible
Perez-Steele postcards	Impossible

Judy Johnson (1900-1989) 1975

Availability: *Plentiful*
Demand: *Little*

Cut signature	$7
Single-signature baseball	$150
3x5" index card	$8
Photograph/baseball card	$35
HOF plaque postcard	$25
Perez-Steele postcards	$80-$100

Walter Johnson (1887-1946) 1946

Availability: *Limited*
Demand: *Strong*

Cut signature	$450
Single-signature baseball	$3,500
3x5" index card	$450-$500
Photograph/baseball card	$1,000
HOF plaque postcard	Unknown
Perez-Steele postcards	Impossible

Addie Joss (1880-1911) 1978

Availability: *Scarce*
Demand: *Strong*

Cut signature	$1,500-$2,200
Single-signature baseball	$5,000-$9,000
3x5" index card	$2,500
Photograph/baseball card	$4,000
HOF plaque postcard	Impossible
Perez-Steele postcards	Impossible

Al Kaline (1934-) 1980

Availability: *Plentiful*
Demand: *Little*

Cut signature	$3
Single-signature baseball	$20-$30
3x5" index card	$4
Photograph/baseball card	$12-$15
HOF plaque postcard	$10-$15
Perez-Steele postcards	$18-$30

Tim Keefe (1857-1933) 1964

Availability: *Scarce*
Demand: *Strong*

Cut signature	$500-$600
Single-signature baseball	$6,500-$7,000
3x5" index card	$750-$1,000
Photograph/baseball card	$2,000
HOF plaque postcard	Impossible
Perez-Steele postcards	Impossible

Wee Willie Keeler (1872-1923) 1939

Availability: *Limited*
Demand: *Strong*

Cut signature	$1,000
Single-signature baseball	$8,000
3x5" index card	$2,000
Photograph/baseball card	$3,000
HOF plaque postcard	Impossible
Perez-Steele postcards	Impossible

George Kell (1922-) 1883

Availability: *Plentiful*
Demand: *Little*

Cut signature	$3
Single-signature baseball	$20
3x5" index card	$5
Photograph/baseball card	$8-$12
HOF plaque postcard	$6-$10
Perez-Steele postcards	$15-$20

Joe Kelley (1871-1943) 1971

Availability: *Limited*
Demand: *Strong*

Cut signature	$800
Single-signature baseball	$8,000
3x5" index card	$1,000-$1,700
Photograph/baseball card	$2,100
HOF plaque postcard	Impossible
Perez-Steele postcards	Impossible

George Kelly (1895-1984) 1973

Availability: *Plentiful*
Demand: *Little*

Cut signature	$8
Single-signature baseball	$325
3x5" index card	$15
Photograph/baseball card	$75
HOF plaque postcard	$25-$30
Perez-Steele postcards	$650-$700

Mike Kelly (1857-1894) 1945

Availability: *Scarce*
Demand: *Strong*

Cut signature	$2,000
Single-signature baseball	$6,950
3x5" index card	$3,500
Photograph/baseball card	$5,000
HOF plaque postcard	Impossible
Perez-Steele postcards	Impossible

Harmon Killebrew (1936-) 1984

Availability: *Plentiful*
Demand: *Little*

Cut signature	$3
Single-signature baseball	$20-$30
3x5" index card	$5
Photograph/baseball card	$15
HOF plaque postcard	$12-$15
Perez-Steele postcards	$18-$25

Ralph Kiner (1922-) 1975

Availability: *Plentiful*
Demand: *Little*

Cut signature	$3
Single-signature baseball	$20
3x5" index card	$5
Photograph/baseball card	$12
HOF plaque postcard	$10
Perez-Steele postcards	$18-$25

Chuck Klein (1904-1958) 1980

Availability: *Average*
Demand: **Average**

Cut signature	$200
Single-signature baseball	$3,000
3x5" index card	$275
Photograph/baseball card	$500
HOF plaque postcard	Impossible
Perez-Steele postcards	Impossible

Bill Klem (1874-1951) 1953

Availability: *Average*
Demand: *Average*

Cut signature	$400
Single-signature baseball	$3,500
3x5" index card	$500
Photograph/baseball card	$1,200
HOF plaque postcard	Impossible
Perez-Steele postcards	Impossible

Sandy Koufax (1935-) 1971

Availability: *Plentiful*
Demand: *Little*

Cut signature	$7
Single-signature baseball	$60
3x5" index card	$12
Photograph/baseball card	$35
HOF plaque postcard	$30
Perez-Steele postcards	$40-$60

Nap Lajoie (1875-1959) 1937

Availability: *Average*
Demand: *Strong*

Cut signature	$250
Single-signature baseball	$4,000-$4,500
3x5" index card	$300-$400
Photograph/baseball card	$800
HOF plaque postcard	$650-$800
Perez-Steele postcards	Impossible

Kenesaw Landis (1866-1944) 1944

Availability: *Above average*
Demand: *Average*

Cut signature	$225
Single-signature baseball	$3,500
3x5" index card	$300
Photograph/baseball card	$650
HOF plaque postcard	Impossible
Perez-Steele postcards	Impossible

Tony Lazzeri (1903-1946) 1991

Availability: *Average*
Demand: *Above average*

Cut signature	$300
Single-signature baseball	$4,000
3x5" index card	$450
Photograph/baseball card	$700
HOF plaque postcard	Impossible
Perez-Steele postcards	Impossible

Bob Lemon (1920-) 1976

Availability: *Plentiful*
Demand: *Little*

Cut signature	$3
Single-signature baseball	$20
3x5" index card	$3
Photograph/baseball card	$13
HOF plaque postcard	$6-$10
Perez-Steele postcards	$15-$25

Buck Leonard (1907-) 1972

Availability: *Plentiful*
Demand: *Little*

Cut signature	$5
Single-signature baseball	$35
3x5" index card	$10
Photograph/baseball card	$12-$18
HOF plaque postcard	$10-$15
Perez-Steele postcards	$20-$35

Freddie Lindstrom (1905-1981) 1976

Availability: *Plentiful*
Demand: *Average*

Cut signature	$12
Single-signature baseball	$600
3x5" index card	$25
Photograph/baseball card	$100
HOF plaque postcard	$40-$45
Perez-Steele postcards	Impossible

John Lloyd (1884-1964) 1977

Availability: *Limited*
Demand: *Above average*

Cut signature	$700
Single-signature baseball	$5,000-$7,000
3x5" index card	$750
Photograph/baseball card	$1,200
HOF plaque postcard	Impossible
Perez-Steele postcards	Impossible

Ernie Lombardi (1908-1977) 1986

Availability: *Above average*
Demand: *Average*

Cut signature	$25
Single-signature baseball	$1,400-$1,500
3x5" index card	$50
Photograph/baseball card	$300
HOF plaque postcard	Impossible
Perez-Steele postcards	Impossible

Al Lopez (1908-) 1977

Availability: *Plentiful*
Demand: *Little*

Cut signature	$5
Single-signature baseball	$75
3x5" index card	$10
Photograph/baseball card	$30
HOF Plaque postcard	$30
Perez-Steele postcards	$50-$100

Ted Lyons (1900-1986) 1955

Availability: *Plentiful*
Demand: *Little*

Cut signature	$8-$10
Single-signature baseball	$175
3x5" index card	$12-$18
Photograph/baseball card	$50
HOF plaque postcard	$25-$35
Perez-Steele postcards	$300

Connie Mack (1862-1956) 1937

Availability: *Average*
Demand: *Average*

Cut signature	$100
Single-signature baseball	$850-$1,000
3x5" index card	$175
Photograph/baseball card	$350
HOF plaque postcard	$600
Perez-Steele postcards	Impossible

Larry MacPhail (1890-1975) 1978

Availability: *Above average*
Demand: *Average*

Cut signature	$60
Single-signature baseball	$2,000
3x5" index card	$175
Photograph/baseball card	$400
HOF plaque postcard	Impossible
Perez-Steele postcards	Impossible

Mickey Mantle (1931-) 1974

Availability: *Plentiful*
Demand: *Average*

Cut signature	$15
Single-signature baseball	$60-$75
3x5" index card	$20-$30
Photograph/baseball card	$45-$55
HOF plaque postcard	$40-$50
Perez-Steele postcards	$100-$275

Heinie Manush (1901-1971) 1964

Availability: *Average*
Demand: *Average*

Cut signature	$30
Single-signature baseball	$2,000
3x5" index card	$50
Photograph/baseball card	$300
HOF plaque postcard	$250-$300
Perez-Steele postcards	Impossible

Rabbit Maranville (1891-1954) 1954

Availability: *Average*
Demand: *Average*

Cut signature	$150
Single-signature baseball	$2,000
3x5" index card	$250
Photograph/baseball card	$350
HOF plaque postcard	Impossible
Perez-Steele postcards	Impossible

Juan Marichal (1938-) 1983

Availability: *Plentiful*
Demand: *Little*

Cut signature	$4
Single-signature baseball	$20
3x5" index card	$8
Photograph/baseball card	$12
HOF plaque postcard	$12
Perez-Steele postcards	$15-$25

Rube Marquard (1889-1980) 1971

Availability: *Plentiful*
Demand: *Little*

Cut signature	$10
Single-signature baseball	$600-$750
3x5" index card	$15
Photograph/baseball card	$150
HOF plaque postcard	$30-$40
Perez-Steele postcards	Impossible

Eddie Mathews (1931-) 1978

Availability: *Plentiful*
Demand: *Little*

Cut signature	$3
Single-signature baseball	$25
3x5" index card	$6
Photograph/baseball card	$12
HOF plaque postcard	$10
Perez-Steele postcards	$15-$25

Christy Mathewson (1880-1925) 1936

Availability: *Limited*
Demand: *Strong*

Cut signature	$800-$1,000
Single-signature baseball	$9,000-$12,000
3x5" index card	$1,200
Photograph/baseball card	$3,000
HOF plaque postcard	Impossible
Perez-Steele postcards	Impossible

Willie Mays (1931-) 1979

Availability: *Plentiful*
Demand: *Little*

Cut signature	$10
Single-signature baseball	$40
3x5" index card	$15
Photograph/baseball card	$25-$35
HOF plaque postcard	$17-$22
Perez-Steele postcards	$30-$65

Joe McCarthy (1887-1978) 1957

Availability: *Average*
Demand: *Average*

Cut signature	$15
Single-signature baseball	$1,000
3x5" index card	$25
Photograph/baseball card	$150
HOF plaque postcard	$30-$80
Perez-Steele postcards	Impossible

Tom McCarthy (1864-1922) 1946

Availability: *Limited*
Demand: *Above average*

Cut signature	$1,500-$2,000
Single-signature baseball	$3,500-$4,250
3x5" index card	$2,000
Photograph/baseball card	$4,000
HOF plaque postcard	Impossible
Perez-Steele postcards	Impossible

Willie McCovey (1938-) 1986

Availability: *Plentiful*
Demand: *Little*

Cut signature	$3
Single-signature baseball	$25
3x5" index card	$7
Photograph/baseball card	$15
HOF plaque postcard	$12
Perez-Steele postcards	$15-$25

Joe McGinnity (1871-1929) 1946

Availability: *Scarce*
Demand: *Above average*

Cut signature	$800
Single-signature baseball	$9,000
3x5" index card	$1,500-$1,900
Photograph/baseball card	$3,500-$5,000
HOF plaque postcard	Impossible
Perez-Steele postcards	Impossible

Bill McGowan (1871-1954) 1992

Availability: *Average*
Demand: *Little*

Cut signature	$300
Single-signature	$3,500
3x5" index card	$400
Photograph/baseball card	$2,000
HOF plaque postcard	Impossible
Perez-Steele postcards	Impossible

John McGraw (1873-1934) 1937

Availability: *Limited*
Demand: *Strong*

Cut signature	$450-$500
Single-signature baseball	$3,500-$5,500
3x5" index card	$750
Photograph/baseball card	$1,500
HOF plaque postcard	Impossible
Perez-Steele postcards	Impossible

Bill McKechnie (1886-1965) 1962

Availability: *Above average*
Demand: *Average*

Cut signature	$75
Single-signature baseball	$2,000
3x5" index card	$150
Photograph/baseball card	$350
HOF plaque postcard	$300-$425
Perez-Steele postcards	Impossible

Ducky Medwick (1911-1975) 1968

Availability: *Above average*
Demand: *Average*

Cut signature	$25
Single-signature baseball	$1,400-$1,700
3x5" index card	$45
Photograph/baseball card	$200
HOF plaque postcard	$125-$150
Perez-Steele postcards	Impossible

Johnny Mize (1913-1993) 1981

Availability: *Plentiful*
Demand: *Little*

Cut signature	$4
Single-signature baseball	$35
3x5" index card	$7
Photograph/baseball card	$20
HOF plaque postcard	$10-$20
Perez-Steele postcards	$20-$40

Joe Morgan (1943-) 1990

Availability: *Plentiful*
Demand: *Little*

Cut signature	$3
Single-signature baseball	$25
3x5" index card	$7
Photograph/baseball card	$15
HOF plaque postcard	$12-$18
Perez-Steele postcards	$20-$30

Stan Musial (1920-) 1969

Availability: *Plentiful*
Demand: *Little*

Cut signature	$8
Single-signature baseball	$40-$50
3x5" index card	$12-$15
Photograph/baseball card	$25
HOF plaque postcard	$20-$30
Perez-Steele postcards	$40-$75

Hal Newhouser (1921-) 1992

Availability: *Average*
Demand: *Average*

Cut signature	$3
Single-signature	$20-$30
3x5" index card	$5
Photograph/baseball card	$10
HOF plaque postcard	$8
Perez-Steele postcards	$20

Kid Nichols (1869-1953) 1949

Availability: *Average*
Demand: *Above average*

Cut signature	$135-$175
Single-signature baseball	$3,500-$4,500
3x5" index card	$250-$325
Photograph/baseball card	$500
HOF plaque postcard	$355-$1,000
Perez-Steele postcards	Impossible

James O'Rourke (1852-1919) 1945

Availability: *Scarce*
Demand: *Strong*

Cut signature	$1,500-$2,100
Single-signature baseball	$10,000
3x5" index card	$2,500-$3,200
Photograph/baseball card	$3,500
HOF plaque postcard	Impossible
Perez-Steele postcards	Impossible

Mel Ott (1909-1958) 1951

Availability: *Average*
Demand: *Above average*

Cut signature	$125-$175
Single-signature baseball	$3,200-$3,500
3x5" index card	$250
Photograph/baseball card	$500
HOF plaque postcard	$425-$700
Perez-Steele postcards	Impossible

Satchel Paige (1906-1982) 1971

Availability: *Above average*
Demand: *Above average*

Cut signature	$30
Single-signature baseball	$675-$750
3x5" index card	$50
Photograph/baseball card	$150-$200
HOF plaque postcard	$100-$125
Perez-Steele postcards	$3,200-$3,500

Jim Palmer (1945-) 1990

Availability: *Plentiful*
Demand: *Little*

Cut signature	$3
Single-signature baseball	$25
3x5" index card	$7
Photograph/baseball card	$10-$15
HOF plaque postcard	$10-$15
Perez-Steele postcards	$25

Herb Pennock (1894-1948) 1948

Availability: *Average*
Demand: *Average*

Cut signature	$175
Single-signature baseball	$2,500
3x5" index card	$200
Photograph/baseball card	$350
HOF plaque postcard	Impossible
Perez-Steele postcards	Impossible

Gaylord Perry (1938-) 1991

Availability: *Plentiful*
Demand: *Little*

Cut signature	$2
Single-signature baseball	$22
3x5" index card	$6
Photograph/baseball card	$12
HOF plaque postcard	$8-$12
Perez-Steele postcards	$20

Ed Plank (1875-1926) 1946

Availability: *Limited*
Demand: *Strong*

Cut signature	$1,500
Single-signature baseball	$7,500
3x5" index card	$2,200
Photograph/baseball card	$3,200
HOF plaque postcard	Impossible
Perez-Steele postcards	Impossible

Charles Radbourne (1854-1897) 1948

Availability: *Scarce*
Demand: *Strong*

Cut signature	$1,600-$2,000
Single-signature baseball	$7,500
3x5" index card	$2,500
Photograph/baseball card	$3,200
HOF plaque postcard	Impossible
Perez-Steele postcards	Impossible

Pee Wee Reese (1918-) 1984

Availability: *Plentiful*
Demand: *Little*

Cut signature	$4
Single-signature baseball	$35
3x5" index card	$9
Photograph/baseball card	$20-$30
HOF plaque postcard	$20
Perez-Steele postcards	$30-$40

Sam Rice (1890-1974) 1963

Availability: *Above average*
Demand: *Average*

Cut signature	$20
Single-signature baseball	$1,400-$1,600
3x5" index card	$35
Photograph/baseball card	$150
HOF plaque postcard	$100-$135
Perez-Steele postcards	Impossible

Branch Rickey (1881-1965) 1967

Availability: *Average*
Demand: *Average*

Cut signature	$175
Single-signature baseball	$2,500
3x5" index card	$200
Photograph/baseball card	$750
HOF plaque postcard	Impossible
Perez-Steele postcards	Impossible

Eppa Rixey (1891-1963) 1963

Availability: *Average*
Demand: *Average*

Cut signature	$60-$70
Single-signature baseball	$2,500
3x5" index card	$100
Photograph/baseball card	$350-$400
HOF plaque postcard	Impossible
Perez-Steele postcards	Impossible

Phil Rizzuto (1918-) 1994

Availability: *Above average*
Demand: *Average*

Cut signature	$2
Single-signature baseball	$33
3x5" index card	$9
Photograph/baseball card	$15

Robin Roberts (1926-) 1976

Availability: *Plentiful*
Demand: *Little*

Cut signature	$4
Single-signature baseball	$20
3x5" index card	$7
Photograph/baseball card	$12
HOF plaque postcard	$8-$12
Perez-Steele postcards	$20-$25

Brooks Robinson (1937-) 1983

Availability: *Plentiful*
Demand: *Little*

Cut signature	$4
Single-signature baseball	$20-$25
3x5" index card	$6
Photograph/baseball card	$12
HOF plaque postcard	$8-$12
Perez-Steele postcards	$18-$25

Frank Robinson (1935-) 1982

Availability: *Plentiful*
Demand: *Little*

Cut signature	$4
Single-signature baseball	$20-$30
3x5" index card	$7
Photograph/baseball card	$15-$20
HOF plaque postcard	$10-$20
Perez-Steele postcards	$25

Jackie Robinson (1919-1972) 1962

Availability: *Above average*
Demand: *Above average*

Cut signature	$175
Single-signature baseball	$2,200-$2,500
3x5" index card	$300
Photograph/baseball card	$700
HOF plaque postcard	$400-$600
Perez-Steele postcards	Impossible

Wilbert Robinson (1863-1934) 1945

Availability: *Limited*
Demand: *Above average*

Cut signature	$700
Single-signature baseball	$6,000
3x5" index card	$750-$1,225
Photograph/baseball card	$2,000
HOF plaque postcard	Impossible
Perez-Steele postcards	Impossible

Edd Roush (1893-1988) 1962

Availability: *Plentiful*
Demand: *Little*

Cut signature	$8
Single-signature baseball	$125
3x5" index card	$15
Photograph/baseball card	$50-$75
HOF plaque postcard	$20-$25
Perez-Steele postcards	$100-$150

Red Ruffing (1904-1986) 1967

Availability: *Plentiful*
Demand: *Little*

Cut signature	$20
Single-signature baseball	$300-$375
3x5" index card	$35
Photograph/baseball card	$50-$80
HOF plaque postcard	$65-$85
Perez-Steele postcards	$650-$800

Amos Rusie (1871-1942) 1977

Availability: *Limited*
Demand: *Above average*

Cut signature	$700
Single-signature baseball	$5,000
3x5" index card	$750
Photograph/baseball card	$2,000-$2,300
HOF plaque postcard	Impossible
Perez-Steele postcards	Impossible

Babe Ruth (1895-1948) 1936

Availability: *Average*
Demand: *Strong*

Cut signature	$700
Single-signature baseball	$3,500
3x5" index card	$1,000
Photograph/baseball card	$3,500-$4,200
HOF plaque postcard	$3,500-$4,500
Perez-Steele postcards	Impossible

Ray Schalk (1892-1970) 1955

Availability: *Above average*
Demand: *Average*

Cut signature	$45
Single-signature baseball	$1,350-$1,700
3x5" index card	$80
Photograph/baseball card	$350
HOF plaque postcard	$225-$300
Perez-Steele postcards	Impossible

Red Schoendienst (1923-) 1989

Availability: *Plentiful*
Demand: *Little*

Cut signature	$4
Single-signature baseball	$22
3x5" index card	$6
Photograph/baseball card	$13
HOF plaque postcard	$10-$20
Perez-Steele postcards	$20

Tom Seaver (1944-) 1992

Availability: *Above average*
Demand: *Above average*

Cut signature	$4
Single-signature baseball	$45
3x5" index card	$15
Photograph/baseball card	$35
HOF plaque postcard	$25
Perez-Steele postcards	$30

Joe Sewell (1898-1990) 1977

Availability: *Plentiful*
Demand: *Little*

Cut signature	$4
Single-signature baseball	$60-$75
3x5" index card	$10
Photograph/baseball card	$25
HOF plaque postcard	$10-$15
Perez-Steele postcards	$50-$75

Al Simmons (1902-1956) 1953

Availability: *Average*
Demand: *Average*

Cut signature	$175
Single-signature baseball	$2,500
3x5" index card	$250
Photograph/baseball card	$225
HOF plaque postcard	$700-$800
Perez-Steele postcards	Impossible

George Sisler (1893-1973) 1939

Availability: *Above average*
Demand: *Average*

Cut signature	$25-$35
Single-signature baseball	$1,400
3x5" index card	$50-$75
Photograph/baseball card	$175
HOF plaque postcard	$100-$125
Perez-Steele postcards	Impossible

Enos Slaughter (1916-) 1985

Availability: *Plentiful*
Demand: *Little*

Cut signature	$2
Single-signature baseball	$18
3x5" index card	$3
Photograph/baseball card	$12
HOF plaque postcard	$6-$10
Perez-Steele postcards	$15-$20

Duke Snider (1926-) 1980

Availability: *Plentiful*
Demand: *Little*

Cut signature	$4
Single-signature baseball	$25
3x5" index card	$7
Photograph/baseball card	$15
HOF plaque postcard	$10-$15
Perez-Steele postcards	$45

Warren Spahn (1921-) 1973

Availability: *Plentiful*
Demand: *Little*

Cut signature	$3
Single-signature baseball	$20
3x5" index card	$6
Photograph/baseball card	$10
HOF plaque postcard	$9-$12
Perez-Steele postcards	$20-$30

Al Spalding (1850-1915) 1939

Availability: *Limited*
Demand: *Strong*

Cut signature	$750-$1,500
Single-signature baseball	$12,000
3x5" index card	$1,750
Photograph/baseball card	$1,800
HOF plaque postcard	Impossible
Perez-Steele postcards	Impossible

Tris Speaker (1888-1958) 1937

Availability: *Average*
Demand: *Above average*

Cut signature	$175-$200
Single-signature baseball	$3,000-$3,200
3x5" index card	$225-$275
Photograph/baseball card	$500
HOF plaque postcard	$525-$600
Perez-Steele postcards	Impossible

Willie Stargell (1940-) 1988

Availability: *Plentiful*
Demand: *Little*

Cut signature	$3
Single-signature baseball	$20-$25
3x5" index card	$4
Photograph/baseball card	$15
HOF plaque postcard	$8-$15
Perez-Steele postcards	$15-$20

Casey Stengel (1890-1975) 1966

Availability: *Average*
Demand: *Above average*

Cut signature	$20-$30
Single-signature baseball	$900-$1,100
3x5" index card	$50-$60
Photograph/baseball card	$150
HOF plaque postcard	$85-$100
Perez-Steele postcards	Impossible

Bill Terry (1898-1989) 1954

Availability: *Plentiful*
Demand: *Little*

Cut signature	$7
Single-signature baseball	$100-$125
3x5" index card	$15
Photograph/baseball card	$25-$30
HOF plaque postcard	$25-$35
Perez-Steele postcards	$65-$100

Sam Thompson (1860-1922) 1974

Availability: *Scarce*
Demand: *Strong*

Cut signature	$1,200
Single-signature baseball	$7,500-$10,000
3x5" index card	$3,250-$3,900
Photograph/baseball card	$6,000
HOF plaque postcard	Impossible
Perez-Steele postcards	Impossible

Joe Tinker (1880-1948) 1946

Availability: *Average*
Demand: *Average*

Cut signature	$300
Single-signature baseball	$6,000
3x5" index card	$375
Photograph/baseball card	$1,200
HOF plaque postcard	$1,000-$1,200
Perez-Steele postcards	Impossible

Pie Traynor (1899-1972) 1948

Availability: *Above average*
Demand: *Average*

Cut signature	$80-$100
Single-signature baseball	$1,000-$1,400
3x5" index card	$125-$175
Photograph/baseball card	$250
HOF plaque postcard	$350-$450
Perez-Steele postcards	Impossible

Dazzy Vance (1891-1961) 1955

Availability: *Average*
Demand: *Average*

Cut signature	$150-$200
Single-signature baseball	$3,200
3x5" index card	$225-$300
Photograph/baseball card	$750
HOF plaque postcard	$600
Perez-Steele postcards	Impossible

Arky Vaughan (1912-1952) 1985

Availability: *Average*
Demand: *Above average*

Cut signature	$150-$175
Single-signature baseball	$3,500
3x5" index card	$250
Photograph/baseball card	$650
HOF plaque postcard	Impossible
Perez-Steele postcards	Impossible

William Veeck (1914-1986) 1991

Availability: *Above average*
Demand: *Average*

Cut signature	$35
Single-signature baseball	$1,000-$2,000
3x5" index card	$75
Photograph/baseball card	$225-$175
HOF plaque postcard	Impossible
Perez-Steele postcards	Impossible

Rube Waddell (1876-1914) 1946

Availability: *Scarce*
Demand: *Strong*

Cut signature	$1,400
Single-signature baseball	$12,500
3x5" index card	$1,500-$2,225
Photograph/baseball card	$4,500
HOF plaque postcard	Impossible
Perez-Steele postcards	Impossible

Honus Wagner (1874-1955) 1936

Availability: *Average*
Demand: *Strong*

Cut signature	$275-$325
Single-signature baseball	$4,000-$4,200
3x5" index card	$350-$400
Photograph/baseball card	$800-$900
HOF plaque postcard	$950-$1,200
Perez-Steele postcards	Impossible

Bobby Wallace (1873-1960) 1953

Availability: *Average*
Demand: *Average*

Cut signature	$225
Single-signature baseball	$3,500-$4,500
3x5" index card	$300
Photograph/baseball card	$700
HOF plaque postcard	$700
Perez-Steele postcards	Impossible

Ed Walsh (1881-1959) 1946

Availability: *Average*
Demand: *Average*

Cut signature	$135-$150
Single-signature baseball	$2,700-$3,600
3x5" index card	$150-$200
Photograph/baseball card	$400
HOF plaque postcard	$350-$400
Perez-Steele postcards	Impossible

Lloyd Waner (1906-1982) 1967

Availability: *Plentiful*
Demand: *Little*

Cut signature	$15
Single-signature baseball	$300
3x5" index card	$20
Photograph/baseball card	$75
HOF plaque postcard	$30-$35
Perez-Steele postcards	$3,200-$3,500

Paul Waner (1903-1965) 1952

Availability: *Average*
Demand: *Above average*

Cut signature	$50-$100
Single-signature baseball	$2,000-$2,500
3x5" index card	$125
Photograph/baseball card	$250-$300
HOF plaque postcard	$275-$350
Perez-Steele postcards	Impossible

Monte Ward (1860-1925) 1964

Availability: *Limited*
Demand: Strong

Cut signature	$1,000-$1,700
Single-signature baseball	$7,500-$12,000
3x5" index card	$1,500-$2,000
Photograph/baseball card	$3,000
HOF plaque postcard	Impossible
Perez-Steele postcards	Impossible

George Weiss (1895-1972) 1971

Availability: *Above average*
Demand: *Average*

Cut signature	$40
Single-signature baseball	$3,500-$5,500
3x5" index card	$75-$100
Photograph/baseball card	$300
HOF plaque postcard Undetermined	
Perez-Steele postcards	Impossible

Mickey Welch (1859-1941) 1973

Availability: *Limited*
Demand: *Strong*

Cut signature	$1,700
Single-signature baseball	$5,700-$8,500
3x5" index card	$2,750
Photograph/baseball card	$4,000
HOF plaque postcard	Impossible
Perez-Steele postcards	Impossible

Zack Wheat (1888-1972) 1959

Availability: *Above average*
Demand: *Average*

Cut signature	$40-$50
Single-signature baseball	$1,500
3x5" index card	$45-$75
Photograph/baseball card	$150-$200
HOF plaque postcard	$175-$350
Perez-Steele postcards	Impossible

Hoyt Wilhelm (1923-) 1985

Availability: *Plentiful*
Demand: *Little*

Cut signature	$3
Single-signature baseball	$20
3x5" index card	$5
Photograph/baseball card	$10
HOF plaque postcard	$8-$15
Perez-Steele postcards	$20

Billy Williams (1938-) 1987

Availability: *Plentiful*
Demand: *Little*

Cut signature	$4
Single-signature baseball	$20
3x5" index card	$7
Photograph/baseball card	$15
HOF plaque postcard	$8-$12
Perez-Steele postcards	$12-$20

Early Wynn (1920-) 1972

Availability: *Plentiful*
Demand: *Little*

Cut signature	$4
Single-signature baseball	$20-$30
3x5" index card	$7
Photograph/baseball card	$15
HOF plaque postcard	$10-$15
Perez-Steele postcards	$20-$35

Ted Williams (1918-) 1966

Availability: *Plentiful*
Demand: *Average*

Cut signature	$20
Single-signature baseball	$125-$150
3x5" index card	$30
Photograph/baseball card	$60-$75
HOF plaque postcard	$50-$65
Perez-Steele postcards	$100-$235

Carl Yastrzemski (1939-) 1989

Availability: *Plentiful*
Demand: *Little*

Cut signature	$4
Single-signature baseball	$35-$45
3x5" index card	$7
Photograph/baseball card	$25
HOF plaque postcard	$15-$20
Perez-Steele postcards	$25-$35

Hack Wilson (1900-1948) 1979

Availability: *Limited*
Demand: *Above average*

Cut signature	$265-$300
Single-signature baseball	$4,000
3x5" index card	$350
Photograph/baseball card	$800
HOF plaque postcard	Impossible
Perez-Steele postcards	Impossible

Tom Yawkey (1903-1976) 1980

Availability: *Average*
Demand: *Average*

Cut signature	$80-$100
Single-signature baseball	$1,200-$2,000
3x5" index card	$125-$175
Photograph/baseball card	$400
HOF plaque postcard	Impossible
Perez-Steele postcards	Impossible

George Wright (1847-1937) 1937

Availability: *Limited*
Demand: *Strong*

Cut signature	$800
Single-signature baseball	$8,000-$10,000
3x5" index card	$1,200-$1,700
Photograph/baseball card	$2,500-$3,000
HOF plaque postcard	Impossible
Perez-Steele postcards	Impossible

Cy Young (1867-1955) 1937

Availability: *Average*
Demand: *Strong*

Cut signature	$175-$275
Single-signature baseball	$3,500
3x5" index card	$350-$400
Photograph/baseball card	$700
HOF plaque postcard	$950-$1,100
Perez-Steele postcards	Impossible

Harry Wright (1835-1895) 1953

Availability: *Scarce*
Demand: *Strong*

Cut signature	$1,200-$1,800
Single-signature baseball	$4,000-$5,000
3x5" index card	$2,000-$2,400
Photograph/baseball card	$3,500
HOF plaque postcard	Impossible
Perez-Steele postcards	Impossible

Ross Youngs (1897-1927) 1972

Availability: *Scarce*
Demand: *Strong*

Cut signature	$800-$1,000
Single-signature baseball	$4,500-$6,500
3x5" index card	$1,200-$1,500
Photograph/baseball card	$2,500
HOF plaque postcard	Impossible
Perez-Steele postcards	Impossible

Gallery of Superstars

Sparky Anderson

Cut signature	$3
Single-signature baseball	$25-$35
3x5" index card	$5
Photograph/baseball card	$11

Jose Canseco

Cut signature	$7
Single-signature	$40
3x5" index card	$15
Photograph/baseball card	$20-$25

Richie Ashburn

Cut signature	$6
Single-signature baseball	$25
3x5" index card	$6
Photograph/baseball card	$10

Orlando Cepeda

Cut signature	$3
Single-signature baseball	$22
3x5" index card	$5
Photograph/baseball card	$14

Vida Blue

Cut signature	$3
Single-signature baseball	$17
3x5" index card	$4
Photograph/baseball card	$10

Will Clark

Cut signature	$9
Single-signature baseball	$35
3x5" index card	$8
Photograph/baseball card	$25-$30

Bert Blyleven

Cut signature	$4
Single-signature baseball	$22-$25
3x5" index card	$9
Photograph/baseball card	$12

Roger Clemens

Cut signature	$7
Single-signature baseball	$40
3x5" index card	$8
Photograph/baseball card	$20-$25

Wade Boggs

Cut signature	$5
Single-signature baseball	$35-$40
3x5" index card	$8
Photograph/baseball card	$20-$25

Andre Dawson

Cut signature	$5
Single-signature baseball	$40
3x5" index card	$6
Photograph/baseball card	$15

George Brett

Cut signature	$10
Single-signature baseball	$50
3x5" index card	$20
Photograph/baseball card	$25-$35

Dwight Evans

Cut signature	$5
Single-signature baseball	$20-$25
3x5" index card	$9
Photograph/baseball card	$12-$15

Jim Bunning

Cut signature	$4
Single-signature baseball	$25
3x5" index card	$5
Photograph/baseball card	$10

Carlton Fisk

Cut signature	$6
Single-signature baseball	$30-$45
3x5" index card	$12
Photograph/baseball card	$20-$30

Nellie Fox

Cut signature	$20
Single-signature baseball	$450
3x5" index card	$46
Photograph/baseball card	$110

Joe Jackson

Cut signature	$1,500
Single-signature baseball	$13,100
3x5" index card	$2,000
Photograph/baseball card	$5,875

Steve Garvey

Cut signature	$4
Single-signature baseball	$20
3x5" index card	$8
Photograph/baseball card	$10-$12

Tommy John

Cut signature	$2
Single-signature baseball	$22
3x5" index card	$4
Photograph/baseball card	$11

Dwight Gooden

Cut signature	$5
Single-signature baseball	$20-$25
3x5" index card	$9
Photograph/baseball card	$15

Jim Kaat

Cut signature	$2
Single-signature baseball	$20
3x5" index card	$4
Photograph/baseball card	$12

Mark Grace

Cut signature	$4
Single-signature baseball	$20-$25
3x5" index card	$10
Photograph/baseball card	$10-$15

Jerry Koosman

Cut signature	$2
Single-signature baseball	$20
3x5" index card	$4
Photograph/baseball card	$8

Ken Griffey Jr.

Cut signature	$6
Single-signature baseball	$35-$40
3x5" index card	$10
Photograph/baseball card	$25

Don Larsen

Cut signature	$2
Single-signature baseball	$22
3x5" index card	$5
Photograph/baseball card	$10

Rickey Henderson

Cut signature	$7
Single-signature baseball	$45
3x5" index card	$20
Photograph/baseball card	$20-$30

Mickey Lolich

Cut signature	$2
Single-signature baseball	$19
3x5" index card	$4
Photograph/baseball card	$10

Gil Hodges

Cut signature	$15
Single-signature baseball	$1,500
3x5" index card	$65
Photograph/baseball card	$325

Roger Maris

Cut signature	$25
Single-signature baseball	$350
3x5" index card	$75
Photograph/baseball card	$175

Bo Jackson

Cut signature	$6
Single-signature baseball	$45
3x5" index card	$15
Photograph/baseball card	$25

Billy Martin

Cut signature	$15
Single-signature baseball	$90
3x5" index card	$29
Photograph/baseball card	$60

Don Mattingly

Cut signature	$9
Single-signature baseball	$40-$45
3x5" index card	$17
Photograph/baseball card	$30

Bill Mazeroski

Cut signature	$9
Single-signature baseball	$25-$35
3x5" index card	$12
Photograph/baseball card	$12

Mark McGwire

Cut signature	$6
Single-signature baseball	$35-$40
3x5" index card	$12
Photograph/baseball card	$20-$25

Thurman Munson

Cut signature	$20
Single-signature baseball	$625
3x5" index card	$70
Photograph/baseball card	$180

Dale Murphy

Cut signature	$7
Single-signature baseball	$25-$30
3x5" index card	$6
Photograph/baseball card	$15

Eddie Murray

Cut signature	$8
Single-signature baseball	$25-$30
3x5" index card	$12
Photograph/baseball card	$18

Phil Niekro

Cut signature	$5
Single-signature baseball	$25
3x5" index card	$9
Photograph/baseball card	$12

Tony Oliva

Cut signature	$4
Single-signature baseball	$19
3x5" index card	$6
Photograph/baseball card	$10

Al Oliver

Cut signature	$2
Single-signature baseball	$15
3x5" index card	$4
Photograph/baseball card	$7

Dave Parker

Cut signature	$6
Single-signature baseball	$25
3x5" index card	$9
Photograph/baseball card	$10

Tony Perez

Cut signature	$2
Single-signature baseball	$25
3x5" index card	$4
Photograph/baseball card	$12-$15

Jim Rice

Cut signature	$2
Single-signature baseball	$20
3x5" index card	$4
Photograph/baseball card	$11

Cal Ripken Jr.

Cut signature	$6
Single-signature baseball	$45
3x5" index card	$12
Photograph/baseball card	$30

Pete Rose

Cut signature	$6
Single-signature baseball	$35
3x5" index card	$10
Photograph/baseball card	$20

Nolan Ryan

Cut signature	$4
Single-signature baseball	$50
3x5" index card	$15
Photograph/baseball card	$30

Ryne Sandberg

Cut signature	$7
Single-signature baseball	$40
3x5" index card	$15
Photograph/baseball card	$30

Dave Winfield

Don Sutton

Mike Schmidt

Cut signature	$10
Single-signature baseball	$45
3x5" index card	$20
Photograph/baseball card	$35

Don Sutton

Cut signature	$4
Single-signature baseball	$25
3x5" index card	$7
Photograph/baseball card	$12

Ted Simmons

Cut signature	$2
Single-signature baseball	$19
3x5" index card	$5
Photograph/baseball card	$9

Luis Tiant

Cut signature	$2
Single-signature baseball	$20
3x5" index card	$4
Photograph/baseball card	$10

Ozzie Smith

Cut signature	$6
Single-signature baseball	$30
3x5" index card	$15
Photograph/baseball card	$25

Earl Weaver

Cut signature	$2
Single-signature baseball	$25-$35
3x5" index card	$4
Photograph/baseball card	$15

Rusty Staub

Cut signature	$2
Single-signature baseball	$23
3x5" index card	$6
Photograph/baseball card	$12

Dave Winfield

Cut signature	$7
Single-signature baseball	$35-$45
3x5" index card	$18
Photograph/baseball card	$25

Darryl Strawberry

Cut signature	$5
Single-signature baseball	$25-$35
3x5" index card	$8
Photograph/baseball card	$16

Robin Yount

Cut signature	$7
Single-signature baseball	$35
3x5" index card	$12
Photograph/baseball card	$20-$25

Inactive Players

Players	Baseball	Photo	Players	Baseball	Photo
Joe Adcock	$25	$10	Bob Friend	$18	$12
Tommie Agee	$20	$9	Jim Gentile	$20	$8
Dick Allen	$20	$10	Cesar Geronimo	$17	$10
Felipe Alou	$20	$10	Al Gionfriddo	$20	$17
Jesus Alou	$20	$10	Mudcat Grant	$15	$5
Matty Alou	$20	$10	Bobby Grich	$22	$10
Dusty Baker	$17	$8	Ken Griffey Sr.	$20	$10
Sal Bando	$15	$8	Dick Groat	$20	$10
Don Baylor	$25	$12	Jerry Grote	$20	$8
Ewell Blackwell	$20	$10	Ron Guidry	$25	$13
Paul Blair	$29	$9	Don Gullet	$19	$9
Johnny Blanchard	$20	$10	Harvey Haddix	$20	$10
Steve Blass	$15	$8	Bud Harrelson	$20	$8
Ron Blomberg	$18	$8	Richie Hebner	$15	$8
Bobby Bonds	$15	$8	Ellie Hendricks	$15	$8
Bob Boone	$20	$10	Tommy Henrich	$22	$10
Larry Bowa	$15	$9	Keith Hernandez	$21	$10
Clete Boyer	$20	$8	Whitey Herzog	$30	$20
Ralph Branca	$20	$8	Bob Horner	$20	$10
Rocky Bridges	$25	$10	Ralph Houk	$21	$8
Bill Buckner	$18	$9	Elston Howard	$30	$18
Lou Burdette	$18	$8	Frank Howard	$35	$15
Johnny Callison	$15	$8	Randy Hundley	$15	$8
Bert Campaneris	$15	$8	Alex Johnson	$15	$8
Gary Carter	$25	$12	Jay Johnstone	$16	$8
Rico Carty	$20	$10	Dave Kingman	$15	$8
Rick Cerone	$15	$8	Ted Kluszewski	$45	$30
Ron Cey	$20	$9	Ray Knight	$11	$5
Chris Chambliss	$15	$8	Ed Kranepool	$15	$7
Jack Clark	$18	$10	Ken Landreaux	$14	$7
Rocky Colavito	$25	$15	Tommy Lasorda	$30	$18
Dave Concepcion	$20	$10	Vern Law	$19	$10
Gene Conley	$17	$8	Bill Lee	$15	$6
Chuck Connors	$150	$23	Ron LeFlore	$15	$8
Cecil Cooper	$18	$9	Johnny Logan	$20	$8
Roger Cramer	$150	$20	Vic Lombardi	$20	$8
Frank Crosetti	$30	$10	Jim Lonborg	$15	$8
Babe Dahlgren	$30	$12	Davey Lopes	$20	$10
Willie Davis	$15	$8	Sparky Lyle	$18	$8
Ron Guidry	$25	$15	Fred Lynn	$21	$12
Bucky Dent	$20	$10	Bill Madlock	$40	$8
Lou Dials	$30	$20	Rick Manning	$17	$8
Dom DiMaggio	$35	$15	John Matlack	$17	$8
Larry Doby	$25	$10	Gene Mauch	$20	$8
Walt Dropo	$20	$8	Carlos May	$15	$8
Ryne Duren	$20	$8	Rudy May	$20	$10
Duffy Dyer	$15	$8	John Mayberry	$20	$10
Dock Ellis	$12	$5	Lee Mazzilli	$15	$8
Darrell Evans	$25	$10	Mickey McDermott	$15	$10
Elroy Face	$25	$10	Gil McDougald	$17	$8
Boo Ferriss	$15	$8	Sam McDowell	$15	$8
Mark Fidrych	$15	$8	Tug McGraw	$25	$13
Ed Figueroa	$15	$8	Denny McLain	$18	$7
Curt Flood	$21	$8	Dave McNally	$20	$10
George Foster	$15	$8	Gene Michael	$15	$8

Autographs

Players	Baseball	Photo	Players	Baseball	Photo
Felix Milan	$15	$7	Ron Santo	$20	$10
Minnie Minoso	$30	$12	Hank Sauer	$18	$9
Wilmer Mizell	$18	$11	George Scott	$17	$8
Don Money	$15	$10	Mike Scott	$19	$7
Bobby Murcer	$18	$10	Roy Sievers	$15	$8
Craig Nettles	$20	$10	Ken Singleton	$20	$10
Don Newcombe	$19	$10	Reggie Smith	$18	$8
Joe Niekro	$17	$9	Bob Stanley	$15	$8
Gary Nolan	$15	$8	Fred Stanley	$22	$9
Blue Moon Odom	$20	$9	Mel Stottleyre	$20	$10
Ben Oglivie	$16	$8	Johnny Temple	$17	$10
Amos Otis	$17	$8	Wayne Terwilliger	$17	$8
Mickey Owen	$20	$8	Bobby Thomson	$20	$8
Joe Pepitone	$20	$8	Marv Throneberry	$20	$8
Jim Perry	$15	$10	Joe Torre	$20	$8
Rico Petrocelli	$15	$8	Virgil Trucks	$25	$8
Billy Pierce	$23	$8	Bob Uecker	$40	$18
Jimmy Piersall	$20	$8	Del Unser	$15	$8
Lou Piniella	$21	$10	Bill Virdon	$15	$8
Vada Pinson	$22	$10	Rube Walker	$50	$15
Boog Powell	$15	$8	Claudell Washington	$16	$8
Willie Randolph	$21	$12	Bob Watson	$15	$8
Allie Reynolds	$20	$10	Earl Weaver	$35	$10
Bobby Richardson	$18	$8	Bill White	$20	$10
Dave Righetti	$20	$10	Roy White	$17	$8
Mickey Rivers	$15	$8	Dick Williams	$20	$11
Preacher Roe	$20	$17	Maury Wills	$30	$9
Stan Rogers	$20	$10	Mookie Wilson	$20	$8
Johnny Roseboro	$20	$10	Steve Yeager	$22	$10
Joe Rudi	$20	$9	Don Zimmer	$20	$10
Johnny Sain	$18	$8			

The Astros' Joe Niekro gets a tip from Hoyt Wilhem.

Active Players

Players	Baseball	Photo	Players	Baseball	Photo
Jim Abbott	$35	$20	Ray Lankford	$20	$12
Roberto Alomar	$27	$14	Barry Larkin	$20	$9
Sandy Alomar	$15	$10	Pat Listach	$28	$18
Steve Avery	$25	$16	Kenny Lofton	$20	$15
Carlos Baerga	$25	$16	Greg Maddux	$28	$15
Jeff Bagwell	$20	$10	Dennis Martinez	$20	$12
Albert Belle	$25	$18	Ben McDonald	$24	$12
Andy Benes	$18	$10	Jack McDowell	$25	$17
Dante Bichette	$15	$8	Fred McGriff	$30	$18
Craig Biggio	$23	$6	Kevin McReynolds	$19	$10
Barry Bonds	$38	$30	Kevin Mitchell	$28	$18
Bobby Bonilla	$26	$18	Paul Molitor	$30	$12
Brett Butler	$25	$12	Jack Morris	$18	$9
Joe Carter	$25	$12	Charles Nagy	$20	$10
David Cone	$18	$10	John Olerud	$20	$14
Darren Daulton	$16	$12	Rafael Palmeiro	$19	$8
Eric Davis	$25	$10	Terry Pendleton	$30	$22
Rob Deer	$18	$8	Kirby Puckett	$35	$22
Delino DeShields	$21	$10	Tim Raines	$20	$8
Mike Devereaux	$18	$10	Jeff Reardon	$25	$15
Rob Dibble	$20	$10	Jose Rijo	$14	$7
Doug Drabek	$25	$12	Bret Saberhagen	$28	$12
Shawon Dunston	$15	$8	Chris Sabo	$25	$10
Len Dykstra	$30	$20	Benito Santiago	$20	$12
Dennis Eckersley	$36	$18	Steve Sax	$25	$18
Cal Eldred	$18	$10	Gary Sheffield	$30	$15
Tony Fernandez	$22	$15	Ruben Sierra	$35	$8
Cecil Fielder	$30	$18	Lee Smith	$20	$10
Julio Franco	$21	$10	John Smoltz	$28	$18
Travis Fryman	$20	$15	Dave Stewart	$28	$15
Andres Galarraga	$24	$15	Dave Stieb	$20	$12
Ron Gant	$24	$12	Greg Swindell	$13	$6
Kirk Gibson	$20	$10	Danny Tartabull	$25	$9
Tom Glavine	$30	$20	Mickey Tettleton	$25	$12
Juan Gonzalez	$30	$12	Frank Thomas	$36	$23
Tom Gordon	$12	$8	Alan Trammell	$19	$15
Goose Gossage	$21	$12	Fernando Valenzuela	$19	$10
Mike Greenwell	$19	$12	Andy Van Slyke	$25	$15
Marquis Grissom	$22	$10	Greg Vaughn	$22	$12
Pedro Guerrero	$20	$8	Mo Vaughn	$19	$10
Tony Gwynn	$26	$10	Robin Ventura	$25	$17
Pete Harnisch	$16	$8	Frank Viola	$20	$10
Charlie Hayes	$18	$12	Bob Welch	$22	$12
Orel Hershiser	$30	$18	Lou Whitaker	$11	$7
Ted Higuera	$15	$8	Matt Williams	$22	$10
Kent Hrbek	$25	$10	Mitch Williams	$45	$35
Pete Incaviglia	$18	$7	Todd Zeile	$17	$6
Gregg Jefferies	$25	$16			
Howard Johnson	$25	$15			
Wally Joyner	$20	$10			
Dave Justice	$33	$18			
Eric Karros	$25	$15			
Chuck Knoblauch	$22	$18			
John Kruk	$22	$15			
Mark Langston	$17	$7			

Autographed Team Baseballs

Key signatures follow each team name

1948 New York Yankees

1920 BOSTON (AL) - Barrow, Hendryx, Hooper, Pennock, Hoyt ....$780-$1170
1920 BOSTON (NL) - Maranville, Powell, Mann ....$512-$768
1920 BROOKLYN - Robinson, Konetchy, Myers, Wheat, Grimes, Marquard
....$1120-$1680
1920 CHICAGO (AL) - Collins, Risberg, Weaver, Leibold, Felsch, Jackson, Schalk, Faber, Williams, Kerr, Cicotte .... $ uncertain
1920 CHICAGO (NL) - Hollocher, Flack, Robertson, Alexander............$880-$1320
1920 CINCINNATI - Daubert, Roush ....$448-$672
1920 CLEVELAND - Wambsganss, Chapman, Gardner, Smith, Speaker, Jamieson, O'Neill, Sewell, Coveleski..$1320-$1980
1920 DETROIT - Jennings, Heilmann, Cobb, Veach ....$1700-$2550

1920 NEW YORK (AL) - Huggins, Pratt, Ruth, Mays, Shawkey ....$2160-$3240

1920 NEW YORK (NL) - McGraw, Kelly, Bancroft, Frisch, Youngs, Toney, Nehf, Barnes ....$1680-$2520

1920 PHILADELPHIA (AL) - Mack...................$560-$840

1920 PHILADELPHIA (NL) - Stengel, Williams, Meusel, Wheat, Rixey ....$784-$1176

1920 PITTSBURGH - Carey, McKechnie, Traynor, Cooper ....$660-$990

1920 ST. LOUIS (AL) - Sisler, Tobin, Jacobson, Williams, Shocker..........$420-$630

1920 ST. LOUIS (NL) - Rickey, Fournier, Hornsby, Stock, Doak, Haines ....$1120-$1680

1920 WASHINGTON - Griffith, Judge, Harris, Rice, Milan, Johnson ...$1320-$1980

1921 BOSTON (AL) - Duffy, McInnis, Pratt, Leibold, Menosky, Jones, Pennock ....$544-$816

1921 BOSTON (NL) - Barbare, Boeckel, Southworth, Powell, Cruise, Oeschger ....$400-$600

1921 BROOKLYN - Robinson, Schmandt, Johnston, Griffith, Wheat, Grimes ....$800-$1200

1921 CHICAGO (AL) - Sheely, Collins, Hooper, Strunk, Schalk, Faber ....$736-$1104

1921 CHICAGO (NL) - Evers, Grimes, Flack, Maisel, Barber, Alexander ....$1200-$1800

1921 CINCINNATI - Daubert, Groh, Bressler, Roush, Duncan, Rixey, Marquard ....$540-$810

1921 CLEVELAND - Speaker, Sewell, Gardner, Jamieson, O'Neill, Coveleski ....$720-$1080

1921 DETROIT - Cobb, Blue, Heilmann, Veach, Bassler, Jones ....$800-$1200

1921 NEW YORK (AL) - Huggins, Ward, Baker, Meusel, Ruth, Mays, Hoyt ....$2500-$3240

1921 NEW YORK (NL) - McGraw, Kelly, Bancroft, Frisch, Youngs, Meusel, Snyder, Stengel, Nehf ....$1920-$2880

1921 PHILADELPHIA (AL) - Mack, Witt, T. Walker...................$496-$744

1921 PHILADELPHIA (NL) - Konetchy, Williams, Meusel, Bruggy, Stengel ....$400-$600

1921 PITTSBURGH - Cuthsaw, Maranville, Carey, Bigbee, Traynor, Cuyler, Cooper ....$800-$1200

1921 ST. LOUIS (AL) - Sisler, Tobin, Jacobson, Williams, Severeid, Shocker ....$420-$630

1921 ST. LOUIS (NL) - Rickey, Fournier, Hornsby, Stock, Smith, Mann, McHenry, Clemons, Dillhoefer, Haines, Doak ....$1080-$1620

1921 WASHINGTON - Judge, Harris, Shanks, Rice, Gharrity, Goslin, Johnson ....$1000-$1500

1922 BOSTON (AL) - Duffy, Burns, Pratt, Harris, Pennock ....$500-$750

1922 BOSTON (NL) - Marquard ....$360-$540

1922 BROOKLYN - Johnston, Robinson, Myers, Wheat, DeBerry, Ruether, Vance, Grimes, T. Griffith ....$1000-$1500

1922 CHICAGO (AL) - Sheely, Collins, Hooper, Mostil, Schalk, Evers, Faber ....$1080-$1620

1922 CHICAGO (NL) - Grimes, Hollocher, Friberg, Miller, O'Farrell, Hartnett,

Alexander...$800-$1200
1922 CINCINNATI - Daubert, Pinelli, Harper, Duncan, Hargrave, Roush, Rixey
....$424-$636
1922 CLEVELAND - Speaker, McGinnis, Sewell, Uhle, Jamieson, O'Neill, Coveleski...$680-$1020
1922 DETROIT - Cobb, Blue, Rigney, Heilmann, Veach, Bassler ....$768-$1152
1922 NEW YORK (AL) - Pipp, Meusel, Ruth, Schang, Baker, Bush, Shawkey, Hoyt, Huggins...$2040-$3060
1922 NEW YORK (NL) - McGraw, Kelly, Frisch, Bancroft, Youngs, Stengel, Meusel, Snyder, Jackson, Nehf ....$1880-$2820
1922 PHILADELPHIA (AL) - Mack, Hauser, Galloway, Rommel, Miller
....$480-$720
1922 PHILADELPHIA (NL) - Walker, Williams, Lee, Henline ....$320-$480
1922 PITTSBURGH - McKechnie, Tierney, Maranville, Traynor, Russell, Carey, Bigbee, Gooch, Cuyler, Cooper...$960-$1440
1922 ST. LOUIS (AL) - Sisler, McManus, Tobin, Jacobson, Williams, Severeid, Shocker ....$420-$630
1922 ST. LOUIS (NL) - Rickey, Hornsby, Toporcer, Stock, Smith, Schultz, Bottomley, Haines..$1280-$1920
1922 WASHINGTON - Harris, Rice, Goslin, Johnson...........................$880-$1320
1923 BOSTON (AL) - Burns, Flagstead, Harris, Ehmke, Chance ....$880-$1320
1923 BOSTON (NL) - McInnis, Southworth, Powell, Marquard...............$360-$540
1923 BROOKLYN - Robinson, Fournier, Johnston, Wheat, Grimes, Vance
....$960-$1440
1923 CHICAGO (AL) - Collins, Hooper, Falk, Schalk, Faber, Lyons .....$688-$1032
1923 CHICAGO (NL) - Grimes, Friberg, Statz, Miller, O'Farrell, Hartnett, Alexander, Aldridge ....$800-$1000
1923 CINCINNATI - Roush, Duncan, Hargrave, Luque, Rixey.................$400-$600
1923 CLEVELAND - Speaker, Sewell, Summa, Jamieson, Uhle, Coveleski
....$680-$1020
1923 DETROIT - Cobb, Rigney, Heilmann, Manush, Daus ....$880-$1320
1923 NEW YORK (AL) - Huggins, Pipp, Ruth, Witt, Meusel, Gehrig, Pennock, Hoyt ....$2500-$3750
1923 NEW YORK (NL) - McGraw, Kelly, Frisch, Bancroft, Youngs, Jackson, Stengel, Terry, Wilson, Ryan..$2100-$3150
1923 PHILADELPHIA (AL) - Mack, Hauser ....$460-$630
1923 PHILADELPHIA (NL) - Holke, Tierney, Mokan, Henline..............$308-$462
1923 PITTSBURGH - McKechnie, Grimm, Maranville, Traynor, Barnhart, Carey, Cuyler, Morrison ....$880-$1320
1923 ST. LOUIS (AL) - McManus, Tobin, Jacobson, Williams, Severeid, Shocker
....$360-$540
1923 ST. LOUIS (NL) - Rickey, Bottomley, Hornsby, Myers, Smith, Haines
....$1200-$1800
1923 WASHINGTON - Judge, Harris, Rice, Leibold, Goslin, Ruel, Johnson
....$840-$1260
1924 BOSTON (AL) - Harris, Boone, Flagstead, Ruffing ....$360-$540
1924 BOSTON (NL) - Stengel, Bancroft, Marquard ....$560-$840
1924 BROOKLYN - Robinson, Fournier, High, Brown, Wheat, Grimes, Vance

....$960-$1440

1924 CHICAGO (AL) - Evers, Sheely, Collins, Hooper, Mostil, Falk, Schalk, Thurston, Lyons, Faber ....$1140-$1710

1924 CHICAGO (NL) - Grantham, Heathcote, Hartnett, Alexander ....$720-$1080

1924 CINCINNATI - Critz, Pinelli, Walker, Roush, Mays, Rixey.............$360-$540

1924 CLEVELAND - Speaker, Burns, Sewell, Jamieson, Myatt, Shaute, Coveleski ....$640-$960

1924 DETROIT - Cobb, Blue, Pratt, Heilmann, Manush, Bassler, Gehringer ....$960-$1440

1924 NEW YORK (AL) - Huggins, Dugan, Ruth, Meusel, Combs, Gehrig, Pennock, Hoyt ....$3000-$4500

1924 NEW YORK (NL) - McGraw, Kelly, Frisch, Jackson, Youngs, Wilson, Snyder, Terry, Lindstrom, Bentley ....$1840-$2760

1924 PHILADELPHIA (AL) - Miller, Simmons, Lamar.........................$560-$840

1924 PHILADELPHIA (NL) - Holke, Wrightstone, Williams.................$300-$450

1924 PITTSBURGH - McKechnie, Maranville, Traynor, Carey, Cuyler, Cooper ....$800-$1225

1924 ST. LOUIS (AL) - Sisler, McManus, Robertson, Jacobson, Williams, Severeid ....$352-$528

1924 ST. LOUIS (NL) - Rickey, Bottomley, Hornsby, Blades, Hafey ....$1120-$1680

1924 WASHINGTON - Harris, Judge, Rice, Goslin, Johnson ....$1000-$1500

1925 BOSTON (AL) - Prothro, Boone, Carlyle, Ruffing.....................$320-$480

1925 BOSTON (NL) - Bancroft, Burrus, Welsh, Felix, Stengel, Marquard ....$552-$828

1925 BROOKLYN - Robinson, Fournier, Stock, Cox, Brown, Wheat, Taylor, Vance, Grimes..$880-$1320

1925 CHICAGO (AL) - Collins, Sheely, Hooper, Falk, Schalk, Lyons, Faber, Bender..$880-$1320

1925 CHICAGO (NL) - Maranville, Grimm, Freigau, Jahn, Hartnett, Alexander ....$800-$1200

1925 CINCINNATI - Walker, Roush, Hargrave, Rixey........................$348-$522

1925 CLEVELAND - Speaker, Burns, Sewell, McNulty, Buckeye..........$560-$840

1925 DETROIT - Cobb, Blue, Heilmann, Wingo, Manush, Gehringer ....$800-$1200

1925 NEW YORK (AL) - Huggins, Gehrig, Ruth, Hoyt, Pennock, Durocher ....$2780-$4170

1925 NEW YORK (NL) - McGraw, Terry, Kelly, Jackson, Lindstrom, Youngs, Meusel, Frisch, Wilson ....$1800-$2700

1925 PHILADELPHIA (AL) - Mack, Hale, Miller, Simmons, Lamar, Cochrane, Foxx, Rommel, Grove..$1360-$2040

1925 PHILADELPHIA (NL) - Hawks, Williams, Harper ....$280-$420

1925 PITTSBURGH - McKechnie, Grantham, Wright, Traynor, Cuyler, Carey, Barnhart, Smith, Meadows ....$720-$1080

1925 ST. LOUIS (AL) - Sisler, Rice, Jacobson, Williams ....$348-$522

1925 ST. LOUIS (NL) - Rickey, Bottomley, Hornsby, Hafey, Mueller, Blades, Haines ....$1200-$1840

1925 WASHINGTON - Harris, Judge, Rice, Goslin, Johnson, Coveleski ....$1000-$1500

1926 BOSTON (AL) - Jacobson, Ruffing...$304-$456

41

1959 New York Yankees

1926 BOSTON (NL) - Bancroft, J. Smith, Brown ....$320-$480
1926 BROOKLYN - Robinson, Herman, Wheat, Maranville, Carey, Grimes, Vance
....$1080-$1620
1926 CHICAGO - McCarthy, Adams, Wilson, Stephenson, Hartnett, Alexander
....$880-$1320
1926 CHICAGO (AL) - Collins, Barrett, Mostil, Falk, Schalk, Lyons, Faber
....$560-$840
1926 CINCINNATI - Walker, Roush, Donahue, Rixey ....$348-$522
1926 CLEVELAND - Speaker, Burns, J. Sewell, Summa, Uhle.................$560-$840
1926 DETROIT - Cobb, Gehringer, Heilmann, Manush, Fothergill ....$720-$1080
1926 NEW YORK (AL) - Huggins, Gehrig, Lazzeri, Ruth, Combs, Meusel, Pennock, Hoyt ....$3200-$4800
1926 NEW YORK (NL) - McGraw, Kelly, Frisch, Jackson, Lindstrom, Youngs, Terry, Ott..$1720-$2580
1926 PHILADELPHIA (AL) - Mack, French, Simmons, Cochrane, Foxx
....$1280-$1920
1926 PHILADELPHIA (NL) - Williams, Leach, Mokan, Wilson.............$272-$408
1926 PITTSBURGH - McKechnie, Grantham, Wright, Traynor, Waner, Carey, Cuyler, Smith, Cronin, Kremer, Meadows...$800-$1200
1926 ST. LOUIS (AL) - Sisler, Miller, Rice, Shang...................................$304-$456
1926 ST. LOUIS (NL) - Hornsby, Bottomley, Bell, Southworth, Douthit, Blades,

Hafey, Rhem, Haines, Alexander ....$1460-$2190
1926 WASHINGTON - Harris, Myer, Rice, McNeely, Goslin, Johnson, Coveleski
....$800-$1200
1927 BOSTON (AL) - Tobin, Ruffing ....$300-$450
1927 BOSTON (NL) - Bancroft, High, Richbourg, Brown ....$300-$450
1927 BROOKLYN - Robinson, Carey, Vance..$760-$1140
1927 CHICAGO (AL) - Schalk, Clancy, Metzler, Falk, Lyons, Faber ......$320-$480
1927 CHICAGO (NL) - McCarthy, Grimm, Webb, Wilson, Stephenson, Hartnett,
Root...$480-$720
1927 CINCINNATI - Hargrave, Kelly, Rixey...$288-$432
1927 CLEVELAND - Burns, Fonseca, J. Sewell, Jamieson, Miller ....$300-$450
1927 DETROIT - Gehringer, Heilmann, Manush, Fothergill, Collins ....$372-$558
1927 NEW YORK (AL) - Gehrig, Lazzeri, Ruth, Combs, Meusel, Hoyt, Moore,
Pennock...$8000-$14000
1927 NEW YORK (NL) - McGraw, Terry, Honrsby, Jackson, Lindstrom, Harper,
Roush, Grimes ....$1800-$2700
1927 PHILADELPHIA (AL) - Mack, Dykes, Hale, Cobb, Simmons, French,
Cochrane, Collins, Wheat, Foxx, Grove ....$2200-$3300
1927 PHILADELPHIA (NL) - Wrightstone, Thompson, Leach ....$252-$378
1927 PITTSBURGH - Harris, Grantham, Traynor, P. Waner, L. Waner, Barnhart,
Cuyler, Groh, Cronin, Kremer ....$620-$930
1927 ST. LOUIS (AL) - Sisler, Miller, Williams, Schang ....$300-$450
1927 ST. LOUIS (NL) - Bottomley, Frisch, Maranville, Haines, Alexander
....$1080-$1620
1927 WASHINGTON - Harris, Judge, Rice, Speaker, Goslin, Ruel, Lisenbee, Had-
ley, Johnson, Coveleski...$1120-$1680
1928 BOSTON (AL) - Myer, Williams, Ruffing ....$280-$420
1928 BOSTON (NL) - Hornsby, Sisler, Richbourg...................................$700-$1050
1928 BROOKLYN - Robinson, Bissonette, Bancroft, Hendrick, Herman, Carey,
Lopez, Vance ....$920-$1380
1928 CHICAGO (AL) - Schalk, Kamm, Metzler, Lyons, Walsh, Faber ....$480-$720
1928 CHICAGO (NL) - McCarthy, Cuyler, Wilson, Stephenson, Hartnett
....$448-$672
1928 CINCINNATI - Kelly, Allen, Rixey ....$280-$420
1928 CLEVELAND - Fonseca, Sewell, Hodapp, Jamieson......................$280-$420
1928 DETROIT - Gehringer, Heilmann, Rice...$320-$480
1928 NEW YORK (AL) - Huggins, Gehrig, Lazzeri, Koenig, Ruth, Combs, Dickey,
Pipgras, Hoyt, Pennock, Coveleski..$3200-$4800
1928 NEW YORK (NL) - McGraw, Terry, Jackson, Lindstrom, Ott, Welsh, O'Doul,
Hogan, Roush, Benton, Fitzsimmons, Hubbell.....................................$1120-$1680
1928 PHILADELPHIA (AL) - Mack, Bishop, Hale, Cobb, Miller, Simmons,
Cochrane, Foxx, Speaker, Collins, Grove, Quinn ....$2000-$3000
1928 PHILADELPHIA (NL) - Whitney, Klein, Leach ....$320-$480
1928 PITTSBURGH - Grantham, Wright, Traynor, P. Waner, L. Waner, Brickell,
Grimes..$500-$750
1928 ST. LOUIS (AL) - Manush, Crowder...$300-$450
1928 ST. LOUIS (NL) - McKechnie, Bottomley, Frisch, Maranville, Hafey, Haines,
Alexander...$1200-$1800

1928 WASHINGTON - Harris, Judge, Reeves, Rice, Barnes, Goslin, Cronin, Sisler, Jones...$480-$720
1929 BOSTON (AL) - Rothrock, Ruffing ....$220-$330
1929 BOSTON (NL) - Sisler, Maranville, Richbourg, Clark, Evers ....$680-$1020
1929 BROOKLYN - Robinson, Bancroft, Gilbert, Herman, Frederick, Bressler, Carey, Vance...$780-$1170
1929 CHICAGO (AL) - Shires, Reynolds, Lyons, Faber.........................$264-$396
1929 CHICAGO (NL) - McCarthy, Hornsby, Cuyler, Wilson, Hartnett, Malone
....$800-$1200
1929 CINCINNATI - Kelly, Dressen, Swanson, Gooch, Rixey ....$260-$390
1929 CLEVELAND - Fonseca, Hodapp, Sewell, Falk, Averill, Sewell, Ferrell
....$320-$480
1929 DETROIT - Harris, Alexander, Gehringer, Heilmann, Rice, Johnson
....$320-$480
1929 NEW YORK (AL) - Huggins, Gehrig, Lazzeri, Ruth, Combs, Dickey, Wells, Hoyt, Pennock ....$2720-$4080
1929 NEW YORK (NL) - McGraw, Terry, Jackson, Lindstrom, Ott, Roush, Hubbell
....$1060-$1590
1929 PHILADELPHIA (AL) - Mack, Foxx, Miller, Haas, Simmons, Cochrane, Cronin, Collins, Earnshaw, Grove...$800-$1200
1929 PHILADELPHIA (NL) - Hurst, Thompson, Thevenow, Whitney, Klein, Sothern, O'Doul...$300-$450
1929 PITTSBURGH - Grantham, Bartell, Traynor, P. Waner, L. Waner, Comorosky, Grimes..$496-$744
1929 ST. LOUIS (AL) - Kress, Schulte, Manush, Ferrell...........................$320-$480
1929 ST. LOUIS (NL) - McKechnie, Bottomley, Frisch, Orsatti, Douthit, Hafey, Wilson, Johnson, Haines, Alexander...$860-$1290
1929 WASHINGTON - Johnson, Judge, Myer, Cronin, Rice, Goslin ....$1160-$1740
1930 BOSTON (AL) - Webb, Ruffing ....$216-$324
1930 BOSTON (NL) - McKechnie, Sisler, Maranville, Grimes................$420-$630
1930 BROOKLYN - Robinson, Bissonette, Wright, Herman, Frederick, Lopez, Vance..$680-$1020
1930 CHICAGO (AL) - Watwood, Jolley, Reynolds, Lyons, Appling, Faber
....$240-$360
1930 CHICAGO (NL) - McCarthy, Grimm, Cuyler, Wilson, Hartnett, Hornsby, Kelly...$880-$1320
1930 CINCINNATI - Durocher, Cuccinello, Heilmann, Walker, Kelly, Rixey
....$880-$1320
1930 CLEVELAND - Morgan, Hodapp, J. Sewell, Porter, Averill, Jamieson, L. Sewell, Ferrell..$280-$420
1930 DETROIT - Harris, Alexander, Gehringer, McManus, Stone, Hoyt, Greenberg
....$292-$438
1930 NEW YORK (AL) - Gehrig, Lazzeri, Chapman, Ruth, Hoyt, Combs, Ruffing, Gomez, Pennock, Dickey..$2720-$4080
1930 NEW YORK (NL) - McGraw, Terry, Jackson, Lindstrom, Ott, Leach, Hogan, Bancroft, Roush, Hubbell...$1160-$1740
1930 PHILADELPHIA, (AL) - Mack, Foxx, Dykes, Miller, Simmons, Cochrane, Collins, Grove...$660-$990

44

1930 PHILADELPHIA (NL) - Hurst, Whitney, O'Doul, Davis, Alexander, Klein
....$688-$1032
1930 PITTSBURGH - Grantham, Bartell, Traynor, P. Waner, L. Waner, Comorosky
....$440-$660
1930 ST. LOUIS (AL) - Kress, Goslin, Ferrell, Manush ....$356-$534
1930 ST. LOUIS (NL) - Street, Bottomley, Frisch, Gelbert, Adams, Watkins, Douthit, Hafey, Wilson, Grimes, Haines, Dean ....$700-$1050
1930 WASHINGTON - Johnson, Judge, Myer, Cronin, Rice, Manush, Goslin, Marberry ....$1360-$2040
1931 BOSTON (AL) - Webb..$216-$324
1931 BOSTON (NL) - Maranville, Schulmerich, Berger, McKechnie ....$320-$480
1931 BROOKLYN - O'Doul, Lopez, Lombardi, Vance, Robinson ....$800-$1200
1931 CHICAGO (AL) - Blue, Appling, Faber, Lyons.............................$240-$360
1931 CHICAGO (NL) - Grimm, Hornsby, English, Cuyler, Wilson, Taylor, Hartnett, Herman ....$700-$1050
1931 CINCINNATI - Hendrick, Cuccinello, Stripp, Roush, Heilmann, Rixey
....$320-$480
1931 CLEVELAND - Morgan, Porter, Averill...$240-$360
1931 DETROIT - Alexander, Gehringer, Rogell, Stone, Hoyt, Harris........$292-$438
1931 NEW YORK (AL) - Gehrig, Lazzeri, Sewell, Ruth, Combs, Chapman, Dickey, Ruffing, Gomez, Pennock, McCarthy ....$2880-$4320
1931 NEW YORK (NL) - Terry, Jackson, Lindstrom, Ott, Leach, Hogan, Walker, Hubbell, McGraw..$960-$1440
1931 PHILADELPHIA (AL) - Mack, Foxx, Simmons, Cochrane, Grove, Earnshaw, Hoyt ....$624-$936
1931 PHILADELPHIA (NL) - Hurst, Mallon, Arlett, Klein, Davis..........$300-$450
1931 PITTSBURGH - Grantham, Traynor, Waner, Waner ....$420-$630
1931 ST. LOUIS (AL) - Melillo, Kress, Schulte, Goslin, Ferrell ....$300-$450
1931 ST. LOUIS (NL) - Bottomley, Frisch, Hafey, Hallahan, Grimes, Haines
....$560-$840
1931 WASHINGTON - Cronin, Rice, West, Manush, Crowder, Marberry, Johnson
....$1200-$1800
1932 BOSTON (AL) - Alexander, Jolley, Morris.......................................$228-$342
1932 BOSTON (NL) - Maranville, Berger, Worthington, McKechnie ....$300-$450
1932 BROOKLYN - Kelly, Wright, Stripp, Wilson, Taylor, O'Doul, Lopez, Clark, Vance, Hoyt, Carey..$580-$870
1932 CHICAGO (AL) - Appling, Lyons, Faber ....$320-$480
1932 CHICAGO (NL) - Grimm, Herman, Cuyler, Moore, Stephenson, Hartnett, Hornsby, Warneke, Grimes ....$700-$1050
1932 CINCINNATI - Hendrick, Durocher, Herman, Lombardi, Hafey, Heilmann, Frey ....$388-$582
1932 CLEVELAND - Cissell, Porter, Averill, Vosmik ....$240-$360
1932 DETROIT - Gehringer, Walker, Harris...$292-$438
1932 NEW YORK (AL) - Gehrig, Lazzeri, Sewell, Ruth, Combs, Dickey, Ruffing, Gomez, Allen, Pennock, McCarthy......................................$4400-$6600
1932 NEW YORK (NL) - Terry, Ott, Lindstrom, McGraw, Hogan, Jackson, Jo-Jo Moore, Hoyt, Hubbell ....$880-$1320
1932 PHILADELPHIA (AL) - Cramer, Haas, Simmons, Cochrane, Grove, Mack

1964 New York Mets

....$500-$750
1932 PHILADELPHIA (NL) - Hurst, Bartell, Klein, Davis, Lee, Davis ..$280-$420
1932 PITTSBURGH - Vaughn, Traynor, Waner, Waner ....$480-$720
1932 ST. LOUIS (AL) - Burns, Scharien, Goslin, Ferrell...........................$292-$438
1932 ST. LOUIS (NL) - Watkins, Martin, Orsatti, Frisch, Bottomley, Medwick, Dean, Haines..$448-$672
1932 WASHINGTON - Cronin, Reynolds, Manush, Rice, Crowder, Johnson
....$1200-$1800
1933 BOSTON (AL) - Hodapp, Johnson, Ferrell....................................$240-$360
1933 BOSTON (NL) - Maranville, Moore, Cantwell, McKechnie ....$300-$450
1933 BROOKLYN - Wright, Frederick, Wilson, Lopez, Mungo, Carey ....$460-$690
1933 CHICAGO (AL) - Appling, Swanson, Simmons, Lyons, Faber........$360-$540
1933 CHICAGO (NL) - Grimm, Stephenson, Hartnett, Cuyler, Bush, Grimes, Billy Herman ....$400-$600
1933 CINCINNATI - Bottomley, Hafey, Lombardi, Durocher, Rixey ....$388-$582
1933 CLEVELAND - Averill, Johnson ....$800-$1200
1933 DETROIT - Greenberg, Gehringer, Harris ....$340-$510
1933 NEW YORK (AL) - Gehrig, Lazzeri, Sewell, Ruth, Combs, Chapman, Dickey, Gomez, Allen, Ruffing, Pennock, McCarthy ....$2780-$4170
1933 NEW YORK (NL) - Terry, Ott, Jackson, Hubbell ....$520-$780
1933 PHILADELPHIA (AL) - Foxx, Higgins, Cochrane, Grove, Mack ..$392-$588

46

1933 PHILADELPHIA (NL) - Klein, Fullis, Schulmerich, Davis ....$300-$450
1933 PITTSBURGH - Piet, Vaughan, Traynor, Waner, Lindstrom, Waner, Hoyt
....$560-$840
1933 ST. LOUIS (AL) - West, Ferrell, Hornsby ....$440-$660
1933 ST. LOUIS (NL) - Collins, Frisch, Durocher, Martin, Medwick, Hornsby,
Haines, Dean, Vance, Grimes ....$920-$1380
1933 WASHINGTON - Kuhel, Myer, Cronin, Goslin, Manush, Rice, Crowder,
Whitehill ....$440-$660
1934 BOSTON (AL) - Harris, Reynolds, Johnson, R. Ferrell, W. Ferrell, Grove, Pen-
nock $340-510
1934 BOSTON (NL) - McKechnie, Jordan, Maranville, Frankhouse.........$280-$420
1934 BROOKLYN - Stengel, Leslie, Stripp, Boyle, Koenecke, Lopez, Mungo
.... $280-$420
1934 CHICAGO (AL) - Appling, Simmons, Conlan ....$376-$564
1934 CHICAGO (NL) - Grimm, Billy Herman, Hack, Cuyler, Klein, Hartnett
....$380-$570
1934 CINCINNATI - Bottomley, Hafey, Lombardi.............................$312-$468
1934 CLEVELAND - Johnson, Trosky, Hale, Knickerbocker, Averill, Vosmik,
Harder .... $760-$1140
1934 DETROIT - Cochrane, Greenberg, Gehringer, Fox, Goslin, Rowe, Bridges
....$488-$732
1934 NEW YORK (AL) - McCarthy, Gomez, Lazzeri, Dickey, Gehrig, Ruffing,
Grimes, Ruth, Combs...$2600-$3900
1934 NEW YORK (NL) - Terry, Jackson, Ott, Hubbell ....$380-$570
1934 PHILADELPHIA (AL) - Mack, Foxx, Higgins, Cramer, Johnson ..$308-$462
1934 PHILADELPHIA (NL) - Chiozza, Bartell, J. Moore, Allen, Todd ..$200-$300
1934 PITTSBURGH - Traynor, Vaughan, P. Waner, L. Waner, Lindstrom, Hoyt,
Grimes..$540-$810
1934 ST. LOUIS (AL) - Hornsby, West, Hemsley ....$408-$612
1934 ST. LOUIS (NL) - Frisch, Collins, Durocher, Martin, Orsatti, Medwick, Davis,
Dean, Haines, Grimes, Vance ....$540-$810
1934 WASHINGTON - Cronin, Manush ....$260-$390
1935 BOSTON (AL) - Cronin, Cooke, R. Johnson, R. Ferrell, W. Ferrell, Grove
....$280-$420
1935 BOSTON (NL) - McKechnie, Lee, Ruth, Maranville....................$1000-$1500
1935 BROOKLYN - Stengel, Leslie, Stripp, Lopez...............................$280-$420
1935 CHICAGO (AL) - Appling, Simmons, Conlan, Lyons, Stratton ....$372-$558
1935 CHICAGO (NL) - Grimm, Herman, Lee, Klein, Demaree, Galan, Hartnett,
Cuyler, Lindstrom, Hack...$460-$690
1935 CINCINNATI - Bottomley, Herman, Lombardi, Cuyler, Hafey, Derringer
....$320-$480
1935 CLEVELAND - Johnson, Averill ....$680-$1020
1935 DETROIT - Cochrane, Greenberg, Gehringer, Goslin.......................$460-$690
1935 NEW YORK (AL) - McCarthy, Gehrig, Lazzeri, Dickey, Combs, Ruffing,
Gomez...$1360-$2040
1935 NEW YORK (NL) - Terry, Jackson, Ott, Leiber, Hubbell ....$360-$540
1935 PHILADELPHIA (AL) - Mack, Foxx, Moses, Cramer ....$292-$438
1935 PHILADELPHIA (NL) - Moore, Allen ....$172-$258

1935 PITTSBURGH - Traynor, Vaughan, P. Waner, L. Waner, Hoyt........$440-$660
1935 ST. LOUIS (AL) - Hornsby, West, Solters, Andrews ....$396-$594
1935 ST. LOUIS (NL) - Frisch, Collins, Durocher, Martin, Medwick, Haines, P. Dean, D. Dean ....$360-$540
1935 WASHINGTON - Harris, Myer, Travis, Powell, Manush, Bolton.....$260-$390
1936 BOSTON (AL) - Cronin, Foxx, R. Ferrell, Hanush, Grove...............$400-$600
1936 BOSTON (NL) - McKechnie, Jordan, Cuccinello, Lopez ....$228-$342
1936 BROOKLYN - Stengel, Hassett, Stripp, Bordagaray, Lindstrom.......$260-$390
1936 CHICAGO (AL) - Appling, Lyons, Stratton....................................$260-$390
1936 CHICAGO (NL) - Grimm, Herman, Demaree, Hartnett, Klein, French
....$300-$450
1936 CINCINNATI - Scarsella, Cuyler, Lombardi, Hafey........................$260-$390
1936 CLEVELAND - Trosky, Hale, Weatherly, Averill, Sullivan, Allen ...$208-$312
1936 DETROIT - Cochrane, Gehringer, Simmons, Goslin, Greenberg ......$376-$564
1936 NEW YORK (AL) - McCarthy, Gehrig, Lazzeri, DiMaggio, Dickey, Ruffing, Gomez...$1360-$2040
1936 NEW YORK (NL) - Terry, Jackson, Ott, Moore, Mancuso, Hubbell $440-$660
1936 PHILADELPHIA (AL) - Mack, Finney, Moses.............................$232-$348
1936 PHILADELPHIA (NL) - Camilli, Klein, Moore.............................$200-$300
1936 PITTSBURGH - Traynor, Suhr, Vaughan, P. Waner, L. Waner, Hoyt
....$420-$630
1936 ST. LOUIS (AL) - Hornsby, Bottomley, Clift, Bell ....$432-$648
1936 ST. LOUIS (NL) - Frisch, Mize, Durocher, Martin, Alston, Dean, Haines
....$420-$630
1936 WASHINGTON - Harris, Travis, Chapman, Stone ....$216-$324
1937 BOSTON (AL) - Foxx, Cronin, Higgins, Chapman, Cramer, Doerr, Ferrell, Grove..$400-$600
1937 BOSTON (NL) - Lopez, McKechnie...$228-$342
1937 BROOKLYN - Hassett, Manush, Phelps, Hoyt, Grimes....................$336-$504
1937 CHICAGO (AL) - Appling, Stratton, Lyons...................................$260-$390
1937 CHICAGO (NL) - Herman, Demaree, Hartnett, Carleton, Grimm .. $260-$390
1937 CINCINNATI - Wallace, Hafey, Cuyler, Lombardi.........................$320-$480
1937 CLEVELAND - Campbell, Sotters, Pytlak, Feller, Averill................$240-$360
1937 DETROIT - Greenberg, Gehringer, Goslin, Cochrane.....................$320-$480
1937 NEW YORK (AL) - Gehrig, Lazzeri, DiMaggio, Dickey, Gomez, Ruffing, McCarthy ....$1360-$2040
1937 NEW YORK (NL) - Bartell, Ott, Ripple, Moore, Hubbell, Melton, Terry
....$400-$600
1937 PHILADELPHIA (AL) - Moses, Johnson, Mack ....$232-$348
1937 PHILADELPHIA (NL) - Camilli, Whitney, Klein..........................$200-$300
1937 PITTSBURGH - Vaughan, Waner, Waner, Todd, Traynor, Hoyt.......$420-$630
1937 ST. LOUIS (AL) - Clift, Bell, West, Vosmik, Hornsby, Bottomley ...$420-$630
1937 ST. LOUIS (NL) - Mize, Durocher, Padgett, Medwick, Martin, Frisch, Dean, Haines...$364-$546
1937 WASHINGTON (AL) - Travis, Lewis, Stone, Almada, Simmons, R. Ferrell, Harris...$276-$414
1938 BOSTON (AL) - Foxx, Doerr, Cronin, Higgins, Chapman, Cramer, Vosmik, Grove..$384-$576

1938 BOSTON (NL) - Stengel, Lopez, MacFayden ....$228-$342
1938 BROOKLYN - Grimes, Durocher, Phelps, Cuyler, Manush, Hoyt ....$392-$588
1938 CHICAGO (AL) - Hayes, Appling, Steinbacher, Walker, Stratton....$260-$390
1938 CHICAGO (NL) - Herman, Hack, Reynolds, Hartnett, Garbark, Lee, Grimm, Dean, Lazzeri................................$376-$564
1938 CINCINNATI - McKechnie, McCormick, Berger, Lombardi, Derringer, Vander Meer ....$252-$378
1938 CLEVELAND - Trosky, Averill, Heath, Pytlak, Boudreau, Feller.....$240-$360
1938 DETROIT - Cochrane, Greenberg, Gehringer, Walker, Bridges ....$260-$390
1938 NEW YORK (AL) - McCarthy, Gehrig, DiMaggio, Dickey, Ruffing, Gomez ....$1200-$1800
1938 NEW YORK (NL) - Terry, Ott, Moore, Danning, Hubbell................$340-$510
1938 PHILADELPHIA (AL) - Mack, Moses, Johnson ....$228-$342
1938 PHILADELPHIA (NL) - Weintraub................................$196-$294
1938 PITTSBURGH - Traynor, Vaughan, Waner, Waner, Rizzo, Manush, Brown ....$420-$630
1938 ST. LOUIS (AL) - McQuinn, Kress, Almada ....$200-$300
1938 ST. LOUIS (NL) - Frisch, Mize, Slaughter, Medwick, Martin..........$336-$504
1938 WASHINGTON - Harris, Myer, Travis, Case, Simmons, Ferrell, Goslin, Ferrell................................$308-$462
1939 BOSTON (AL) - Cronin, Foxx, Doerr, Williams, Cramer, Grove......$420-$630
1939 BOSTON (NL) - Stengel, Hassett, Cuccinello, Lopez, Simmons ......$288-$432
1939 BROOKLYN - Durocher, Lazzeri................................$368-$552
1939 CHICAGO (AL) - Kuhel, Appling, McNair, Lyons..........................$216-$324
1939 CHICAGO (NL) - Hartnett, Herman, Leiber, Galan, Hartnett, Dean $240-$360
1939 CINCINNATI - McKechnie, McCormick, Goodman, Lombardi, Simmons, Walters, Derringer ....$320-$480
1939 CLEVELAND - Trosky, Hale, Keltner, Boudreau, Feller ....$220-$330
1939 DETROIT - Greenberg, Gehringer, McCosky, Averill, Bridges ....$252-$378
1939 NEW YORK (AL) - McCarthy, Rolfe, Keller, DiMaggio, Selkirk, Dickey, Ruffing, Gehring, Gomez................................$480-$720
1939 NEW YORK (NL) - Terry, Bonura, Ott, Demaree, Danning, Lazzeri, Hubbell ....$384-$576
1939 PHILADELPHIA (AL) - Mack, Moses, Johnson, Collins................$272-$408
1939 PHILADELPHIA (NL) - Suhr, Arnovich, Davis ....$172-$258
1939 PITTSBURGH - Traynor, Fletcher, Vaughan, P. Waner, L. Waner, Manush ....$384-$576
1939 ST. LOUIS (AL) - McQuinn, Laabs................................$180-$270
1939 ST. LOUIS (NL) - Mize, Slaughter, Medwick, P. Martin ....$316-$474
1939 WASHINGTON - Harris, Vernon, Lewis, Case, Wright, Ferrell, Leonard ....$200-$300
1940 BOSTON (AL) - Cronin, Foxx, Doerr, Williams, Wilson, Grove......$400-$600
1940 BOSTON (NL) - Stengel, Rowell, Cooney, Lopez ....$240-$360
1940 BROOKLYN - Durocher, Reese, Medwick................................$336-$504
1940 CHICAGO (AL) - Appling, Wright, Solters, Lyons..........................$208-$312
1940 CHICAGO (NL) - Hartnett, Herman, Dean................................$212-$318
1940 CINCINNATI - McKechnie, F. McCormick, Lombardi ....$360-$540
1940 CLEVELAND - Boudreau, Weatherly, Feller, Smith ....$200-$300

1965 New York Mets

1940 DETROIT - York, Gehringer, McCosky, Greenberg, Averill, Newsom
....$336-$504
1940 NEW YORK (AL) - McCarthy, DiMaggio, Dickey, Ruffing, Gomez
....$420-$630
1940 NEW YORK (NL) - Terry, Ott, Demaree, Danning, Hubbell...........$320-$480
1940 PHILADELPHIA (AL) - Mack, Moses, Hayes, Simmons...............$260-$390
1940 PHILADELPHIA (NL)-...$160-$240
1940 PITTSBURGH - Frisch, Vaughan, P. Waner, L. Waner, Lopez.........$316-$474
1940 ST. LOUIS (AL) - Judnich, Radcliff..$180-$270
1940 ST. LOUIS (NL) - Mize, Slaughter, P. Martin, Medwick...................$288-$432
1940 WASHINGTON - Harris, Lewis, Ferrell, Vernon...............................$192-$288
1941 BOSTON (AL) - Cronin, Foxx, Doerr, DiMaggio, Williams, Grove.$440-$660
1941 BOSTON (NL) - Cooney, Waner, Stengel................................$240-$360
1941 BROOKLYN - Durocher, Camilli, Herman, Reese, Medwick, Waner
....$372-$558
1941 CHICAGO (AL) - Appling, Lyons..$220-$330
1941 CHICAGO (NL) - Hack, Herman, Dean ....$180-$270
1941 CINCINNATI - McKechnie, Lombardi, Waner...................................$252-$378
1941 CLEVELAND - Boudreau, Heath, Lemon, Feller ....$184-$276
1941 DETROIT - Gehringer, McCosky, Radcliff, Greenberg, Benton ....$220-$330
1941 NEW YORK (AL) - McCarthy, Rizzuto, DiMaggio, Dickey, Gomez, Ruffing

....$640-$960

1941 NEW YORK (NL) - Terry, Bartell, Ott, Hubbell..............................$320-$480

1941 PHILADELPHIA (AL) - Mack, Siebert, Moses, Chapman, Collins, Simmons
....$320-$480

1941 PHILADELPHIA (NL) - Litwhiler, Etten ....$160-$240

1941 PITTSBURGH - Frisch, Vaughan, Lopez, Waner ....$252-$378

1941 ST. LOUIS (AL) - Ferrell..$192-$288

1941 ST. LOUIS (NL) - Mize, Brown, Slaughter, Hopp, Musial..............$300-$450

1941 WASHINGTON - Harris, Vernon, Travis, Ferrell, Wynn...................$224-$336

1942 BOSTON (AL) - Cronin, Doerr, Williams, Foxx ....$380-$570

1942 BOSTON (NL) - Stengel, Lombardi, Sain, Spahn ....$248-$372

1942 BROOKLYN - Durocher, Herman, Reese, Vaughan, Reiser, Medwick, Wyatt,
French ....$320-$480

1942 CHICAGO (AL) - Appling, Lyons...$220-$330

1942 CHICAGO (NL) - Cavarretta, Hack, Novikoff, Foxx ....$224-$336

1942 CINCINNATI - McKechnie, Vander Meer ....$208-$312

1942 CLEVELAND - Boudreau..$188-$282

1942 DETROIT - Gehringer, Trucks, Newhouser................................$208-$312

1942 NEW YORK (AL) - McCarthy, Gordon, Rizzuto, DiMaggio, Dickey, Ruffing,
Gomez..$600-$900

1942 NEW YORK (NL) - Ott, Mize, Hubbell ....$320-$480

1942 PHILADELPHIA (AL) - Mack, Collins.......................................$280-$420

1942 PHILADELPHIA (NL) - Waner ....$192-$288

1942 PITTSBURGH - Frisch, Lopez ....$200-$300

1942 ST. LOUIS (AL) - Ferrell..$196-$294

1942 ST. LOUIS (NL) - Slaughter, Musial, W. Cooper, M. Cooper, Beazley
....$360-$540

1942 WASHINGTON - Harris, Vernon, Wynn......................................$200-$300

1943 BOSTON (AL) - Cronin, Doerr ....$208-$312

1943 BOSTON (NL) - Stengel, McCarthy ....$220-$330

1943 BROOKLYN - Durocher, Herman, Vaughan, Bordagaray, Walker, Olmo,
Waner, Hodges, Medwick, Wyatt ....$320-$480

1943 CHICAGO (AL) - Appling, Grove ....$196-$294

1943 CHICAGO (NL) - Cavarretta, Nicholson, Goodman..........................$196-$294

1943 CINCINNATI - McKechnie, McCormick, Vander Meer ....$208-$312

1943 CLEVELAND - Boudreau, Smith ....$188-$282

1943 DETROIT - Cramer, Wakefield, Trout, Trucks ....$196-$294

1943 NEW YORK (AL) - McCarthy, Dickey, Chandler............................$380-$570

1943 NEW YORK (NL) - Ott, Witek, Medwick, Lombardi, Adams ....$320-$480

1943 PHILADELPHIA (AL) - Mack, Kell..$208-$312

1943 PHILADELPHIA (NL) - Rowe, Barrett ....$184-$276

1943 PITTSBURGH - Frisch, Elliott, Lopez, Sewell ....$200-$300

1943 ST. LOUIS (AL) - Ferrell, Dean ....$196-$294

1943 ST. LOUIS (NL) - Musial, W. Cooper......................................$308-$462

1943 WASHINGTON - Vernon, Wynn, Gomez ....$220-$330

1944 BOSTON (AL) - Cronin, Doerr, Fox, Johnson, Hughson..................$208-$312

1944 BOSTON (NL) - Holmes ....$184-$276

1944 BROOKLYN - Durocher, Walker, Galan, P. Waner, L. Waner, Vaughan

....$260-$390
1944 CHICAGO (AL) - Schalk...$208-$312
1944 CHICAGO (NL) - Grimm, Cavarretta, Dallessandro, Foxx ....$208-$312
1944 CINCINNATI - McKechnie, McCormick, Tiptop, Walters ....$208-$312
1944 CLEVELAND - Boudreau...$188-$282
1944 DETROIT - Wakefield, Newhouser.....................................$220-$330
1944 NEW YORK (AL) - McCarthy, Lindell, Martin, Waner...................$212-$318
1944 NEW YORK (NL) - Ott, Weintraub, Medwick, Lombardi, Voiselle
....$320-$480
1944 PHILADELPHIA (AL) - Mack, Simmons ....$248-$372
1944 PHILADELPHIA (NL) ....$184-$276
1944 PITTSBURGH - Russell, Lopez, Sewell, Frisch ....$208-$312
1944 ST. LOUIS (AL) - Kreevich, Potter.................................$220-$330
1944 ST. LOUIS (NL) - Marion, Musial, Hopp, W. Cooper, Martin, M. Cooper
....$340-$510
1944 WASHINGTON - Spence, Ferrell, Wynn ....$204-$306
1945 BOSTON (AL) - Cronin...$200-$300
1945 BOSTON (NL) - Holmes ....$184-$276
1945 BROOKLYN - Durocher, Galan, Walker, Rosen, Olmo...................$180-$270
1945 CHICAGO (AL) - Appling...$192-$288
1945 CHICAGO (NL) - Grimm, Cavarretta, Johnson, Hack, Wyse.........$220-$330
1945 CINCINNATI - McKechnie...$208-$312
1945 CLEVELAND - Boudreau, Feller.......................................$188-$282
1945 DETROIT (AL) - Greenberg, Newhouser................................$260-$390
1945 NEW YORK (AL) - McCarthy, Waner, Ruffing ....$212-$318
1945 NEW YORK (NL) - Ott, Lombardi, Mungo.............................$288-$432
1945 PHILADELPHIA (AL) - Mack, Kell....................................$208-$312
1945 PHILADELPHIA (NL) - Wasdell, Foxx ....$208-$312
1945 PITTSBURGH - Frisch, Lopez, Waner.................................$228-$342
1945 ST. LOUIS (AL) - Muncrief ....$188-$282
1945 ST. LOUIS (NL) - Kurowski, Schoendienst, Barrett, Burkhart, Brecheen
....$192-$288
1945 WASHINGTON - Lewis, Ferrell, Wolff.................................$200-$300
1946 BOSTON (AL) - Cronin, Doerr, Pesky, DiMaggio, Williams, Ferriss
....$320-$480
1946 BOSTON (NL) - Holmes, Herman, Sain, Spahn.........................$212-$318
1946 BROOKLYN - Durocher, Reese, Medwick, Higbe ....$240-$360
1946 CHICAGO (AL) - Lyons, Appling, Caldwell...........................$208-$312
1946 CHICAGO (NL) - Grimm, Waitkus.....................................$180-$270
1946 CINCINNATI - McKechnie, Walters ....$208-$312
1946 CLEVELAND - Boudreau, Edwards, Lemon, Feller ....$212-$318
1946 DETROIT - Kell, Newhouser ....$212-$318
1946 NEW YORK (AL) - McCarthy, Rizzuto, DiMaggio, Dickey, Berra, Ruffing,
Chandler...$460-$690
1946 NEW YORK (NL) - Ott, Mize, Lombardi ....$340-$510
1946 PHILADELPHIA (AL) - Mack, Valo, McCosky, Kell ....$212-$318
1946 PHILADELPHIA (NL) - Ennis, Rowe...................................$196-$294
1946 PITTSBURGH - Frisch, Kiner, Lopez ....$212-$318

1946 ST. LOUIS (AL) - Stephens..$188-$282
1946 ST. LOUIS (NL) - Musial, Schoendienst, Kurowski, Slaughter, Walker, Garagiola, Pollet...$380-$570
1946 WASHINGTON - Vernon, Grace, Leonard, Wynn.............................$188-$282
1947 BOSTON (AL) - Cronin, Doerr, Pesky, Williams, Dobson................$220-$330
1947 BOSTON (NL) - Elliott, Holmes, Spahn, Sain...................................$208-$312
1947 BROOKLYN - Robinson, Reese, Vaughan, Snider, Hodges, Branca, Hatten
....$560-$840
1947 CHICAGO (AL) - Lyons, Appling, Wright......................................$204-$306
1947 CHICAGO (NL) - Grimm, Pafko, Cavarretta...................................$180-$270
1947 CINCINNATI - Galan, Kluszewski, Blackwell................................$180-$270
1947 CLEVELAND - Boudreau, Mitchell, Feller, Lemon.........................$212-$318
1947 DETROIT - Kell...$212-$318
1947 NEW YORK (AL) - McQuinn, Rizzuto, DiMaggio, Berra, Reynolds, Shea
....$600-$900
1947 NEW YORK (NL) - Ott, Mize, Cooper, Jansen...............................$320-$480
1947 PHILADELPHIA (AL) - Mack, Valo, Fox, Marchildon.................$212-$318
1947 PHILADELPHIA (NL) - Walker, Leonard, Rowe.........................$200-$300
1947 PITTSBURGH - Herman, Greenberg, Kiner...................................$208-$312
1947 ST. LOUIS (AL) - Dean...$216-$324
1947 ST. LOUIS (NL) - Musial, Schoendienst, Garagiola, Medwick, Munger
....$260-$390
1947 WASHINGTON - Vernon, Wynn...$188-$282
1948 BOSTON (AL) - McCarthy, Doerr, Pesky, Williams.......................$212-$318
1948 BOSTON (NL) - Dark, Sain, Spahn..$260-$390
1948 BROOKLYN - Durocher, Hodges, Robinson, Reese, Furillo, Campanella, Roe, Vaughan, Snider, Branca, Erskine..$560-$840
1948 CHICAGO (AL) - Lyons, Appling..$204-$306
1948 CHICAGO (NL) - Grimm..$180-$270
1948 CINCINNATI - Kluszewski...$180-$270
1948 CLEVELAND - Boudreau, Mitchell, Bearden, Lemon, Feller, Paige
....$360-$540
1948 DETROIT - Kell, Cramer, Newhouser, Trucks...............................$212-$318
1948 NEW YORK (AL) - Rizzuto, DiMaggio, Berra, Raschi...................$420-$630
1948 NEW YORK (NL) - Ott, Durocher, Mize...$320-$480
1948 PHILADELPHIA (AL) - Mack, Fox...$212-$318
1948 PHILADELPHIA (NL) - Sisler, Ashburn, Leonard, Rowe, Roberts
....$200-$300
1948 PITTSBURGH - Kiner...$184-$276
1948 ST. LOUIS (AL) -..$188-$282
1948 ST. LOUIS (NL) - Schoendienst, Slaughter, Musial, Garagiola, Medwick
....$260-$390
1948 WASHINGTON - Vernon, Wynn...$188-$282
1949 BOSTON (AL) - McCarthy, Doerr, Williams, Parnell.....................$212-$318
1949 BOSTON (NL) - Spahn, Sain...$200-$300
1949 BROOKLYN - Hodges, Robinson, Reese, Furillo, Roe, Newcombe, Campanella, Snider, Connors..$600-$900
1949 CHICAGO (AL) - Appling..$200-$300

1969 Atlanta Braves

1949 CHICAGO (NL) - Grimm, Frisch, Burgess.......................................$200-$300
1949 CINCINNATI - Kluszewski..$180-$270
1949 CLEVELAND - Boudreau, Vernon, Mitchell, Lemon, Feller, Wynn
....$200-$300
1949 DETROIT - Kell, Wertz, Evers, Trucks..$212-$318
1949 NEW YORK (AL) - Stengel, Rizzuto, Berra, DiMaggio, Mize, Raschi, Reynolds $640-$960
1949 NEW YORK (NL) - Durocher, Mize, Marshall, Thomson, Irvin......$260-$390
1949 PHILADELPHIA (AL) - Mack, Fox ....$212-$318
1949 PHILADELPHIA (NL) - Sisler, Meyer, Roberts...............................$208-$312
1949 PITTSBURGH - Hopp, Kiner ....$192-$288
1949 ST. LOUIS (AL) - Dillinger, Sievers...$188-$282
1949 ST. LOUIS (NL) - Schoendienst, Musial, Slaughter, Garagiola, Pollet
....$220-$330
1949 WASHINGTON ....$180-$270
1950 BOSTON (AL) - McCarthy, Dropo, Doerr, Pesky, Williams ....$212-$318
1950 BOSTON (NL) - Jethroe, Spahn, Sain..$180-$270
1950 BROOKLYN - Hodges, Robinson, Reese, Furillo, Roe, Campanella, Newcombe, Snider..$560-$840
1950 CHICAGO (AL) - Fox, Appling ....$200-$300
1950 CHICAGO (NL) - Frisch, Pafko ....$200-$300

1950 CINCINNATI - Kluszewski, Adcock..$180-$270
1950 CLEVELAND - Boudreau, Rosen, Doby, Mitchell, Lemon, Wynn, Feller
....$200-$300
1950 DETROIT - Kell, Wertz, Groth, Evers ....$192-$288
1950 NEW YORK (AL) - Stengel, Martin, Rizzuto, Bauer, DiMaggio, Woodling,
Berra, Mize, Ford ....$688-$1032
1950 NEW YORK (NL) - Dark, Irvin, Jansen, Maglie ....$300-$450
1950 PHILADELPHIA (AL) - Mack, Dillinger, Lehner ....$208-$312
1950 PHILADELPHIA (NL) - Ennis, Ashburn, Roberts, Simmons, Konstanty
....$288-$432
1950 PITTSBURGH - Hopp, Kiner ....$192-$288
1950 ST. LOUIS (AL) -...$184-$276
1950 ST. LOUIS (NL) - Musial, Schoendienst, Garagiola ....$200-$300
1950 WASHINGTON - Vernon ....$180-$270
1951 BOSTON (AL) - Doerr, Pesky, Boudreau ....$212-$318
1951 BOSTON (NL) - Spahn, Sain...$180-$270
1951 BROOKLYN - Hodges, Robinson, Reese, Snider, Campanella, Roe, New-
combe.. $560-$840
1951 CHICAGO (AL) - Fox, Minoso ....$192-$288
1951 CHICAGO (NL) - Frisch, Connors, Burgess.................................$208-$312
1951 CINCINNATI - Kluszewski, Adcock...$180-$270
1951 CLEVELAND - Lopez, Avila, Feller, Wynn, Lemon ....$200-$300
1951 DETROIT - Kell, Trucks..$184-$276
1951 NEW YORK (AL) - Stengel, Mize, Rizzuto, Brown, DiMaggio, Mantle,
McDougald, Berra, Martin...$720-$1080
1951 NEW YORK (NL) - Durocher, Dark, Mays, Irvin, Maglie...............$380-$570
1951 PHILADELPHIA (AL) - Fain, Shantz...$184-$276
1951 PHILADELPHIA (NL) - Ashburn, Roberts ....$180-$270
1951 PITTSBURGH - Kiner, Garagiola..$192-$288
1951 ST. LOUIS (AL) - Paige, Gaedel..$224-$336
1951 ST. LOUIS (NL) - Schoendienst, Slaughter, Musial, Garagiola.........$200-$300
1951 WASHINGTON - Vernon ....$160-$240
1952 BOSTON (AL) - Boudreau, Goodman, Kell, Williams.....................$192-$288
1952 BOSTON (NL) - Grimm, Mathews, Spahn......................................$200-$300
1952 BROOKLYN - Hodges, Robinson, Reese, Furillo, Snider, Campanella, Black,
Erskine ....$600-$900
1952 CHICAGO (AL) - Fox, Minoso ....$200-$300
1952 CHICAGO (NL) - Fondy, Baumholtz, Sauer, Hacker.......................$176-$264
1952 CINCINNATI - Hornsby, Kluszewski, Adcock...............................$256-$384
1952 CLEVELAND - Avila, Rosen, Mitchell, Wynn, Garcia, Lemon, Feller
....$200-$300
1952 DETROIT - Kell, Kuenn...$180-$270
1952 NEW YORK (AL) - Stengel, Martin, Reynolds, Mantle, Berra, Raschi, Woo-
dling, Brown, Mize, Rizzuto...$520-$780
1952 NEW YORK (NL) - Durocher, Dark, Irvin, Maglie, Wilhelm ....$280-$420
1952 PHILADELPHIA (AL) - Fain, Shantz...$180-$270
1952 PHILADELPHIA (NL) - Ashburn, Roberts ....$180-$270
1952 PITTSBURGH - Groat, Kiner, Garagiola ....$200-$300

1952 ST. LOUIS (AL) - Hornsby, Paige..$280-$420
1952 ST. LOUIS (NL) - Schoendienst, Slaughter, Musial............................$200-$300
1952 WASHINGTON - Vernon ....$160-$240
1953 BOSTON - Boudreau, Goodman, Kell, Williams, Parnell ....$192-$288
1953 BROOKLYN - Hodges, Meyer, Reese, Furillo, Snider, Robinson, Campanella, Erskine, Gilliam...$640-$960
1953 CHICAGO (AL) - Fox, Minoso, Trucks..$220-$330
1953 CHICAGO (NL) - Fondy, Baumholtz, Kiner, Garagiola, Banks ....$200-$300
1953 CINCINNATI - Hornsby, Kluszewski, Bell...$256-$384
1953 CLEVELAND - Lopez, Rosen, Westlake, Mitchell, Lemon, Wynn, Feller
....$236-$354
1953 DETROIT - Kuenn, Boone, Kaline ....$180-$270
1953 MILWAUKEE - Grimm, Adcock, Mathews, Spahn, Burdette ....$220-$330
1953 NEW YORK (AL) - Stengel, Martin, Rizzuto, Mantle, Berra, Mize, Ford
....$540-$810
1953 NEW YORK (NL) - Durocher, Dark, Mueller, Thomson, Irvin ....$260-$390
1953 PHILADELPHIA (AL) - Philley...$160-$240
1953 PHILADELPHIA (NL) - Ashburn, Roberts ....$176-$264
1953 PITTSBURGH - Kiner, Garagiola..$200-$300
1953 ST. LOUIS (AL) -...$160-$240
1953 ST. LOUIS (NL) - Schoendienst, Slaughter, Musial, Haddix, Staley
....$192-$288
1953 WASHINGTON - Vernon, Busby, Porterfield...$160-$240
1954 BALTIMORE -...$144-$216
1954 BOSTON - Boudreau, Jensen, Williams ....$184-$276
1954 BROOKLYN - Alston, Hodges, Gilliam, Reese, Furillo, Lasorda, Robinson, Campanella, Erskine, Newcombe, Snider...$480-$720
1954 CHICAGO (AL) - Fox, Kell, Trucks, Minoso..$208-$312
1954 CHICAGO (NL) - Banks, Kiner, Garagiola ....$200-$300
1954 CINCINNATI - Kluszewski, Temple ....$176-$264
1954 CLEVELAND - Lopez, Avila, Lemon, Wynn, Feller.........................$300-$450
1954 DETROIT - Kuenn, Kaline ....$180-$270
1954 MILWAUKEE - Grimm, Adcock, Mathews, Aaron, Spahn, Burdette
....$240-$360
1954 NEW YORK (AL) - Stengel, Rizzuto, Mantle, Berra, Slaughter, Grim, Ford
....$460-$690
1954 NEW YORK (NL) - Durocher, Mays, Irvin, Antonelli, Maglie, Wilhelm
....$400-$600
1954 PHILADELPHIA - Ashburn, Burgess, Roberts.....................................$168-$252
1954 PHILADELPHIA (AL) - Finigan...$160-$240
1954 PITTSBURGH - Gordon ....$160-$240
1954 ST. LOUIS - Schoendienst, Musial, Moon ....$180-$270
1954 WASHINGTON - Vernon, Killebrew...$152-$228
1955 BALTIMORE - Robinson ....$152-$228
1955 BOSTON - Goodman, Jensen, Piersall, Williams...................................$184-$276
1955 BROOKLYN - Hodges, Gilliam, Reese, Labine, Furillo, Snider, Campanella, Newcombe, Robinson, Erskine, Koufax ....$960-$1440
1955 CHICAGO (AL) - Fox, Kell, Donovan, Trucks ....$200-$300

1955 CHICAGO (NL) - Banks..$160-$240
1955 CINCINNATI - Kluszewski, Burgess ....$180-$270
1955 CLEVELAND - Lopez, Smith, Kiner, Colavito, Lemon, Wynn, Score, Feller
....$240-$360
1955 DETROIT - Kuenn, Kaline, Bunning...$180-$270
1955 KANSAS CITY - Boudreau, Slaughter.....................................$168-$252
1955 MILWAUKEE - Mathews, Aaron, Adcock, Spahn, Burdette...........$260-$390
1955 NEW YORK (AL) - Stengel, Mantle, Slaughter, Howard, Martin, Berra, Rizzuto, Ford, Larsen...$580-$870
1955 NEW YORK (NL) - Durocher, Mays, Irvin, Antonelli.....................$260-$390
1955 PHILADELPHIA - Ashburn, Roberts..$160-$240
1955 PITTSBURGH - Groat, Clemente, Friend..............................$480-$720
1955 ST. LOUIS - Musial, Schoendienst, Boyer, Virdon, Haddix.............$180-$270
1955 WASHINGTON - Vernon, Killebrew...$140-$210
1956 BALTIMORE - Kell, Gastall, Robinson ....$160-$240
1956 BOSTON - Vernon, Jensen, Williams ....$184-$276
1956 BROOKLYN - Hodges, Gilliam, Reese, Furillo, Snider, Campanella, Koufax, Newcombe, Erskine, Drysdale, Robinson...$600-$900
1956 CHICAGO (AL) - Fox, Aparicio, Kell ....$200-$300
1956 CHICAGO (NL) - Banks, Irvin...$160-$240
1956 CINCINNATI - Kluszewski, Robinson....................................$220-$330
1956 CLEVELAND - Lopez, Colavito, Lemon, Wynn, Score, Feller ....$220-$330
1956 DETROIT - Kuenn, Kaline, Bunning..$180-$270
1956 KANSAS CITY - Boudreau, Slaughter, Lasorda....................$180-$270
1956 MILWAUKEE - Grimm, Adcock, Mathews, Aaron, Spahn, Burdette
....$264-$396
1956 NEW YORK (AL) - Stengel, Martin, Mantle, Howard, Rizzuto, Slaughter, Berra, Bauer, Ford ....$640-$960
1956 NEW YORK (NL) - White, Schoendienst, Mays, Antonelli.............$220-$330
1956 PHILADELPHIA - Ashburn, Roberts..$144-$216
1956 PITTSBURGH - Mazeroski, Groat, Clemente, Virdon.....................$512-$768
1956 ST. LOUIS - Musial, Boyer, Schoendienst, Peete ....$192-$288
1956 WASHINGTON - Killebrew..$144-$216
1957 BALTIMORE - Kell, Robinson..$152-$228
1957 BOSTON - Jensen, Williams, Vernon ....$180-$270
1957 BROOKLYN - Hodges, Gilliam, Reese, Furillo, Snider, Campanella, Koufax, Drysdale...$400-$600
1957 CHICAGO (AL) - Lopez, Fox, Aparicio ....$200-$300
1957 CHICAGO (NL) - Banks..$160-$240
1957 CINCINNATI - Robinson, Kluszewski....................................$220-$330
1957 CLEVELAND - Colavito, Maris, Wynn, Wilhelm ....$180-$270
1957 DETROIT - Kuenn, Kaline, Bunning..$180-$270
1957 KANSAS CITY - Martin...$180-$270
1957 MILWAUKEE - Schoendienst, Mathews, Aaron, Adcock, Spahn ....$360-$540
1957 NEW YORK (AL) - Stengel, Slaughter, Berra, Howard, Sturdivant, Ford
.... $460-$690
1957 NEW YORK (NL) - Mays, Schoendienst, McCormick, White.........$220-$330
1957 PHILADELPHIA - Ashburn, Sanford, Roberts...............................$140-$210

1973 Oakland A's

1957 PITTSBURGH - Mazeroski, Groat, Clemente, Friend......................$512-$768
1957 ST. LOUIS - Musial, Boyer, Wilhelm...$192-$288
1957 WASHINGTON - Killebrew..$140-$210
1958 BALTIMORE - Robinson, Wilhelm...$152-$228
1958 BOSTON - Runnels, Williams..$180-$270
1958 CHICAGO (AL) - Fox, Aparicio, Cash, Wynn ....$200-$300
1958 CHICAGO (NL) - Banks..$160-$240
1958 CINCINNATI - Robinson, Pinson..$220-$330
1958 CLEVELAND - Vernon, Colavito, Maris, Wilhelm, Lemon ....$180-$270
1958 DETROIT - Martin, Kaline, Kuenn, Bunning....................................$180-$270
1958 KANSAS CITY - Maris ....$180-$270
1958 LOS ANGELES - Alston, Hodges, Furillo, Snider, Reese, Drysdale, Koufax,
Howard ....$280-$420
1958 MILWAUKEE - Schoendienst, Mathews, Aaron, Spahn, Burdette
....$288-$432
1958 NEW YORK - Kubek, Mantle, Berra, Howard, Slaughter, Turley, Ford, Larsen
....$480-$720
1958 PHILADELPHIA - Ashburn, Roberts..$120-$180
1958 PITTSBURGH - Kluszewski, Mazeroski, Groat, Clemente, Friend
....$540-$810
1958 SAN FRANCISCO - Cepeda, Mays, White, McCormick ....$224-$336

1958 ST. LOUIS - Musial, Boyer...$160-$240
1958 WASHINGTON - Pearson, Killebrew...$140-$210
1959 BALTIMORE - Robinson, Wilhelm..$160-$240
1959 BOSTON - Runnels, Williams..$180-$270
1959 CHICAGO (AL) - Lopez, Fox, Aparicio, Cash, Kluszewski, Wynn
....$340-$510
1959 CHICAGO (NL) - Banks, Williams...$160-$240
1959 CINCINNATI - Robinson, Pinson..$220-$330
1959 CLEVELAND - Martin, Colavito, Perry, Score...............................$160-$240
1959 DETROIT - Kuenn, Kaline, Bunning..$140-$210
1959 KANSAS CITY - Maris...$180-$270
1959 LOS ANGELES - Alston, Hodges, Gilliam, Snider, Koufax, Furillo, Drysdale,
Howard, Wills...$320-$480
1959 MILWAUKEE - Adcock, Mathews, Aaron, Vernon, Slaughter, Schoendienst,
Spahn ....$240-$360
1959 NEW YORK - Stengel, Kubek, Mantle, Berra, Howard, Slaughter, Ford,
Larsen ....$388-$582
1959 PHILADELPHIA - Sparky Anderson, Ashburn, Roberts ....$120-$180
1959 PITTSBURGH - Stuart, Mazeroski, Groat, Clemente, Kluszewski, Friend
....$540-$810
1959 SAN FRANCISCO - Cepeda, Mays, McCovey, McCormick ....$240-$360
1959 ST. LOUIS - Musial, Boyer, White, McDaniel, Gibson....................$160-$240
1959 WASHINGTON - Killebrew, Allison, Kaat......................................$140-$210
1960 BALTIMORE - Hansen, Robinson, Wilhelm ....$160-$240
1960 BOSTON - Runnels, Williams..$180-$270
1960 CHICAGO (AL) - Lopez, Fox, Aparicio, Kluszewski, Wynn, Score
....$160-$240
1960 CHICAGO (NL) - Grimm, Boudreau, Banks, Santo, Ashburn, Williams
....$160-$240
1960 CINCINNATI - Robinson, Martin, Pinson.....................................$240-$360
1960 CLEVELAND - Aspromonte, Kuenn, Piersall, Perry.......................$100-$150
1960 DETROIT - Cash, Colavito, Kaline, Bunning.................................$140-$210
1960 KANSAS CITY -...$100-$150
1960 LOS ANGELES - Alston, Wills, Howard, Davis, Snider, Hodges, Davis, Kou-
fax, Drysdale, Gilliam ....$260-$390
1960 MILWAUKEE - Adcock, Mathews, Aaron, Schoendienst, Spahn, Burdette,
Torre...$208-$312
1960 NEW YORK - Stengel, Kubek, Maris, Mantle, Howard, Berra, Ford
....$500-$750
1960 PHILADELPHIA - Roberts ....$100-$150
1960 PITTSBURGH - Stuart, Mazeroski, Clemente, Law, Vernon.........$800-$1200
1960 SAN FRANCISCO - McCovey, Mays, Cepeda, McCormick, Marichal
....$240-$360
1960 ST. LOUIS - White, Boyer, Musial, McCarver, Gibson....................$228-$342
1960 WASHINGTON - Killebrew, Versalles, Kaat ....$140-$210
1961 BALTIMORE - Robinson, Powell, Wilhelm ....$144-$216
1961 BOSTON - Jensen, Yastrzemski ....$160-$240
1961 CHICAGO (AL) - Lopez, Fox, Aparicio, Pierce, Wynn...................$148-$222

1961 CHICAGO (NL) - Banks, Santo, Ashburn, Hubbs, Brock, Williams
....$176-$264
1961 CINCINNATI - Robinson, Pinson, Jay ....$320-$480
1961 CLEVELAND - Piersall, McDowell ....$92-$138
1961 DETROIT - Cash, Kaline, Colavito, Bunning, Freehan ....$136-$204
1961 KANSAS CITY -...$100-$150
1961 LOS ANGELES (AL) -...$200-$300
1961 LOS ANGELES (NL) - Alston, Wills, T. Davis, W. Davis, Howard, Snider, Drysdale, Koufax..$240-$360
1961 MILWAUKEE - Adcock, Mathews, Aaron, Torre, Spahn, Martin ....$180-$270
1961 MINNESOTA - Lavagetto, Killebrew, Martin, Versalles, Kaat.........$200-$300
1961 NEW YORK - Kubek, Maris, Mantle, Berra, Howard, Tresh, Ford
....$880-$1320
1961 PHILADELPHIA -..$96-$144
1961 PITTSBURGH - Stuart, Mazeroski, Clemente, Clendenon, Friend
....$540-$810
1961 SAN FRANCISCO - McCovey, Mays, Cepeda, Marichal, McCormick
....$232-$348
1961 ST. LOUIS - White, Boyer, Musial, Schoendienst, McCarver, Gibson
....$220-$330
1961 WASHINGTON - Vernon ....$128-$192
1962 BALTIMORE - Robinson, Powell, Roberts, Wilhelm ....$160-$240
1962 BOSTON - Yastrzemski..$160-$240
1962 CHICAGO (AL) - Lopez, Fox, Wynn, Peters, DeBusschere............$140-$210
1962 CHICAGO (NL) - Banks, Hubbs, Santo, Brock, Williams...............$172-$258
1962 CINCINNATI - Robinson, Pinson..$176-$264
1962 CLEVELAND - McDowell ....$92-$138
1962 DETROIT - Cash, Kaline, Colavito, Bunning.................................$120-$180
1962 HOUSTON - Aspromonte ....$208-$312
1962 KANSAS CITY ....$92-$138
1962 LOS ANGELES (AL) - Lee Thomas, Fregosi ....$140-$210
1962 LOS ANGELES (NL) - Alston, Gilliam, Wills, Howard, W. Davis, T. Davis, Snider, Drysdale, Koufax ....$240-$360
1962 MILWAUKEE - Adcock, Mathews, Aaron, Uecker, Spahn ....$152-$228
1962 MINNESOTA - Versalles, Killebrew, Oliva, Kaat............................$176-$264
1962 NEW YORK (AL) - Tresh, Maris, Mantle, Howard, Berra, Kubek, Terry, Ford
....$460-$690
1962 NEW YORK (NL) - Stengel, Hodges, Kranepool............................$300-$450
1962 PHILADELPHIA -..$92-$138
1962 PITTSBURGH - Mazeroski, Groat, Clemente, Clendenon, Stargell.$500-$750
1962 SAN FRANCISCO - Cepeda, Mays, McCovey, Marichal, McCormick, Perry
....$368-$552
1962 ST. LOUIS - White, Boyer, Musial, Schoendienst, Gibson ....$220-$330
1962 WASHINGTON - Vernon ....$128-$192
1963 BALTIMORE - Aparicio, Robinson, Powell, Roberts ....$160-$240
1963 BOSTON - Yastrzemski...$168-$252
1963 CHICAGO (AL) - Lopez, Fox, Peters, Wilhelm, DeBusschere ....$116-$174
1963 CHICAGO (NL) - Banks, Hubbs, Santo, Brock, Williams...............$160-$240

1980 Kansas City Royals

1963 CINCINNATI - Rose, Harper, Pinson, Robinson ....$176-$264
1963 CLEVELAND - Adcock, McDowell, John...$92-$138
1963 DETROIT - Cash, Kaline, Colavito, Lolich, McLain ....$120-$180
1963 HOUSTON - Staub, Aspromonte, Morgan, Umbricht.....................$152-$228
1963 KANSAS CITY -...$88-$132
1963 LOS ANGELES (AL) - Fregosi, Chance ....$80-$120
1963 LOS ANGELES (NL) - Alston, Gilliam, Wills, Howard, W. Davis, T. Davis, Koufax, Drysdale...$320-$480
1963 MILWAUKEE - Mathews, Aaron, Torre, Uecker, Spahn ....$144-$216
1963 MINNESOTA - Versalles, Killebrew, Oliva, Kaat............................$168-$252
1963 NEW YORK (AL) - Maris, Howard, Mantle, Berra, Ford ....$380-$570
1963 NEW YORK (NL) - Stengel, Snider, Kranepool, Hodges ....$240-$360
1963 PHILADELPHIA - Allen...$88-$132
1963 PITTSBURGH - Clendenon, Mazeroski, Clemente, Stargell, Mota .$480-$720
1963 SAN FRANCISCO - Cepeda, Mays, McCovey, Marichal, Larsen, Perry ....$220-$330
1963 ST. LOUIS - Groat, Boyer, McCarver, Musial, Gibson ....$240-$360
1963 WASHINGTON - Vernon, Hodges...$104-$156
1964 BALTIMORE - Aparicio, Robinson, Powell, Piniella, Roberts.........$160-$240
1964 BOSTON - Herman, Yastrzemski..$176-$264
1964 CHICAGO (AL) - Lopez, Wilhelm..$104-$156

1964 CHICAGO (NL) - Banks, Santo, Williams, Brock, Kessinger ....$140-$210
1964 CINCINNATI - Rose, Robinson, Pinson, Perez ....$160-$240
1964 CLEVELAND - McDowell, Tiant, John......................................$92-$138
1964 DETROIT - Cash, Kaline, Freehan, Lolich, McLain........................$128-$192
1964 HOUSTON - Fox, Aspromonte, Staub, Morgan ....$88-$132
1964 KANSAS CITY - Colavito, Campaneris, Odom................................$88-$132
1964 LOS ANGELES (AL) - Adcock, Fregosi, Chance.......................$80-$100
1964 LOS ANGELES (NL) - Alston, Wills, Howard, W. Davis, T. Davis, Koufax, Drysdale ....$240-$360
1964 MILWAUKEE - Mathews, Aaron, Carty, Torre, Spahn, Niekro.......$160-$240
1964 MINNESOTA - Versalles, Oliva, Killebrew, Kaat ....$180-$270
1964 NEW YORK (AL) - Berra, Maris, Mantle, Howard, Ford, Stottlemyre
....$320-$480
1964 NEW YORK (NL) - Stengel, Kranepool ....$200-$300
1964 PHILADELPHIA - Allen, Bunning...$88-$132
1964 PITTSBURGH - Clendenon, Mazeroski, Clemente, Mota ....$420-$630
1964 SAN FRANCISCO - Cepeda, Mays, McCovey, Snider, Marichal, Perry, Larsen...$200-$300
1964 ST. LOUIS - White, Boyer, Brock, McCarver, Uecker, Gibson ....$368-$552
1964 WASHINGTON - Hodges ....$104-$156
1965 BALTIMORE - Powell, Aparicio, Robinson, Blefary, Palmer, Roberts
....$184-$276
1965 BOSTON - Herman, Yastrzemski..$184-$276
1965 CALIFORNIA - Fregosi ....$80-$120
1965 CHICAGO (AL) - Lopez, John, Wilhelm.....................................$100-$150
1965 CHICAGO (NL) - Banks, Santo, Williams....................................$104-$156
1965 CINCINNATI - Rose, Robinson, Pinson, Perez ....$144-$216
1965 CLEVELAND - Colavito, McDowell, Tiant....................................$92-$138
1965 DETROIT - Cash, Kaline, Freehan, McLain, Lolich........................$128-$192
1965 HOUSTON - Morgan, Staub, Fox, Roberts....................................$96-$144
1965 KANSAS CITY - Campaneris, Hunter, Paige, Odom ....$96-$144
1965 LOS ANGELES - Alston, Lefebvre, Wills, W. Davis, Koufax, Drysdale
....$320-$480
1965 MILWAUKEE - Mathews, Aaron, Torre, Niekro ....$160-$240
1965 MINNESOTA - Versalles, Oliva, Killebrew, Kaat ....$236-$354
1965 NEW YORK (AL) - Mantle, Howard, Maris, Murcer, Stottlemyre, Ford
....$296-$444
1965 NEW YORK (NL) - Stengel, Kranepool, Swoboda, Berra, Spahn ...$240-$360
1965 PHILADELPHIA - Allen, Bunning, Jenkins ....$88-$132
1965 PITTSBURGH - Mazeroski, Clemente, Stargell ....$408-$612
1965 SAN FRANCISCO - McCovey, Mays, Cepeda, Marichal, Perry, Spahn
....$176-$264
1965 ST. LOUIS - Schoendienst, White, Boyer, Brock, McCarver, Uecker, Gibson, Carlton ....$200-$300
1965 WASHINGTON - Hodges, Howard, McCormick ....$120-$180
1966 ATLANTA - Mathews, Aaron, Torre, Niekro..................................$152-$228
1966 BALTIMORE - Aparicio, B. Robinson, F. Robinson, Palmer ....$308-$462
1966 BOSTON - Herman, Yastrzemski, Lonborg....................................$208-$312

1966 CALIFORNIA - Fregosi ....$80-$120
1966 CHICAGO (AL) - Agee, John, Wilhelm ....$100-$150
1966 CHICAGO (NL) - Banks, Santo, Jenkins, Roberts ....$120-$180
1966 CINCINNATI - Perez, Rose, Helms, Harper, Pinson ....$144-$216
1966 CLEVELAND - Colavito, Tiant, McDowell...$92-$138
1966 DETROIT - Cash, Kaline, Freehan, McLain, Lolich.........................$128-$192
1966 HOUSTON - Morgan, Staub, Roberts ....$96-$144
1966 KANSAS CITY - Campaneris, Hunter, Odom......................................$96-$144
1966 LOS ANGELES - Wills, W. Davis, T. Davis, Koufax, Drysdale, Sutton
....$292-$438
1966 MINNESOTA - Killebrew, Oliva, Kaat...$160-$240
1966 NEW YORK (AL) - Maris, Mantle, Howard, Stottlemyre, Ford ......$272-$408
1966 NEW YORK (NL) - Kranepool, Boyer, Swoboda, Ryan...................$224-$336
1966 PHILADELPHIA - White, Allen, Uecker, Bunning, Jenkins ....$88-$132
1966 PITTSBURGH - Clendenon, Mazeroski, Clemente, Stargell, Mota .$400-$600
1966 SAN FRANCISCO - McCovey, Mays, Cepeda, Marichal, Perry......$160-$240
1966 ST. LOUIS - Schoendienst, Cepeda, Brock, McCarver, Gibson, Carlton
....$200-$300
1966 WASHINGTON - Hodges, Howard ....$116-$174
1967 ATLANTA - Aaron, Carty, Uecker, Niekro ....$144-$216
1967 BALTIMORE (AL) - Powell, Aparicio, B. Robinson, F. Robinson, Palmer
....$180-$270
1967 BOSTON (AL) - Yastrzemski, Howard, Lonborg, Lyle ....$308-$462
1967 CALIFORNIA (AL) - Fregosi ....$80-$120
1967 CHICAGO (AL) - Colavito, Boyer, John, Wilhelm..........................$100-$150
1967 CHICAGO (NL) - Durocher, Banks, Santo, Williams, Jenkins.........$120-$180
1967 CINCINNATI - Pinson, Rose, Bench..$144-$216
1967 CLEVELAND (AL) - Adcock, McDowell, Tiant ....$88-$132
1967 DETROIT (AL) - Cash, Kaline, Freehan, Mathews, McLain, Lolich
....$140-$210
1967 HOUSTON - Mathews, Morgan, Staub...$96-$144
1967 KANSAS CITY (AL) - Appling, Jackson, Hunter, Odom.................$136-$204
1967 LOS ANGELES - Alston, Davis, Drysdale, Sutton............................$192-$288
1967 MINNESOTA (AL) - Killebrew, Carew, Oliva, Kaat ....$160-$240
1967 NEW YORK (AL) - Mantle, Howard, Stottlemyre, Ford ....$228-$342
1967 NEW YORK (NL) - Kranepool, Harrelson, Swoboda, Seaver, Koosman
....$320-$480
1967 PHILADELPHIA - White, Allen, Uecker, Groat, Bunning ....$88-$132
1967 PITTSBURGH - Mazeroski, Wills, Clemente, Stargell ....$400-$600
1967 SAN FRANCISCO (NL) - McCovey, Mays, McCormick, Perry, Marichal
....$160-$240
1967 ST. LOUIS - Schoendienst, Cepeda, Maris, Brock, McCarver, Carlton, Gibson
....$288-$432
1967 WASHINGTON (AL) - Hodges, Howard ....$116-$174
1968 ATLANTA - Aaron, Torre, Niekro...$144-$216
1968 BALTIMORE - Weaver, Powell, B. Robinson, F. Robinson.............$180-$270
1968 BOSTON - Yastrzemski, Howard, Lyle ....$120-$180
1968 CALIFORNIA - Fregosi ....$80-$120

1986 Los Angeles Dodgers

1968 CHICAGO (AL) - Lopez, Aparicio, John..$100-$150
1968 CHICAGO (NL) - Durocher, Banks, Santo, Williams, Jenkins.........$120-$180
1968 CINCINNATI - Perez, Rose, Pinson, Bench......................................$160-$240
1968 CLEVELAND - Tiant, McDowell...$80-$120
1968 DETROIT - Cash, Freehan, Kaline, McLain, Lolich........................$232-$348
1968 HOUSTON - Staub, Morgan ....$80-$120
1968 LOS ANGELES - Alston, Davis, Drysdale, Sutton...........................$168-$252
1968 MINNESOTA - Carew, Oliva, Killebrew, Kaat ....$160-$240
1968 NEW YORK (AL) - Mantle, Bahnsen ....$188-$282
1968 NEW YORK (NL) - Hodges, Kranepool, Harrelson, Swoboda, Koosman,
Seaver, Ryan ....$380-$570
1968 OAKLAND - Bando, Jackson, Odom, Hunter, Fingers ....$136-$204
1968 PHILADELPHIA - White, Allen..$80-$120
1968 PITTSBURGH - Mazeroski, Wills, Clemente, Stargell, Oliver, Bunning
....$400-$600
1968 SAN FRANCISCO - McCovey, Bonds, Mays, Marichal, Perry, McCormick
....$160-$240
1968 ST. LOUIS - Schoendienst, Cepeda, Maris, Brock, Simmons, Gibson, Carlton,
McCarver...$208-$312
1968 WASHINGTON - Howard..$88-$132
1969 ATLANTA - Cepeda, Aaron, Evans, Niekro, Wilhelm ....$160-$240

1969 BALTIMORE - Weaver, Powell, B. Robinson, F. Robinson, Cueller, Palmer
....$220-$330
1969 BOSTON - Yastrzemski, Lyle...$116-$174
1969 CALIFORNIA - Fregosi, Wilhelm...$80-$120
1969 CHICAGO (AL) - Lopez, Aparicio, John.................................$100-$150
1969 CHICAGO (NL) - Durocher, Banks, Santo, Williams, Jenkins.........$120-$180
1969 CINCINNATI - Perez, Rose, Bench..$160-$240
1969 CLEVELAND - McDowell, Tiant..$80-$120
1969 DETROIT - Cash, Kaline, Freehan, McLain, Lolich.........................$120-$180
1969 HOUSTON - Morgan...$80-$120
1969 KANSAS CITY - Piniella ....$240-$360
1969 LOS ANGELES - Alston, Sizemore, Wills, Davis, Drysdale, Bunning, Buckner, Garvey...$160-$240
1969 MINNESOTA - Carew, Killebrew, Oliva, Nettles, Kaat.....................$176-$264
1969 MONTREAL - Staub ....$180-$270
1969 NEW YORK (AL) - Murcer, Munson, Stottlemyre ....$180-$270
1969 NEW YORK (NL) - Harrelson, Swoboda, Seaver, Koosman, Ryan.$420-$630
1969 OAKLAND - Bando, Jackson, Odom, Hunter, Fingers, Blue ....$144-$216
1969 PHILADELPHIA - Allen...$88-$132
1969 PITTSBURGH - Oliver, Mazeroski, Clemente, Stargell, Bunning....$380-$570
1969 SAN DIEGO - ....$200-$300
1969 SAN FRANCISCO - McCovey, Bonds, Mays, Marichal, Perry ....$160-$240
1969 SEATTLE - Harper...$320-$480
1969 ST. LOUIS - Pinson, Torre, Simmons, Gibson, Carlton, Schoendienst, Brock,
McCarver..$140-$210
1969 WASHINGTON - Williams, Howard..$128-$192
1970 ATLANTA - Cepeda, Aaron, Evans, Niekro, Wilhelm ....$120-$180
1970 BALTIMORE - Weaver, Powell, B. Robinson, F. Robinson, Palmer $260-$390
1970 BOSTON - Yastrzemski, Lyle...$116-$174
1970 CALIFORNIA - Fregosi ....$76-$114
1970 CHICAGO (AL) - Aparicio, John...$92-$138
1970 CHICAGO (NL) - Durocher, Banks, Santo, Williams, Jenkins, Wilhelm
....$120-$180
1970 CINCINNATI - Anderson, Concepcion, Perez, Rose, Bench ....$192-$288
1970 CLEVELAND - Nettles, Pinson, McDowell.................................$80-$120
1970 DETROIT - Cash, Kaline, Freehan, Lolich ....$104-$156
1970 HOUSTON - Morgan...$76-$114
1970 KANSAS CITY - Lemon, Piniella...$12-$180
1970 LOS ANGELES - Alston, Wills, Garvey, Buckner, Sutton.................$160-$240
1970 MILWAUKEE - Harper ....$76-$114
1970 MINNESOTA - Killebrew, Oliva, Carew, Perry, Kaat, Tiant ....$140-$210
1970 MONTREAL - Staub, Morton...$104-$156
1970 NEW YORK (AL) - Murcer, Munson, Stottlemyre ....$180-$270
1970 NEW YORK (NL) - Hodges, Koosman, Harrelson, Swoboda, Kranepool,
Seaver, Ryan, Clendenon ....$248-$372
1970 OAKLAND - Bando, Jackson, Hunter, Fingers.............................$148-$222
1970 PHILADELPHIA - Bowa, McCarver, Bunning, Luzinski ....$100-$150
1970 PITTSBURGH - Mazeroski, Clemente, Stargell, Oliver..................$440-$660

1970 SAN DIEGO - ....$100-$150
1970 SAN FRANCISCO - McCovey, Bonds, Mays, Foster, Perry, Marichal
....$160-$240
1970 ST. LOUIS - Allen, Torre, Brock, Simmons, Gibson, Carlton............$128-$192
1970 WASHINGTON - Williams, Howard..$128-$192
1971 ATLANTA - Aaron, Evans, Williams, Cepeda, Niekro, Wilhelm......$120-$180
1971 BALTIMORE - Weaver, Powell, B. Robinson, F. Robinson, Palmer
....$200-$300
1971 BOSTON - Aparicio, Fisk, Lyle, Tiant....................................$128-$192
1971 CALIFORNIA - Fregosi ....$76-$114
1971 CHICAGO (AL) - John ....$80-$120
1971 CHICAGO (NL) - Santo, Williams, Banks, Jenkins ....$100-$150
1971 CINCINNATI - Concepcion, Perez, Rose, Foster, Bench ....$180-$270
1971 CLEVELAND - Chambliss, Nettles, Pinson, McDowell ....$80-$120
1971 DETROIT - Martin, Cash, Kaline, Freehan, Lolich........................$128-$192
1971 HOUSTON - Morgan..$72-$108
1971 KANSAS CITY - Lemon, Piniella..$80-$120
1971 LOS ANGELES - Alston, Wills, Garvey, Buckner, Sutton, Wilhelm
....$160-$240
1971 MILWAUKEE - Harper ....$76-$114
1971 MINNESOTA - Killebrew, Carew, Oliva, Blyleven, Kaat ....$104-$156
1971 MONTREAL - Staub..$72-$108
1971 NEW YORK (AL) - Murcer, Munson, Stottlemyre ....$180-$270
1971 NEW YORK (NL) - Hodges, Kranepool, Harrelson, Seaver, Ryan, Koosman
....$220-$330
1971 OAKLAND - Bando, Jackson, Hunter, Blue, Fingers.......................$180-$270
1971 PHILADELPHIA - Bowa, McCarver, Luzinski, Bunning ....$104-$156
1971 PITTSBURGH - Clemente, Oliver, Stargell, Mazeroski....................$520-$780
1971 SAN DIEGO - ....$72-$108
1971 SAN FRANCISCO - McCovey, Bonds, Mays, Kingman, Foster, Marichal,
Perry..$160-$240
1971 ST. LOUIS - Schoendienst, Torre, Brock, Simmons, Carlton, Gibson
....$120-$180
1971 WASHINGTON - Williams, Harrah, Howard, McLain ....$160-$240
1972 ATLANTA - Mathews, Aaron, Evans, Cepeda, Niekro ....$120-$180
1972 BALTIMORE - Weaver, Powell, Robinson ....$108-$162
1972 BOSTON - Aparicio, Yastrzemski, Fisk, Tiant ....$128-$192
1972 CALIFORNIA - Pinson, Ryan..$80-$120
1972 CHICAGO (AL) - Allen, Gossage..$80-$120
1972 CHICAGO (NL) - Durocher, Santo, Williams, Jenkins ....$92-$138
1972 CINCINNATI - Anderson, Perez, Morgan, Concepcion, Rose, Bench, Foster
....$240-$360
1972 CLEVELAND - Nettles, Bell, Perry...$80-$120
1972 DETROIT - Cash, Northrup, Freehan, Kaline, Lolich ....$140-$210
1972 HOUSTON - Durocher..$72-$108
1972 KANSAS CITY - Piniella ....$80-$120
1972 LOS ANGELES - Alston, Garvey, Robinson, Davis, Sutton, John, Wilhelm
....$160-$240

1972 MILWAUKEE - Scott .... $76-$114
1972 MINNESOTA - Killebrew, Carew, Oliva, Blyleven, Kaat .... $104-$156
1972 MONTREAL - Singleton, McCarver .... $68-$102
1972 NEW YORK (AL) - Murcer, Munson, Stottlemyre .... $180-$270
1972 NEW YORK (NL) - Hodges, Berra, Kranepool, Harrelson, Mays, Staub, Seaver, Matlack, Koosman .... $200-$300
1972 OAKLAND - Bando, Jackson, Cepeda, Hunter, Fingers, Blue .... $272-$408
1972 PHILADELPHIA - Bowa, Luzinski, McCarver, Boone, Schmidt, Carlton
.... $104-$156
1972 PITTSBURGH - Stargell, Clemente, Oliver, Mazeroski .... $480-$720
1972 SAN DIEGO - .... $72-$108
1972 SAN FRANCISCO - McCovey, Bonds, Mays, Marichal .... $120-$180
1972 ST. LOUIS - Schoendienst, Torre, Brock, Simmons, Gibson .... $100-$150
1972 TEXAS - Williams, Howard, Harrah .... $140-$210
1973 ATLANTA - Mathews, Aaron, P. Niekro, J. Niekro .... $120-$180
1973 BALTIMORE - Weaver, Powell, Robinson, Bumbry, Palmer .... $208-$312
1973 BOSTON - Yastrzemski, Aparicio, Fisk, Cepeda, Evans, Tiant .... $140-$210
1973 CALIFORNIA - Pinson, Robinson, Ryan .... $92-$138
1973 CHICAGO (AL) - Kaat, Gossage .... $80-$120
1973 CHICAGO (NL) - Kessinger, Williams, Jenkins .... $68-$102
1973 CINCINNATI - Anderson, Perez, Concepcion, Rose, Bench, Foster $220-$330
1973 CLEVELAND - Perry .... $80-$120
1973 DETROIT - Martin, Cash, Northrup, Freehan, Kaline, Lolich, Perry $120-$180
1973 HOUSTON - Richard .... $68-$102
1973 KANSAS CITY - Piniella, Brett .... $92-$138
1973 LOS ANGELES - Alston, Buckner, Cey, Davis, Garvey, Sutton, John
.... $120-$180
1973 MILWAUKEE - Thomas .... $80-$120
1973 MINNESOTA - Carew, Oliva, Killebrew, Blyleven, Kaat .... $104-$156
1973 MONTREAL - Singleton .... $68-$102
1973 NEW YORK (AL) - Nettles, Murcer, Munson, Stottlemyre, McDowell, Lyle
.... $188-$282
1973 NEW YORK (NL) - Berra, Harrelson, Staub, Jones, Kranepool, Seaver, Koosman .... $200-$300
1973 OAKLAND - Bando, Jackson, Hunter, Blue, Fingers .... $280-$420
1973 PHILADELPHIA - Bowa, Schmidt, Luzinski, Boone, Carlton .... $100-$150
1973 PITTSBURGH - Oliver, Stargell, Parker .... $108-$162
1973 SAN DIEGO - Winfield .... $76-$114
1973 SAN FRANCISCO - McCovey, Bonds, Matthews, Marichal .... $100-$150
1973 ST. LOUIS - Schoendienst, Torre, Brock, Simmons, McCarver, Gibson
.... $96-$144
1973 TEXAS - Martin, Harrah, Burroughs, Madlock .... $96-$144
1974 ATLANTA - Mathews, Evans, Aaron, P. Niekro .... $120-$180
1974 BALTIMORE - Weaver, Powell, Robinson, Palmer .... $208-$312
1974 BOSTON - Yastrzemski, Evans, Fisk, Cooper, Rice, Lynn, McCarver, Marichal
.... $140-$210
1974 CALIFORNIA - Robinson, Ryan .... $92-$138
1974 CHICAGO (AL) - Allen, Kaat, Gossage .... $80-$120

1983 Detroit Tigers

1974 CHICAGO (NL) - Kessinger, Madlock ....$68-$102
1974 CINCINNATI - Anderson, Perez, Morgan, Concepcion, Foster, Rose, Bench
....$220-$330
1974 CLEVELAND - G. Perry, J. Perry ....$100-$150
1974 DETROIT - Freehan, Horton, Kaline, Lolich......................................$92-$138
1974 HOUSTON - Wilson, Richard..$68-$102
1974 KANSAS CITY - Brett, Pinson ....$88-$132
1974 LOS ANGELES - Alston, Garvey, Cey, Buckner, Sutton, Marshall, John
....$200-$300
1974 MILWAUKEE - Yount..$80-$120
1974 MINNESOTA - Carew, Oliva, Killebrew, Blyleven ....$100-$150
1974 MONTREAL - Singleton, Davis, Carter ....$68-$102
1974 NEW YORK (AL) - Nettles, Murcer, Munson, Lyle, McDowell......$188-$282
1974 NEW YORK (NL) - Harrelson, Staub, Jones, Kranepool, Koosman, Seaver
....$128-$192
1974 OAKLAND - Bando, Jackson, Hunter, Blue, Fingers........................$272-$408
1974 PHILADELPHIA - Bowa, Schmidt, Luzinski, Boone ....$100-$150
1974 PITTSBURGH - Oliver, Stargell, Parker, Tekulve ....$140-$210
1974 SAN DIEGO - McCovey, Winfield..$80-$120
1974 SAN FRANCISCO - Kingman, Bonds..$68-$102
1974 ST LOUIS - Torre, McBride, Brock, Simmons, McCarver, Gibson.....$92-$138

1974 TEXAS - Martin, Hargrove, Harrah, Burroughs, Jenkins.....................$96-$144
1975 ATLANTA - Evans, Niekro...$68-$102
1975 BALTIMORE - Weaver, Robinson, Palmer..................................$104-$156
1975 BOSTON - Yastrzemski, Evans, Lynn, Rice, Fisk, Cooper, Conigliaro, McCarver, Tiant...$220-$330
1975 CALIFORNIA - Ryan...$80-$120
1975 CHICAGO (AL) - Kaat, Gossage ....$72-$108
1975 CHICAGO (NL) - Madlock...$68-$102
1975 CINCINNATI - Anderson, Perez, Morgan, Concepcion, Rose, Foster, Bench
....$320-$480
1975 CLEVELAND - Robinson ....$104-$156
1975 DETROIT - Freehan, Horton, Lolich...$76-$114
1975 HOUSTON - Richard..$64-$96
1975 KANSAS CITY - Brett, Killebrew ....$88-$132
1975 LOS ANGELES - Alston, Garvey, Cey, Buckner, Sutton, John ....$104-$156
1975 MILWAUKEE - Yount, Aaron...$100-$150
1975 MINNESOTA - Carew, Bostock, Oliva, Blyleven...........................$88-$132
1975 MONTREAL - Carter ....$68-$102
1975 NEW YORK (AL) - Martin, Nettles, Bonds, Munson, Piniella, Hunter, Lyle, Guidry..$192-$288
1975 NEW YORK (NL) - Kranepool, Staub, Kingman, Grote, Seaver, Koosman
....$120-$180
1975 OAKLAND - Bando, Jackson, Williams, Blue, Fingers, Odom.........$140-$210
1975 PHILADELPHIA - Allen, Schmidt, Luzinski, Boone, McCarver, Carlton
....$100-$150
1975 PITTSBURGH - Stargell, Parker, Oliver, Candelaria, Tekulve ....$140-$210
1975 SAN DIEGO - McCovey, Winfield...$76-$114
1975 SAN FRANCISCO - Murcer, Clark..$72-$108
1975 ST LOUIS - Schoendienst, Brock, Simmons, Hernandez, Gibson.......$88-$132
1975 TEXAS - Martin, Harrah, Jenkins, Perry..$96-$144
1976 ATLANTA - Murphy, Niekro ....$64-$96
1976 BALTIMORE - Weaver, Jackson, Robinson, Palmer.......................$104-$156
1976 BOSTON - Yastrzemski, Evans, Lynn, Rice, Fisk, Cooper, Tiant, Jenkins
....$108-$162
1976 CALIFORNIA - Ryan...$80-$120
1976 CHICAGO (AL) - Gossage ....$60-$90
1976 CHICAGO (NL) - Madlock..$60-$90
1976 CINCINNATI - Anderson, Perez, Morgan, Concepcion, Rose, Griffey, Foster, Bench, Zachry...$260-$390
1976 CLEVELAND - Robinson, Powell, Bell ....$68-$102
1976 DETROIT - Staub, Freehan, Horton, Fidrych ....$76-$114
1976 HOUSTON - Richard..$60-$90
1976 KANSAS CITY - Brett..$120-$180
1976 LOS ANGELES - Alston, Garvey, Cey, Buckner, Sutton, John ....$104-$156
1976 MILWAUKEE - Yount, Aaron, Frisella ....$100-$150
1976 MINNESOTA - Carew, Bostock, Oliva, Blyleven............................$72-$108
1976 MONTREAL - Carter, Dawson..$72-$108
1976 NEW YORK (AL) - Martin, Nettles, Munson, Hunter, Lyle ....$216-$324

1976 NEW YORK (NL) - Kranepool, Harrelson, Kingman, Torre, Koosman, Seaver, Lolich .... $116-$174
1976 OAKLAND - Williams, Blue, Fingers .... $76-$114
1976 PHILADELPHIA - Allen, Bowa, Schmidt, Luzinski, Boone, McCarver, Carlton, Kaat .... $120-$180
1976 PITTSBURGH - Stargell, Parker, Oliver, Candelaria, Tekulve .... $116-$174
1976 SAN DIEGO - Winfield, McCovey, Jones, Metzger .... $88-$132
1976 SAN FRANCISCO - Evans, Murcer, Clark .... $68-$102
1976 ST. LOUIS - Schoendienst, Hernandez, Brock, Simmons .... $88-$132
1976 TEXAS - Harrah, Thompson, Perry, Blyleven .... $72-$108
1977 ATLANTA - Niekro .... $60-$90
1977 BALTIMORE - Weaver, Murray, Robinson, Palmer .... $100-$150
1977 BOSTON - Evans, Lynn, Yastrzemski, Fisk, Rice, Tiant, Jenkins ..... $108-$162
1977 CALIFORNIA - Grich, Bonds, Ryan .... $80-$120
1977 CHICAGO (AL) - B. Lemon .... $60-$90
1977 CHICAGO (NL) - Buckner, Trillo, Murcer, R. Reuschel .... $60-$90
1977 CINCINNATI - Anderson, Morgan, Concepcion, Rose, Griffey, Foster, Bench, Seaver .... $116-$174
1977 CLEVELAND - Robinson, Bell, Eckersley .... $68-$102
1977 DETROIT - Staub, Trammell, Whitaker, Morris .... $100-$150
1977 HOUSTON - Richard .... $60-$90
1977 KANSAS CITY - Brett .... $120-$180
1977 LOS ANGELES - Lasorda, Garvey, Cey, Mota, John, Sutton .... $172-$258
1977 MILWAUKEE - Cooper, Yount .... $76-$114
1977 MINNESOTA - Carew, Bostock .... $68-$102
1977 MONTREAL - Perez, Dawson, Carter .... $80-$120
1977 NEW YORK (AL) - Martin, Nettles, Jackson, Munson, Piniella, Guidry, Lyle, Hunter .... $260-$390
1977 NEW YORK (NL) - Harrelson, Kranepool, Kingman, Grote, Koosman, Seaver .... $100-$150
1977 OAKLAND - Allen, Armas, Blue .... $60-$90
1977 PHILADELPHIA - Bowa, Schmidt, Luzinski, Boone, McCarver, Carlton, Kaat .... $120-$180
1977 PITTSBURGH - Stargell, Parker, Oliver, Gossage, Tekulve .... $116-$174
1977 SAN DIEGO - Winfield, Kingman, Fingers .... $88-$132
1977 SAN FRANCISCO - McCovey, Madlock, Clark .... $88-$132
1977 SEATTLE - .... $120-$180
1977 ST. LOUIS - Hernandez, Brock, Simmons .... $80-$120
1977 TEXAS - Perry, Blyleven .... $68-$102
1977 TORONTO - .... $140-$210
1978 ATLANTA - Murphy, Horner, Neikro .... $72-$108
1978 BALTIMORE - Weaver, Murray, Palmer .... $108-$162
1978 BOSTON - Evans, Lynn, Yastrzemski, Fisk, Rice, Eckersley .... $96-$144
1978 CALIFORNIA - Bostock, Ryan .... $80-$120
1978 CHICAGO (AL) - Bob Lemon .... $60-$90
1978 CHICAGO (NL) - Murcer, Kingman .... $60-$90
1978 CINCINNATI - Anderson, Morgan, Concepcion, Rose, Foster, Bench, Seaver
.... $116-$174

1978 CLEVELAND - Bell ....$60-$90
1978 DETROIT - Whitaker, Trammell, Staub, Morris ....$100-$150
1978 HOUSTON - Richard...$60-$90
1978 KANSAS CITY - Brett...$120-$180
1978 LOS ANGELES - Lasorda, Garvey, Cey, Guerrero, John, Sutton .....$172-$258
1978 MILWAUKEE - Molitor, Yount ....$80-$120
1978 MINNESOTA - Carew ....$68-$102
1978 MONTREAL - Perez, Dawson, Carter.......................................$80-$120
1978 NEW YORK (AL) - Martin, Jackson, Lyle, Munson, Guidry, Hunter, Gossage, Lemon, Piniella...$260-$390
1978 NEW YORK (NL) - Kranepool, Koosman...................................$72-$108
1978 OAKLAND - Armas ....$60-$90
1978 PHILADELPHIA - Schmidt, Luzinski, Boone, Carlton, Kaat...........$12-$180
1978 PITTSBURGH - Stargell, Parker, Blyleven, Candelaria, Tekulve.....$116-$174
1978 SAN DIEGO - Smith, Winfield, Perry, Fingers ....$104-$156
1978 SAN FRANCISCO - McCovey, Clark, Blue ....$88-$132
1978 SEATTLE - ....$60-$90
1978 ST. LOUIS - Boyer, Hernandez, Brock, Simmons ....$80-$120
1978 TEXAS - Harrah, Oliver, Jenkins..$64-$96
1978 TORONTO - ....$112-$168
1979 ATLANTA - Murphy, Horner, Niekro..$72-$108
1979 BALTIMORE - Weaver, Murray, Flanagan, Palmer....................$160-$240
1979 BOSTON - Lynn, Rice, Fisk, Yastrzemski, Eckersley.........................$96-$144
1979 CALIFORNIA - Carew, Lansford, Baylor, Ryan ....$116-$174
1979 CHICAGO (AL) - ....$60-$90
1979 CHICAGO (NL) - Buckner, Kingman, Sutter ....$60-$90
1979 CINCINNATI - Morgan, Concepcion, Griffey, Foster, Bench, Seaver $88-$132
1979 CLEVELAND - Harrah..$60-$90
1979 DETROIT - Anderson, Whitaker, Trammell, Staub, Morris ....$100-$150
1979 HOUSTON - Richard...$72-$108
1979 KANSAS CITY - Brett, Quisenberry ....$100-$150
1979 LOS ANGELES - Lasorda, Garvey, Cey, Guerrero, Sutcliffe, Sutton
....$100-$150
1979 MILWAUKEE - Molitor, Yount ....$80-$120
1979 MINNESOTA - Castino, Koosman ....$60-$90
1979 MONTREAL - Perez, Dawson, Carter, Staub, Raines ....$100-$150
1979 NEW YORK (AL) - Martin, Nettles, Jackson, Munson, Murcer, John, Guidry, Tiant, Gossage, Kaat, Hunter ....$168-$252
1979 NEW YORK (NL) - Kranepool ....$72-$108
1979 OAKLAND - Armas, Henderson ....$72-$108
1979 PHILADELPHIA - Rose, Trillo, Bowa, Schmidt, Luzinski, Boone, Carlton, Kaat..$112-$168
1979 PITTSBURGH - Stargell, Madlock, Parker, Candelaria, Blyleven, Tekulve
....$240-$360
1979 SAN DIEGO - Smith, Winfield, Perry, Fingers, Lolich ....$104-$156
1979 SAN FRANCISCO - McCovey, Clark, Madlock, Blue ....$88-$132
1979 SEATTLE - ....$60-$90
1979 ST. LOUIS - Boyer, Hernandez, Brock, Simmons ....$80-$120

1988 San Diego Padres

1979 TEXAS - Bell, Oliver, Jenkins, Lyle...$64-$96
1979 TORONTO - Griffin, Stieb..$60-$90
1980 ATLANTA - Horner, Murphy, Niekro...$72-$108
1980 BALTIMORE - Weaver, Murray, Stone, Palmer ....$100-$150
1980 BOSTON - Perez, Evans, Lynn, Rice, Fisk, Yastrzemski, Eckersley .$120-$180
1980 CALIFORNIA - Carew, Lansford ....$60-$90
1980 CHICAGO (AL) - Baines..$60-$90
1980 CHICAGO (NL) - Buckner, Kingman ....$60-$90
1980 CINCINNATI - Concepcion, Griffey, Foster, Bench, Seaver...............$72-$108
1980 CLEVELAND - Harrah, Charboneau...$64-$96
1980 DETROIT - Anderson, Whitaker, Trammell, Gibson, Morris............$100-$150
1980 HOUSTON - Morgan, Ryan ....$116-$174
1980 KANSAS CITY - Brett, Quisenberry ....$172-$258
1980 LOS ANGELES - Lasorda, Garvey, Guerrero, Welch, Sutton, Howe, Valenzu-
ela... $100-$150
1980 MILWAUKEE - Molitor, Yount ....$80-$120
1980 MINNESOTA - Koosman..$60-$90
1980 MONTREAL - Dawson, Carter, Raines...$100-$150
1980 NEW YORK (AL) - Nettles, Jackson, Piniella, Murcer, Guidry, Tiant, Gos-
sage, John, Perry, Kaat ....$160-$240
1980 NEW YORK (NL) - Wilson ....$72-$108

1980 OAKLAND - Martin, Henderson..$140-$210
1980 PHILADELPHIA - Rose, Bowa, Schmidt, Luzinski, Boone, Carlton, Lyle
....$252-$378
1980 PITTSBURGH - Stargell, Madlock, Parker, Candelaria, Tekulve, Blyleven
....$100-$150
1980 SAN DIEGO - Smith, Winfield, Fingers...$80-$120
1980 SAN FRANCISCO - Clark, McCovey, Blue ....$80-$120
1980 SEATTLE - ....$60-$90
1980 ST. LOUIS - Schoendienst, Hernandez, Simmons, Kaat ....$80-$120
1980 TEXAS - Bell, Oliver, Staub, Jenkins, Perry, Lyle..............................$64-$96
1980 TORONTO - Stieb...$60-$90
1981 ATLANTA - Murphy, Butler, Perry, Niekro ....$100-$150
1981 BALTIMORE - Weaver, Murray, Ripken, Palmer...........................$100-$150
1981 BOSTON - Lansford, Rice, Yastrzemski, Eckersley ....$100-$150
1981 CALIFORNIA - Carew, Lynn ....$60-$90
1981 CHICAGO (AL) - Baines, Fisk, Luzinski, Hoyt ....$72-$108
1981 CHICAGO (NL) - Buckner ....$60-$90
1981 CINCINNATI - Concepcion, Griffey, Foster, Bench, Seaver..............$72-$108
1981 CLEVELAND - Harrah, Blyleven..$60-$90
1981 DETROIT - Anderson, Whitaker, Trammell, Gibson, Morris...........$100-$125
1981 HOUSTON - Ryan, Sutton ....$72-$108
1981 KANSAS CITY - Brett, Quisenberry ....$64-$96
1981 LOS ANGELES - Garvey, Cey, Guerrero, Sax, Valenzuela, Stewart $236-$354
1981 MILWAUKEE - Yount, Molitor, Fingers ....$100-$150
1981 MINNESOTA - ....$60-$90
1981 MONTREAL - Dawson, Raines, Carter..$116-$174
1981 NEW YORK - Kingman, Staub ....$76-$114
1981 NEW YORK (AL) - Nettles, Jackson, Winfield, Murcer, Piniella, Guidry, John,
Gossage..$200-$300
1981 OAKLAND - Martin, Henderson ....$140-$210
1981 PHILADELPHIA - Rose, Bowa, Schmidt, Boone, Sandberg, Carlton, Lyle
....$100-$150
1981 PITTSBURGH - Parker, Stargell, Madlock.....................................$72-$108
1981 SAN DIEGO - Smith, Kennedy ....$72-$108
1981 SAN FRANCISCO - Morgan, Clark, Blue ....$64-$96
1981 SEATTLE - Henderson...$56-$84
1981 ST. LOUIS - Hernandez, Kaat ....$88-$132
1981 TEXAS - Bell, Oliver, Jenkins ....$64-$96
1981 TORONTO - Bell, Barfield, Stieb..$60-$108
1982 ATLANTA - Murphy, Butler, Niekro ....$116-$174
1982 BALTIMORE - Weaver, Murray, Ripken, Palmer...........................$104-$156
1982 BOSTON - Lansford, Rice, Yastrzemski, Boggs, Perez, Eckersley....$100-$150
1982 CALIFORNIA - Carew, Jackson, Lynn, Boone, John, Tiant ....$120-$180
1982 CHICAGO (AL) - Baines, Fisk, Luzinski, Hoyt, Lyle ....$72-$108
1982 CHICAGO (NL) - Buckner, Sandberg, Jenkins, Hernandez................$80-$120
1982 CINCINNATI - Concepcion, Bench, Seaver ....$68-$102
1982 CLEVELAND - Harrah, Blyleven...$60-$90
1982 DETROIT - Anderson, Whitaker, Trammell, Gibson, Johnson, Morris

1982 HOUSTON - Ryan, Sutton ....$100-$150
1982 KANSAS CITY - Brett, Quisenberry ....$72-$108
1982 LOS ANGELES - Garvey, Sax, Guerrero, Valenzuela, Stewart ....$100-$150
1982 MILWAUKEE - Yount, Molitor, Vuckovich, Fingers, Sutton............$160-$240
1982 MINNESOTA - Hrbek, Brunansky, Viola...$60-$90
1982 MONTREAL - Oliver, Dawson, Raines, Carter, Reardon....................$72-$108
1982 NEW YORK (AL) - Lemon, Nettles, Winfield, Piniella, Murcer, Mattingly, John, Guidry, Gossage...$120-$180
1982 NEW YORK (NL) - Kingman, Foster ....$80-$120
1982 OAKLAND - Martin, Henderson...$120-$180
1982 PHILADELPHIA - Rose, Schmidt, Carlton, Lyle ....$100-$150
1982 PITTSBURGH - Madlock, Parker, Stargell, Candelaria, Tekulve ......$72-$108
1982 SAN DIEGO - Kennedy, Gwynn ....$72-$108
1982 SAN FRANCISCO - Robinson, Morgan, Clark, Leonard ....$60-$90
1982 SEATTLE - Perry...$60-$90
1982 ST. LOUIS - Hernandez, Smith, McGee...$260-$390
1982 TEXAS - Bell...$60-$90
1982 TORONTO - Barfield, Stieb...$60-$90
1983 ATLANTA - Murphy, Butler, Niekro ....$60-$90
1983 BALTIMORE - Murray, Ripken, Palmer ....$240-$360
1983 BOSTON - Boggs, Rice, Yastrzemski, Eckersley............................$100-$150
1983 CALIFORNIA - Carew, Lynn, Boone, Jackson, John.........................$80-$120
1983 CHICAGO (AL) - Baines, Kittle, Fisk, Hoyt ....$120-$180
1983 CHICAGO (NL) - Buckner, Sandberg, Jenkins, Hernandez.............$100-$150
1983 CINCINNATI - Concepcion, Bench..$60-$90
1983 CLEVELAND - Franco, Harrah, Blyleven ....$60-$90
1983 DETROIT - Anderson, Whitaker, Trammell, Johnson, Morris ....$100-$150
1983 HOUSTON - Ryan...$72-$108
1983 KANSAS CITY - Brett, Quisenberry, Perry.......................................$80-$120
1983 LOS ANGELES - Sax, Guerrero, Valenzuela, Welch, Stewart, Hershiser
....$116-$174
1983 MILWAUKEE - Yount, Molitor, Simmons, Fingers...........................$72-$108
1983 MINNESOTA - Hrbek, Brunansky, Viola ....$60-$90
1983 MONTREAL - Oliver, Dawson, Raines, Carter ....$72-$108
1983 NEW YORK (AL) - Martin, Nettles, Winfield, Piniella, Murcer, Guidry, Gossage ....$160-$240
1983 NEW YORK (NL) - Strawberry, Foster, Staub, Kingman, Seaver ....$100-$150
1983 OAKLAND - Lansford, Henderson ....$60-$90
1983 PHILADELPHIA - Rose, Morgan, Schmidt, Perez, Denny, Hernandez
....$200-$300
1983 PITTSBURGH - Madlock, Parker, Candelaria, Tekulve.......................$60-$90
1983 SAN DIEGO - Garvey, Gwynn ....$100-$150
1983 SAN FRANCISCO - Robinson ....$60-$90
1983 SEATTLE - Perry..$60-$90
1983 ST. LOUIS - Smith, McGee, Hernandez..$100-$150
1983 TEXAS - Bell, Stewart ....$60-$90
1983 TORONTO - Bell, Fernandez, Stieb..$60-$90

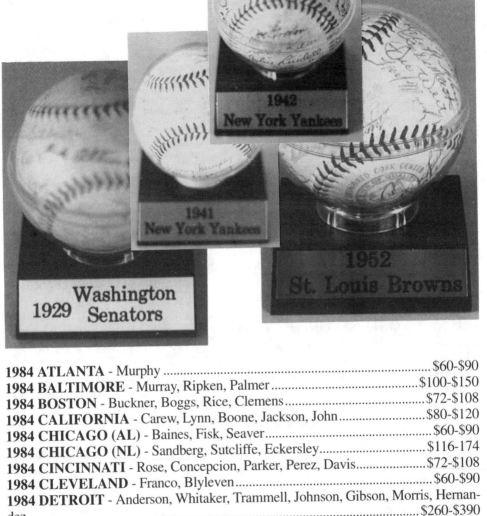

1984 ATLANTA - Murphy .... $60-$90
1984 BALTIMORE - Murray, Ripken, Palmer ....$100-$150
1984 BOSTON - Buckner, Boggs, Rice, Clemens..$72-$108
1984 CALIFORNIA - Carew, Lynn, Boone, Jackson, John........................$80-$120
1984 CHICAGO (AL) - Baines, Fisk, Seaver..$60-$90
1984 CHICAGO (NL) - Sandberg, Sutcliffe, Eckersley.............................$116-174
1984 CINCINNATI - Rose, Concepcion, Parker, Perez, Davis....................$72-$108
1984 CLEVELAND - Franco, Blyleven...$60-$90
1984 DETROIT - Anderson, Whitaker, Trammell, Johnson, Gibson, Morris, Hernandez ....$260-$390
1984 HOUSTON - Davis, Ryan ....$72-$108
1984 KANSAS CITY - Brett, Saberhagen ....$100-$150
1984 LOS ANGELES - Sax, Guerrero, Valenzuela, Hershiser ....$100-$150
1984 MILWAUKEE - Yount, Sutton ....$72-$108
1984 MINNESOTA - Hrbek, Puckett, Viola ....$72-$108
1984 MONTREAL - Dawson, Raines, Carter, Rose.....................................$72-$108
1984 NEW YORK (AL) - Berra, Mattingly, Winfield, Piniella, Niekro, Guidry ....$120-$180
1984 NEW YORK (NL) - Hernandez, Strawberry, Foster, Gooden...........$100-$150
1984 OAKLAND - Morgan, Lansford, Henderson ....$72-$108
1984 PHILADELPHIA - Schmidt, Carlton..$100-$150

1984 PITTSBURGH - Madlock, Candelaria, Tekulve ....$60-$90
1984 SAN DIEGO - Garvey, Nettles, Gwynn, Gossage ....$180-$270
1984 SAN FRANCISCO - Oliver, Leonard, Clark................................$60-$90
1984 SEATTLE - Davis, Tartabull, Langston................................$60-$90
1984 ST. LOUIS - O. Smith, McGee ....$100-$150
1984 TEXAS - Stewart ....$60-$90
1984 TORONTO - Bell, Fernandez, Stieb....................................$80-$120
1985 ATLANTA - Murphy ....$60-$90
1985 BALTIMORE - Weaver, Murray, Ripken, Lynn............................$60-$90
1985 BOSTON - Boggs, Rice, Clemens.......................................$60-$90
1985 CALIFORNIA - Carew, Jackson, Boone, Sutton, John....................$80-$120
1985 CHICAGO (AL) - Guillen, Baines, Fisk, Seaver ....$60-$90
1985 CHICAGO (NL) - Sandberg, Eckersley..................................$60-$90
1985 CINCINNATI - Rose, Concepcion, Parker, Perez, Davis.................$72-$108
1985 CLEVELAND - Franco, Carter, Blyleven................................$56-$84
1985 DETROIT - Anderson, Whitaker, Trammell, Gibson, Morris.............$72-$108
1985 HOUSTON - Davis, Ryan...$72-$108
1985 KANSAS CITY - Brett, Saberhagen ....$236-$354
1985 LOS ANGELES - Sax, Oliver, Hershiser, Valenzuela....................$116-$174
1985 MILWAUKEE - Yount, Fingers..$60-$90
1985 MINNESOTA - Hrbek, Puckett, Viola, Blyleven.........................$72-$108
1985 MONTREAL - Dawson, Raines...$60-$90
1985 NEW YORK (AL) - Berra, Martin, Mattingly, Winfield, Henderson, Guidry, Niekro ....$120-$180
1985 NEW YORK (NL) - Hernandez, Johnson, Strawberry, Foster, Carter, Gooden ....$108-$162
1985 OAKLAND - Lansford, Kingman, Sutton ....$60-$90
1985 PHILADELPHIA - Schmidt, Carlton.....................................$60-$90
1985 PITTSBURGH - Madlock ....$60-$90
1985 SAN DIEGO - Garvey, Nettles, Gwynn, Gossage ....$72-$108
1985 SAN FRANCISCO - Leonard ....$60-$90
1985 SEATTLE - Tartabull, Langston ....$60-$90
1985 ST. LOUIS - Clark, McGee, Coleman ....$160-$240
1985 TEXAS - Harrah..$60-$90
1985 TORONTO - Fernandez, Bell, Fielder, Stieb ....$100-$150
1986 ATLANTA - Murphy ....$48-$72
1986 BALTIMORE - Weaver, Murray, Ripken, Lynn............................$48-$72
1986 BOSTON - Boggs, Rice, Clemens, Seaver ....$160-$240
1986 CALIFORNIA - Joyner, Boone, Jackson, Sutton ....$56-$84
1986 CHICAGO (AL) - Baines, Fisk, Carlton, Seaver ....$60-$90
1986 CHICAGO (NL) - Sandberg, Palmeiro, Eckersley........................$48-$72
1986 CINCINNATI - Parker, Davis, Concepcion, Perez, Rose.................$60-$90
1986 CLEVELAND - Franco, Carter, Niekro ....$48-$72
1986 DETROIT - Anderson, Whitaker, Trammell, Gibson, Morris.............$80-$120
1986 HOUSTON - Davis, Scott, Ryan..$100-$150
1986 KANSAS CITY - Howser, Brett, Jackson, Saberhagen....................$60-$90
1986 LOS ANGELES - Guerrero, Valenzuela, Hershiser ....$68-$102
1986 MILWAUKEE - Yount...$48-$72

1986 MINNESOTA - Hrbek, Puckett, Blyleven, Viola.................................$80-$120
1986 MONTREAL - Dawson, Raines...$48-$72
1986 NEW YORK (AL) - Mattingly, Winfield, Henderson, Guidry, John...$80-$120
1986 NEW YORK (NL) - Hernandez, Strawberry, Carter, Mitchell, Foster, Gooden
....$236-$354
1986 OAKIAND - Canseco, McGwire, Stewart...$80-$120
1986 PHILADELPHIA - Schmidt, Carlton..$56-$84
1986 PITTSBURGH - Bonds, Bonilla..$48-$72
1986 SAN DIEGO - Garvey, Gwynn, Gossage...$48-$72
1986 SAN FRANCISCO - Clark, Carlton...$48-$72
1986 SEATTLE - Tartabull, Langston...$48-$72
1986 ST. LOUIS - Smith, McGee...$48-$72
1986 TEXAS - Sierra...$48-$72
1986 TORONTO - Fernandez, Bell, Stieb...$48-$72
1987 ATLANTA - Murphy, Niekro...$48-$72
1987 BALTIMORE - Murray, Ripken, Lynn..$48-$72
1987 BOSTON - Boggs, Rice, Clemens...$48-$72
1987 CALIFORNIA - Joyner, Boone, Buckner, Sutton...................................$52-$78
1987 CHICAGO - Sandberg, Dawson, Palmeiro...$48-$72
1987 CHICAGO (NL) - Fisk, Baines...$48-$72
1987 CINCINNATI - Rose, Parker, Davis, Concepcion..................................$56-$84
1987 CLEVELAND - Carter, Franco, Niekro, Carlton....................................$60-$90
1987 DETROIT - Anderson, Whitaker, Trammell, Gibson, Morris...........$128-$192
1987 HOUSTON - Davis, Ryan...$56-$84
1987 KANSAS CITY - Brett, Tartabull, Jackson, Saberhagen.......................$60-$90
1987 LOS ANGELES - Lasorda, Sax, Guerrero, Hershiser, Valenzuela......$80-$120
1987 MILWAUKEE - Yount...$48-$72
1987 MINNESOTA - Hrbek, Puckett, Viola, Blyleven, Carlton.................$236-$354
1987 MONTREAL - Raines...$48-$72
1987 NEW YORK (AL) - Mattingly, Henderson, Winfield, John, Guidry..$80-$120
1987 NEW YORK (NL) - Hernandez, Johnson, Strawberry, Carter, Gooden
....$108-$162
1987 OAKLAND - McGwire, Canseco, Jackson, Stewart, Eckersley........$100-$150
1987 PHILADELPHIA - Schmidt..$48-$72
1987 PITTSBURGH - Bonilla, Van Slyke, Bonds...$48-$72
1987 SAN DIEGO - Gwynn, Garvey, Gossage..$48-$72
1987 SAN FRANCISCO - Clark, Mitchell, Williams...................................$100-$150
1987 SEATTLE - Langston...$48-$72
1987 ST. LOUIS - Smith, McGee...$160-$240
1987 TEXAS - Sierra...$48-$72
1987 TORONTO - Fernandez, Bell, McGriff, Stieb, Niekro..........................$52-$78
1988 ATLANTA - Murphy..$48-$72
1988 BALTIMORE - Robinson, Murray, Ripken, Lynn..................................$48-$72
1988 BOSTON - Boggs, Rice, Clemens...$100-$150
1988 CALIFORNIA - Joyner, Boone, Buckner...$48-$72
1988 CHICAGO (AL) - Fisk, Baines..$48-$72
1988 CHICAGO (NL) - Grace, Sandberg, Dawson, Palmeiro, Gossage.......$52-$78
1988 CINCINNATI - Sabo...$56-$84

1988 CLEVELAND - Franco, Carter ....$48-$72
1988 DETROIT - Whitaker, Trammell, Lynn, Morris ....$48-$72
1988 HOUSTON - Davis, Ryan ....$56-$84
1988 KANSAS CITY - Brett, Tartabull, Jackson, Buckner, Saberhagen........$60-$90
1988 LOS ANGELES - Sax, Gibson, Hershiser, Valenzuela ....$236-$354
1988 MILWAUKEE - Yount...$48-$72
1988 MINNESOTA - Hrbek, Puckett, Viola, Blyleven, Carlton ....$48-$72
1988 MONTREAL - Raines...$48-$72
1988 NEW YORK (AL) - Martin, Mattingly, Winfield, Henderson, John, Guidry
....$100-$150
1988 NEW YORK (NL) - Hernandez, Johnson, Strawberry, Carter, Gooden
....$100-$150
1988 OAKLAND - McGwire, Lansford, Canseco, Parker, Stewart, Welch, Eckersley
....$160-$240
1988 PHILADELPHIA - Schmidt..$48-$72
1988 PITTSBURGH - Bonilla, Van Slyke, Bonds, Drabek ....$48-$72
1988 SAN DIEGO - Gwynn...$48-$72
1988 SAN FRANCISCO - Clark, Mitchell, Williams................................$56-$84
1988 SEATTLE - Langston ....$48-$72
1988 ST. LOUIS - Smith, McGee, Guerrero..$48-$72
1988 TEXAS - Sierra...$48-$72
1988 TORONTO - McGriff, Fernandez, Bell, Stieb ....$48-$72
1989 ATLANTA - Murphy ....$40-$60
1989 BALTIMORE - Robinson, Ripken ....$48-$72
1989 BOSTON - Boggs, Clemens ....$48-$72
1989 CALIFORNIA - Joyner, Blyleven..$40-$60
1989 CHICAGO (AL) - Fisk, Baines..$48-$72
1989 CHICAGO (NL) - Grace, Sandberg, Dawson ....$100-$150
1989 CINCINNATI - Davis ....$48-$72
1989 CLEVELAND - Carter..$40-$60
1989 DETROIT - Anderson, Trammell, Lynn, Morris ....$48-$72
1989 HOUSTON - Davis ....$40-$60
1989 KANSAS CITY - Brett, Jackson, Boone, Tartabull, Saberhagen..........$60-$90
1989 LOS ANGELES - Lasorda, Murray, Randolph, Gibson, Hershiser, Valenzuela
....$80-$120
1989 MILWAUKEE - Yount..$48-$72
1989 MINNESOTA - Hrbek, Puckett, Viola ....$48-$72
1989 MONTREAL - Raines...$48-$72
1989 NEW YORK (AL) - Mattingly, Sax, Winfield, Gossage....................$80-$120
1989 NEW YORK (NL) - Johnson, Strawberry, Hernandez, Carter, Gooden
....$80-$120
1989 OAKLAND - LaRussa, McGwire, Canseco, D. Henderson, R. Henderson, Parker, Stewart, Eckersley ....$236-$354
1989 PHILADELPHIA - Dykstra, Schmidt ....$40-$60
1989 PITTSBURGH - Bonilla, Van Slyke, Bonds ....$48-$72
1989 SAN DIEGO - Clark, Gwynn..$48-$72
1989 SAN FRANCISCO - Clark, Williams, Mitchell, Gossage.................$160-$240
1989 SEATTLE - Griffey Jr...$48-$72

1989 St. Louis Cardinals

1989 ST. LOUIS - Guerrero, Smith, McGee...$48-$72
1989 TEXAS - Palmeiro, Franco, Sierra, Baines, Ryan.................................$60-$90
1989 TORONTO - McGriff, Fernandez, Stieb...$100-$150
1990 ATLANTA - Justice, Murphy ....$40-$60
1990 BALTIMORE - F. Robinson, C. Ripken Jr..$48-$72
1990 BOSTON - Boggs, Clemens ....$88-$132
1990 CALIFORNIA - Joyner, Winfield, Blyleven ....$40-$60
1990 CHICAGO (AL) - Fisk ....$48-$72
1990 CHICAGO (NL) - Dawson, Grace, Sandberg ....$56-$84
1990 CINCINNATI - Larkin, Davis, Piniella...$200-$300
1990 CLEVELAND - Hernandez ....$40-$60
1990 DETROIT - Anderson, Fielder, Morris, Trammell, Whitaker ....$48-$72
1990 HOUSTON - Davis..$40-$60
1990 KANSAS CITY - Brett, Tartabull, Jackson, Saberhagen........................$60-$90
1990 LOS ANGELES - Lasorda, Murray, Gibson, Valenzuela....................$80-$120
1990 MILWAUKEE - Yount, Molitor, Parker...$48-$72
1990 MINNESOTA - Hrbek, Puckett ....$48-$72
1990 MONTREAL - Raines...$48-$72
1990 NEW YORK (AL) - Mattingly...$80-$120
1990 NEW YORK (NL) - Strawberry, Johnson, Viola, Gooden...................$80-$120
1990 OAKLAND - McGwire, Randolph, Canseco, R. Henderson, D. Henderson,

1990 Pittsburgh Pirates

Baines, McGee, Welch, Stewart, Eckersley ....$160-$240
1990 PHILADELPHIA - Dykstra, Murphy...$40-$60
1990 PITTSBURGH - Bonds, Bonilla, Van Slyke, Drabek ....$80-$100
1990 SAN DIEGO - Gwynn, Carter, Clark...$48-$72
1990 SAN FRANCISCO - Clark, Mitchell, Williams ....$56-$84
1990 SEATTLE - Ken Griffey Jr., Ken Griffey Sr...$56-$84
1990 ST. LOUIS - Guerrero, Smith, McGee...$48-$72
1990 TEXAS - Palmeiro, Franco, Sierra, Ryan ....$60-$90
1990 TORONTO - McGriff, Stieb, Fernandez ....$48-$72
1991 ATLANTA - Glavine, Pendleton ....$140-$210
1991 BALTIMORE - F. Robinson, C. Ripken ....$44-$66
1991 BOSTON - Boggs, Clemens ....$60-$90
1991 CALIFORNIA - Joyner, Winfield ....$32-$48
1991 CHICAGO (AL) - Fisk, Thomas..$60-$90
1991 CHICAGO (NL) - Sandberg, Dawson ....$56-$84
1991 CINCINNATI - Larkin, Davis, Piniella..$60-$90
1991 CLEVELAND - Swindell ....$32-$48
1991 DETROIT - Anderson, Whitaker, Trammell, Fielder ....$36-$54
1991 HOUSTON - Bagwell, Harnisch ....$48-$72
1991 KANSAS CITY - Brett, Saberhagen, Tartabull.....................................$36-$54
1991 LOS ANGELES - Lasorda, Murray, Strawberry ....$64-$96

1991 MILWAUKEE - Yount, Molitor ....$32-$48
1991 MINNESOTA - Knoblauch, Morris, Puckett, Hrbek ....$160-$240
1991 MONTREAL - Calderon..$32-$48
1991 NEW YORK (AL) - Mattingly...$60-$90
1991 NEW YORK (NL) - Johnson, Gooden, Viola ....$60-$90
1991 OAKLAND - R. Henderson, Stewart, Eckersley, Canseco ....$80-$120
1991 PHILADELPHIA - Dykstra, Murphy..$32-$48
1991 PITTSBURGH - Bonds, Bonilla ....$80-$120
1991 SAN DIEGO - Gwynn, McGriff, Fernandez ....$32-$48
1991 SAN FRANCISCO - Mitchell, Clark ....$40-$60
1991 SEATTLE - Griffey Jr., Griffey Sr. ....$48-$72
1991 ST. LOUIS - O. Smith, L. Smith ....$32-$48
1991 TEXAS - Franco, Ryan, Sierra, Palmeiro..$60-$90
1991 TORONTO - Carter, Alomar, Stieb ....$80-$120
1992 ATLANTA - Pendleton, Justice, Glavine.. $250
1992 BALTIMORE - Devereaux, Ripken, Mussina.. $110
1992 BOSTON - Boggs, Clemens $90
1992 CALIFORNIA - Langston $50
1992 CHICAGO (AL) - Thomas, McDowell $65
1992 CHICAGO (NL) - Maddux, Grace, Dawson, Sandberg.......................... $95
1992 CINCINNATI - Larkin, Rijo... $85
1992 CLEVELAND - Baerga, Belle, Nagy.. $85
1992 DETROIT - Fryman, Whitaker, Trammell, Fielder $75
1992 HOUSTON - Biggio, Bagwell.. $40
1992 KANSAS CITY - Brett, Jefferies, Joyner... $65
1992 LOS ANGELES - Karros, Butler $60
1992 MILWAUKEE - Listach, Yount, Eldred, Molitor $60
1992 MINNESOTA - Puckett, Knoblauch $80
1992 MONTREAL - Grissom, Walker, Martinez $50
1992 NEW YORK (AL) - Mattingly.. $85
1992 NEW YORK (NL) - Murray, Bonilla, Cone $85
1992 OAKLAND - Eckersley, McGwire, Henderson, Canseco $95
1992 PHILADELPHIA - Hollins, Dykstra, Kruk, Schilling, Daulton $100
1992 PITTSBURGH - Bonds, Van Slyke, Drabek $125
1992 SAN DIEGO - Gwynn, Sheffield, McGriff $75
1992 SAN FRANCISCO - Clark, Williams... $110
1992 SEATTLE - Griffey Jr., Martinez... $75
1992 ST. LOUIS - O. Smith, L. Smith, Lankford $60
1992 TEXAS - Sierra, Gonzalez $125
1992 TORONTO - Alomar, Carter, Winfield, Morris $200
1993 ATLANTA - Maddux, McGriff $250
1993 BALTIMORE - Ripken, Mussina... $95
1993 BOSTON - Dawson, Clemens, Vaughn.. $90
1993 CALIFORNIA - Salmon, Langston $75
1993 CHICAGO (AL) - Thomas, McDowell $150
1993 CHICAGO (NL) - Sandberg, Grace.. $85
1993 CINCINNATI - Larkin, Rijo.. $50
1993 CLEVELAND - Baerga, Belle, Nagy... $75

1993 COLORADO - Galarraga, Hayes $150
1993 DETROIT - Whitaker, Trammell, Fielder $80
1993 FLORIDA - Harvey, Weiss, Destrade $150
1993 HOUSTON - Swindell, Drabek, Bagwell $40
1993 KANSAS CITY - Brett, Cone $75
1993 LOS ANGELES - Piazza, Karros $100
1993 MILWAUKEE - Listach, Hamilton, Vaughn, Yount $50
1993 MINNESOTA - Puckett, Winfield $95
1993 MONTREAL - D. Martinez, Grissom, Walker $50
1993 NEW YORK (AL) - Boggs, Mattingly $90
1993 NEW YORK (NL) - Bonilla, Murray, Gooden $75
1993 OAKLAND - Sierra, McGwire, Eckersley $85
1993 PHILADELPHIA - Schilling, Dykstra, Kruk, Daulton $195
1993 PITTSBURGH - Van Slyke, Bell $95
1993 SAN DIEGO - Gwynn, Sheffield $60
1993 SAN FRANCISCO - Bonds, Clark $150
1993 SEATTLE - Griffey Jr., R. Johnson $70
1993 ST. LOUIS - O. Smith, Lankford $50
1993 TEXAS - Ryan, Gonzalez, Canseco $150
1993 TORONTO - Alomar, Molitor, Carter, Olerud, Stewart $225

Autographed All-Star Baseballs

Key signatures follow each team name

1937 American League All-Stars

1933 American League All-Star Team - Mack, Collins, Gehrig, Ruth
....$6400-$9600
1933 National League All-Star Team - McGraw, Traynor, Waner, Frisch
....$2240-$3360
1934 American League All-Star Team - Gehrig, Ruth, Foxx ....$5600-$8400
1934 National League All-Star Team - Ott, Traynor, Vaughan, Waner
....$2000-$3000
1935 American League All-Star Team - Foxx, Gehrig, Hornsby.........$4000-$6000
1935 National League All-Star Team - Frisch, Ott, Vaughan ....$1360-$2040
1936 American League All-Star Team - Foxx, Gehrig, DiMaggio......$4800-$7200
1936 National League All-Star Team - Ott, Vaughan, Traynor ....$1200-$1800

1954 National League All-Stars

1937 American League All-Star Team - Foxx, DiMaggio, Gehrig......$4400-$6600
1937 National League All-Star Team - Frisch, Ott, Vaughan ....$1440-$2160
1938 American League All-Star Team - Foxx, DiMaggio, Gehrig......$4400-$6600
1938 National League All-Star Team - Ott, Vaughan, Frisch ....$1200-$1800
1939 American League All-Star Team - Foxx, DiMaggio, Gehrig......$4000-$6000
1939 National League All-Star Team - Ott, Vaughan ....$800-$1200
1940 American League All-Star Team - Foxx, Williams, DiMaggio ......$520-$780
1940 National League All-Star Team - Ott, Vaughan ....$720-$1080
1941 American League All-Star Team - Foxx, Williams, DiMaggio ......$560-$840
1941 National League All-Star Team - Ott, Vaughan ....$640-$960
1942 American League All-Star Team - Williams, Joe DiMaggio ....$480-$720
1942 National League All-Star Team - McKechnie, Frisch, Ott, Vaughan
....$680-$1020
1943 American League All-Star Team - McCarthy.................................$400-$600
1943 National League All-Star Team - Frisch, Ott, Musial ....$480-$720
1944 American League All-Star Team - McCarthy, Cronin....................$400-$600
1944 National League All-Star Team - Wagner, Ott, Musial....................$480-$720
1945 (There was no All-Star Game)
1946 American League All-Star Team - Williams, DiMaggio.................$440-$660
1946 National League All-Star Team - Musial..$480-$720
1947 American League All-Star Team - Williams, DiMaggio.................$460-$690

1971 American League All-Stars

1947 National League All-Star Team - Ott, Musial ....$520-$780
1948 American League All-Star Team - Williams, DiMaggio.................$460-$690
1948 National League All-Star Team - Ott, Musial ....$520-$780
1949 American League All-Star Team - Williams, DiMaggio.................$460-$690
1949 National League All-Star Team - Campanella, Robinson, Musial ..$540-$810
1950 American League All-Star Team - Williams, DiMaggio.................$480-$720
1950 National League All-Star Team - Campanella, Robinson, Musial ..$540-$810
1951 American League All-Star Team - Williams, J. DiMaggio ....$480-$720
1951 National League All-Star Team - Campanella, Robinson, Musial ..$540-$810
1952 American League All-Star Team - Mantle, Paige ....$792-$1188
1952 National League All-Star Team - Campanella, Robinson, Musial ..$540-$810
1953 American League All-Star Team - Mantle, Williams, Paige ....$480-$720
1953 National League All-Star Team - Campanella, Robinson, Musial ..$540-$810
1954 American League All-Star Team - Williams, Mantle ....$440-$660
1954 National League All-Star Team - Campanella, Robinson, Musial ..$540-$810
1955 American League All-Star Team - Williams, Mantle ....$400-$600
1955 National League All-Star Team - Musial...$380-$570
1956 American League All-Star Team - Williams, Mantle, Berra, Martin, Ford
....$440-$660
1956 National League All-Star Team - Campanella, Musial ....$480-$720
1957 American League All-Star Team - Williams, Mantle ....$380-$570

1957 National League All-Star Team - Musial...$380-$570
1958 American League All-Star Team - Williams, Mantle, Martin, Berra, Ford
....$380-$570
1958 National League All-Star Team - Musial...............................$360-$540
1959 American League All-Star Team - Williams, Mantle ....$400-$600
1959 American League 2nd Game All-Stars - Mantle, Maris, Williams
....$460-$690
1959 National League All-Star Team - Musial...............................$380-$570
1959 National League 2nd Game All-Stars - Musial ....$380-$570
1960 American League All-Star Team, both teams - Mantle, Maris........$460-$690
1960 National League All-Star Team, both teams - Clemente ....$420-$630
1961 American League All-Star Team - Mantle, Maris ....$480-$720
1961 American League 2nd Game All-Stars - Mantle, Maris ....$480-$720
1961 National League All-Star Team - Clemente ....$420-$630
1961 National League 2nd Game All-Stars - Clemente.........................$420-$630
1962 American League All-Star Team - Mantle, Maris ....$400-$600
1962 American League 2nd Game All-Stars - Mantle, Maris ....$400-$600
1962 National League All-Star Team - Clemente ....$420-$630
1962 National League 2nd Game All-Stars - Clemente.........................$420-$630
1963 American League All-Star Team - Fox, Yastrzemski ....$280-$420
1963 National League All-Star Team - Musial, Clemente.......................$360-$540
1964 American League All-Star Team - Mantle ....$320-$480
1964 National League All-Star Team - Clemente ....$400-$600
1965 American League All-Star Team - Kaline, Killebrew ....$280-$420
1965 National League All-Star Team - Clemente ....$440-$660
1966 American League All-Star Team -.......................................$360-$540
1966 National League All-Star Team - Clemente ....$400-$600
1967 American League All-Star Team - Mantle ....$360-$540
1967 National League All-Star Team - Clemente ....$400-$600
1968 American League All-Star Team - Mantle ....$340-$510
1968 National League All-Star Team -.......................................$340-$510
1969 American League All-Star Team - Williams...............................$340-$510
1969 National League All-Star Team - Clemente ....$380-$570
1970 American League All-Star Team - ....$320-$480
1970 National League All-Star Team - Hodges, Clemente.......................$380-$570
1971 American League All-Star Team - Munson, Martin ....$360-$540
1971 National League All-Star Team - Clemente ....$380-$570
1972 American League All-Star Team - ....$300-$450
1972 National League All-Star Team - Clemente ....$400-$600
1973 American League All-Star Team - Munson ....$320-$480
1973 National League All-Star Team - ....$300-$450
1974 American League All-Star Team - ....$320-$480
1974 National League All-Star Team - ....$320-$480
1975 American League All-Star Team - Munson, Martin ....$320-$480
1975 National League All-Star Team -.......................................$280-$420
1976 American League All-Star Team - Munson ....$320-$480
1976 National League All-Star Team - ....$280-$420
1977 American League All-Star Team - Munson, Martin ....$340-$510

1977 National League All-Star Team - ....$260-$390
1978 American League All-Star Team - Martin.......................................$300-$450
1978 National League All-Star Team - ....$260-$390
1979 American League All-Star Team - ....$280-$420
1979 National League All-Star Team - ....$288-$432
1980 American League All-Star Team -...$280-$420
1980 National League All-Star Team - ....$240-$360
1981 American League All-Star Team -...$280-$420
1981 National League All-Star Team - ....$280-$420
1982 American League All-Star Team - ....$300-$450
1982 National League All-Star Team - ....$252-$378
1983 American League All-Star Team -...$240-$360
1983 National League All-Star Team - ....$240-$360
1984 American League All-Star Team -...$240-$360
1984 National League All-Star Team - ....$240-$360
1985 American League All-Star Team -...$240-$360
1985 National League All-Star Team -...$260-$390
1986 American League All-Star Team -...$240-$360
1986 National League All-Star Team -...$240-$360
1987 American League All-Star Team -...$240-$360
1987 National League All-Star Team -...$240-$360
1988 American League All-Star Team -...$220-$330
1988 National League All-Star Team -...$220-$330
1989 American League All-Star Team -...$220-$330
1989 National League All-Star Team -...$220-$330
1990 American League All-Star Team -...$220-$330
1990 National League All-Star Team - ....$220-$330
1990 American League All-Star Team -...$220-$330
1990 National League All-Star Team - ....$220-$330
1991 American League All-Star Team - R. Henderson, Puckett, Boggs,
Clemens, Ripken ....$120-$180
1991 National League All-Star Team - O. Smith, Sandberg, Murray, Dawson,
Gwynn.. $120-$180
1992 American League All-Star Team - Boggs, Puckett, Molitor, Ripken,
Griffey Jr. ....$140-$210
1992 National League All-Star Team - O. Smith, Gwynn, Bonds, McGriff,
Sandberg ....$136-$204
1993 American League All-Star Team -..$100-$150
1993 National League All-Star Team - ....$100-$150

Uniforms

Some collectors may opt to pursue a "set" of jerseys from New York teams.

"Flannels," which often contain other materials such as wool, cotton or a blend of various fibers, are the pot of gold at the end of the uniform rainbow. In today's marketplace, more than 80 percent of the flannels offered for sale or trade were not used before 1960. Flannels were used in major league baseball until 1973, when doubleknits, made primarily of polyester-based fabrics, were introduced over three seasons (1970-1972). Since that time, mesh jerseys, not unlike those used by many teams in the other major sports, have been worn, too, generally as pregame jerseys for batting practice or spring training exhibition contests.

Pregame jerseys are not as sought-after as game-used jerseys, due to the lack of names on backs, the pullover design, and screened-on logos and numbers. Plus, the cheaper quality fabric on many styles, individually or in combinations, leaves the genre relegated to team collectors and budget-minded collectors unable to afford authentic game garb. Lack of year/set/etc. tagging in most teams' offerings hurts the demand as well, although pregame jerseys, due to lack of demand, are far less likely to be forged.

Until the early 1980s, most baseball teams held an elitist mindset - making uniforms available to regular fans was off-base; the average fan was not worthy of owning a hallowed piece of history. Some jerseys made it into circulation through charity auctions or the occasional lucky fan who wrote to a team and actually got one back in the mail. But, unfortunately, much of what made it into circulation in those days was either stolen or obtained through bribes and payoffs to clubhouse people and security personnel. Thus, many authentic shirts were "hot."

Changes in that elitist mindset began to occur in 1978, when the Philadelphia Phillies sold an entire lot of 1977 game-used jerseys to a New Jersey dealer, who then advertised them in hobby papers. This practice of bulk sales to dealers has been continued by many teams in all sports today, allowing the team to sell all of the items at once, at a set price per shirt. This has eliminated the need to have team employees individually price the items. Some teams, however, also filter individually-priced items into the market through their own outlets and shops, publicity caravans, or through charity auctions, which are not as popular with mainstream collectors because oftentimes bidding escalates to ridiculously high levels.

Shirts bought in bulk from the teams generally make their way to buyers at baseball card shows, through mail order catalogs, and in advertisements in hobby publications. Because the initial seller was the team itself, the authenticity of these jerseys is virtually uncontested.

Game-used equipment collectors consider a truly authentic item as having been issued by the team whose logo or name appears on the jersey and must have been worn by the player in question discernibly. It doesn't have to be falling apart, but it shouldn't be fresh off the rack, either, and should show some evidence of laundering.

Two points to consider in establishing authenticity include wear and tagging. A jersey used for an entire season should show some sort of visible wear. The collar and perhaps the armpits should indicate sweat, or laundering out of that perspiration. Letters and numbers on the jersey should feature an even degree of wear; the edges of the characters may be a bit frayed, the letters and numbers may be loose in one or several locations, and the numbers or scripting may be wrinkled or shrunken a wee bit.

Several types of tags exist, and vary in color, design and location. Year tags depicts depict the year of issuance for a jersey. Most often, these embroideries are done on a piece of fabric that is then affixed to the jersey itself. Strip tags are either embroidered or printed (screened) and are shaped in strip fashion, that is, an accentuated rectangular shape with a line of information running horizontally on an even plane. Flag tags are any tags attached to the jersey on only one edge, normally underneath an adjoining, larger tag (such as a manufacturer's label). In some instances, it may be attached underneath a jersey seam or even occasionally be attached to the jersey.

Name tags identify the name of a player who was originally issued the jersey. With only rare exceptions, name tags have only a player's last name. They are generally embroidered, and affixed to a strip-style tag that itself is sewn into the jersey. Name tags come in two varieties, based on their location on the jersey. Tags affixed to the inside back of the shirt collar are classified as "name in collar" tags, usually referred to on sale lists and in inventories as "NIC." Or, the tag may be included in the shirt's tail, with the corresponding notation being "NIT," for "name in tail." Variations of "NIT" include "NOT" (name on tail) and "NIF" or "NOF" (name in/on flap).

Extra length tags, used mainly by Rawlings, were of the flag variety for several years after their late-1970s introduction and are attached on all sides thereafter. They denote extra inches added into a jersey's sizing, done usually for taller players.

Before 1987, several manufacturers supplied major league teams with their game jerseys. Wilson, a Chicago-based firm, was predominant. Notable runnersup included Rawlings, Sand-Knit, Goodman, McAuliffe, and, in the flannel era, MacGregor and Spalding. However, in 1987, Rawlings stepped up as the first designated "official" supplier of Major League Baseball, done at Commissioner Peter Ueberroth's request.

Rawlings, based in the St. Louis area, emerged victorious, and, from 1987-91, made all game attire for 21 of the 26 teams and some for three others. At the end of 1991, Rawlings' agreement with the major leagues ended and Russell, an Atlanta-based firm with experience in football and basketball, but not major league baseball, was awarded the new contract.

Your best bet for obtaining authentic items secondhand (i.e., not from the team directly nor from team outlets) is to visit experienced dealers in the field, whose identities can be learned through reading hobby publications and magazines, or visiting card conventions and through recommendations from card and hobby shops. Dealers who have made bulk purchases of numerous items from one or several teams are a good bet, as are dealers with proven experience and longevity in the field. A dealer with an inventory featuring a varied mix of commons, minor stars and superstars is a better possibility than someone who only carries top-of-the-line players in ample quantities.

Uniform dealers, of course, are still the most frequent and diversely inventoried source for game-used uniform acquisitions. Many such dealers advertise through display or classified advertising in hobby papers and magazines. Most issue mail order catalogs, often available for as little as a self-addressed, stamped envelope. The names you see regularly advertising in hobby periodicals, or set up at shows on the regional or national level, are generally going to be good people with whom to deal.

Most dealers utilize straight sales, although some will auction rare or unusual pieces. Major consignment dealers with multi-page advertisements for phone auctions of all types of memorabilia often include some uniforms and equipment in their ads. These, as well as auction house events, are generally geared towards higher-end material, although some mainstream, affordable equipment may also be included.

If questions arise concerning a jersey's authenticity, seek a second opinion. Most dealers will not object to having another party examine items to ensure authenticity, but the allowed time to gain an outside appraisal should be agreed upon beforehand, and stressed to the third party whose opinions are being sought.

Many forged jerseys, normally knits, are subject to "simulated" wear, such as a uniform forger using sandpaper, a sharp instrument, or other foreign object to abrade and damage portions of the jersey to give it the appearance of moderate to extreme game usage.

Jersey tags may be clandestinely doctored by removing legitimate tags from a lesser-valued authentic jersey and placing them into a phony item capable of being passed off as a high-ticket item. Doctoring is defined as taking an authentic jersey of a common player and changing tagging, numbering, or other factors pertinent to the jersey to upgrade the identity of the advertiser (i.e. doctoring the collar strip tag in a 1964 Andre Rodgers Cubs flannel jersey to a "14" or a "26" to make the jersey appear as if it was worn by Ernie Banks or Billy Williams).

Restoration, however, involves attempting to bring jerseys (especially flannels) back to their original appearance as close as possible. Where restorations differ from doctoring and gain acceptability in the majority of hobby quarters is that, first, no attempt is made to change or upgrade the identity of the major league wearer.

Legitimate restorations never attempt to restructure or refurbish tags, because too much potential for having a restoration slip into the dark side of the realm (doctoring) exists. Tagging is generally what is used to establish just who wore an item in the first place, and how to go about arranging the restoration process - what year and player were involved - so that the proper script or insignia or numbers can be used. A legitimate restoration tries to put things back the way they originally were, not embellish identities or years of usage to make an item more attractive or saleable.

Restorations are generally accepted by hobbyists if four conditions are met: 1) The restoration is true and accurate to the original identity of the jersey's wearer, with no illicit attempts to upgrade that wearer's identity. 2) The restoration should try to match as closely as possible the original appearance of the item being restored. 3) Potential buyers or traders should know in advance about any restorations. 4) Restorations should have a slight markdown in price, depending on how many were done and the degree of quality of them.

Although there are often telltale clues for detecting certain companies' replicated jerseys, some instances of fakery center around styles, teams and years, or specific players. Some of them include: Hank Aaron 1972-74 Atlanta Braves knits; Hank Aaron 1975-76 Milwaukee Brewers; Don Mattingly 1984 New York Yankees jerseys; pre-1987 Detroit Tigers jerseys of Al Kaline, Norm Cash, Mark Fidrych, Alan Trammell and Lance Parrish; mid-1970s Boston Red Sox and Oakland A's jerseys for Fred Lynn, Jim Rice, Carl Yastrzemski, Luis Tiant, Carlton Fisk, Reggie Jackson and Vida Blue; 1970s Houston Astros jerseys for Cesar Cedeno and Bob Watson; and 1970s Cincinnati Reds jerseys for members of the "Big Red Machine" - Pete Rose, Johnny Bench, Joe Morgan and Tony Perez.

Other forgery targets include: Braves (Dale Murphy, Phil Niekro); Reds (Eric Davis); Dodgers (Steve Garvey); Padres (Tony Gwynn, Ozzie Smith, Garry Templeton); Giants (Vida Blue, Will Clark, Dave Kingman, Bill Madlock); Cubs (Ryne Sandberg); Expos (Gary Carter, Andre Dawson); Mets (Gary Carter, Dwight Gooden, Darryl Strawberry, Tom Seaver); Phillies (Steve Carlton, Pete Rose, Mike Schmidt); Pirates (Bill Madlock, Willie Stargell); Cardinals (Keith Hernandez, Ozzie Smith); Orioles (Reggie Jackson, Jim Palmer, Boog Powell, Cal Ripken Jr., Brooks Robinson); Red Sox (Wade Boggs, Roger Clemens, Carl Yastrzemski); Indians (Warren Spahn); Yankees (Reggie Jackson, Thurman Munson, Graig Nettles, Mickey Rivers); Blue Jays (Ron Fairly, Lloyd Moseby); Angels (Frank Robinson, Nolan Ryan); White Sox (Dick Allen, Harold Baines, Carlton Fisk, Ralph Garr, Rich Gossage, Greg Luzinski, Jorge Orta); Royals (George Brett); Twins (Rod Carew, Kent Hrbek, Harmon Killebrew, Kirby Puckett); A's (Jose Canseco, Rickey Henderson, Billy Martin); Mariners (Ken Griffey Jr.).

In most instances, teams issue two of each jersey style to players under their employment. Three sets of attire is not uncommon, but this practice of three homes/three roads is not as common. In rare instances, set 4 and even set 5 shirts have surfaced. Apart from that, extra shirts tend to appear only when replacements are needed for damaged or stolen uniforms, or, in the 1980s especially, some stars have had several jerseys issued to them for several reasons, such as to be used as donations to fund-raisers and charity auctions, to be given to friends, or for team employees to perhaps barter with collectors. Thus, some star jerseys from the last several years may exist in more common than twos or threes for a given style, and some may only evidence minor wear.

The jersey market has a wide variety of dollar amounts assigned to its items. Certain common knits of less popular teams and styles can be had for well under $200, while some totally original, authentic flannels have commanded five-figure sums in highly publicized auctions.

Basically speaking, the price range for a "common" knit usually falls in the $100 to $200 range. However, many exceptions exist. Rather than presenting a yearly, team-by-team price guide, this text will examine situations that may cause a jersey price to exceed $200, or perhaps cause a noticeable markup in a jersey from the lower end of the scale.

Scarcity: Supply/demand considerations affect the price guide scale in the equipment market. The highest dollars come with teams whose jerseys are not only scarce, but also sought by a wide range of collectors.

New releases: Higher prices are generally seen for styles that have recently been introduced and whose numbers within the hobby are restricted due to limited time for release, until greater quantities appear.

Sleeve adornments: Although a regularly-issued logo patch will only minimally increase a shirt's price, a commemorative, memoriam, or other specially-issued patch often creates a notable price increase.

High popularity: Some teams' prices, even though their attire is readily available, are driven up due to longstanding fan following or current popularity due to recent on-field success.

Striking styles: Other times, a style, be it rare, common or in-between, hits a chord with collectors and finds a niche as a high-priced item, due to demand for the style itself.

Early 1970s knits: Since the uniform hobby didn't begin hitting full stride until the end of the 1970s, many teams that wore styles for a short time in the 1972-76 time frame may have allowed only a small quantity of styles into the hobby. The focus on preserving jerseys was almost nonexistent in many quarters at that time.

The availability of jerseys in the marketplace varies from team to team.

Spring training/old-timers day jerseys: This is an area in which documentation and history of an item is more important than one may assume. Although prices for such items are lower, proving their origins is often more difficult, and sometimes not provable.

Many collectors don't realize that knits, and even newer and better conditioned flannels, can be machine washed for laundering. This can be done safely if a few key points are heeded about the laundering process.

First, never, ever bleach the jerseys. Chlorine bleach will often drastically fade the letters and numbers on a jersey, so a bleached 1977 Dave Concepcion shirt may as well have had him playing for the Cincinnati Pinks! A no-bleach detergent such as Wisk is recommended.

Secondly, hot water cycles are a definite no-no; the heat in the wash cycle will shrink a jersey. If you own a Carlton Fisk jersey, you're built like Carlton Fisk, and you wash the jersey in hot water, pretty soon you'll need to be built like Ozzie Guillen to fit into it. Cold water is recommended, but lukewarm water is also acceptable in many instances.

Finally, don't use a hot dry cycle; it may cause shrinkage. If you must use an automatic dryer, use an air setting, or the lowest setting. If you have the means, and your neighbors aren't into scavenging your back yard, then a closeline and sunshine will do the rest.

Tags bearing an inscription "wash separately by color" are not a concern when repeatedly done. That inscription is to warn parties about the possible fading of the new jersey's coloring onto other items it is washed with.

Simply put, those who follow the laundry tags in a jersey, and don't try to innovate or discard the information those tags offer for caring for jerseys, should have very few problems.

— Dave Miedema

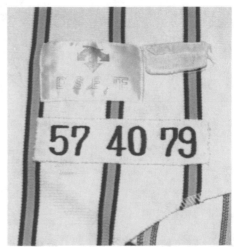

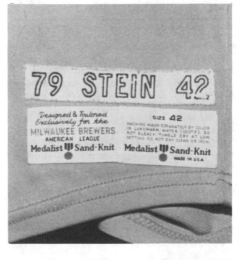

Clockwise, from top left:

1) This 1963 A's gold vest shows a 1959-66 Wilson company label.

2) Harvey Haddix's 1979 Descente Pittsburgh Pirates pinstripe knit jersey shows the label and strip tag — uniform #, size, year.

3) Randy Stein's 1979 Milwaukee Brewers road knit shows a strip tag (year/name/size) and exclusive tag.

4) Rick Reichardt's Washington Senators road flannel has the year tag embroidered directly into the tail.

5) Joe Kerrigan's 1985 Montreal Expos knit shows a Rawlings strip tag (size/year) and flag tag.

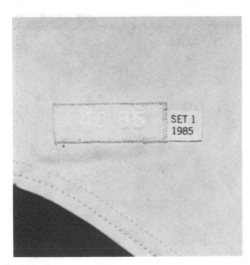

Clockwise, from top left:

1) Rawlings' extra-length tags are attached on the jersey sides.

2) John Henry Johnson's 1987 Milwaukee Brewers road knit shows the occasionally-used 1987 Rawlings company label with flag and strip tags.

3) Sid Monge's 1978 Cleveland Indians road knit shows Rawlings' 1971-88 company label with flag tag.

4) Carlton Fisk's 1991 Chicago White Sox road knit shows a 1989-91 Rawlings company label with flag tag, extra-length tag and tapered tag.

5) Dave Pavlas' 1989 Texas Rangers home spring training knit shows a 1988-89 Rawlings company label with strip tag.

Clockwise, from top left:

1) This jersey is an example of a strip tag showing uniform number, year, set and size.

2) Rick Reichardt's Senators flannel shows a 1967-73 Wilson company label, type 1 small.

3) Ray Burris' 1976 Chicago Cubs home knit shows a 1974-78 Wilson company label (type 2 small) with a strip tag (uniform #/year/set/size).

4) Tom Dettore's 1975 Chicago Cubs road knit shows a 1974-78 Wilson company label with strip tag (uniform #/year/set/size).

5) Bobby Jones' 1984 Texas Rangers blue knit shows a 1979-86 Wilson company label (type 3 small) with year/set tag.

Game-used jerseys

Sparky Anderson: 1974 Cincinnati Reds home, game worn, NOB, signed $1,000
Luis Aparicio: 1968 Chicago White Sox home, with pants, NOB, signed $8,500
Dusty Baker: 1970 Atlanta Braves away, game worn $1,250
Johnny Bench: 1971 Cincinnati Reds road, NIC, NOB, signed $7,500
Tony Bernazard: 1980 Montreal Expos road, game worn, NOB $195
Bert Blyleven: 1987 Minnesota Twins home, game worn, NOB $950
Wade Boggs: 1984 Boston Red Sox road, game worn $1,490
Barry Bonds: 1989 Pittsburgh Pirates road, game worn, NOB $3,000
Bobby Bonilla: 1988 Pittsburgh Pirates road, game worn, NOB $495
Bob Boone: 1980s California Angels road, game worn, NOB, signed $775
Bob Boone: 1990 Kansas City Royals away, game worn, NOB $475
Lou Brock: 1964 St. Louis Cardinals road, NIT, restored, signed $2,500
Hubie Brooks: 1991 New York Mets road, game worn, NOB $295
Jose Canseco: 1986 Oakland A's yellow, game worn, NOB $1,600
Rod Carew: California Angels Old-Timers Game jersey, game worn $250
Steve Carlton: 1977 Philadelphia Phillies home, game worn $2,800
Orlando Cepeda: 1961 San Francisco Giants away, game worn $3,500
Orlando Cepeda: 1971 Atlanta Braves home, game worn $1,395
Jack Clark: 1989 San Diego Padres road, game worn, NOB, signed $195
Will Clark: 1988 San Francisco Giants home, game worn, NOB $1,500
Roger Clemens: 1988 Boston Red Sox home, signed $1,995
Roberto Clemente: 1957 Pittsburgh Pirates road, restored $15,000
Vince Coleman: 1986 St. Louis Cardinals knit, game worn, NOB $375
David Cone: 1989 New York Mets road, NOB, game worn, signed $350
Eric Davis: 1985 Cincinnati Reds knit, game worn $400
Glenn Davis: 1988 Houston Astros knit, game worn, NOB $400
Andre Dawson: 1984 Montreal Expos road, game worn $1,595
Andre Dawson: complete 1988 Chicago Cubs home uniform, game worn $2,500
Rob Dibble: 1988 Cincinnati Reds road, All-Star Game patch, signed $350
Rollie Fingers: 1970 Oakland A's road flannel, game worn, signed $2,500
Chuck Finley: 1987 California Angels road, game worn, NOB $295
Carlton Fisk: 1993 Chicago White Sox road, NOB $1,095
Ray Fosse: 1978 Milwaukee Brewers road, game worn $295
Julio Franco: 1984 Cleveland Indians home, game worn, NOB $495
Ron Gant: 1992 Atlanta Braves home, game worn, NOB $600
Steve Garvey: 1976 Los Angeles Dodgers home, game worn $1,600
Steve Garvey: 1981 Los Angeles Dodgers home, game worn, NOB, signed $850
Bob Gibson: 1968 St. Louis Cardinals road, NOB, restored, signed $7,500
Kirk Gibson: 1989 Los Angeles Dodgers home, game worn, NOB, signed $350
Mike Greenwell: 1986 Boston Red Sox road, game worn $595
Ken Griffey Jr.: 1990 Seattle Mariners road, game worn, NOB $2,400
Ozzie Guillen: 1988 Chicago White Sox road, game worn $495
Tony Gwynn: 1989 San Diego Padres road, game worn, NOB, signed $1,195
Moose Haas: 1978 Milwaukee Brewers home, game worn $185

Richie Hebner: 1977 Philadelphia Phillies road, NOB, NIC...................................$375
Tommy Helms: 1972 Houston Astros home, game worn $1,200
Dave Henderson: 1988 Oakland A's home, game worn, NOB $295
Rickey Henderson: 1991 Oakland A's road, game worn, NOB, signed $1,995
Rickey Henderson: 1993 Oakland A's road, game worn $800
Orel Hershiser: 1984 Los Angeles Dodgers home, NOB, signed....................... $550
Whitey Herzog: 1983 St. Louis Cardinals home, game worn, NOB $375
Burt Hooten: 1983 Los Angeles Dodgers home, NOB, 25th anniversary patch....... $350
Kent Hrbek: 1988 Minnesota Twins road, game worn, NOB $450
Catfish Hunter: 1971 Oakland A's road, game worn, NOB.................................$2,800
Catfish Hunter: 1974 Oakland A's home, game worn $1,950
Bo Jackson: 1989 Kansas City Royals home, game worn, NOB $1,495
Gregg Jefferies: 1990 New York Mets home, game worn, NOB.........................$450
Fergie Jenkins: 1980 Texas Rangers home, game worn, signed......................... $1,095
Tommy John: 1974 Los Angeles Dodgers away, game worn................................$1,100
Cliff Johnson: 1979 Cleveland Indians blue, game worn, NOB.......................... $195
Wally Joyner: 1987 California Angels road, game worn, NOB, signed................ $495
Dave Justice: 1992 Atlanta Braves home, game worn, NOB...............................$1,200
Eric Karros: 1992 Los Angeles Dodgers road, game worn, NOB, signed $695
Harmon Killebrew: 1969 Minnesota Twins home flannel, game worn, NIC...... $6,995
Ken Landreaux: 1977 California Angeles road, game worn $225
Mark Langston: 1984 Seattle Mariners, road, game worn, NOB $650
Tony LaRussa: 1993 Oakland A's home, game worn.. $200
Tommy Lasorda: 1988 Los Angeles Dodgers home, game worn, NOB, signed $450
Ron LeFlore: 1980 Montreal Expos away, game worn, NOB $250
Charlie Leibrandt: 1979 Cincinnati Reds away, game worn, NOB $150
Davey Lopes: 1986 Chicago Cubs home, game worn $395
Fred Lynn: 1975 Boston Red Sox home, game worn $495
Bill Madlock: 1977 San Francisco Giants away, game worn, NOB........................$350
Juan Marichal: 1966 San Francisco Giants home, NIC, signed $9,500
Billy Martin: 1958 Detroit Tigers home, game worn $2,200
Eddie Mathews: 1967 Houston Astros home, game worn...................................$7,500
Gene Mauch: 1972 Montreal Expos home flannel, game worn $1,695
Lee May: 1977 Baltimore Orioles road, game worn, NOB $750
Jack McDowell: 1988 Chicago White Sox road, game worn.............................. $995
Willie McGee: 1984 St. Louis Cardinals knit, game worn.................................. $400
Lynn McGlothen: 1978 Chicago Cubs road, game worn $175
Mark McGwire: Oakland A's road, game worn, NOB $900
Hal McRae: 1986 Kansas City Royals away, game worn, NOB $275
Kevin Mitchell: 1989 San Francisco Giants, for 1989 All-Star Game.................... $695
Paul Molitor: 1983 Milwaukee Brewers road, game worn, NIT $1,500
Paul Molitor: 1988 Milwaukee Brewers road, game worn $975
Joe Morgan: 1968 Houston Astros road, game worn $5,500
Joe Morgan: 1969 Houston Astros home, restored $1,800
Joe Morgan: 1982 San Francisco Giants home, game worn, NOB, signed $1,950
Joe Morgan: 1984 Oakland A's road, game worn, NOB, signed $850
Jack Morris: 1983 Detroit Tigers road, game worn, NOB.................................. $850

Manny Mota: 1971 Los Angeles Dodgers road, game worn, NIT $2,500
Eddie Murray: 1988 Baltimore Orioles road, game worn $1,300
Dale Murphy: 1988 Atlanta Braves home, game worn, signed.............................. $895
Stan Musial: 1953 St. Louis Cardinals home, signed... $20,000
Craig Nettles: 1985 San Diego Padres home, game worn, NOB $595
Phil Niekro: 1968 Atlanta Braves home, NIC, restored, signed $2,800
Mike Norris: 1990 Oakland A's home, game worn, NOB $250
Tony Oliva: 1967 Minnesota Twins home flannel, game worn, NIC...................... $1,800
Gene Oliver: 1966 Atlanta Braves home, game worn, signed.............................. $650
Dave Parker: 1984 Cincinnati Reds road, signed, NOB..................................... $395
Dave Parker: 1990 Milwaukee Brewers home, game worn $550
Dan Pasqua: 1985 New York Yankees road, game worn $395
Terry Pendleton: 1991-93 Atlanta Braves road, game worn $200
Tony Perez: 1971 Cincinnati Reds home, game worn $2,850
Gaylord Perry: 1982 Seattle Mariners home, game worn, NOB, signed................. $995
Boog Powell: 1967 Baltimore Orioles home flannel, game worn, NOB............... $1,095
Kirby Puckett: 1988 Minnesota Twins road, game worn, NOB $1,300
Tim Raines: 1987 Montreal Expos road, game worn, NOB, signed..................... $595
Pee Wee Reese: 1956 Brooklyn Dodgers home, NIC, restored, signed................ $2,800
Cal Ripken Jr.: 1993 Baltimore Orioles road, NOB, All-Star Game patch $2,295
Brooks Robinson: 1957 Baltimore Orioles road, signed $5,000
Brooks Robinson: 1973 Baltimore Orioles road, game worn, NOB $3,750
Frank Robinson: 1975 Cleveland Indians away, game worn, NOB...................... $1,950
Frank Robinson: 1982 San Francisco Giants home, game worn, NOB, signed...... $850
Pete Rose: 1965 Cincinnati Reds home, game worn, NOB $8,250
Pete Rose: 1970 Cincinnati Reds road, game worn, NOB.................................. $2,000
Nolan Ryan: 1984 Houston Astros road, NOB $3,495
Bret Saberhagen: 1988 Kansas City Royals road, game worn, NOB, signed......... $350
Benito Santiago: 1988 San Diego Padres road, game worn, NOB, signed $395
Steve Sax: 1984 Los Angeles Dodgers road, game worn, NOB $550
Mike Schmidt: 1989 Philadelphia Phillies road, NOB, signed........................... $1,750
Red Schoendienst: 1957 New York Giants flannel, game worn, NIC................... $3,000
Tom Seaver: 1974 New York Mets home, game worn, signed............................. $5,500
Lee Smith: 1988 Boston Red Sox road, game worn... $425
Ozzie Smith: 1982 St. Louis Cardinals World Series home, game worn............... $1,895
Reggie Smith: 1978 Los Angeles Dodgers road, game worn, NOB $450
Willie Stargell: 1970 Pittsburgh Pirates home, signed.................................... $8,000
Darryl Strawberry: 1986 New York Mets road, game worn, NOB $600
Don Sutton: 1974 Los Angeles Dodgers home, NOB, signed............................. $1,995
Greg Swindell: 1991 Cleveland Indians road, game worn, NOB, signed................ $495
Danny Tartabull: 1987 Kansas City Royals home, game worn, NOB.................... $695
Frank Thomas: Black mesh Chicago White Sox warm-up jersey, signed.............. $995
Joe Torre: 1981 New York Mets road, game used, NOB $225
Fernando Valenzuela: 1981 Los Angeles Dodgers road, game worn, NOB $895
Frank Viola: 1990 New York Mets home, game worn, NOB $350
Earl Weaver: 1976 Baltimore Orioles, game worn, NOB.................................. $1,195
Bob Welch: 1988 Oakland A's World Series home, 1988 W.S. patch, game worn $595

Mitch Williams: 1989 Chicago Cubs road, game worn, NOB, signed $295
Maury Wills: 1981 Seattle Mariners road, manager, NOB $750
Todd Worrell: 1982 St. Louis Cardinals road, game worn $250
Early Wynn: 1955 Cleveland Indians home, game worn, NIC, signed................. $6,000
Carl Yastrzemski: 1969 Boston Red Sox home, signed..................................... $5,000
Robin Yount: 1991 Milwaukee Brewers road, complete uniform, signed $1,500
Robin Yount: 1992 Milwaukee Brewers warm up... $1,295

Replica jerseys

Hank Aaron: Late 1950s Milwaukee Braves tomahawk, signed $350
Hank Aaron: Late 1960s Atlanta Braves flannel, signed $295
Sparky Anderson: Detroit Tigers home #11 .... $185
Luis Aparicio: Chicago White Sox flannel, signed... $275
Steve Avery: Atlanta Braves home #33.. $165
Johnny Bench: 1969 Cincinnati Reds home, signed $295
Yogi Berra: 1952 New York Yankees home flannel, signed $300
Vida Blue: San Francisco Giants home, signed $175
Barry Bonds: Pittsburgh Pirates home, signed.. $275
Barry Bonds: San Francisco Giants road, signed.. $275
George Brett: Kansas City Royals home, signed... $395
Lou Brock: St. Louis Cardinals road, signed $250
Bill Buckner: Chicago Cubs home, signed... $185
Roy Campanella: Brooklyn Dodgers, signed $895
Rod Carew: California Angels home, signed... $395
Steve Carlton: St. Louis Cardinals flannel, signed $325
Will Clark: San Francisco Giants home, signed $275
Roger Clemens: Boston Red Sox home, signed $295
Roberto Clemente: Pittsburgh Pirates home, flannel $195
Eric Davis: Cincinnati Reds home, signed $185
Joe DiMaggio: 1939 New York Yankees pinstripe, signed $2,495
Don Drysdale: Los Angeles Dodgers grey flannel, signed $750
Dennis Eckersley: Oakland A's home #43... $185
Cal Eldred: Milwaukee Brewers home #21 .... $140
Bob Feller: Cleveland Indians flannel, signed $225
Cecil Fielder: Detroit Tigers road, signed $275
Rollie Fingers: Oakland A's road flannel, signed... $275
Rollie Fingers: Milwaukee Brewers home, signed $275
Carlton Fisk: Chicago White Sox road, signed.. $300
Lou Gehrig: 1930s New York Yankees pinstripe flannel..................................... $210
Charlie Gehringer: Detroit Tigers home, signed.. $575
Bob Gibson: St. Louis Cardinals home, signed $295
Juan Gonzalez: Texas Rangers home, signed... $295
Dwight Gooden: New York Mets pinstripe, signed.. $160
Ken Griffey Jr.: Seattle Mariners home, signed.. $325
Tony Gwynn: San Diego Padres home, signed... $250

Rickey Henderson: New York Yankees pinstripe, signed $275
Keith Hernandez: New York Mets road, signed $150
Orel Hershiser: Los Angeles Dodgers home, signed $325
Bo Jackson: Chicago White Sox road, signed $350
Reggie Jackson: 1969 Oakland A's road, flannel, signed $375
Reggie Jackson: New York Yankees grey, signed $295
Fergie Jenkins: Chicago Cubs home, signed $295
Al Kaline: Detroit Tigers grey flannel, signed $275
Harmon Killebrew: Minnesota Twins road, signed $295
Barry Larkin: Cincinnati Reds home, signed.. $225
Pat Listach: Milwaukee Brewers home #16 .... $140
Bill Madlock: Pittsburgh Pirates away $85
Mickey Mantle: 1951 New York Yankees pinstripe, signed $695
Juan Marichal: San Francisco Giants road, signed..................................... $275
Roger Maris: New York Yankees home $185
Eddie Mathews: 1957 Milwaukee Braves tomahawk, signed $295
Don Mattingly: New York Yankees road, signed $300
Willie Mays: San Francisco Giants flannel, signed..................................... $450
Willie McCovey: San Francisco Giants road, signed $250
Joe Morgan: 1969 Houston Astros flannel, signed..................................... $295
Stan Musial: 1942 St. Louis Cardinals flannel, signed.................................. $325
Stan Musial: St. Louis Cardinals home #6 .... $175
Phil Niekro: 1969 Atlanta Braves flannel, signed..................................... $300
Jim Palmer: Baltimore Orioles home, signed.. $275
Terry Pendleton: Atlanta Braves home #9.. $165
Gaylord Perry: 1962 San Francisco Giants flannel, signed $275
Kirby Puckett: Minnesota Twins home, signed... $350
Pee Wee Reese: Brooklyn Dodgers away flannel, signed $295
Cal Ripken Jr.: Baltimore Orioles home #8 .... $225
Brooks Robinson: Baltimore Orioles grey flannel, signed $275
Frank Robinson: Cincinnati Reds flannel, signed $295
Pete Rose: 1963 Cincinnati Reds flannel vest, signed $295
Babe Ruth: 1920s New York Yankees flannel... $200
Ryne Sandberg: Chicago Cubs road, signed $350
Mike Schmidt: Philadelphia Phillies grey flannel, signed $350
Tom Seaver: 1969 New York Mets home, signed....................................... $350
Ozzie Smith: St. Louis Cardinals home, signed.. $295
Duke Snider: Los Angeles Dodgers flannel, signed $250
Warren Spahn: Milwaukee Braves home, signed $325
Darryl Strawberry: New York Mets road, signed $150
Don Sutton: Los Angeles Dodgers home, signed $275
Frank Thomas: Chicago White Sox road, signed $350
Alan Trammell: Detroit Tigers home #3 .... $175
Ted Williams: 1939 Boston Red Sox home flannel, signed $750
Dave Winfield: New York Yankees road, signed $350
Carl Yastrzemski: Boston Red Sox home flannel, signed............................... $350
Robin Yount: Milwaukee Brewers home #19 .... $220

Equipment

Lack of information to identify a bat often hinders beginning collectors.

There are basically four categories of bats which collectors pursue. They are:

1) Authentic cracked vs. uncracked, but game-used bat: The player has actually used the bat in a game; it shows wear and tear from use, including scuffs, dents, tape, filing of the handle, uniform #s on the handles, use of pine tar, hollowed ends and cracks. The value of a bat decreases according to the size of the crack.

Companies make store model bats with players' endorsements on them.

This bat is made to a player's specifications, with his name and signature on it, or it could be a bat ordered by the team, with the team name branded into it. Pitchers and coaches generally use these bats. Coaches' bats may carry the player's name, but are not necessarily made according to the specifics he used as an active player.

2) Authentic bats, made to the player's specifications, but which have not been used in a game: It's possible the player didn't even own the bat, which could have been ordered by the team for promotions or giveaways, or made for other businesses for resale. These bats are often used for autographing.

3) Retail or store model bats are those which are purchased in sporting goods stores. They are not made according to the player's specifications, but often carry his name as an endorsement. Vintage model bats of stars before the 1950s generally sell well. Naive collectors can end up purchasing these bats for $100 to $200, thinking they are game-used bats when they aren't. Store models can be distinguished from game-used bats because the knobs carry inch markings, a single-digit number, or both initials of the player whose name is on the barrel. Also, if the bat number in the brand oval is followed by any letters, probably player initials, it's likely the bat is a store model.

4) Commemoratives: These bats are made to recognize a particular person, place or event in baseball history, such as a World Series or Hall of Fame induction. These customized bats, generally more desirable than store models, are often created for display purposes and are suitable for autographing, which makes them more valuable. Black Sharpie pens work best.

According to Mark Allen Baker, author of the second edition of the **Baseball Autograph Handbook**, "lack of accurate information to identify particular bats, along with sources to purchase them from, have been the two greatest obstacles for beginning collectors. Also complicating the hobbyist's acquisition is the lack of the proper terminology to describe a bat. Novice collectors often incorrectly mistake store-bought or retail bats for authentic game-used models. Both collectors and dealers simply do not take enough time to research the background of their acquisitions, often resulting in false advertising of the bat and a worthless acquisition by a novice collector."

The complexities of bat markings will not be delved into, but some general guidelines follow:

Baseball's rules limit the length of bats to 42 inches long and 2 3/4 inches wide. Generally, bats weigh between 30-50 ounces.

These are the most common bat brands used by major leaguers:

1) Hillerich & Bradsby: This company has undergone several name modifications since 1884 until 1979, when its bats became more commonly known as Louisville Sluggers, H&B's most popular style. Since 1945 H&B has labeled bats with player initials and a model number on the knob, which is an identifying number for each individual style. In 1976 those numbers were moved to the barrel of the bat. If the player is contracted with the manufacturer his name is burned into the bat barrel in autograph form. If he isn't, his name is in block letters.

Hillerich & Bradsby adopted the slogan "Powerized" in 1932 and began putting model numbers - which have one letter and at least one number - on the knob in 1944. Those numbers were removed beginning in 1976 and then placed on the barrel. The H&B logo was dropped in 1979, with Louisville Slugger becoming the brand label.

2) A.G. Spalding & Bros. bats, used primarily before the turn of the century.

3) A.J. Reach bats, which were prominent at the beginning of the century.

4) Rawlings, which labels its bats as Adirondacks, and feature a single-colored ring around the neck and a diamond-shaped trademark.

5) Worth, which entered the market in the 1970s and offers its Tennessee Thumper bats.

6) Cooper bats, produced in Canada since 1986.

7) Mizuno bats, made in Japan.

A final caveat, as offered by noted dealer Alan "Mr. Mint" Rosen in his book **Mr. Mint's Insider's Guide To Investing in Baseball Cards and Collectibles**: "Caveat emptor. It is very difficult to verify a bat actually used by a player in a major-league game. (Was it scuffed at a softball game last week? Did the player himself use it, or did one of his teammates? Was it used only in batting practice? Often, players themselves cannot remember which stick they used.) If you invest in one of these bats, deal only with a dealer who is an expert in the area and insist on written documentation. Reliable dealers usually get these items from unimpeachable sources - the player's attorney or agent, a family member, the clubhouse attendant, or a batboy."

The following are examples of styles and brands of game-used bats and the prices for which they've been listed for sale in *Sports Collectors Digest*.

Hank Aaron: Hillerich & Bradsby, game used, 1964 .... $2,850

Hank Aaron: Adirondack, game used, 1961-67, signed $2,350

Hank Aaron: Adirondack, game used, uncracked, early 1970s $2,295

Hank Aaron: Hillerich & Bradsby, game used, 1973-75 .... $1,295

Shawn Abner: Cooper, game used, cracked.. $40

Dick Allen: Hillerich & Bradsby, game used, 1973-75, signed................................ $695

Bill Almon: Louisville Slugger, game used, cracked $25

Roberto Alomar: Cooper, game used, cracked, 1993 .... $295

Sandy Alomar: Adirondack, game used, 1970s... $95

Sandy Alomar Jr.: Cooper, game used, cracked, 1993 .... $145

Matty Alou: Hillerich & Bradsby, game used, early 1960s $175

Jesus Alou: Hillerich & Bradsby, game used, pre-1965, cracked $75

Moises Alou: Adirondack, game used, 1992... $140

Ryne Sandberg signs a bat during one of his baseball card show appearances.

Brady Anderson: Louisville Slugger, game used, 1986-89 .... $90

Luis Aparicio: Hillerich & Bradsby, game used, 1960s $795

Tony Armas: Louisville Slugger, game used, cracked, 1986-89 .... $45

Richie Ashburn: Hillerich & Bradsby, game used, cracked, 1948-49 .... $1,695

Benny Ayala: Hillerich & Bradsby, game used, cracked $35

Carlos Baerga: Adirondack, game used, 1991 .... $295

Harold Baines: Adirondack, game used, uncracked, 1991, signed $110

Dusty Baker: Adirondack, game used, 1970s $150

Steve Balboni: Louisville Slugger, game used, 1986-89 .... $30

Chris Bando: Louisville Slugger, game used, 1984-85 .... $20

Ernie Banks: Hillerich & Bradsby, game used, 1960-64, signed $5,400

Ernie Banks: Hillerich & Bradsby, game used, uncracked, pre-1972 .... $2,495

Jesse Barfield: Adirondack, game used, 1986 .... $70

Don Baylor: Adirondack, game used, 1968-71 .... $110

Mark Belanger: new label Louisville Slugger, uncracked, signed $125

Albert Belle: Louisville Slugger, game used, 1991-93 .... $295

Johnny Bench: Louisville Slugger, game used, uncracked, 1972-75, signed $695

Tony Bernazard: Louisville Slugger, game used, two-tone, 1984-85 .... $35

Yogi Berra: Hillerich & Bradsby, game used, uncracked, 1950s, signed $2,500

Ron Blomberg: Hillerich & Bradsby, game used, cracked, 1977-79 .... $90

Wade Boggs: Cooper, game used, uncracked, pine tar, 1991, signed $295
Wade Boggs: Louisville Slugger, game used, cracked, 1993................................... $495
Barry Bonds: Louisville Slugger, game used, uncracked, 1992 .... $750
Bobby Bonds: Adirondack, game used, 1971-79... $195
Bobby Bonilla: Louisville Slugger, game used, 1986-89.. $175
Bob Boone: Hillerich & Bradsby, game used, 1972-75, signed $325
Lyman Bostock: Hillerich & Bradsby, game used, uncracked.................................. $85
Larry Bowa: Hillerich & Bradsby, game used, uncracked...................................... $125
Clete Boyer: Hillerich & Bradsby, game used, 1965-72.. $225
Phil Bradley: Louisville Slugger, game used, cracked.. $40
Glenn Braggs: Adirondack, game used, 1989... $30
Sid Bream: new label Louisville Slugger, cracked, 1991....................................... $70
George Brett: Louisville Slugger, game used, uncracked, 1977-79, signed $1,850
George Brett: Louisville Slugger, game used, uncracked, early 1980s................. $1,150
Lou Brock: Hillerich & Bradsby, game used, 1965-72.. $625
Lou Brock: Adirondack, game used, 1971-79, signed $495
Jack Brohamer: new label Louisville Slugger, game used, cracked....................... $30
Hubie Brooks: Worth, game used, uncracked $75
Gates Brown: Hillerich & Bradsby, game used, 1960-64 .... $395
Ollie Brown: Hillerich & Bradsby, game used, 1965-72 .... $125
Bill Buckner: Hillerich & Bradsby, game used, cracked, pre-1972, signed $100
Bill Buckner: Adirondack, game used, uncracked, black, 1988............................. $90
Al Bumbry: Louisville Slugger, game used, uncracked, signed $65
Jeff Burroughs: Adirondack, game used, 1977... $75
Brett Butler: Louisville Slugger, game used, 1980s.. $150
Enos Cabell: Hillerich & Bradsby, game used, 1973-75 .... $60
Ken Caminiti: Adirondack, game used, 1992... $70
Jose Canseco: Louisville Slugger, game used, uncracked, 1986-89, signed $395
Bernie Carbo: Louisville Slugger, game used, cracked, early 1980s $30
Rod Carew: Hillerich & Bradsby, game used, 1973-75.. $595
Rod Carew: Louisville Slugger, game used, uncracked, 1984-85, signed............... $450
Steve Carlton: Louisville Slugger, game used, 1980-83, signed $795
Gary Carter: Louisville Slugger, game used, 1980-83 .... $165
Gary Carter: Adirondack, game uesd, uncracked, mid-1980s............................... $275
Joe Carter: Louisville Slugger, game used, 1986-89... $195
Rico Carty: Hillerich & Bradsby, game used, 1972-75, signed $295
Dave Cash: Adirondack, game used, cracked 1970s
Cesar Cedeno: Hillerich & Bradsby, game used, 1977-79, signed.......................... $55
Orlando Cepeda: Hillerich & Bradsby, game used, 1973-75 .... $495
Rick Cerone: Louisville Slugger, game used, cracked 1986-89.............................. $45

Ron Cey: Hillerich & Bradsby, game used, 1973-75 .... $150
Jack Clark: Louisville Slugger, 1984-85 .... $60
Will Clark: Adirondack, game used, uncracked, 1992 .... $325
Roberto Clemente: Hillerich & Bradsby, game used, cracked, 1960 .... $3,295
Roberto Clemente: Adirondack, game used, 1968-70 .... $2,495
Rocky Colavito: Hillerich & Bradsby, game used, 1949-65 .... $995
Alex Cole: new label Louisville Slugger, game used, cracked $45
Darnell Coles: Worth, game used, cracked $15
Cecil Cooper: Hillerich & Bradsby, game used, 1977-79 .... $50
Joey Cora: Louisville Slugger, game used, 1993 .... $45
Al Cowens: Louisville Slugger, game used, 1986-89 .... $25
Roger "Doc" Cramer: Hillerich & Bradsby, game used, handle crack $850
Kal Daniels: Rawlings, uncracked, #28 on knob, signed $95
Alvin Dark: Hillerich & Bradsby, game used, 1946-65 .... $395
Jack Daubert: Hillerich & Bradsby, game used, 1921-31 .... $595
Chili Davis: Worth, game used, 1991 .... $75
Eric Davis: Louisville Slugger, uncracked, #44 at both ends $135
Glenn Davis: Louisville Slugger, game used, uncracked, 1986-89 .... $55
Tommy Davis: Hillerich & Bradsby, used in 1962 All-Star Game, cracked $795
Andre Dawson: Louisville Slugger, game used, 1980-83, signed $395
Rob Deer: Louisville Slugger, game used, cracked, 1993 .... $50
Jose DeLeon: new label Louisville Slugger, game used, uncracked $30
Bucky Dent: Adirondack, 1980, game used $95
Joe DiMaggio: Hillerich & Bradsby, game used, 1949-60 .... $1,695
Al Downing: Hillerich & Bradsby, 1965-72 .... $275
Jim Dwyer: Hillerich & Bradsby, game used $45
Len Dykstra: Louisville Slugger, game used, 1993, signed $295
Jim Eisenrich: new label Louisville Slugger, game used, cracked $40
Nick Esasky: Louisville Slugger, game used, 1990 .... $35
Dwight Evans: Hillerich & Bradsby, 1977-79 .... $295
Ron Fairly: Hillerich & Bradsby, 1973-75 .... $125
Tony Fernandez: Louisville Slugger, 1992, game used, pine tar $60
Cecil Fielder: Cooper, game used, cracked, 1992 .... $295
Carlton Fisk: Adirondack, game used, 1971-79, signed $995
Scott Fletcher: new label Louisville Slugger, game used, cracked $50
Tim Foli: Louisville Slugger, game used, 1984-85 .... $25
Julio Franco: Louisville Slugger, game used, 1986-89 .... $60
Bill Freehan: Hillerich & Bradsby, game used, 1960-64, signed $795
Jim Fregosi: Hillerich & Bradsby, game used, handle crack, 1960-64 .... $350
Tito Fuentes: Adirondack, game used, 1970s, uncracked $85

Gary Gaetti: Louisville Slugger, game used, cracked, 1986-89 .... $50

Ron Gant: Louisville Slugger, game used, 1993 .... $450

Pedro Garcia: Hillerich & Bradsby, game used, cracked $30

Phil Garner: Louisville Slugger, game used, 1986-89 .... $40

Ralph Garr: Hillerich & Bradsby, game used, 1977-79 .... $95

Steve Garvey: Hillerich & Bradsby, game used, 1969-72 .... $525

Steve Garvey: Louisville Slugger, game used, uncracked, 1986-87 .... $275

Cito Gaston: Adirondack, game used, 1970s $225

Bob Gibson: Hillerich & Bradsby, game used, 1972-75, signed $1,500

Kirk Gibson: Louisville Slugger, game used, 1993 .... $100

Juan Gonzalez: Louisville Slugger, game used, uncracked, 1993, signed $595

Goose Gossage: Louisville Slugger, game used, 1984-85 .... $125

Mark Grace: Adirondack, game used, 1993 .... $295

Mike Greenwell: Louisville Slugger, game used, cracked, 1993 .... $85

Ken Griffey Jr.: Louisville Slugger, game used, cracked, 1992 .... $795

Charlie Grimm: Hillerich & Bradsby, game used, 1921-31 .... $650

Marquis Grissom: Adirondack, game used, 1993 .... $115

Johnny Grubb: Hillerich & Bradsby, game used, 1973-75 .... $60

Pedro Guerrero: Louisville Slugger, game used, 1984-85 .... $50

Tony Gwynn: Louisville Slugger, game used, uncracked, 1986-89, signed $395

Jerry Hairston: Louisville Slugger, game used, 1986-89 .... $15

Toby Harrah: Hillerich & Bradsby, game used, cracked, 1984, signed $40

Bud Harrelson: Hillerich & Bradsby, game used, 1977-79 .... $135

Von Hayes: Louisville Slugger, game used, 1986-89 .... $40

Harry Heilmann: Hillerich & Bradsby, game used, 1921-31 .... $1,600

Rickey Henderson: Louisville Slugger, game used, 1980-83 .... $495

Rickey Henderson: Louisville Slugger, game used, uncracked, 1984-85, signed . $375

George Hendrick: Louisville Slugger, cracked, #25 on knob, signed $90

Keith Hernandez: Louisville Slugger, game used, cracked, 1980s $150

Babe Herman: Hillerich & Bradsby, game used, 1943-45 .... $495

Whitey Herzog: Hillerich & Bradsby, fungo bat, 1972-75, signed $295

Marc Hill: Adirondack, game used $45

Ron Hodges: Louisville Slugger, game used, 1980-83 .... $40

Burt Hooten: Hillerich & Bradsby, game used, 1971-72 .... $125

Willie Horton: Adirondack, game used, 1971-79 .... $195

Elston Howard: Hillerich & Bradbsy, uncracked, 1958 World Series $3,000

Frank Howard: Hillerich & Bradsby, game used, 1965-72 .... $550

Kent Hrbek: Louisville Slugger, game used, 1980-83 .... $75

Bruce Hurst: Louisville Slugger, game used, 1990 .... $45

Mike Ivie: Hillerich & Bradsby, game used, cracked $35

Bo Jackson: Louisville Slugger, game used, uncracked, 1993 .... $250

Reggie Jackson: Adirondack, game used, 1971-79 .... $695

Reggie Jackson: Adirondack, game used, 1971-79, signed $995

Fergie Jenkins: Louisville Slugger, game used, 1980-83, signed $495

Jackie Jensen: Hillerich & Bradsby, used in 1952 All-Star Game $1,695

Tommy John: Hillerich & Bradsby, game used, 1977-79 .... $295

Cliff Johnson: Louisville Slugger, game used, cracked, early 1980s $40

Jay Johnstone: Hillerich & Bradsby, game used, 1965-72 .... $115

Wally Joyner: Louisville Slugger, uncracked, 1993 .... $95

Dave Justice: Louisville Slugger, game used, 1993 .... $295

Jim Kaat: Louisville Slugger, game used, 1980-83 .... $195

Al Kaline: Hillerich & Bradsby, game used, 1965-72 .... $995

Eric Karros: Louisville Slugger, game used, 1992, uncracked $250

Steve Kemp: Hillerich & Bradsby, game used, 1977-79 .... $30

Fred Kendall: Adirondack, game used, cracked $35

Ralph Kiner: Hillerich & Bradsby, game used, 1949 .... $1,695

Mickey Klutts: Hillerich & Bradsby, game used, uncracked $40

Ray Knight: Louisville Slugger, game used, 1986-89 .... $70

Chuck Knoblauch: Louisville Slugger, game used, 1992-93 .... $225

Ed Kranepool: Adirondack, game used, 1971-79 .... $295

Harvey Kuenn: Hillerich & Bradsby, game used, 1965-72 .... $550

Ray Lankford: Louisville Slugger, game used, 1993, cracked $75

Carney Lansford: Hillerich & Bradsby, game used, 1977-79 .... $125

Carney Lansford: Louisville Slugger, game used, 1984-85 .... $65

Ron LeFlore: Hillerich & Bradsby, game used, 1977-79 .... $75

Mark Lemke: Louisville Slugger, game used, 1993 .... $95

Chet Lemon: Louisville Slugger, game used, 1990 .... $35

Sixto Lezcano: Hillerich & Bradsby, game used, 1977-79 .... $40

Pat Listach: Cooper, game used, cracked, 1992 .... $65

Davey Lopes: Hillerich & Bradsby, game used, 1973-75 .... $175

Davey Lopes: Adirondack, game used, 1986 .... $65

Greg Luzinski: Adirondack, 1982, signed $100

Fred Lynn: Adirondack, game used, 1990 .... $100

Bill Madlock: Hillerich & Bradsby, 1977, signed $295

Pepe Mangual: Hillerich & Bradsby, game used, cracked $35

Mickey Mantle: Hillerich & Bradsby, 1964 .... $9,995

Mickey Mantle: Adirondack, game used, handle crack, 1961-67 .... $8,500

Eddie Mathews: Hillerich & Bradsby, uncracked, 1968, signed $4,500

Don Mattingly: Louisville Slugger, game used, 1984 .... $795

Carlos May: Hillerich & Bradsby, game used, uncracked $50

Dave May: Adirondack, game used, 1970s $35

John Mayberry: Adirondack, game used, cracked, signed $75

Willie Mays: Adirondack, game used, uncracked, 1971 .... $1,850

Bill Mazeroski: Hillerich & Bradsby, game used, pre-1960, signed $995

Dick McAuliffe: Hillerich & Bradsby, game used, 1960-64 .... $195

Tim McCarver: Hillerich & Bradsby, game used, 1965-72 .... $495

Willie McCovey: Hillerich & Bradsby, game used, 1973-79 .... $1,200

Oddibe McDowell: Louisville Slugger, game used, 1990 .... $20

Fred McGriff: Louisville Slugger, game used, 1986-89 .... $295

Mark McGwire: Adirondack, game used, uncracked, 1992 .... $350

Hal McRae: Hillerich & Bradsby, game used, 1973-75 .... $45

Bill Melton: Adirondack, game used, 1970 .... $110

Minnie Minoso: Hillerich & Bradsby, game used, piece missing, cracked, 1960-64
.... $695

Kevin Mitchell: Louisville Slugger, game used, 1984-85 .... $295

Paul Molitor: Hillerich & Bradsby, game used, 1977-79 .... $695

Paul Molitor: Cooper, game used, cracked, 1992 .... $275

Rick Monday: Hillerich & Bradsby, game used, handle crack, 1965-72 .... $295

Mike Morgan: Louisville Slugger, game used, 1986-89 .... $50

Joe Morgan: Adirondack, game used, slightly cracked, 1979-83 .... $375

Manny Mota: Hillerich & Bradsby, game used, 1977-79 .... $120

Thurman Munson: Hillerich & Bradsby, game used, cracked, 1977-79 .... $550

Bobby Murcer: Hillerich & Bradsby, game used, cracked $175

Dale Murphy: Louisville Slugger, game used, 1986-89, signed $225

Dwayne Murphy: Hillerich & Bradsby, game used, 1977-79 .... $30

Eddie Murray: Louisville Slugger, game used, uncracked, 1986-89 .... $450

Stan Musial: Hillerich & Bradsby, cracked, 1950s, signed $5,500

Stan Musial: Adirondack, game used, 1960 .... $5,000

Stan Musial: Hillerich & Bradsby, uncracked, 1960-63, signed $4,500

Matt Nokes: Louisville Slugger, game used, 1984-85 .... $80

Matt Nokes: Adirondack, game used, 1992 .... $45

Ben Oglivie: Louisville Slugger, game used, 1980-83 .... $85

John Olerud: Adirondack, game used, 1993 .... $395

Tony Oliva: Hillerich & Bradsby, game used, missing knob, early 1970s $175

Bob Oliver: Hillerich & Bradsby, game used, 1965-72 .... $75

Spike Owen: new label Louisville Slugger, game used, cracked $40

Rafael Palmeiro: Cooper, game used, 1993 .... $150

Dave Parker: Rawlings Black Belt, game used, cracked $140

Tony Pena: Louisville Slugger, game used, 1986-89 .... $50

Terry Pendleton: Louisville Slugger, game used, cracked, 1986-89 .... $175

Gaylord Perry: Louisville Slugger, game used, 1980-83, signed $625

Jim Piersall: Hillerich & Bradsby, game used, handle crack, 1960-64 .... $495

Lou Piniella: Hillerich & Bradsby, game used, 1973-75 .... $85

Vada Pinson: Hillerich & Bradsby, game used, 1965-72 .... $295

Darrell Porter: Louisville Slugger, game used, 1980s $40

Boog Powell: Adirondack, game used, 1971-79, signed $295

Boog Powell: Hillerich & Bradsby, used in 1968 All-Star Game, signed $1,295

Vic Power: Hillerich & Bradsby, game used, handle crack, 1960-64 .... $495

Kirby Puckett: Louisville Slugger, game used, uncracked, 1986-89 .... $395

Doug Rader: Hillerich & Bradsby, game used, 1973-75 .... $55

Tim Raines: Louisville Slugger, game used, early 1980s, signed $175

Willie Randolph: Adirondack, game used, 1990 .... $95

Harold Reynolds: Adirondack, game used, uncracked, 1993 .... $55

Dave Revering: Adirondack, game used, uncracked $30

Rick Rhoden: Louisville Slugger, game used, 1984-85 .... $30

Jim Rice: Louisville Slugger, game used, uncracked, early 1980s $125

Cal Ripken Jr.: Louisville Slugger, game used, cracked,1990 .... $725

Brooks Robinson: Adirondack, game used, slightly cracked, 1971-77, signed $895

Don Robinson: Louisville Slugger, game used, 1984-85 .... $20

Frank Robinson: Hillerich & Bradsby, game used, 1977 .... $795

Bob Rodgers: Hillerich & Bradsby, game used, handle crack $295

Ivan Rodriguez: Adirondack, game used, 1992 .... $200

Pete Rose: Hillerich & Bradsby, game used, 1972-75, signed $1,595

Pete Rose: Mizuno, game used, uncracked, 1985-86, signed $1,050

Nolan Ryan: Louisville Slugger, game used, 1983-85, signed $2,995

Tim Salmon: Adirondack, game used, 1992 .... $350

Ryne Sandberg: Louisville Slugger, game used, 1980-83, signed $1,295

Ryne Sandberg: Adirondack, game used, 1992 .... $625

Ryne Sandberg: Adirondack, game used, 1991, uncracked, signed $795

Deion Sanders: Louisville Slugger, game used, 1993 .... $325

Ron Santo: Hillerich & Bradsby, game used, 1965-72, signed $795

Benito Santiago: Adirondack, game used, 1990 .... $70

Steve Sax: Worth, game used, 1992 .... $75

Mike Schmidt: Hillerich & Bradsby, game used, 1973-79 .... $2,000

Mike Schmidt: Hillerich & Bradsby, game used, 1977-79 .... $1,395

Mike Schmidt: Adirondack, game used, cracked, 1983, signed $995

Red Schoendienst: Adirondack, game used, cracked, 1950s $995

George Scott: Adirondack, game used, 1970s $35

Tom Seaver: Hillerich & Bradsby, game used, uncracked, 1977-79 .... $1,625

Kevin Seitzer: Louisville Slugger, game used, 1986-89 .... $60

Gary Sheffield: Adirondack, game used, cracked, 1990..$175
Ruben Sierra: Louisville Slugger, game used, 1990..$175
Ted Simmons: Louisville Slugger, game used, 1984-85 ....$150
Ken Singleton: Hillerich & Bradsby, game used, 1977-79 ....$65
George Sisler: Hillerich & Bradsby, game used, 1921..$995
Roy Smalley: Louisville Slugger, game used, 1986-89 ....$40
Ozzie Smith: Louisville Slugger, game used, slightly cracked, 1977-79 ....$495
Ozzie Smith: Louisville Slugger, game used, repaired, 1984-85, signed $395
Reggie Smith: Louisville Slugger, game used, 1980-83, signed $95
Eddie Stanky: Hillerich & Bradsby, game used 1944-49 ....$495
Willie Stargell: Hillerich & Bradsby, used in 1964 All-Star Game, signed.......... $2,495
Willie Stargell: Louisville Slugger, game used, uncracked, 1965-71, signed.......... $395
Willie Stargell: Hillerich & Bradsby, game used, 1973-75, signed $495
Rusty Staub: Adirondack, game used, 1971-79 ....$295
John Stearns: Louisville Slugger, game used, cracked..$40
Rennie Stennett: Hillerich & Bradsby, game used, 1973-75 ....$65
Darryl Strawberry: Adirondack, game used, uncracked, 1985, signed $225
Don Sutton: Louisville Slugger, game used, 1984-85, signed $395
Danny Tartabull: Worth, game used, 1992..$125
Frank Taveras: Louisville Slugger, game used, cracked $25
Garry Templeton: Adirondack, game used, 1990 ....$50
Gene Tenace: Hillerich & Bradsby, game used, 1973-75......................................$95
Mickey Tettleton: Louisville Slugger, game used, cracked, 1984-85, signed $145
Frank Thomas: Worth, game used, two-toned, 1993 ....$425
Bobby Thomson: Hillerich & Bradsby, 1949-60 ....$495
Dickie Thon: new label Louisville Slugger, game used, cracked $40
Luis Tiant: Hillerich & Bradsby, game used, 1965-72, signed $595
Bob Tolan: Hillerich & Bradsby, game used, 1965-72...$110
Joe Torre: Hillerich & Bradsby, game used, pre-1965, signed..............................$195
Cesar Tovar: Hillerich & Bradsby, game used, 1965-72.......................................$110
Alan Trammell: Worth, game used, signed $160
Alan Trammell: Louisville Slugger, game used, cracked, 1980-83 ....$295
Tom Tresh: Hillerich & Bradsby, game used, handle crack, 1960-64......................$450
Fernando Valenzuela: Louisville Slugger, game used, 1980-83 ....$100
Andy Van Slyke: Louisville Slugger, game used, 1984-85 ....$195
Greg Vaughn: Louisville Slugger, game used, cracked, 1992 ....$85
Robin Ventura: Cooper, game used, 1989..$295
Mickey Vernon: Hillerich & Bradsby, used in 1955 All-Star Game....................$1,995
Mickey Vernon: Adirondack, game used, uncracked, 1952-57...............................$750
Tim Wallach: Louisville Slugger, game used, cracked, 1992 ....$85

Bob Watson: Adirondack, game used, 1971-79..$85
Bob Watson: Adirondack, game used, 1980...$70
Lou Whitaker: Hillerich & Bradsby, game used, cracked, 1977-79 ....$495
Lou Whitaker: Louisville Slugger, game used, 1980-83....................................$295
Lou Whitaker: Louisville Slugger, game used, 1980-83....................................$295
Lou Whitaker: Louisville Slugger, game used, 1991-93......................................$95
Frank White: Adirondack, game used, cracked, 1971-79....................................$95
Roy White: Adirondack, game used, uncracked $125
Bump Wills: Hillerich & Bradsby, game used, cracked.......................................$30
Maury Wills: Hillerich & Bradsby, game used, cracked, 1972, signed..................$325
Dave Winfield: Adirondack, game used, 1984, signed $695
Dave Winfield: Adirondack, game used, cracked, 1993 ....$425
Rick Wise: Adirondack, game used, uncracked, 1970s................................... $90
Jimmy Wynn: Hillerich & Bradsby, game used, 1973-75, signed..........................$125
Carl Yastrzemski: Hillerich & Bradsby, game used, cracked, 1960-64.............$1,695
Carl Yastrzemski: Hillerich & Bradsby, game used, 1977-79, signed................$795
Steve Yeager: Louisville Slugger, game used, 1984-85....................................$50
Rudy York: Hillerich & Bradsby, game used, 1937-43 ....$495
Ed Yost: Hillerich & Bradsby, used in 1952 All-Star Game....................................$895
Joel Youngblood: new label Louisville Slugger, game used, cracked $30
Robin Yount: Hillerich & Bradsby, game used, uncracked, 1977-79......................$995
Robin Yount: Louisville Slugger, game used, 1984-85, signed $595
Richie Zisk: Adirondack, game used, cracked, 1971-79..$40

Unused game bats

Roberto Alomar: Cooper, C243, 1992..$150
Jeff Bagwell: Cooper, C235 ....$95
Albert Belle: Cooper, B343..$125
Wade Boggs: Louisville Slugger, 1982, signed..$750
Wade Boggs: Louisville Slugger, R161, 1984-85 ....$195
Barry Bonds: Cooper, H176..$295
Barry Bonds: Louisville Slugger 1990, signed $350
Bobby Bonilla: Cooper, S318..$85
Bobby Bonilla: Louisville Slugger, 1990, signed..$95
Tom Brunansky: Louisville Slugger, C243, 1986-89 ....$50
Jose Canseco: Cooper...$150
Gary Carter: Louisville Slugger, P89, 1984-85 ....$135
Joe Carter: Cooper, B343, 1992 ....$95
Jack Clark: Louisville Slugger, 1986-89, signed...$40

Will Clark: Adirondack, 1989, signed $195
Roger Clemens: Louisville Slugger, C243, 1986-89, signed $175
Vince Coleman: Louisville Slugger, 1990, signed.................................... $50
Eric Davis: Louisville Slugger, 1986-89, signed...................................... $40
Glenn Davis: Louisville Slugger, M253, 1986-89, signed......................... $60
Andre Dawson: Louisville Slugger, R43, 1986-89................................... $150
Dwight Evans: Louisville Slugger, C271, 1986-89.................................. $75
Cecil Fielder: Cooper, C271 .... $150
Kirk Gibson: Worth, 1988, signed... $95
Juan Gonzalez: Cooper, P72... $200
Ken Griffey Jr.: Louisville Slugger, C271, 1986-89, signed.................... $395
Pedro Guerrero: Louisville Slugger, M110, signed................................ $40
Tony Gwynn: Louisville Slugger, C253, 1986-89, signed $175
Orel Hershiser: Louisville Slugger, H248, 1986-89, signed $150
Bo Jackson: Louisville Slugger, J93, 1990 .... $125
Gregg Jefferies: Worth, 1990, signed $75
Howard Johnson: Adirondack, 1990, signed $75
Pat Listach: Cooper, C243, 1992 .... $65
Don Mattingly: Cooper, T141... $150
Kevin McReynolds: Adirondack, 1990.. $50
Kevin Mitchell: Cooper, K55.. $85
Eddie Murray: Louisville Slugger, M272, 1986-89, signed $175
Rafael Palmeiro: Cooper, S329.. $85
Dave Parker: Cooper, C243 .... $60
Terry Pendleton: Louisville Slugger, 1990, signed $60
Tim Raines: Cooper, TR4 .... $40
Jim Rice: Cooper, R206 .... $85
Pete Rose: Hillerich & Bradsby, signed.. $200
Ryne Sandberg: Louisville Slugger, B267, 1986-89.............................. $295
Mike Schmidt: Adirondack, 154B, 1988, signed.................................. $495
Ruben Sierra: Louisville Slugger, T141, 1991-92................................. $125
Darryl Strawberry: Adirondack, 1990, signed...................................... $50
Fernando Valenzuela: Louisville Slugger, 1986-89, signed $75
Andy Van Slyke: Louisville Slugger, 1990, signed............................... $75
Tim Wallach: Cooper, 1990, signed $75

Basic tips on bat collecting

Not a week goes by that I don't receive a call regarding the status of a bat in someone's possession. "Is it a game bat or a store bat" is the usual question, followed immediately by "How much is it worth?"

Then there is the myriad of bat companies, ie. Adirondack, Hillerich & Bradsby, Spalding, Worth, Hanna-Batrite, just to name a few. Which companies made game bats? What length bat did a player use?

So many questions, so little space. But I will try to clarify a few basic tips that may make bat collecting a little less painful, and hopefully, a little more profitable.

First, this article will deal mainly with Hillerich & Bradsby, hereafter H&B bats, since this is what most collectors, especially collectors of older bats, prefer. Adirondack started making bats around 1946 and are now owned by Rawlings. Simple deduction would eliminate Ruth or Cobb Adirondacks from the game bat category. Many players, such as Willie Mays, Gil Hodges and Joe Adcock, started using Adirondack bats during the 1950s.

Hanna Bat Co., of Athens, Ga., also found favor with ballplayers, especially the Yankees of the 1930s. In a legal fight with H&B during that time, Lou Gehrig stated that he occasionally used Hanna Bats. The difficulty lies in knowing which ones are game bats. In regards to Hanna bats of the period, it is almost impossible. You can decipher whether or not the wood is of top quality, whether the dimensions are proper, or if the bat dates from the correct period, but that's about as close as it gets without actual provenance.

Spalding is another popular company that made bats for several players from the late 1870s until World War II. These bats were the preferred tool of men such as Frank Chance, Sam Crawford, Fred Clarke, and a host of others. Again, to tell if you have a game bat or a store model would take an entire article in itself, since there are so many variables.

But on to the subject of H&B bats and why they are probably the easiest of all to decipher, if any of this might be considered easy. I will touch on the quick, generally accepted guidelines for dating and determining possible professional game use. Then, if a bat warrants further examination as to its game possibilities, at least one will know it's worth getting it to an expert for a closer examination.

The place to start looking at any H&B bat, to decide whether the bat has even the remotest possibility of being a game model, is on the knob. The year 1943 is generally considered the first year H&B applied players' model numbers to the bat's knob.

Professional players' bats from 1943 through 1975 will have this number on the knob. These codes will be a letter followed by three or fewer numbers, ie. S2, D29, O1, K55, etc. No professional bat may have more than one letter unless it is an "L", which must come at the end, thus designating a large knob. Joe DiMaggio used a D29 early in his career, then switched to a D29L, which was simply a bat with the same dimensions except for the large knob. H&B bats made during and after 1976 will find the model number moved to the barrel above the player's name.

If your bat has inch marks, a single digit, or two letters followed by a number, they are most likely a store model bat. A single digit, ie. 4, would indicate the length which would be 34". If your Hank Aaron bat has HA3, it is a Hank Aaron store model with a length of 33".

Bats made prior to the 1943 will be void of model designations unless they returned to the factory. If this was the case, the code would be found on both ends of the bat and filled with white paint. If a pre-1943 bat has inch markings, it must be considered a store model bat unless accompanied by a letter from a primary source, ie. ballplayer, family etc., and even then, its value would be a fraction of one without inch marks.

The center label of an H&B bat tells the rest of the story. Let's start with a point that must be made right off. A game model H&B bat made after 1918 must be a model 125. You will find this number in the center of the logo under the slogan "Louisville Slugger".

Prior to 1918, many bats have no model number at all, with only a "dash, dot, dash" where the 125 would normally appear. Other numbers, such as 40, 8, 250, 14, etc., must for general purposes be considered store model designations.

Next, all game model bats made on or after 1931 must have the slogan "Powerized" to the right of the label. This will be found in conjunction with "Bone Rubbed" or "Oil Tempered" which is fine. If you see the slogan "Flame Tempered", again, it must be considered a store model bat.

For dating purposes, I will list the major general center label changes and their respective dates as

Top left: barrel marks from a 1921-31 era Paul Waner game bat. Above: the center label of a 1921-31 Waner game-used bat.

Left: The K34 mark, filled in with white paint, is on the knob and also the end of the barrel. The mark was applied to pre-1943 bats when they were returned to the factory for duplication. Above: the center label of a 1921-31 Hillerich & Bradsby Tris Speaker store bat. The T.S. in the label are the player's initials.

At right: the block letter name means the player was not under contract with H&B. Below: the center label of the first model H&B bat. Bradsby's name was added in 1916; the -.- was added around 1917 or 1918.

accurately as I can determine at this time:

1. J.F. Hillerich & Son with a "dash, dot, dash" beneath, 1897-1905.

2. J.F. Hillerich & Son Co., the world "Co." added, 1906-1915.

3. Bradsby name incorporated - Hillerich & Bradsby Co., but with the "dash, dot, dash" still below the name in the center, 1916-1921.

4. Same as above but with the words "Made In USA" added under Hillerich & Bradsby, 1922-1979.

5. The number "2" of 125 will be found above the "&" in the center label on bats made after 1960. The "1" will be above 125s made before.

This is called the Malta theory named after bat dating "Columbus," Vince Malta. This theory seems to hold water for all game bats made after 1949 and is used by most collectors and dealers to date labels.

6. A small "r" in a circle after the words "Louisville Slugger" replaced the legend that until then was under the oval. This is assumed to have taken place sometime after the All-Star break in 1964. Any bat with the small "r" is considered a post-1964 bat.

7. Another small "r" found its way above the "d" of Powerized, sometime in 1973.

8. The Hillerich & Bradsby Co. center logo was changed to Louisville Slugger in 1980.

9. "Trade Mark Reg. U.S. Pat. Off." is found under the oval of all H&B bats from 1906 until about 1937, when the "U.S. Pat. Off." was dropped, leaving only the "Trade Mark Reg." This mark continued until sometime around 1943-44 when it was again switched, this time to "Reg. U.S. Pat. Off" which was removed and replaced after 1964 by the small "r".

10. The Liberty Bell Bi-Centennial bats are only from 1976.

Now if that's not enough to confuse anybody who's still awake, consider that the words "Powerized" and it's lightning bolts and assorted accompanying legends changed constantly, and you have real confusion. But that's nothing to what the barrel markings are doing to theories and sanity.

The player's name should appear on the barrel, in script if he had a player's contract with H&B, in block if he did not. What appears above and below this name is enough to drive one mad, but I will list a few supposed "givens."

1. It is assumed that the word "Genuine" appeared above the player's name sometime in 1936, with "Louisville Slugger" appearing below the name sometime in 1937. Prior to that one might find the word "Trade Mark" either above or below with nothing else, "Trade Mark" above with "Reg. U.S. Pat. Off." below, or just the player's name with nothing above or below it, a practice which seems to date from the 1932-36 period.

2. Player model number, ie. S2, moved to barrel above name in 1976.

3. If you see something under the player's name, such as U.C.L.A. or Illinois State, you have a pro-model bat made for a college. They are not considered game-used bats and sell for a slight premium over store models.

And what does all this have to do with anything? If you have a professional model Babe Ruth bat with Genuine above his name and Louisville Slugger below, the bat is 35" in length, a model 125, weighing 40 oz., with no model number on the knob, what do you have?

Ruth retired after the 1935 season, but the word Genuine is not supposed to have been added to bats until 1936. What if that date is wrong and it was actually added at the end of the 1935 season? Is this a game-used bat or a coaches bat? Using the dating technique I've just laid out, it would have to be a coaches bat.

What difference does it make, you may ask? Well, if you were the owner of the above bat, the difference would be about $10,000 that wouldn't end up in your pocket if you went to sell it. So you can see how crucial some of these dating techniques are in relation to certain players and the dates in which they played.

Use the above guidelines to decide whether or not you have a possible game-used H&B bat. If your bat falls into the game category, get it to someone who knows bats. There are lots of ingredients that will help a dealer access the possibility of game use - the proper dating period for a certain player,

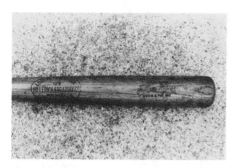

Store model bats

Honus Wagner game bat, 1921-31. The "MADE IN USA" in the center didn't start until 1921; Wagner retired as a player in 1917, so he could only have used the bat as a coach. The difference in value - $15,000.

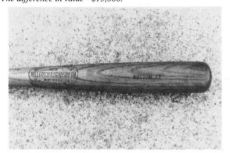

This Jim Bottomley game-used bat from 1921-31 has block letters; the last name only indicates a pre-contract bat.

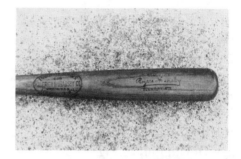

This 1921-31 Roger Hornsby game-used bat lacks the "Powerized" stamp, but does have a "MADE IN USA" logo.

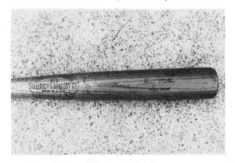

This Bing Miller game-used bat from 1932-36 has the "Powerized" stamp.

This Bill Terry game-used bat from 1937-43 has "TRADE MARK REG." under the label.

Notice that the 2 in 125 is above the & between H&B on this 1960-64 Stan Musial game-used bat. Musial had block letter bats for most of his career.

This is a 1965-72 game-used Luis Aparicio bat. Notice the small trademark symbol after Slugger in the center label, but there is none above the d in "Powerized."

the correct dimensions (most factory records are incomplete prior to 1930 and sketchy even after that), proper game use, correct model numbers, high quality wood, finish, and on and on and on.

And even after all of this, in most cases, we can only reasonably ascertain that a bat was game used by the player whose name appears on the barrel, and only that the bat was proper for one ordered by him at the time in which he played.

If you venture into the world of collecting game-used bats, get acquainted with a reputable dealer who knows what he is doing and will stand behind his product. Learn as much as you can yourself; an educated collector is good for the hobby. Don't be afraid to ask questions, no matter how trivial they may seem; that's how you learn. Most dealers will share their knowledge because they know that once that confidence is built up, you will become a good customer.

—David Bushing

Store model bats

Dick Allen: Adirondack $35

Ernie Banks: Louisville Slugger $45

Hank Bauer: Adirondack $45

Johnny Bench: Louisville Slugger $50

Yogi Berra: Hillerich & Bradsby $65

Roberto Clemente: Hillerich & Bradsby $75

Eddie Collins: Louisville Slugger $95

Rocky Colavito: Spalding $50

Joe DiMaggio: JC Higgens $125

Joe DiMaggio: Louisville Slugger $200

Carlton Fisk: Adirondack $50

Jimmie Foxx: JC Higgens $85

Jimmie Foxx: Hanna Batrite $150

Jimmie Foxx: Louisville Slugger $125

Joe Gordon: Louisville Slugger $100

Ken Harrelson: Louisville Slugger $55

Cleon Jones: Adirondack $25

George Kell: Spalding $135

George Kelly: Louisville Slugger $100

Mickey Mantle: Adirondack Big Stick $75

Mickey Mantle: Louisville Slugger $100

Eddie Mathews: Hillerich & Bradsby $45

Willie Mays: Adirondack $60

Willie McCovey: Adirondack $40

Joe Medwick: Hanna Batrite $35

Felix Milan: Adirondack $25

Joe Morgan: Hillerich & Bradsby $35

Mel Ott: MacGregor Gold Smith $150

Vada Pinson: Adirondack $50

Frank Robinson: Hillerich & Bradsby $65

At left, Bill Williams, of Hillerich & Bradsby Co. Inc., makers of Louisville Slugger bats, compares the finishing stain on a modern bat (closest to him) to the original master copy of Babe Ruth's bat. H&B stores thousands of "master model" professional baseball players' bats in a fire-proof vault deep within its plant near Louisville, Ky. The master models are used to pre-set wood lathes when copies are ordered. Below, Gary Brown, of H&B, brands a series of bats prior to the staining process. Goodyear produces a water-based resin, used in the stain, specifically in three current pro model bats because it can penetrate the branded areas on the bat. H&B produces more than 1.4 million wooden bats a year. The knob on the end of the bat allows the bat to be handled during the production process without touching the bat and is removed before the staining process. - Photos courtesy Goodyear

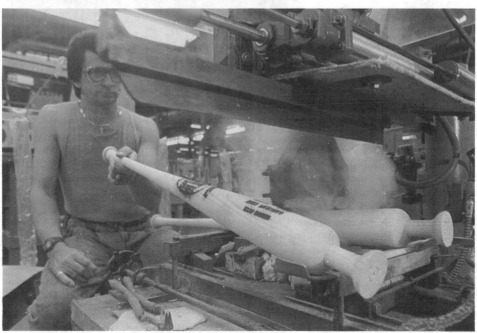

Jackie Robinson: Hillerich & Bradsby $75
Pete Rose: Hillerich & Bradsby $60
Babe Ruth: Revelation Bat Co. $95
Babe Ruth: Louisville Slugger $95
Ron Santo: Adirondack $35
Al Simmons: JC Higgens $125
Tris Speaker: Hanna Batrite $95
Willie Stargell: Louisville Slugger $65
Vern Stephens: MacGregor Gold Smith $100
Joe Torre: Adirondack $30
Paul Waner: Louisville Slugger $125
Ted Williams: Hillerich & Bradsby $125
Carl Yastrzemski: Louisville Slugger $65

Cooperstown Bat Co. commemorative bats

Cooperstown Bat Co., Cooperstown, N.Y., has produced several limited-edition bats (500) to commemorate several players, stadiums and teams. Recent prices and/or minimum bids for some of the bats, signed, will be listed.

C.B.C.'s 10 Stadium Series bats include: 1) Fenway Park, 1986; 2) Wrigley Field, 1986; 3) Ebbets Field, 1987; 4) Polo Grounds, 1987; 5) Yankee Stadium, 1987; 6) Forbes Field, 1988; 7) Shibe Park, 1988; 8) Briggs/Tiger Stadium, 1989; 9) Sportsman's Park, 1989; and 10) Comiskey Park, 1990. As of late 1991, only two bats from the series were still available from the company - Shibe Park and Forbes Field.

C.B.C.'s Famous Players Series includes five players: Pee Wee Reese, 1988; Ted Williams, 1989; Yogi Berra, 1990; Ernie Banks, 1991; and Carl Yastrzemski, 1992.

C.B.C. was commissioned by the National Baseball Hall of Fame to produce a limited edition of 500 sets of five bats and a display rack for the inaugural "Class of 1936" - Ty Cobb, Walter Johnson, Christy Mathewson, Babe Ruth and Honus Wagner.

The company also makes bats for autographing. A C.B.C. 1989 Cooperstown Hall of Fame autograph model bat, signed by 18 greats (including Stan Musial, Tom Seaver, Bob Gibson, Steve Carlton, Luis Aparicio, Willie Stargell and Enos Slaughter), has been offered in an auction for a minimum bid of $350.

Another C.B.C. Hall of Fame autograph model bat, signed by 24 Hall of Famers (including Stan Musial, Ted Williams, Mike Schmidt, Willie Mays, Hank Aaron, Pete Rose, Johnny Bench, Lefty Gomez, Jocko Conlan, Happy Chandler, Duke Snider, Willie McCovey, Ernie Banks and Lou Brock), has been offered in an auction for a minimum bid of $900.

C.B.C.'s Vintage Club Series includes bats for three teams - Brooklyn Dodgers, 1990; Boston Braves, 1991; and Milwaukee Braves, 1992. A Brooklyn Dodgers bat, signed by 34 Dodger greats (including Sandy Koufax, Andy Pafko, Duke Snider, Carl Abrams, Ralph Branca, Don Drysdale, Billy Herman, Mickey Owen and Chuck Connor) has been offered in an auction for a minimum bid of $250.

C.B.C. also creates bats for team autograph collectors. The 1992 Major League Team Series was scheduled to have bats for seven teams - California Angels, Chicago White Sox, Cincinnati Reds, Detroit Tigers, Pittsburgh Pirates, San Francisco Giants and Toronto Blue Jays.

The 1991 Major League Team Series features six teams - Chicago Cubs, Kansas City Royals, Los

Angeles Dodgers, Oakland Athletics, Philadelphia Phillies and St. Louis Cardinals.

The 1990 Major League Team Series included four teams - Baltimore Orioles, Boston Red Sox, New York Mets and New York Yankees.

C.B.C. has also created three Doubleday Field Bats - in 1983, 1985 and 1989. The 1983 bat is red and brown. Twenty have a plain red band at the throat of the bat; the remaining 124 had a red ring with a brown center stripe. The 1985 version was also red and brown and featured an enlarged drawing of the stadium compared to the first bat. The company has not limited production on these bats, and estimates about 1,900 have been made. About 900 of these were made before 1988 and have the red and brown stripe. Those after 1988 have a red and brown band art reading "Stadium Series."

A limited edition of 1,000 bats were issued 1989 in red and blue to commemorate the 150th anniversary of baseball in America. The text was changed to give the history of the stadium, beginning with the Phinney Lot in 1839 and ending with the 1939 "all-star" game for the dedication of the Hall of Fame. The company did not number the bats in this edition, so there is not an edition number stamped into the knob of the bat.

Louisville Slugger Hall of Fame Induction Bats

Since 1983, Louisville Slugger, in conjunction with the Baseball Hall of Fame, has issued limited-edition bats commemorating the inductions of players, executives, managers and umpires into the Hall of Fame. Their names are engraved into the bat barrels with gold lettering.

Five hundred bats, each numbered, were made per induction ceremony from 1936-87. From 1988 on there have been 1,000 bats made per ceremony. The first 500 are sold through subscription. The Hall of Fame sells the others during the induction ceremonies.

1936 - Ty Cobb, Walter Johnson, Christy Mathewson, Babe Ruth, Honus Wagner $600

1937 - Morgan Bulkeley, Ban Johnson, Nap Lajoie, Connie Mack, John McGraw, Tris Speaker, George Wright, Cy Young.. $275-$325

1938 - Grover Alexander, Alexander Cartwright, Henry Chadwick .... $150-$200

1939 - Cap Anson, Eddie Collins, Charles Comiskey, Candy Cummings, Buck Ewing, Lou Gehrig, Willie Keeler, Charles Radbourn, George Sisler, Al Spalding .... $275-$350

1942 - Rogers Hornsby .... $125-$200

1944 - Kenesaw Landis.. $100-$175

1945 - Roger Bresnahan, Dan Brouthers, Fred Clarke, Jimmy Collins, Ed Delahanty, Hugh Duffy, Hugh Jennings, Mike Kelly, James O'Rourke, Wilbert Robinson... $75-$150

1971 - Dave Bancroft, Chick Hafey, Harry Hooper, Rube Marquard, Satchel Paige, George Weiss .... $150-$225

1972 - Yogi Berra, Josh Gibson, Lefty Gomez, Will Harridge, Sandy Koufax, Buck Leonard, Ross Youngs, Early Wynn.. $425-$500

1973 - Roberto Clemente, Billy Evans, Monte Irvin, George Kelly, Warren Spahn, Mickey Welch .... $350-$500

1974 - Cool Papa Bell, Jim Bottomley, Jocko Conlan, Whitey Ford, Mickey Mantle, Sam Thompson .... $350-$500

1975 - Earl Averill, Bucky Harris, Billy Herman, Judy Johnson, Ralph Kiner............... $100-$175

1976 - Oscar Charleston, Roger Connor, Cal Hubbard, Bob Lemon, Freddie Linstrom, Robin Roberts .... $125-$175

1977 - Ernie Banks, Martin Dihigo, John Lloyd, Al Lopez, Amos Rusie, Joe Sewell..... $150-$175

1978 - Addie Joss, Larry MacPhail, Eddie Mathews... $125-$175

1979 - Warren Giles, Willie Mays, Hack Wilson .... $125-$175

1980 - Al Kaline, Chuck Klein, Duke Snider, Tom Yawkey .... $150-$200

1981 - Rube Foster, Bob Gibson, Johnny Mize.. $150-$175

1982 - Hank Aaron, Happy Chandler, Travis Jackson, Frank Robinson .... $200-$250
1983 - Walter Alston, George Kell, Juan Marichal, Brooks Robinson .... $375-$450
1984 - Luis Aparicio, Don Drysdale, Wes Ferrell, Harmon Killebrew, Pee Wee Reese .. $175-$250
1985 - Lou Brock, Enos Slaughter, Arky Vaughan, Hoyt Wilhelm .... $150-$175
1986 - Bobby Doerr, Willie McCovey, Ernie Lombardi .... $150-$175
1987 - Ray Dandridge, Jim Hunter, Billy Williams .... $150-$175
1988 - Willie Stargell .... $150-$200
1989 - Al Barlick, Johnny Bench, Red Schoendienst, Carl Yastrzemski .... $175-$225
1990 - Joe Morgan, Jim Palmer .... $125-$175
1991 - Rod Carew, Fergie Jenkins, Tony Lazzeri, Gaylord Perry, Bill Veeck .... $200-$250

World Series Black Bats

    World Series Black Bats, created by Hillerich and Bradsby, are given to participating players and dignitaries from teams in the Series. They have facsimile signatures of the entire team in gold on a dark black ebony bat.

1937 New York Yankees World Series Black Bat .... $2,250-$3,000
1947 New York Yankees World Series Black Bat .... $500-$600
1949 New York Yankees World Series Black Bat .... $475-$550
1951 New York Yankees World Series Black Bat .... $1,000-$1,500
1952 New York Yankees World Series Black Bat .... $375-$500
1953 New York Yankees World Series Black Bat .... $425-$500
1955 Brooklyn Dodgers World Series Black Bat .... $1,300-$1,600
1955 New York Yankees World Series Black Bat .... $375-$450
1957 Milwaukee Braves World Series Black Bat .... $550-$700
1957 New York Yankees World Series Black Bat .... $400-$500
1958 Milwaukee Braves World Series Black Bat .... $450-$500
1959 Los Angeles Dodgers World Series Black Bat .... $500-$600
1960 New York Yankees World Series Black Bat .... $350-$475
1961 New York Yankees World Series Black Bat .... $900-$1,000
1961 Cincinnati Reds World Series Black Bat .... $250-$350
1962 New York Yankees World Series Black Bat .... $500-$600
1964 St. Louis Cardinals World Series Black Bat .... $700-$900
1965 Los Angeles Dodgers World Series Black Bat .... $350-$450
1965 Minnesota Twins World Series Black Bat .... $475-$550
1966 Baltimore Orioles World Series Black Bat .... $300-$375
1966 Los Angeles Dodgers World Series Black Bat .... $250-$300
1967 Boston Red Sox World Series Black Bat .... $475-$550
1967 St. Louis Cardinals World Series Black Bat .... $450-$550
1968 Detroit Tigers World Series Black Bat .... $550-$650
1969 Baltimore Orioles World Series Black Bat .... $275-$350
1970 Baltimore Orioles World Series Black Bat .... $250-$300
1970 Cincinnati Reds World Series Black Bat .... $225-$275
1971 Pittsburgh Pirates World Series Black Bat .... $325-$375
1971 Baltimore Orioles World Series Black Bat .... $200-$250
1972 Oakland A's World Series Black Bat .... $175-$225

Notice the different labeling on these old-time Hillerich & Bradsby bats.

This 1916-21 era Honus Wagner 40W decal bat is from one of the most beautiful series of store bats ever made.

This is an early JF Hillerich & Son Co. Ty Cobb decal bat, circa 1911-15.

This special bat commemorates the 1971 Baltimore Orioles as American League playoff winners.

This is a 1941 New York Yankees World Series Black Bat.

Cooperstown Bat Co. has produced several limited-edition commemorative bats.

1973 Oakland A's World Series Black Bat .... $175-$225
1973 New York Mets World Series Black Bat .... $350-$450
1974 Oakland A's World Series Black Bat .... $200-$275
1974 Los Angeles Dodgers World Series Black Bat .... $175-$225
1975 Cincinnati Reds World Series Black Bat .... $375-$450
1975 Boston Red Sox World Series Black Bat .... $275-$350
1976 Cincinnati Reds World Series Black Bat .... $275-$350
1977 Los Angeles Dodgers World Series Black Bat .... $250-$325
1978 Los Angeles Dodgers World Series Black Bat .... $250-$325
1979 Baltimore Orioles World Series Black Bat .... $200-$275
1979 Pittsburgh Pirates World Series Black Bat .... $275-$350
1980 Kansas City Royals World Series Black Bat .... $200-$275
1981 Los Angeles Dodgers World Series Black Bat .... $275-$350
1982 St. Louis Cardinals World Series Black Bat .... $300-$350
1984 Detroit Tigers World Series Black Bat .... $450-$550
1984 San Diego Padres World Series Black Bat .... $200-$275
1985 St. Louis Cardinals World Series Black Bat .... $250-$350
1985 Kansas City Royals World Series Black Bat .... $275-$350
1986 New York Mets World Series Black Bat .... $500-$750
1986 Boston Red Sox World Series Black Bat .... $450-$525
1987 Minnesota Twins World Series Black Bat .... $350-$400
1987 St. Louis Cardinals World Series Black Bat .... $250-$300
1989 San Francisco Giants World Series Black Bat .... $175-$250
1989 Oakland A's World Series Black Bat .... $175-$250
1990 Oakland A's World Series Black Bat .... $175-$250
1992 Toronto Blue Jays World Series Black Bat .... $350-$450
1992 Atlanta Braves World Series Black Bat .... $450-$550

Pro Insignia Inc.

Pro Insignia Inc. is a Hudson, Wis.-based company which produces regulation and miniature laser-engraved baseball bats. The bats, which are black Rawlings/Adirondack professional model bats, are produced in limited editions and generally have an issue price of about $50. They are suitable for autographing. Among others, the company has produced commemorative bats for the 1989, 1990 and 1991 World Series champions, the 1990 and 1991 All-Star games, the 100th anniversary of the Dodgers and the closing of Comiskey Park in Chicago, Ill. Laser-engraved northern white ash Adirondack bats have also been created to commemorate the 1955 World Champion Brooklyn Dodgers and the 1957 World Series between the Milwaukee Braves and New York Yankees.

Equipment

While jerseys, bats and autographed baseballs bring the high-end prices for game-used equipment collectibles, there are other avenues for collectors to pursue, although they are not as abundant. These areas include caps, pants, jackets, helmets, shoes, batting gloves, gloves, and miscellaneous items, such as shin guards, equipment bags and wrist bands.

The items in these categories which show the highest prices are usually those which have been obtained in an auction, primarily because of who the player was who used the equipment. Hobby publications such as *Sports Collectors Digest* offer several ads each issue for equipment. One example offers a 1959 Ted Williams Boston Red Sox game-used team undershirt, grey with navy blue sleeves, and Williams' name in collar, for $2,250.

Caps

Carlos Baerga: 1990s Cleveland Indians, game used, Sports Specialties $145
Vida Blue: 1970s Oakland A's cap, game used, New Era................................. $225
Wade Boggs: 1980s Boston Red Sox, game used, New Era.................................... $185
George Brett: 1990s Kansas City Royals, game used, New Era, signed $425
Lou Brock: 1970s St. Louis Cardinals, game used, New Era $425
Jose Canseco: 1990s Oakland A's, game used, New Era, signed............................. $245
Gary Carter: Montreal Expos cap, #8 under bill, game used, signed...................... $250
Chili Davis: San Francisco Giants, game used... $40
Andre Dawson: 1993 Boston Red Sox, game used, New Era, signed...................... $175
Cecil Fielder: 1990s Detroit Tigers, game used, New Era, signed.......................... $165
Steve Finley: 1990s Houston Astros, game used, New Era, signed........................... $70
Travis Fryman: 1990s Detroit Tigers, game used, New Era $145
Mike Greenwell: 1992 Boston Red Sox, game used, New Era, signed $95
Ken Griffey Jr.: 1993 Seattle Mariners cap, game used, New Era, signed $325
Kelly Gruber: Toronto Blue Jays, game used, New Era, signed................................. $75
Rickey Henderson: 1980s New York Yankees, game used, New Era, signed $325
Bo Jackson: Chicago White Sox cap, #8 under bill, game used, signed................... $295
Reggie Jackson: 1970s Oakland A's, game used, New Era.................................... $595
Harmon Killebrew: 1970s Minnesota Twins, game used, KM Pro........................ $595
Pat Listach: 1992 Milwaukee Brewers, game used, Sports Specialties $120
Billy Martin: 1970s New York Yankees, game used, New Era, signed $425
Billy Martin: 1982 Oakland A's, game worn, signed $550
Don Mattingly: New York Yankees cap, game used, signed................................ $195
Jack McDowell: 1992 Chicago White Sox cap, game used, New Era, signed........ $140
Kevin Mitchell: 1980s San Francisco Giants, game used, New Era, signed $90
Thurman Munson: New York Yankees cap, game used, #15.............................. $650
Eddie Murray: 1992 New York Mets cap, game used, signed.............................. $175
Jim Palmer: 1970s Baltimore Orioles cap, game used, AJD, signed $475
Lou Piniella: 1990s Cincinnati Reds cap, game used, New Era, signed $95
Vada Pinson: 1968 Cincinnati Reds cap, game used, Wilson................................. $250
Kirby Puckett: 1992 Minnesota Twins cap, game used, New Era, signed............. $345
Merv Rettenmund: 1970s Baltimore Orioles, game used $125
Cal Ripken Jr.: 1993 Baltimore Orioles cap, game used, New Era, signed $395
Pete Rose: Montreal Expos cap, game used, New Era, signed $425

Nolan Ryan: 1992 Texas Rangers, game used, New Era, signed............................ $695

Chris Sabo: Cincinnati Reds cap, game used, signed $95

Ryne Sandberg: Chicago Cubs cap, game used, New Era, signed........................ $345

Ruben Sierra: Texas Rangers cap, #21 under bill, game used, signed $250

Ruben Sierra: 1992 Oakland A's cap, game used, New Era, signed $195

Bob Stanley: Boston Red Sox cap, #46, game used $45

Darryl Strawberry: Los Angeles Dodgers cap, #44 under bill, game used, signed
.... $250

B.J. Surhoff: Milwaukee Brewers 1993 Turn Back the Clock cap, game used.......... $95

Greg Vaughn: 1991 Milwaukee Brewers cap, Sports Specialties, game used, signed$85

Mitch Williams: Chicago Cubs cap, "Thing" under bill, game used $125

Dave Winfield: California Angels cap, game used, New Era, signed...................... $425

Robin Yount: 1990s Milwaukee Brewers, Sports Specialties, signed..................... $295

Pants

Bob Allison: 1967 Minnesota Twins flannel pants, home $125

Yogi Berra: 1968 New York Mets road pants, signed $220

Wade Boggs: 1990 Boston Red Sox road pants $125

Steve Carlton: 1986 Chicago White Sox road pants... $175

Gary Carter: 1980 Montreal Expos road pants, #8... $100

Roger Clemens: 1988 Boston Red Sox road pants $145

Mike Greenwell: 1989 Boston Red Sox road pants $65

Rick Honeycutt: 1986 Los Angeles Dodgers home pants.. $50

Tony Perez: 1973 Cincinnati Reds home pants... $90

Bill Russell: 1971 Los Angeles Dodgers home pants.. $75

Tim Wallach: 1981 Montreal Expos road pants, #29 .... $40

Maury Wills: 1973 Los Angeles Dodgers home pants... $125

Umpire shirts

Rich Garcia: #19 American League umpire shirt... $150

Bill Haller: #1 American League umpire shirt $150

Paul Runge: #17 National League umpire shirt... $150

Marty Springstead: #4 American League umpire shirt... $150

Billy Williams: #24 National League jacket, pants, cap $400

Jackets

Buddy Bell: 1980s Starter Texas Rangers heavy jacket $295

Jose Canseco: 1993 Texas Rangers warm-up jacket $295

Rod Carew: California Angels light jacket, name stitched inside $495

Gary Carter: Montreal Expos heavy jacket, signed............................ $475

Al Downing: 1970s Goodman & Sons Los Angeles Dodgers heavy jacket $295

Cecil Fielder: Detroit Tigers heavy jacket, number stitched inside...................... $525

Phil Garner: 1977 Pittsburgh Pirates heavy jacket, signed $495

Ron Guidry: Yankee Starter warm-up jacket, signed $200

Ozzie Guillen: Chicago White Sox jacket, #13 inside $200

Kent Hrbek: Minnesota Twins jacket, 1980s $250

Reggie Jackson: 1987 Starter Oakland A's jacket, signed...................... $1,250

Bill Madlock: Los Angeles Dodgers jacket, knit Goodman, NOB.......................... $300

Tug McGraw: New York Mets jacket #45, Aladen.............................. $495

Joe Morgan: San Francisco Giants jacket $415

Frank Robinson: Baltimore Orioles light jacket............................. $425

Lou Whitaker: Detroit Tigers Starter heavy jacket, number inside........................ $650

Nolan Ryan: 1993 Texas Rangers warm-up jacket $950

Frank Viola: New York Mets Starter windbreaker, NOB.............................. $395

Houston Colt 45s heavyweight jacket, #38 written inside $3,495

Game-used batting helmets

Wade Boggs: Boston Red Sox batting helmet, #23, signed $750

Jose Canseco: Texas Rangers batting helmet, #33, signed..................................... $750

Ron Cey: Los Angeles Dodgers batting helmet, #10, signed.................................... $275

Roberto Clemente: Pittsburgh Pirates batting helmet $3,025

Chili Davis: San Francisco Giants batting helmet, cracked/repaired $80

Rob Deer: 1990 Rawlings Milwaukee Brewers batting helmet.............................. $110

George Foster: New York Mets batting helmet, name on helmet, cracked............. $175

Cesar Geronimo: 1970s Cincinnati Reds batting helmet, no flaps........................ $190

Ken Griffey Jr.: Seattle Mariners batting helmet, #24, signed.............................. $995

Rickey Henderson: Oakland A's batting helmet, signed.................................... $500

Reggie Jackson: California Angels batting helmet, #44, signed $1,750

Pat Listach: 1992 Milwaukee Brewers batting helmet $135

Fred Lynn: California Angels batting helmet $195

Kevin Mitchell: San Francisco Giants batting helmet $275

Paul Molitor: Milwaukee Brewers batting helmet, #4, signed.............................. $750

Don Money: 1970 KM-Pro Milwaukee Brewers helmet, flapless $185

Dale Murphy: Atlanta Braves batting helmet, #3, signed $575
Dave Parker: Milwaukee Brewers batting helmet, #39 .... $275
Terry Pendleton: St. Louis Cardinals batting helmet, cracked, #9 .... $325
Kirby Puckett: Minnesota Twins batting helmet, #34, signed $995
Pete Rose: Cincinnati Reds batting helmet, #14, signed $1,750
Steve Sax: New York Yankees batting helmet, #9, signed $425
Gary Sheffield: Milwaukee Brewers batting helmet, #1, ... $350
Willie Stargell: 1960s Pittsburgh Pirates helmet, flapless $350
Greg Vaughn: 1990 Rawlings Milwaukee Brewers helmet $175
Carl Yastrzemski: Boston Red Sox batting helmet, game used $1,065
Robin Yount: 1970s Milwaukee Brewers batting helmet, blue with gold M $1,325
1993 Toronto Blue Jays autographed batting helmet, signed by the entire team (Carter, Alomar, Olerud, White, Morris, Stewart) $195
1993 California Angels autographed batting helmet, signed by the entire team (Langston, Snow, Finley, Salmon) $150

Replica batting helmets

Ken Griffey Jr.: Seattle Mariners batting helmet, signed $125
Tony Gwynn: San Diego Padres batting helmet, signed $85
Eric Karros: Los Angeles Dodgers batting helmet, signed $80
Carl Yastrzemski: Boston Red Sox batting helmet, signed $150

Game-worn shoes

Dick Allen: Philadelphia Phillies Adidas cleats $210
Roberto Alomar: Reebok cleats $195
Jay Bell: Pony cleats $95
Bob Boone: Nike, maroon and white, game used, #8 on each heel, signed $195
Ellis Burks: Boston Red Sox Nike cleats $75
Rod Carew: Nike, red and white, game used, #29 on each heel, signed $325
Gary Carter: Nike, blue and white, game used, signed $195
Joe Carter: Nike cleats $110
Cecil Cooper: Pony cleats $40
Chili Davis: Nike cleats $89
Eric Davis: Brooks spikes, signed $150
Lenny Dykstra: Philadelphia Phillies cleats, signed $120
Cecil Fielder: Pony, black and white, game used $195
Ray Fosse: Puma cleats $60
Dwight Gooden: Nike, blue and white, game used, signed $225
Dick Groat: 1966-67 Philadelphia Phillies Riddell spikes $350

Rickey Henderson: turf black Mizuno, game used, signed.....................................$295
Reggie Jackson: navy Pony, signed..$650
Jerry Koosman: Philadelphia Phillies Adidas cleats $60
Pat Listach: Reebok high tops, blue and white, game used....................................$95
Mickey Lolich: San Diego Padres Adidas cleats $100
Paul Molitor: Milwaukee Brewers Pony cleats..$250
Joe Morgan: Mizuno, maroon and white, game used...$325
Rafael Palmeiro: Nike turf shoes $125
Dave Parker: Adidas cleats, #39 ....$125
Terry Pendleton: red Pony turf shoes $95
Tony Perez: Bauer, blue and white, game used, signed..$195
Dave Parker: Adidas, scarlet, signed $150
Kirby Puckett: Nike cleats, game used, signed...$350
Tim Raines: blue Mizuno Montreal Expos cleats signed.....................................$150
Steve Sax: Nike, black and white, game used, signed..$75
Mike Schmidt: Converse, #20, signed $600
Ozzie Smith: San Diego Padres Brooks cleats..$250
Cesar Tovar: Philadelphia Phillies Adidas cleats..$45
Dave Winfield: New York Yankees Brooks cleats $250
Carl Yastrzemski: Spot-Bilt cleats, black and white, game used $495
Robin Yount: Mizuno cleats, blue and white, game used, signed $350

Batting gloves

Roberto Alomar: Mizuno batting gloves, signed...$145
Sandy Alomar Jr.: Mizuno batting gloves, black and white, signed........................$50
Carlos Baerga: Franklin batting gloves, orange and white, signed $150
Barry Bonds: Franklin batting gloves, signed..$195
Jose Canseco: Mizuno, blue and white...$110
Will Clark: black Easton batting gloves...$50
Eric Davis: Mizuno batting gloves, scarlet, signed $50
Andre Dawson: Mizuno batting gloves, black, signed $60
Cecil Fielder: Louisville batting gloves and wrist band $110
Carlton Fisk: Saranac #72 batting glove $45
Julio Franco: Franklin batting gloves, red and white..$45
Juan Gonzalez: batting gloves, signed $175
Ken Griffey Jr.: Franklin batting gloves, name printed on $145
Ken Griffey Sr.: Franklin batting glove, #30, signed $30
Tony Gwynn: Franklin batting gloves, blue, number printed on..............................$95

Rickey Henderson: Mizuno batting gloves, fluorescent, signed $90
John Kruk: maroon Saranac batting glove, #19 .... $20
Barry Larkin: Franklin batting glove, #11 .... $25
Don Mattingly: Franklin batting glove, #23, torn, signed $100
Kevin McReynolds: Wilsons, orange and white, signed.. $35
Paul Molitor: Saranac batting gloves, signed.. $100
Dale Murphy: Saranac batting glove $90
Rafael Palmeiro: Franklin batting glove, white $30
Kirby Puckett: Franklin batting gloves, name printed on $125
Tim Raines: black Worth batting gloves $40
Harold Reynolds: Franklin batting glove, blue and silver...................................... $25
Cal Ripken Jr.: Franklin batting gloves, black and white, signed $200
Ruben Sierra: Easton batting gloves, green and white $65
Darryk Strawberry: Saranac batting glove, #18, signed $65
Mickey Tettleton: Franklin batting gloves, orange and white $50
Frank Thomas: Mizuno batting gloves, signed... $85
Robin Yount: Easton batting gloves, blue and white, signed $200

Equipment bags

Eric Davis: Worth bat bag, scarlet, #44, signed.. $160
Dwight Gooden: blue/orange bat bag, signed.. $150
Bill Madlock: Pittsburgh Pirates large equipment bag, #5, circa 1979.................... $150
Deion Sanders: Easton black bat bag, signed $150

Miscellaneous

D&M celluloid umpire indicator, turn-of-the-century, dog logo on the back $80
Turn-of-century reach umpire indicator in original box, celluloid plastic $150
Circa 1915 wire catcher's mask, "goggle eyes," $225
1930s-style catcher's mask $145
Turn-of-the-century wire catcher's mask, rectangular eye openings, bird-cage style.... $200
Circa 1880s baseball handmade ball, thick brown leather $175
Turn-of-the-century chest protector, very crude, narrow protector $200
1975 Boston Red Sox catcher's helmet, Carlton Fisk $450
Dusty Baker Los Angeles Dodgers home run #139 baseball, 1979, signed.................... $195
Davey Lopes Los Angeles Dodgers home run #19 baseball, 1975, signed..................... $150
Joe Morgan Cincinnati Reds home run #163 baseball, 1976, signed............................. $395
Reggie Smith Los Angeles Dodgers home run #255 baseball, 1978, signed.................. $195

Store-bought gloves

One of the hottest collectibles on the market today seems to be the baseball glove. But what makes a glove collectible? Is it the maker or the style of glove? Is it the player's name who appears embossed on it or is it the condition? The answer is all of the above.

But which of the criteria is most important? Well, in this case, it depends. Baseball gloves, much like baseball cards, derive their value based on several features, which will all be defined.

Let's begin by explaining that this is a treatise on store-bought, over-the-counter gloves, and has little or nothing to do with game-used gloves which may be worth thousands of dollars and must be evaluated individually as to provenance and value. A store-bought glove is just that, an over-the-counter purchase. Those which bear a facsimile autograph of a player will herewith be called an autograph model.

The most important factor in determining the value of a glove is the player's name which appears embossed somewhere on the face of the glove. For example, if you had two identical Draper Maynard G41 gloves in the same condition, one bearing the facsimile autograph of Babe Ruth and the other bearing the facsimile autograph of Babe Young, presuming they are both in used but Excellent condition with all markings easily read, then the Ruth glove would bring in excess of $800, while the identical Young glove would probably sell in the $75 range.

The reason is as obvious as in baseball card collecting. All the 1952 Topps cards are made of the same material and share the same printing process. But the one that illustrates the image of Mickey Mantle is worth thousands of dollars, while the card of Howie Pollet, only one number away from Mantle, would bring less than $100 in any condition. And so it is with glove collecting - the bigger the name, the higher the price, given that all other variants are the same.

The second most important consideration when determining glove value is the condition. Even a relatively common player, if I may borrow the vernacular of the card collecting fraternity, may be worth hundreds of dollars if in Near Mint to Mint condition. This is especially true with older gloves, because it is much harder to find a Near Mint to Mint common player from the 1920s or 1930s than it is to find a similar condition glove from the 1960s or 1970s.

Given this criteria, a Mint condition glove of a relatively obscure player from the 1920s, ie. Bibb Falk, would be worth more than $200, probably much more, while a Mint condition glove of a Hall of Fame member, such as Luis Aparicio, might only bring the same amount or less. It may seem ridiculous, to those who collect more modern era items, that a glove of a Hall of Fame player would bring less than a glove of a player of whom many readers have never heard.

To justify this, one need look no further than any baseball card price guide. Look up the price of any Near Mint E97 Briggs card from 1909-10, then look up the Near Mint price of a 1974 Topps card of Hall of Fame member Reggie Jackson.

That brings us right into the next two very important factors in determining value; supply and demand, or the relative scarcity of some gloves versus the seemingly endless supply of others. Let's take two gloves of players from relatively the same era, Grover C. Alexander and Dave Bancroft.

Both are Hall of Famers and both of their gloves are in great demand amongst serious pre-war glove collectors. Given that both are in Near Mint condition, the Alexander glove, even though he is arguably the more renowned of the two, might bring $500-$700, while a Bancroft would probably bring $800-$1,200. The reason behind the disparity is that Alexander gloves are fairly easy to locate; they appear on the market from time to time. However, there are only a couple of Bancroft models known in private collections.

If a signature model Joe Jackson baseman's mitt exists that was made before his banishment from the major leagues (as a result of the Black Sox scandal in 1919) and it became available on the public market, especially in the auction arena, it would undoubtedly set a new record price paid for a store model glove, regardless of its condition.

While we have already touched on another important factor in determining glove values - age - it deserves its own category. It is impossible to discuss value without the age factor being present. Until recently, very early gloves, because they lacked player endorsements, commanded very little collector attention, which computed to very weak prices as well.

All this is changing now as more and more collectors are beginning to realize how truly scarce the pre-World War I era gloves are in today's marketplace. Two sets of turn-of-the-century fingerless gloves, gloves that were worn either individually or in pairs and had no fingers, traded hands within the last two years for prices in excess of $3,000. Another recent sale of an 1890s baseman's mitt, one which was dated in pen and bore the player's name and college, broke the four digit barrier as well.

Another area in which age plays an important role has to do with the date of manufacture as compared to when the player whose name appears on the glove was active. For example, a Jimmie Foxx baseman's mitt, circa 1930, in Excellent condition, might bring around $500-$600, while a more recently manufactured Jimmie Foxx glove, one made well into the 1960s, sold last year for less than $100. This is an important factor to consider when purchasing a glove - make sure that the date of manufacture corresponds with the time frame in which a player was active.

Rarely, if ever, is a post period glove of any player worth the same amount as one manufactured while the player was still on the diamond. There are dozens of players whose names appeared on gloves long after their playing days ended - Foxx, Ruth, Bill Dickey, Lefty Gomez, Joe DiMaggio, just to name a few. In fact, just like early, or rookie cards, of a player are worth more than later cards of the same player, even while he was still active, so too are earlier model gloves of certain players.

Take Joe DiMaggio, for example. He played in the major leagues from the 1930s until 1951. It is generally accepted that fielders gloves with unlaced fingers are pre-war models or styles, while gloves with the fingers laced are considered post-war models or styles. Various companies produced both laced and unlaced gloves prior to and after World War II, but the terms pre-war and post-war are used to determine the relative era of a fielder's glove using the criteria of whether or not the glove is laced.

If you had two identical Joe DiMaggio gloves, yet one was the laced variation and the other was not, as was the case in 1950 when Spalding manufactured both the earlier style, or unlaced version, as well as the laced model, the earlier would bring a premium, even though both were made the same year, simply because it is the split finger model.

Now, using the same Joe DiMaggio glove as an example, let's discuss two other very important factors in determining glove values. First, does the name Joe DiMaggio appear in cursive, facsimile autograph style, or is it a block style name, each letter independent of the other? Facsimile autograph gloves will always command a higher price than their block style counterparts.

While an excellent condition DiMaggio pre-war style with facsimile autograph may sell somewhere in the $400-$500 range, a like condition and era glove bearing a block stamp might only bring $250-$350. This difference is magnified when the scarcity of a certain player's glove is greater, ie. Lou Gehrig gloves. A signature model Ken-Wel in Excellent condition would sell for $1,500-$2,000; a like conditioned model bearing a block name recently brought $750. All Gehrig gloves are very scarce; less than half a dozen currently reside in private collections. But, as you can see, a signature model glove brings twice the price of its block style counterpart.

Another important value factor has to do with which hand the glove fits on. This is the area that seems to cause the most confusion, even among advanced collectors. The factories, and hence the sporting good stores, used to designate a glove either right hand or left hand by determining which hand the glove actually fit, indicating right hand for a left-handed thrower. As a result, one might find the letters RH somewhere on the box label.

Because of the confusion amongst today's collectors, most now call a glove that fits on the left hand, for a right-handed thrower, a right-handed glove. The best rule of thumb is if you're ordering a glove from a mail order dealer, ask which hand the glove actually fits on. If you see the letters LH in a description of a glove for sale in a mail order ad, it most likely means that the glove is for a left-handed thrower, but always check just to be sure.

And why all this dribble about which hand a glove fits on? The reason is simple economics. Take Mickey Mantle gloves, for example. A recent price paid for a Mickey Mantle MM personal model glove made for right-handed thrower and in Mint condition surpassed the $800 mark. However, a Personal Model Mantle glove in the same Mint condition, but for a left-handed thrower, sold for a mere $175. That's a substantial difference for two almost identical gloves except that one was what collectors call "off-handed."

But what about left-handed gloves of left-handed players, ie. Stan Musial. A Near Mint Heart of the Hide Rawlings Musial baseman's mitt, for a left-handed thrower, sells for $200-250. But the same glove for a right-handed thrower, even though Musial was left handed, would still sell in the same price range, maybe 10 percent less, even though a right-handed Musial would be considered "off-handed."

The reason for this is simple - most collectors are right handed and they want to put the glove on and feel comfortable, so they will buy a nice right-handed model of a left-handed player for nearly the same price, yet they refuse to pay anywhere near the same price for a left-handed glove of a right-handed player.

Does all this make sense, even if left-handed gloves are scarcer? No, but it has to do with supply and demand, and that's what sets the market. What this also means is that if you are left handed, there are some absolute bargains out there on top-of-the-line gloves if you don't mind "off-handed" player's models.

One item we haven't discussed is the quality of the different models. Some players' endorsements may have only been offered on limited versions or models. Still others, like Mantle or Musial, were available on many different models, running the gamut from cheap, dime-store-quality kids gloves to professional, top-of-the-line, leather trimmed, deluxe models. In all instances, the higher the quality, if the player and condition are equal, the higher the price.

We have discussed several factors that determine the actual value and desirability of a collectible glove. There are many more that haven't been discussed, such as how to grade a glove, or how to determine its age, or what's the best marketplace for buying and selling.

Each of these areas might constitute an entire article to completely define, but the above information should help you get a feel for the hobby and how to approach it with some confidence.

- David Bushing

The following information is taken from David Bushing's Vintage Baseball Glove 1994 Pocket Price Guide. Bushing's comprehensive guide to valuation of vintage gloves estimates there are nearly 1,500 persons involved in the glove collecting hobby. The prices given reflect retail prices based on what dealers or collectors might sell their gloves for and should not be considered as absolute, fixed prices.

Often, gloves were sold in individual boxes and with "hang tags" which were used to price and/or describe the features of the glove. Having them with the glove adds to the overall value of the glove. Pre-war hang tags add $30 with a player photo and can add $50-$150 depending on the player. Post-war tags add $15, and can add $25-$75 depending on the player.

Plain boxes, those without pictures on them, in Good condition (intact, some corners may be split, light scuffing, small surface tears, slight soiling) can add 20-50 percent in value. Post-war plain boxes add 20 percent, 1930-45 add 30 percent, 1920-30 add 40 percent and pre-1920 boxes add 50 percent.

Picture boxes (those with a photo or illustration of the player either posed or in action) in Good condition can add two to six times to the price of the glove. Pre-war boxes of Hall of Famers add four to six times the price, post-war boxes Hall of Famers add two to four times the value, while post-war boxes of non-Hall of Famers adds no more than two times the value.

Other factors involved in value include player popularity and condition of the glove. Bushing's guide has established the following grading scale:

Fair/Poor: Gloves in this condition are generally not collectible and often are only good for parts. Irreparable tears, holes, severe magic marker, dry rot, water damage, and any other major problem.

Good: Glove that has been used considerably. Most of the stamping will be gone or barely visible. Leather very chaffed, thinned in spots, no form left, may still be serviceable but only collectible if an extremely rare model, usually used as a filler until a better similar type is available.

Very Good: Well used but most stamping visible, no form but intact, cloth label gone or worn out, piping frayed and worn.

Excellent: Well used but cared for. Stamping visible. Dark with age but nice patina. Cloth label intact, minor piping wear. Some form left.

Excellent/Mint: The most confusing grade. Much stronger than an Excellent glove but not Near Mint. It is an Excellent glove with certain strong characteristics of a higher grade glove, i.e. super strong, bright signature, perfect cloth label, no oil stains, perfect insides, etc.

Near Mint: A glove that has seen almost no use. Still stiff in form, all stamping strong, most original silver or black ink still within stamping. Perfect insides, perfect cloth patch, has caught but a few balls. Some otherwise Mint gloves may not have been used but have significant enough blemishes such as staining, cracking from dryness, scratches from some handling, to drop it into this category.

Mint: Just that, stone cold new, never played with. This is regardless of age. A Mint glove may show some shelf wear due to years, for example minute piping wear, oxidation around brass grommets, stiff due to no use, slight fading of original color, all of which must be minute and from storage, not from use.

Terms used in the following charts include:

None Known: No glove has been discovered in a manufacturer's catalog or personally.

None Found: These gloves have been found to exist in a manufacturer's catalog, but have not been mentioned as been having been owned or sold by a collector or dealer.

Very Rare: For pre-war gloves, four or less gloves have turned up. For post-war models, eight or less have turned up.

Rare: For pre-war model gloves, five to 10 gloves have turned up. For post-war gloves, 10 to 20 have been found.

Common: For pre-war, this is 11 to 20 gloves. For post-war models this is 21-35.

Very Common: For pre-war gloves, 21 or more have been found. For post-war gloves, 36 or more have been found.

Pre-war gloves (Hall of Famers)

Mint: Add 50 percent to Near Mint values
Joe Jackson is not a Hall of Famer, but his items are highly sought.
+ (increase) or - (decrease) indicates recent trends in the value.
Prices are for USA-made gloves, full size.
* Also have imported models

Player	Very Good	Excellent	Near Mint	Supply
Grover Alexander (+)	$250	$350	$500	Common
Luke Appling (-)	$50	$100	$150	Very Common
Earl Averill	$75	$150	$200	Very Common
Frank Baker (+)	$500	$800	$1,200	None Known
Dave Bancroft	$400	$650	$850	Very Rare
Chief Bender (+)	$500	$800	$1,200	Very Rare
Jim Bottomley (LH) (+)	$250	$350	$500	Rare
Roger Breshnahan (+)	$500	$800	$1,200	Very Rare
Mordecai Brown (+)	$500	$800	$1,200	None Known
Max Carey (+)	$250	$350	$500	Rare
Frank Chance (+)	$500	$800	$1,200	None Known
Jack Chesbro (+)	$500	$800	$1,200	None Known
Fred Clarke (+)	$500	$800	$1,200	None Known

Ty Cobb	$750	$1,000	$1,500	Very Rare
Mickey Cochrane (+)	$250	$350	$500	Rare
Eddie Collins (+)	$250	$350	$500	Rare
Jimmy Collins	$400	$650	$850	None Known
Earle Combs (+)	$250	$350	$500	Very Rare
Stan Coveleski	$400	$650	$850	None Known
Sam Crawford (LH) (+)	$500	$800	$1,200	Very Rare
Joe Cronin (-)	$50	$100	$150	Very Common
Kiki Cuyler (-)	$125	$250	$375	Common
Dizzy Dean	$500	$800	$1,200	Very Rare
Bill Dickey (-)	$50	$100	$150	Very Common
Joe DiMaggio (-)	$250	$350	$500	Very Common
Bobby Doerr (-)	$50	$100	$150	Very Common
Johnny Evers (+)	$500	$800	$1,200	None Known
Red Faber	$400	$650	$850	Very Rare
Bob Feller (-)	$50	$100	$150	Very Common
Rick Ferrell (+)	$250	$350	$500	Very Rare
Elmer Flick	$400	$650	$850	None Known
Jimmie Foxx (+)	$250	$350	$500	Common
Frankie Frisch (-)	$125	$250	$375	Common
Lou Gehrig (LH) (+)	$850	$1,000	$1,500	Common
Charlie Gehringer (-)	$125	$250	$375	Very Common
Lefty Gomez (LH) (-)	$125	$250	$375	Rare
Goose Goslin	$75	$150	$200	Very Common
Hank Greenberg (-)	$125	$250	$375	Common
Burleigh Grimes	$400	$650	$850	None Known
Lefty Grove (LH) (-)	$125	$250	$375	Rare
Chick Hafey (+)	$250	$350	$500	Very Rare
Jesse Haines (+)	$250	$350	$500	Very Rare
Bucky Harris	$75	$150	$200	Common
Gabby Hartnett (-)	$125	$250	$375	Common
Harry Heilmann (+)	$250	$350	$500	Common
Billy Herman (-)	$50	$100	$150	Very Common
Harry Hooper (LH) (+)	$500	$800	$1,200	None Known
Rogers Hornsby (-)	$125	$250	$375	Very Common
Waite Hoyt	$400	$650	$850	Very Rare
Carl Hubbell (LH) (+)	$250	$350	$500	Rare
Joe Jackson *	$850	$1,000	$1,500	Vere Rare
Travis Jackson (-)	$125	$250	$375	Common
Walter Johnson (+)	$250	$350	$500	Common
George Kelly (+)	$250	$350	$500	Very Rare
Chuck Klein (-)	$125	$250	$375	Common
Nap Lajoie	$850	$1,000	$1,500	None Knonw
Tony Lazzeri (+)	$250	$350	$500	Very Rare
Freddie Lindstrom (+)	$250	$350	$500	None Found
Ernie Lombardi (-)	$75	$150	$200	Very Common
Al Lopez (-)	$50	$100	$150	Very Common
Ted Lyons (-)	$75	$150	$200	Very Common
Heinie Manush (LH)	$75	$150	$200	Very Common
Rube Marquard (LH) (+)	$500	$800	$1,200	None Known
Rabbit Maranville (+)	$250	$350	$500	Rare

Christy Mathewson	$750	$1,000	$1,500	Very Rare
Joe McGinnity	$500	$800	$1,200	None Known
Ducky Medwick (-)	$50	$100	$150	Very Common
Johnny Mize (-)	$50	$100	$150	Very Common
Mel Ott (-)	$75	$150	$200	Very Common
Herb Pennock (LH) (+)	$250	$350	$500	None Found
Eddie Plank (LH) (+)	$500	$800	$1,200	None Known
Pee Wee Reese (-)	$50	$100	$150	Very Common
Sam Rice (+)	$250	$350	$500	Very Rare
Eppa Rixey (LH) (+)	$250	$350	$500	Very Rare
Edd Roush (LH) (-)	$250	$350	$500	Very Rare
Red Ruffing (-)	$125	$250	$375	Common
Babe Ruth (LH) (-)	$500	$800	$1,200	Common
Ray Schalk (-)	$125	$250	$375	Common
Joe Sewell (+)	$250	$350	$500	Very Rare
Al Simmons (-)	$125	$250	$375	Common
George Sisler (LH) (-)	$125	$250	$375	Common
Tris Speaker (LH)	$750	$1,000	$1,500	Very Rare
Bill Terry (LH) (+)	$250	$350	$500	Rare
Joe Tinkers (+)	$500	$800	$1,200	None Known
Pie Traynor (-)	$125	$250	$375	Very Common
Dazzy Vance (-)	$125	$250	$375	Common
Arky Vaughn (+)	$250	$350	$500	None Found
Rube Waddell (LH) (+)	$500	$800	$1,200	None Known
Honus Wagner	$750	$1,000	$1,500	Very Rare
Bobby Wallace (+)	$500	$800	$1,200	None Known
Ed Walsh (+)	$500	$800	$1,200	None Known
Lloyd Waner (-)	$125	$250	$375	Common
Paul Waner (LH) (+)	$250	$350	$500	Very Rare
Zack Wheat (+)	$500	$800	$1,200	Very Rare
Ted Williams (-)	$125	$250	$375	Very Common
Hack Wilson (+)	$250	$350	$500	Very Rare
Cy Young (-)	$250	$350	$500	Very Common
Ross Youngs	$400	$650	$850	None Found

Post-war gloves (Hall of Famers)

Player	Very Good	Excellent	Mint	Supply
Hank Aaron *	$100	$150	$300	Rare
Luis Aparicio (-)	$30	$50	$85	Common
Ernie Banks (-)	$50	$85	$125	Common
Johnny Bench * (-)	$30	$50	$85	Very Common
Yogi Berra * (-)	$50	$85	$125	Very Common
Lou Boudreau	$30	$50	$85	Very Common
Lou Brock	$65	$125	$175	Very Rare
Roy Campanella (-)	$50	$85	$125	Very Common
Rod Carew	$40	$75	$95	Very Rare
Roberto Clemente (-)	$30	$50	$85	Very Common
Steve Carlton *	$50	$85	$125	Very Rare

Joe DiMaggio * (+)	$150	$250	$375	Common
Don Drysdale *	$40	$75	$95	Common
Bob Feller	$40	$75	$95	Very Common
Rollie Fingers	$40	$75	$95	Very Rare
Whitey Ford (LH) *	$40	$75	$95	Very Common
Bob Gibson	$40	$75	$95	Common
Lefty Gomez	$40	$75	$95	Common
Catfish Hunter *	$40	$75	$95	Common
Monte Irvin	$65	$125	$175	Rare
Joe Jackson	$150	$250	$375	Very Rare
Reggie Jackson	$30	$50	$85	Common
Fergie Jenkins	$40	$75	$95	Rare
Al Kaline * (-)	$30	$50	$85	Very Common
George Kell	$30	$50	$85	Common
Harmon Killebrew (-)	$40	$75	$95	Common
Ralph Kiner	$30	$50	$85	Common
Sandy Koufax (LH) * (+)	$85	$150	$200	Rare
Bob Lemon (-)	$30	$50	$85	Rare
Mickey Mantle * (-)	$225	$350	$500	Rare
Juan Marichal * (-)	$40	$75	$95	Common
Eddie Mathews * (+)	$50	$85	$125	Common
Willie Mays * (-)	$125	$175	$350	Rare
Willie McCovey (-) (LH)	$65	$125	$175	Rare
Joe Morgan *	$40	$75	$95	Very Rare
Stan Musial (LH) *	$100	$150	$300	Common
Hal Newhouser (LH)	$50	$85	$125	Rare
Jim Palmer *	$40	$75	$95	None Known
Gaylord Perry	$40	$75	$95	Rare
Pee Wee Reese	$30	$50	$85	Very Common
Robin Roberts	$30	$50	$85	Very Common
Brooks Robinson * (-)	$30	$50	$85	Common
Frank Robinson * (-)	$40	$75	$95	Common
Red Schoendienst	$30	$50	$85	Very Common
Tom Seaver * (-)	$40	$75	$95	Common
Enos Slaughter	$30	$50	$85	Very Common
Duke Snider (+)	$50	$100	$150	Common
Warren Spahn (LH) (+)	$50	$100	$150	Common
Willie Stargell (LH) *	$40	$75	$95	Rare
Hoyt Wilhelm	$85	$150	$200	Very Rare
Billy Williams *	$40	$75	$95	Rare
Ted Williams *	$100	$150	$300	Rare
Early Wynn	$30	$50	$85	Very Common
Carl Yastrzemski *	$30	$50	$85	Common

Pre-war gloves (star players)

Player	Very Good	Excellent	Near Mint	Supply
Adams, Charles "Babe"	$100	$175	$250	None Known
Archer, Jimmy	$150	$250	$375	None Known

Equipment

Austin, Jimmy (+)	$150	$250	$375	None Known
Bagby, Jim	$75	$150	$200	None Known
Bartell, Dick (-)	$50	$85	$175	Very Common
Berg, Moe (+)	$500	$800	$1,200	None Known
Berger, Wally (-)	$50	$85	$175	Very Common
Bishop, Max (+)	$100	$175	$250	Very Rare
Blue, Lu (+)	$150	$250	$375	None Known
Bluege, Ossie (+)	$100	$175	$250	Very Rare
Bodie, Ping (+)	$150	$250	$375	None Known
Bonura, Zeke (-)	$75	$150	$200	Rare
Bressler, Rube (+)	$225	$350	$500	None Known
Bridges, Tommy (+)	$100	$175	$250	Very Rare
Brown, Mace (-)	$50	$85	$175	Very Common
Bush, Guy (+)	$75	$150	$200	Rare
Bush, Joe	$150	$250	$375	Very Rare
Camilli, Dolf (-)	$50	$85	$175	Very Common
Carleton, James "Tex"	$75	$150	$200	Rare
Case, George (+)	$150	$250	$375	None Known
Chapman, Ray (+)	$400	$650	$850	None Known
Chase, Hal	$400	$650	$850	None Known
Cicotte, Eddie (+)	$500	$800	$1,200	None Known
Clift, Harlond	$100	$175	$250	Very Rare
Collins, Rip (-)	$35	$65	$125	Very Common
Cooper, Mort	$75	$150	$200	Common
Cooper, Walker	$75	$150	$200	Common
Craft, Harry	$50	$85	$175	Very Common
Cramer, Doc (-)	$75	$150	$200	Common
Cravath, Clifford, "Gravy"	$150	$250	$375	None Known
Crosetti, Frank (-)	$75	$150	$200	Very Common
Crowder, General	$150	$250	$375	None Known
Danning, Harry (-)	$50	$85	$175	Very Common
Daubert, Jake (+)	$225	$350	$500	None Found
Davis, Harry (+)	$225	$350	$500	Very Rare
Dean, Paul (Daffy) (-)	$75	$150	$200	Common
Derringer, Paul	$75	$150	$200	Rare
DiMaggio, Vince (-)	$35	$65	$125	Very Common
Doak, Bill (+15% early models)	$75	$150	$200	Very Common
Doyle, Larry (+)	$225	$350	$500	None Known
Dugan, Joe (+)	$225	$350	$500	None Known
Durocher, Leo (-)	$50	$85	$175	Very Common
Dykes, Jimmy (+)	$150	$250	$375	Very Rare
Earnshaw, George (+)	$100	$175	$250	Very Rare
Falk, Bibb (+)	$150	$250	$375	None Known
Felsch, Hap (+)	$500	$800	$1,200	None Known
Ferrell, Wes (-)	$150	$250	$375	None Found
Fitzsimmons, Fred (+)	$150	$250	$375	Very Rare
Flagstead, Ira (+)	$150	$250	$375	Very Rare
Fournier, Jack (+)	$150	$250	$375	None Found
French, Larry (-)	$35	$65	$125	Very Common
Galehouse, Denny (+)	$100	$175	$250	None Found
Gandil, Chick (+)	$500	$800	$1,200	None Known

Gerber, Wally (+)	$150	$250	$375	None Found
Gibson, George (+)	$100	$175	$250	Very Rare
Goodman, Ival (-)	$35	$65	$125	Very Common
Gowdy, Hank (-)	$35	$65	$125	Very Common
Gray, Pete	$225	$350	$500	None Known
Groh, Heinie	$225	$350	$500	Very Rare
Haas, Mule (-)	$50	$85	$175	Very Common
Hack, Stan (-)	$35	$65	$125	Very Common
Hadley, Bump	$100	$175	$250	None Found
Hale, Sammy (+)	$150	$250	$375	None Found
Harder, Mel (+)	$150	$250	$375	None Found
Hargrave, Bubbles (-)	$100	$175	$250	Very Common
Hemsley, Rollie (-)	$35	$65	$125	Very Common
Henrich, Tommy (-)	$50	$85	$175	Rare
Herman, Babe (+)	$100	$175	$250	Very Rare
Higgins, Pinky (-)	$35	$65	$125	Very Common
Johnson "Indian Bob"	$75	$150	$200	None Found
Jones, Sam	$150	$250	$375	None Known
Judge, Joe (+)	$150	$250	$375	Very Rare
Kamm, Willie	$150	$250	$375	None Found
Keller, Charlie (-)	$35	$65	$125	Very Common
Keltner, Ken	$100	$175	$250	Common
Kerr, Dickie (+)	$225	$350	$500	None Known
Koenig, Mark (+)	$225	$350	$500	Very Rare
Kuehl, Joe (+)	$100	$175	$250	Rare
Kurowski, Whitey	$50	$85	$175	Rare
Leach, Tommy	$225	$350	$500	None Known
Leonard, Dutch (+)	$225	$350	$500	None Known
Lewis, Duffy (+)	$225	$350	$500	None Known
Lobert, Hans	$100	$175	$250	None Found
Mancuso, Gus (-)	$50	$85	$175	Very Common
Marberry, Firpo (+)	$225	$350	$500	Very Rare
Martin, Pepper (+)	$150	$250	$375	Very Rare
Mays, Carl	$225	$350	$500	Rare
McInnis, Snuffy J. (+)	$225	$350	$500	None Known
Meyers, Chief (+)	$400	$650	$850	Very Rare
Miller, Bing	$150	$250	$375	Very Rare
Moore, Terry (-)	$35	$65	$125	Very Common
Moses, Wally (-)	$50	$85	$175	Very Common
Mostil, Johnny (-)	$50	$85	$175	Common
Muesel, Bob (+)	$225	$350	$500	Very Rare
Muesel, Irish (+)	$150	$250	$375	Very Rare
Mungo, Van Lingle (+)	$100	$175	$250	Very Rare
Myer, Buddy	$75	$150	$200	Very Rare
Nickelson, Swish	$50	$85	$175	Common
O'Doul, Lefty (-)	$75	$150	$200	Common
O'Farrell, Bob (-)	$75	$150	$200	Common
Owen, Mickey (-)	$35	$65	$125	Very Common
Pearson, Monte	$35	$65	$125	Very Common
Peckinpaugh, Roger (+)	$225	$350	$500	None Known
Pipp, Wally	$100	$175	$250	Very Rare

Equipment

Risberg, Swede (+)	$500	$800	$1,200	None Known
Rolfe, Red	$100	$175	$250	Very Common
Rommel, Eddie	$100	$175	$250	Common
Root, Charlie	$75	$150	$200	Common
Rowe, Schoolboy (-)	$50	$85	$175	Common
Ruel, Muddy (+)	$225	$350	$500	Very Rare
Ruether, Dutch (+)	$225	$350	$500	None Known
Schang, Wally (+)	$225	$350	$500	Very Rare
Schocker, Urban (+)	$400	$650	$850	None Known
Schulte, Wildfire (+)	$225	$350	$500	None Known
Schumacher, Hal	$150	$250	$375	None Found
Selkirk, George (-)	$50	$85	$175	Common
Sewell, Luke	$100	$175	$250	Common
Smith, Elmer (+)	$150	$250	$375	None Known
Snodgrass, Fred (+)	$225	$350	$500	None Known
Southworth, Billy (+)	$150	$250	$375	None Found
Stahl, Jake (+)	$225	$350	$500	None Known
Stephenson, Riggs (+)	$150	$250	$375	Rare
Tobin, Jake (+)	$150	$250	$375	None Known
Toporcer, Specs	$150	$250	$375	None Known
Trosky, Hal	$75	$150	$200	Rare
Trout, Dizzy	$75	$150	$200	Rare
Uhle, George (+)	$150	$250	$375	None Known
Vander Meer, Johnny	$75	$150	$200	Rare
Vaughn, Jim (Hippo) (+)	$400	$650	$850	None Known
Veach, Bobby (+)	$150	$250	$375	None Known
Walker, Dixie (-)	$35	$65	$125	Very Common
Waker, Harry (The Hat) (-)	$50	$85	$175	Very Common
Walters, Bucky (-)	$50	$85	$175	Common
Wambsganss, Bill (+)	$400	$650	$850	None Known
Warneke, Lon (-)	$50	$85	$175	Very Common
Weaver, Buck (+)	$500	$800	$1,200	None Known
Whitehill, Earl (+)	$150	$250	$375	Very Rare
Williams, Claude (+)	$500	$800	$1,200	None Known
Williams, Cy (+)	$150	$250	$375	None Known
Williams, Ken	$75	$150	$200	Rare
Willis, Vic (-)	$150	$250	$375	None Known
Wilson, Jimmie (+)	$100	$175	$250	Rare
Wood, Joe (+)	$400	$650	$850	None Known
York, Rudy (-)	$35	$65	$125	Very Common
Zimmerman, Heinie (+)	$225	$350	$500	None Known

Post-war gloves (star players)

Player	Very Good	Excellent	Near Mint	Supply
Abrams, Cal (+)	$45	$65	$95	Common
Adams, Bobby	$30	$45	$60	Rare
Adcock, Joe (+)	$45	$65	$95	Common
Agee, Tommy	$35	$55	$75	None Known

Agganis, Harry	$55	$75	$100	Rare
Allen, Richie	$35	$55	$75	Common
Alley, Gene	$35	$55	$75	None Known
Allison, Bob	$25	$35	$50	Common
Alou, Felipe (+)	$25	$35	$50	Rare U.S.A.
Alou, Matty	$25	$35	$50	Common
Amoros, Sandy	$45	$65	$95	Very Rare
Anderson, Sparky	$45	$65	$95	None Known
Antonelli, Johnny (-)	$30	$45	$60	Common
Ashburn, Richie (-)	$30	$45	$60	Very Common
Avila, Bobby (-)	$35	$55	$75	Common
Bailey, Ed (-)	$35	$55	$75	Very Common
Barber, Steve	$35	$55	$75	None Known
Barney, Rex	$35	$55	$75	None Known
Battey, Earl	$30	$45	$60	Common
Bauer, Hank (+)	$45	$65	$95	Common
Baumhohz, Frank	$35	$55	$75	Very Rare
Beckert, Glenn	$25	$35	$50	Common
Beggs, Joe	$35	$55	$75	Rare
Bell, Gus (-)	$25	$35	$50	Common
Berry, Ken	$35	$55	$75	None Known
Bevins, Floyd	$35	$55	$75	None Known
Bickford, Vern	$35	$55	$75	None Known
Black, Joe (+)	$75	$150	$200	None Known
Blackwell, Ewell	$45	$65	$95	Rare
Blair, Paul	$30	$45	$60	Common
Blasingame, Don	$30	$45	$60	Very Common
Blefary, Curt	$30	$45	$60	Common
Bolling, Frank (+)	$30	$45	$60	None Found
Bolling, Milt	$35	$55	$75	None Found
Boone, Ray	$35	$55	$75	Rare
Boros, Steve	$30	$45	$60	Common
Bouton, Jim	$40	$60	$85	Rare
Boyer, Clete	$35	$55	$75	Rare U.S.A.
Boyer, Ken (+)	$45	$65	$95	Common
Bragan, Bobby	$35	$55	$75	Very Rare
Branca, Ralph	$45	$65	$95	Rare
Brandt, Jackie	$30	$45	$60	Common
Brazle, Al	$35	$55	$75	None Found
Brecheen, Harry	$35	$55	$75	Common
Broglio, Ernie	$25	$35	$50	Rare
Brosnan, Jim (+)	$30	$45	$60	None Found
Brown, Bobby	$35	$55	$75	None Found
Bruton, Bill	$35	$55	$75	Rare
Buhl, Bob (-)	$30	$45	$60	Common
Bunning, Jim	$35	$55	$75	Common
Burdette, Lew (-)	$35	$55	$75	Common
Burgess, Smoky	$35	$55	$75	Common
Busby, Jim	$30	$45	$60	Common
Byrne, Tommy	$25	$35	$50	None Found
Callison, John	$30	$45	$60	Rare

Equipment

Campaneris, Bert	$30	$45	$60	Rare
Carey, Andy	$30	$45	$60	Rare
Carlton, Steve	$35	$55	$75	Very Rare USA
Carrasquel, Chico	$30	$45	$60	Very Common
Casey, Hugh	$35	$55	$75	None Known
Cash, Norm	$30	$45	$60	Rare U.S.A.
Cavaretta, Phil	$35	$55	$75	Common
Cepeda, Orlando (-)	$35	$55	$75	Rare U.S.A.
Cerv, Bob	$25	$35	$50	Rare
Cimoli, Gino (+)	$35	$55	$75	Very Rare
Colavito, Rocky	$50	$70	$95	Common
Coleman, Jerry (-)	$35	$55	$75	Common
Collins, Joe	$30	$45	$60	Common
Conigliaro, Tony	$35	$55	$75	Common
Conley, Gene (+)	$55	$75	$100	Very Rare
Connors, Chuck	$100	$175	$300	Very Rare
Consolo, Billy	$35	$55	$75	None Known
Cooper, Walker	$75	$150	$200	Rare
Cottier, Chuck	$35	$55	$75	Very Rare
Courtney, Clint	$30	$45	$60	Common
Covington, Wes (+)	$35	$55	$75	None Found
Cox, Billy	$35	$55	$75	Rare
Craig, Roger	$30	$45	$60	Common
Crandall, Del	$35	$55	$75	Very Common
Crowe, George	$35	$55	$75	None Known
Cuellar, Mike	$35	$55	$75	None Found
Cullenbine, Roy	$35	$55	$75	None Known
Culp, Ray	$35	$55	$75	Rare
Cunningham, Joe	$30	$45	$60	Common
Dark, Al (-)	$30	$45	$60	Very Common
Davalillo, Vic	$35	$55	$75	None Known
Davenport, Jim (-)	$25	$35	$50	Very Common
Davis, Tommy	$30	$45	$60	Rare U.S.A.
Davis, Willie	$30	$45	$60	Rare U.S.A.
DeBusschere, Dave	$35	$55	$75	None Known
Dickson, Murry	$35	$55	$75	None Found
Dierker, Larry	$35	$55	$75	None Known
Dillinger, Bob	$55	$75	$100	Common
DiMaggio, Dom (+)	$55	$75	$100	Very Rare
Doby, Larry (+)	$75	$150	$200	Very Rare
Donovan, Dick	$30	$45	$160	Common
Dropo, Walt	$30	$45	$60	Common
Duren, Ryne	$25	$35	$50	Common
Easter, Luke (+)	$55	$75	$100	None Found
Edwards, John	$25	$35	$50	Common
Elliott, Bob	$35	$55	$75	Common
Ellsworth, Dick	$30	$45	$60	Rare
Ennis, Del (-)	$30	$45	$60	Common
Epstein, Mike	$30	$45	$60	Rare U.S.A.
Erskine, Carl	$55	$75	$100	Common
Evers, Hoot	$30	$45	$60	Common

Face, Elroy	$35	$55	$75	Common
Fain, Ferris (-)	$30	$45	$60	Common
Flood, Curt	$40	$60	$85	None Found
Fondy, Dee	$25	$35	$50	Common
Fosse, Ray	$35	$55	$75	Very Rare
Fox, Nelson * Deduct Higgins	$40	$60	$85	Common Wilson
Francona, Tito	$25	$35	$50	Common
Freehan, Bill	$40	$60	$85	Common
Freese, Gene	$35	$55	$75	Rare
Fregosi, Jim	$30	$45	$60	Rare
Friend, Bob	$35	$55	$75	Rare U.S.A.
Furillo, Carl (-)	$40	$60	$85	Very Common
Garagiola, Joe	$55	$75	$100	Common
Garcia, Mike	$45	$65	$95	None Known
Garver, Ned (-)	$30	$45	$60	Very Rare
Gentile, Jim	$30	$45	$60	Rare
Gilliam, Jim (+)	$75	$150	$200	Very Rare
Goodman, Billy	$30	$45	$60	Very Common
Gordon, Joe (-)	$25	$35	$50	Very Common
Gordon, Sid	$35	$55	$75	Rare
Grim, Bob	$45	$45	$60	Common
Groat Dick	$35	$55	$75	Common
Groth, Johnny	$30	$45	$60	Common
Gustine, Frank	$25	$35	$50	Common
Haddix, Harvey	$45	$65	$95	Common
Hanson, Ron	$25	$35	$50	Common
Harrelson, Ken	$35	$55	$75	None Known
Hart, Jim Ray	$35	$55	$75	None Known
Hartung, Clint	$35	$55	$75	None Known
Hegan, Jim (-)	$30	$45	$60	Common
Hemus, Jim (-)	$30	$45	$60	Common
Henrich, Tommy	$40	$60	$85	Common
Herzog, Whitey (+)	$75	$150	$200	Very Rare
Hoak, Don	$35	$55	$75	Common
Hodges, Gil (-)	$40	$60	$85	Very Common
Hoeft Billy	$35	$55	$75	None Known
Holmes, Tommy	$40	$60	$85	Common
Hopp, Johnny	$35	$55	$75	Common
Houk, Ralph	$35	$55	$75	None Known
Howard, Elston (-)	$40	$60	$85	Common
Howard, Frank	$40	$60	$85	Rare
Howell, Dixie	$45	$65	$95	None Found
Hubbs, Ken	$35	$55	$75	Rare
Hutchinson, Fred	$45	$65	$95	None Known
Jackson, Larry (-)	$25	$35	$50	Very Common
Janowicz, Vic	$35	$55	$75	None Known
Jansen, Larry	$35	$55	$75	Very Rare
Jay, Joey	$25	$35	$50	Rare
Jenson, Jackie (-)	$30	$45	$60	Common
Jethroe, Sam	$40	$60	$85	None Known
Johnson, Dave	$35	$55	$75	Very Rare

Equipment

Jones, Sam	$35	$55	$75	None Known
Jones, Willie (-)	$40	$60	$85	Common
Kaat, Jim	$40	$60	$85	Rare
Kerr, Buddy	$25	$35	$50	Common
Kessinger, Don	$30	$45	$60	Rare U.S.A.
Kinder, Ellis (+)	$35	$55	$75	None Known
Kline, Ron	$35	$55	$75	None Known
Klipstein, Johnny (+)	$35	$55	$75	None Known
Kluszewski, Ted (-)	$40	$60	$85	Common
Knoop, Bobby	$35	$55	$75	Very Rare
Konstanty, Jim	$35	$55	$75	None Known
Koslo, Dave	$35	$55	$75	None Known
Kubek, Tony	$45	$65	$95	Common
Kucks, Johnny	$25	$35	$50	Rare
Kuenn, Harvey (-)	$30	$45	$60	Very Common
Kurowski, Whitey	$35	$55	$75	Rare
Labine, Clem	$45	$65	$95	Rare
Landis, Jim	$30	$45	$60	Common
Lanier, Max	$45	$65	$95	Rare
Larsen, Don (-)	$40	$60	$85	Common
Lary, Frank	$30	$45	$60	Very Common
Lasorda, Tommy (+)	$75	$150	$200	None Known
Law, Vern	$35	$55	$75	Rare
Lawrence, Brooks	$30	$45	$60	Very Rare
Leja, Frank	$25	$35	$50	Common
Lemon, Jim	$25	$35	$50	Common
Leonard, Dutch	$75	$150	$200	None Known
Lewis, Buddy	$30	$45	$60	Very Rare
Lockman, Whitey	$35	$55	$75	Common
Loes, Billy	$45	$65	$95	Rare
Logan, Johnny (-)	$35	$55	$75	Common
Lolich, Mickey	$35	$55	$75	Rare
Lollar, Sherm (-)	$35	$55	$75	Common
Long, Dale	$35	$55	$75	Common
Lopat, Eddie	$35	$55	$75	None Known
Lopata, Stan	$30	$45	$60	Rare
Lopez, Hector	$35	$55	$75	None Known
Lowrey, Peanuts	$30	$45	$60	Common
Lynch, Jerry	$25	$35	$50	Common
Maglie, Sal	$35	$55	$75	Rare
Maloney, Jim	$35	$55	$75	Rare
Malzone, Frank	$35	$55	$75	Rare
Mantilla, Felix	$35	$55	$75	None Known
Marion, Marty (-)	$35	$55	$75	Very Common
Maris, Roger	$55	$75	$100	Common
Marshall, Willard	$25	$35	$50	None Known
Martin, Billy (-)	$35	$55	$75	Very Common
Mauch, Gene	$35	$55	$75	None Known
Maxvill, Dal	$30	$45	$60	Rare
Maxwell, Charlie	$25	$35	$50	Rare
Mazeroski, Bill	$45	$65	$95	Rare U.S.A.

McCarver, Tim	$40	$60	$85	Common
McCormick, Mike F.	$35	$55	$75	Rare
McCormick, Myron (Mike)	$40	$60	$85	Rare
McCosky, Barney	$40	$60	$85	Common
McCullough, Clyde (-)	$25	$35	$50	Very Common
McDaniel, Lindy	$45	$65	$95	None Known
McDermott, Mickey	$45	$65	$95	None Known
McDougald, Gil (-)	$30	$45	$60	Very Common
McDowell, Sam	$35	$55	$75	None Known
McLain, Denny	$45	$65	$95	Rare U.S.A.
McMillan, Ray (-)	$30	$45	$60	Common
McOuinn, George (Claw)	$55	$75	$100	Common
Meyer, Russ (+)	$25	$35	$50	None Known
Miller, Eddie (-)	$30	$45	$60	None Known
Millan, Felix	$35	$55	$75	None Known
Miller, Eddie (-)	$30	$45	$60	Very Common
Miller, Stu	$40	$60	$85	None Known
Milliken, Bob	$45	$65	$95	Common
Minoso, Minnie	$65	$95	$125	Rare
Mitchell, Dale (-)	$45	$65	$95	Common
Mizell, Wilmer	$45	$65	$95	Common
Moon, Wally (-)	$35	$55	$75	Common
Moore, Terry	$40	$60	$85	Common
Moryn, Walt (-)	$30	$45	$60	Common
Mossi, Don (-)	$30	$45	$60	Common
Mueller, Don (-)	$30	$45	$60	Common
Murtaugh, Danny	$35	$55	$75	None Known
Narleski, Ray	$35	$55	$75	None Known
Neal, Charlie	$35	$55	$75	Common
Newcombe, Don	$65	$95	$125	Very Rare
Newsom, Bobo	$45	$65	$95	None Known
Nicholson, Bill	$40	$60	$85	Rare
Niekro, Phil	$45	$65	$95	None Known
Nieman, Bob	$35	$55	$75	Very Rare
Noren, Irv (-)	$30	$45	$60	Common
Nuxall, Joe	$35	$55	$75	Rare
Oliva, Tony	$35	$55	$75	None Known
Osteen, Claude	$35	$55	$75	None Known
Otis, Amos	$30	$45	$60	Common
O'Toole, Jim	$30	$45	$60	Common
Pafko, Andy (-)	$30	$45	$60	Common
Page, Joe	$45	$65	$95	None Known
Pappas, Milt (+)	$35	$55	$75	None Known
Parker, Wes	$30	$45	$60	Common
Parnell, Mel	$45	$65	$95	Very Rare
Pascual, Camilo	$35	$55	$75	None Known
Pearson, Albie	$30	$45	$60	Rare
Pepitone, Joe	$35	$55	$75	None Known
Perranowsk, Ron	$25	$35	$50	Common
Perez, Tony	$30	$45	$60	Common
Pesky, John (-)	$30	$45	$60	Very Common

Equipment

Peters, Gary	$35	$55	$75	Rare
Philley, Dave	$30	$45	$60	Rare
Pierce, Billy (-)	$30	$45	$60	Very Common
Piersall, Jimmy	$35	$55	$75	Very Common
Pinson, Vada	$30	$45	$60	Common
Podres, Johnny (-)	$30	$45	$60	Very Common
Pollet, Howie	$40	$60	$85	Rare
Post, Wally	$30	$45	$60	Common
Powell, Boog (+)	$30	$45	$60	Common
Power, Vic (-)	$30	$45	$60	Common
Priddy, Jerry	$30	$45	$60	Rare
Purkey, Bob	$30	$45	$60	Rare
Raffensberger, Ken	$40	$60	$85	None Known
Raschi, Vic	$40	$60	$85	None Known
Reiser, Pete (-)	$30	$45	$60	Very Common
Repulski, Rip (-)	$30	$45	$60	Common
Reynolds, Allie (+)	$75	$150	$200	None Known
Rhodes, Dusty (+)	$40	$60	$85	None Known
Rice, Del (-)	$30	$45	$60	Very Common
Richardson, Bobby	$40	$60	$85	Very Common
Rivera, Jim	$35	$55	$75	Rare
Rizzuto, Phil	$25	$35	$50	Very Common
Robinson, Eddie (+)	$40	$60	$85	Very Rare
Roe, Preacher (-)	$40	$60	$85	Very Common
Roebuck, Ed	$35	$55	$75	None Known
Romano, John	$35	$55	$75	Common
Rosar, Buddy	$30	$55	$75	Rare
Rose, Pete	$40	$60	$85	Rare U.S.A.
Roseboro, John	$35	$55	$75	Common
Rosen, Al (-)	$40	$60	$85	Common
Rowe, Schoolboy	$40	$60	$85	Rare
Runnels, Pete (-)	$25	$35	$50	Very Common
Rush, Bob (-)	$30	$45	$60	Very Rare
Rutherford, John	$25	$35	$50	Common
Sain, Johnny (-)	$40	$60	$85	Rare
Sanford, Jack	$35	$55	$75	Very Rare
Santo, Ron	$30	$45	$60	Common
Sauer, Hank (-)	$25	$35	$50	Very Common
Schmitz, Johnny	$25	$35	$50	Rare
Schofield, Dick	$30	$45	$60	None Known
Score, Herb	$45	$65	$95	Rare
Scott, George	$25	$35	$50	Common
Seminick, Andy (-)	$25	$35	$50	Very Rare
Shannon, Mike	$25	$35	$50	Common
Shantz, Bobby (-)	$25	$35	$50	V. Common/Non USA
Shea, Frank	$40	$60	$85	None Known
Sherry, Larry	$25	$35	$50	Common
Sherry, Norm	$30	$45	$60	Rare
Shuba, George	$45	$65	$95	Rare
Siebern, Norm	$30	$45	$60	Rare
Sievers, Roy (-)	$25	$35	$50	Very Common

Simmons, Curt (-)	$30	$45	$60	Very Common
Sisler, Dick	$30	$45	$60	Rare
Skinner, Bob	$30	$45	$60	Rare
Skowron, Moose (-)	$30	$45	$60	Very Common
Smalley, Roy	$30	$45	$60	Rare
Smith, Al	$30	$45	$60	Common
Spooner, Karl	$45	$65	$95	Common
Staley, Gerry	$40	$60	$85	None Known
Stanky, Eddie	$35	$55	$75	Common
Stanley, Mickey	$30	$45	$60	Rare
Staub, Rusty	$25	$35	$50	Common
Stephens, Vern (-)	$30	$45	$60	Very Common
Stirnweiss, Snuffy (-)	$30	$45	$60	Very Common
Stuart, Dick (+)	$40	$60	$85	Very Rare
Susce, George	$30	$45	$60	Rare
Sullivan, Haywood	$25	$35	$50	Common
Tanner, Chuck	$35	$55	$75	None Known
Tebbetts, Birdie	$40	$60	$85	Common
Temple, Johnny (-)	$25	$35	$50	Very Common
Terry, Ralph	$30	$45	$60	Common
Terwilliger, Wayne	$35	$55	$75	None Known
Thomas, Frank (-)	$25	$35	$50	Very Common
Thompson, Hank (-)	$25	$35	$50	Very Common
Thomson, Bobby (-)	$30	$45	$60	Common
Tiant, Luis	$35	$55	$75	None Known
Torgeson, Earl (-)	$30	$45	$60	Very Common
Torre, Frank	$30	$45	$60	Very Rare
Torre, Joe	$30	$45	$60	Very Rare USA
Tresh, Tom	$35	$55	$75	Common
Triandos, Gus	$35	$55	$75	Common
Trucks, Virgil	$35	$55	$75	Rare
Turley, Bob	$40	$60	$85	Common
Tuttle, Bill	$25	$35	$50	Very Common
Uecker, Bob	$75	$150	$200	None Known
Valo, Elmer	$30	$45	$60	Very Rare
Verban, Emil	$35	$55	$75	Common
Vernon, Mickey	$35	$55	$75	Common
Versalles, Zolio	$35	$55	$75	None Known
Virdon, Bill	$30	$45	$60	Rare
Waitkus, Eddie	$30	$45	$60	Common
Wakefield, Dick (-)	$30	$45	$60	Common
Walker, Rube (+)	$40	$60	$85	Common
Wertz, Vic (+)	$75	$150	$200	Rare
Westrum Wes	$40	$60	$85	Very Rare
White, Bill (-)	$35	$55	$75	Rare
Williams, Dave	$35	$55	$75	Common
Williams, Dick	$35	$55	$75	Common
Wills, Maury	$35	$55	$75	Rare
Wilson, Earl (+)	$25	$35	$50	None Known
Wooding, Gene	$40	$60	$85	Rare
Yost, Eddie	$35	$55	$75	Rare

Young, Babe	$35	$55	$75	Common
Zarilla, Al (-)	$30	$45	$60	Common
Zernial, Gus (+)	$35	$55	$75	Very Rare
Zimmer, Don (-)	$30	$45	$60	Very Common

Additional player model gloves

Ted Abernathy: 1960s Hollander model, signed $65

Hank Bauer: 1950s Hurricane model, signed $85

Gus Bell: 1950s MacGregor model, signed $75

Johnny Bench: 1970s Rawlings catcher's mitt, signed $150

George Brett: 1970s Wilson model, signed $175

Roy Campanella: 1950s Wilson catcher's mitt $135

Steve Carlton: 1970s Rawlings model, right-handed, signed $85

Roberto Clemente: 1950s Franklin model $150

Tony Conigliaro: 1970s Hurricane model $110

Alvin Dark: 1950s Spalding model $60

Joe DiMaggio: 1950s Spalding model, signed $895

Don Drysdale: 1960s Spalding model, signed $450

Dwight Evans: 1980s Wilson black model, signed $85

Carlton Fisk: 1970s Wilson catcher's mitt $85

George Foster: 1970s MacGregor model, signed $40

Catfish Hunter: 1970s Wilson model $40

Harvey Kuenn: 1950s Wilson model $125

Bob Lemon: 1950s Hurricane model $50

Billy Martin: 1950s Wilson model $100

John Mayberry: 1970s MacGregor first baseman's mitt $35

Bill Mazeroski: 1950s MacGregor model $50

Joe Morgan: 1970s MacGregor model, signed $60

Stan Musial: 1960s Hawthorne model, signed $140

Gaylord Perry: 1960s Wilson model, signed $90

Jimmy Piersall: 1950s Wilson model $60

Del Rice: 1960s black Denkert catcher's mitt, 1960s $100

Jim Rice: 1970s Wilson model $40

Ron Santo: 1960s Wilson model, signed $75

Tom Seaver: 1970s MacGregor model, signed $100

Enos Slaughter: 1950s J.C. Higgins model, signed $125

Ozzie Smith: 1970s Rawlings model, signed $125

Bill Virdon: 1950s Denkert model $65

Carl Yastrzemski: 1970s Spalding, signed twice $125

Pep Young: 1940s Hutch model $75

Robin Yount: 1970s Rawlings model $150

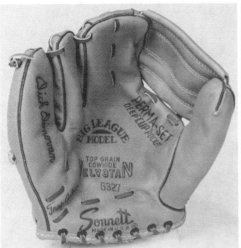

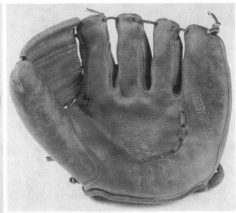

Sonnett, F4F Bobby Thomson model.

Sonnett, G327 Dick Donovan model.

This Hutch cloth label (above) and Sonnett label (right) were attached to gloves produced by the Ohio-based companies.

Sonnett, TW55 Gil Hodges model.

Hutch, 180 Ted Kluszewski model.

Hutch Joe DiMaggio model.

At left is a Bill Dickey glove from the mid-1930s, made for Montgomery Wards stores. At right is a 1920s infielder's glove for a right-handed thrower. Notice the 1-inch web sewed to the thumb and finger.

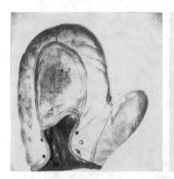  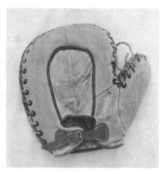

Left to right: late 1800s baseman's mitt without any webbing; 1910-era fielder's glove with a full web between thumb and finger; a pre-WWII Spalding baseman's mitt with a small cloth patch.

At left is a WWI-era fielder's glove made by Folsom Sporting Goods. Notice the Horsehide mark; horsehide gave way to cowhide during the 1930s. At right is a Rick Ferrell Reach mitt from the 1930s; notice the lack of webbing or break action.

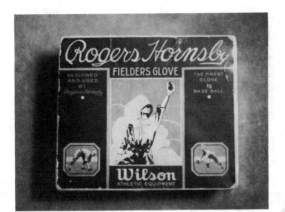

At left, a Rogers Hornsby glove box, circa 1930. Early boxed gloves featuring pictures or illustrations of pre-war Hall of Famers are worth hundreds, even thousands of dollars, with or without the glove.

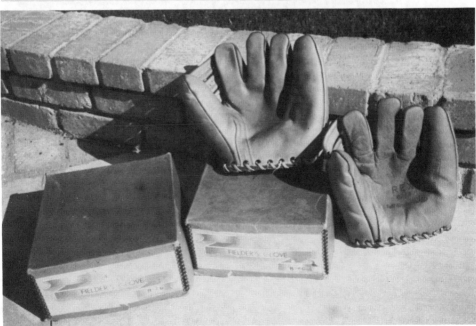

These two Mint pre-war gloves have unlaced fingers and generic boxes.

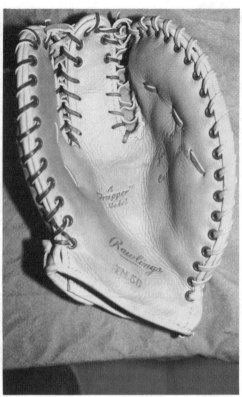

These photos show the front and back of a Joe Adcock Rawlings Trapper mitt, circa 1956-58.

At left is a Rawlings box for the Adcock Trapper mitt; at right is a Wes Parker baseman's mitt, made in Japan, circa 1970.

Statues/Figurines

Hartland Plastics Inc.

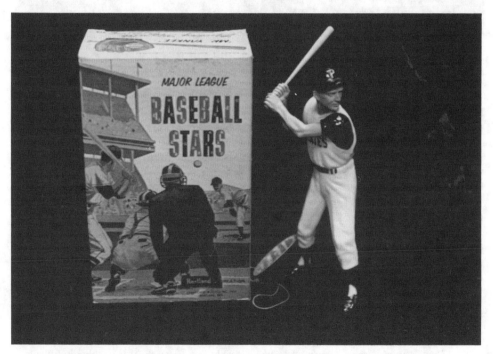

A Dick Groat Hartland statue with box and tag will sell for $1,800-$2,000.

From 1960-1963, Hartland Plastics Co. in Wisconsin offered a line of molded plastic statues featuring 18 baseball stars.

The approximately 8-inch statues sold well at baseball stadium concession stands and retail stores, for between $2-$4. Up to 150,000 of some players (Babe Ruth, Willie Mays, Mickey Mantle, Yogi Berra, Hank Aaron, Ted Williams and Eddie Mathews) were sold.

There were 5,000 Pittsburgh Pirates Dick Groat statues made. However, although he is considered the most valuable in the set, he wasn't a big seller at the time because he, the 1960 National League

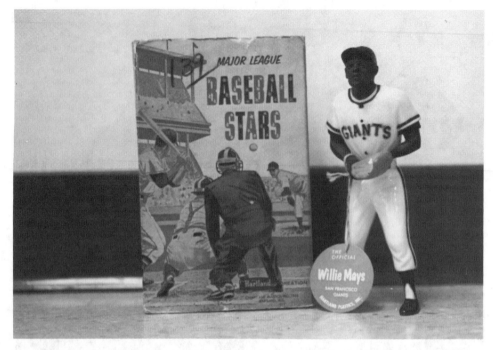

Willie Mays' glove comes in different colors depending on how long it was dyed.

MVP, was a one-year wonder. Rocky Colavito's statue, of which about 10,000 were sold, is the second most valuable.

Others in the line were Warren Spahn, Duke Snider, Don Drysdale, Roger Maris, Harmon Killebrew, Luis Aparicio, Nellie Fox, Ernie Banks, and Stan Musial. Twelve statues were hitting poses, two were pitching poses and five were fielding poses. The players, who negotiated contracts with Hartland to use their likenesses, received $500 as royalties, plus 5 percent of gross sales.

Artists created sculptures from countless sketches, then made plastic molds from the sculptures. Details were hand-painted, and intricate paint-spray masks were also used.

Hartland placed its trade stamp on the back belt loop of the player's pants. However, the Ted Williams statue had the stamp printed behind the shoulder and the Rocky Colavito statue had the stamp underneath a shoulder. The Mickey Mantle statue has its stamp on the inside of Mantle's right forearm.

Variations among the statues include:
- Aaron, Mantle, Mathews, Ruth, Spahn and Williams — with or without magnets.
- Willie Mays — his glove and bat come in a variety of colors, depending upon how long they were left in a dye tank.
- Hank Aaron — some early models have his right foot up on the toes, making it difficult for the statue to stand up; later models made his left foot flatter for more support.
- Aparicio, Drysdale, Colavito, Williams — original platforms were dark purple; later models are white.
- Luis Aparicio and Nellie Fox — uniforms have the word "Sox" written in either red (more common) or black.

In addition to baseball players, Hartland, formed in 1950, made western and religious statues, football players and beer signs, which were the company's best sellers. About 25,000 each of a little leaguer and smaller minor leaguer were also created.

In 1963, the firm was sold to Revlon, and production of the statues ceased. After a series of sales of the company to different conglomerates, Hartland closed its plant in 1978. The original molds were taken to the city dump and are buried under a subdivision.

In 1988 William Alley bought the rights to the Hartland name. In 1989-90 the company retooled the original molds and produced a 25th commemorative edition of the 18 stars, 10,000 each, at $25 each. Each figure has a 25th-anniversary label on the back of the belt. The original designer, Frank Fulop, helped in the reproductions as well. A new line of figures began in 1990; there were 10,000 statues each made for each of the original players, plus Roberto Clemente. These generally sell for $50 each. In 1993 Hartland produced statues for Nolan Ryan, Honus Wagner and Cy Young.

In addition to condition (having paint intact, without marks, and including all original parts, including bats) prices for the original Hartland statues are based on the degree of whiteness the statue has maintained - has it stayed white, or faded to cream or yellow?

The Hartland statues were packaged in cardboard boxes. A hang tag was also included on a string. Having these two items also adds to the price of the statue.

Yogi Berra and Stan Musial Hartland statues sell for between $250-$350 each.

These prices are ranges for white (in Excellent to Near Mint) statues; lower-priced off-whites are generally about 50 percent less of the starting range for whites.

- Hank Aaron .... $275-$350.
- Luis Aparicio .... $250-$400.
- Ernie Banks .... $275-$400.
- Yogi Berra .... $250-$350.
- Rocky Colavito .... $1,000-$1,300.
- Don Drysdale .... $350-$525.
- Nellie Fox .... $250-$350.
- Dick Groat .... $1,800-$2,000.
- Harmon Killebrew .... $500-$650.

- Mickey Mantle .... $300-$400.
- Roger Maris .... $450-$600.
- Willie Mays .... $300-$400.
- Eddie Mathews .... $175-$250.
- Stan Musial .... $250-$350.
- Babe Ruth .... $200-$300.
- Duke Snider .... $450-$650.
- Warren Spahn .... $150-$225.
- Ted Williams .... $250-$350.
- Little leaguer (bat boy) .... $200-250.
- 4" Batter (Minor Leaguer) .... $150-175.

Complete sets of 18 can be found for between $6,000 and $8,000.

Kenner Starting Lineup statues

Prices include the cards which come with each statue

1994 Kenner American League All-Stars (33)

Kevin Appier
Carlos Baerga
Albert Belle
Wade Boggs
Joe Carter
Roger Clemens
David Cone
Chad Curtis
Alex Fernandez
Cecil Fielder
Juan Gonzalez

Ken Griffey Jr.
Brian Harper
Chris Hoiles
Randy Johnson
Jimmy Key
Chuck Knoblauch
Mark Langston
Kenny Lofton
Don Mattingly
Paul Molitor
Mike Mussina

John Olerud
Tony Phillips
Cal Ripken Jr.
Ivan Rodriquez
Tim Salmon
J.T. Snow
Frank Thomas
Greg Vaughn
Mo Vaughn
Robin Ventura
Dave Winfield

1994 Kenner National League All-Stars (26)

Steve Avery
Jeff Bagwell
Derek Bell
Jay Bell
Barry Bonds
John Burkett
Darren Daulton
Delino DeShields
Andres Galarraga

Mark Grace
Tommy Greene
Bryan Harvey
Charlie Hayes
Dave Hollins
Gregg Jefferies
Dave Justice
Eric Karros
Darryl Kile

Orlando Merced
Mike Piazza
Jose Rijo
Ryne Sandberg
Curt Schilling
Gary Sheffield
Robbie Thompson
Matt Williams

1994 Kenner Stadium Stars (8)

Barry Bonds
Will Clark
Dennis Eckersley

Tom Glavine
Juan Gonzalez
Bo Jackson

Kirby Puckett
Deion Sanders

1994 Kenner Cooperstown Collection (8)

Ty Cobb
Lou Gehrig
Reggie Jackson

Willie Mays
Jackie Robinson
Babe Ruth

Honus Wagner
Cy Young

1993 Kenner statues checklist (45)

Roberto Alomar $7

Carlos Baerga $16

Jeff Bagwell $24

Barry Bonds $14

Barry Bonds (SF) $12

Kevin Brown $6

Jose Canseco $6

Will Clark $6

Roger Clemens $9

David Cone $6

Carlton Fisk $9

Travis Fryman $7

Tom Glavine $13

Juan Gonzalez $12

Ken Griffey Jr. $7

Marquis Grissom $7

Juan Guzman $8

Bo Jackson $8

Eric Karros $14

Roberto Kelly $6

John Kruk $10

Ray Lankford $6

Barry Larkin $6

Shane Mack $6

Greg Maddux $10

Jack McDowell $9

Fred McGriff $7

Mark McGwire $6

Mike Mussina $15

David Nied $12

Dean Palmer $8

Terry Pendleton $6

Kirby Puckett $10

Cal Ripken Jr. $11

Bip Roberts $9

Nolan Ryan $17

Nolan Ryan (retire) $24

Ryne Sandberg $6

Benito Santiago $8

Gary Sheffield $9

John Smoltz $10

Frank Thomas $12

Andy Van Slyke $6

Robin Ventura $8

Larry Walker $8

1992 Kenner statues checklist (46)

Atlanta Braves
Steve Avery $9
Tom Glavine $20
Dave Justice $15

Baltimore Orioles
Cal Ripken Jr. $22

Boston Red Sox
Roger Clemens $15

California Angels
Chuck Finley $11

Chicago Cubs
George Bell $10
Ryne Sandberg $15

Chicago White Sox
Bo Jackson spring $10
Bo Jackson running $10
Frank Thomas $30
Frank Thomas $25

Cincinnati Reds
Rob Dibble $8
Chris Sabo $10

Cleveland Indians
Albert Belle $15

Detroit Tigers
Cecil Fielder $20

Houston Astros
Craig Biggio $10

Kansas City Royals
Brian McRae $10

Los Angeles Dodgers
Eric Davis $10
Ramon Martinez $9
Darryl Strawberry $10

Milwaukee Brewers

Minnesota Twins
Scott Erickson $9
Kirby Puckett $15

Montreal Expos
Ivan Calderon $10

New York Mets
Bobby Bonilla $9
Howard Johnson $12
Bret Saberhagen $8

New York Yankees
Kevin Maas $9
Danny Tartabull $12

Oakland A's
Jose Canseco $10
Dave Henderson $8
Rickey Henderson $10
Todd Van Poppel $12

Philadelphia Phillies

Pittsburgh Pirates
Barry Bonds $18

St. Louis Cardinals
Felix Jose $15

San Diego Padres
Tony Gwynn $15
Fred McGriff $15

San Francisco Giants
Will Clark $12
Malt Williams $10

Seattle Mariners
Ken Griffey Jr. $15
Ken Griffey Jr. $15

Texas Rangers
Juan Gonzalez $25
Nolan Ryan $15
Ruben Sierra $12

Toronto Blue Jays
Roberto Alomar $15
Tom Seaver $17

157

1991 Kenner statues (55)

Commons are generally between $8-$12, unless noted.

Atlanta Braves
Dave Justice $27

Baltimore Orioles
Glenn Davis $10
Ben McDonald $12

Boston Red Sox

California Angels
Jim Abbott $17

Chicago Cubs
George Bell $10
Andre Dawson $11
Shawon Dunston $12
Mark Grace $12
Ryne Sandberg $15

Chicago White Sox
Ozzie Guillen $14
Bo Jackson $18
Tim Raines $15

Cincinnati Reds
Jack Armstrong $12
Tom Browning $10
Eric Davis $12
Barry Larkin $11
Chris Sabo $8

Cleveland Indians
Sandy Alomar Jr. $15

Detroit Tigers
Cecil Fielder $12
Alan Trammell $15

Houston Astros

Kansas City Royals
Bo Jackson $15

Los Angeles Dodgers
Ramon Martinez $15
Darryl Strawberry $20

Milwaukee Brewers

Kenner has offered statues of baseball players since 1988.

Minnesota Twins
Kirby Puckett $20

Montreal Expos
Delino DeShields $18

New York Mets
Vince Coleman $10
John Franco $10
Dwight Gooden $9
Gregg Jefferies $15
Howard Johnson $15
Dave Magadan $10
Darryl Strawberry $12
Frank Viola $11

New York Yankees
Roberto Kelly $14
Kevin Maas $18
Don Mattingly $12
Steve Sax $13

Oakland A's
Jose Canseco $12
Rickey Henderson $12
Mark McGwire $10
Dave Stewart $15

Philadelphia Phillies
Len Dykstra $13

Pittsburgh Pirates
Barry Bonds $22
Bobby Bonilla $15
Doug Drabek $15

St. Louis Cardinals
Todd Zeile $20

San Diego Padres
Benito Santiago $10

San Francisco Giants
Will Clark $12
Kevin Mitchell $8
Matt Williams $20

Seattle Mariners
Ken Griffey Jr. batting $12
Ken Griffey Jr. $12
Ken Griffey Sr. $17

Texas Rangers
Nolan Ryan $25

Toronto Blue Jays
Kelly Gruber $10

1990 Kenner statues (92)

Commons are generally between $8-$12, unless noted.

Atlanta Braves

Baltimore Orioles
Jeff Ballard $11
Ben McDonald $25
Cal Ripken Jr. $35
Mickey Tettleton $14

Boston Red Sox
Wade Boggs $18
Ellis Burks $14
Roger Clemens $23
Nick Esasky $28
Mike Greenwell $10
Jody Reed $15

California Angels
Jim Abbott $25

Chicago Cubs
Damon Berryhill $12
Andre Dawson $15
Mark Grace batting $27
Mark Grace power $15
Greg Maddux $25
Ryne Sandberg $25
Rick Sutcliffe $14
Jerome Walton $8
Mitch Williams $11

Chicago White Sox

Cincinnati Reds
Todd Benzinger $13
Eric Davis $12
Rob Dibble $20

Cincinnati Reds
Barry Larkin $25
Paul O'Neill $15
Chris Sabo $8

Cleveland Indians
Sandy Alomar $18

Detroit Tigers
Matt Nokes $13
Gary Pettis $30
Alan Trammell $13
Lou Whitaker $13

Houston Astros
Mike Scott $9

Kansas City Royals
Bo Jackson $12

Los Angeles Dodgers
Kirk Gibson $10
Orel Hershiser $15
Eddie Murray $20
Willie Randolph $15

Milwaukee Brewers
Chris Bosio $12
Paul Molitor $14
Gary Sheffield $25
Robin Yount $40

Minnesota Twins
Alan Anderson $12
Wally Backman $17
Gary Gaetti $12

Minnesota Twins
Kent Hrbek $10
Kirby Puckett $20

Montreal Expos
Andres Galarraga $20

New York Mets
Ron Darling $11
Dwight Gooden $12
Gregg Jefferies $12
Howard Johnson $17
Kevin McReynolds $15
Juan Samuel $12
Darryl Strawberry batting $12
Darryl Strawberry fielding $18
Frank Viola $15

New York Yankees
Jesse Barfield $10
Roberto Kelly $18
Don Mattingly batting $20
Don Mattingly power $25
Dave Righetti $10
Steve Sax $9
Dave Winfield $25

Oakland A's
Jose Canseco $14
Dennis Eckersley $27
Dave Henderson $15
Rickey Henderson $15
Mark McGwire $15
Dave Stewart $15

Philadelphia Phillies
Len Dykstra $27
Von Hayes $15
Tom Herr $11
Ricky Jordan $14

Pittsburgh Pirates
Barry Bonds $17
Bobby Bonilla $17
John Smiley $14
Andy Van Slyke $15

St. Louis Cardinals
Vince Coleman $11
Pedro Guerrero $10
Joe Magrane $12
Jose Oquendo $10
Ozzie Smith $14

San Diego Padres
Joe Carter $30

San Francisco Giants
Steve Bedrosian $12
Will Clark power $25
Will Clark stance $15
Kevin Mitchell $10
Rick Reuschel $12

Seattle Mariners
Ken Griffey Jr. slide $60
Ken Griffey Jr. jump $40

Texas Rangers
Nolan Ryan $40

Toronto Blue Jays
Fred McGriff $20

1989 Kenner (168) Commons are generally between $12-$16, unless noted.

Atlanta Braves
Ron Gant $60
Albert Hall $17
Dion James $12
Dale Murphy $14
Gerald Perry $16
Zane Smith $15
Bruce Sutter $25

Baltimore Orioles
Brady Anderson $22
Cal Ripken Jr. $55
Larry Sheets $12
Pete Stanicek $13

Boston Red Sox
Marty Barrett $14
Wade Boggs $20
Ellis Burks $20
Roger Clemens $25
Mike Greenwell $12
Jim Rice $15
Lee Smith $25

California Angels
Chili Davis $35
Jack Howell $35
Wally Joyner $13
Johnny Ray $45
Dick Schofield $40
Devon White $30
Mike Witt $25

Chicago Cubs
Damon Berryhill $15
Andre Dawson $15
Shawon Dunston $17
Mark Grace $28
Greg Maddux $22
Ryne Sandberg $26
Rick Sutcliffe $18

Chicago White Sox
Harold Baines $15
Ivan Calderon $22
Ozzie Guillen $20
Dan Pasqua $18
Melido Perez $20
Bobby Thigpen $25
Greg Walker $19

Cincinnati Reds
Kal Daniels $16
Eric Davis $13
Bo Diaz $15

Cincinnati Reds
John Franco $14
Danny Jackson $15
Barry Larkin $30
Chris Sabo $25
Jeff Treadway $32

Cleveland Indians
Joe Carter $15
Mel Hall $10
Brook Jacoby $12
Doug Jones $16
Cory Snyder $15
Greg Swindell $18

Detroit Tigers
Tom Brookens $12
Mike Henneman $11
Chet Lemon $14
Jack Morris $23
Matt Nokes $12
Luis Salazar $18
Alan Trammell $14
Lou Whitaker $20

Houston Astros
Kevin Bass $13
Glenn Davis $13
Billy Doran $20
Billy Hatcher $12
Mike Scott $12
Dave Smith $14
Gerald Young $12

Kansas City Royals
George Brett $35
Mark Gubicza $10
Bo Jackson $45
Bret Saberhagen $20
Kevin Seitzer $12
Kurt Stillwell $11
Pat Tabler $13
Danny Tartabull $15

Los Angeles Dodgers
Kirk Gibson $15
Orel Hershiser $20
Mike Marshall $11
Mike Scioscia $15
John Shelby $12
Fernando Valenzuela $15

Milwaukee Brewers
Glenn Braggs $14
Rob Deer $14
Ted Higuera $15

Milwaukee Brewers
Paul Molitor $20
Dan Plesac $12
B.J. Surhoff $20
Robin Yount $65

Minnesota Twins
Gary Gaetti $12
Dan Gladden $15
Kent Hrbek $12
Tim Laudner $13
Kirby Puckett $22
Jeff Reardon $23
Frank Viola $14

Montreal Expos
Tim Raines $11

New York Mets
Gary Carter $13
David Cone $20
Len Dykstra $15
Kevin Elster $13
Dwight Gooden $15
Keith Hernandez $11
Gregg Jefferies $22
Kevin McReynolds $20
Randy Myers $20
Darryl Strawberry $15

New York Yankees
Rickey Henderson $25
Al Leiter $12
Don Mattingly $15
Mike Pagliarulo $13
Dave Righetti $14
Don Slaught $12
Dave Winfield $25

Oakland A's
Jose Canseco $14
Dennis Eckersley $25
Carney Lansford $20
Mark McGwire $20
Dave Parker $20
Terry Steinbach $30
Dave Stewart $23
Walt Weiss $35
Bob Welch $20

Philadelphia Phillies
Phil Bradley $30
Steve Bedrosian $10
Von Hayes $10
Chris James $10

Philadelphia Phillies
Juan Samuel $13
Mike Schmidt $62
Milt Thompson $18

Pittsburgh Pirates
Barry Bonds $40
Bobby Bonilla $22
Doug Drabek $25
Mike LaValliere $15
Jose Lind $20
Andy Van Slyke $20
Bob Walk $13

St. Louis Cardinals
Tom Brunansky $15
Vince Coleman $12
Pedro Guerrero $10
Willie McGee $15
Tony Pena $17
Terry Pendleton $28
Ozzie Smith $18
Todd Worrell $16

San Diego Padres
Roberto Alomar $50
Mark Davis $15
Tony Gwynn $35
John Kruk $22
Benito Santiago $22
Marvell Wynne $18

San Francisco Giants
Brett Butler $20
Will Clark $17
Candy Maldonado $12
Kevin Mitchell $20
Robby Thompson $15
Jose Uribe $14

Seattle Mariners
Mickey Brantley $16
Alvin Davis $17
Mark Langston $25
Harold Reynolds $18
Rey Quinones $18

Texas Rangers
Steve Buechele $20
Scott Fletcher $12
Pete Incaviglia $12
Jeff Russell $17
Ruben Sierra $33

Toronto Blue Jays
George Bell $15

1988 Kenner Starting Lineup (124)

Commons are generally between $15-$17, unless noted. Cards were included with the statues, and the prices for these and the previous statues include the card.

Atlanta Braves
Ken Griffey Sr. $33
Dale Murphy $15
Ken Oberkfell $17
Zane Smith $15
Ozzie Virgil $14

Baltimore Orioles
Mike Boddicker $18
Terry Kennedy $20
Fred Lynn $25
Eddie Murray $18
Cal Ripken Jr. $75

Boston Red Sox
Wade Boggs $20
Ellis Burks $42
Roger Clemens $28
Dwight Evans $22
Jim Rice $22

California Angels
Brian Downing $15
Wally Joyner $14
Donnie Moore $20
Devon White $20
Mike Witt $15

Chicago Cubs
Jody Davis $15
Andre Dawson $22
Shawon Dunston $25
Leon Durham $15
Ryne Sandberg $50
Rick Sutcliffe $17

Chicago White Sox
Harold Baines $15
Carlton Fisk $50
Ozzie Guillen $20
Gary Redus $19
Greg Walker $15

Cincinnati Reds
Buddy Bell $22

Cincinnati Reds
Kal Daniels $17
Eric Davis $13
John Franco $20
Pete Rose $25

Cleveland Indians
Joe Carter $25
Julio Franco $20
Mel Hall $17
Cory Snyder $15
Pat Tabler $15

Detroit Tigers
Willie Hernandez $20
Jack Morris $25
Matt Nokes $19
Alan Trammell $15
Lou Whitaker $20

Houston Astros
Alan Ashby $20
Kevin Bass $14
Glenn Davis $15
Billy Hatcher $20
Nolan Ryan $200
Mike Scott $12

Kansas City Royals
George Brett $40
Dan Quisenberry $20
Bret Saberhagen $24
Kevin Seitzer $20
Danny Tartabull $20

Los Angeles Dodgers
Pedro Guerrero $13
Mike Marshall $12
Steve Sax $15
Franklin Stubbs $16
Fernando Valenzuela $12

Milwaukee Brewers
Rob Deer $18

Milwaukee Brewers
Ted Higuera $18
Paul Molitor $30
B.J. Surhoff $23
Robin Yount $65

Minnesota Twins
Tom Brunansky $25
Gary Gaetti $17
Kent Hrbek $18
Kirby Puckett $28
Jeff Reardon $25
Frank Viola $20

Montreal Expos
Tim Raines $15

New York Mets
Gary Carter $18
Len Dykstra $25
Dwight Gooden $16
Keith Hernandez $18
Howard Johnson $30
Kevin McReynolds $20
Darryl Strawberry $15

New York Yankees
Jack Clark $22
Rickey Henderson $25
Don Mattingly $18
Willie Randolph $17
Dave Righetti $15
Dave Winfield $26

Oakland A's
Jose Canseco $45
Carney Lansford $30
Mark McGwire $45
Dave Parker $27

Philadelphia Phillies
Steve Bedrosian $16

Philadelphia Phillies
Von Hayes $15
Shane Rawley $15
Juan Samuel $15
Mike Schmidt $42

Pittsburgh Pirates
Barry Bonds $48
Bobby Bonilla $28
Sid Bream $18
Mike Dunne $17
Andy Van Slyke $33

St. Louis Cardinals
Vince Coleman $16
Tommy Herr $15
Willie McGee $18
Ozzie Smith $20
Todd Worrell $20

San Diego Padres
Chris Brown $18
Tony Gwynn $24
John Kruk $33
Benito Santiago $20

San Francisco Giants
Will Clark $35
Jeffrey Leonard $15
Candy Maldonado $16
Rick Reuschel $15

Seattle Mariners
Alvin Davis $15
Mark Langston $29
Ken Phelps $16
Jim Presley $15

Texas Rangers
Charlie Hough $17
Pete Incaviglia $16
Pete O'Brien $15
Larry Parrish $13
Ruben Sierra $42

Toronto Blue Jays
George Bell $19

1993 Kenner Headliners (8)

Jim Abbott	$13	Cal Ripken Jr.	$16
Roberto Alomar	$13	Nolan Ryan	$26
Tom Glavine	$16	Deion Sanders	$12
Mark McGwire	$12	Frank Thomas	$15

1993 Kenner Stadium Stars (6)

Roger Clemens	$25	Nolan Ryan	$36
Cecil Fielder	$18	Ryne Sandberg	$24
Ken Griffey Jr.	$18	Frank Thomas	$42

1992 Kenner Headliners (7)

George Brett	$25	Bo Jackson	$17
Cecil Fielder	$17	Nolan Ryan	$20
Ken Griffey Jr.	$18	Ryne Sandberg	$23
Rickey Henderson	$18		

1991 Kenner Headliners (7)

Jose Canseco	$18	Bo Jackson	$15
Will Clark	$25	Don Mattingly	$25
Ken Griffey Jr.	$30	Nolan Ryan	$40
Rickey Henderson	$22.50		

1990 Kenner Team Lineup & Award Winners

Boston Red Sox	$75	Oakland A's	$200
Chicago Cubs	$50	American League Lineup	$50
New York Mets	$50	National League Lineup	$50
New York Yankees	$50		

1989 Kenner One-On-One

Jose Canseco/Alan Trammell	$30	Don Mattingly/Wade Boggs	$40
Gary Carter/Eric Davis	$25	Ryne Sandberg/Vince Coleman	$40

1989 Kenner Baseball Greats (10)

This set included a pair of great players from one team per package, with two collector cards also.

1) Willie Mays/Willie McCovey	$16
2) Johnny Bench/Pete Rose	$22
3) Ernie Banks/Billy Williams	$15
4) Stan Musial/Bob Gibson	$20
5) Roberto Clemente/Willie Stargell	$18
6) Babe Ruth/Lou Gehrig	$22
7) Hank Aaron/Eddie Mathews	$16
8) Mickey Mantle/Joe DiMaggio	$35
9) Don Drysdale/Reggie Jackson	$22
10) Carl Yastrzemski/Hank Aaron	$25

Salvino Sports Legends

This Salvino statue shows Rickey Henderson about to steal second.

Many of the sporting world's greatest superstars are honored on hand-signed, limited-edition figurines offered by Salvino Inc. of Corona, Calif.

Original artwork is cast by mold makers to insure an exact reproduction of the original artwork. Every figurine is individually cast by artisans in cold-cast porcelain and inspected for defects. Every casting is then hand-painted by professionals.

The honored athlete personally autographs signature plaques which are permanently mounted to the figurine base. The authenticity of the autograph is guaranteed and endorsed with a certificate of authenticity numbered to match the figurine.

Brooklyn Dodger Collection: Sandy Koufax, 1st, 2,500 made $225
Sandy Koufax, 2nd, 500 .... $325
Don Drysdale, 3rd, 2,500 .... $185
Don Drysdale, 4th, 300 .... $250
Roy Campanella, 5th, 2,000 .... $400
Roy Campanella, 6th, 200 .... $600
Heroes of the Diamond: Rickey Henderson home, 1st, 600 .... $275
Rickey Henderson away, 2nd, 600 .... $275
Rickey Henderson, 3rd, 550 .... $375
Mickey Mantle fielding, 4th, 682 .... $400
Mickey Mantle batting, 5th, 682 .... $400
Mickey Mantle batting, 10" #6, 368 .... $700
Mickey Mantle batting, 7" #7, 368 .... $700

Gartlan Statues

Gartlan USA is based in Huntington Beach, Calif., and produces limited-edition ceramic and porcelain sports collectibles, including hand-signed plates and figurines. The larger versions of the statues are about 8 inches tall each; the smaller ones are about 5 inches tall and sell for about $75 each. Plates range in size from 10 1/4" diameter ($45 each), to 8 1/2" diameter, to 3 1/4" diameter plates ($20 each).

Statues

This list of players includes the number made, issue price, and a current selling price. Artist's proofs are signed by the artist and player:

- Hank Aaron: 1,982; $225; $225.
- Luis Aparicio: 1,984; $225; $225.
- Al Barlick: 1,989; $175; $175.
- "Cool Papa" Bell: 1,499; $195; $195.
- Johnny Bench: 1,989; $150; $350.
Bench artist proof: 250; $350; $550.
- Yogi Berra: 2,150; $225; $225.
Berra artist proof: 250; $350; $375.
- George Brett: 2,250; $225; $225.
- Rod Carew: 1,991; $225; $225.
- Steve Carlton: 3,290; $175; $215.
Carlton artist proof: 300; $350; $350.

- Ray Dandridge: 1,987; $195; $195.
- Joe DiMaggio: 2,214; $275; $1,275.
DiMaggio pinstripe: 325; $695; $2,000.
- Carlton Fisk: 1,972; $225; $225.
- Whitey Ford: 2,360; $225; $225.
Ford artist proof: 250; $350; $350.
- Ken Griffey Jr.: 1,989; $225; $225.
- Monte Irvin: 1,973; $225; $225.
- Buck Leonard: 1,972; $195; $195.
- Pete Rose: 4,192; $125; $1,375.
- Mike Schmidt: 1,987; $150; $950.
Schmidt artist proof: 20; $275; $1,500.
- Warren Spahn: 1,973; $225; $225.
- Darryl Strawberry: 2,500; $225; $225.
- Ted Williams: 2,654; $295; $550.
Williams artist proof: 250; $650; $700.
- Carl Yastrzemski: 1,989; $150; $425.
Yaz artist proof: 250; $150; $495.

Plates (10 1/4")

This list of players includes the number made, issue price, and a current selling price. Artist's proofs are signed by the artist and the player:

- Luis Aparicio: 1,984; $125; $125.
Aparicio proof: 250; $150; $150.
- Johnny Bench: 1,989; $100; $175.
- Yogi Berra: 2,150; $125; $125.
Berra proof: 250, $175; $175.
- George Brett: 2,000; $100; $275.
- Rod Carew: 950, $150; $150.

- Carlton Fisk: 950; $150; $150.
- Whitey Ford: 2,360; $125; $125.
- Ken Griffey: 1,992; $125; $125.
- Pete Rose farewell: 50; $300; $550.
Pete Rose diamond: 950; $195; $385.
Pete Rose platinum: 4,192; $100; $650.
- Mike Schmidt: 1,987; $100; $500.
Schmidt proof: 56; $150; $750.
- Tom Seaver: 1,992; $125; $125.
- Darryl Strawberry: 1,979; $100; $125.

Mini plates, worth $19 each, have been made for Reggie Jackson and Al Barlick.

ProSport Creations

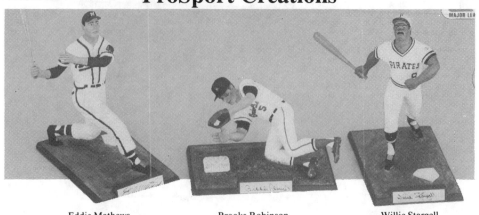

Eddie Mathews	Brooks Robinson	Willie Stargell
edition size: 1,978	edition size: 1,983	edition size: 1,988
issue price: $175	issue price: $200	issue price: $175

	# Issued	Issue Price	Value
Richie Ashburn hand-signed	1,962	$175	$85
mini	3,000	$60	$50
Bill Dickey hand-signed	1,954	$150	$100
mini	3,000	$60	$55
artist proof	200	$190	$140
Whitey Ford hand-signed	1,974	$225	$100
mini	3,000	$55	$55
Steve Garvey hand-signed	1,987	$175	$100
artist proof hand-signed	200	$215	$100
Bob Gibson hand-signed	1,981	$200	$140
mini	3,000	$55	$55
Tony Gwynn hand-signed	1,989	$175	$125
artist proof hand-signed	200	$215	$140
Harmon Killebrew hand-signed	1,984	$175	$125
artist proof hand-signed	200	$215	$150
Eddie Mathews hand-signed	1,978	$175	$100
artist proof hand-signed	200	$215	$140
Jim Palmer hand-signed	1,990	$225	$125
artist proof hand-signed	200	$265	$165
mini	3,000	$200	$125
Brooks Robinson hand-signed	1,983	$200	$125
artist proof hand-signed	200	$240	$140
Willie Stargell hand-signed	1,988	$175	$100
artist proof hand-signed	200	$215	$140

Sports Impressions

Sports Impressions offers a wide variety of players who have been featured on plates and as figurines. Mini 5-inch figurines generally have a price range of $35 to $45. Regular figurines (7") range from $90 to $100. Mini plates generally sell for $20. Regular-size (10 1/4") plates generally range from $75 to $150, while a

Sports Impressions Statues and Plates

Mickey Mantle gold plate sells for up to $300.

Mickey Mantle

- "Switch Hitter" mini plate; 4 1/4" diameter; porcelain; by artist Joseph Catalano.
- Mickey Mantle figurine; porcelain bisque/wood; 5 inches; first in Yesterday's Stars Series.
- "The Life of a Legend" collectoval; a gold plate; porcelain/gold; 12" diameter; limited edition of 1,968; artist Terrence Fogarty.
- "Mickey 7" gold edition plate; porcelain/gold; 1) 1/4" diameter; limited edition of 1,500.
- "Golden Years" mini plate; 4 1/4" diameter; porcelain; artist Mike Petronella.
- "Golden Years" plate; porcelain; 8 1/2" diameter; limited edition of 5,000; artist Mike Petronella.

Duke Snider

- "Boys of Summer" Duke Snider figurine; porcelain bisque/wood; 7 inches; limited edition of 2,500.
- Duke Snider mini plate; 4 1/4" diameter, porcelain; artist Brian Johnson.
- Duke Snider regular plate; 10 1/4" diameter; porcelain; limited edition of 5,000; artist Brian Johnson.
- Duke Snider gold plate; "Boys of Summer"; 10 1/4 diameter; porcelain, gold; limited edition of 1,500; artist Brian Johnson.
- Duke Snider figurine; 5 inches; porcelain bisque/wood; third in Yesterday's Stars Series.
- "Golden Years" mini plate; porcelain; 4 1/4" diameter; artist Mike Petronella.

Willie Mays

- Willie Mays figurine; porcelain bisque/wood; 7 inches; limited edition of 5,600.
- Willie Mays "Famous Catch" mini plate; 4 1/4" diameter; porcelain; artist Ron Lewis.
- Willie Mays gold plate; porcelain/gold; 10 1/4" diameter; limited edition of 2,500; artist Ron Lewis.
- Willie Mays figurine; porcelain/wood; 5 inches; second in Yesterday's Stars Series.
- Willie Mays "Famous Catch" figurine; porcelain bisque/wood; 7 inches; limited edition of 5,000.
- "Golden Years" Mays mini plate; 4 1/4" diameter; porcelain; artist Mike Petronella.

• "Golden Years" Mays regular plate; porcelain; 8 1/2" diameter; limited edition of 5,000; artist Mike Petronella.

Babe Ruth

• Babe Ruth figurine; porcelain bisque/wood; 7 inches; limited edition of 5,000.
• Babe Ruth mini plate; 4 1/4" diameter; porcelain; artist Brian Johnson.
• Babe Ruth regular plate; 10 1/4" diameter; limited edition of 10,000; artist Brian Johnson.

Lou Gehrig

• Lou Gehrig figurine; 7 inches; porcelain bisque/wood; limited edition of 5,000.
• Lou Gehrig mini plate; 4 1/4" diameter; porcelain; artist Brian Johnson.
• Lou Gehrig regular plate; porcelain; 10 1/4" diameter; limited edition of 10,000; artist Brian Johnson.

Ted Williams

• Ted Williams figurine; 5 inches; porcelain bisque/wood.
• Ted Williams "Splendid Splinter" mini plate; 4 1/4" diameter; artist Joseph Catalano.
• Ted Williams "Splendid Splinter"; gold plate; porcelain, gold; 10 1/4" diameter; limited edition of 1,960; artist Joseph Catalano.
• Ted Williams 500 HR Club figurine; porcelain bisque/wood; 7 inches; limited edition of 5,521.

Jackie Robinson

• Jackie Robinson figurine; porcelain bisque/wood; 7 inches; limited edition of 5,042.
• Jackie Robinson mini plate; porcelain; 4 1/4" diameter; artist Joseph Catalano.
• Jackie Robinson gold edition plate; 10 1/4" diameter; porcelain/gold; limited edition of 1,956; artist Joseph Catalano.
• Jackie Robinson figurine; 5 inches; porcelain bisque/wood.

Thurman Munson

• Thurman Munson figurine; porcelain bisque/wood; 7 inches; limited edition of 5,000.

• Thurman Munson mini plate; 4 1/4" diameter; porcelain; artist R. Simon.
• Thurman Munson regular plate; 10 1/4" diameter; porcelain; limited edition of 10,000; artist R. Simon.
• Thurman Munson figurine; porcelain bisque/wood; 5 inches.

Tom Seaver

• Tom Seaver mini plate; 4 1/4" diameter; porcelain; artist Ron Lewis.
• Tom Seaver gold plate; porcelain/gold; 10 1/4" diameter; limited edition of 3,311; artist Ron Lewis,
• Tom Seaver figurine; porcelain bisque/wood; 5 inches.
• Tom Seaver large figurine; porcelain bisque/wood; 8 inches; limited edition of 2,000.

Joe Morgan

• Joe Morgan figurine; 7 inches; porcelain bisque/wood; limited edition of 1,900.
• Joe Morgan mini plate; porcelain; 4 1/4" diameter; artist Joseph Catalano.
• Joe Morgan gold edition plate; porcelain/gold; 10 1/4" diameter; limited edition of 1,990; artist Joseph Catalano.
• Joe Morgan figurine; 5 inches; porcelain bisque/wood.

Al Kaline

• Al Kaline figurine; 7 inches; porcelain bisque/wood; limited edition of 2,500.
• Al Kaline mini plate; 4 1/4" diameter; porcelain; artist Ed Lapere.
• Al Kaline regular plate; 10 1/4" diameter; porcelain; limited edition of 10,000; artist Ed Lapere.
• Al Kaline gold plate; porcelain/gold; 10 1/4" diameter; limited edition of 1,000; artist Ed Lapere.

Brooks Robinson

• Brooks Robinson figurine; porcelain bisque/wood; 7 inches; limited edition of 2,848.
• Brooks Robinson mini plate; 4 1/4" diameter; porcelain; artist R. Simon.
• Brooks Robinson gold plate; porcelain/gold; 10 1/4" diameter; limited edition of 1,000; artist R. Simon.

• Brooks Robinson figurine; porcelain bisque/wood; 5 inches.

Bob Feller

• Bob Feller figurine; porcelain bisque/wood; 7 inches; limited edition of 2,500.

• Bob Feller mini plate; 4 1/4" diameter; porcelain; artist Ed Lapere.

• Bob Feller regular plate; porcelain; 10 1/4" diameter; limited edition of 10,000; artist Ed Lapere.

• Bob Feller gold plate; porcelain/gold; 10 1/4" diameter; limited edition of 2,500; artist Ed Lapere.

Carl Yastrzemski

• Carl Yastrzemski mini plate; porcelain; 4 1/4" diameter; artist R. Simon.

• Carl Yastrzemski regular plate; porcelain; 10 1/4" diameter; limited edition of 1,500.

• Carl Yastrzemski gold plate; porcelain/gold; 10 1/4" diameter; limited edition of 1,500; artist R. Simon.

Cy Young

• Cy Young figurine; 7 inches; porcelain bisque/wood; limited edition of 5,000.

• Cy Young mini plate; porcelain; 4 1/4" diameter; artist Ron Lewis.

• Cy Young regular plate; porcelain; 10 1/4" diameter; limited edition of 10,000; artist Ron Lewis.

Honus Wagner

• Honus Wagner figurine; porcelain bisque/wood; 7 inches; limited edition of 5,000.

• Honus Wagner mini plate; porcelain; 4 1/4" diameter; artist Ron Lewis.

• Honus Wagner regular plate; porcelain; 10 1/4" diameter; limited edition of 10,000; artist Ron Lewis.

Roberto Clemente

• Roberto Clemente figurine; porcelain bisque/wood; 7 inches; limited edition of 5,000.

• Roberto Clemente mini plate; porcelain; 4 1/4" diameter; artist Ron Lewis.

• Roberto Clemente regular plate; porcelain; 10 1/4" diameter; limited edition of 10,000; artist Ron Lewis.

Stan Musial

• Stan Musial mini plate; porcelain; 4 1/4" diameter; Ed Lapere.

• Stan Musial gold plate; porcelain; 10 1/4" diameter; limited edition of 1,963; artist Ed Lapere.

Ty Cobb

• Ty Cobb figurine; porcelain bisque/wood; 7 inches; limited edition of 5,000.

• Ty Cobb mini plate; 4 1/4" diameter; porcelain; artist Ron Lewis.

• Ty Cobb plate; porcelain; 10 1/4" diameter; limited edition of 10,000; artist Ron Lewis.

Golden Years Series

• Duke Snider figurine; porcelain bisque/wood; 5 inches.

• Mickey Mantle figurine; porcelain bisque/wood; 5 inches.

• "Golden Years" collectoval plate; features Snider, Mays, Mantle; porcelain/gold; 12" diameter; limited edition of 1,000; artist Mike Petronella.

• "Golden Years" Willie Mays mini plate; porcelain; 4 1/4" diameter; artist Mike Petronella.

• "Golden Years" Willie Mays regular plate; porcelain; 8 1/2" diameter; limited edition of 5,000; artist Mike Petronella.

• "Golden Years" Mickey Mantle mini plate; porcelain; 4 1/2" diameter; artist Mike Petronella.

• "Golden Years" Mickey Mantle regular plate; porcelain; 8 1/2" diameter; limited edition of 5,000; artist Mike Petronella.

• "Golden Years" Duke Snider mini plate; porcelain; 4 1/4" diameter; artist Mike Petronella.

• "Golden Years" Duke Snider regular plate; porcelain; 8 1/2" diameter; limited edition of 5,000; artist Mike Petronella.

The Greatest Centerfielders

• Mini plate featuring Willie Mays, Duke Snider, Mickey Mantle; 4 1/4" diameter; porcelain; artist Ron Lewis.

• "The Greatest Centerfielders" porcelain/gold plate; 10 1/4" diameter; limited edition of 3,500; artist Ron Lewis.

• "Mickey, Willie & Duke" mini plate; porcelain; 4 1/4" diameter; artist R. Simon.

• "Mickey, Willie & Duke" regular plate; porcelain; 10 1/4" diameter; limited edition of 3,500; artist R. Simon.

• "Mickey, Willie & Duke" gold plate; porcelain; 10 1/4" diameter; limited edition of 1,500; artist R. Simon.

Yesterday's Stars Series

• Hank Aaron figurine; porcelain bisque; 5 inches.

• Reggie Jackson (Yankees) figurine; porcelain bisque; 5 inches.

• Steve Garvey figurine; porcelain bisque; 5 inches.

• Ted Williams figurine; porcelain bisque; 5 inches.

• Thurman Munson figurine; porcelain bisque; 5 inches.

• Tom Seaver figurine; porcelain bisque; 5 inches.

• Brooks Robinson figurine; porcelain bisque; 5 inches.

• Duke Snider figurine; porcelain bisque; 5 inches.

• Ernie Banks figurine; porcelain bisque; 5 inches.

• Jackie Robinson figurine; porcelain bisque; 5 inches.

• Mickey Mantle figurine; porcelain bisque; 5 inches.

• Willie Mays figurine; porcelain bisque; 5 inches.

The 500 Home Run Club

• Ernie Banks figurine; porcelain bisque/wood; 7 inches; limited edition of 5,512.

• Frank Robinson (Orioles) figurine; porcelain bisque/wood; 7 inches; limited edition of 5,586.

• Hank Aaron figurine; porcelain bisque/wood; 7 inches; limited edition of 5,755.

• Willie Mays figurine; porcelain bisque/wood; 7 inches; limited edition of 5,660.

• Harmon Killebrew figurine; porcelain bisque/wood; 7 inches; limited edition of 5,573.

• Willie McCovey figurine; porcelain bisque/wood; 7 inches; limited edition of 5,521.

• Jimmie Foxx (A's) figurine; porcelain bisque/wood; 7 inches; limited edition of 1,008.

• Mel Ott figurine; porcelain bisque/wood; 7 inches; limited edition of 1,008.

• Ted Williams figurine; porcelain bisque/wood; 7 inches; limited edition of 25,000.

• Eddie Mathews figurine; porcelain bisque/wood; 7 inches; limited edition of 5,512.

Yesterday's Legends

• Al Kaline figurine; porcelain bisque/wood; 7 inches; limited edition of 2,500.

• Babe Ruth figurine; porcelain bisque/wood; 7 inches; limited edition of 5,000.

• Bob Feller figurine; porcelain bisque/wood; 7 inches; limited edition of 2,500.

• Cy Young figurine; porcelain bisque/wood; 7 inches; limited edition of 5,000.

• Lou Gehrig figurine; porcelain bisque/wood; 7 inches; limited edition of 5,000.

• Roberto Clemente figurine; porcelain bisque/wood; 7 inches; limited edition of 5,000.

• Rod Carew (Angels) figurine; porcelain bisque/wood; 7 inches; limited edition of 3,053.

• Thurman Munson figurine; porcelain bisque/wood; 7 inches; limited edition of 5,000.

Yesterday's Superstars

• Brooks Robinson figurine; 7 inches; porcelain bisque/wood; limited edition of 2,848.

• Steve Garvey figurine; 7 inches; porcelain bisque/wood; limited edition of 2,599.

Miscellaneous

• "Dem Bums" mini plate; 4 1/4" diameter; Brooklyn Dodgers; porcelain; artist R. Simon.

• "Dem Bums" regular plate; porcelain; Brooklyn Dodgers; 10 1/4" diameter; limited edition of 10,000; artist R. Simon.

• Duke Snider figurine; "Boys of Summer"; porcelain/bisque/wood; 7 inches; limited edition of 2,500.

• Honus Wagner figurine; "Legendary Hitters"; porcelain bisque/wood; 7 inches; limited edition of 5,000.

• Jackie Robinson figurine; "Boys of Summer"; porcelain bisque/wood; 7 inches; limited edition of 5,042.

• "Living Triple Crown" mini plate; features Frank Robinson, Ted Williams, Mickey Mantle and Carl Yastrzemski; 4 1/4" diameter; artist Ron Lewis.

• "Living Triple Crown" regular plate, features Frank Robinson, Ted Williams, Mickey Mantle and Carl Yastrzemski; porcelain; 10 1/4" diameter; limited edition of 10,000; artist Ron Lewis.

• "Living Triple Crown" gold edition plate; features Frank Robinson, Ted Williams, Mickey Mantle and Carl Yastrzemski; gold/porcelain; 10 1/4" diameter; limited edition of 1,000; artist Ron Lewis.

• Ty Cobb figurine; "Legendary Hitters"; porcelain bisque/wood; 7 inches; limited edition of 5,000.

• "Wait Till Next Year" mini plate; porcelain; 4 1/4" diameter; Brooklyn Dodgers; artist Ron Lewis.

• "Wait Till Next Year" regular plate; porcelain; 10 1/4" diameter; limited edition of 5,000; artist Ron Lewis.

• Yankee Stadium mini plate; porcelain; 4 1/4" diameter; artist Ron Lewis.

• Yankee Stadium regular plate; porcelain; 10 1/2" diameter; limited edition of 5,000; artist Ron Lewis.

• "Yankee Tradition" double figurine; Mickey Mantle and Don Mattingly; porcelain bisque/wood; 7 1/2 inches; limited edition of 900.

• "Yankee Tradition" mini plate of Mantle and Mattingly; porcelain; 4 1/4" diameter; artist Joseph Catalano.

• "Yankee Tradition" regular plate of Mantle and Mattingly; porcelain; 10 1/4" diameter; limited edition of 10,000; artist Joseph Catalano.

• "Yankee Tradition" artist proof figurine; of Mattingly and Mantle; 7 1/2 inches; porcelain bisque/wood; limited edition of 90.

Collectovals

• "Life of A Legend" collectoval plate for Mickey Mantle; porcelain/gold; 12" diameter; artist Terrence Fogarty.

• "Kings of K" collectoval plate for Steve Carlton, Tom Seaver and Nolan Ryan; porcelain/gold; 12" diameter; limited edition of 1,990; artist J. Catalano.

• "Fenway Tradition" collectoval plate of Wade Boggs, Carl Yastrzemski, Ted Williams; porcelain/gold; 12" diameter; limited edition of 1,000; artist Brian Johnson.

• "The Golden Years" collectoval plate of Willie Mays, Mickey Mantle and Duke Snider; porcelain/gold; 12" diameter; limited edition of 1,000; artist Mike Petronella.

King of Kings Series

• Steve Carlton figurine; porcelain bisque/wood; 9 inches; limited edition of 500.

• "Kings of K" set of three figurines; feature Steve Carlton, Nolan Ryan and Tom Seaver; porcelain bisque/wood; 9 inches; limited edition of 995.

• "Kings of K" collectoval plate; features Carlton, Ryan and Seaver; porcelain/gold; 12" diameter; limited edition of 1,900; artist Joseph Catalano.

• Nolan Ryan (Rangers) figurine; porcelain bisque/wood; 9 inches; limited edition of 500.

• Tom Seaver figurine; porcelain bisque/wood; 9 inches; limited edition of 500.

Living Legends

• Nolan Ryan 5000 K mini plate; porcelain; 4 1/4" diameter; artist Ron Lewis.

• Nolan Ryan 5,000 K gold plate; porcelain/gold; 10 1/4" diameter; limited edition of 5,000; artist Ron Lewis.

- Nolan Ryan figurine; porcelain bisque/wood; 5 inches.
- Nolan Ryan figurine; porcelain bisque/wood 9 inches; limited edition of 1,990.
- Nolan Ryan 300 Wins mini plate; porcelain; 4 1/4" diameter; artist Joseph Catalano.
- Nolan Ryan 300 Wins; gold edition; porcelain gold; 10 1/4" diameter; limited edition of 1,990; artist Joseph Catalano.
- Nolan Ryan (Rangers) figurine; fifth in the series; 5 inches; porcelain bisque/wood; limited edition of 2,950.
- Rickey Henderson (A's) figurine; "Stolen Base King"; porcelain wood/bisque; 8 inches; limited edition of 939.
- Rickey Henderson mini plate; porcelain; 4 1/4" diameter; artist Ron Lewis.
- Rickey Henderson gold plate; "Born to Steal"; 10 1/4" diameter; porcelain/gold; limited edition of 1,990; artist Ron Lewis.
- Rickey Henderson artist proof figurine; "Stolen Base King"; porcelain bisque/wood; 8 1/4" diameter; limited edition of 94.
- Nolan Ryan artist proof figurine; porcelain bisque; 7 inches; limited edition of 500.
- Don Mattingly figurine; porcelain bisque/wood; 7 inches; limited edition of 1,990.
- Don Mattingly figurine; porcelain bisque/wood; 5 inches.
- Don Mattingly supersize figurine; porcelain/wood; 10 inches; limited edition of 1,990.
- Don Mattingly artist proof doll with stand; porcelain, fabric, fiber, metal; 15 inches; limited edition of 200.
- Don Mattingly figurine; porcelain/wood; 5 inches; limited edition of 2,950.
- Don Mattingly "Player of the Year" mini plate; porcelain; 4 1/4" diameter; artist Brian Johnson.
- Don Mattingly "Player of the Year" regular plate; porcelain; 10 1/4" diameter; limited edition of 5,000; artist Brian Johnson.
- Don Mattingly "Player of the Year" gold plate; porcelain/gold; limited edition of 2,500; artist Brian Johnson.

- "Yankee Pride" mini plate of Don Mattingly; porcelain; 4 1/4" diameter; artist Joseph Catalano.
- Yankee Pride gold edition; porcelain/gold; 10 1/4" diameter; limited edition of 3,500; artist Joseph Catalano.
- Don Mattingly "23" gold mini plate; porcelain/gold; 4 1/4" diameter; artist Mike Petronella.
- Don Mattingly "23" gold plate; porcelain/gold; 10 1/4" diameter; limited edition of 1,991; artist Mike Petronella.
- Will Clark mini plate; porcelain; 4 1/4" diameter; artist Joseph Catalano.
- Will Clark regular plate; porcelain; 10 1/4" diameter; limited edition of 10,000; Joseph Catalano.
- Will Clark gold plate; porcelain/gold; 10 1/4" diameter; limited edition of 2,500; artist Joseph Catalano.
- Will Clark figurine; porcelain bisque/wood; 5 inches.
- Will Clark supersize figurine; porcelain bisque/wood; 10" diameter; limited edition of 1,990.

Stars of Today

- Mark McGwire figurine; porcelain/wood; 7 inches; limited edition of 2,500.
- Mark McGwire mini plate; porcelain; 4 1/4" diameter; Terrence Fogarty.
- Mark McGwire gold plate; porcelain/gold; 10 1/4" diameter; limited edition of 2,500; artist Terrence Fogarty.
- Mark McGwire figurine; porcelain bisque/wood; 5 inches.
- Mark McGwire superstar figurine; 10 inches; porcelain bisque/wood; limited edition of 1,990.
- Orel Hershiser figurine; porcelain bisque/wood; 7 inches; limited edition of 5,055.
- Orel Hershiser mini plate; porcelain bisque/wood; 4 1/4" diameter; artist Joseph Catalano.
- Orel Hershiser regular plate; porcelain; 10 1/4" diameter; limited edition of 1,000; artist Joseph Catalano.
- Orel Hershiser gold plate; porcelain/gold; 10 1/4" diameter; limited edition of 2,500; artist Joseph Catalano.

• Orel Hershiser figurine; porcelain bisque/wood; 5 inches.

• Alan Trammell figurine; porcelain bisque/wood; 7 inches; limited edition of 2,500.

• Alan Trammell mini plate; porcelain; 4 1/4" diameter; artist Ed Lapere.

• Alan Trammell regular plate; porcelain; 10 1/4" diameter; limited edition of 10,000; artist Ed Lapere.

• Alan Trammell gold plate; porcelain/gold; 10 1/4" diameter; limited edition of 1,000; artist Ed Lapere.

• Darryl Strawberry figurine; porcelain bisque/wood; 7 inches; limited edition of 5,018.

• Darryl Strawberry gold plate; porcelain/gold; 10 1/4" diameter; limited edition of 3,500; artist Terrence Fogarty.

• Darryl Strawberry figurine; porcelain bisque/wood; 5 inches; limited edition of 2,950.

• Dwight Gooden figurine; porcelain bisque/wood; 7 inches; limited edition of 5,016.

• Dwight Gooden mini plate; porcelain; 4 1/4" diameter; artist Terrence Fogarty.

• Dwight Gooden gold plate; porcelain bisque/wood; 10 1/4" diameter; limited edition of 3,500; artist Terrence Fogarty.

• Dwight Gooden figurine; porcelain bisque/wood; 5 inches; limited edition of 2,950.

• Jose Canseco mini plate; porcelain; 4 1/4" diameter; artist Joseph Catalano.

• Jose Canseco regular plate; porcelain; 10 1/4" diameter; limited edition of 10,000; artist Joseph Catalano.

• Jose Canseco figurine; porcelain bisque/wood; 5 inches.

• Paul Molitor figurine; porcelain bisque/wood; 7 inches; limited edition of 2,500.

• Paul Molitor regular plate; porcelain; 10 1/4" diameter; limited edition of 10,000; artist Terrence Fogarty.

• Paul Molitor mini plate; porcelain; 4 1/4" diameter; artist Terrence Fogarty.

• Paul Molitor gold plate; porcelain/gold; 10 1/4" diameter; limited edition of 1,000; Terrence Fogarty.

• Andre Dawson figurine; porcelain bisque/wood; 7 inches; limited edition of 2,500.

• Andre Dawson mini plate; porcelain; 4 1/4" diameter; artist Ron Lewis.

• Andre Dawson regular plate; porcelain; 10 1/4" diameter; limited edition of 10,000; artist Ron Lewis.

• Andre Dawson gold plate; porcelain/gold; 10 1/4" diameter; limited edition of 1,000; artist Ron Lewis.

Today's Stars Series

• Dodgers Darryl Strawberry; third in series; porcelain bisque/wood; 5 inches; limited edition of 2,950.

• Mets Dwight Gooden; fifth in series; porcelain bisque/wood; 5 inches; limited edition of 2,950.

• Twins Frank Viola figurine; porcelain bisque/wood.

• Twins Frank Viola mini plate; porcelain; artist Terrence Fogarty.

* Twins Frank Viola gold edition plate; porcelain/gold; artist Terrence Fogarty.

* N.Y. Mets Gary Carter figurine; porcelain bisque/wood.

• N.Y. Mets Gary Carter mini plate; porcelain/gold; artist R. Simon.

• Mets Gregg Jefferies figurine; porcelain bisque/wood.

• Mets Gregg Jefferies mini plate; porcelain; artist Terrence Fogarty.

• Mets Gregg Jefferies gold edition plate; porcelain/gold; artist Terrence Fogarty.

• Dodgers Kirk Gibson mini plate; porcelain; artist Terrence Fogarty.

• Dodgers Kirk Gibson regular plate; porcelain; artist Terrence Fogarty.

• Dodgers Kirk Gibson gold edition plate; porcelain/gold; artist Terrence Fogarty.

• Yankees Don Mattingly; forth in series; porcelain bisque/wood; limited edition of 2,950.

• Red Sox Wade Boggs mini plate; porcelain; artist Brian Johnson.

• Red Sox Wade Boggs regular plate; porcelain; artist Brian Johnson.

• Red Sox Wade Boggs gold edition plate; porcelain/gold; Brian Johnson.

- Phillies Lenny Dykstra; second in series; porcelain bisque/wood; 5 inches; limited edition of 2,950.
- Mariners Ken Griffey Jr.; first in series; porcelain bisque/wood; 5 inches; limited edition of 2,950.
- Rangers Nolan Ryan; sixth in series; porcelain bisque/wood; 5 inches; limited edition of 2,950.
- Royals Bo Jackson figurine; porcelain bisque/wood; 5 inches.
- Orioles Cal Ripken Jr. figurine; porcelain bisque/wood; 5 inches.
- Giants Will Clark figurine; porcelain bisque/wood; 5 inches.
- Yankees Don Mattingly figurine; porcelain bisque/wood; 5 inches.
- Mets Howard Johnson figurine; porcelain bisque/wood; 5 inches.
- A's Jose Canseco figurine; porcelain bisque/wood; 5 inches.
- Giants Kevin Mitchell figurine; porcelain bisque/wood; 5 inches.
- Twins Kirby Puckett figurine; porcelain bisque/wood; 5 inches.
- A's Mark McGwire figurine; porcelain bisque/wood; 5 inches.
- Rangers Nolan Ryan figurine; porcelain bisque/wood; 5 inches.
- Dodgers Orel Hershiser figurine; porcelain bisque/wood; 5 inches.
- Padres Tony Gwynn figurine; porcelain bisque/wood; 5 inches.

Team of Dreams Series

- Orioles Cal Ripken Jr. figurine; porcelain bisque/wood; 7 inches; limited edition of 1,990.
- Yankees Don Mattingly figurine; porcelain bisque/wood; 7 inches; limited edition of 1,990.
- Giants Kevin Mitchell figurine; porcelain bisque/wood; 7 inches; limited edition of 1,990.
- Twins Kirby Puckett figurine; porcelain bisque/wood; 7 inches; limited edition of 1,990.
Phillies Lenny Dykstra figurine; porcelain bisque/wood; 7 inches; limited edition of 1,990.

- Reds Eric Davis figurine; porcelain bisque/wood; 7 inches; limited edition of 1,990.
- Mariners Ken Griffey Jr. figurine; porcelain bisque/wood; 7 inches; limited edition of 1,990.
- Mariners Ken Griffey Jr. figurine; 5 inches; porcelain bisque/wood.
- Angels Mark Langston figurine; porcelain bisque/wood; 7 inches; limited edition of 1,990.
- Team Griffey mini plate; 4 1/4" diameter; porcelain; both Griffeys; artist Ron Lewis.
- Team Griffey gold plate; 10 1/4" diameter; porcelain/gold; artist Ron Lewis.

Supersize Figurines

- Pirates Andy Van Slyke figurine; porcelain bisque/wood; 7 inches; limited edition of 2,500.
- K.C. Royals Bo Jackson figurine; porcelain bisque/wood; 7 inches; limited edition of 2,950.
- Royals Bo Jackson supersize figurine, 10 inches; porcelain bisque/wood; limited edition of 2,950.
- Giants Will Clark supersize figurine; porcelain bisque/wood; 10 inches; limited edition of 1,990.
- Yankees Dave Winfield figurine; 7 inches; porcelain bisque/wood; limited edition of 2,500.
- Yankees Don Mattingly supersize figurine; porcelain bisque/wood; 10 inches; limited edition of 1,990.
- Mets Dwight Gooden supersize figurine; porcelain bisque/wood; 10 inches; limited edition of 1,990.
- A's Mark McGwire figurine; porcelain bisque/wood; 7 inches; limited edition of 2,500.
- A's Mark McGwire supersize figurine; porcelain bisque/wood; 10 inches; limited edition of 1,990.
- Red Sox Mike Greenwell figurine; porcelain bisque/wood; 7 inches; limited edition of $2,500.
- Rangers Nolan Ryan supersize figurine; porcelain bisque/wood; 10 inches; limited edition of 1,990.

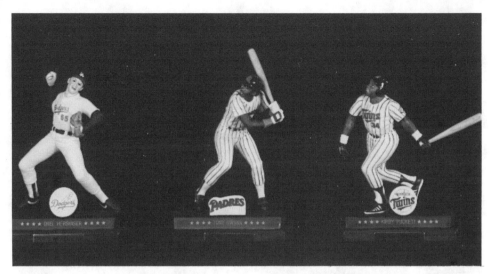

• Dodgers Orel Hershiser figurine; porcelain bisque/wood; 7 inches; limited edition of 5,055.

• Yankees Thurman Munson supersize figurine; porcelain bisque/wood; 10 inches; limited edition of 995.

• Padres Tony Gwynn figurine; porcelain bisque/wood; 7 inches; limited edition of 2,500.

• Tigers Alan Trammel figurine; porcelain bisque/wood; 7 inches; limited edition of 2,500.

• Mets Darryl Strawberry figurine; porcelain bisque/wood; 7 inches; limited edition of 5,018.

• Mets Dwight Gooden figurine; porcelain bisque/wood; 7 inches; limited edition of 5,016.

• Twins Frank Viola figurine; porcelain bisque/wood; 7 inches; limited edition of 2,500.

• Mets Gary Carter figurine; porcelain bisque/wood; 7 inches; limited edition of 5,009.

• Mets Gregg Jefferies figurine; porcelain bisque/wood; 7 inches; limited edition of 5,009.

• Mets Howard Johnson figurine; porcelain bisque/wood; 7 inches; limited edition of 5,020.

• Mets Keith Hernandez figurine; porcelain bisque/wood; 7 inches; limited edition of 2,500.

• Mets Kevin McReynolds figurine; porcelain bisque/wood; 7 inches; limited edition of 5,022.

• Brewers Paul Molitor figurine; porcelain bisque/wood; 7 inches; limited edition of 2,500.

• Cubs Andre Dawson figurine; porcelain bisque/wood; 7 inches; limited edition of 2,500.

Porcelain Dolls

• Don Mattingly doll with stand; porcelain, fabric, fiber, metal; 15 inches; limited edition of 1,991.

• Don Mattingly artist proof doll with stand; porcelain, fabric, fiber, metal; 15 inches; limited edition of 199.

• Mickey Mantle doll with stand; porcelain, fabric, fiber, metal; 15 inches; limited edition of 1,956.

• Mickey Mantle artist proof doll with stand; porcelain, fabric, fiber, metal; 15 inches; limited edition of 195.

• Nolan Ryan doll with stand; porcelain, fabric, fiber, metal; 15 inches; limited edition of 1,992.

• Nolan Ryan artist proof doll with stand; porcelain, fabric, fiber, metal; 15 inches; limited edition of 199.

Bobbing Head Dolls

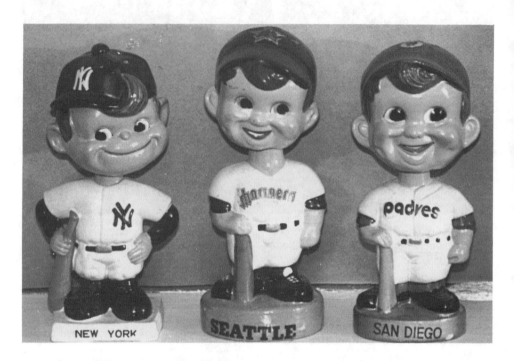

Although bobbing head dolls didn't necessarily garner much respect when they first came over from Japan in 1960, today people are shaking their heads over how much those $2.95 dolls have appreciated in value since then.

Over the years the supply has decreased; the bobbers were not built to last, a factor which contributes to their values. It's rare when a now-scarce bobbing head doll does not have a small crack or paint chip in it.

It's even been reported in *Sports Collectors Digest* that some of the paper mache dolls sold at major league stadiums in the early 1970s were used as bowling pins by stadium vendors. Others were smashed by baseball bats.

The dolls were originally sold at major league ball parks and through mail orders.

But they can be found today, if a collector is patient and persistent. Thorough perusal of a hobby publication such as *Sports Collectors Digest* may turn up a doll or two, especially in auction or classified ads. Card shows, garage sales, flea markets and antique shops are also good places to find these dolls.

Options to pursue in collecting bobbers would be by base color, by team, or by head type, which is either a mascot or boy's head.

The heads, attached by the neck with a spring to the body, bob, or nod, up and down at the slightest vibration. They were originally produced by Lego (a Swiss firm) and imported exclusively by Sports Specialties of Los Angeles. Many gold-based dolls still have stickers on the base which read "Sports Specialties 10203

Santa Monica Blvd. Los Angeles Calif. 67." The 67 represented a postal code.

Generally, eight categories, based on the doll's base color, are used when listing bobbing head dolls. They are: 1) Square colored bases, 1960-61; 2) Square white bases, 1961-62; 3) Caricatures, 1961-62; 4) White round miniatures, 1961-62; 5) Round green bases, 1962-64; 6) Green round bases, black players, 1962-64; 7) Round gold bases, 1965-72; and 8) Others.

In the following charts, the type of base is listed first, followed by the head types, which are represented by M, meaning team mascot head, or B, meaning boy's head. Team or city names are represented by embossed hand-painted letters, as E, or D, for paper decals. Scarcity is represented by ER, which means Extremely Rare; R, for Rare; S, for Scarce; D, for Difficult; and C, for Common. The last column represents a value range for dolls in Mint condition.

I. Square colored bases 1960-61

These dolls were the first dolls ever made. Every franchise from 1960-61 is represented, including the expansion teams of the Minnesota Twins, New York Mets, Houston Colts and Los Angeles Angels. The Twins dolls apparently were produced in great abundance. Four teams from the minor league's Pacific Coast League were also created.

1. Baltimore Orioles	green diamond (Lego on base)	M (large)	D/E	ER	$175-$200
2. Boston Red Sox	green square	B	D/E	ER	$175-$200
3. Chicago Cubs	light blue sq.	B	D/E	ER	$200-$225
4. Cincinnati Reds	red square	B	D/E	ER	$200-$225
5. Detroit Tigers	green square	M	D/E	ER	$200-$225
6. Los Angeles Angels	blue square	B	D/E	R	$85-$100
7. Los Angeles Dodgers	blue square	B	D/E	R	$90-$100
8. Minnesota Twins	blue square	B	D	C	$30-$35
9. New York Mets	blue square	B	D/E	ER	$200-$225
10. New York Yankees	orange sq.	B	D/E	R	$125-$150
11. Pittsburgh Pirates	orange sq.	B	D/E	R	$175-$200
12. San Francisco Giants	orange sq.	B	D/E	ER	$175-$200
13. Houston Colts	light blue sq.	B	E	ER	$150-$200
14. Washington Senators	blue square	B	E	ER	$175-$225

Minor League subset, Pacific Coast League teams, same design, 1960-61.

15. Hawaii	xxxx	B	D	ER	$100-$150
16. Portland Beavers	orange square	B	D	ER	$110-$150
17. Tacoma Giants	orange square	B	D	ER	$110-$150
18. Seattle	xxxx	B	D	ER	$110-$150

II. Square white bases 1961-62.

This series, the most difficult to complete, features 22 dolls, including the Anaheim (California) Angels and Houston Colts. The dolls in this series are perhaps the most beautiful and most desirable of all dolls. They are colorfully hand-painted, with embossed team logos on the uniform's chest.

Nine teams are represented with figural head mascots: Chicago Cubs, Cub head; Detroit Tigers, Tiger head; Cincinnati Reds, ball head; Cleveland Indians, "Wahoo" Indian head; Milwaukee Braves, Braves Indian head; Pittsburgh Pirates, Pirate head; Houston Colts, boy head with 10 gallon hat; Baltimore Orioles, Oriole bird head; and St. Louis Cardinals, Cardinal bird head.

This series is most difficult to find, especially the figurals and bobbers for the Chicago White Sox, New York Mets, Minnesota Twins, San Francisco Giants and defunct teams of the Milwaukee Braves, Los Angeles Angels, Washington Senators, Houston Colts and Kansas City A's. The Colt 45's in a blue uniform is super rare. Scarcity is represented by ER, which means Extremely Rare, or R, which means Rare.

1. Anaheim Angels	Boy's head	Decals	ER	$120-$145
2. Baltimore Orioles	Mascot	Embossed	ER	$200-$265
3. Boston Red Sox	Mascot	Embossed	ER	$200-$240
4. Chicago Cubs	Mascot	Embossed	ER	$240-$300
5. Chicago White Sox	Boy's head	Embossed	R	$135-$185
6. Cincinnati Reds	Mascot	Embossed	ER	$300-$375
7. Cleveland Indians	Mascot	Embossed	ER	$200-$285
8. Detroit Tigers	Mascot	Embossed	ER	$175-$225
9. Houston Colts	Boy's head	Embossed	R	$120-$165
10. Houston Colts (blue uniform)	Boy's head	Embossed	ER	$480-$600
11. Kansas City A's	Boy's head	Decals	ER	$275-$350
12. Los Angeles Angels	Boy's head	Decals	R	$120-$145
13. Los Angeles Dodgers	Boy's head	Decals	R	$120-$145
14. Milwaukee Braves	Mascot	Embossed	ER	$180-$240
15. Minnesota Twins	Boy's head	Decals	ER	$200-$285
16. New York Mets	Boy's head	Decals	ER	$200-$275
17. New York Yankees	Boy's head	Embossed	R	$120-$145
18. Philadelphia Phillies	Boy's head	Embossed	R	$120-$175
19. Pittsburgh Pirates	Mascot	Embossed	ER	$180-$240
20. St. Louis Cardinals	Mascot	Embossed	ER	$250-$325
21. San Francisco Giants	Boy's head	Embossed /Decals	ER	$180-$240
22. Washington Senators	Boy's head	Embossed	R	$180-$240

III. Caricatures 1961-62
Clemente, Mantle, Maris, Mays

Four dolls, fairly accurate and pretty realistic in likeness, were made of individual players - Roberto Clemente, Mickey Mantle, Roger Maris and Willie Mays. Both round and square white bases were made, with the player's facsimile autograph on the front of the base. All dolls are extremely rare and very much sought after.

A) *Clemente* is the rarest of all the caricatures. He wasn't the most popular player of that time, but his doll is the most expensive of all dolls to locate. Only a few surface every year. No box was made with this doll, and there was no miniature made for Clemente. This 7" doll commands a hefty price of $1,100-$1,600; perhaps as few as 40 exist in any condition.

B) *Mantle* is not the rarest doll but certainly the most popular. It has an embossed "N.Y." or "Yankee" decal on chest. The doll was originally issued with a box, which is worth $50-$150. The Mantle is worth $375-500 and can often be found at most major card shows. A miniature Mantle was also made and is very difficult to find. An embossed "N.Y." or "Yankee" decal is on the chest. The mini Mantle is worth $600-$800.

C) *Maris* is rarer than Mantle, due to far less distribution than Mantle. It also includes an original box, worth $50-$100, with color pictures of the doll/player on it. An embossed "N.Y." or "Yankee" decal is on the chest. Maris is worth $450-$550. A miniature Maris was also made and is very difficult to locate. It's worth between $650-$900.

D) *Mays* is the most common of the caricatures but is found in two variations, made with either a bat or ball. A "dark variation" (the skin tone is darker) of the two types is far more difficult to find. Its value is $300-$450. The "light variation" (with a lighter skin tone) has Oriental-like eyes. This is the most common of the types and is worth between $175-$275.

IV. White round miniatures 1961-62

White rounds were intended to sit on car dashes. These dolls are extremely fragile, especially near the neck.

There are 10 National League and 10 American League dolls. None appear to be more rarer than the others. They were boxed individually or were packaged by a league, 10 to a large box.

A few variations exist; dolls hold either a bat or ball. Reportedly some mavericks with green bases also exist. Some team decals come in script and block.

Scarcity is represented by R, which represents Rare, or ER, which means Extremely Rare.

1. Baltimore Orioles	Mascot	Decals	ER	$150-$285
2. Boston Red Sox	Boy's head	Decals	R	$125-$220
3. Chicago Cubs	Mascot	Decals	ER	$225-$325
4. Chicago White Sox	Boy's head	Decals	R	$100-$165
5. Cincinnati Reds	Mascot	Decals	ER	$275-$350
6. Cleveland Indians	Mascot	Decals	ER	$150-$285
7. Detroit Tigers	Mascot	Decals	ER	$200-$300
8. Houston Colts	Boy's head	Decals	ER	$125-$215
9. Kansas City A's	Boy's head	Decals	R	$120-$230
10. Los Angeles Angels	Boy's head	Decals	R	$120-$150
11. Los Angeles Dodgers	Boy's head	Decals	R	$120-$150
12. Milwaukee Braves	Mascot	Decals	ER	$225-$300
13. Minnesota Twins	Boy's head	Decals	R	$125-$185
14. Minneapolis Twins (Var.)	Boy's head	Decals	ER	$150-$200
15. New York Mets	Boy's head	Decals	ER	$225-$325
16. New York Yankees	Boy's head	Decals	ER	$200-$240
17. Philadelphia Phillies	Boy's head	Decals	R	$125-$200
18. Pittsburgh Pirates	Mascot	Decals	ER	$225-$275
19. St. Louis Cardinals	Mascot	Decals	ER	$225-$300
20. San Francisco Giants	Boy's head	Decals	R	$125-$180
21. Washington Senators	Boy's head	Decals	R	$200-$230

V. Round green bases 1962-64

The green round series continued with the same teams as the white base series but reduced the number of variations of curls. One major change featured the Houston Colts doll which was made with a pistol, not a bat, in its hand. This doll is one of the more popular green base bobbers. Most dolls were made with decals, not embossed team logos. Scarcer issues are for the Pirates, Cubs and Orioles. Scarcity is represented by R, which means Rare, ER, which represents Extremely Rare, S, which represents Scarce, or D, which represents Difficult.

1. Baltimore Orioles	Mascot	Decals		
		/Embossed	ER	$100-$130
2. Boston Red Sox	Boy's head	Decals	R	$65-$85
3. Chicago Cubs	Mascot	Decals	ER	$200-$250
4. Chicago White Sox	Boy's head	Decals	S	$50-$65
5. Cincinnati Reds	Mascot	Decals		
		/Embossed	ER	$120-$160
6. Cleveland Indians	Mascot	Decals	ER	$125-$200
7. Detroit Tigers	Mascot	Embossed	ER	$130-$160
8. Houston Colts	Boy's head	Embossed	ER	$100-$125
9. Kansas City A's	Boy's head	Decals	ER	$125-$225
10. Los Angeles Angels	Boy's head	Decals	D	$75-$150
11. Los Angeles Dodgers	Boy's head	Decals	D	$40-$60
12. Milwaukee Braves	Mascot	Decals	ER	$135-$160
13. Minnesota Twins	Boy's head	Decals	D	$40-$60
14. New York Mets	Boy's head	Decals	S	$50-$70
15. New York Yankees	Boy's head	Decals		
		/Embossed	R	$90-$110
16. Philadelphia Phillies	Boy's head	Decals		
		/Embossed	R	$60-$80
17. Pittsburgh Pirates	Mascot	Decals	ER	$135-$160
18. St. Louis Cardinals	Mascot	Decals	ER	$135-$160
19. San Francisco Giants	Boy's head	Decals	S	$60-$90
20. Washington Senators	Boy's head	Decals	R	$85-$150

VI. Green round base, black players 1962-64

This series, an offshoot of the green series, is by far the most difficult and rarest series to complete. There are no mascots in the series, but the Houston Colts is different; it has a cowboy hat. Each black, boyish face is not simply a white face painted black; these bobbers have distinctive features, including larger eyes, thicker, redder lips and curly hair. All dolls are extremely rare.

1. Baltimore Orioles .... $350-$400
2. Boston Red Sox .... $450-$600
3. Chicago Cubs .... $450-$500
4. Chicago White Sox .... $250-$300
5. Cincinnati Reds .... $500-$600
6. Cleveland Indians .... $250-$300
7. Detroit Tigers .... $450-$550
8. Houston Colts .... $800-$900
9. Kansas City A's .... $850-$1,000
10. Los Angeles Angels .... $425-$650
11. Los Angeles Dodgers .... $250-$300
12. Milwaukee Braves .... $600-$700

13. Minnesota Twins .... $450-$500
14. New York Mets .... $300-$400
15. New York Yankees .... $450-$625
16. Philadelphia Phillies .... $350-$400
17. Pittsburgh Pirates .... $500-$600
18. St. Louis Cardinals .... $450-$525
19. San Francisco Giants .... $600-$650

VII. Round gold bases 1965-72

This set is the easiest and most reasonable to obtain. Most dolls are abundant and common. The series, which contains the largest number of dolls, is the last series of Japanese-made dolls. It includes teams that moved and expansion teams. The rarest, most expensive, doll in the series is the Seattle Pilot, made for a team which existed only one year. The Kansas City A's is also popular and scarce, because it is one of few to have a uniform entirely in its team colors - green jersey and gold pants. The new Oakland A's issue in a white uniform is also quite rare. But an A's doll with a yellow uniform also exists; it is exceedingly common. Two Astros dolls - a plain white uniform with blue trim and hat, or the famous "shooting star" insignia with orange hat - exist. The Padres, Cubs and Kansas City A's are tricky, but popular, as are the figurals. This series marked the end of the Japanese era of bobbers; companies in Hong Kong, Korea and Taiwan attempted to revive with plastic, but were not well distributed. From 1983 on the present Taiwan-made dolls brought back the nationwide ballpark/mail order concept. Scarcity is represented by ER, which means Extremely Rare; R, which means Rare; S, which means Scarce; D, which represents Difficult; or C, for Common.

1. Atlanta Braves	Mascot	Decals	D	$40-$60
2. Baltimore Orioles	Mascot	Decals	S	$60-$80
3. Boston Red Sox	Boy's head	Decals	D	$40-$60
4. California Angels	Boy's head	Decals	D	$40-$60
5. Chicago Cubs	Mascot	Decals	D	$70-$90
6. Chicago White Sox	Boy's head	Decals	C	$35-$40
7. Cincinnati Reds	Mascot	Decals	R	$70-$90
8. Cleveland Indians	Mascot	Decals	R	$70-$90
9. Detroit Tigers	Mascot	Decals	R	$80-$100
10. Houston Astros	Boy's head	Decals	S	$50-$70
11. Kansas City Royals	Boy's head	Decals	S	$50-$70
12. Los Angeles Angels	Boy's head	Decals	C	$40-$50
13. Los Angeles Dodgers	Boy's head	Decals	C	$35-$45
14. Milwaukee Brewers	Boy's head	Decals	C	$30-$35
15. Minnesota Twins	Boy's head	Decals	S	$50-$70
16. Montreal Expos	Boy's head	Decals	C	$25-$30
17. New York Mets	Boy's head	Decals	S	$50-$70
18. New York Yankees	Boy's head	Decals	S	$60-$80

19. Oakland A's (gold)	Boy's head	Decals	C	$20-$25
20. Oakland A's (white)	Boy's head	Decals	ER	$125-$150
21. Philadelphia Phillies	Boy's head	Decals	C	$65-$85
22. Pittsburgh Pirates	Mascot	Decals	R	$70-$90
23. St. Louis Cardinals	Mascot	Decals	R	$70-$90
24. San Diego Padres	Boy's head	Decals	S	$70-$90
25. San Francisco Giants	Boy's head	Decals	S	$60-$80
26. Seattle Pilots	Boy's head	Decals	R	$225-$300
27. Texas Rangers	Boy's head	Decals	D	$45-$65
28. Washington Senators	Boy's head	Decals	R	$70-$90

VIII. Other bobbing heads

A) *Little League baseball boy, early 1960s.* This features a boy sitting on half a baseball. The ball is a bank. It's rare, and worth $100-$150.

B) *Weirdos Los Angeles Dodgers, early 1960s.* The dolls on these white bases feature silly expressions. The dolls are holding various items, and wearing uniforms with fractions as numbers. They go for $150 and up.

C) *Pitcher/Catcher/Umpire set, early 1960s.* They are extremely rare and feature blinking eyes, freckles, and feet bases. The players sell for about $100 each; the umpire is worth $150-$200.

D) *Umpires, early 1960s.* Several variations exist, including a square base with a scowling umpire holding a mask and broom in each hand. Another umpire has a boyish grin and is wearing a curved hat. The last is a Little League miniature on a green round base. These dolls are highly desirable, worth at least $100.

E) *Green square bases, rounded corners, 1962.* These are similar to the white bases, but it's doubtful there is a complete set. Dolls for the Tigers, Red Sox, Twins and Senators are known to exist, but all dolls are rare and demand prices between whites and greens.

F) *Cleveland Indians, miniature boy head, late 1960s,* Japanese. These 4 1/2-inch tall dolls are rare, worth between $50-$70, and were evidently given away at ballparks with a purchase.

G) *Mr. and Mrs. Met gold round base, 1969.* These beautiful, extremely rare dolls commemorate the Mets participation in the World Series. Mr. and Mrs. (more expensive) were made. The doll features a ball head logo/mascot, with legs crossed, leaning on a bat. It's valued at $200-$250. One (of two varieties) is a bank with a coin slot on the back.

H) *Gold square bases, early 1970s.* All dolls feature boy heads. The Houston Astros "shooting star" (worth $125-$175) and the Kansas City A's green jersey/gold pants ($125-$175) are extremely rare, but the most popular.

I) *Series of plastic dolls, mid-1970s, with boxes.* These dolls were never too popular, hence are worth $5-$10.

J) *Plastic Henry Aaron caricature, with box, 1975.* This doll, worth between $14-$18, is very common, due to overproduction.

K) *Modern heavy ceramics, by Twins Enterprises, 1983-84.* The 1983 series came with a ball; the 1984 set had bats. All dolls were boxed. The dolls, made in

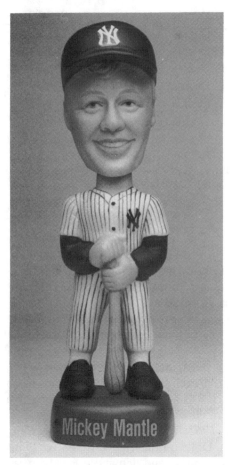

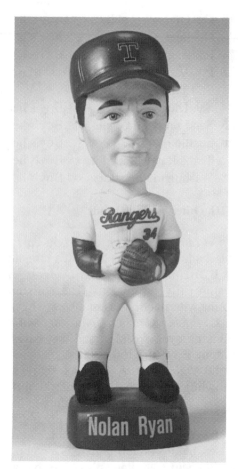

Taiwan, have round green bases which are thicker and heavier than the 1960s Japaneses dolls. Eight dolls are mascots. The dolls are in the $5-$10 range.

L) *Modern heavy ceramic, Twins Enterprises, 1988-89*. These dolls, also made in Taiwan, have new designs for the eight mascots and are larger than the 1983-84 versions. They sell for between $5-$8.

M) *Modern porcelain, Sports Accessories & Memorabilia Inc., 1993-present*. Each doll is hand painted and resembles the player whose name is painted on the base of the eight-inch statue. Issue prices were $40 each, with 3,000 made for each player. Baseball players done by SAM include, with current values: Johnny Bench, Joe Morgan, Tony Perez and Pete Rose (sold as a set of four as the Big Red Machine for an initial release price of $175); Ted Williams, Carl Yastrzemski and Roger Clemens (three generations of Boston Red Sox players, due for spring 1994 release); Yogi Berra (sold out, $50); Roberto Clemente ($49.95 issue price); Ty Cobb (sold out, $50); Rollie Fingers ($40); Whitey Ford (sold out, $50); Ken Griffey Jr. (sold out, $50); Martinez Jackson ($40); Reggie Jackson ($40); Mickey Mantle ($99.95 issue price); Roger Maris (sold out, $80); Willie Mays ($40); Satchel Paige ($40); Brooks Robinson ($40); Babe Ruth (sold out, $50); Nolan Ryan (sold out, $80) and Tom Seaver (sold out, $50).

Yearbooks

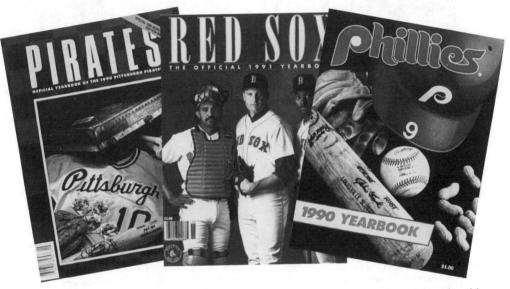

It wasn't until the 1940s and 1950s that what we now consider as yearbooks were produced by teams on a regular basis. During the 1950s many teams didn't do the actual publishing, but instead had the Jay Publishing Co. of New York put out a series of what were called "Big League Books," which served as the official yearbooks for the clubs. Jay Publishing stopped issuing them in 1965.

The main problem in creating a yearbook checklist is that there is not a general consensus as to whether a certain publication should be considered a yearbook or something else; many teams have labeled their publications with a variety of other names - magazines, roster books, photo albums and sketchbooks.

Two collectors, Ralph Deptolla and Dennis Sell, contributed a yearbook checklist which appeared in the Aug. 3, 1984, issue of Sports Collectors Digest. The two agree that in order to be classified as a yearbook, a publication must at the very least have photographs of every player on the 25-man roster, plus biographies and player statistics. If, however, a publication has photos, stats and biographies, but is labeled as a media guide, scorecard or program, then it's obviously something other than a year-book.

Most yearbooks from the 1960s offer collectors an affordable alternative for under $100. Those from the 1950s bring the top dollars, depending on scarcity and age, while those which are auto-graphed are even more valuable. Yearbooks should be stored in plastic holders and kept out of sun-light.

Angels Yearbooks

Los Angeles Angels

1962 Angels baby with cake ....$85-$100
1963 ....$50-$60
1964 Angels in action.....................................$30-$45
1965 Angels in action.....................................$30-$45

California Angels

1966 Anaheim Stadium....................................$40-$65
1967 "All About the Angels," with logo ....$30-$40
1968 .... None issued
1969 .... None issued
1970 .... None issued
1971 .... None issued
1972 .... None issued
1973 .... None issued
1974 .... None issued
1975 .... None issued
1976 .... None issued
1977 .... None issued
1978 .... None issued
1979 .... None issued
1980 .... None issued
1981 .... None issued
1982 .... None issued
1983 Lynn, Carew, Jackson, others ....$7-$12
1984 Anaheim Stadium......................................$7-$9
1985 25th Anniversary, Angel greats.................$7-$8
1986 .... None issued
1987 .... None issued
1988 .... None issued
1989 .... None issued
1990 .... None issued

1991 .... None issued
1992 Abbott, Langston, Harvey, Finley $12
1993 Nolan Ryan...$6

Astros Yearbooks

Houston Colt 45s

1962 Baseball, pistol, Texas ....$175-$200
1963 .... $175
1964 ....$125-$150

Houston Astros

1965 "Inside the Astrodome"...............................$100
1966 Astrodome $45
1967 .... None issued
1968 .... None issued
1969 .... None issued
1970 .... None issued
1971 .... None issued
1972 .... None issued
1973 .... None issued
1974 .... None issued
1975 .... None issued
1976 .... None issued
1977 Photo album...$20
1978 Photo album...$20
1979 Photo album...$20
1980 .... None issued
1981 .... None issued
1982 Nolan Ryan...$15
1983 .... None issued
1984 .... None issued
1985 .... None issued

Astros Yearbooks

1986 .... None issued
1987 .... None issued
1988 .... None issued
1989 .... None issued
1990 .... None issued
1991 .... None issued
1992 Luis Gonzalez $12
1993 .... None issued

Athletics Yearbooks

Philadelphia Athletics

1949 Connie Mack ....$135-$200
1950 Connie Mack Golden Jubiliee ....$135-$175
1951 Team mascot (elephant).....................$110-$150
1952 Team mascot (elephant).....................$110-$150
1953 Elephant pitching baseball...........................$100
1954 Play at first base...$95

Kansas City Athletics

1955 A's batter ripping through map ....$160-$200
1956 Elephant mascot ....$100-$150
1957 Kansas City Municipal Stadium...................$95
1958 Play at first $90
1959 Kansas City Municipal Stadium...................$80
1960 Baseball wearing Athletics hat ....$60-$80
1961 Pitcher and baseball......................................$45
1962 A's players in action $45
1963 ....$45
1964 Player making a catch...................................$45
1965 A's donkey, Finley flag $45
1966 ....$45-$75
1967 Athletics pitcher $50

Oakland Athletics

1968 Oakland Coliseum ....$100-$125
1969 Connie Mack ....$45-$60
1970 Monday, Odom, Jackson, others ....$45-$75
1971 Sal Bando, Bert Campaneris ....$35-$65
1972 Dick Williams, Vida Blue....................$25-$50
1973 Rudi, Fingers, Williams, Hunter............$25-$40
1974 "One More in 74," two trophies ....$22.50-$30
1975 "Keep it Alive in 75"............................$20-$25
1976 Bicentennial celebration ....$15-$20
1977 A's logo, arch of baseballs.....................$15-$18
1978 .... None issued
1979 "The Swingin 'A's," with logo $18
1980 .... None issued
1981 .... None issued
1982 Billy Ball baseball $15
1983 A's baseball card collage $10
1984 .... None issued
1985 .... None issued
1986 .... None issued
1987 .... None issued
1988 .... None issued
1989 .... None issued
1990 .... None issued
1991 .... None issued

1993 TORONTO BLUE JAYS YEARBOOK
SCOREBOOK MAGAZINE $59.00

1992 .... None issued
1993 .... None issued

Blue Jays Yearbooks

1977 "The First Year," fans ....$35-$45
1978 .... None issued
1979 ....$15
1980 ....$10-$12
1981 Ernie Whitt, Jim Clancy ....$8-$12
1982 Martinez, Moseby, Whitt.........................$7-$10
1983 Blue Jays baseball ....$7-$10
1984 Exhibition Stadium..................................$7-$10
1985 Logo and year..$6-$10
1986 American League baseball, bat ....$6-$10
1987 Barfield, Clancy, Whitt.............................$6-$9
1988 Blue Jay player batting ....$6-$8
1989 ....$6-$8
1990 George Bell...$6-$8
1991 Player drawing..$5-$6
1992 Roberto Alomar...$5-$6
1993 Trophy $6

Braves Yearbooks

Boston Braves

1946 ....$350
1947 Billy Southworth ....$200-$225
1948 .... None issued
1949 .... None issued
1950 Smiling Brave...$150
1951 Baseball diamond and ball $150
1952 Braves players talking $150

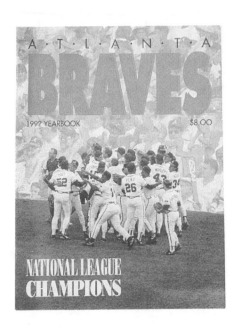

Milwaukee Braves

1953 Runner sliding into home ....$150-$175
1954 "To the People of Milwaukee" ....$75-$100
1955 Fans and stadium ....$85-$100
1956 Cartoon of Braves fans $75
1957 Braves logo in crystal ball ....$85-$100
1958 Brave raising World Series pennant ....$75-$80
1959 Brave in hot-air balloon..........................$65-$70
1960 Brave with two baseball bats.................$60-$65
1961 Braves player, other N.L. players ....$45-$55
1962 Braves logo..$45
1963 Braves player, other N.L. players $40
1964 Aaron, Mathews, Torre, Spahn..............$35-$55
1965 Bobby Bragan, Felipe Alou...................$35-$45

Atlanta Braves

1966 Aaron, Mathews, others.......................$60-$100
1967 Play at home plate ....$35-$75
1968 Play at second base................................$25-$60
1969 Braves infielder......................................$25-$55
1970 Braves in action ....$20-$45
1971 Hank Aaron, Babe Ruth ....$25-$35
1972 Five Braves...$18-$25
1973 Braves pitcher..$18-$25
1974 Hank Aaron, Babe Ruth $20
1975 Four Braves ....$15-$18
1976 Niekro, Cepeda, Aaron, others $18
1977 Former Braves, Hank Aaron $15
1978 Spahn, Niekro, Burdette $12
1979 Garber stops Rose's streak ....$12-$15
1980 Bob Horner, Bobby Cox...............................$10
1981 Dale Murphy, Bob Horner, others $10

1982 Spahn, Horner, Aaron, others ....$12-$15
1983 Phil Niekro in an Uncle Sam outfit ....$6-$10
1984 Horner, Murphy, Aaron ....$5-$8
1985 Aaron, Murphy, 20th Anniversary ....$5-$8
1986 Dale Murphy, Chuck Tanner ....$5-$8
1987 Dale Murphy...$5-$9
1988 "Braves Illustrated" ....$5-$8
1989 .... None issued
1990 25 years in Atlanta...................................$5-$6
1991 .... None issued
1992 N.L. Champions $10
1993 .... None issued

Brewers Yearbooks

Seattle Pilots

1969 Pilot logos, 10 pictures ....$175-$200

Milwaukee Brewers

1970 Brewers hitter ....$50-$75
1971 .... None issued
1972 .... None issued
1973 .... None issued
1974 .... None issued
1975 .... None issued
1976 .... None issued
1977 .... None issued
1978 .... None issued
1979 Larry Hisle...$12
1980 Gorman Thomas $10
1981 Molitor, Fingers, Yount, others.....................$12
1982 Crowd celebrating $10
1983 Robin Yount and fans $12

Brewers Yearbooks

1984 County Stadium	$10
1985 George Bamberger and fans	$9
1986 Brewers locker room	$8
1987 Brewers baseball cards	$8
1988 Paul Molitor hologram	$10
1989 Brewer greats, Hank Aaron	$10
1990 Brewers logo, Milwaukee skyline	$10
1991 Paul Molitor	$10
1992 Molitor, Yount, Gantner	$10
1993	None issued

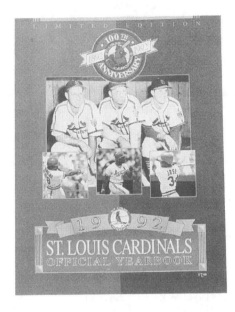

Cardinals Yearbooks

1951 Cardinal in bottom right	$200
1952 Cardinal and soldier	$110-$150
1953 Stan Musial	$75-$100
1954 Red Schoendienst	$95
1955 Cardinal pitcher gets the sign	$75-$85
1956 Cardinal pitcher gets the sign	$75-$85
1957 Cardinal circles the bases	$55-$65
1958 Cardinal circles the bases	$50-$60
1959 Stan Musial	$45-$55
1960 Cardinal catches a ball	$40-$50
1961 Simmons, Sadecki, others	$35-$45
1962 Stan Musial and his milestones	$35-$40
1963 Musial slides into second	$30-$35
1964 Groat, Boyer, Javier, White	$40-$50
1965 Bob Gibson	$30-$45
1966 New Busch Stadium photo	$30-$35
1967 World Champs	$50-$75

1968 Busch Stadium	$40
1969 Brock, Flood, Gibson, others	$18-$25
1970 Five Cardinal drawings	$20
1971 Brock, Torre, Gibson, others	$18-$25
1972 Cardinals fielder	$18-$20
1973 Cardinals batter	$15-$18
1974 Simmons, Torre	$15-$20
1975 Brock, Gibson, others	$12-$18
1976 Centennial Yearbook	$12-$15
1977 Brock, Ty Cobb	$12-$15
1978	None issued
1979 St. Louis city skyline	$12
1980 Simmons, Hernandez	$10
1981	None issued
1982	None issued
1983	None issued
1984	None issued
1985	None issued
1986	None issued
1987	None issued
1988 Wraparound team photo	$8
1989 Coleman, Worrell	$5-$9
1990 Herzog, Busch Stadium	$5-$7
1991 Lee Smith	$5-$6
1992 Moore, Slaughter, Musial, Guerrero, Lankford, Jose	$5
1993 Ozzie Smith	$5

Cubs Yearbooks

1934 Wraparound batting scene	$275-$350
1939 Players' records	$200-$300
1941 Players' history/record book	$175-$250
1942 Roster/record book	$150-$200
1948 Logo and blue "1948"	$100-$150
1949 Logo and blue "1949"	$100-$125
1950 Hat and red "1950"	$90-$100
1951 Ball in center of red glove	$90
1952 Logo, year in red and blue	$80-$90
1953 Cubs logo	$80
1954 Name and year	$70-$80
1955 Name and year	$70-$75
1956	$65-$75
1957 Head with Cubs hat	$65
1958	None issued
1959	None issued
1960	None issued
1961	None issued
1962	None issued
1963	None issued
1964	None issued
1965	None issued
1966	None issued
1967	None issued
1968	None issued
1969	None issued
1970	None issued
1971	None issued
1972	None issued
1973	None issued
1974	None issued
1975	None issued

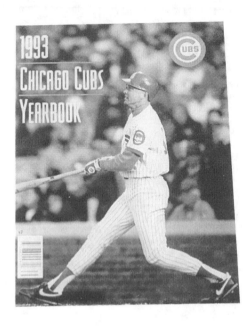

Cubs Yearbooks

1976	None issued
1977	None issued
1978	None issued
1979	None issued
1980	None issued
1981	None issued
1982	None issued
1983	None issued
1984	None issued
1985 Wrigley photo	$8-$10
1986 70th Anniversary, Ryne Sandberg	$8-$10
1987 Billy Williams, Ryne Sandberg	$6-$10
1988 Andre Dawson	$6-$9
1989	$8
1990 Photo of players' bats	$5-$7
1991 Ryne Sandberg	$5-$6
1992 Scoreboard, celebration	$5
1993 Mark Grace	$5

Dodgers Yearbooks

Brooklyn Dodgers

1947 League Champs	$275
1948	None issued
1949 League Champs	$225-$325
1950	$200-$250
1951	$175-$185
1952 "The Bum" holding a sign	$150-$185
1953 "The Bum" holding a bat	$150-$185
1954 "The Bum" with saw, hammer	$125-$170
1955 "The Bum" reaching for a star	$175-$240
1956 "The Bum" holding #6	$150-$165
1957 "The Bum" holding pennants	$150-$165

Los Angeles Dodgers

1958 Autographed team baseball	$150
1959 Play at second base	$95-$135
1960 Dodger stadium drawing	$50-$100
1961	$35-$75
1962	$35-$60
1963 Maury Wills	$50-$65
1964 1963 World Champions banner	$20-$45
1965 Dodger Stadium	$50
1966 Walter Alston	$30-$35
1967 Dodger juggling crowns	$25
1968 Drysdale, Koufax, others	$25
1969 Baseball's centennial logo	$20-$35
1970 Dodgers and Mets mascots	$20-$25
1971 10th Anniversary of stadium	$18-$22
1972 Dodger Stadium	$15-$22
1973 Maury Wills, Walter Alston	$15-$25
1974 Jimmy Wynn	$18-$20
1975 Steve Garvey/N.L. Champions	$12-$18
1976 Davey Lopes	$12-$18
1977 20th Anniversary, players	$12-$22
1978 Lasorda, Garvey, Cey, others	$12-$15
1979 Tom Lasorda	$10-$12
1980 Dodger baseball cards	$10
1981 Dusty Baker, Steve Garvey	$10-$12
1982 World Series trophy	$8-$12
1983 25th Anniversary in Los Angeles	$10
1984 "A Winning Tradition," Lasorda	$7-$10
1985 Russell, Valenzuela, Garvey	$9-$10
1986 Guerrero, Hershiser, Marshall	$7-$10
1987 24 previous Los Angeles yearbooks	$7-$10
1988 "Blueprint for Success"	$8-$9
1989 World Series trophy	$6-$7
1990 Dodger greats painting	$6

Dodgers Yearbooks

1991 Dodgers Field of Dreams ....$5-$6
1992 Dodger greats ....$5-$6
1993 Hershiser, Lasorda, collage $6

Expos Yearbooks

1969 Larry Jaster......................................$45-$100
1970 Expos equipment and fan ....$25-$70
1971 Fan with Expos pennant ....$20-$50
1972 Four different covers, each....................$20-$50
1973 .... None issued
1974 .... None issued
1975 .... None issued
1976 .... None issued
1977 .... None issued
1978 .... None issued
1979 .... None issued

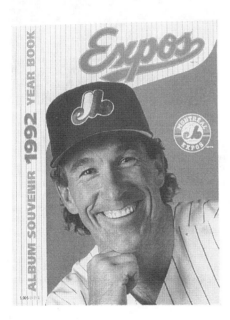

1980 .... None issued
1981 .... None issued
1982 Expos celebration, All-Star logo ....$8-$10
1983 Dawson, Carter, Oliver, others ....$7-$12
1984 Raines, Rose, Dawson, others ....$6-$12
1985 Wallach, Raines, Dawson, others ....$6-$10
1986 Baseball in hand ....$6-$8
1987 .... None issued
1988 .... None issued
1989 .... None issued
1990 .... None issued
1991 .... None issued
1992 Gary Carter $5
1993 .... None issued

Giants Yearbooks
New York Giants

1947 First Year ....$185-$200
1948 .... None issued
1949 .... None issued
1950 .... None issued
1951 ....$100-$150
1952 Durocher and Giant ....$100-$125
1953 Polo Grounds photo.............................$75-$100
1954 Giant cutting a "1951" book..............$100-$125
1955 Giant holding other mascots................$75-$100
1956 Giants cap ....$75-$90
1957 Photo of play at second ....$75-$85

San Francisco Giants

1958 Giant with a load of books $250
1959 Photo of a play at third ....$75-$85
1960 Al Dark, play at first..............................$40-$75
1961 Giants hat...$35-$55
1962 N.L. Champs...$40-$50
1963 Trolley car with Giants pennant ....$30-$40
1964 Child looking at Candlestick ....$30-$40
1965 Painting of a play at second....................$30-$40
1966 Willie Mays with S.F. baseball..............$25-$45
1967 Willie Mays, Juan Marichal...................$25-$45
1968 Willie Mays ....$25-$35
1969 Mays, Bonds, McCovey ....$25-$35
1970 Photos of Mays, McCovey ....$20-$30
1971 Willie McCovey ....$25-$30
1972 Willie Mays sliding into third...............$18-$25
1973 Marichal, Bonds, Speier ....$15-$20
1974 "Young Giants '74" ....$15-$18
1975 Gary Matthews, Mike Caldwell $15
1976 ....$12-$15
1977 .... None issued
1978 .... None issued
1979 .... None issued
1980 Giant batter...$8-$10
1981 Frank Robinson ....$12-$14
1982 Silver Anniversary yearbook...................$8-$10
1983 Frank Robinson ....$8-$12
1984 Giants All-Star memorabilia ....$7-$10
1985 Horizontal "A History of..." ....$7-$9
1986 .... None issued
1987 .... None issued
1988 .... None issued
1989 .... None issued
1990 .... None issued
1991 .... None issued
1992 Will Clark $7.50
1993 .... None issued

Indians Yearbooks

1948 World Champs....................................$100-$150
1949 Logo wearing crown............................$65-$100
1950 Fans entering stadium..........................$75-$100
1951 50th Anniversary with logo.................$75-$100
1952 Chain with Indians logo ....$65-$85
1953 Umpire yelling "Play ball" ....$65-$80
1954 Lemon, Wynn, Doby, Rosen................$95-$110
1955 Indian wearing crown..........................$90-$200

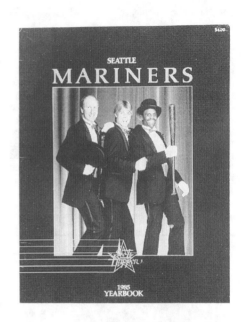

Indians Yearbooks

1956 Indian mascot ....$60-$75
1957 Indian mascot ....$60-$75
1958 Herb Score.......................................$100-$180
1959 Indians logo ....$55-$60
1960 Jim Perry, Indians pitcher ....$50-$60
1961 ....$50-$75
1962 ....$50-$75
1963 ....$50-$75
1964 Indian sliding into home........................$40-$45
1965 Past and present uniforms......................$40-$45
1966 Sam McDowell......................................$40-$45
1967 Picture set ....$45-$50
1968 Baseball and year..................................$25-$40
1969 Runner sliding into base ....$25-$35
1970 Sam McDowell......................................$25-$30
1971 Indians in action ....$20-$25
1972 Indians in action ....$20-$25
1973 Jim Perry, others $18
1974... None issued
1975... None issued
1976... None issued
1977... None issued
1978... None issued
1979... None issued
1980... None issued
1981... None issued
1982... None issued
1983... None issued

1984 Franco, Sutcliffe, others ....$6-$10
1985... None issued
1986... None issued
1987... None issued
1988... None issued
1989 Autographed team baseball ....$5-$7
1990 90th Anniversary in Cleveland.................$5-$6
1991 Score, Alomar, Chambliss.........................$5-$6
1992 Alomar, Hargrove...$5
1993... None issued

Mariners Yearbooks

1977... None issued
1978... None issued
1979... None issued
1980... None issued
1981... None issued
1982... None issued
1983... None issued
1984... None issued
1985 Davis, Beattie, Langston $10
1986... None issued
1987... None issued
1988... None issued
1989... None issued
1990... None issued
1991... None issued
1992... None issued
1993... None issued

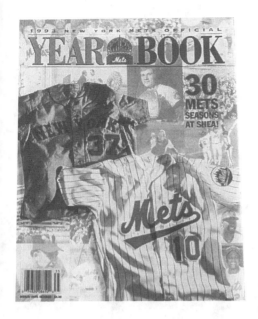

Mets Yearbooks

1962 First year	$300-$400
1963	$125-$150
1964 Cartoon	$85-$100
1965	$60-$90
1966	$60-$80
1967 Cartoon	$45-$70
1968 Gil Hodges	$45-$70
1969	$85-$100
1970 Film strips, World Series celebration	$25-$50
1971 Play at the plate	$20-$50
1972 Harrelson, McGraw, Seaver	$30-$40
1973 All-Star gallery with Mays, Seaver	$45
1974 N.L. Champions pennant	$20-$35
1975 Tom Seaver	$20-$35
1976 Mr. Met	$15-$30
1977 Jerry Koosman	$15-$18
1978	$15
1979 Mets logo	$12-$15
1980 Mazzilli with fan, others	$15
1981 Joe Torre, All-Time Mets	$10-$12
1982 George Foster, George Bamberger	$10-$12
1983 Foster, M. Wilson, Seaver	$10-$15
1984 Orosco, Hernandez, Stawberry	$10-$15
1985 Hernandez, Gooden, D. Johnson	$12-$15
1986 25th Anniversary logo	$7-$12
1987 World Champions logo	$7-$10
1988 Strawberry, Gooden, Johnson, others	$7-$9
1989 Strawberry, Gooden, Carter, others	$7-$8
1990 Mets starting pitchers	$7
1991 Shea Stadium	$6
1992 Bonilla, Saberhagen, Murray, Torborg	$6-$7
1993 30 years at Shea	$7

Orioles Yearbooks

St. Louis Browns

1944	$335
1945	$275
1946	$250
1947	$225
1948	$200
1949	$200
1950 Browns sketchbook	$175-$325
1951 Browns logo	$175-$300
1952	$150-$275
1953	$150-$275

Baltimore Orioles

1954 Orioles mascot in spotlight	$200-$225
1955 Oriole mascot batting	$125-$150
1956 Oriole mascot on deck	$100-$125
1957 Oriole mascot pitching	$85-$115
1958 Oriole mascot riding a rocket	$80-$110
1959 Oriole mascot with report	$75-$100
1960 Oriole mascot sitting on eggs	$70-$90
1961 Oriole mascot hitting opponent	$75
1962 Jim Gentile	$60-$75
1963	$50-$55
1964 Orioles catcher	$40-$55
1965 B. Robinson, Bauer, Bunker	$45
1966 Robinsons, Blefary, Powell	$40-$65
1967 Frank Robinson and fans	$35-$40
1968 Brooks and Frank Robinson	$37.50
1969 Dave McNally	$30-$35
1970 Boog Powell	$25-$40
1971 B. Robinson, Palmer, others	$25
1972 Palmer, McNally, Cuellar	$25
1973 Orioles player	$18-$20
1974 Orioles jukebox	$18-$20

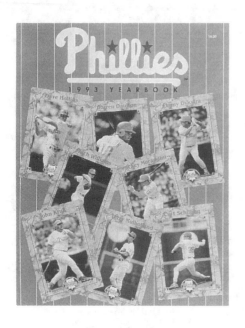

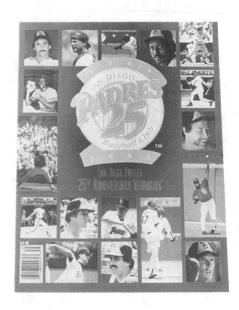

Orioles Yearbooks

1975 .... $15
1976 .... None issued
1977 .... None issued
1978 .... None issued
1979 .... None issued
1980 Orioles mascot .... $10-$12
1981 Orioles players .... $8-$10
1982 Frank Robinson, Earl Weaver .... $8-$12
1983 Brooks Robinson .... $12-$15
1984 30th Anniversary in Baltimore .... $7-$10
1985 .... None issued
1986 Robinsons, Ripken, Murray .... $7-$10
1987 .... None issued
1988 .... None issued
1989 .... None issued
1990 .... None issued
1991 .... None issued
1992 .... None issued
1993 Camden Yards $10

Padres Yearbooks

1969 Jack Murphy Stadium $75
1970 .... None issued
1971 .... None issued
1972 .... None issued
1973 .... None issued
1974 .... None issued
1975 .... None issued
1976 .... None issued
1977 .... None issued
1978 .... None issued
1979 Dave Winfield .... $12-$14
1980 Dave Winfield .... $10-$14
1981 .... None issued
1982 .... $9-$10
1983 Dick Williams, Steve Garvey .... $9-$10
1984 Templeton, Williams, Garvey .... $10-$12
1985 Padres hat, N.L. Championship ring .... $6-$9
1986 Padres memorabilia .... $6-$9
1987 .... None issued
1988 .... None issued
1989 .... None issued
1990 .... None issued
1991 .... None issued
1992 Fernandez, Gwynn, Santiago $5
1993 25th Anniversary $5

Phillies Yearbooks

1949 Batting scene .... $175-$200
1950 Phillie and sheet music $150
1951 Six player drawings .... $500-$600
1952 Color stadium photo .... $110-$125
1953 Phillie batter .... $50-$100
1954 Smiling Phillie (head only) .... $100-$150
1955 Phillie pitcher .... $85-$100
1956 Robin Roberts, Richie Ashburn .... $100-$125
1957 Ball wearing a Phillies hat .... $75-$100
1958 Hat on pinstriped background .... $75-$90
1959 Five balls, one with a logo .... $60-$90
1960 "New Faces of 1960," eleven photos ..... $60-$90
1961 First edition $250

Phillies Yearbooks

1961 Second edition $75
1962 Four balls and logo .... $45-$80
1963 Bat, ball and logo.................................... $40-$75
1964 First or second edition $40
1964 Third edition, Bunning, others $80
1965 Richie Allen, Jim Bunning .... $40-$75
1966 Stadium photo.. $35-$65
1967 Child eating a hot dog .... $35-$55
1968 Phillie ballplayers .... $25-$50
1969 Connie Mack Stadium .... $30-$45
1970 Veterans Stadim in tree bark.................. $20-$40
1971 Veterans Stadium drawing.................... $20-$40
1972 Stadium, fans and players...................... $20-$30
1973 12 drawings, with Carlton $25
1974 12 drawings, with Carlton, Bowa.................. $20
1975 Schmidt, Carlton.. $18
1976 Drawings with Schmidt, Carlton $18
1977 Larry Bowa... $15-$18
1978 Schmidt, Carlton, photos .... $15-$18
1979 Schmidt, Rose, Carlton........................ $15-$18
1980 Schmidt, Rose, Carlton........................ $16-$25
1981 World Series ring photo......................... $10-$25
1982 Schmidt, Rose, Carlton.......................... $7-$12
1983 Centennial celebration $10
1984 Schmidt, Carlton, 20 others .... $5-$12
1985 Schmidt, Carlton, Samuel, Hayes............. $5-$12
1986 Mike Schmidt at bat .... $5-$12
1987 Schmidt, Samuel, others......................... $8-$12
1988 Veterans Stadium photo............................. $5-$8
1989 Jordan, V. Hayes, Schmidt...................... $5-$9
1990 Photo of John Kruk's equipment $7
1991 Veteran's Stadium................................... $5-$6
1992 Kruk, Dykstra, Daulton, others $5
1993 Kruk, Dykstra, Daulton, others $5

Pirates Yearbooks

1951 Forbes Field photo............................ $175-$225
1952 Pirate with sword and pistol .... $100-$125
1953 "Buc youngster" in sailboat.................. $90-$110
1954 Honus Wagner statue .... $90-$100
1955 Pirate batter - "It's a hit!" .... $85-$95
1956 Pirate swinging at "1956" ball............... $75-$85
1957 Pirate winding up......................... $70-$85
1958 Pirate head between two bats .... $60-$80
1959 Pirate with "Pa Pitt" .... $55-$70
1960 Pirate in sailboat .... $65-$75
1961 Pirate on a treasure chest .... $45-$60
1962 Ball wearing bandana and cap.............. $45-$55
1963 Pirate batter... $35-$50
1964 Pirate sliding into third .... $35-$45
1965 Manager Harry Walker and coaches........ $30-$45
1966 Wraparound Forbes Field photo .... $25-$40
1967 Clemente, Mazeroski, others .... $40-$40
1968 Clemente, Stargell, others...................... $25-$45
1969 Wraparound Forbes Field photo .... $25-$30
1970 Three Rivers Stadium .... $25-$50
1971 Three Rivers Stadium .... $20-$50
1972 Clemente, Stargell, others...................... $20-$35
1973 Clemente, Stargell, others...................... $25-$35

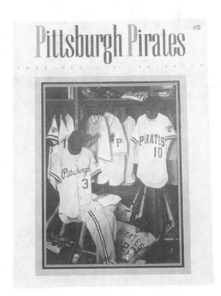

1974 Stargell, Parker, others............................ $20-$25
1975 Historical photos.................................... $16-$20
1976 Yosemite Sam cartoon .... $12-$16
1977 Pirate baseball cards .... $12-$15
1978 .... $10-$15
1979 Dave Parker $15
1980 "The Family of Stars".......................... $8-$14
1981 Lacy, Rhoden, Madlock, others................... $10
1982 Stargell, Madlock, others......................... $7-$12
1983 Chuck Tanner.. $7-$10
1984 Madlock, Pena, Ray, others .... $7-$10
1985 Painting of Maz's '60 homer .... $5-$12
1986 Leland, Pena, Ray, M. Brown .... $5-$9
1987 Centennial yearbook.............................. $5-$8
1988 Bonds, Bonilla, Van Slyke, others............. $5-$9
1989 Photo of official N.L. balls .... $5-$8
1990 Van Slyke bat, Leyland uniform................ $5-$7
1991 Pirates greats.. $5-$6
1992 Lockerroom/uniforms.................................... $5
1993 Jay Bell $5

Rangers Yearbooks

1972 .... None issued
1973 .... None issued
1974 .... None issued
1975 .... None issued
1976 Rangers cowgirl on horse .... $20-$30
1977 Autographed Rangers ball .... $15-$20
1978 .... $15
1979 Jenkins, Oliver, others .... $12-$14
1980 Arlington Stadium .... $10-$12
1981 Rangers hitter $8-12
1982 Rangers baseball...................................... $8-$10

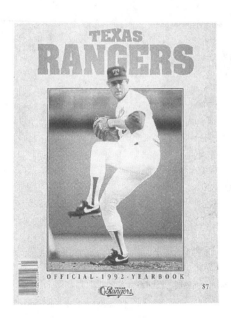

Rangers Yearbooks

1983 .... None issued
1984 George Wright ....$5-$10
1985 Pete O'Brien equipment ....$5-$9
1986 .... None issued
1987 .... None issued
1988 Ruben Sierra $9
1989 .... None issued
1990 Rangers helmet rack ....$5-$6
1991 20 Years in Texas...$5
1992 Nolan Ryan $5
1993 Arlington Stadium tribute...............................$5

Nationals/Senators Yearbooks

1947 ....$250-$400
1948 .... None issued
1949 ....$150-$350
1950 ....$125-$300
1951 .... None issued
1952 National's batter ....$95-$100
1953 Capitol building and baseball $95
1954 Bob Porterfield, Mickey Vernon..........$70-$100
1955 National with four bats..........................$65-$85
1956 Clark C. Griffith memorial ....$60-$85
1957 Senators pitcher ....$60-$95
1958 Roy Sievers...$60-$90
1959 ....$55-$80
1960 Harmon Killebrew ....$55-$80

Becomes Minnesota Twins

1961 "A Team is Born" ....$65-$100
1962 Washington Stadium...............................$50-$55
1963 Red cover with dedication.....................$40-$55
1964 "Off the Floor in '64"............................$35-$50

Nationals/Senators Yearbooks

1965 Senator signing autograph ....$30-$50
1966 Senators in action ....$25-$45
1967 Capitol and Washington Monument.......$25-$45
1968 Pitcher delivering ....$20-$35
1969 Ted Williams..$20-$45
1970 .... None issued
1971 .... None issued

Becomes Texas Rangers

Reds Yearbooks

1948 Ewell Blackwell, Ray Lamanno ....$175-$200
1949 Bucky Walters, Harry Gumbert ....$150-$175
1950 .... None issued
1951 75th Anniversary of N.L. $125
1952 Crosley Field ....$115-$125
1953 Reds mascot leaning on bat $100
1954 Reds mascot swinging bat ....$90-$95
1955 Reds mascot rising on bat............................$90
1956 Reds mascot swinging bat ....$75-$90
1957 Reds mascot in space ship ....$75-$80
1958 Reds mascot in orbit...............................$65-$75
1959 Vander Meer, Lombardi, others....................$60
1960 Reds mascot, Goodman, Rixey ....$55-$60
1961 Reds mascot running after ball..............$45-$65
1962 Reds mascot raising pennant $45
1963 Reds mascot yelling "Charge".....................$45
1964 Reds mascot in action................................$35
1965 Reds mascot making catch $35
1966 Reds mascot reaching for ball $30
1967 Reds mascot, Crosley Field $30

Reds Yearbooks

1968 Autographed team baseball ....$25-$30
1969 Perez, Rose, Bench, others ....$25-$30
1970 Johnny Bench ....$25-$30
1971 Rose, Bench, Anderson, others ....$20-$25
1972 Bench, Perez, other film strips.....................$25
1973 Morgan, Bench, others ....$15-$25
1974 Pete Rose sliding into home ....$15-$25
1975 Joe Morgan ....$18-$20
1976 Morgan, Rose, Perez.............................$15-$18
1977 Morgan, Bench, Foster, others...............$12-$15
1978 Pete Rose $12
1979 Bench, Perez, Griffey, Foster ....$10-$14
1980 Reds equipment ....$8-$10
1981 Riverfront Stadium and baseball ....$8-$10
1982 Binoculars on stadium seat......................$6-$10
1983 Red player signing autographs ....$6-$10
1984 Bats and baseball equipment ....$5-$10
1985 Pete Rose, Ty Cobb ....$5-$12
1986.. None issued
1987 Rose, Parker, E. Davis, others ....$5-$9
1988 All-Star Game logo ....$5-$8
1989 Baseball with Reds logo ....$5-$7
1990 Red player with fans..................................$6-$7
1991 World Series trophy $5
1992 Equipment collage...$5
1993 Barry Larkin's jersey $5

Red Sox Yearbooks

1951 Fenway Park ....$175-$200
1952 Red Sox sliding into home ....$175-$200

Red Sox Yearbooks

1953 .... None issued
1954 .... None issued
1955 Red Sox fielder ....$100-$165
1956 Red Sox owners....................................$80-$150
1957 Fenway Park ....$80-$130
1958 Red Sox signing autograph...................$70-$120
1959 Red Sox pitcher ....$70-$100
1960 Gary Geiger ....$60-$75
1961 Red Sox batter ....$45-$65
1962 Carl Yastrzemski....................................$45-$65
1963 ....$40-$55
1964 ....$40-$55
1965 Dick Radatz ....$40-$45
1966 Fenway Park ....$35-$45
1967 Scott, T. Conigliaro, Yastrzemski...........$50-$75
1968 Yastrzemski, Lonborg, D. Williams ....$30-$45
1969 Fenway Park ....$25-$30
1970 Lyle, Petrocelli, Yastrzemski ....$25-$30
1971 Scott, Yastrzemski, Petrocelli....................$5.00
1972 Carl Yastrzemski and fans ....$20-$30
1973 Carlton Fisk and fans..............................$20-$25
1974 Carlton Fisk, with Thurman Munson .....$20-$25
1975 Foxx, Williams, Yastrzemski, Fisk.........$20-$25
1976 Fred Lynn $15
1977 Carl Yastrzemski.............................$15-$17.50
1978 Jim Rice, Carl Yastrzemski ....$12-$15
1979 Jim Rice..$12
1980 Fred Lynn ....$10-$12
1981 Rice, Yastrzemski, Eckersley ....$9-$12
1982 Yastrzemski, Evans, Rice, Lansford.......$10-$12
1983 Carl Yastrzemski....................................$10-$12
1984 Jim Rice..$7-$10
1985 Tony Armas ....$7-$10
1986 Wade Boggs...$7-$10
1987 Roger Clemens and Fenway Park ....$7-$9
1988 Wade Boggs, Roger Clemens ....$7-$9
1989 Dwight Evans ....$6-$7
1990 Mike Greenwell, Ellis Burks ....$6-$7
1991 Pena, Clemens, Burks...............................$5-$7
1992 Clemens, Reardon, Viola..........................$5-$7
1993 Roger Clemens $7

Royals Yearbooks

1969 Pitcher inside large "R" $50
1970 Piniella, Otis, others ....$25-$40
1971 Piniella, Otis, others ....$25-$35
1972 Catcher's mitt with face.........................$22-$30
1973 Mayberry, Splittorff, others ....$15-$25
1974 Otis, Mayberry, Splittorff ....$18-$20
1975 Killebrew, McRae, Mayberry $18
1976.. None issued
1977.. None issued
1978.. None issued
1979.. None issued
1980.. None issued

Royals Yearbooks

1981	None issued
1982	None issued
1983 Bronze Royals statue	$7-$10
1984 Royals jacket and equipment	$7-$10
1985 Division championship celebration	$10-$12
1986 Hand wearing World Series ring	$5-$10
1987 Royals championship pennants	$5-$8
1988 Fireworks over Royals Stadium	$5-$8
1989 Royals player locker	$5-$7
1990 Royals in action	$5-$6
1991 Scoreboard replay	$5-$6
1992 Newspaper format	$5
1993 Memorabilia collage	$5

Tigers Yearbooks

1955	$250-$275
1956	None issued
1957 Tiger sliding into home	$125-$175
1958 Tiger Hall of Famers, with Cobb	$125-$150
1959 Tiger batting and logo	$85-$125
1960 Tiger Stadium	$70-$100
1961 Tiger head and five baseballs	$55-$80
1962 Tiger head and nine players	$55-$80
1963 Tiger head	$45-$75
1964 Tiger head	$45-$60
1965 Bill Freehan	$40-$60
1966 Willie Horton	$35-$50
1967 Denny McLain	$40-$45

Tigers Yearbooks

1968 Al Kaline	$40-$60
1969 World Series trophy	$30-$40
1970 Tiger hat, bats, baseballs	$20-$40
1971 Billy Martin, Kaline, Horton	$25-$35
1972 Mickey Lolich	$15-$30
1973 Tiger infielder in action	$15-$25
1974 Tiger sliding into home	$12-$20
1975 Ron LeFlore	$12-$20
1976 75th Anniversary	$15
1977 Fidrych, Staub, LeFlore	$10-$12
1978	$8-$12
1979 Alan Trammell, Lou Whitaker	$8-$18
1980 Trammell, Whitaker, Morris, others	$8-$15
1981 Trammell, Whitaker, Morris, others	$7-$15
1982 Clubhouse photo with Gibson	$7-$12
1983 Hank Greenberg, Charlie Gehringer	$7-$10
1984 Morris, Whitaker, Trammell, others	$10-$12
1985 World Championship trophy	$5-$10
1986 Sparky Anderson	$5-$10
1987 Tiger on top of baseball	$7-$8
1988 Tiger face, "Eye of the Tiger"	$5-$8
1989 "Intend-a-Pennant"	$5-$7
1990 Roaring into the '90s Tiger	$5-$6
1991 Whitaker, Trammell, Fielder, others	$5
1992 Anderson, Stengel	$5
1993	None issued

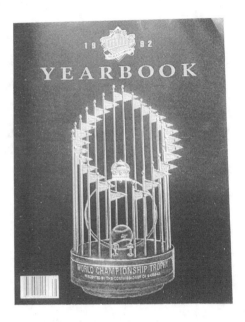 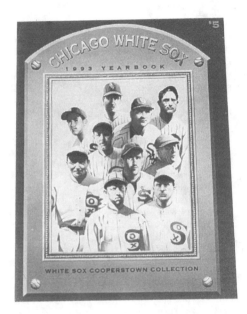

Twins Yearbooks

1961 Twins batters	$185-$200
1962 Metropolitan Stadium	$50-$95
1963 Harmon Killebrew	$55-$85
1964 Gloved hand and baseball	$40-$75
1965 Autographed Twins ball	$40-$80
1966 Tony Oliva, A.L. Champions	$45-$60
1967 Killebrew, Kaat, Oliva	$40-$60
1968 Jim Kaat, Harmon Killebrew	$35-$50
1969 Killebrew, Carew, Oliva, others	$35-$55
1970 Rod Carew	$20-$50
1971 Carew, Killebrew, Oliva, others	$25-$30
1972 Tony Oliva, Harmon Killebrew	$30
1973 Frank Quilici	$20-$25
1974 Rod Carew	$20-$25
1975 Rod Carew	$15-$20
1976 Rod Carew	$15-$20
1977 Past Twins yearbooks	$12-$16
1978 Rod Carew	$12
1979 Twins batting helmet	$10-$12
1980 Twins baseball cards	$10
1981 20th Anniversary, Rod Carew	$8-$12
1982 Metrodome	$8-$10
1983	None issued
1984	None issued
1985 Yearbook/scorecard	$6-$10
1986 25th Anniversary celebration	$6-$10
1987 Twins uniforms	$7-$8
1988 World Champions celebration	$5-$8
1989 Viola, Puckett, Gaetti, Reardon	$5-$7
1990 Carew, Puckett, Oliva	$5-$6
1991 Uniform collage	$5-$6
1992 World Series trophy	$5
1993	None issued

White Sox Yearbooks

1952	$90-$100
1953 Comiskey Park	$90-$95
1954 White Sox batter	$75-$85
1955 White Sox batter	$70-$80
1956 White Sox sliding into home	$70-$75
1957 White Sox fielder	$70-$75
1958 White Sox batter	$60-$65
1959 White Sox mascot with hat	$70-$80
1960 White Sox fielding	$50-$55
1961 White Sox pitching	$40-$45
1962 White Sox batting	$40-$45
1963 White Sox fielding	$30-$40
1964 Fireworks over Comiskey Park	$30-$40
1965 White Sox uniform #80	$25-$35
1966 White Sox batter swinging	$20-$35
1967 White Sox in action	$20-$30
1968 White Sox batter at plate	$20-$25
1969 Tommy John	$20-$25
1970 White Sox in action	$18-$20
1971	None issued
1972	None issued
1973	None issued
1974	None issued
1975	None issued
1976	None issued
1977	None issued
1978	None issued
1979	None issued
1980	None issued
1981	None issued
1982 LaRussa, Luzinski, Fisk	$7-$10
1983 All-Star Game with Fisk, others	$8-$10
1984 Hoyt, LaRussa, Kittle, Luzinski	$6-$10

White Sox Yearbooks

1985 .... None issued
1986 Walker, Guillen, J. Davis, Baines $9
1987 .... None issued
1988 White Sox memorabilia $8
1989 .... None issued
1990 Comiskey Park .... $5-$6
1991 Comiskey Park $5
1992 Good Guys Wear Black $5
1993 Cooperstown Collection $5

Yankees Yearbooks

1950 Big League Books .... $275-$325
1951 Big League Books $250
1952 Big League Books .... $200-$250
1953 Big League Books $225
1954 Yankee with World Series bats .... $125-$200
1955 Three Yankees .... $125-$175
1956 Yankee sliding into home .... $100-$150
1957 Yankee batting .... $100-$125
1958 Yankee fielding .... $90-$100
1959 Big League Books .... $80-$90
1960 Artwork, batter .... $75-$90
1961 Artwork, pitcher .... $100-$125
1962 Yankee Stadium $65
1963 Yankee holding bats $60
1964 .... $35-$60
1965 .... $50
1966 Two autographed balls .... $40-$50
1967 Mickey Mantle .... $40-$70
1968 Mantle, Stottlemyre, others .... $25-$50
1969 Mantle, Stottlemyre, others .... $25-$45
1970 Murcer, Stottlemyre, others .... $30-$35
1971 Murcer, White, others .... $20-$25
1972 Murcer, White, Stottlemyre .... $20-$25
1973 Ruth, DiMaggio, Mantle, Gehrig .... $20-$35
1974 Bobby Murcer, Thurman Munson .... $20-$35
1975 25th Annual with past yearbooks .... $15-$18
1976 Yankees Stadium .... $20-$25
1977 Chris Chambliss $20
1978 World Series trophy .... $15-$20
1979 World Series celebration .... $10-$15

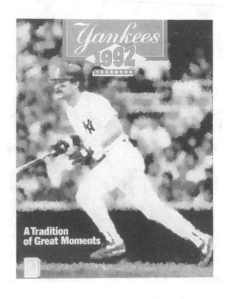

1980 Yankee Stadium .... $10-$12
1981 Yankees Big Apple .... $8-$12
1982 Winfield, Guidry, Gossage, others .... $7-$12
1983 Billy Martin .... $7-$15
1984 Yankee greats .... $7-$10
1985 Maris, Mantle, Ruth, Gehrig .... $6-$12
1986 Yankees MVPs .... $6-$12
1987 Gehrig, Mattingly, Mantle .... $6-$12
1988 Mattingly, Clark, Randolph .... $5-$10
1989 Yankees memorabilia .... $5-$8
1990 Don Mattingly .... $5-$7
1991 Pitcher vs. batter $5
1992 Don Mattingly $5
1993 Team photo $5

Media guides

Media guides, which, as we know them today, debuted in the late 1940s, are presented to the radio, television and newspaper beat reporters who cover major league teams throughout the season. They are designed to provide the reporters with almost every imaginable kind of biographical and statistical tidbits to liven up a broadcast or story, from who's on first, to what his favorite hobby is. Farm teams are also covered and, coupled with the chronologies of team histories, have contributed to the guides' increases in page size from the 1950s to the 1990s.

The guides are not found on newsstands or bookstores; they are generally available only from the reporters, who sell or give them to memorabilia dealers, or from the teams, which in recent years have given them to season ticket holders or have sold them at the stadiums, by mail or during year-end promotional sales.

The press guide provides far more extensive coverage of the team but, although it does contain profile shots of the players and key people in the organization, lacks the colorful photographs that would appear in a team yearbook.

Angels Media Guides

Los Angeles Angels

1961 Player emerging from baseball
.... $30-$50
1962 Baby with Angels logo .... $20-$45
1963 Angels logo, Rigney, Haney .... $15-$40
1964 Angels in action .... $15-$25
1965 Dean Chance/Cy Young Award
.... $18-$25

California Angels

1966 Anaheim Stadium .... $15-$20
1967 League logos and Anaheim .... $12-$20
1968 Anaheim Stadium and logo .... $12-$20
1969 New-look A.L. West .... $12-$15
1970 Press box and player .... $12-$15
1971 Four Angels in California .... $12-$15
1972 Del Rice .... $10-$12
1973 Nolan Ryan .... $10-$20
1974 Anaheim Stadium .... $10-$15
1975 Dick Williams .... $8-$15
1976 Angels baseball cards .... $8-$12

1977 Frank Tanana .... $8-$12
1978 Tanana, Ryan, Rudi .... $8-$14
1979 Anaheim Stadium .... $10-$12
1980 Don Baylor .... $6-$7
1981 Angels equipment .... $6-$7
1982 Angels logo .... $7-$8
1983 Angels in action, R. Jackson .... $4-$8
1984 Angels celebrating, R. Jackson .... $4-$7
1985 .... $4-$7
1986 DeCinces, Schofield, Downing .... $5-$6
1987 Donnie Moore .... $4-$6
1988 Wally Joyner, Brian Downing .... $4-$5
1989 All-Star Game logo .... $4-$5
1990 Angels stars, Joyner, Finley .... $4-$5
1991 Pitcher in action .... $4-$5
1992 Bryan Harvey .... $4-$5
1993 Old Angels uniforms $4

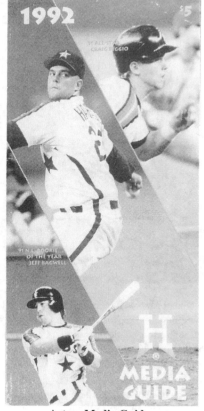

Astros Media Guides

Houston Colt 45's

1962 45's logo .... $35-$55
1963 45's logo .... $25-$30
1964 Player art .... $20-$30

Houston Astros

1965 New logo .... $15-$20
1966 Catcher's mask .... $15-$20
1967 Astroturf .... $12-$17
1968 Astrodome art............................... $12-$17
1969 Baseball anniversary .... $12-$15
1970 Team roster................................... $12-$15
1971 Locker room scene $12
1972 Ball, bat as pool cue $12
1973 Zodiac signs................................. $10-$12
1974 Big orange $10
1975 Equipment .... $8-$10
1976 Bicentennial logo........................... $8-$10
1977 Player art .... $7-$10
1978 Art.. $7-$10
1979 Art.. $6-$10
1980...$6
1981...$6
1982.. $5-$6
1983.. $5-$6
1984.. $5-$6
1985.. $4-$6
1986...$6
1987.. $4-$6
1988.. $4-$6
1989.. $4-$6
1990.. $4-$6
1991 Helmet, bat, ball .... $4-$5
1992 Craig Biggio, Pete Harnisch..................$5
1993 Luis Gonzalez, Jeff Bagwell $4

Athletics Media Guides
Philadelphia Athletics

1930 Team mascot (elephant) .... $75-$100
1931 Team mascot (elephant) .... $70-$100
1932 Team mascot (elephant) .... $65-$125
1933 Team mascot (elephant) .... $60-$100
1934 Team mascot (elephant) .... $60-$100
1935 Team mascot (elephant) .... $55-$100
1936 Team mascot (elephant) .... $55-$75
1937 Team mascot (elephant) .... $50-$75
1938 Team mascot (elephant) .... $50-$75
1939 "A's" and elephant........................ $50-$75
1940 Pennant and elephant.................... $45-$75
1941 "A's" and baseball .... $45-$75
1942.. $40-$45
1943 Team mascot with flag.................. $40-$60
1944 Team mascot with flag.................. $40-$60
1945.. $40-$60
1946 Connie Mack .... $45-$60

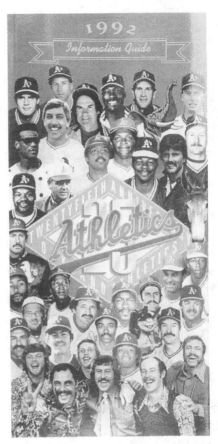

1947..$35-$60
1948 Baseball and elephant ....$35-$60
1949..$30-$60
1950 Connie Mack..................................$45-$50
1951..$30-$50
1952 Team mascot (elephant) ....$25-$50
1953..$25-$50
1954 Eddie Joost....................................$25-$65

Kansas City Athletics

1955 K.C. Municipal Stadium ....$40-$65
1956 Elephant logo ....$20-$40
1957 Elephant logo ....$20-$40
1958 Elephant logo ....$20-$40
1959 "A's" baseball.................................$20-$40
1960 Baseball and A's hat......................$20-$40
1961 K.C. Municipal Stadium ....$15-$40
1962..$15-$30
1963 Player sliding, baseball ....$15-$30
1964 1964 and A's logo..........................$15-$30
1965 1965 and A's logo..........................$15-$20
1966 1966 and A's logo..........................$15-$20

Kansas City Athletics

1967 1967 and A's logo .... $12-$20

Oakland Athletics

1968 Oakland Stadium, ball, logo .... $25-$50
1969 Bando, Campaneris, Hunter .... $15-$18
1970 Player at bat .... $12-$15
1971 A's logo and 1971 ....$12
1972 A's logo and 1972 .... $12-$14
1973 A's logo and 1973 .... $12-$14
1974 A's logo and 1974 .... $12-$14
1975 A's logo and 1975 .... $8-$10
1976 A's logo and 1976 .... $8-$10
1977 A's logo and 1977 .... $7-$10
1978 A's logo and 1978 .... $7-$10
1979 A's logo and 1979 .... $6-$10
1980 A's logo and 1980 .... $6-$7
1981 Billy Ball baseball .... $6-$9
1982 Running spikes .... $5-$7
1983 A's jukebox .... $5-$7
1984 Oakland sportswriters...................... $5-$6
1985 Athletics memorabilia .... $4-$6
1986.. $4-$6
1987 All-time Athletics team .... $4-$7
1988 Batter hitting.................................... $5-$6
1989 Canseco, Eckersley, Weiss $6
1990 World Series trophy......................... $5-$6
1991 Team memorabilia............................ $4-$5
1992 25th anniversary, A's greats.................. $4
1993 Dennis Eckersley.....................................$4

Blue Jays Media Guides

1977 Toronto Exhibition Stadium .... $20-$22
1978 Blue Jays pitcher .... $7-$10
1979 Blue Jays in action.......................... $6-$12
1980 Alfredo Griffin................................. $6-$7
1981 Blue Jays equipment........................ $6-$7
1982 Blue Jays in action, Bobby Cox
.... $5-$7
1983 Blue Jays equipment and hat........... $5-$7
1984 Blue Jays in action........................... $5-$6
1985 Blue Jays logo $6
1986 Blue Jays 10th anniversary.............. $4-$6
1987 Bell, Barfield, Fernandez............. $4-$6.50
1988 George Bell .... $4-$6
1989 Blue Jays stars, McGriff........................$6
1990 Blue Jays, McGriff, Gruber............. $4-$6
1991 Dave Stieb .... $5-$6
1992 Roberto Alomar................................ $5-$6
1993 World Series trophy.............................. $5

TORONTO BLUE JAYS OFFICIAL GUIDE 1992

ROBERTO ALOMAR
1991 Labatt's Blue Jays MVP
and Rawlings Gold Glove Winner

Braves Media Guides

Boston Braves

1931 Roster, Indian head $80
1932 Indian head.................................. $60-$100
1933 Indian head.................................. $60-$100
1934 Indian head.................................. $55-$100
1935 Indian head.................................. $55-$100
1936 Roster...$55-$75
1937 Roster...$50-$75
1938 "Bees" Baseball ....$50-$75
1939..$50-$75
1940 Casey Stengel................................$60-$75
1941 Casey Stengel.......................................$60
1942 Indian head....................................$45-$60
1943 Indian head....................................$40-$60
1944 Bat, flag, airplane ....$40-$60
1945 Indian Head....................................$40-$60
1946 Billy Southworth............................$40-$60
1947 Billy Southworth............................$40-$60
1948 Bob Elliott.....................................$40-$60
1949 Billy Southworth............................$35-$60
1950 Braves Logo ....$30-$50
1951...$30-$50
1952 Baseball and Indian head ....$25-$50

Atlanta Braves

1966 Player hitting ....$20-$30
1967 Felipe Alou...................................$14-$20
1968 Hands gripping bat.......................$12-$18
1969 Players in action...........................$12-$20
1970 Hank Aaron..................................$15-$18
1971 Foot sliding into base ....$12-$15
1972 Players in action...........................$12-$15
1973 Players in action...........................$10-$12
1974 Players in action................................$10
1975 "Knit" baseballs $10
1976 Dave Bristol ....$8-$10
1977 Braves hat.....................................$8-$10
1978 Atlanta-Fulton Co. Stadium................$10
1979 Phil Niekro, All-Stars.....................$7-$12
1980 Baseball and stadium $7
1981 Bob Horner, Dale Murphy ....$6-$8
1982 Joe Torre..$7-$8
1983 Bedrosian, Murphy, Niekro, Torre
....$5-$7
1984 Braves logo ....$5-$6
1985 Dale Murphy, Bruce Sutter ....$5-$6
1986 Bobby Cox, Chuck Tanner...............$5-$6
1987 Braves uniform................................$5-$6
1988...$5
1989 Gant, Glavine, Perry, Smith, Thomas
.... $5
1990 25th anniversary logo............................$5
1991 Ron Gant, Dave Justice....................$5-$6
1992 Greg Olson, John Smoltz ....$5-$6
1993 N.L. Champions $4

Brewers Media Guides

Seattle Pilots

1969 Pilots logo ....$45-$75
1970 Pilots logo $20

Milwaukee Brewers

1971 Newspaper clipping ....$12-$20
1972 State of Wisconsin ....$12-$15
1973 Del Crandall, George Scott ....$10-$12
1974 Team mascot ....$10-$12
1975 Team mascot ....$8-$10
1976 Baseball glove................................$8-$10
1977 Robin Yount ....$7-$15
1978 Larry Hisle ....$7-$10
1979 George Bamberger ....$6-$10
1980 Cooper, Lezcano, Thomas ....$6-$8
1981 Cooper, Oglivie, Yount ....$6-$8
1982 Rollie Fingers..................................$7-$8

Milwaukee Braves

1953 State of Florida.............................$35-$55
1954...$25-$50
1955...$20-$50
1956...$20-$40
1957...$25-$45
1958...$25-$45
1959...$20-$40
1960 Pennant and Indian head ....$20-$40
1961 Pennant and Indian head ....$15-$40
1962 Pennant and Indian head ....$15-$40
1963 Pennant and Indian head ....$15-$40
1964 Aaron, Alou, Mathews, Spahn
.... $20-$40
1965 Felipe Alou, Bobby Bragan
....$17.50-$30

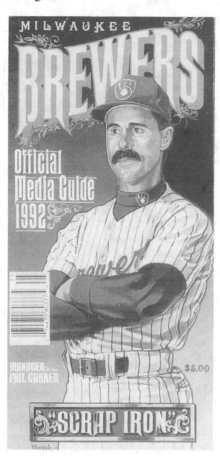

1937 Team logo and 1937 ....$50-$75
1938...$50-$75
1939 Name and year ....$50-$75
1940 Team logo and 1940 ....$45-$75
1941 Team logo and 1941 ....$45-$60
1942 Logo, Statue of Liberty ....$45-$65
1943 Flag and team logo........................$40-$70
1944 Victory V and logo........................$40-$70
1945 Team logo and 1945 ....$40-$60
1946...$35-$70
1947 Team logo...$35-$60
1948 Team logo and baseball................$35-$60
1949 Team logo and baseball................$30-$60
1950 Baseball and players ....$30-$50
1951 25th anniversary of World Champs
....$30-$50
1952 Team logo...$25-$50
1953 "It's the Cardinals"........................$25-$50
1954 Team logo...$25-$50
1955 Team logo...$20-$50
1956 Team logo...$20-$40
1957 Team logo...$20-$40
1958 Team mascot ....$20-$40
1959 Stan Musial ....$35-$40
1960 Team mascot ....$20-$40
1961 Broglio, McDaniel, Sadecki, Simmons
....$15-$40
1962 Stan Musial $30
1963 Player in action ....$15-$30
1964 Boyer, Groat, Javier, White..........$20-$35
1965 Team logo...$15-$20
1966 Busch Stadium, team logo ....$15-$20
1967 Busch Stadium ....$12-$25
1968 World Series trophy ....$12-$25
1969 Bob Gibson ....$15-$16
1970 Joe Torre..$14-$15
1971 Bob Gibson, Joe Torre ....$12-$18
1972 Red Schoendienst, Joe Torre........$12-$15
1973 Brock, Gibson, Simmons, Torre
....$10-$16
1974 Cardinals uniform and hat...................$10
1975 Lou Brock and team logo...............$8-$15
1976 Busch Stadium ....$8-$10
1977 Lou Brock, Vern Rapp ....$7-$12
1978 Cardinals equipment ....$7-$10
1979 St. Louis Arch ....$6-$12
1980 Keith Hernandez ....$6-$8
1981 Whitey Herzog............................$6-$7.50
1982 Whitey Herzog.......................................$7
1983 World Series celebration ....$5-$7
1984 Player running.................................$5-$6

1983 Kuenn, Vuckovich, Yount .... $5-$8
1984 County Stadium................................$5-$6
1985 Brewers uniform #85........................ $4-$6
1986 Brewers pitcher in action..................$4-$6
1987 Ted Higuera ....$4-$6
1988 Player running ....$4-$5
1989 20th anniversary logo ....$4-$5
1990 Player running ....$4-$5
1991 Team logo...$4-$5
1992 Phil Garner ....$4-$5
1993 Pat Listach $4

Cardinals Media Guides

1930 Team logo and 1930 .... $75-$115
1931 ....$70-$115
1932 Team logo and 1932 ....$65-$125
1933 Team logo and 1933 ....$60-$125
1934 Team logo and 1934 ....$60-$115
1935 Team logo and 1935 ....$55-$100
1936 Team logo and 1936 ....$55-$75

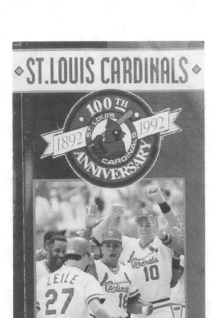

1985 Busch Stadium, St. Louis Arch ....$4-$6
1986 Coleman, Herzog, McGee...........$4-$6.50
1987 Whitey Herzog, former managers
.... $4-$6
1988 N.L. Champions celebrate................ $4-$5
1989 Action photos, Whitey Herzog......... $4-$6
1990 Team logo.. $4-$5
1991 Joe Torre... $4-$5
1992 Todd Ziele .... $4-$5
1993 Team logo...$4

Cubs Media Guides

1926 The year...$70
1927 The year.................................... $70-$175
1928 The year.................................... $65-$150
1929 The year.................................... $65-$150
1930 The year.................................... $65-$100
1931 Rogers Hornsby.......................... $75-$100
1932 Rogers Hornsby.......................... $75-$125
1933 Team mascot.............................. $60-$100

1934 Team mascot ....$55-$100
1935 Team mascot ....$55-$115
1936 Team mascot ....$55-$75
1937 Team mascot throwing.................$50-$75
1938 Team mascot hitting.....................$50-$80
1939 Team mascot with pennant...........$50-$65
1940...$45-$65
1941 Jimmy Wilson ....$45-$65
1942...$45-$65
1943...$40-$65
1944...$40-$65
1945...$40-$70
1946 Charlie Grimm ....$35-$65
1947 Team mascot ....$35-$65
1948...$35-$65
1949...$30-$55
1950...$30-$55
1951...$30-$55
1952...$25-$45
1953...$25-$45
1954...$25-$45
1955...$20-$45
1956...$20-$35
1957...$20-$35
1958 Team logo....................................$20-$35
1959 Team logo....................................$20-$35
1960 Team logo....................................$20-$35
1961 Team logo....................................$15-$35
1962 Team logo....................................$15-$30
1963 Team logo....................................$15-$30
1964 Team logo....................................$15-$30
1965 Team logo....................................$15-$20
1966 Team logo....................................$15-$20
1967 Team logo....................................$12-$17
1968 Team logo....................................$12-$17
1969 Team logo....................................$12-$15
1970 Team logo....................................$12-$15
1971 Team logo....................................$12-$17
1972 Team logo...$12
1973 Team logo....................................$10-$12
1974 Team logo...$10
1975 Team logo.....................................$8-$10
1976 Team logo.....................................$8-$10
1977 Team logo.....................................$7-$10
1978 Team logo.....................................$7-$10
1979 Team logo.....................................$6-$10
1980 Team logo.......................................$6-$7
1981 Team logo.......................................$6-$7
1982 Team logo.......................................$5-$7
1983 Wrigley Field, celebration...............$5-$7
1984 Autographed baseballs $6

1985 Frey, Green, Sandberg, Sutcliffe
.... $4-$7
1986 Cubs second baseman (Sandberg)
.... $4-$6
1987 Billy Williams .... $4-$7
1988 Andre Dawson............................ $4-$5.50
1989 Wrigley Field.................................. $5-$6
1990 Wrigley Field.................................. $4-$5
1991 Ryne Sandberg............................ $4-$5.50
1992 Wrigley Field.................................. $4-$5
1993 Wrigley Field.......................................$4

Dodgers Media Guides
Brooklyn Dodgers
1928 Name and 1928........................... $80-$150
1929 Name and 1929........................... $75-$100
1930 Name and 1930........................... $75-$100
1931 Name and 1931........................... $70-$100

1932 Name and 1932 ....$70-$100
1933 Team logo and 1933...................$65-$100
1934 Team logo and 1934...................$65-$100
1935 Team logo and 1935...................$65-$100
1936 Team logo and 1936.....................$55-$75
1937 Team logo and 1937.....................$55-$75
1938 Team logo and 1938.....................$50-$75
1939 100th anniversary logo.................$50-$75
1940 50th anniversary in Brooklyn
....$45-$75
1941 Team airplane..............................$45-$85
1942 "V" logo ....$45-$65
1943...$40-$65
1944...$40-$65
1945...$40-$65

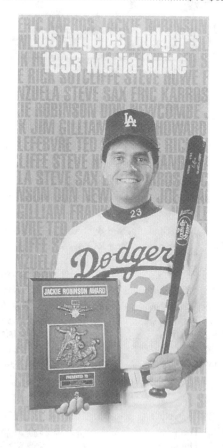

1946...$35-$65
1947...$35-$70
1948...$35-$65
1949...$30-$70
1950 "The Bum" ....$30-$55

1951 "The Bum" .... $30-$55
1952 .... $25-$60
1953 "The Bum" .... $25-$60
1954 .... $25-$50
1955 Walter Alston .... $25-$60
1956 Walter Alston .... $25-$55
1957 Walter Alston .... $25-$55

Los Angeles Dodgers

1958 Walter Alston .... $45-$100
1959 L.A. Coliseum .... $20-$50
1960 Dodger Stadium drawing $20
1961 Dodger Stadium .... $15-$40
1962 Cartoon and airplane .... $15-$30
1963 T. Davis, Drysdale, Koufax, Wills
.... $20-$35
1964 Players celebrating .... $15-$30
1965 Championship pennants .... $15-$25
1966 Mascot climbing mountains .... $15-$20
1967 Mascot juggling crowns .... $12-$17
1968 Walter Alston .... $16-$17
1969 100th anniversary .... $12-$15
1970 W. Davis, Osteen, Singer, Sizemore
.... $12-$15
1971 Dodgers in action $12
1972 Dodgers in action $12
1973 Dodgers in action .... $10-$12
1974 Dodgers in action .... $10-$12
1975 Steve Garvey .... $8-$12
1976 Buckner, Cey, Garvey, Lopes, Sutton
.... $8-$14
1977 Tom Lasorda .... $9-$12
1978 Baker, Cey, Garvey, Smith .... $9-$14
1979 Dodger Stadium .... $6-$12
1980 Team logo .... $6-$7
1981 1980 highlights .... $7-$8
1982 World Series trophy, Howe, Yeager
.... $5-$8
1983 Sax, Guerrero, Valenzuela .... $7-$8
1984 Fireworks over Dodger Stadium
.... $5-$6
1985 Bill Russell .... $6-$7
1986 Player swinging bat .... $4-$6
1987 Dodger Stadium .... $4-$6
1988 Baseballs .... $5-$7
1989 World Series trophy .... $4-$5
1990 100th anniversary pins and pins
.... $4-$5
1991 Name and 1991 .... $4-$5
1992 Team stadium .... $4-$5
1993 Eric Karros $4

Expos Media Guides

1969 Team logo .... $20-$50
1970 Jarry Park $15
1971 Baseball $12
1972 Action photos, Jarry Park $12
1973 Montreal photos .... $10-$12
1974 Gene Mauch $10
1975 Players in action .... $8-$10
1976 Players in action .... $8-$10
1977 Cash, McEnaney, Perez, D. Williams
.... $7-$12
1978 Gary Carter, Andre Dawson .... $7-$14
1979 Team logo .... $6-$10
1980 Locker with uniform .... $6-$7
1981 Pennant .... $6-$7
1982 Players in action .... $5-$7
1983 Hands holding a bat .... $5-$7
1984 Team hats .... $5-$6
1985 Olympic Stadium with dome .... $4-$6
1986 Baseball and team logo .... $4-$6
1987 Olympic Stadium with dome .... $4-$6

1988 20th anniversary bat .... $4-$5
1989 Hands giving hi-five .... $4-$5
1990 Team logo .... $4-$5
1991 Team logo .... $4-$5
1992 Dennis Martinez .... $4-$5
1993 25th anniversary $4

Giants Media Guides

New York Giants

1927 Name and 1927 .... $90-$150
1928 Name and 1928 .... $85-$100
1929 Name and 1929 .... $80-$100
1930 Name and 1930 .... $75-$100
1931 Name and 1931 .... $70-$100
1932 Name and 1932 .... $65-$100
1933 Name and 1933 .... $65-$125
1934 Name and 1934 .... $60-$100
1935 Name and 1935 .... $60-$100
1936 Name and 1936 .... $55-$85
1937 Name and 1937 .... $55-$85
1938 Name and 1938 .... $50-$75
1939 New York World's Fair .... $50-$75
1940 Name and 1940 .... $45-$75
1941 Name and 1941 .... $45-$60
1942 Name and 1942 .... $45-$60
1943 Name and 1943 .... $40-$60
1944 Name and 1944 .... $40-$60
1945 Name and 1945 .... $40-$60
1946 Name and 1946 .... $35-$60
1947 Baseball with 1947 .... $35-$60
1948 Baseball with 1948 .... $35-$60
1949 Baseball with 1949 .... $30-$60
1950 Polo Grounds .... $30-$50
1951 Team logo .... $30-$55
1952 Leo Durocher, a "Giant" .... $30-$50
1953 Polo Grounds .... $25-$50
1954 Team logo .... $25-$60
1955 The "Giant" .... $20-$50
1956 Team hat .... $20-$40
1957 Team hat .... $20-$40

San Francisco Giants

1958 Candlestick Park drawing .... $40-$50
1959 Players in action .... $20-$40
1960 Team logo .... $20-$40
1961 Giants in action .... $15-$40
1962 Players in action .... $15-$35
1963 Candlestick Park .... $15-$30
1964 Candlestick Park .... $15-$30
1965 Candlestick Park .... $15-$20
1966 Baseball and team logo .... $15-$20

SAN FRANCISCO
GIANTS
1992
INFORMATION
GUIDE

1967 Team logo .... $12-$17
1968 Team logo .... $12-$17
1969 Team logo .... $12-$15
1970 Willie Mays, Willie McCovey
.... $15-$20
1971 Year of the Fox .... $12-$15
1972 "Best in the West" $12
1973 Candlestick Park .... $10-$12
1974 Matthews, Bryant, Bonds .... $10-$15
1975 Team logo .... $8-$10
1976 Team logo .... $8-$10
1977 Joe Altobelli, John Montefusco
.... $7-$10
1978 Players in action .... $7-$10
1979 Blue, Clark, Giants management
.... $6-$11
1980 On deck circle with team logo .... $6-$7
1981 Golden Gate Bridge .... $6-$7
1982 25th anniversary in city .... $5-$7
1983 Team logo .... $5-$7
1984 Team logo .... $5-$6

1985 Team logo ....$4-$6
1986 Team logo ....$4-$6
1987 Team logo $6
1988 Team logo ....$4-$5
1989 Team logo ....$5-$6
1990 Team logo ....$4-$5
1991 Team logo ....$4-$5
1992 Team uniform ....$4-$5
1993 Team logo $4

Indians Media Guides

1936 Indian chief and 1936 ....$55-$75
1937 Indian chief and 1937 ....$50-$75
1938 Indian chief and 1938 ....$50-$75
1939 Indian chief and 1939 ....$50-$75
1940 Indian chief and 1940 ....$50-$75
1941 Indian chief and 1941 ....$50-$60
1942 Lou Boudreau ....$55-$60
1943 Lou Boudreau ....$50-$60
1944 Team mascot and year ....$40-$60
1945 Team mascot and year ....$40-$60
1946 Lou Boudreau ....$45-$60
1947 Team mascot ....$35-$60
1948 Team mascot with media ....$35-$150
1949 Team mascot ....$30-$60
1950 Team mascot at bat ....$30-$50
1951 Team mascot ....$30-$50
1952 Garcia, Wynn, Lemon, Feller ....$35-$50
1953 Press box and media ....$25-$50
1954 Al Rosen ....$35-$60
1955 ....$20-$40
1956 ....$20-$40
1957 Kirby Farrell ....$20-$40
1958 Bobby Bragan, Frank Lane ....$25-$40
1959 Rocky Colavito ....$25-$40
1960 Tito Francona ....$25-$40
1961 Jim Perry ....$17.50-$40
1962 Team mascot ....$15-$30
1963 Team uniform #20 ....$15-$30
1964 Team mascot ....$15-$30
1965 Team mascot ....$15-$20
1966 Baseball with feather ....$15-$20
1967 Cleveland Stadium ....$12-$17
1968 Autographed baseball ....$12-$17
1969 100th anniversary, mascot ....$12-$15
1970 Team mascot ....$12-$15
1971 Team hat, feather ....$12-$15
1972 Players in action $12
1973 Team logo ....$10-$12
1974 Team logo $10
1975 Frank Robinson ....$8-$10

**CLEVELAND INDIANS
1992 MEDIA GUIDE $6**

1976 Baseball with feather ....$8-$16
1977 Player hitting ....$7-$10
1978 Baseball, logo, glove ....$7-$12
1979 Team logo ....$6-$12
1980 Fireworks over stadium...................$6-$7
1981 Team logo.......................................$6-$7
1982 Cleveland Stadium ....$5-$7
1983 Team logo.......................................$5-$7
1984 Team memorabilia ....$5-$6
1985 Bert Blyleven, Andre Thornton
....$4-$6
1986 Past team uniforms...........................$4-$6
1987 Joe Carter ....$4-$6
1988 Indians uniform #88.........................$4-$5
1989 Candiotti, Farrell, Jones, Swindell
....$4-$5
1990 90 Years of Cleveland baseball ....$4-$5
1991 Jacoby, Jones, Alomar......................$4-$5
1992 60 years at Cleveland Stadium..........$4-$5
1993 Memorabilia collage $4

211

Mariners Media Guides

1977 Kingdome $20
1978 Baseball with team logo .... $7-$10
1979 Kingdome .... $6-$10
1980 Mariners equipment.......................... $6-$7
1981 Maury Wills..................................... $6-$7
1982 Team logo....................................... $5-$7
1983 Gaylord Perry, team equipment .... $5-$8
1984 Team logo....................................... $5-$7
1985 Beattie, Davis, Henderson, Langston
.... $4-$7
1986 Team memorabilia...................... $4-$6.50
1987 Team logo....................................... $4-$6
1988 Team bat .... $4-$5
1989 Kingdome, baseball, logo................. $4-$5
1990 A.L. baseballs, team logo .... $4-$5
1991 Highlights...................................... $4-$5
1992 Team logo....................................... $4-$5
1993 Team logo/Kingdome .... $4-$5

Mets Media Guides

1962 First year $100
1963 ....$50
1964 Shea Stadium ....$35-$50
1965 Mr. Met ....$20-$25
1966 Mass media ....$15-$25
1967 Donald Grant, George Weiss
....$20-$25
1968 Gil Hodges, crowd shot................$12-$22
1969 Gil Hodges ....$18-$25
1970 World Series ticket, action photos
....$12-$15
1971 Scoreboard $12
1972 Tom Seaver ....$12-$18
1973 Yogi Berra and pennant................$12-$15
1974 N.L. Champs flag $10
1975 Mets general managers ....$8-$10
1976 Joe Frazier...................................$8-$10
1977 Mets uniform #77.........................$7-$10
1978 Team logo, hat, glove.....................$7-$10

Mets Media Guides

1979 Willie Mays .... $6-$12
1980 Team logo .... $6-$7
1981 New York City, baseball .... $6-$7
1982 George Bamberger locker .... $5-$7
1983 Tom Seaver, others .... $5-$8
1984 Davey Johnson .... $5-$6
1985 Tom Seaver, Mets stars .... $4-$7
1986 R. Craig, Gooden, Shea Stadium
.... $6-$7
1987 World Series ring .... $4-$6
1988 Shea 25th anniversary .... $4-$5
1989 Frank Cashen, Howard Johnson
.... $4-$5.50
1990 Howard Johnson .... $4-$5
1991 Bud Harrelson .... $4-$5
1992 Bonilla, Murray, Saberhagen, Torborg
.... $4-$5
1993 Team uniform #93 ....$4

Orioles Media Guides

St. Louis Browns

1927 Name and 1927 .... $80-$150
1928 Name and 1928 .... $75-$125
1929 .... $75-$125
1930 .... $75-$125
1931 Sportsman's Park .... $70-$125
1932 Sportsman's Park .... $70-$100
1933 Sportsman's Park .... $70-$100
1934 .... $65-$100
1935 .... $65-$100
1936 Rogers Hornsby .... $75-$80
1937 Team logo .... $60-$75
1938 .... $60-$75
1939 .... $60-$75
1940 Fred Haney .... $55-$75
1941 Statue and 1941 .... $55-$60
1942 .... $55-$60
1943 Team logo .... $50-$60
1944 .... $50-$70
1945 .... $50-$60
1946 Team logo .... $45-$60
1947 Baseball, logo .... $45-$60
1948 Meet the Brownies .... $40-$60
1949 .... $40-$60
1950 Team logo .... $30-$50
1951 Team logo .... $30-$50
1952 Team mascot .... $25-$50
1953 Team mascot .... $25-$50

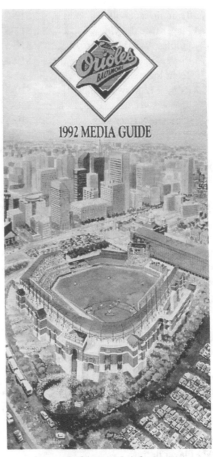

1992 MEDIA GUIDE

Baltimore Orioles

1954 Team mascot .... $45-$75
1955 Team mascot .... $25-$50
1956 Team mascot .... $25-$45
1957 Team mascot .... $25-$40
1958 Team mascot .... $20-$35
1959 Team mascot .... $20-$30
1960 Team mascot $20
1961 Team mascot .... $15-$20
1962 Team mascot .... $15-$20
1963 Team mascot .... $15-$20
1964 Team mascot .... $15-$20
1965 Hank Bauer .... $17.50-$20
1966 Team mascot .... $15-$20
1967 Dave McNally, Brooks Robinson
.... $18-$20
1968 Memorial Stadium .... $12-$20
1969 View from press box .... $12-$25
1970 Orioles dugout .... $12-$20
1971 World Series celebration .... $12-$20

1972 Team mascot with pennants .... $12-$15
1973 Player face drawing...................... $12-$15
1974 Orioles Award Winners .... $10-$15
1975 Players in action .... $10-$15
1976 Team logo $10
1977 Palmer, L. May, Belanger............. $10-$12
1978 Earl Weaver .... $10-$12
1979 25th anniversary hats.................... $10-$12
1980 Players celebrating .... $6-$7
1981 Orioles locker room....................... $6-$7
1982 Team logo and mascot..................... $6-$8
1983 Frank and Brooks Robinson..................$8
1984 World Series celebration .... $4-$6
1985 Bumbry, Palmer, Singleton .... $4-$7
1986 Eddie Murray, Cal Ripken............... $4-$7
1987 Cal Ripken Sr. .... $4-$6
1988 Team logo....................................... $4-$5
1989 New team uniforms .... $4-$5
1990 1989 highlights................................ $4-$5
1991 Team stadium drawing .... $4-$5
1992 Team stadium .... $4-$5
1993 Team stadium .... $4-$5

Padres Media Guides

1969 Preston Gomez, stadium............... $25-$30
1970 Jack Murphy Stadium...........................$15
1971 Jack Murphy Stadium...........................$12
1972 Padres vs. Dodgers, July 3, 1971 ....$12
1973 Nate Colbert .... $10-$14
1974 Player hitting $10
1975 Players in action .... $8-$10
1976 Randy Jones.................................. $8-$10
1977 Randy Jones, Butch Metzger.......... $7-$10
1978 Batter, pitcher in action .... $7-$10
1979 Roger Craig, Padres stars .... $6-$10
1980 Jerry Coleman, Dave Winfield .... $6-$8
1981 Frank Howard, stadium .... $5-$8
1982 Dick Williams.................................. $5-$7
1983 Padres memorabilia.......................... $5-$7
1984 Team logo, Ray Kroc memorabilia
.... $6.50-$7
1985 N.L. Champions trophy .... $6-$7
1986 Team logo....................................... $4-$6
1987 Larry Bowa...................................... $4-$6
1988 Tony Gwynn, Benito Santiago .... $4-$6
1989 Team logo, stadium .... $4-$5
1990 Players in action .... $4-$5
1991 Padres uniform, ball, glove .... $4-$5
1992 All-Star Game .... $4-$5
1993 Gary Sheffield, Fred McGriff..............$4

1993 MEDIA GUIDE

Rangers Media Guides

1972 Team logo.................................... $15-$20
1973 Burke, Herzog, Short $15
1974 Billy Martin................................... $10-$15
1975 Hargrove, Jenkins, Martin............. $10-$14
1976 Toby Harrah, old-timers.................. $8-$10
1977 Team equipment, hat .... $8-$12
1978 Billy Hunter .... $7-$10
1979 Baseball and 1979 .... $7-$10
1980 Rangers catcher............................ $6-$10
1981 Fireworks over scoreboard................ $6-$7
1982 Baseball with logo............................ $5-$7
1983 Baseball glove .... $5-$7
1984 Buddy Bell, others .... $4-$6
1985 Team hat... $4-$6
1986 Arlington Stadium............................. $4-$6
1987 Bobby Valentine............................... $4-$6
1988 Team logo and baseball..................... $4-$5
1989 Rangers uniforms............................. $4-$7
1990 Home plate with team logo .... $4-$5

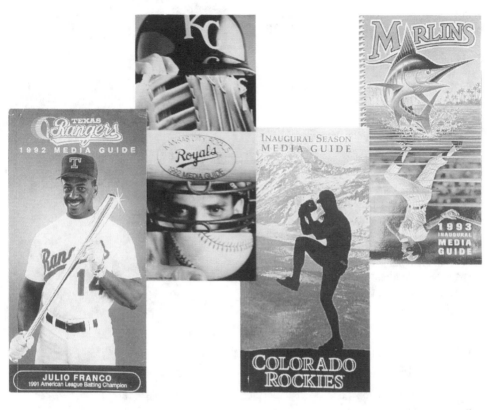

1991 Nolan Ryan.......................................$4-$5
1992 Julio Franco.....................................$4-$5
1993 Arlington Stadium..................................$4

Royals Media Guides

1969 Team logo.....................................$20-$30
1970 Player hitting...............................$15-$30
1971 Team bat rack.......................................$12
1972 Royals Stadium....................................$12
1973 Players in action...........................$10-$12
1974 Royals Stadium............................$10-$15
1975 Player hitting..................................$8-$10
1976 Whitey Herzog............................$10-$12
1977 Players in action...........................$10-$12
1978 Players hitting, pitching...............$10-$12
1979 1976-1978 A.L. West Champions
....$6-$10
1980 Team logo, scoreboard....................$7-$8
1981 Players in action, logo......................$5-$7

1982 Team logo, pitcher.............................$5-$7
1983 Statue of hitter..................................$5-$6
1984 George Brett and fans.......................$5-$7
1985 Scoreboard (A.L. West Champions)
....$6-$8
1986 World Series trophy.........................$4-$6
1987 Players in action...............................$4-$7
1988 Fireworks over scoreboard...............$4-$5
1989 Team equipment................................$4-$5
1990 Players in action...............................$4-$5
1991 George Brett......................................$4-$5
1992 Equipment...$4-$5
1993 25th anniversary....................................$4

Colorado Rockies

1993 Silhouette..$5

Florida Marlins

1993 Logo, player...$5

Phillies Media Guides

1930 Team logo....................................$75-$100
1931..$70-$100
1932 Team logo....................................$65-$125
1933 Phillies golden anniversary
....$60-$100
1934 Team logo....................................$60-$100
1935 Team logo....................................$55-$100
1936 Team logo.....................................$55-$75
1937 Team logo.....................................$50-$75
1938..$50-$75
1939..$50-$75
1940..$45-$75
1941 Player hitting.................................$45-$60
1942 Soldier with crossed bats.............$45-$60
1943..$40-$60
1944..$40-$60
1945..$40-$60
1946 Team logo, Shibe Park.................$35-$60
1947 Team logo, Shibe Park.................$35-$60
1948 Team logo, Shibe Park.................$35-$60
1949..$30-$70
1950..$30-$50
1951..$30-$50
1952 Shibe Park....................................$25-$50
1953 Player hitting.................................$25-$50
1954 Robin Roberts...............................$35-$50
1955 "Get Set To Go In '55".................$20-$50
1956 Crowd photo.................................$20-$40
1957 Crowd photo.................................$20-$40
1958 Crowd photo.................................$20-$40
1959 Team logo....................................$20-$40
1960 Team logo....................................$20-$40
1961 Team logo....................................$14-$40
1962..$15-$20
1963..$15-$20
1964 Team hat......................................$15-$20
1965 Team hat......................................$15-$20
1966 Team hat......................................$15-$20
1967 Team hat......................................$12-$17
1968 Team hat......................................$12-$17
1969 Team hat......................................$12-$15
1970 Phillies "P"..................................$12-$15
1971 Frank Luchessi.................................$12
1972 Team logo.......................................$12
1973 Steve Carlton/Cy Young Award
....$10-$18
1974 Players in action.............................$10
1975 Players in action..........................$8-$10
1976 Players in action..........................$8-$15
1977 Division champs pennant..............$7-$10

1992 MEDIA GUIDE

1978 Fireworks over stadium...................$7-$10
1979 Team logo.......................................$6-$12
1980 Team logo, baseball..............................$8
1981 World Series trophy..........................$6-$7
1982 Basket of baseballs...........................$5-$7
1983 100th anniversary logo.....................$5-$7
1984 N.L. Championship trophy...............$5-$6
1985 Hands holding bat.............................$4-$6
1986 Home plate with team logo..............$4-$6
1987 Mike Schmidt, trophies.....................$4-$7
1988 Steve Bedrosian, Mike Schmidt
....$4-$6.50
1989 Nick Leyva, Lee Thomas.................$4-$5
1990 Ashburn, Carlton, Roberts, Schmidt
....$4-$5.50
1991 Catcher's mask, baseball...................$4-$5
1992 Memorabilia collage.........................$4-$5
1993 Phillies league leaders..........................$4

Pirates Media Guides

1930 Pirate and 1930	$75-$100
1931 Pirate and 1931	$65-$100
1932 Pirate and 1932	$65-$125
1933 Pirate and 1933	$60-$100
1934 Pirate and 1934	$60-$100
1935 Pirate and 1935	$55-$100
1936 Pirate and 1936	$55-$75
1937 Pirate and 1937	$50-$75
1938 Pirate and 1938	$50-$75
1939 100th anniversary, Pirate	$50-$75
1940 Pirate and 1940	$45-$75
1941 Pirate and 1941	$45-$60
1942 Pirate, Remember Pearl Harbor	$45-$60
1943 Pirate, Buy War Bonds, Stamps	$40-$60
1944 Pirate and 1944	$40-$60
1945 Pirate and 1945	$40-$60
1946 Pirate, Buy Victory Bonds	$35-$60
1947 Billy Herman	$40-$60
1948 William Meyer	$40-$60
1949 40th anniversary	$30-$60
1950 Baseballs	$30-$50
1951 Logo and 1951	$30-$50
1952 Baseball and 1952	$25-$50
1953 Fred Haney	$25-$50
1954 Honus Wagner statue	$40-$50
1955 Baseball diamond and 1955	$20-$50
1956 Pirate cartoon	$20-$40
1957 Pirate cartoon	$20-$40
1958 Danny Murtaugh	$25-$40
1959 Pirate cartoon	$20-$40
1960 Pirate cartoon	$20-$45
1961 Pirate cartoon	$15-$40
1962 Pitcher	$15-$30
1963 Baseballs	$15-$30
1964 Logo and 1964	$15-$30
1965 Harry Walker	$18-$20
1966 Pirate cartoon	$15-$20
1967 Pirate cartoon	$12-$17
1968 Larry Shepard and coaches	$12-$17
1969 100th anniversary, Forbes	$12-$15
1970 Three River Stadium model	$12-$17
1971 Danny Murtaugh	$12-$15
1972 World Series celebration	$12-$15
1973 Clemente memorial	$10-$25
1974 Three Rivers Stadium	$10-$12
1975 Championship Stars, logo	$10-$12
1976 Rennie Stennett	$8-$10
1977 Players in action	$7-$10

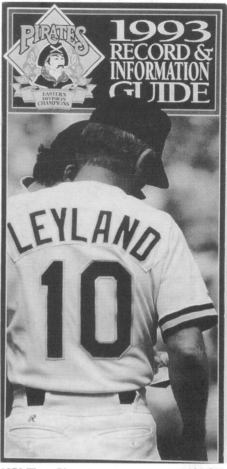

1978 Three Pirates	$7-$10
1979 Team uniform	$8-$10
1980 Willie Stargell	$6-$9
1981 Team logo	$6-$7
1982 Team hat	$5-$7
1983 Team logo	$5-$7
1984 Bill Madlock	$5-$6
1985 Tony Pena	$4-$6
1986 Three Rivers Stadium	$4-$6
1987 100th anniversary logo	$4-$6
1988 Pirates memorabilia	$4-$5
1989 Bonilla, LaValliere, Van Slyke	$4-$6
1990 Bonds, Bonilla, Drabek, Van Slyke	$4-$5.50
1991 N.L. Champions, logo	$4-$5
1992 Doug Drabek, Don Slaught	$4-$5
1993 Jim Leyland	$4

Reds Media Guides

1930 Team logo .... $65-$100
1931 Team logo .... $60-$100
1932 Team logo .... $60-$100
1933 .... $60-$100
1934 Cincinnati Reds .... $55-$100
1935 Team logo .... $55-$100
1936 Team logo .... $55-$75
1937 Team logo .... $50-$75
1938 Bill McKechnie .... $50-$75
1939 1869 Reds .... $50-$85
1940 Team logo .... $45-$85
1941 Baseball, champions pennant
.... $45-$60
1942 Team logo, eagle .... $45-$60
1943 Team logo, eagle .... $40-$60
1944 Team logo, hitter .... $40-$60
1945 Baseball, eagle .... $40-$60
1946 Catcher and batter .... $35-$60
1947 Baseball and eagle .... $35-$60
1948 Team logo, batter .... $35-$60
1949 City, team logo .... $30-$60
1950 Cartoon sportswriter .... $30-$50
1951 75th anniversary logo .... $30-$50
1952 Team logo, eagle .... $25-$50
1953 .... $25-$50
1954 .... $25-$50
1955 Team mascot .... $20-$50
1956 Birdie Tebbetts .... $20-$40
1957 Schedule .... $20-$40
1958 Team mascot batting .... $20-$40
1959 Mayo Smith .... $20-$40
1960 Fred Hutchinson .... $20-$40
1961 Fred Hutchinson, Bill DeWitt
.... $18-$45
1962 Team mascot .... $15-$30
1963 Team mascot .... $15-$30
1964 Team mascot .... $15-$30
1965 Team mascot .... $15-$20
1966 Team mascot .... $15-$20
1967 .... $12-$17
1968 .... $12-$17
1969 100th anniversary logo .... $12-$17
1970 N.L. hats .... $12-$20
1971 .... $12
1972 Baseball field .... $12-$15
1973 Sparky Anderson .... $12-$15
1974 Jack Billingham, Don Gullett $10
1975 Johnny Bench .... $12-$14
1976 Joe Morgan, MVP Trophy $12
1977 Johnny Bench .... $7-$14

1992 CINCINNATI REDS MEDIA GUIDE

$6

1978 George Foster .... $7-$10
1979 John McNamara .... $9-$10
1980 Riverfront Stadium .... $6-$7
1981 Players in action .... $6-$7
1982 Team uniform .... $6-$7
1983 Russ Nixon .... $5-$7
1984 Team logo .... $5-$6
1985 Riverfront Stadium .... $5-$6
1986 Pete Rose .... $4-$7.50
1987 N.L. logos .... $4-$6
1988 All-Star Game logo .... $4-$5
1989 Autographed bats .... $4-$5
1990 Lou Piniella .... $5-$6
1991 World Series trophy .... $3-$5
1992 Equipment .... $3-$5
1993 Reds locker .... $3-$5

Red Sox Media Guides

1939 Jimmie Foxx .... $65-$70
1940 Team logo .... $45-$65

$6.00

1941 Fenway Park .... $45-$60
1942 Baseball bats and 1942 .... $45-$60
1943 Tufts College batting cage .... $40-$60
1944 .... $40-$60
1945 Name and 1945 .... $40-$60
1946 Player in action .... $35-$70
1947 World Series pennant .... $35-$60
1948 Joe McCarthy .... $45-$60
1949 .... $30-$60
1950 Team mascot .... $30-$50
1951 Old-timer, current player .... $30-$50
1952 Fenway Park .... $25-$50
1953 Team logo .... $25-$50
1954 Team logo .... $25-$50
1955 Team logo .... $25-$50
1956 Name and 1956 .... $20-$40
1957 Player in action .... $20-$40
1958 Red Sox media .... $20-$40
1959 Player in mirror .... $20-$40
1960 Player on horse .... $20-$40

1961 Baseball glove, ball .... $15-$40
1962 Carl Yastrzemski, others .... $22.50-$30
1963 Johnny Pesky .... $15-$30
1964 Team logo .... $15-$30
1965 Team logo .... $15-$20
1966 Showerhead, team logo .... $15-$20
1967 Team logo .... $17-$18
1968 A.L. Championship pennant .... $12-$17
1969 100th anniversary .... $12-$15
1970 Fenway Park .... $12-$15
1971 Red Sox stars $12
1972 Cheering fan $12
1973 Player in action .... $10-$12
1974 Darrell Johnson $10
1975 Fenway Park $10
1976 A.L. Championship pennant .... $7-$10
1977 Don Zimmer .... $7-$12
1978 Carl Yastrzemski, Jim Rice .... $7-$15
1979 Jim Rice .... $6-$11
1980 Carl Yastrzemski .... $6-$12
1981 Ralph Houk .... $6-$7
1982 Ralph Houk and players .... $5-$7
1983 Dwight Evans, Bob Stanley .... $5-$7
1984 Wade Boggs, Jim Rice .... $5-$7
1985 Tony Armas .... $5-$6
1986 Boggs, Boyd, Buckner, Gedman $6
1987 Roger Clemens, John McNamara
.... $4-$7
1988 Dwight Evans, Roger Clemens $6
1989 Joe Morgan .... $4-$5
1990 Fenway Park $5
1991 Ellis Burks, Tony Pena .... $4-$5
1992 Roger Clemens, Butch Hobson .... $4-$5
1993 Red Sox baseball $4

Senators Media Guides

1933 Capitol and 1933 .... $80-$115
1934 Capitol and 1934 .... $80-$100
1935 Capitol and 1935 .... $75-$100
1936 Capitol and 1936 .... $75
1937 Capitol and 1937 .... $75
1938 Capitol and 1938 .... $70-$75
1939 Capitol and 1939 .... $70-$75
1940 Capitol and 1940 .... $70-$75
1941 Capitol and 1941 .... $60-$65
1942 Capitol and 1942 .... $60-$65
1943 Capitol and 1943 .... $60-$65
1944 Capitol and 1944 .... $60
1945 Capitol and 1945 .... $60
1946 Capitol and 1946 .... $60
1947 Capitol and 1947 .... $55-$60

1948 Capitol and 1948 .... $55-$60
1949 Capitol and 1949 .... $55-$60
1950 Capitol and 1950 .... $50
1951 Capitol and 1951 .... $50
1952 Capitol and 1952 .... $50
1953 Capitol, bat, baseball .... $45-$50
1954 Capitol, bat, baseball .... $45-$50
1955 Capitol, bat, baseball .... $45-$50
1956 Sportswriter $40
1957 Team mascot pitching............................ $40
1958 Golden anniversary of BBWAA.......... $40
1959 Mascot blowing out candles......... $35-$40
1960 Home run celebration................... $35-$40

Becomes Minnesota Twins

1961 Doherty, Quesada, Vernon............ $35-$40
1962 Stadium and team logo........................ $30
1963 Stadium and team logo........................ $30
1964 Stadium and team logo........................ $30
1965 Stadium and team logo........................ $30
1966 Stadium and team logo................ $20-$25
1967 Pitcher and baseball...................... $17-$25
1968 Batter and baseball .... $17-$22
1969 Frank Howard............................... $15-$25
1970 Bob Short, Ted Williams .... $15-$25
1971 Stadium and team logo................ $12-$18

Becomes Texas Rangers

Twins Media Guides

1961 Metropolitan Stadium drawing..... $30-$50
1962 Metropolitan Stadium.................. $20-$30
1963 Player hitting .... $15-$30
1964 Baseball and 1964 .... $15-$30
1965 All-Star Game hosts .... $15-$30
1966 Player fielding .... $15-$20
1967 Twins uniform .... $12-$17
1968 Pitcher throwing .... $12-$17
1969 Metropolitan Stadium.................. $12-$20
1970 Rod Carew, Twins stars .... $16-$20
1971 Jim Perry $12
1972 Minnesota media $12
1973 Rod Carew.. $15
1974 Baseballs.. $10
1975 Rod Carew, Ty Cobb .... $8-$15
1976 Rod Carew, Harmon Killebrew, others
.... $8-$14
1977 Old press guide covers .... $7-$10
1978 Rod Carew...................................... $7-$12
1979 Metropolitan Stadium.................... $6-$12
1980 Twins baseball cards........................ $6-$7
1981 Twins bats, hats, uniforms............... $6-$7

1982 Metrodome....................................... $5-$7
1983 Kent Hrbek...................................... $5-$7
1984 Twins uniforms .... $5-$6
1985 All-Star Game logo.......................... $4-$6
1986 25th anniversary logo...................... $4-$6
1987 Gary Gaetti, Kirby Puckett $6
1988 World Series trophy .... $4-$5
1989 Kirby Puckett, Frank Viola .... $4-$6
1990 Carew, Oliva, Puckett .... $4-$5
1991 Drawings of Carew, Killebrew .... $5-$6
1992 Celebration, World Series trophy
.... $4-$5
1993 Kirby Puckett $4

Tigers Media Guides

1933 Tiger head and 1933................... $60-$100
1934 Tiger head and 1934................... $55-$110
1935 Tiger head and 1935................... $55-$115
1936 Tiger head and 1936..................... $55-$75
1937... $50-$75
1938 Tiger head and 1938..................... $50-$75
1939 Tiger head and 1939..................... $50-$75
1940... $45-$85
1941 Briggs Stadium .... $45-$60
1942 Flag over Briggs Stadium .... $45-$60
1943 Tiger head and 1943..................... $40-$60
1944 Tiger head and 1944..................... $40-$60
1945 Tiger head and 1945..................... $40-$70

1946 Tiger head and 1946 .... $35-$60
1947 Tiger head and 1947 .... $35-$60
1948 Tiger head and 1948 .... $35-$60
1949 Tiger head and 1949 .... $30-$60
1950 Tiger head and 1950 .... $30-$50
1951 Tiger head and 1951 .... $30-$50
1952 Tiger head and 1952 .... $25-$50
1953 Tiger head and 1953 .... $25-$50
1954 Tiger head and 1954 .... $25-$50
1955 Tiger head and 1955 .... $20-$50
1956 Ray Boone, Al Kaline .... $25-$40
1957 Frank Lary .... $20-$40

1958 Jim Bunning .... $25-$40
1959 Tiger head and 1959 .... $20-$40
1960 Tiger head and 1960 .... $20-$40
1961 Tiger Stadium .... $15-$40
1962 Players and team logo .... $15-$30
1963 Team logo .... $15-$30
1964 Team logo .... $15-$30
1965 Team logo .... $15-$20
1966 Team mascot and 1966 .... $15-$20
1967 Team mascot and 1967 .... $12-$20
1968 Team mascot and 1968 .... $12-$25
1969 Team mascot .... $12-$15
1970 Team mascot fielding .... $12-$15
1971 Team mascot throwing .... $12-$15
1972 Team mascot fielding .... $12-$17
1973 Team mascot fielding .... $10-$12
1974 Team mascot sliding .... $10-$12
1975 Team mascot in field .... $8-$10
1976 Team mascot pitching .... $8-$10
1977 Team mascot catching .... $7-$10
1978 Team mascot hitting .... $7-$12
1979 Team logo and 1979 .... $6-$10
1980 Team mascot in action .... $6-$10
1981 Tigerjumping .... $6-$7
1982 Team logo .... $5-$7
1983 Greenberg and Gehringer uniforms
.... $5-$8
1984 Team mascot boxing $6
1985 World Series trophy, logo .... $4-$6
1986 Team mascot in stadium .... $4-$6
1987 Baseball and Tiger $6
1988 .... $4-$5
1989 "The Press Guide" and logo .... $4-$5
1990 Uniform "D" .... $4-$5
1991 "And Once Again" .... $4-$5
1992 Alan Trammell, Lou Whitaker
.... $4-$5
1993 Tiger greats $4

White Sox Media Guides

1933 Name and 1933 .... $60-$100
1934 Name and 1934 .... $55-$100
1935 Name and 1935 .... $55-$100
1936 Name and 1936 .... $55-$75
1937 Name and 1937 .... $50-$75
1938 Name and 1938 .... $50-$75
1939 Name and 1939 .... $50-$75
1940 Name and 1940 .... $45-$75
1941 Ted Lyons .... $50-$60
1942 Jimmy Dykes .... $45-$60
1943 Buy More War Bonds .... $40-$60

CHICAGO
WHITE SOX

1993

MEDIA GUIDE

1944 Back the attack .... $40-$60
1945 .... $40-$60
1946 Name and 1946 .... $35-$60
1947 Ted Lyons .... $40-$60
1948 Team mascot and 1948 .... $35-$60
1949 Team logo and 1949 .... $30-$60
1950 Luke Appling .... $35-$50
1951 Paul Richards .... $30-$50
1952 Carrasquel, Fox, Minoso, Rogovin
.... $30-$50
1953 Player in action .... $25-$50
1954 Team mascot .... $25-$50

1955 Team mascot .... $20-$50
1956 Team mascot .... $20-$50
1957 Team mascot .... $20-$50
1958 Team mascot .... $20-$50
1959 Team mascot .... $20-$60
1960 Team mascot .... $20-$40
1961 Name and 1961 .... $15-$40
1962 Player in action .... $15-$30
1963 Player in action .... $15-$30
1964 Player in action .... $15-$30
1965 Pitcher throwing .... $15-$20
1966 Batter hitting .... $15-$20
1967 Player in action .... $12-$17
1968 Hitter up to bat .... $12-$17
1969 Batter hitting .... $12-$15
1970 Fielder in action .... $12-$15
1971 Chuck Tanner $12
1972 Player in action $12
1973 Allen, Tanner, Wood .... $10-$14
1974 Team logo .... $10-$15
1975 A.L. 75th anniversary .... $8-$10
1976 Team logo .... $8-$10
1977 Team logo .... $7-$10
1978 Team logo, hitter .... $7-$12
1979 Don Kessinger .... $6-$10
1980 Fans in crowd .... $6-$7
1981 Pitcher in action .... $6-$7
1982 Team logo .... $6-$7
1983 Sportswriter equipment .... $7-$8
1984 Scoreboard, A.L. West Champs
.... $5-$6
1985 Comiskey Park .... $5-$6
1986 Aparicio, Appling, Guillen .... $4-$7
1987 New White Sox uniform #87 .... $4-$6
1988 Player in action .... $4-$5
1989 Former White Sox stars .... $4-$5
1990 Comiskey Park 80 years .... $4-$5
1991 Catcher's mask, uniform, bat .... $4-$5
1992 Team logo .... $4-$5
1993 Team logo .... $4-$5

Yankees Media Guides

1936 Joe McCarthy .... $70-$100
1937 Joe McCarthy .... $65-$100
1938 Joe McCarthy .... $65-$100
1939 Joe McCarthy .... $65-$100
1940 Joe McCarthy .... $60-$75
1941 Joe McCarthy .... $60-$65
1942 Joe McCarthy .... $60-$65
1943 .... $45-$65
1944 .... $45-$60

1955 Team logo and 1955.......................$20-$55
1956 Team logo and 1956.......................$20-$45
1957 Team logo and 1957.......................$20-$45
1958 Team logo and 1958.......................$20-$45
1959 Team logo and 1959.......................$20-$40
1960 Yankee Stadium.............................$20-$45
1961 Team logo and 1961.......................$15-$45
1962 Team logo and 1962.......................$15-$35
1963 Team logo and 1963.......................$15-$35
1964 Yogi Berra and logo.......................$18-$35
1965 Team logo..$15-$20
1966 Yankee Stadium and logo.............$15-$20
1967 Team logo and hitter.....................$12-$17
1968 Yankee Stadium.............................$12-$17
1969 Yankee glove and hat....................$12-$15
1970 Mel Stottlemyre.............................$12-$15
1971 Logo and players in action...................$12
1972 Bobby Murcer, Roy White............$12-$14
1973 Yankee Stadium.............................$10-$12
1974 Whitey Ford, Mickey Mantle
....$10-$18
1975 Bobby Bonds, Catfish Hunter.........$8-$15
1976 Yankee Stadium....................................$10
1977 Chris Chambliss, Thurman Munson
....$9-$12
1978 Reggie Jackson, Babe Ruth.............$9-$15
1979 Goose Gossage, Thurman Munson
....$6-$12
1980 Dick Howser, Gene Michael.............$6-$7
1981 Team logo...$7-$8
1982 Team logo...$5-$7
1983 Billy Martin with umpire..................$5-$8
1984 Righetti, Yankee no-hitters...............$5-$7
1985 Don Mattingly......................................$4-$7
1986 Guidry, Henderson, Mattingly, Niekro
....$4-$7
1987 Lou Piniella and team.........................$4-$6
1988 Team logo...$4-$5
1989 Dallas Green...$4-$5
1990 Baseball bat and ball..........................$4-$5
1991 Maas, Mattingly, Meulens, Sax
....$4-$5
1992 A tradition of great moments............$4-$5
1993 Collage..$4

1945 Victory "V" and 1945................... $40-$60
1946 Team logo and 1946...................... $40-$60
1947 Team logo and 1947..................... $35-$65
1948 Team logo and 1948..................... $35-$60
1949 Team logo and 1949..................... $30-$65
1950 Team logo and 1950..................... $30-$55
1951 Team logo and 1950..................... $30-$55
1952 Team logo and 1952..................... $25-$55
1953 Team logo and 1953..................... $25-$55
1954 Team logo and 1954..................... $25-$50

Programs

World Series programs

1903
Pittsburgh $25,000-$35,000
Boston $20,000-$30,000

1905
Philadelphia $12,000-$20,000
New York Giants $12,000-$23,000

1906
Chicago Cubs $12,000-$15,000
Chicago White Sox $12,000-$16,000

1907
Detroit $10,000-$14,000
Chicago Cubs $10,000-$14,000

1908
Detroit $8,000-$12,000
Chicago Cubs $8,000-$12,500

1909
Detroit $8,000-$10,000
Pittsburgh $8,000-$12,000

1910
Chicago Cubs $5,000-$7,000
Philadelphia $5,000-$6,500

1911
Philadelphia $5,000-$6,000
New York Giants $3,500-$5,000

1912
New York Giants $3,000-$5,000
Boston Red Sox $3,500-$4,500

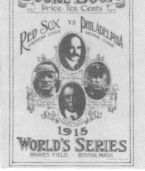

1913
New York Giants $3,000-$4,000
Philadelphia $3,000-$4,500

1914
Boston Braves $2,000-$3,000
Philadelphia $2,000-$3,000

1915
Philadelphia $2,500-$3,500
Boston Red Sox $3,000-$3,500

1916
Brooklyn $4,000-$6,000
Boston Red Sox $3,000-$4,500

1917
New York Giants $2,500-$3,000
Chicago $3,500-$4,500

1918
Boston Red Sox $5,000-$5,500
Chicago Cubs $4,000-$5,000

1919
Cincinnati $3,000-$6,000
Chicago $5,000-$7,000

1920
Brooklyn $3,500-$4,500
Cleveland $3,000-$4,000

1921
New York Yankees $2,000-$3,250
New York Giants $2,000-$3,250

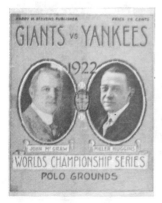

1922
New York Yankees $2,000-$2,750
New York Giants $2,000-$2,750

1923
New York Yankees $2,000-$4,000
New York Giants $2,000-$3,000

1924
New York Giants $2,000-$3,000
Washington $1,000-$2,000

1925
Pittsburgh $3,000-$4,000
Washington $700-$1,000

1926
St. Louis $800-$1,750
New York Yankees $600-$1,500

1927
Pittsburgh $3,000-$4,000
New York Yankees $2,000-$3,000

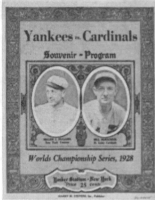

1928
St. Louis $1,000-$1,500
New York Yankees $1,500-$2,750

1929
Chicago Cubs $750-$1,000
Philadelphia $800-$1,250

1930
St. Louis $600-$800
Philadelphia $750-$800

1931
St. Louis $500-$750
Philadelphia $500-$750

1932
Chicago Cubs $600-$1,000
New York Yankees $1,000-$1,250

1933
New York Giants $500-$850
Washington $600-$700

1934
St. Louis $350-$500
Detroit $450-$550

1935
Chicago Cubs $450-$500
Detroit $500-$600

1936
New York Giants $375-$400
New York Yankees $300-$400

227

1937
New York Giants $350-$375
New York Yankees $350-$375

1938
Chicago Cubs $350-$425
New York Yankees $350-$425

1939
Cincinnati Reds $350-$425
New York Yankees $300-$350

1940
Cincinnati $300-$350
Detroit $275-$325

1941
Brooklyn $325-$475
New York Yankees $250-$300

1942
St. Louis $200-$250
New York Yankees $150-$250

1943
St. Louis $200-$250
New York Yankees $200-$250

1944
St. Louis Cardinals $200-$300
St. Louis Browns $250-$325

1945
Chicago Cubs $150-$200
Detroit $250-$350

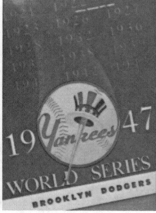

1946
St. Louis $175-$200
Boston $175-$200

1947
Brooklyn $250-$300
New York Yankees $225-$250

1948
Boston $175-$200
Cleveland $75-$150

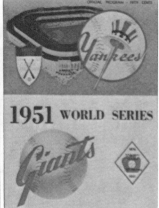

1949
Brooklyn $200-$250
New York Yankees $175-$200

1950
Philadelphia $125-$175
New York Yankees $150-$200

1951
New York Giants $150-$225
New York Yankees $150-$225

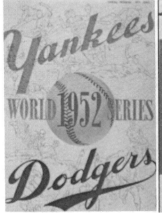

1952
Brooklyn $200-$275
New York Yankees $150-$200

1953
Brooklyn $150-$200
New York Yankees $125-$175

1954
New York Giants $150-$200
Cleveland $125-$200

1955
Brooklyn $200-$275
New York Yankees $150-$225

1956
Brooklyn $150-$250
New York Yankees $125-$200

1957
Milwaukee $100-$150
New York Yankees $75-$100

1958
Milwaukee $75-$150
New York Yankees $75-$150

1959
Los Angeles $75-$125
Chicago $100-$150

1960
Pittsburgh $100-$125
New York Yankees $75-$100

1961
Cincinnati $100-$125
New York Yankees $125-$150

1962
San Francisco Giants $125-$200
New York Yankees $75-$100

1963
Los Angeles $40-$60
New York Yankees $60-$75

1964
St. Louis $100-$125
New York Yankees $60-$75

1965
Los Angeles $30-$40
Minnesota $75-$100

1966
Los Angeles $40-$50
Baltimore $75-$125

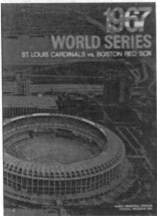

1967
St. Louis $100-$125
Boston $100-$125

1968
St. Louis $100-$125
Detroit $125-$200

1969
New York Mets $125-$150
Baltimore $50-$70

1970
Cincinnati $50-$75
Baltimore $30-$50

1971
Pittsburgh $50-$100
Baltimore $25-$50

1972
Cincinnati $50-$75
Oakland $60-$75

Programs

1973
New York Mets $20-$30
Oakland $50-$75

1974
Los Angeles $35-$60
Oakland $35-$60

1975
Cincinnati $25-$50
Boston $25-$50

1976
Cincinnati $20-$40
New York Yankees $20-$40

1977
Los Angeles $15-$25
New York Yankees $15-$40

1978
Los Angeles $15-$20
New York Yankees $15-$35

1979
Pittsburgh $15-$20
Baltimore $15-$20

1980
Philadelphia $10-$15
Kansas City $15-$30

1981
Los Angeles $10-$18
New York Yankees $10-$20

World Series Programs

1982
St. Louis $15-$25
Milwaukee $15-$25

1983
Philadelphia $12-$15
Baltimore $10-$12

1984
San Diego $10-$15
Detroit $10-$15

1985
Kansas City $10-$15
St. Louis $10-$15

1986
New York Mets $10-$15
Boston $10-$15

1987
St. Louis $10-$15
Minnesota $10-$15

1988
Oakland $10-$15
Los Angeles $10-$15

1989
San Francisco $10-$15
Oakland $10-$15

1990
Cincinnati $10-$15
Oakland $10-$15

1991
Atlanta $10-$12
Minnesota $10-$12

1992
Toronto $10-$12
Atlanta $10-$12

1993
Toronto $10
Philadelphia $10

The Pittsburgh Pirates played the Cincinnati Reds in the 1974 National League Championship Series.

World Series programs

World Series programs have been published every year since 1903, except for in 1904, when none were printed. A different program, each full of statistics, pictures, biographies and having special covers, was offered for both teams in the series until 1974. Since that time the programs have been a joint effort of the teams and have been distributed by Major League Promotion Corp. Robert D. Opie, a publisher from San Jose, Calif., reprinted classic programs in 1981 in his The Great World Series Program Collection. The programs' print runs are limited to 1,000 each. This information, and edition number, along with the indication that the program is a reprint, is contained within one of the last pages of the program. These programs generally can be purchased for between $10 to $20. The price range for original World Series programs in Excellent condition is from $10 to $15 for issues from the 1980s and 1990s, to $25,000-$35,000 for a 1903 Pittsburgh program and $20,000-$30,000 for a 1903 Boston program. Programs for the teams which win the series generally are more valuable than those for the losers. World Series programs generally command higher prices compared to those from All-Star games, regular season games, record-breaking games and playoff games. The best programs are not torn or faded, unscored, and have the original inserts.

American League
Championship programs

1969 Baltimore	$50-$75
1969 Minnesota	$60-$125
1970 Baltimore	$25-$50
1970 Minnesota	$100-$150
1971 Baltimore	$20-$50
1971 Oakland	$20-$50
1972 Detroit	$85-$115
1972 Oakland	$20-$30
1973 Baltimore	$30-$40
1973 Oakland	$15-$25
1974 Baltimore	$15-$40
1974 Oakland	$325-$375
1975 Boston	$40-$60
1975 Oakland	$40-$60
1976 New York	$15-$25
1976 Kansas City	$5-$15
1977 New York	$12-$18
1977 Kansas City	$10-$20
1978 New York	$12-$20
1978 Kansas City	$10-$20
1979 Baltimore	$60-$85
1979 California	$5-$15
1980 New York	$10-$18
1980 Kansas City	$5-$15
1981 N.Y. at Oakland	$10-$20
1981 Oakland at N.Y.	$10-$20
1981 K.C. at Oakland	$10-$20
1981 Oakland at K.C.	$40-$60
1981 Milwaukee at N.Y.	$10-$20
1981 N.Y. at Milwaukee	$30-$50
1982 Milwaukee	$60-$85
1982 California	$5-$10
1983 Baltimore	$5-$15
1983 Chicago	$10-$20
1984 Detroit	$5-$10
1984 Kansas City	$10-$20
1985 Toronto	$25-$35
1985 Kansas City	$25-$35
1986 Boston	$5-$10
1986 California	$8-$20
1987 Detroit	$8-$20
1987 Minnesota	$10-$20
1988 Boston	$5-$10
1988 Oakland	$75-$125
1989 Toronto	$20-$30
1989 Oakland	$20-$30
1990 Boston	$20-$30
1990 Oakland	$20-$30
1991 Toronto	$20-$30
1991 Minnesota	$20-$30
1992 Toronto	$20-$30
1992 Oakland	$20-$30
1993 Toronto	$10-$20
1993 Chicago	$10-$20

National League
Championship programs

1969 New York	$75-$100
1969 Atlanta	$50-$75
1970 Pittsburgh	$30-$45
1970 Cincinnati	$40-$75
1971 Pittsburgh	$30-$50
1971 San Francisco	$300-$400
1972 Pittsburgh	$25-$50
1972 Cincinnati	$20-$30
1973 New York	$50-$85
1973 Cincinnati	$20-$25
1974 Pittsburgh	$15-$20
1974 Los Angeles	$150-$275
1975 Pittsburgh	$5-$15
1975 Cincinnati	$5-$15
1976 Philadelphia	$5-$15
1976 Cincinnati	$20-$60
1977 Philadelphia	$5-$15
1977 Los Angeles	$20-$60
1978 Philadelphia	$5-$12
1978 Los Angeles	$5-$15
1979 Pittsburgh	$5-$15
1979 Cincinnati	$10-$20
1980 Philadelphia	$10-$20
1980 Houston	$40-$50
1981 Houston at L.A.	$10-$20
1981 Philadelphia at Montreal	$15-$25
1981 Montreal at Philadelphia	$15-$25
1981 L.A. at Montreal	$30-$75
1981 Montreal at L.A.	$10-$35
1982 St. Louis	$10-$25
1982 Atlanta	$5-$15
1983 Philadelphia	$5-$15
1983 Los Angeles	$60-$85
1984 Chicago	$10-$20
1984 San Diego	$10-$25
1985 St. Louis	$10-$25
1985 Los Angeles	$40-$60
1986 Houston	$10-$20
1986 New York	$15-$30
1987 St. Louis	$5-$15
1987 San Francisco	$15-$30
1988 New York	$5-$15
1988 Los Angeles	$5-$15
1989 Chicago	$10-$20
1989 San Francisco	$10-$20
1990 Pittsburgh	$15-$30
1990 Cincinnati	$15-$30
1991 Pittsburgh	$10-$20
1991 Atlanta	$20-$40
1992 Pittsburgh	$5-$20
1992 Atlanta	$20-$40
1993 Philadelphia	$10-$20
1993 Atlanta	$10-$20

All-Star Game programs

1933 Chicago .... $1,900-$2,000	1956 Washington .... $125-$175	1975 Milwaukee .... $35-$65
1934 New York N.L........ $1,500-$3,200	1957 St. Louis .... $150-$225	1976 Philadelphia .... $20-$30
1935 Cleveland .... $450-$600	1958 Baltimore .... $175-$250	1977 New York A.L................. $10-$20
1936 Boston .... $3,250-$3,750	1959 Pittsburgh .... $150-$250	1978 San Diego........................ $30-$50
1937 Washington .... $600-$800	1959 Los Angeles .... $75-$125	1979 Seattle............................. $10-$25
1938 Cincinnati.................. $750-$1,000	1960 Kansas City .... $125-$175	1980 Los Angeles .... $25-$50
1939 New York A.L............. $800-$900	1960 New York A.L.............. $75-$125	1981 Cleveland .... $15-$30
1940 St. Louis........ $800-$900	1961 San Francisco .... $275-$400	1982 Montreal.......................... $25-$50
1941 Detroit.......................... $500-$800	1961 Boston .... $450-$550	1983 Chicago A.L.................... $10-$20
1942 New York N.L........ $4,250-$4,750	1962 Washington .... $100-$175	1984 San Francisco................. $5-$15
1943 Philadelphia .... $650-$750	1962 Chicago N.L................. $100-$150	1985 Minnesota......................... $5-$15
1944 Pittsburgh.............. $1,150-$1,350	1963 Cleveland .... $75-$125	1986 Houston .... $5-$15
1945 ....no game	1964 New York N.L.............. $175-$275	1987 Oakland........................... $10-$20
1946 Boston .... $900-$1,100	1965 Minnesota .... $60-$85	1988 Cincinnati....................... $10-$20
1947 Chicago N.L................ $325-$500	1966 St. Louis .... $75-$175	1989 California .... $10-$20
1948 St. Louis .... $375-$600	1967 California .... $100-$200	1990 Chicago .... $10-$20
1949 Brooklyn .... $900-$1,000	1968 Houston .... $75-$125	1991 Toronto........................... $10-$20
1950 Chicago A.L............... $375-$550	1969 Washington .... $60-$85	1992 San Diego....................... $10-$20
1951 Detroit.......................... $125-$175	1970 Cincinnati.................... $125-$175	1993 Baltimore .... $12-$15
1952 Philadelphia .... $125-$175	1971 Detroit.......................... $100-$200	
1953 Cincinnati.................... $175-$300	1972 Atlanta............................. $20-$40	
1954 Cleveland .... $175-$275	1973 Kansas City .... $125-$175	
1955 Milwaukee .... $125-$175	1974 Pittsburgh .... $20-$40	

Regular programs

Many of those who have attended a major league game have purchased a souvenir program to keep score in. Others have purchased them as reading or historical material, or perhaps to have it autographed by a player during pregame warm-ups or after the game, which increases its value. Although unscored ones are preferred, a scored program, if done neatly, does have an intrinsic value; it provides a history of what happened for that particular game, and can trigger fond memories for fans who were there. Programs from games when a record was broken or a significant event happened command premium prices.

Program design and attractiveness add to the value of a program, especially the front cover. Condition is an important factor in determining a program's value. Most collectors want them to be in nice condition, hence it will have a higher value than one which is torn, stained or missing pages. Values given in this guide are for programs in Excellent condition, those which show little wear and tear. Other factors in determining a program's value include scarcity and rarity (teams have been issuing them since the 1850s, primarily as vehicles for advertising revenue).

In general, here are the price ranges for regular season programs, with exceptions in parentheses:

Year	Price	Exceptions
pre-1900	$500-$750	(only Braves, Cardinals, Dodgers, Giants, Indians, Orioles, Phillies, Pirates, Reds, Senators and Tigers have pre-1900s programs)
1900-1910	$200-$500	
1910-1919	$75-$200	(certain Cubs, Indians, Reds, Senators and Tigers programs can be up to $250)
1920-1929	$35-$75	(certain Indians, Phillies, Pirates, Reds, Senators, Tigers and Yankees programs can be up to $100; 1920 Dodgers and Indians programs can be up to $135 each; Giants programs from 1921-24 are $80-$85)
1930-1939	$20-$35	(certain Indians, Phillies, Pirates, Tigers and Braves programs can be up to $40; certain Reds, Yankees and Dodgers programs have reached $50; Cubs programs from 1930-40 are $35-$50; A's programs from 1930-31 can be up to $75)
1940-1949	$15-$25	(certain Dodgers programs are up to $30; certain Yankees programs have reached $35)
1950-1959	$10-$25	(Baltimore programs from 1954-56 are $55-$75; 1953 Milwaukee Braves programs are $75; 1958 San Francisco Giants programs are $35; 1969 Seattle Pilots programs are $55)
1960-1969	$5-$25	(Houston Colt 45's programs can be up to $35; 1962 New York Mets programs are $60; 1961 Los Angeles Angels programs are $40; 1961 Minnesota Twins programs are $35; 1969 Montreal Expos programs are $30)
1970-1979	$5-$7.50	(1970 Milwaukee Brewer programs are $25; 1972 Texas Rangers programs are $20; 1977 Seattle Mariners programs are $15; 1977 Toronto Blue Jays programs are $12)

Periodicals

The Sporting News

The first issue of *The Sporting News*, an eight-page newspaper, was published by Alfred Henry Spink of St. Louis in 1886. Although other professional and collegiate sports are covered, baseball has always been *TSN's* primary attraction, with each weekly issue devoting coverage to every major league team. Often called the Bible of Baseball, *The Sporting News* has included box scores of all major league games, and has offered several attractive baseball-related photographic and artistic covers throughout the years. In the late 1960s, *TSN* began using color on its covers.

During the 1970s, most front covers were devoted to baseball players, with collegiate and professional football and basketball following. This continued throughout the decade, until the 1980s, when the paper began featuring more than one sport on its covers.

Those who collect *TSNs*, which should have its pages intact and be in at least in Very Good condition, often seek those which feature one player, members of one team, or superstars. Some people collect issues from an entire memorable season, or try to collect as many issues as possible, for the publication's historical information.

Pete Rose, Steve Carlton, Reggie Jackson and Carl Yastrzemski are among the leaders of those who have appeared on the cover the most times. Rose, Yastrzemski, Willie Mays, Hank Aaron and Roberto Clemente remain among the most popular players pictured.

Many times collectors have the covers autographed and framed. *TSN* did not start putting mailing labels on the front cover until the Nov. 28, 1981, issue. However, the labels are positioned so as to not detract from the cover photo.

TSN has also devoted space to the sports memorabilia hobby, with occasional ads for sports books, publications, baseball cards and memorabilia, and baseball card shows.

Common issues from the 1910s in Very Good condition sell for about $50 each; all issues thereafter until the 1960s fall in a range from $10-$30. Issues from the 1970s-1990s generally sell for $15 or less.

Issues during the regular season (April-October), as do commemorative, Opening Day, All-Star and World Series and superstar issues, generally have higher prices than those from the off-season (November-March) and have more investment potential.

These superstars are among the leaders in number of times appearing on selected *TSN* covers in the 1940s-1990s (Prices are given for some of the higher-priced issues):

Hank Aaron — 10/10/56 ($50), 09/24/58, 06/03/59, 07/20/63, 10/12/63, 11/23/63, 04/25/64, 07/03/65, 05/23/70, 07/29/72, 04/20/74, 08/02/82

Joe DiMaggio — 11/29/34, 10/29/36, 03/25/37, 04/29/37 ($100, with Doerr, Mungo, Gehrig), 09/30/37, 11/25/37, 12/28/39, 07/18/40, 10/24/40, 11/13/41 ($100), 02/25/43, 04/01/43, 06/17/43, 05/04/44, 01/31/46, 01/15/47, 12/03/47, 02/16/49, 04/13/49 ($200, with Ted Williams), 04/20/49, 07/06/49, 09/07/49, 01/04/50, 12/19/51 ($100), 12/26/51, 03/12/52, 02/02/55, 07/04/56 ($100, with Ted Williams, Musial), 03/22/61

Mickey Mantle — 01/3/51 ($100), 04/04/51, 04/25/51 ($300), 10/22/52, 11/12/52, 04/29/53 ($100), 06/17/53, 07/01/53, 09/14/55, 06/13/56, 10/10/56, 11/14/56, 11/28/56, 01/02/57, 01/23/57, 01/08/58, 03/29/61, 06/28/61 ($100, with Maris), 07/12/61, 09/06/61, 09/27/61 ($100, with Maris, Ruth), 03/07/62, 07/21/62, 09/22/62, 03/16/63, 04/06/68

Roger Maris — 05/01/57, 05/25/60, 07/13/60, 08/31/60, 11/16/60, 06/28/61 ($100, with Mantle), 07/12/61, 09/06/61, 09/27/61 ($100, with Mantle, Ruth), 10/11/61, 11/22/61, 01/03/62, 02/28/62, 04/29/67, 10/12/68

Willie Mays - 08/15/51, 02/24/54, 07/07/54, 07/21/54, 09/15/54, 10/13/54 ($100, with Antonelli, Avila, Lemon), 01/05/55, 02/26/58, 09/24/58, 01/28/59, 01/20/60, 03/07/62, 07/21/62, 03/16/63, 05/02/64, 07/11/64, 10/30/65, 05/21/66, 03/01/69, 01/17/70, 07/25/70, 07/17/71, 10/06/73, 07/19/75, 10/08/84

Stan Musial — 02/05/42, 10/15/42, 11/04/43, 12/09/43, 07/13/44, 11/08/45, 09/25/46, 11/27/46, 01/01/47, 02/12/47, 03/05/47, 08/20/47, 06/02/48, 12/08/48, 08/03/49, 02/28/51, 03/14/51, 10/10/51 ($200, with Feller, Fain, Roe), 11/14/51, 01/02/52, 05/12/54, 06/23/54, 07/13/55, 03/28/56, 07/04/56 ($100, with DiMaggio, Williams), 07/11/56 ($100), 02/06/57, 06/19/57, 07/10/57, 10/09/57, 05/14/58, 09/24/58, 11/05/58, 12/09/59, 09/28/60, 03/07/62, 11/24/62, 10/12/63, 10/07/67, 07/19/75, 06/20/81

Jackie Robinson — 09/11/46, 09/17/47 ($75), 11/23/49, 02/01/50, 04/19/50, 05/30/51, 12/10/52, 12/19/56, 01/16/57

Pete Rose — 10/26/63 ($30), 08/21/65, 04/20/68, 07/18/70, 07/28/73, 10/23/76, 5/20/78, 04/21/79, 07/21/79, 10/20/79, 12/29/79, 10/04/80, 06/20/81, 04/10/82, 07/25/83, 04/02/84, 09/16/85, 01/06/86, 05/26/86, 05/18/87, 04/24/89, 09/04/89, 03/12/90

Babe Ruth — 10/06/32 ($350, with Gehrig), 12/24/36, 06/23/38, 07/14/38, 10/13/38, 07/02/42, 08/13/42, 10/08/42, 10/28/43, 06/12/46, 04/23/47 ($300), 05/07/47, 03/24/48, 06/23/48 ($300), 08/25/48 ($500, death), 07/12/50, 07/26/50, 03/12/52, 09/26/56, 09/27/61, 04/20/74, 07/19/75, 07/09/84

Ted Williams — 04/13/39, 08/22/40, 06/19/41, 11/20/41, 01/01/42, 01/29/42, 12/31/42, 06/17/43, 01/31/46, 03/14/46, 05/23/46, 07/17/46, 09/18/46, 09/25/46, 11/20/46, 03/05/47, 12/31/47, 06/30/48, 04/13/49 ($200), 10/05/49, 11/30/49, 12/07/49, 12/28/49, 11/14/51, 08/05/53, 04/21/54, 07/04/56, 08/15/56, 02/20/57, 04/10/57, 05/15/57, 05/22/57, 07/10/57, 10/09/57, 01/01/58, 01/08/58, 08/27/58, 07/08/59, 12/09/59, 06/29/60, 08/17/60, 03/07/62, 01/22/66, 03/15/69, 07/19/75

The following is a list of covers with baseball players, or the main baseball story or photo contained within the issue (generally page 3):

THE SPORTING NEWS

1932

01/02/32 Bud Tinning	$30
01/14/32 Les Mallon	$30
01/21/32 Oscar Roettger	$30
01/28/32 Joyner White	$30
02/04/32 Horace Ford	$30
02/11/32 Lee Mangum	$30
02/18/32 Cubs prepare for Catalina Island	$30
02/25/32 Marv Olson, Bill Terry	$35
03/03/32 Sam Gibson, Waite Hoyt	$35
03/10/32 Edward Madjeski	$30
03/17/32 Leonard Koenecke	$30
03/24/32 William Brenzel	$30
03/31/32 Smead Jolley	$32
04/07/32 Burleigh Grimes	$35
04/14/32 Monte Weaver	$30
04/21/32 Harold Anderson	$30
04/28/32 Samuel Byrd	$30
05/05/32 William Rogell	$30
05/12/32 Walter Betts	$30
05/19/32 Ernie Lombardi	$35
05/26/32 Bill Dickey	$50
06/02/32 Fritz Knothe, Pie Traynor	$35
06/09/32 Jimmie Foxx, Bill Terry	$65
06/16/32 Mel Ott	$65
06/23/32 Dizzy Dean	$75
06/30/32 Lefty Gomez	$50
07/07/32 William Clark	$30
07/14/32 Larry French	$30
07/21/32 Oscar Melillo	$30
07/28/32 Lloyd Brown	$30
08/04/32 Earl Grace	$30
08/11/32 John Jones	$30
08/18/32 Ernie Orsatti	$30
08/25/32 Baxter Jordan	$30
09/01/32 Pepper Martin, Red Ruffing	$45
09/08/32 Tony Freitas	$30
09/15/32 Billy Herman, Joe Medwick	$35
09/22/32 Evar Swanson	$30
09/29/32 Yankees vs. Cubs	$150
10/06/32 Lou Gehrig, Babe Ruth	$350
10/13/32 Joe Cronin, Hal Smith	$32
10/20/32 Howard Maple	$30
10/27/32 John Hogan	$30
11/03/32 Del Bissonette	$30
11/10/32 Fred Lindstrom	$32
11/17/32 George Susce	$30
11/24/32 George Grantham	$30
12/01/32 Harry Taylor	$30
12/08/32 Babe Herman	$32
12/15/32 Travis Jackson	$32
12/22/32 Hal Rhyne	$30
12/29/32 Sam West	$30

1933

01/05/33 Henry Johnson $30
01/12/33 Gus Mancuso $30
01/19/33 Paul Andrews $30
01/26/33 Woody English..............................$30
02/02/33 Ossie Bluege $30
02/09/33 Joe Moore, Honus Wagner $35
02/16/33 Harry Rice $30
02/23/33 Carl Reynolds $30
03/02/33 Bud Parmelee $30
03/09/33 Bob Boken...................................$30
03/16/33 Beryl Richmond.............................$30
03/23/33 Hal Schumacher, Luke Appling.....$35
03/30/33 Don Brennan $30
04/06/33 Frank Reiber $30
04/13/33 Bill Werber..................................$30
04/20/33 Schoolboy Rowe $35
04/27/33 Clinton Brown $30
05/04/33 Carl Hubbell, Luke Appling $45
05/11/33 Pete Fox, Schoolboy Rowe.............$35
05/18/33 Russell Van Atta...........................$30
05/25/33 Wally Berger $32
06/01/33 Jake Miller...................................$30
06/08/33 Bobby Coombs $30
06/15/33 Harley Boss $30
06/22/33 Bill McAfee $30
06/29/33 John Jackson $30
07/06/33 First All-Star issue.......................$300
07/13/33 Chuck Fullis $30
07/20/33 Dib Williams $30
07/27/33 Rogers Hornsby, Sam Leslie $45
08/03/33 Dizzy Dean...................................$50
08/10/33 Carl Hubbell, Monte Pearson $40
08/17/33 D. Chapman (Nationals), Mel Ott.$40
08/24/33 Dolph Camilli $32
08/31/33 Dizzy and Paul Dean......................$50
09/07/33 Gus Mancuso $30
09/14/33 Travis Jackson...............................$32
09/21/33 Joey Kuhel $30
09/28/33 Al Lopez $32
10/05/33 World Series, Nationals/Giants ...$125
10/12/33 Giants team photo..........................$85
10/19/33 Babe Phelps $30
10/26/33 Fritz Ostermueller $30
11/02/33 Tony Piet $30
11/09/33 Red Rolfe $35
11/16/33 John Pomorski $30
11/23/33 Spud Davis....................................$30
11/30/33 George Steinback............................$30
12/07/33 Reggie Grabowski...........................$30
12/14/33 Raymond Prim $30
12/21/33 John Stone $30
12/28/33 Joseph Glenn $30

1934

01/04/34 Lou Chiozza $28

01/11/34 Pete Fox.......................................$28
01/18/34 Benny Tate $28
01/25/34 Glenn Spencer...............................$28
02/01/34 Forrest Twogood.............................$28
02/08/34 Edward Baecht...............................$28
02/15/34 Henry Johnson $28
02/22/34 Cy Blanton $28
03/01/34 Dick Ward....................................$28
03/08/34 John Krider $28
03/15/34 Giants' catchers.............................$28
03/22/34 Otho Nitcholas, Lee Stine $28
03/29/34 Al Lopez $30
04/05/34 Bill and George Dickey.................$40
04/12/34 Augie Galan..................................$28
04/19/34 Jack Rothrock $28
04/26/34 Johnny Pasek $28
05/03/34 Al Spohrer $28
05/10/34 Daniel MacFayden $28
05/17/34 Carl Reynolds $28
05/24/34 Joe Cascarella $28
05/31/34 Curt Davis $28
06/07/34 Linus Frey $28
06/14/34 Al Benton.....................................$28
06/21/34 William Urbanski............................$28
06/28/34 Billy Knickerbocker $28
07/05/34 Second All-Star issue...................$250
07/12/34 Johnny Broaca $28
07/19/34 Fred Ostermueller $28
07/26/34 Hal Lee $28
08/02/34 James Weaver $28
08/09/34 Alex Kampouris $28
08/16/34 Bill Myers.....................................$28
08/23/34 Zeke Bonura $28
08/30/34 Buzz Boyle....................................$28
09/06/34 Jo Jo White...................................$28
09/13/34 Leslie Tietje..................................$28
09/20/34 Johnny McCarthy $28
09/27/34 Beryl Richmond.............................$28
10/04/34 World Series, Tigers/Cardinals $25
10/11/34 Cards win World Series $75
10/18/34 George Hockette.............................$28
10/25/34 Pat Malone $28
11/01/34 Oscar Melillo $28
11/08/34 Lynford Lary..................................$28
11/15/34 George Watkins $28
11/22/34 Dick Bartell, Johnny Vergez..........$28
11/29/34 Joe DiMaggio, Al Todd $50
12/06/34 George Stumpf $28
12/13/34 Bill Dietrich..................................$28
12/20/34 Dutch Leonard $28
12/27/34 Marvin Duke $28

1935

01/03/35 Wally Moses...................................$28
01/10/35 Steve Sundra.................................$28
01/17/35 Roy Hansen $28

01/24/35 Hal Finney $28
01/31/35 Walter Millies $28
02/07/35 Francis Parker...............................$28
02/14/35 Larry Bettencourt $28
02/21/35 Edward Durham.............................$28
02/28/35 Eugene Schott $28
03/07/35 Leon Chagnon................................$28
03/14/35 Cliff Bolton $28
03/21/35 Todd Moore $28
03/28/35 Luke Sewell $28
04/04/35 Clyde Hatter $28
04/11/35 Babe Dahlgren...............................$28
04/18/35 Leslie Tietje $28
04/25/35 Tony Lazzeri $35
05/02/35 Joseph Stripp..................................$28
05/09/35 Johnny Whitehead $28
05/16/35 Dolph Camilli $30
05/23/35 Whitey Whitehead..........................$28
05/30/35 Bucky Harris, Bobo Newsom........$30
06/06/35 Whitey Wilshere.............................$28
06/13/35 Pep Young $28
06/20/35 Leon Chagnon................................$28
06/27/35 Tommy Bridges...............................$28
07/04/35 Cleveland Municipal Stadium All-Star issue..$50
07/11/35 Slick Castleman..............................$28
07/18/35 William Myers $28
07/25/35 Pete Fox $28
08/01/35 Roy Henshaw..................................$28
08/08/35 Lewis Riggs.....................................$28
08/15/35 Jose Gomez $28
08/22/35 Joe Vosmik......................................$28
08/29/35 Joseph Bowman..............................$28
09/05/35 Roxie Lawson..................................$28
09/12/35 Bud Hafey $28
0? 19/35 Ivy Andrews.....................................$28
09/26/35 Paul Derringer $28
10/03/35 World Series, Tigers/Cubs..............$95
10/10/35 Tigers win World Series.................$75
10/17/35 Hal Lee...$28
10/24/35 William McGee $28
10/31/35 Henry Coppola................................$28
11/07/35 Eugene Lillard.................................$28
11/14/35 Dennis Galehouse............................$28
11/21/35 Frank Pytlok...................................$28
11/28/35 Whitey Whitehead..........................$28
12/05/35 Donald McNair $28
12/12/35 Leroy Parmelee $28
12/19/35 Marcellus Monte Pearson $28
12/26/35 Monte Pearson................................$28

1936

01/02/36 George McQuinn $28
01/09/36 Frank Gabler...................................$28
01/16/36 Jack Knott $28
01/23/36 Roy Johnson $28

01/30/36 Babe Phelps....................................$28
02/06/36 Elburt Fletcher $28
02/13/36 James DeShong................................$28
02/20/36 Orville Jorgens...............................$28
02/27/36 Roy Hughes $28
03/05/36 Samuel Leslie $28
03/12/36 Rudy York $28
03/19/36 Alfred Todd.....................................$28
03/26/36 James Oglesby $28
04/02/36 Hank Greenberg $50
04/09/36 Lee John Norris $28
04/16/36 Albert Butcher $28
04/23/36 Charlie Grimm................................$28
04/30/36 Bill and George Dickey $45
05/07/36 Bill Terry $40
05/14/36 Dusty Rhodes $28
05/21/36 50th Anniversary issue....................$75
05/28/36 Frankie Frisch $40
06/04/36 Steve O'Neill $28
06/11/36 Stuart Martin..................................$28
06/18/36 Gabby Hartnett................................$35
06/25/36 Monte Pearson $28
07/02/36 All-Star Game issue........................$50
07/09/36 Augie Galan, Lou Gehrig...............$85
07/16/36 Jimmie Foxx, Lefty Grove $75
07/23/36 Dizzy Dean $45
07/30/36 Jimmie Foxx....................................$50
08/06/36 Tom Yawkey $28
08/13/36 Italo Chelini $28
08/20/36 Rip Radcliff.....................................$28
08/27/36 Women baseball fans $28
09/03/36 Jimmie Foxx, Joe McCarthy $50
09/10/36 Bob Feller $100
09/17/36 Branch Rickey................................$35
09/24/36 John McCarthy $28
10/01/36 Yankees (Gehrig) vs. Giants........$200
10/08/36 Lou Gehrig, Yankees win Series ...$50
10/15/36 James Mosolf....................................$28
10/22/36 Earl Averill, other Indians $35
10/29/36 Joe DiMaggio, family......................$25
11/05/36 Six comeback players $28
11/12/36 Burleigh Grimes..............................$32
11/19/36 American League officials...............$28
11/26/36 Lou Gehrig, Lefty Gomez...............$100
12/03/36 George Caster.................................$28
12/10/36 Winter meetings..............................$28
12/17/36 Cookie Lavagetto $30
12/24/36 Cronin, D. Dean, Ruth...................$30
12/31/36 Hubbell, McCarthy, Rickey, Vander Meer..$100

1937

01/07/37 Cuyler, Frisch, Goslin, others........$40
01/14/37 M. Cochrane, P. Dean, other injured players $35
01/21/37 Ival Goodman.................................$26

01/28/37 Paul Dean, Branch Rickey.............$30

02/04/37 Vince DiMaggio, other minor leaguers
....$28

02/11/37 P. Dean, Goslin, P. Waner.............$40

02/18/37 Gabby Hartnett $28

02/25/37 St. Louis Browns $28

03/04/37 Giants in Havana $28

03/11/37 Bob Feller......................................$75

03/18/37 A's, White Sox in spring training...$26

03/25/37 DiMaggio, Greenberg, others........$75

04/01/37 Jeff Heath $26

04/08/37 Pepper Martin $28

04/15/37 Roxie Lawson.................................$26

04/22/37 Hefty ballplayers...........................$36

04/29/37 DiMaggio, Doerr, Gehrig, Mungo
....$100

05/06/37 Mickey Cochrane, Hank Greenberg
....$50

05/13/37 Lamar Newsome $26

05/20/37 Gerry Walker $26

05/27/37 Cubs trainer $26

06/03/37 Lloyd Waner $35

06/10/37 Branch Rickey $28

06/17/37 Dick Bartell $26

06/24/37 Jimmy Dykes..................................$26

07/01/37 Griffith Stadium, All-Star issue ..$100

07/08/37 Paul Dean, Carl Hubbell...............$40

07/15/37 Gabby Hartnett, Charlie Root $28

07/22/37 Bucky Jordan.................................$26

07/29/37 Del Baker $26

08/05/37 Heinie Manush $28

08/12/37 John Wilson $26

08/19/37 Gabby Hartnett, Mel Ott $40

08/26/37 Jim Turner......................................$26

09/02/37 Rudy York $26

09/09/37 Joe Medwick $30

09/16/37 Kid fans..$26

09/23/37 Lou Gehrig.....................................$100

09/30/37 Body parts of the stars - DiMaggio's
eyes, Gehrig's legs, etc. $75

10/07/37 Yankees vs. Giants........................$50

10/14/37 Yankees win World Series............$100

10/21/37 Major League trainers $26

10/28/37 Ossie Vitt $26

11/04/37 Pirate bosses $26

11/11/37 Charlie Gehringer...........................$35

11/18/37 Dodger bosses $26

11/25/37 Joe DiMaggio, Tony Lazzeri..........$60

12/02/37 Indian bosses $26

12/09/37 Milwaukee winter meetings $26

12/16/37 More winter meetings.....................$26

12/23/37 Joe Medwick MVP celebration $30

12/30/37 J.T. Allen, Keller, Barrow $75

1938

01/06/38 Florida players at home.................$26

01/13/38 Like father, like son $26

01/20/38 Grover Alexander HOF election.... $35

01/27/38 Cecil Travis....................................$26

02/03/38 St. Petersburg players at home $26

02/10/38 August Mancuso $26

02/17/38 Joe Gordon, other rookies.............$35

02/24/38 Harry Danning...............................$26

03/03/38 Lefty Gomez $32

03/10/38 Cubs at Catalina Island $26

03/17/38 Indians in New Orleans.................$26

03/24/38 St. Louis Browns players...............$26

03/31/38 Spalding factory making balls $26

04/07/38 Vince DiMaggio, other Bees $28

04/14/38 Clay Bryant....................................$26

04/21/38 First pitch presidents, Taft to FDR
....$32

04/28/38 Bobby Doerr $30

05/05/38 Bobo Newsom $26

05/12/38 Bob Feller in action.......................$65

05/19/38 Three umpires................................$26

05/26/38 Bill Dickey.....................................$35

06/02/38 Tot Pressnell..................................$26

06/09/38 Casey Stengel managing Bees $45

06/16/38 Sam Chapman, Dick Siebert.........$26

06/23/38 Babe Ruth, Dodger coach $125

06/30/38 All-Star issue.................................$150

07/07/38 Crosley Field $26

07/14/38 John Gee, Babe Ruth.....................$25

07/21/38 Fastest ballplayers........................$26

07/28/38 Ballplayers' wives $28

08/04/38 Hank Greenberg $45

08/11/38 Ernie Lombardi $30

08/18/38 Major League musicians................$26

08/25/38 Joe Glenn.......................................$26

09/01/38 Lynn Myers $26

09/08/38 Vance Page $26

09/15/38 Miguel Gonzalez.............................$26

09/22/38 Red Ruffing....................................$35

09/29/38 Hank Greenberg $40

10/06/38 Yankee team picture $100

10/13/38 Faces in World Series crowd, with
Ruth $75

10/20/38 Major league scouts $26

10/27/38 Off-season hunting, with Jimmie
Foxx $35

11/03/38 Jimmie Foxx, Ernie Lombardi $35

11/10/38 Mack's 1913 $100,000 infield.........$28

11/17/38 PCL presidents...............................$26

11/24/38 Gehrig, Goslin, Simmons, vets $75

12/01/38 New Orleans winter meetings.......$26

12/08/38 MLB President Bramham $26

12/15/38 New Orleans winter meetings.......$26

12/22/38 New York winter meetings............$26

12/29/38 Giles, McCarthy, VanderMeer.......$50

1939

01/05/39 Dizzy Dean, Paul Waner $35
01/12/39 Baseball historians.........................$24
01/19/39 Triumvirate to rule Yankees..........$24
01/26/39 New owners of Yankees..................$24
02/02/39 Dizzy Trout $24
02/09/39 Off-season player homes...............$24
02/16/39 Tris Speaker $30
02/23/39 Rogers Hornsby, AA managers......$28
03/02/39 Hot Springs, Ariz., Giants camp....$24
03/09/39 Cubs at Catalina Island.................$24
03/16/39 Camilli, Lavagetto, Lazzeri $30
03/23/39 "Identify these Yankees" $24
03/30/39 Marty Marion $26
04/06/39 Browns photos $24
04/13/39 ROY favorites, with Ted Williams.$25
04/20/39 Bill McKechnie, Reds coaches $24
04/27/39 Zeke Bonura $24
05/04/39 Barney McCosky $24
05/11/39 Babe Dahlgren...............................$24
05/18/39 Traded Tigers, Browns...................$24
05/25/39 Lon Warneke and father $24
06/01/39 Cardinals manager.........................$24
06/08/39 Bill Cissell.....................................$24
06/15/39 Doubleday Field $24
06/22/39 Greenberg, Ruffing, Terry, others..$40
06/29/39 St. Louis Browns firemen $24
07/06/39 All-Star issue $50
07/13/39 Players with complicated names...$24
07/20/39 Johnny Mize $30
07/27/39 Donald McNair $24
08/03/39 Paul Derringer, Bucky Walters $24
08/10/39 Tony Cuccinello $24
08/17/39 Jimmie Dykes $24
08/24/39 Branch Rickey $26
08/31/39 Boudreau, Mack, Vitt.....................$28
09/07/39 Gabby Hartnett $26
09/14/39 Bob Feller $60
09/21/39 AA pitchers....................................$24
09/28/39 White Sox coaches.........................$24
10/05/39 World Series, Yankees/Reds.........$100
10/12/39 World Series fans $50
10/19/39 Yankee minor leaguers...................$24
10/26/39 Leo Durocher, the Waners $50
11/02/39 Minor league managers $24
11/09/39 Hank Greenberg.............................$26
11/16/39 Bullpen buddies.............................$24
11/23/39 Connie Mack alumni $26
11/30/39 Cincinnati winter meetings $24
12/07/39 Larry MacPhail $24
12/14/39 Winter meetings $24
12/21/39 Lefty Grove $28
12/28/39 DiMaggio, Durocher, MacPhail $25

1940

01/04/40 Redbirds on the rise $24

01/11/40 Yankee talent scouts $24
01/18/40 Judge Landis..................................$24
01/25/40 Reds to stay in pink $24
02/01/40 Judge Landis' minor league plan..$24
02/08/40 Bucky Walters $24
02/15/40 Anaheim photos $24
02/22/40 Winter Haven, Giants camp.........$24
02/29/40 Nationals training in Orlando.......$24
03/07/40 Dodgers in Belleair, Fla. $24
03/14/40 Reds in Tampa $24
03/21/40 Indians in Ft. Myers, Fla...............$24
03/28/40 Minor league managers $24
04/04/40 Hank Greenberg, others $30
04/11/40 Mickey Harris, Mickey Witek........$24
04/18/40 Gabby Hartnett..............................$26
04/25/40 Managers' wives.............................$24
05/02/40 Goose Goslin, others $26
05/09/40 Pee Wee Reese...............................$28
05/16/40 Hal Newhouser $28
05/23/40 Clyde Shown..................................$24
05/30/40 Athletics infield..............................$24
06/06/40 Vince DiMaggio, Paul Waner, others
....$26
06/13/40 Ballplayers' fathers........................$24
06/20/40 Ducky Medwick..............................$28
06/27/40 Rollie Hemsley $24
07/04/40 All-Star issue.................................$150
07/11/40 "Return Selections of All-Star Game
to Fans" $26
07/18/40 DiMaggio, Greenberg, Mize..........$85
07/25/40 Billy Southworth............................$24
08/01/40 Female fans' clothing.....................$24
08/08/40 Frankie Frisch $28
08/15/40 Barney McCosky $24
08/22/40 Ted Williams..................................$80
08/29/40 Learning from their dads $24
09/05/40 Gerald Priddy, Phil Rizzuto..........$30
09/12/40 Lou Novikoff, Lou Stringer $24
09/19/40 Texas League standouts $24
09/26/40 Jimmie Foxx...................................$40
10/03/40 Schoolboy Rowe, World Series.......$45
10/10/40 Reds win World Series...................$65
10/17/40 Jimmy Wilson.................................$24
10/24/40 Joe DiMaggio, Bob Feller $75
10/31/40 Dodgers of yesteryear $24
11/07/40 Hank Greenberg..............................$40
11/14/40 Frank McCormick $24
11/21/40 Ray Schalk.....................................$24
11/28/40 Atlanta winter meetings................$24
12/05/40 Charlie Grimm $24
12/12/40 Winter meetings..............................$24
12/19/40 Bob Feller $50
12/26/40 Debs Garms....................................$24

1941

01/02/41 Bob Feller, Phil Rizzuto, others $80

01/09/41 Bill Klem $24
01/16/41 Leading relief pitchers $24
01/23/41 William C. Tuttle $24
01/30/41 Ted Lyons $24
02/06/41 Cardinal newcomers $24
02/13/41 Bobo Newsom $24
02/20/41 Bobo Newsom, Al Simmons, others
....$25
02/27/41 Dodgers in Cuba $24
03/06/41 Giants in Miami $24
03/13/41 Reds in Tampa $24
03/20/41 Browns, Bees in San Antonio $24
03/27/41 Front-office families $24
04/03/41 Minor league managers $24
04/10/41 Ty Cobb, Frankie Frisch, others....$35
04/17/41 FDR throws out the first pitch $30
04/24/41 Bramham, Frick, Harridge, Landis
....$24
05/01/41 Bob Feller $45
05/08/41 Larry MacPhail, others $24
05/15/41 Baseball husbands and wives........$24
05/22/41 Connie Mack $30
05/29/41 Branch Rickey $28
06/05/41 Jimmy Dykes $24
06/12/41 Brooklyn Dodgers issue $65
06/19/41 Ted Williams $75
06/26/41 Appling, Boudreau, Reese, Rizzuto,
others $45
07/03/41 Briggs Stadium, All-Star issue......$85
07/10/41 Jeff Heath $24
07/17/41 Sportsman's Park scoreboard $24
07/24/41 Foxx, Gehrig, Mize, others............$80
07/31/41 300 game winners: Grove, Johnson,
Mathewson, Young, others...........................$50
08/07/41 Relief pitchers................................$24
08/14/41 Honus Lobert..................................$24
08/21/41 "All-Star Noisomatics" $24
08/28/41 Joe Gordon, Phil Rizzuto $30
09/04/41 Lon Warneke $24
09/11/41 Hal Chase $24
09/18/41 Hal Chase $24
09/25/41 Joe McCarthy $28
10/02/41 World Series issue $75
10/09/41 World Champion Yankees..............$75
10/16/41 Baker, Roffe, Traynor, others.........$28
10/23/41 John Wyatt $24
10/30/41 Minor league managers $24
11/06/41 Dolph Camilli...................................$24
11/13/41 Joe DiMaggio $100
11/20/41 Cobb, Hornsby, Jackson, T. Williams,
others $75
11/27/41 Jacksonville winter meetings $24
12/04/41 Lou Boudreau $35
12/11/41 Winter meetings $24
12/18/41 Hank Greenberg.............................$40
12/25/41 Rogers Hornsby $35

1942

01/01/42 Ted Williams, others $100
01/08/42 Mel Ott $40
01/15/42 Frisch, Gehringer, Hornsby, others
....$40
01/22/42 FDR to Landis: Keep Playing........$30
01/29/42 Ted Williams.................................$75
02/05/42 Musial, others as minor leaguers..$35
02/12/42 Jimmie Foxx, others $40
02/19/42 Mickey Cochrane, Bill Dickey, others
....$35
02/26/42 Bill McKechnie..............................$24
03/05/42 Yankee pitchers............................$24
03/12/42 Bruce Campbell.............................$24
03/19/42 Lou Boudreau, Burt Shotton.........$28
03/26/42 Mrs. McGraw, Mel Ott...................$35
04/02/42 Ty Cobb...$45
04/09/42 Nine major league coaches $24
04/16/42 FDR: "Play Ball" $28
04/23/42 Vern Stephens $24
04/30/42 Player-managers: Boudreau, Cronin,
Ott, others $35
05/07/42 Bob Feller, Hank Greenberg, others
....$40
05/14/42 Navy photos...................................$24
05/21/42 Four players wearing #3................$24
05/28/42 Bobby Doerr $26
06/04/42 Three Phillies with glasses............$24
06/11/42 Joe Gordon....................................$26
06/18/42 Edgar Smith $24
06/25/42 Paul Waner....................................$26
07/02/42 All-Star issue: Gehrig, Foxx, Ruth $50
07/09/42 Don Gutteridge $24
07/16/42 Players at new positions $24
07/23/42 Chet Laabs $24
07/30/42 Rollie Hemsley $24
08/06/42 Lou Boudrea, others $30
08/13/42 Hitting pitchers: Ruth, others.......$60
08/20/42 Headhunting cartoon......................$24
08/27/42 Lou Novikoff caricature $24
09/03/42 Reese, Rizzuto, others...................$30
09/10/42 Close plays....................................$24
09/17/42 James Sewell..................................$24
09/24/42 Joe Jackson $50
10/01/42 World Series issue, Joe McCarthy
....$100
10/08/42 Famous "Babes": Ruth, others $65
10/15/42 Stan Musial....................................$40
10/22/42 Ossie Bluege..................................$24
10/29/42 Mort Cooper $24
11/05/42 Branch Rickey $26
11/12/42 Bobo Newsom $24
11/19/42 Sam Breadon $24
11/26/42 Nick Altrock $24
12/03/42 Judge Landis $26
12/10/42 Al Schacht $24

12/17/42 Lefty Grove $28

12/24/42 Major leaguers' war efforts............$24

12/31/42 Southworth, Veeck, Williams, others $100

1943

01/07/43 Steve O'Neill....................................$22

01/14/43 Map of Northeastern U.S...............$22

01/21/43 Sylvester Goedde............................$22

01/28/43 Bob Feller in Navy uniform $40

02/04/43 Ty Cobb as WWI captain................$30

02/11/43 Cubs uniform changes....................$22

02/18/43 Joe Cronin......................................$22

02/25/43 Joe DiMaggio joins the Army $75

03/04/43 Griffith, Harris, Hornsby $30

03/11/43 Bear Mountain (Dodgers training site) $22

03/18/43 Babe Dahlgren...............................$22

03/25/43 Paul, Lloyd Waner..........................$22

04/01/43 Joe DiMaggio $60

04/08/43 Carl Hubbell $35

04/15/43 Franklin D. Roosevelt $30

04/22/43 Soldier reading sports page $22

04/29/43 Case, Johnson, Spence....................$22

05/06/43 Etten, Gordon, Johnson, Stirnweiss $25

05/13/43 "Front-Row Hits for Home Fronters" $22

05/20/43 Garbs, Simmons, Weatherly..........$24

05/27/43 Five new Cardinals $22

06/03/43 Jesse S. Flores $22

06/10/43 Dutch Leonard with rookies $22

06/17/43 Army (DiMaggio, Slaughter) vs. Navy (Mize, Williams) $75

06/24/43 Dixie, Harry, G. Walker $22

07/01/43 American flag $22

07/08/43 Shibe Park: All-Star issue $24

07/15/43 Durocher, Newsom, Rickey............$22

07/22/43 Dodger Bum, Giant.........................$25

07/29/43 Gus Mancuso $22

08/05/43 Mike Naymick $22

08/12/43 Ford Frick $22

08/19/43 Nick Etten $22

08/26/43 Dodger Bum playing with kids......$24

09/02/43 Howie Schultz, Dodgers.................$22

09/09/43 Beauregard, W. Johnson $22

09/16/43 Cardinals team photo.....................$75

09/23/43 World Series issue, Mort Cooper ...$45

09/30/43 Joe McCarthy, Billy Southworth ...$25

10/07/43 Red Barber.......................................$35

10/14/43 Joe McCarthy, World Series...........$95

10/21/43 "Break up the Yanks!"....................$75

10/28/43 Judge Landis, Babe Ruth $65

11/04/43 Stan Musial $50

12/02/43 Winter meetings $22

12/09/43 Frisch, Musial, Walker...................$35

12/16/43 Herb Pennock.................................$22

12/30/43 Chandler, Griffith, McCarthy, others $60

1944

01/06/44 Carl Hubbell....................................$35

01/13/44 Wrigley Field, Los Angeles............$22

01/20/44 Branch Rickey, other owners.........$25

01/27/44 Babe Dahlgren, Bobo Newsom $22

02/03/44 Baseball team owners.....................$22

02/10/44 "Little Lamzeetivee" $22

02/17/44 Clark Griffith $25

02/24/44 Ty Cobb..$45

03/02/44 1944 A.L. schedule.........................$22

03/09/44 1994 N.L. schedule.........................$22

03/16/44 Durocher, C. Mack, McCarthy......$30

03/23/44 Ralph Siewart, Joe Wood...............$22

03/30/44 Giants jogging $22

04/06/44 Spring training photos...................$22

04/13/44 Full page soldier cartoon $22

04/20/44 Stadium photo.................................$22

04/27/44 Servicemen at a game.....................$22

05/04/44 Joe DiMaggio in an Army helmet .$60

05/11/44 Scorecard vendor............................$22

05/18/44 Nick Etten $22

05/25/44 No-hit Hall of Fame $25

06/01/44 Thomas Edison and night ball $30

06/08/44 George Sisler $22

06/15/44 Dixie Walker....................................$22

06/22/44 Cy Young...$40

06/29/44 Browns mascot $22

07/06/44 Pirates mascot, All-Star issue.......$75

07/13/44 Stan Musial, Dixie Walker $50

07/20/44 Dodger Bum $22

07/27/44 Team mascots playing cards..........$22

08/03/44 Connie Mack $25

08/10/44 Browns mascot $22

08/17/44 Mel Ott $35

08/24/44 Browns mascot $22

08/31/44 Hal Newhouser, Dizzy Trout $30

09/07/44 Browns mascot $22

09/14/44 A.L. pennant race $22

09/21/44 Newhouser, O'Neill, Trout.............$28

09/28/44 Cardinals end season......................$22

10/05/44 Browns mascot $65

10/12/44 Browns mascot getting shot $50

10/19/44 Marty Marion, Vern Stephens.......$35

11/02/44 Doc Blanchard.................................$26

11/09/44 Dodger Bum.....................................$24

11/23/44 Marty Marion $24

11/30/44 Judge Landis dies $35

12/14/44 Baseball winter meetings..............$22

12/28/44 Marty Marion, Luke Sewell, others $50

1945

01/04/45 Dodger Bum "This IS Next Year!". $25

243

01/11/45 Hall of Fame balloting process $20
01/18/45 Willard Mullin cartoon..................$20
01/25/45 American Legion cartoon $20
02/01/45 Larry MacPhail $20
02/08/45 Abbott and Costello, Durocher, McCarthy, Ott...$35
02/15/45 Commissioner search committee...$20
02/22/45 Search for a new commissioner $20
03/01/45 Dodger Bum...............................$22
03/08/45 Lou Novikoff $20
03/15/45 1945 A.L. schedule $20
03/22/45 1945 N.L. schedule $20
03/29/45 Larry MacPhail $20
04/05/45 Leo Durocher $25
04/12/45 Browns mascot $20
04/19/45 Presidents at baseball games $20
04/26/45 Yankee and Brown mascots $20
05/03/45 Happy Chandler, Judge Landis $22
05/10/45 New York Giants $20
05/17/45 Phillie rhubarb $20
05/24/45 Giants mascot...............................$22
05/31/45 Mort Cooper $20
06/07/45 Dave Ferriss $20
06/14/45 Howard Schultz.............................$20
06/21/45 Indian with tomahawk...................$20
06/28/45 Dodger Bum..................................$22
07/05/45 Hank Greenberg...........................$35
07/12/45 Fans discuss the All-Star Game $50
07/19/45 Al Benton $20
07/26/45 Charlie Grimm $20
08/02/45 Larry MacPhail $20
08/09/45 Major League managers $20
08/16/45 Al Rosen $25
08/23/45 Joe McCarthy $24
08/30/45 Bob Feller $35
09/06/45 Leo Durocher $25
09/13/45 Browns, Indians, Senators, Tigers, Yankees mascots..$20
09/20/45 Dick Fowler $20
09/27/45 Happy Chandler $22
10/04/45 Briggs Stadium, D. Eisenhower $85
10/11/45 Tiger licking Cub's bones, World Series $70
10/25/45 Clarence "Ace" Parker...................$20
11/01/45 Bill Veeck $25
11/08/45 Breadon, Musial, Slaughter, others $35
11/15/45 Happy Chandler $22
11/29/45 Happy Chandler, Muddy Ruel $20
12/06/45 Player returning from war............$25
12/13/45 Two baseball owners $20
12/27/45 Hal Newhouser, Player of the Year $30

1946

01/03/46 Hall of Fame elections $22

01/10/46 Sam Breadon................................$20
01/17/46 Larry MacPhail $22
01/24/46 Happy Chandler............................$22
01/31/46 Joe DiMaggio, Ted Williams..........$50
02/07/46 Mel Ott $25
02/14/46 Grapefruit League $20
02/21/46 Hank Greenberg $30
02/28/46 Mexican League $20
03/07/46 Bob Feller $30
03/14/46 Ted Williams................................$50
03/21/46 Leo Durocher $25
03/28/46 Cardinal outfielders $20
04/04/46 Johnny Mize $25
04/11/46 Mickey Owen $20
04/18/46 Peacetime baseball begins............$50
04/25/46 Spud Chandler $25
05/02/46 Tommy Henrich..............................$25
05/09/46 Joe Cronin, Joe McCarthy $25
05/16/46 1946 Red Sox sluggers...................$25
05/23/46 Ted Williams................................$30
06/05/46 Bill Dickey, Ted Lyons...................$28
06/12/46 Babe Ruth....................................$50
06/19/46 Red Sox tear apart the league.......$20
06/26/46 Joe Garagiola $25
07/03/46 Veeck buys the Cleveland Indians $20
07/10/46 Bill Veeck, All-Star issue...............$50
07/17/46 Ted Williams................................$40
07/24/46 Larry MacPhail $20
07/31/46 Hal Newhouser $25
08/07/46 Dizzy Dean $25
08/14/46 Mickey Owen, Mexican League.....$20
08/21/46 Mickey Owen $20
08/28/46 Feller's 98 mph pitch $30
09/04/46 Larry MacPhail $20
09/11/46 Jackie Robinson $50
09/18/46 Mickey Vernon, Ted Williams........$30
09/25/46 Stan Musial, Ted Williams $60
10/02/46 Eddie Collins $20
10/09/46 Frankie Frisch, World Series $60
10/16/46 DiMaggio, Gordon, MacPhail $50
10/23/46 Harry "The Cat" Brecheen, World Series $50
10/30/46 *TSN* 60-year chronology $250
11/06/46 Bob Feller $25
11/13/46 Bucky Harris $20
11/20/46 Ted Williams MVP $50
11/27/46 Stan Musial MVP..........................$50
12/04/46 Leo Durocher................................$40
12/18/46 Walter Johnson $40
12/25/46 Billy Evans $20

1947

01/01/47 Dyer, Musial, Yawkey $60
01/08/47 Little stars...................................$20
01/15/47 Joe DiMaggio.................................$40
01/22/47 Branch Rickey $30

01/29/47 Bob Feller $30
02/05/47 Pepper Martin $25
02/12/47 Sam Breadon, Stan Musial............$25
02/19/47 Hank Greenberg............................$25
02/26/47 Hornsby, McKechnie, Speaker.......$25
03/05/47 Stan Musial, Ted Williams.............$40
03/12/47 Leo Durocher, Happy Chandler.....$40
03/19/47 Leo Durocher, Larry MacPhail......$40
03/26/47 Chandler, Durocher, MacPhail $40
04/02/47 Hank Greenberg............................$30
04/09/47 Yogi Berra, Joe Medwick................$25
04/16/47 Leo Durocher $60
04/23/47 Babe Ruth....................................$300
04/30/47 Pete Reiser..................................$20
05/07/47 Babe Ruth Day $50
05/14/47 Hank Greenberg...........................$25
05/21/47 Johnny Mize $25
05/28/47 Hal Chase $20
06/04/47 Dugout jockeys $20
06/11/47 George McQuinn...........................$20
06/18/47 Bobby Thomson $22
06/25/47 Warren Spahn $35
07/02/47 Ewell Blackwell $20
07/09/47 Phil Wrigley, All-Star issue............$60
07/16/47 Larry Doby....................................$60
07/23/47 Bobo Newsom $25
07/30/47 Hall of Fame inductees $25
08/06/47 Burt Shotton $20
08/13/47 Harry "The Hat" Walker $20
08/20/47 Stan Musial $35
08/27/47 Connie Mack.................................$25
09/03/47 Dan Bankhead...............................$25
09/10/47 Frank McCormick $20
09/17/47 Jackie Robinson............................$75
09/24/47 Dixie and Harry Walker.................$20
10/01/47 Bucky Harris, Burt Shotton $75
10/08/47 Joe McCarthy, Tom Yawkey...........$60
10/15/47 George Weiss $50
10/22/47 Joe Kuhel $20
10/29/47 Larry MacPhail $20
11/05/47 Red Ruffing $20
11/12/47 Muddy Ruel, Zack Taylor...............$20
11/19/47 Snuffy Stirnweiss $20
11/26/47 Bob Elliott....................................$20
12/03/47 Joe DiMaggio................................$50
12/10/47 Sam Breadon $25
12/17/47 Leo Durocher $25
12/24/47 Hugh Casey $20
12/31/47 Harris, Rickey, T. Williams............$75

1948

01/07/48 Phil Masi......................................$35
01/14/48 Stars' salaries $20
01/21/48 Sam Breadon $20
01/28/48 Bob Feller, Bill Veeck $30
02/04/48 Joe McCarthy $20

02/11/48 Herb Pennock $20
02/18/48 Eddie Miller $20
02/25/48 Spring training..............................$20
03/03/48 Herb Pennock, Pie Traynor $25
03/10/48 Joe McCarthy................................$22
03/17/48 Pat Seerey $20
03/24/48 Babe Ruth....................................$30
03/31/48 Pesky, McCarthy, Stephens $22
04/07/48 Hank Greenberg $30
04/14/48 Joe McCarthy $22
04/21/48 1948 predictions $50
04/28/48 Dixie Walker.................................$20
05/05/48 Schoolboy Rowe $20
05/12/48 Bill Meyer $20
05/19/48 Blackwell, Branca, Feller, Newhouser
....$30
05/26/48 Ken Kellner $20
06/02/48 Stan Musial..................................$35
06/09/48 50 Home Run Club........................$30
06/16/48 25th anniversary of Yankee Stadium
....$25
06/23/48 Babe Ruth...................................$300
06/30/48 Ted Williams................................$40
07/07/48 Bob Lemon....................................$20
07/14/48 Roy Campanella $40
07/21/48 Vic Raschi $25
07/28/48 Leo Durocher................................$22
08/04/48 Joe Tinker....................................$20
08/11/48 Tinker, Evers, Chance...................$22
08/18/48 Lou Boudreau...............................$24
08/25/48 Babe Ruth....................................$500
09/01/48 Carl Erskine $100
09/08/48 Phil Rizzuto..................................$22
09/15/48 Richie Ashburn $22
09/22/48 Satchel Paige................................$25
09/29/48 Billy Southworth, George Stallings
....$20
10/06/48 1914 Miracle Braves, World Series
....$50
10/13/48 *TSN* All-Star team, World Series..$50
10/20/48 Casey Stengel, George Weiss $20
10/27/48 Casey Stengel................................$25
11/03/48 Happy Chandler............................$20
11/10/48 Lefty Gomez $20
11/17/48 Steve O'Neill.................................$20
11/24/48 Red Rolfe......................................$20
12/01/48 Lou Boudreau................................$25
12/08/48 Stan Musial...................................$35
12/15/48 Baseball winter meetings..............$20
12/22/48 Baseball winter meetings..............$20
12/29/48 Boudreau, Meyer, Veeck $40

1949

01/05/49 Pete Reiser $30
01/12/49 20 game winners $18
01/19/49 Earl Torgeson $18

245

01/26/49 Dick Manville $18
02/02/49 Bill Veeck $20
02/09/49 Murray Dickson........................... $18
02/16/49 Joe DiMaggio, Bob Feller.............. $30
02/23/49 Spring training............................. $18
03/02/49 Honus Wagner $20
03/09/49 Casey Stengel, 1949 Yankees $20
03/16/49 Fred Sanford................................. $18
03/23/49 George Earnshaw $18
03/30/49 Joe McCarthy $18
04/06/49 Gene Woodling............................. $18
04/13/49 Joe DiMaggio, Ted Williams $200
04/20/49 Joe DiMaggio $50
04/27/49 Lou Boudreau $20
05/04/49 Chuck Connors $18
05/11/49 Charlie Gehringer $20
05/18/49 Bobby Shantz............................... $18
05/25/49 Sam Breadon $18
06/01/49 Sam Breadon $18
06/08/49 Sam Breadon $18
06/15/49 Mexican Leaguers reinstated $18
06/22/49 Frankie Frisch.............................. $18
06/29/49 Ray Boone $18
07/06/49 Joe DiMaggio $50
07/13/49 Ebbets Field, All-Star issue........... $50
07/20/49 Billy Southworth $20
07/27/49 Casey Stengel $25
08/03/49 Stan Musial $30
08/10/49 Joe Page $25
08/17/49 Luke Appling $20
08/24/49 Yogi Berra $25
08/31/49 Connie Mack Day $18
09/07/49 Joe DiMaggio $50
09/14/49 Bill Klem.................................... $18
09/21/49 Enos Slaughter.............................. $22
09/28/49 Billy Southworth $18
10/05/49 Enos Slaughter, Ted Williams $50
10/12/49 Casey Stengel, World Series $45
10/19/49 Branch Rickey, World Series.......... $50
10/26/49 Casey Stengel $30
11/02/49 Phil Rizzuto $20
11/09/49 Leo Durocher $18
11/16/49 Yogi Berra, Joe Garagiola $25
11/23/49 Jackie Robinson............................ $40
11/30/49 Ted Williams $40
12/07/49 Vern Stephens, Ted Williams......... $25
12/14/49 Bobby Thomson $18
12/21/49 *TSN* All-Star team $20
12/28/49 Carpenter, Stengel, Williams......... $60

1950

01/04/50 Joe DiMaggio................................ $35
01/11/50 Branch Rickey $18
01/18/50 Bob Dillinger $18
01/25/50 Virgil Trucks................................ $18
02/01/50 Jackie Robinson............................ $25

02/08/50 Gerry Priddy $18
02/15/50 Ty Cobb...................................... $30
02/22/50 Spiraling salaries $18
03/01/50 Hank Greenberg $22
03/08/50 Del Crandall................................. $20
03/15/50 Branch Rickey............................... $20
03/22/50 Connie Mack $20
03/29/50 Sam Jethroe $20
04/05/50 Connie Mack $20
04/12/50 Jackie Jensen, Billy Martin $25
04/19/50 Branch Rickey, Jackie Robinson ... $35
04/26/50 Luke Easter $20
05/03/50 Jack Banta $20
05/10/50 Yogi Berra................................... $25
05/17/50 Edward Barrow $18
05/24/50 Ty Cobb...................................... $25
05/31/50 Robin Roberts, Curt Simmons....... $20
06/07/50 Phil Rizzuto $20
06/14/50 Bob Feller $25
06/21/50 Boston 29, Browns 4 .... $18
06/28/50 Joe McCarthy $20
07/05/50 George Kell $20
07/12/50 Babe Ruth, All-Star game $50
07/19/50 Luke Easter $25
07/26/50 Ty Cobb, Babe Ruth $30
08/02/50 Casey Stengel............................... $25
08/09/50 Eddie Collins, Larry Lajoie $18
08/16/50 Sam Jethroe $18
08/23/50 Vern Bickford $25
08/30/50 Preacher Roe $20
09/06/50 Hank Bauer.................................. $18
09/13/50 Gil Hodges $20
09/20/50 Lou Boudreau $20
09/27/50 Sal Maglie.................................... $20
10/04/50 Branch Rickey, World Series $50
10/11/50 Whitey Ford, World Series $50
10/18/50 Jerry Coleman, World Series........ $40
10/25/50 Connie Mack $18
11/01/50 Walter O'Malley, Branch Rickey ... $25
11/08/50 Jim Konstanty, Phil Rizzuto.......... $20
11/15/50 Grover Cleveland Alexander $30
11/22/50 Honus Wagner $22
11/29/50 Al Lopez...................................... $18
12/06/50 Baseball winter meetings.............. $18
12/13/50 Marty Marion $18
12/20/50 Happy Chandler............................ $18
12/27/50 Happy Chandler............................ $18

1951

01/03/51 Rizzuto, Rolfe, Weiss..................... $40
01/10/51 Yogi Berra, Phil Rizzuto $25
01/17/51 Phil Rizzuto.................................. $20
01/24/51 Tom Henrich.................................. $18
01/31/51 Mickey Mantle $100
02/07/51 Jimmie Foxx, Mel Ott.................... $25
02/14/51 National League's 75th................. $25

02/21/51 Happy Chandler $18
02/28/51 Stan Musial $25
03/07/51 Red Ruffin....................................$18
03/14/51 Stan Musial $25
03/21/51 Happy Chandler $18
03/28/51 Fred Clarke....................................$18
04/04/51 Mickey Mantle..............................$50
04/11/51 Bobby Avila $25
04/18/51 Play Ball $40
04/25/51 Mickey Mantle.............................$300
05/02/51 Grover Alexander $25
05/09/51 Leo Durocher $18
05/16/51 Gil McDougald..............................$18
05/23/51 Leo Durocher $20
05/30/51 Furillo, Hodges, Robinson, Snider.$35
06/06/51 Branch Rickey $18
06/13/51 Ed Lopat $18
06/20/51 Minnie Minoso..............................$18
06/27/51 Walter O'Malley, Buzzie Bavasi $20
07/04/51 1926 Cardinals $18
07/11/51 Cobb, Cochrane, Gehringer............$50
07/18/51 Roy Campanella $25
07/25/51 Allie Reynolds...............................$18
08/01/51 Dizzy and Paul Dean.................... $20
08/08/51 1951 Dodgers $25
08/15/51 Willie Mays..................................$50
08/22/51 Charlie Gehringer $30
08/29/51 Bob Feller $30
09/05/51 Casey Stengel $30
09/12/51 Johnny Sain..................................$18
09/19/51 Bobby Thomson $25
09/26/51 Bill Klem......................................$18
10/03/51 Home Run Baker, World Series.....$50
10/10/51 Fain, Feller, Musial, Roe..............$200
10/17/51 Warren Giles, World Series $45
10/24/51 Gabe Paul $18
10/31/51 Lou Boudreau $20
11/07/51 Alvin Dark $18
11/14/51 Stan Musial, Ted Williams............$45
11/21/51 Yogi Berra $25
11/28/51 Gil Hodges....................................$20
12/05/51 Bill Bevins $18
12/12/51 Minnie Minoso...............................$25
12/19/51 Joe DiMaggio...............................$100
12/26/51 Joe DiMaggio.................................$40

1952

01/02/52 Durocher, Musial, Weiss $75
01/09/52 Leo Durocher, Eddie Stanky..........$18
01/16/52 Tommy Holmes..............................$16
01/23/52 Walter Briggs.................................$16
01/30/52 Gus Zernial $16
02/06/52 Negro ballplayers $30
02/13/52 Ralph Branca, Bobby Thomson $30
02/20/52 Johnny Mize $20
02/27/52 Paul Waner $16

03/05/52 Casey Stengel.................................$18
03/12/52 Dickey, DiMaggio, Ruth................$30
03/19/52 Ty Cobb...$25
03/26/52 Ty Cobb...$25
04/02/52 Clem Labine $16
04/09/52 Monte Irvin $18
04/16/52 Play Ball $40
04/23/52 Wilmer Mizell................................$16
04/30/52 Walter O'Malley $20
05/07/52 Walter O'Malley $20
05/14/52 Ty Cobb...$22
05/21/52 Jackie Jensen $15
05/28/52 Dale Mitchell.................................$15
06/04/52 Davey Williams $15
06/11/52 Ty Cobb, Rogers Hornsby $25
06/18/52 Rogers Hornsby, Bill Veeck...........$18
06/25/52 Jimmy Piersall $15
07/02/52 Carl Erskine...................................$15
07/09/52 Leo Durocher, Casey Stengel.........$35
07/16/52 Solly Hemus $20
07/23/52 Clark Griffith $16
07/30/52 Clark Griffith $16
08/06/52 Clark Griffith $16
08/13/52 Jackie Jensen $16
08/20/52 Bill Veeck......................................$18
08/27/52 Bill Loes..$16
09/03/52 Robin Roberts................................$16
09/10/52 Early Wynn $18
09/17/52 Hank Sauer $16
09/24/52 Joe Black, Clint Courtney $16
10/01/52 1941 Dodgers, World Series $40
10/08/52 1952 Yankees, 1952 Dodgers.........$40
10/15/52 Johnny Mize, World Series............$40
10/22/52 Mickey Mantle $40
10/29/52 Phil Rizzuto...................................$18
11/05/52 Frank Lane, Bill Veeck $16
11/12/52 Mickey Mantle...............................$50
11/19/52 Duke Snider...................................$25
11/26/52 *TSN* All-Star team $20
12/03/52 Del Webb $16
12/10/52 Jackie Robinson $25
12/17/52 Ferris Fain $16
12/24/52 Johnny Allen $16
12/31/52 Roberts, Stanky, Weiss $30

1953

01/07/53 1952 Baseball thrills section $30
01/14/53 Johnny Mize...................................$18
01/21/53 Eddie Stanky..................................$16
01/28/53 Johnny Mize...................................$18
02/04/53 Dizzy Dean, Al Simmons $20
02/11/53 Ed Yost..$16
02/18/53 Eddie Robinson $16
02/25/53 August A. Busch Jr. $16
03/04/53 Russ Meyer....................................$16
03/11/53 Mickey Grasso................................$16

03/18/53 Browns move to Baltimore, Braves move to Milwaukee $16
03/25/53 Braves and Browns shift...............$16
04/01/53 Garcia, Lemon, Wynn....................$20
04/08/53 Casey Stengel $18
04/15/53 Play Ball $30
04/22/53 Milwaukee opener $16
04/29/53 Mickey Mantle.............................$100
05/06/53 Clint Courtney, Billy Martin $16
05/13/53 Bobo Holloman $16
05/20/53 Cobb, Mize, Slaughter....................$20
05/27/53 Dave Philley $16
06/03/53 Roy Campanella $25
06/10/53 Hoyt Wilhelm................................$16
06/17/53 Mickey Mantle...............................$45
06/24/53 1953 Yankees winning streak.......$16
07/01/53 Mickey Mantle, Ed Mathews........$45
07/08/53 Doby, Easter, Rosen.......................$20
07/15/53 Charlie Dressen, Casey Stengel $30
07/22/53 Carl Furillo, Monte Irvin $20
07/29/53 Robin Roberts $18
08/05/53 Ted Williams.................................$30
08/12/53 Mickey Vernon...............................$18
08/19/53 Allie Reynolds...............................$18
08/26/53 1953 Dodger sluggers.....................$20
09/02/53 Vic Raschi, Preacher Roe $18
09/09/53 Red Schoendienst $18
09/16/53 Ed Mathews..................................$25
09/23/53 Yankees, Dodgers clinch $20
09/30/53 1949-53 Yankees, World Series issue
....$45
10/07/53 Junior Gilliam, Harvey Kuenn......$20
10/14/53 Bill Veeck, World Series................$40
10/21/53 Rogers Hornsby $18
10/28/53 Rogers Hornsby $18
11/04/53 Jimmy Piersall...............................$18
11/11/53 Nap Lajoie....................................$18
11/18/53 Jimmie Dykes $18
11/25/53 Eddie Joost...................................$18
12/02/53 Atlanta Crackers $16
12/09/53 Walter Alston................................$18
12/16/53 Bob Feller $20
12/23/53 Ed Barrow....................................$16
12/30/53 Perini, Rosen, Stengel...................$35

1954

01/06/54 1953 Baseball thrills $20
01/13/54 Bobo Newsom $16
01/20/54 Danny O'Connell $16
01/27/54 Dickey, Maranville, Terry $20
02/03/54 Spring training..............................$16
02/10/54 Bobby Thomson $18
02/17/54 Paul Krichell.................................$16
02/24/54 Willie Mays...................................$30
03/03/54 Enos Slaughter..............................$16
03/10/54 Johnny Antonelli $16

03/17/54 Walter Alston $18
03/24/54 J.A. Robert Quinn $16
03/31/54 Don Newcombe...............................$18
04/07/54 1954 Dodgers..................................$16
04/14/54 Baseball returns to Baltimore.......$35
04/21/54 Ted Williams.................................$30
04/28/54 Hal Jeffcoat $16
05/05/54 Bucky Harris $16
05/12/54 Stan Musial $75
05/19/54 Johnny Temple $16
05/26/54 Gene Baker, Ernie Banks.............$22
06/02/54 Art Houtteman $16
06/09/54 Ed Lopat $16
06/16/54 Roy Campanella $25
06/23/54 Hornsby, Musial, Wagner $25
06/30/54 Frank Thomas................................$16
07/07/54 Willie Mays, Duke Snider.............$45
07/14/54 Dusty Rhodes, All-Star issue $30
07/21/54 Willie Mays...................................$35
07/28/54 Eddie Stanky.................................$16
08/04/54 Bob Feller $25
08/11/54 Branch Rickey $16
08/18/54 Bob Lemon......................................$16
08/25/54 Don Mueller $16
09/01/54 Jack Harshman...............................$16
09/08/54 Smokey Burgess.............................$16
09/15/54 Johnny Antonelli, Willie Mays......$50
09/22/54 Casey Stengel.................................$18
09/29/54 Leo Durocher, Al Lopez, World Series
....$45
10/06/54 Bob Grim, Wally Moon, World Series
....$25
10/13/54 Antonelli, Avila, Lemon, Mays....$100
10/20/54 Pinky Higgins................................$16
10/27/54 Connie Mack $16
11/03/54 Joe McCarthy $16
11/10/54 Joe McCarthy $16
11/17/54 A's move to Kansas City.................$16
11/24/54 Joe Garagiola................................$16
12/01/54 Bob Turley $16
12/08/54 Bob Feller $15
12/15/54 *TSN* All-Star team.........................$20
12/22/54 Ted Kluszweski $18
12/29/54 Stan Lopata $16

1955

01/05/55 Durocher, Mays, Stoneham $60
01/12/55 Nellie Fox $16
01/19/55 Ken Boyer......................................$18
01/26/55 Joe Nuxhall $16
02/02/55 DiMaggio, Hartnett, Lyons, Vance $25
02/09/55 Home Run Baker, Ray Schalk.......$16
02/16/55 Home Run Baker $16
02/23/55 Sad Sam Jones $16
03/02/55 Roy Campanella............................$20
03/09/55 Jim Busby......................................$16

03/16/55 Gil Hodges $18
03/23/55 Herb Score $16
03/30/55 Mike Higgins $16
04/06/55 Warren Spahn $20
04/13/55 Ken Boyer, Herb Score $35
04/20/55 Ralph Kiner $18
04/27/55 25 game winners $16
05/04/55 1955 Yankees................................$20
05/11/55 Don Mueller $16
05/18/55 Harvey Kuenn $16
05/25/55 Duke Snider...................................$20
06/01/55 Harry Chiti $16
06/08/55 Al Kaline.......................................$25
06/15/55 Yogi Berra, Roy Campanella..........$25
06/22/55 Don Newcombe...............................$25
06/29/55 Jim Konstanty $16
07/06/55 Dick Donovan $16
07/13/55 Stan Musial, All-Star issue $30
07/20/55 Ernie Banks..................................$25
07/27/55 Preacher Roe $20
08/03/55 Sherm Lollar..................................$50
08/10/55 Spitball debate $16
08/17/55 Jimmy Piersall $16
08/24/55 Del Ennis $16
08/31/55 Hank Bauer $18
09/07/55 Al Smith...$16
09/14/55 Mickey Mantle...............................$30
09/21/55 Don Mossi, Ray Narleski $18
09/28/55 Previous Yankees/Dodgers World
Series $60
10/05/55 Herb Score, Bill Virdon $25
10/12/55 Johnny Podres, World Series.......$200
10/19/55 Ford, Kaline, Roberts, Snider........$35
10/26/55 Roy Campanella $20
11/02/55 Clark Griffith.................................$16
11/09/55 Bobby Bragan $16
11/16/55 Cy Young $18
11/23/55 Double play combos........................$16
11/30/55 Bucky Walters................................$16
12/07/55 *TSN* All-Star team $18
12/14/55 Roy Campanella $20
12/21/55 Earl Torgeson $16
12/28/55 Bob Feller $20

1956

01/04/56 Alston, O'Malley, Snider $60
01/11/56 Gil Coan $14
01/18/56 Randy Jackson $14
01/25/56 Pepper Martin $14
02/01/56 Joe Cronin, Hank Greenberg.........$15
02/08/56 Joe Cronin, Hank Greenberg.........$18
02/15/56 Connie Mack...................................$16
02/22/56 Calvin Griffith $14
02/29/56 Robin Roberts $16
03/07/56 Hank Greenberg.............................$18
03/14/56 Vern Law..$14

03/21/56 Greatest players from 1946-55......$25
03/28/56 Stan Musial....................................$25
04/04/56 Earl Averill.....................................$14
04/11/56 Marty Marion $14
04/18/56 Yankees vs. Dodgers $35
04/25/56 Minnie Minoso $14
05/02/56 Top relievers...................................$14
05/09/56 Bob Friend......................................$14
05/16/56 Bill Sarni $14
05/23/56 Vic Wertz $14
05/30/56 Dale Long $14
06/06/56 Murray Dickson $14
06/13/56 Mickey Mantle $75
06/20/56 Gabe Paul $14
06/27/56 Alvin Dark.......................................$14
07/04/56 DiMaggio, Musial, Williams........$100
07/11/56 Stan Musial $100
07/18/56 Gabe Paul, All-Star issue $20
07/25/56 Tigers sold for $5.5 million............$20
08/01/56 Bill Skowron....................................$20
08/08/56 Fred Haney......................................$14
08/15/56 Ted Williams....................................$25
08/22/56 Braves pitchers $20
08/29/56 Joe Adcock $20
09/05/56 Luis Aparicio, Frank Robinson $25
09/12/56 The home run $20
09/19/56 Birdie Tebbets $25
09/26/56 Babe Ruth.......................................$45
10/03/56 Casey Stengel, World Series issue $60
10/10/56 Aaron, Mantle, Newcombe, Pierce $50
10/17/56 Don Larsen......................................$400
10/24/56 Luis Aparicio, Frank Robinson $20
10/31/56 No-hit pitchers $14
11/07/56 Al Lopez..$14
11/14/56 Mickey Mantle................................$30
11/21/56 Frank Lary $30
11/28/56 Mickey Mantle................................$30
12/05/56 Baseball's 5 greatest feats $15
12/12/56 Bob Scheffing..................................$14
12/19/56 Jackie Robinson $14
12/26/56 Harvey Kuenn.................................$14

1957

01/02/57 Mantle, Paul, Tebbetts..................$75
01/09/57 Bob Feller $18
01/16/57 Jackie Robinson $20
01/23/57 Mickey Mantle, George Weiss $30
01/30/57 Duke Snider $18
02/06/57 Stan Musial.....................................$20
02/13/57 Sam Crawford, Joe McCarthy.......$15
02/20/57 Ted Williams....................................$25
02/27/57 Yankees/A's trade $14
03/06/57 Phil Rizzuto $15
03/13/57 Gil Hodges $15
03/20/57 Frank Sullivan $14
03/27/57 Marv Throneberry $14

04/03/57 Ty Cobb $16
04/10/57 Ted Williams...............................$20
04/17/57 Tony Kubek, Andre Rodgers.........$30
04/24/57 Roy Campanella $20
05/01/57 Roger Maris $25
05/08/57 Tom Yawkey..................................$14
05/15/57 Ted Williams.................................$25
05/22/57 Ted Williams.................................$20
05/29/57 Whitey Ford...................................$18
06/05/57 Dodgers, Giants to move $25
06/12/57 Walter O'Malley.............................$14
06/19/57 Stan Musial $20
06/26/57 Baseball brawls, beanballs $14
07/03/57 Danny McDevitt $14
07/10/57 Stan Musial, Ted Williams............$30
07/17/57 Ford Frick $15
07/24/57 Yankees success system $14
07/31/57 Giants to move to San Francisco...$14
08/07/57 Polo Grounds history $15
08/14/57 Polo Grounds history $20
08/21/57 Roy Sievers $14
08/28/57 Giants shift.....................................$14
09/04/57 Nellie Fox..$14
09/11/57 Frank Malzone $14
09/18/57 Walt Moryn......................................$14
09/25/57 Al Kaline $20
10/02/57 Warren Spahn, World Series issue $35
10/09/57 Stan Musial, Ted Williams.............$35
10/16/57 Dodgers to move to Los Angeles....$30
10/23/57 Lew Burdette.....................................$14
10/30/57 L.A. franchise battle.......................$15
11/06/57 Yogi Berra $18
11/13/57 Yogi Berra $18
11/20/57 Frank Lane $14
11/27/57 Frank Lane $20
12/04/57 Baseball winter meetings $14
12/11/57 MVP balloting...................................$14
12/18/57 Al Lopez $14
12/25/57 L.A. Dodgers $15

1958

01/01/58 Hutchinson, Lane, Williams $35
01/08/58 Mickey Mantle, Ted Williams $15
01/15/58 Ed Mathews.....................................$18
01/22/58 Frank Lane, George Weiss.............$14
01/29/58 L.A. Dodgers $14
02/05/58 Roy Campanella $20
02/12/58 Stars' salaries then and now $14
02/19/58 Billy Martin $15
02/26/58 Willie Mays $20
03/05/58 Gil Hodges, Duke Snider $18
03/12/58 Deron Johnson...............................$14
03/19/58 Leadoff hitters $14
03/26/58 1958 Braves $15
04/02/58 1958 Giants $15
04/09/58 1958 batting race...........................$15

04/16/58 California here we come $30
04/23/58 Eisenhower at season opener........$14
04/30/58 L.A. Dodgers....................................$16
05/07/58 Chinese home runs $14
05/14/58 Stan Musial......................................$60
05/21/58 Branch Rickey $14
05/28/58 1958 Yankee pitchers.....................$14
06/04/58 San Francisco Giants......................$14
06/11/58 Ryne Duren $14
06/18/58 Yankees/Kansas City trades..........$14
06/25/58 Walter O'Malley $14
07/02/58 Gabe Paul $14
07/09/58 All-Time All-Stars..........................$25
07/16/58 Casey Stengel..................................$15
07/23/58 Jackie Jensen $14
07/30/58 Phil Wrigley.....................................$14
08/06/58 Bob Turley $14
08/13/58 Philly Whiz Kids $14
08/20/58 Yankees old-timers.........................$15
08/27/58 Ted Williams....................................$25
09/03/58 Ernie Banks $18
09/10/58 Banks, Jensen, Spahn, Turley.......$16
09/17/58 Pete Runnels $14
09/24/58 Aaron, Ashburn, Mays, Musial $35
10/01/58 George Weiss, World Series issue .$30
10/08/58 Top Rookies in 1958 ....$16
10/15/58 Player/managers, World Series.....$25
10/22/58 Mighty Mites $14
10/29/58 Casey Stengel..................................$15
11/05/58 Stan Musial $20
11/12/58 Max Carey $14
11/19/58 Lee MacPhail...................................$14
11/26/58 Houston bids for franchise.............$14
12/03/58 Baseball winter meetings $14
12/10/58 Will Harridge $14
12/17/58 Joe Cronin, Will Harridge $14
12/24/58 New York Yankees' homes $14
12/31/58 Brown, Stengel, Turley..................$25

1959

01/07/59 Will Harridge $14
01/14/59 Marty Marion...................................$14
01/21/59 Bill Norman......................................$14
01/28/59 Willie Mays......................................$20
02/04/59 Soaring player salaries...................$14
02/11/59 Zack Wheat.......................................$14
02/18/59 Spring training.................................$14
02/25/59 Bill Veeck...$15
03/04/59 Durocher, Frisch, McGraw, Stallings
....$15
03/11/59 Solly Hemus $14
03/18/59 Frank Lary $14
03/25/59 Ty Cobb $18
04/01/59 Don Mossi, Ray Narleski................$14
04/08/59 Play Ball $25
04/15/59 Hall of Fame historian Lee Allen..$14

04/22/59 Clint Courtney...............................$14
04/29/59 Woodie Held...............................$14
05/06/59 Paul Richards $14
05/13/59 1959 Yankees woes........................$14
05/20/59 Ernie Banks..................................$18
05/27/59 1925 Yankees................................$14
06/03/59 Hank Aaron $20
06/10/59 Rocky Colavito, Ed Mathews.........$16
06/07/59 Hoyt Wilhelm...............................$14
06/24/59 Roy Face......................................$14
07/01/59 Harmon Killebrew.........................$15
07/08/59 Carl Hubbell, Ted Williams $25
07/15/59 Billy Jurges..................................$14
07/22/59 Senators sluggers $14
07/29/59 Orioles staff $14
08/05/59 Don Drysdale................................$15
08/12/59 Willie McCovey.............................$20
08/19/59 Eppa Rixey..................................$14
08/26/59 Al Lopez $14
09/02/59 Ty Cobb $18
09/09/59 1959 White Sox, Bill Veeck...........$20
09/16/59 Tony Cuccinello, Al Lopez.............$14
09/23/59 1959 Yankees fall $15
09/30/59 Bill Veeck, World Series issue $30
10/07/59 Early Wynn...................................$15
10/14/59 1959 World Series summary..........$25
10/21/59 Larry Sherry.................................$14
10/28/59 Wally Moon $14
11/04/59 Chuck Dressen..............................$14
11/11/59 *TSN's* 1959 All-Stars $18
11/18/59 Nellie Fox....................................$15
11/25/59 Bob Allison $14
12/02/59 Baseball winter meetings $14
12/09/59 Stan Musial, Ted Williams.............$15
12/16/59 Billy Jurges..................................$15
12/23/59 Hall of Fame first basemen $18
12/30/59 Alston, Bavasi, Wynn....................$30

1960

01/06/60 Walter Alston.................................$14
01/13/60 Joe Cronin....................................$12
01/20/60 Willie Mays...................................$25
01/27/60 Clark Griffith................................$12
02/03/60 Johnny Temple $12
02/10/60 Rice, Rixey, Roush $12
02/17/60 Ernie Banks..................................$18
02/24/60 Walter O'Malley.............................$12
03/02/60 Pete Reiser....................................$12
03/09/60 1960 White Sox.............................$12
03/16/60 Walter Alston................................$12
03/23/60 Chuck Dressen $12
03/30/60 1960 Yankees analysis $15
04/06/60 Eddie Lopat $12
04/13/60 Play Ball $25
04/20/60 Johnson, Mathewson, Spahn, Wynn, Young $20

04/27/60 Rocky Colavito, Harvey Kuenn.....$14
05/04/60 Bill DeWitt $12
05/11/60 Ken Boyer.....................................$12
05/18/60 Lou Boudreau................................$12
05/25/60 Roger Maris...................................$25
06/01/60 Bill Veeck.....................................$12
06/08/60 Frank Howard...............................$12
06/15/60 Bill Mazeroski...............................$13
06/22/60 Comiskey dynasty.........................$12
06/29/60 Ted Williams.................................$40
07/06/60 Roberto Clemente $25
07/13/60 Roger Maris, All-Star issue...........$25
07/20/60 New franchises for 1962 ....$15
07/27/60 Del Crandall..................................$12
08/03/60 Cookie Lavagetto $12
08/10/60 Jim Piersall, Casey Stengel...........$12
08/17/60 Ted Williams.................................$100
08/24/60 Dick Groat $12
08/31/60 Dick Groat, Roger Maris...............$20
09/07/60 Roy Sievers...................................$12
09/14/60 1890s stars $12
09/21/60 Hemus, Lavagetto, Murtaugh, Richards $12
09/28/60 Stan Musial..................................$25
10/05/60 1927 Yankees, World Series issue.$30
10/12/60 Mike Fornieles, Lindy McDaniel...$15
10/19/60 Bobby Richardson, World Series...$25
10/26/60 Casey Stengel...............................$15
11/02/60 American League expansion $12
11/09/60 George Weiss $12
11/16/60 Roger Maris...................................$25
11/23/60 Roy Harney...................................$12
11/30/60 Baseball winter meetings $12
12/07/60 Ralph Houk $12
12/14/60 Los Angeles Angels $12
12/21/60 John Galbreath $12
12/28/60 Billy Bruton...................................$12

1961

01/04/61 Mazeroski, Murtaugh, Weiss........$30
01/11/61 Ted Kluszewski..............................$13
01/18/61 Dazzy Vance, Johnny Vander Meer $12
01/25/61 Max Carey, Billy Hamilton............$12
02/01/61 Walter Alston $12
02/08/61 Lindy McDaniel.............................$12
02/15/61 Stars swan songs $14
02/22/61 Max Carey $12
03/01/61 Ralph Houk $12
03/08/61 Leo Durocher................................$13
03/15/61 Yankees, Tigers outfielders...........$15
03/22/61 Joe DiMaggio................................$18
03/29/61 Mickey Mantle $30
04/05/61 1961 managers...............................$12
04/12/61 Presidents/Opening Day...............$40
04/19/61 Willie Davis, Carl Yastrzemski $30

04/26/61 Whitey Ford....................................$16
05/03/61 Babe Herman $14
05/10/61 Wally Moon $25
05/17/61 Jim Gentile $14
05/24/61 Alvin Dark $14
05/31/61 Charles Finley $14
06/07/61 Pitching coach Jim Turner.............$14
06/14/61 Johnny Temple $14
06/21/61 Sandy Koufax $20
06/28/61 Mickey Mantle, Roger Maris $100
07/05/61 300 game winners $20
07/12/61 Cash, Cepeda, Ford, Jay, Koufax,
Mantle, Maris, F. Robinson...........................$60
07/19/61 George Weiss $20
07/26/61 Ty Cobb $50
08/02/61 Red Sox immortals $40
08/09/61 Ford Frick $25
08/16/61 Elston Howard.................................$15
08/23/61 Whitey Ford.....................................$25
08/30/61 Top 1961 rookies............................$30
09/06/61 Mickey Mantle, Roger Maris $75
09/13/61 Arroyo, Ford, Spahn......................$40
09/20/61 Ralph Houk......................................$40
09/27/61 Mantle, Maris, Ruth....................$100
10/04/61 1939 Yankees vs. Reds, World Series
.... $50
10/11/61 Casey Stengel, New York Mets....$200
10/18/61 Hail to the champs $45
10/25/61 Yogi Berra $15
11/01/61 Top 1961 rookies............................$15
11/08/61 Ron Santo $12
11/15/61 Johnny Temple $12
11/22/61 Roger Maris $60
11/29/61 Baseball winter meetings $12
12/06/61 Walter O'Malley...............................$12
12/13/61 Ty Cobb $14
12/20/61 Best No. 2 hitters $14
12/27/61 George Sisler $12

1962

01/03/62 Houk, Maris, Spahn, Topping........$40
01/10/62 Al Kaline..$18
01/17/62 Rogers Hornsby $14
01/24/62 Hall of Fame candidates.................$15
01/31/62 Pie Traynor $12
02/07/62 Elston Howard.................................$13
02/14/62 Gil Hodges $13
02/21/62 Sophomore jinx................................$12
02/28/62 Roger Maris $18
03/07/62 Mantle, Mays, Musial, Spahn, Will-
iams...$50
03/14/62 Hall of Famers who stayed with one
team $25
03/21/62 Braves infielders $12
03/28/62 Ray Schalk......................................$12
04/04/62 Minnie Minoso.................................$12

04/11/62 Play Ball $20
04/18/62 1962 Giants....................................$12
04/25/62 Ford Frick..$12
05/02/62 Felipe and Matty Alou..................$12
05/09/62 Casey Stengel.................................$12
05/16/62 Ralph Terry $12
05/23/62 Sandy Koufax $15
06/02/62 Luis Aparicio, Dick Howser..........$12
06/09/62 1962 Giants pitchers......................$12
06/16/62 Bob Purkey......................................$12
06/23/62 Carl Sawatski..................................$12
06/30/62 Don Drysdale..................................$14
07/07/62 All-Star goats $18
07/14/62 Maury Wills.....................................$12
07/21/62 Davis, Mantle, Mays, Wagner $25
07/28/62 Chicago Cubs immortals $20
08/04/62 Bob Gibson $20
08/11/62 1962 Reds $12
08/18/62 Yogi Berra.......................................$20
08/25/62 Juan Marichal..................................$20
09/01/62 Tom Tresh.......................................$12
09/08/62 New York Mets................................$20
09/15/62 Ron Fairly, Frank Howard $12
09/22/62 Donovan, Mantle, Marichal, Wills $20
09/29/62 George Weiss $12
10/06/62 Walter O'Malley, World Series issue
....$20
10/13/62 Ralph Houk $20
10/20/62 1962 baseball thrills $20
10/27/62 Ken Hubbs, Tom Tresh $20
11/03/62 Birdie Tebbetts $12
11/10/62 Brooks and Frank Robinson..........$30
11/17/62 Don Drysdale...................................$14
11/24/62 Stan Musial $18
12/01/62 George Sisler Jr..............................$12
12/08/62 Tom Tresh $12
12/15/62 Jack Sanford $12
12/22/62 Walter O'Malley $12
12/29/62 Don Drysdale, Maury Wills...........$25

1963

01/05/63 1962 World Series Game 7 ....$15
01/12/63 1963's top rookie prospects...........$14
01/19/63 Jim Piersall $12
01/26/63 Dean Chance $12
02/02/63 Sam Mele $12
02/09/63 Chicago White Sox $12
02/16/63 Sandy Koufax..................................$16
02/23/63 Johnny Pesky $12
03/02/63 Dan Topping $12
03/09/63 Johnny Sain $12
03/16/63 Mickey Mantle, Willie Mays..........$35
03/23/63 1963 Yankees..................................$15
03/30/63 Ralph Terry $12
04/06/63 Don Hoak..$12
04/13/63 Play Ball $18

04/20/63 Duke Snider.....................................$14
04/27/63 Ernie Broglio $12
05/04/63 Tony Kubek, Bobby Richardson.....$14
05/11/63 Luis Aparicio, Al Smith..................$13
05/18/63 Cubs pitchers.................................$12
05/25/63 Sandy Koufax $16
06/01/63 Ron Fairly......................................$12
06/08/63 Jim Piersall, Casey Stengel..........$12
06/15/63 Gil Hodges $13
06/22/63 Billy O'Dell $12
06/29/63 Juan Marichal $14
07/06/63 New York Yankees.........................$14
07/13/63 Casey Stengel, All-Star issue $18
07/20/63 Aaron, Ford, Koufax, Wagner
....$20
07/27/63 Hal Woodenshick...........................$12
08/03/63 Rich Rollins $12
08/10/63 Frank Malzone, Carl Yastrzemski
....$16
08/17/63 Dick Ellsworth................................$12
08/24/63 1963 Dodgers.................................$12
08/31/63 Warren Spahn $14
09/07/63 Dick Groat $12
09/14/63 Jimmy Hall.....................................$12
09/21/63 1963's top rookies $14
09/28/63 20 game winners $12
10/05/63 Yankees vs. Dodgers/prior World
Series $25
10/12/63 Aaron, Ford, Kaline, Koufax.........$30
10/19/63 Dodgers sweep the Yankees...........$25
10/26/63 Pete Rose $30
11/02/63 Dick Stuart $12
11/09/63 Yogi Berra $14
11/16/63 Carl Yastrzemski $16
11/23/63 Hank Aaron $18
11/30/63 Elston Howard................................$12
12/07/63 Rocky Colavito................................$12
12/14/63 Sandy Koufax $25
12/21/63 Leon Wagner...................................$12
12/28/63 Jim Bouton $12

1964

01/04/64 1963 Los Angeles Dodgers.............$20
01/11/64 Albie Pearson..................................$10
01/18/64 Sandy Koufax $18
01/25/64 Walter Alston.................................$10
02/01/64 Jim "Mudcat" Grant.....................$10
02/08/64 Lum Harris.....................................$15
02/15/64 Chuck Hinton $10
02/22/64 Eddie Mathews..............................$12
02/29/64 Casey Stengel $12
03/07/64 Burleigh Grimes............................$10
03/14/64 Al Kaline..$15
03/21/64 Willie McCovey.............................$14
03/28/64 Branch Rickey $10
04/04/64 Jim Gilliam....................................$10

04/11/64 Don Drysdale, Sandy Koufax $20
04/18/64 Play Ball..$18
04/25/64 Aaron, Mathews, Spahn $20
05/02/64 Cepeda, Mays, McCovey...............$20
05/09/64 Frank Howard...............................$10
05/16/64 Tony Oliva $12
05/23/64 Richie Allen..................................$12
05/30/64 Ron Hansen...................................$10
06/06/64 Dave Wickersham $10
06/13/64 Ron Santo......................................$10
06/20/64 Wally Bunker $10
06/27/64 Whitey Ford $15
07/04/64 Billy Williams...............................$12
07/11/64 Willie Mays....................................$25
07/25/64 Gene Mauch $10
08/01/64 Boog Powell $10
08/08/64 Ron Hunt.......................................$10
08/15/64 Bill Freehan $10
08/22/64 Johnny Callison $10
08/29/64 Bob Allison, Harmon Killebrew $14
09/05/64 Roberto Clemente $20
09/12/64 Elston Howard $12
09/19/64 Brooks Robinson $15
09/26/64 Ken Boyer......................................$12
10/03/64 Dean Chance $10
10/10/64 Allen, Bunker, Oliva, World Series
....$20
10/17/64 Yankees vs. Cardinals, World Series
....$15
10/24/64 Bing Devine, World Series.............$20
10/31/64 Johnny Keane $10
12/05/64 Mel Stottlemyre, Harry Walker $10

1965

01/02/65 Ken Boyer, Bob Gibson $16
02/06/65 Baseball to select new commissioner
....$12
02/27/65 Spring training..............................$10
03/20/65 Rocky Colavito $10
03/27/65 Juan Marichal................................$14
04/03/65 Bo Belinsky, Dick Stuart $10
04/10/65 Houston Astrodome $10
04/17/65 Play Ball..$15
04/24/65 President Johnson visits the Astro-
dome $12
05/01/65 John Romano.................................$10
05/08/65 Eddie Mathews $12
05/15/65 Tony Conigliaro.............................$10
05/22/65 Frank Robinson.............................$15
05/29/65 White Sox pitchers........................$10
06/05/65 Bob Gibson....................................$15
06/12/65 Felix Mantilla................................$10
06/19/65 Wes Parker $10
06/26/65 Vic Davalillo..................................$10
07/03/65 Hank Aaron....................................$18
07/10/65 Eddie Fisher..................................$10

07/17/65 Don Drysdale, Sandy Koufax $20
07/24/65 Willie Horton $10
07/31/65 Deron Johnson.............................$10
08/07/65 Sonny Siebert $10
08/14/65 Richie Allen $12
08/21/65 Pete Rose $25
08/28/65 Curt Blefary.................................$10
09/04/65 Vern Law......................................$10
09/11/65 Sam McDowell $10
09/18/65 Jim Bunning.................................$10
09/25/65 Sandy Koufax $25
10/02/65 Willie McCovey.............................$12
10/09/65 Jim "Mudcat" Grant, World Series$12
10/16/65 Lou Johnson $10
10/23/65 Maury Wills, World Series............$12
10/30/65 Grant, Koufax, Mays, Oliva..........$20
11/06/65 Cal Grifffth $10

1966

01/08/66 Sandy Koufax $20
01/22/66 Ted Williams.................................$10
03/05/66 Hank Aquirre $10
03/19/66 Dick Stuart....................................$10
03/26/66 Willie Davis $10
04/02/66 Camilo Pascual.............................$10
04/09/66 Brooks and Frank Robinson $20
04/16/66 Atlanta and Anaheim stadiums $15
04/30/66 Milwaukee Braves move to Atlanta
....$10
05/07/66 Larry Brown, Fred Whitfield.........$10
05/14/66 Don Sutton.....................................$10
05/21/66 Willie Mays....................................$20
05/28/66 Luis Tiant $10
06/04/66 Rick Reichardt...............................$10
06/11/66 Joe Morgan $12
06/18/66 Sandy Koufax, Juan Marichal.......$18
06/25/66 Sonny Siebert $10
07/02/66 Richie Allen $10
07/09/66 Jim Northrup.................................$10
07/16/66 August A. Busch Jr. $15
07/23/66 Gaylord Perry $12
07/30/66 Jack Aker......................................$10
08/06/66 Woodie Fryman $10
08/13/66 Boog Powell $10
08/20/66 Orlando Cepeda.............................$10
08/27/66 Baltimore Orioles $12
09/03/66 Phil Regan $10
09/10/66 Jim Kaat $10
09/17/66 Willie Stargell................................$14
09/24/66 Felipe and Matty Alou $10
10/01/66 Jim Nash...$10
10/08/66 Hank Bauer, World Series issue....$15
10/15/66 Jim Lefebvre...................................$10
10/22/66 Luis Aparicio $12

1967

02/25/67 Baseball cartoons $10

03/18/67 Hoyt Wilhelm $8
03/25/67 Andy Etchebarren...........................$8
04/01/67 Chance, Grant, Kaat.......................$9
04/08/67 Frank Robinson.............................$15
04/15/67 Play Ball $12
04/22/67 Jim Fregosi......................................$8
04/29/67 Roger Maris $25
05/06/67 Whitey Ford $12
05/13/67 Steve Hargan $8
05/20/67 Rick Reichardt $8
05/27/67 Walter Alston $8
06/03/67 Gary Nolan $8
06/10/67 Rod Carew $10
06/17/67 Juan Marichal..................................$9
06/24/67 Al Dark, Eddie Stanky $8
07/01/67 Jim Lonborg $8
07/08/67 Bob Veale $8
07/15/67 Jim McGlothlin, All-Star issue $15
07/22/67 Tim McCarver $10
07/29/67 Tommy John, Gary Peters...............$8
08/05/67 Dick Williams...................................$8
08/12/67 Joe Torre...$9
08/19/67 Paul Blair $8
08/26/67 Mike McCormick...............................$8
09/02/67 Gil Hodges, Frank Howard $9
09/09/67 Rusty Staub.......................................$8
09/23/67 Carl Yastrzemski..............................$12
09/30/67 Earl Wilson $8
10/07/67 Stan Musial, Red Schoendienst $12
10/14/67 Carl Yastrzemski..............................$25
10/21/67 Jim Lonborg, World Series $15
10/28/67 Bob Gibson, World Series $20

1968

03/02/68 Carl Yastrzeniski $15
03/09/68 Dick Hughes.....................................$8
03/16/68 Mark Belanger $8
03/23/68 Jim Bunning......................................$8
03/30/68 Don Wert $8
04/06/68 Mickey Mantle and family.............$25
04/13/68 Lou Brock $12
04/20/68 Pete Rose $25
04/27/68 Jim Fregosi, Bobby Knoop..............$8
05/04/68 Harmon Killebrew $12
05/11/68 Jerry Koosman $8
05/18/68 Mickey Lolich $8
05/25/68 Orlando Cepeda $9
06/01/68 Frank Howard....................................$8
06/08/68 Don Drysdale.....................................$9
06/15/68 Woody Fryman $8
06/22/68 Jim Hardin $8
06/29/68 Tony Horton..$8
07/06/68 Denny McLain.....................................$8
07/13/68 Willie McCovey, All-Star issue $12
07/20/68 Willie Horton.....................................$9
07/27/68 Matty Alou $8

08/03/68 Luis Tiant $8
08/10/68 Glenn Beckert..................................$8
08/17/68 Reggie Jackson, Rick Monday $25
08/24/68 Dal Maxvill $8
08/31/68 Ted Uhlaender $8
09/07/68 Phil Regan $8
09/21/68 Bill Freehan......................................$8
09/28/68 Mike Shannon $8
10/05/68 Denny McLain, Lefty Grove, World Series $15
10/12/68 Roger Maris and family, World Series $25
10/19/68 Bob Gibson, World Series $8

1969

01/04/69 Denny McLain $12
03/01/69 Willie Mays....................................$15
03/15/69 Ted Williams $15
03/22/69 Denny McLain $12
03/29/69 Tony Conigliaro $12
04/05/69 100 Years of Baseball $15
04/12/69 Brock, Flood, Pinson $15
04/19/69 Don Buford $10
04/26/69 Tug McGraw $10
05/03/69 Mel Stottlemyre............................$10
05/10/69 Bill Sudakis $10
05/17/69 Dave McNally.................................$10
05/24/69 Richie Hebner.................................$10
05/31/69 Bobby Murcer $10
06/07/69 Don Kessinger $10
06/14/69 Blue Moon Odom...........................$10
06/21/69 Lee May $10
06/28/69 Ray Culp $10
07/05/69 Ken Holtzman $10
07/12/69 Rod Carew $15
07/19/69 Powell, B. Robinson, F. Robinson ..$20
07/26/69 Reggie Jackson $30
08/02/69 Matty Alou $10
08/09/69 Willie McCovey $15
08/16/69 Rico Petrocelli.................................$10
08/23/69 Phil Niekro $12
08/30/69 Steve Carlton...................................$15
09/06/69 Ron Santo $12
09/13/69 Mike Cuellar $10
09/27/69 Bobby Tolan $10
10/04/69 Billy Martin $15
10/11/69 Tom Seaver $20
10/18/69 Boog Powell $15
10/25/69 Harmon Killebrew...........................$15
11/01/69 David (Mets)/Goliath (Orioles) $20

1970

01/17/70 Willie Mays.....................................$15
02/28/70 Roberto Clemente...........................$20
04/11/70 T. Conigliaro, R. Smith, Yastrzemski $25
04/18/70 Johnny Bench.................................$20

04/25/70 Bert Campaneris............................$7
05/02/70 Rusty Staub....................................$8
05/09/70 Brant Alyea $7
05/16/70 Tony Perez.....................................$10
05/23/70 Hank Aaron...................................$15
05/30/70 Dave Johnson $7
06/06/70 Richie Allen....................................$8
06/13/70 Vada Pinson....................................$8
06/20/70 Jim Merritt.....................................$7
06/27/70 Danny Walton $8
07/04/70 Rico Carty.......................................$8
07/11/70 Felipe Alou $7
07/18/70 Pete Rose $20
07/25/70 Willie Mays....................................$15
08/01/70 Billy Grabarkewitz $7
08/08/70 Al Kaline.......................................$20
08/15/70 Ray Fosse $7
08/22/70 Roy White $7
08/29/70 Dave Giusti $7
09/05/70 Bud Harrelson.................................$7
09/12/70 Bernie Carbo $7
09/26/70 Joe Pepitone $7
10/03/70 Gaylord Perry/Jim Perry..............$10
10/10/70 Danny Murtaugh $7
10/17/70 Cuellar, McNally, Palmer $12
10/24/70 Johnny Bench.................................$15
10/31/70 World Series wrap-up $10

1971

02/27/71 Bamberger, Etchebarren, Palmer .$10
04/10/71 Johnny Bench, Boog Powell $10
04/17/71 Reggie Jackson...............................$15
04/24/71 Tony Conigliaro $10
05/01/71 Manny Sanguillen...........................$5
05/08/71 Steve Carlton $10
05/22/71 Willie Stargell $8
06/05/71 Vida Blue..$5
06/12/71 Jerry Grote $5
06/19/71 Sonny Siebert...................................$5
06/26/71 Dick Dietz...$5
07/03/71 Fergie Jenkins.................................$8
07/10/71 Bobby Murcer...................................$8
07/17/71 Willie Mays.....................................$12
07/24/71 Joe Torre $5
07/31/71 Frank Robinson...............................$8
08/07/71 Tony Oliva $7
08/14/71 Amos Otis $5
08/21/71 Dock Ellis $5
09/04/71 Bill Melton $5
09/25/71 Mickey Lolich $8
10/02/71 Wilbur Wood $5
10/09/71 Al Downing.......................................$5
10/16/71 Brooks Robinson $12
10/23/71 Joe Torre...$5
10/30/71 Roberto Clemente $15

1972

03/04/72 Cuellar, Dobson, McNally, Palmer ..$8
04/08/72 Roberto Clemente...........................$15
04/29/72 Play Ball $7
05/13/72 Don Sutton.....................................$7
05/27/72 Milt Wilcox.....................................$5
06/03/72 Dave Kingman...............................$5
06/10/72 Mickey Lolich $7
06/17/72 Gary Nolan $5
06/24/72 D. Baylor, T. Crowley, Grich $7
07/01/72 Danny Frisella, Tug McGraw $6
07/08/72 Lou Piniella $6
07/15/72 Manny Sanguillen $5
07/22/72 Joe Rudi $5
07/29/72 Hank Aaron $10
08/12/72 Sparky Lyle...................................$5
08/19/72 Cesar Cedeno................................$5
09/02/72 Steve Carlton...............................$10
09/23/72 Carlton Fisk..................................$8
09/30/72 Al Oliver $5
10/14/72 Luis Tiant $6
10/21/72 Billy Williams...............................$7
10/28/72 Johnny Bench $12
11/04/72 Dick Williams $5

1973

01/06/73 Charlie Finley..............................$5
03/03/73 Rollie Fingers $6
04/14/73 Steve Carlton..............................$10
04/28/73 Chris Speier.................................$5
05/05/73 Nolan Ryan.................................$15
05/12/73 Fred Patek, Cookie Rojas.................$5
05/19/73 Joe Morgan..................................$7
06/02/73 Wilbur Wood $5
06/09/73 Joe Ferguson $5
06/16/73 Joe Coleman $5
06/23/73 Ron Santo $6
06/30/73 Ron Blomberg...............................$5
07/07/73 Bobby Bonds................................$5
07/14/73 John Mayberry $5
07/21/73 Bob Watson $5
07/28/73 Bench, Morgan, Rose $15
08/04/73 Bert Byleven $5
08/11/73 Bobby Bonds $5
08/18/73 Thurman Munson $15
08/25/73 Del Unser....................................$5
09/01/73 Orlando Cepeda............................$5
09/08/73 Darrell Evans $5
09/29/73 Lou Brock $8
10/06/73 Willie Mays..................................$10
10/13/73 Jim Palmer $8
10/20/73 Blue, Holtzman, Hunter $10
10/27/73 Jon Matlack.................................$5
11/03/73 Mike Andrews...............................$5

1974

03/02/74 Dick Green $4
04/06/74 Play Ball.......................................$6
04/20/74 Hank Aaron, Babe Ruth $15
04/27/74 Ted Simmons $4
05/04/74 Roy White $4
05/11/74 Jim Wynn $4
05/18/74 Jeff Burroughs $4
05/25/74 Ken Singleton................................$4
06/01/74 John Hiller $4
06/08/74 Mike Schmidt................................$20
06/15/74 Gaylord Perry................................$5
06/22/74 Tommy John..................................$5
06/29/74 Rod Carew $7
07/06/74 Ralph Garr $4
07/13/74 Carlton Fisk $6
07/20/74 Dick Williams................................$4
07/27/74 Mike Marshall................................$4
08/03/74 Steve Busby..................................$4
08/10/74 Greg Gross....................................$4
08/17/74 Reggie Jackson..............................$12
08/24/74 Jorge Orta $4
09/14/74 Richie Zisk....................................$4
09/28/74 Reggie Smith $4
10/19/74 Bill Virdon $4
10/26/74 Steve Garvey $7
11/02/74 Brock, Burroughs, Hunter, M. Marshall $7

1975

01/04/75 Lou Brock $6
03/08/75 Bobby Bonds, Jim Hunter $7
04/12/75 Opening Day $5
04/26/75 Dave Concepcion $5
05/03/75 Frank Robinson.............................$6
05/10/75 Greg Luzinski................................$5
05/17/75 Nolan Ryan...................................$12
05/24/75 Ken Reitz.....................................$4
05/31/75 Jim Palmer $6
06/07/75 Madlock, Monday, Morales.............$6
06/14/75 Ron LeFlore...................................$5
06/21/75 Andy Messersmith $4
06/28/75 Hal McRae...................................$4
07/05/75 Joe Morgan...................................$6
07/12/75 Fred Lynn $6
07/19/75 Mays, Musial, Ruth, Williams, Feller, Hubbell, Kaline, Marichal $10
07/21/75 Robin Yount..................................$15
08/02/75 Dave Parker $5
08/09/75 Claudell Washington $4
08/16/75 Al Hrabosky $4
08/23/75 Jim Kaat......................................$4
08/30/75 Larry Bowa, Dave Cash...................$4
09/06/75 Randy Jones $4
09/20/75 John Mayberry $4
10/04/75 Fingers, Lindblad, Todd..................$6

10/11/75 Sparky Anderson $5
10/18/75 Fred Lynn $6

1976

03/06/76 Fred Lynn $6
04/10/76 Fergie Jenkins $5
04/17/76 Don Gullett $4
04/24/76 Frank Tanana..................................$4
05/01/76 Larry Bowa $4
05/08/76 Dave Kingman.................................$4
05/15/76 Toby Harrah $4
05/22/76 Willie Horton $8
05/29/76 Ron Cey..$5
06/05/76 George Brett $12
06/12/76 Chris Chambliss..............................$4
06/19/76 Randy Jones $4
06/26/76 Ron LeFlore $5
07/03/76 George Foster $4
07/10/76 John Montefusco $4
07/17/76 Johnny Bench..................................$8
07/24/76 Jim Slaton.......................................$4
07/31/76 Al Oliver..$4
08/07/76 Dennis Leonard $4
08/14/76 Mark Fidrych...................................$5
08/21/76 Dave Cash.......................................$4
08/28/76 Rico Carty $4
09/18/76 Rick Rhoden....................................$4
09/25/76 Mickey Rivers..................................$4
10/16/76 Rawly Eastwick...............................$4
10/23/76 Cincinnati's "Big Red Machine:"
Anderson, Bench, Concepcion, Foster, Geronimo, Griffey, Morgan, Perez, Rose $15

1977

03/05/77 Baylor, Grich, Rudi...........................$5
03/26/77 Wayne Garland................................$4
04/02/77 Mike Schmidt $10
04/09/77 Don Gullett, Reggie Jackson $10
04/16/77 Bert Campaneris $4
04/23/77 Rick Monday...................................$4
04/30/77 Rollie Fingers $4
05/07/77 Amos Otis $4
05/14/77 Joe Rudi $4
05/21/77 Ted Simmons $4
05/28/77 Ron Cey..$4
06/04/77 Mitchell Page..................................$4
06/11/77 Dave Parker....................................$4
06/18/77 Richie Zisk $4
06/25/77 Bruce Sutter $4
07/09/77 Butch Wynegar $4
07/16/77 Jeff Burroughs.................................$4
07/23/77 Frank Tanana $4
07/30/77 Steve Carlton...................................$7
08/06/77 Joe Morgan $6
08/13/77 Jim Rice $6
08/20/77 Cromartie, Dawson, Valentine $6
08/27/77 Billy Hunter, Bump Wills $4

09/03/77 Tommy John....................................$4
09/24/77 Graig Nettles....................................$5
10/01/77 Greg Luzinski...................................$5
10/08/77 Al Cowens..$4
10/15/77 Rod Carew $7
10/22/77 Baker, Cey, Garvey, Smith..............$8

1978

03/04/78 Rod Carew, George Foster $7
04/08/78 Salute To 1978 Season.....................$4
04/15/78 Lyman Bostock.................................$4
04/22/78 Garry Templeton $4
04/29/78 Steve Kemp, Jason Thompson $4
05/06/78 Don Money $4
05/13/78 Ross Grimsley $4
05/20/78 Pete Rose $9
05/27/78 Jim Rice..$6
06/03/78 Barr, Blue, Knepper, Montefusco....$5
06/10/78 Gary Alexander $4
06/17/78 Ron Guidry $6
06/24/78 Vic Davalillo, Manny Mota............$4
07/01/78 Paul Splittorff $4
07/08/78 Flanagan, Martinez, McGregor,
Palmer $7
07/15/78 Carew, Foster, Garvey, Guidry,
Seaver, Rice $8
07/22/78 Larry Bowa......................................$4
07/29/78 Jim Sundberg...................................$4
08/05/78 Terry Puhl $4
08/12/78 Paul Molitor $8
08/19/78 Jack Clark $4
08/26/78 Davey Lopes $4
09/16/78 Carlton Fisk $6
09/23/78 Dave Parker $4
09/30/78 Rich Gossage $5
10/21/78 Steve Garvey $5
10/28/78 Ron Guidry $6

1979

01/06/79 Ron Guidry $6
03/03/79 Spring Training issue $5
04/07/79 Guidry, Madlock, Perry, Rice...........$6
04/21/79 Pete Rose $7
04/28/79 Rod Carew $6
05/05/79 Reggie Jackson................................$8
05/12/79 Vida Blue..$4
05/19/79 Al Oliver $4
05/26/79 J.R. Richard......................................$4
06/02/79 Mike Marshall....................................$4
06/09/79 Gary Carter $7
06/16/79 Fred Lynn $6
06/23/79 Brock, Hendrick, Hernandez, Sim-
mons, Templeton $7
06/30/79 Tommy John......................................$4
07/07/79 Roy Smalley......................................$4
07/21/79 Brett, Lynn, Parker, Rose...............$8
07/28/79 Joe Niekro $4

08/04/79 Don Baylor...$4
08/11/79 Willie Stargell..................................$6
08/18/79 Mike Flanagan $4
08/25/79 Dave Kingman, Mike Schmidt $8
09/15/79 Carl Yastrzemski............................$7
09/22/79 Lou Brock.......................................$6
09/27/79 Tom Seaver $8
10/06/79 Darrell Porter.................................$4
10/20/79 Bench, Dent, Fingers, Jackson, Rose
....$8
12/29/79 Pete Rose $8

1980

01/12/80 Willie Stargell................................$5
03/08/80 Keith Hernandez............................$5
04/12/80 Mike Flanagan, Dave Winfield.......$6
04/19/80 Nolan Ryan...................................$12
04/26/80 George Brett $10
05/10/80 Kent Tekulve $4
05/17/80 George Foster $4
05/24/80 Gorman Thomas.............................$4
05/31/80 Ken Reitz, Champ Summers $4
06/07/80 Dave Kingman................................$4
06/14/80 Carlton Fisk....................................$6
06/21/80 Steve Carlton..................................$7
06/28/80 Reggie Smith $4
07/05/80 Billy Martin.....................................$6
07/12/80 Steve Garvey $6
07/26/80 Jim Palmer, Earl Weaver.................$6
08/02/80 Reggie Jackson $8
08/09/80 Willie Wilson...................................$4
08/16/80 Lee Mazzilli $4
08/23/80 Jim Bibby, Steve Stone $4
08/30/80 Andre Dawson, Ron LeFlore............$5
09/20/80 George Brett $8
09/27/80 Jose Cruz $8
10/04/80 Pete Rose $8
10/25/80 Dan Quisenberry, Mike Schmidt $8
11/01/80 Willie Aikens....................................$4

1981

01/10/81 George Brett $8
03/07/81 Rick Langford, Billy Martin $5
03/28/81 Fred Lynn, Don Sutton $5
04/11/81 Cooper, Oglivie, Simmons, Thomas,
Yount..$8
04/18/81 Ty Cobb, Nap Lajoie $4
04/25/81 Bruce Sutter $5
05/09/81 Tony Armas, Matt Keough...............$4
05/16/81 Fisk, LeFlore, Luzinski....................$6
05/23/81 Tim Raines, Fernando Valenzuela ..$5
05/30/81 Ray Grebey, Bowie Kuhn, Marvin
Miller $4
06/06/81 Gary Matthews.................................$4
06/13/81 Ken Singleton $4
06/20/81 Stan Musial, Pete Rose....................$8
06/27/81 On Strike $4

07/25/81 Chuck Tanner...................................$4
08/07/81 R. Foster, B. Gibson, Mize $4
08/14/81 Baseball's Back $4
08/22/81 Goose Gossage..................................$4
08/29/81 Bench, Concepcion, Seaver..............$6
10/31/81 Dave Winfield...................................$6

1982

03/06/82 Steve Garvey $5
03/27/82 Ozzie Smith, Garry Templeton........$4
04/10/82 Perry, Rose, Stargell, Yastrzemski ..$8
04/17/82 Collins, Foster, Griffey.....................$4
04/24/82 Al Oliver $4
05/03/82 Rafael Ramirez..................................$4
05/10/82 Eddie Murray $6
05/17/82 Keith Hernandez...............................$5
05/31/82 LaMarr Hoyt, Keith Moreland........$4
06/14/82 Rickey Henderson $7
06/28/82 Carl Yastrzemski...............................$6
07/05/82 Gene Mauch $4
07/12/82 Gary Carter, Andre Dawson.............$6
07/26/82 Earl Weaver.......................................$4
08/02/82 Aaron, Chandler, T. Jackson, F. Rob-
inson $6
08/09/82 Cecil Cooper, Robin Yount $7
08/23/82 Reggie Jackson, Steve Sax $7
09/06/82 Rickey Henderson $4
09/20/82 Dale Murphy......................................$4
10/11/82 Don Sutton, Robin Yount..................$7
10/18/82 Cecil Cooper, Bruce Sutter $4
10/25/82 Lonnie Smith, Robin Yount $7

1983

01/03/83 Whitey Herzog $4
03/07/83 Billy Martin.......................................$4
03/21/83 Steve Garvey $4
04/04/83 Porter, L. Smith, O. Smith, Sutter
....$4
04/11/83 Carl Yastrzemski...............................$6
04/18/83 Steve Kemp $4
05/02/83 Reggie Jackson..................................$7
05/09/83 Nolan Ryan......................................$10
05/16/83 George Brett $5
05/23/83 Greg Brock, Mike Marshall..............$4
06/06/83 Steve Carlton $5
06/13/83 Dave Stieb $4
06/20/83 Rod Carew $6
06/27/83 Darrell Evans.....................................$4
07/04/83 *TSN's* All-Time All-Stars $5
07/11/83 Fernando Valenzuela $4
07/25/83 Pete Rose $5
08/01/83 Alston, Kell. Marichal, B. Robinson $5
08/08/83 Brett, MacPhail, Martin, McClelland
....$5
08/22/83 Ray Knight $4
09/12/83 Floyd Bannister $4
09/26/83 Cecil Cooper, Andre Dawson $5

10/10/83 Alexander, Fisk, Larsen, Mazeroski$5
10/24/83 Cal Ripken Jr., Lenn Sakata $10

1984

01/02/84 Bowie Kuhn $4
03/05/84 Cal Ripken Jr. $10
04/02/84 Pete Rose $7
04/09/84 Goose Gossage $4
04/23/84 Wade Boggs......................................$6
04/30/84 Bill Madlock......................................$4
05/07/84 Phil Niekro, Jose Rijo......................$5
05/14/84 Dave Kingman..................................$5
05/21/84 Darryl Strawberry............................$8
05/28/84 Lemon, Parrish, Trammell, Whitaker
....$8
06/11/84 Mike Schmidt...................................$8
06/18/84 Leon Durham $4
06/25/84 Eddie Murray $6
07/02/84 Rickey Henderson $6
07/09/84 Cronin, Foxx, Gehrig, Hubbell, Simmons, Ruth $6
07/23/84 Tony Gwynn.....................................$8
08/06/84 Aparicio, Drysdale, Killebrew, Reese
....$10
08/20/84 Ryne Sandberg $10
09/17/84 Kirk Gibson, Willie Hernandez $7
09/24/84 Kirby Puckett $10
10/08/84 Willie Mays......................................$7
10/15/84 Steve Garvey, Alan Trammell......... $7
10/22/84 Gibson, Trammell, Whitaker...........$7
12/31/84 Peter Ueberroth..............................$4

1985

02/11/85 Berra, Henderson, Steinbrenner, Armstrong, Montefusco, Torborg....................$4
03/04/85 Ryne Sandberg $8
03/25/85 Bruce Sutter $4
04/08/85 Rickey Henderson, Don Mattingly ..$8
04/15/85 Anderson, Gibson, Hernandez, Morris, Trammell $7
04/22/85 LaMarr Hoyt....................................$4
04/29/85 Dale Murphy.....................................$4
05/13/85 Armas, Boggs, Easler, Evans, Rice..$4
05/20/85 Billy Martin $4
05/27/85 Terry Whitfield $4
06/10/85 Brett, Quisenberry, Schuerholz, Wilson $4
06/17/85 Joaquin Andujar, Mario Soto...........$4
06/24/85 Jack Clark, David Green baseball cards..$4
06/31/85 Dale Murphy, Eddie Murray............$5
07/08/85 Vince Coleman...................................$4
07/15/85 Bill Caudill, Gary Lavelle.................$4
07/29/85 Gooden, Brock, Slaughter, Vaughan, Wilhelm..$7
08/12/85 Tom Seaver $5
08/19/85 Peter Ueberroth...............................$4

09/09/85 Pittsburgh Pirates franchise $4
09/16/85 Pete Rose $7
09/30/85 Mets-Yankees battle for Big Apple.. $6
10/07/85 Pedro Guerrero $5
10/14/85 Cardinals celebrate pennant...........$4
11/04/85 George Brett, Bret Saberhagen $6
12/09/85 Kirk Gibson $5

1986

01/06/86 Pete Rose, Whitey Herzog $6
02/10/86 Ken "Hawk" Harrelson....................$4
02/17/86 Candlestick Park $4
03/03/86 Brett, J. Clark, R. Henderson $6
03/17/86 Reggie Jackson.................................$4
03/24/86 Dave Parker, Darryl Strawberry.....$4
04/07/86 Ozzie Smith......................................$6
04/21/86 Canseco, W. Clark, Galarraga, Incaviglia, Carew $7
04/28/86 Hoyt, D. Williams, Guidry.............$4
05/12/86 Boone, R. Jackson, Sutton..............$6
05/19/86 P. Niekro, Martin, Schmidt $4
05/26/86 Carlton, Rose, Ryan, Puckett.........$6
06/02/86 Robin Yount, Hubie Brooks $6
06/09/96 Gooden, K. Hernandez, Leonard.....$7
06/16/86 Don Sutton $4
06/23/86 Hal Lanier, Bobby Valentine $4
06/30/86 George Steinbrenner.........................$6
07/07/86 Mike Krukow.....................................$4
07/14/86 Wade Boggs, Bo Jackson $7
07/21/86 Darling, Fernandez, Orosco.............$4
07/28/86 Bankhead, Clark, McDowell, Snyder, Witt, Clemens..$6
08/04/86 Glenn Davis, Mike Scott..................$6
08/18/86 Jose Canseco, Tim Raines $6
08/25/86 Earl Weaver, Tom Lasorda $4
09/01/86 Don Mattingly, Rickey Henderson ..$8
09/08/86 Jack Morris $4
09/15/86 Rob Deer..$5
09/29/86 G. Carter, Clemens, Ashburn..........$8
10/13/86 G. Davis, DeCinces, K. Hernandez, Rice $6
10/27/86 Len Dykstra, Mike Schmidt $5
10/03/86 Marty Barrett, Gary Carter $4
10/24/86 Lance Parrish...................................$5
12/15/86 Roger Clemens $5

1987

03/02/87 Dwight Gooden..................................$4
03/30/87 Mike Schmidt....................................$4
04/06/87 Reggie Jackson..................................$4
04/13/87 Ron Guidry $3.50
05/11/87 Andre Dawson $3.75
05/18/87 Pete Rose $4
05/25/87 Bret Saberhagen $3.50
06/01/87 Rickey Henderson, Charles Hudson$4
06/08/87 Jack Clark $3.50
06/15/87 Eric Davis $3.75

07/06/87 Harold Baines, Jody Davis $3.50
07/13/87 Jack Morris, Alan Trammell......$3.75
07/27/87 Bert Blyleven, Jeff Reardon........$3.50
08/03/87 Whitey Herzog.............................$3.50
08/10/87 Coleman, Durham, Guidry, R. Henderson, Pettis, Strawberry.................................$4
08/24/87 Cal Ripken Sr. $3.50
08/31/87 G. Bell, J. Clark, E. Davis, Dawson, Mattingly, McGwire $4
09/07/87 Will Clark $4
10/05/87 George Bell, Alan Trammell $3.50
10/19/87 Boston Red Sox, New York Mets $3.50
10/26/87 Greg Gagne, Willie McGee..........$3.50
11/02/87 Kent Hrbek, Kirby Puckett.............$4
12/14/87 George Bell $3.50

1988

02/01/88 Yankees, Mets hats $3.50
03/07/88 Kirk Gibson, Tommy Lasorda.....$3.75
04/11/88 Kent Hrbek, Wayne Garland $3.50
04/25/88 Eddie Murray, Frank Robinson ..$3.50
05/02/88 Billy Martin, Dave Winfield.............$4
05/09/88 Roger Clemens................................$4
05/16/88 Canseco, Parker, McGwire..........$4.50
05/30/88 Wrigley Field $3.50
06/06/88 Gooden, D. Robinson, Ryan $6.50
06/20/88 Greg Maddux, Mark Grace.........$3.50
07/04/88 Andres Galarraga, Billy Martin......$4
07/11/88 Baseball cards, Andy Van Slyke......$4
07/25/88 Brett, Sabo, Steinbach $3.50
08/01/88 Frank Viola...................................$3.50
08/08/88 Darryl Strawberry...........................$4
08/15/88 Joe Morgan $3.50
08/22/88 Alan Trammell............................$3.50
09/05/88 Kirby Puckett, Dennis Rasmussen
....$3.75
10/17/88 Boggs, Canseco, Gibson, Strawberry
....$4.50
10/24/88 Kirk Gibson, Orel Hershiser............$4
10/31/88 Orel Hershiser.................................$4

1989

01/23/89 Johnny Bench, Carl Yastrzemski
....$4.50
03/06/89 Molitor, Murray, Valentine, Van Slyke
....$3.50
04/03/89 J. Clark, Hurst, McKeon.............$3.50
04/10/89 Ken Griffey Jr., Ken Griffey Sr...$6.50
04/24/89 Ellis Burks, Pete Rose......................$4
05/01/89 Gregg Jefferies $4.50
05/08/89 Kevin Mitchell $3.75
05/15/89 Brady Anderson, Cal Ripken Jr..$3.75
05/22/89 Tommy John, Jose DeLeon $3.50
06/05/89 Ernie Whitt, Fred McGriff.........$3.50
06/12/89 Blyleven, D. Sanders, Schmidt........$4
07/03/89 John Franco, Don Zimmer $3.50
07/24/89 Orel Hershiser, Howard Johnson $4

07/31/89 J. Franco, Palmeiro, Sierra $4
08/07/89 Lonnie Smith................................$3.50
08/14/89 Will Clark, Kevin Mitchell $4
08/21/89 Nolan Ryan..$5
08/28/89 Jose Oquendo, Mike Scott $3.50
09/04/89 Pete Rose $3.75
09/18/89 Wade Boggs, Tony Gwynn $4
10/16/89 McGriff, McGwire, Mitchell, Sandberg $4
10/23/89 Terry Kennedy, Terry Steinbach
....$3.50
10/30/89 San Francisco earthquake...............$4
11/06/89 Oakland A's...................................$3.50
12/11/89 Kevin Mitchell.............................$3.50

1990

01/08/90 J. Carter, M. Davis, Langston, Parker
....$3.50
01/29/90 Mike Schmidt.................................$4
03/05/90 Baseball lockout..........................$3.50
03/12/90 Dwight Gooden, Pete Rose $3.75
04/09/90 Jack McKeon, Darryl Strawberry
....$3.50
04/30/90 G. Davis, Hrbek, Puckett............$3.50
05/07/90 E. Davis, Larkin, O'Neill, Piniella, Sabo $3.50
05/21/90 Jose Canseco, Will Clark $4
06/04/90 Cecil Fielder $4
06/11/90 Schooler, Viola, M. Williams.......$3.50
06/18/90 Len Dykstra $3.50
06/25/90 Nolan Ryan......................................$4
07/02/90 Barry Bonds, Charlie Fox...........$3.50
07/09/90 Dwight Gooden, Bret Saberhagen
....$3.50
07/23/90 Bert Blyleven, Don Drysdale......$3.50
07/30/90 M. Davis, Heaton, Parker, Wells $3.50
08/06/90 Gant, Strawberry, Tapani...........$3.75
08/13/90 Nolan Ryan, George Steinbrenner..$4
08/20/90 Comiskey Park, Hurst, Mattingly...$4
08/27/90 Bob Welch....................................$3.50
09/03/90 Jeff Ballard, Ramon Martinez....$3.50
09/10/90 Jose Canseco, Barry Larkin $4
09/24/90 Rickey Henderson.......................$3.50
10/01/90 Baines, Canseco, Lansford, McGee, McGwire, Welch, Weiss..............................$3.50
10/15/90 Chris Sabo, Andy Van Slyke.......$3.50
10/22/90 Dennis Eckersley $3.50
10/29/90 Rob Dibble, Lou Piniella.............$3.50
12/17/90 Joe Carter, Fred McGriff $3.50
12/31/90 Glove of money $3.50

1991

01/07/91 Nolan Ryan...................................$3.50
03/04/91 Dave Parker $3.50
03/11/91 Jim Palmer $3
04/01/91 Umpire Bruce Froemming..............$3

04/22/91 G. Bell, J. Clark, R. Henderson, Sanderson...$3
05/13/91 Rickey Henderson, Nolan Ryan..$3.50
05/20/91 Rob Dibble $3
05/27/91 Dave Justice $3
06/17/91 Andre Dawson $3
07/01/91 Gambling in baseball $3
07/08/91 Hundley, Lankford, Van Poppel.......$3
07/29/91 Peter Ueberroth...............................$3
08/05/91 Tiger Stadium.................................$3
08/12/91 Lineups, Dennis Martinez $3
08/19/91 Wounded baseball $3
08/26/91 Pedro Guerrero...............................$3
09/09/91 Bobby Cox $3
09/16/91 Bobby Bonilla $3
09/23/91 Terry Pendleton $3
10/14/91 John Smoltz....................................$3
10/21/91 Kirby Puckett $3
11/04/91 Jack Morris.....................................$3
11/11/91 Bobby Bonilla.................................$3
12/16/91 Bobby Bonilla $3
12/23/91 Steve Palermo, Whitey Herzog........$3

1992

03/02/92 Tom Glavine...............................$2.50
03/09/92 Kirby Puckett $2.50
03/16/92 George Brett $2.50
03/30/92 Cal Ripken Jr.............................$2.50
04/06/92 Joe Carter, Rob Dibble $2.50
04/13/92 Jose Canseco...............................$2.50
04/20/92 Camden Yards $2.50
04/27/92 Butch Hobson $2.50
05/04/92 Barry Bonds................................$2.50
05/11/92 Tony Gwynn $2.50
05/18/92 Craig Biggio................................$2.50
05/25/92 Lenny Harris $2.50
06/01/92 Todd Hundley $2.50
06/08/92 Jeff Reardon $2.50

06/15/92 Gary Sheffield $3
06/22/92 David Cone.................................$2.50
06/29/92 Leo Durocher, Willie Randolph ..$2.50
07/06/92 Norm Charlton, Rob Dibble........$2.50
07/20/92 Carlton Fisk $2.50
07/27/92 Robin Yount................................$2.50
08/03/92 El Beisbol $2.50
08/31/92 John Smoltz....................................$3
09/14/92 Joe Carter....................................$2.50
09/21/92 Fay Vincent $2.50
09/28/92 Jay Bell, Darrin Fletcher $2.50
10/05/92 Tom Glavine, Frank Thomas......$2.50
10/12/92 Dennis Eckersley $2.50
10/19/92 Steve Avery.................................$2.50
10/26/92 Ed Sprague..................................$2.50
11/02/92 Joe Carter, Otis Nixon $2.50
11/23/92 Mark McGwire $2.50

1993

02/01/93 George Brett
02/22/93 How We'd Fix Baseball
03/01/93 Joe Siddall
04/05/93 Dave Winfield
04/19/93 Roger Clemens
05/17/93 Carlton Fisk
05/31/93 Gregg Jefferies
06/14/93 Barry Bonds
07/05/93 Barry Bonds
07/19/93 Jim Abbott
07/26/93 Jack McDowell
08/02/93 Dave Justice
08/09/93 Wade Boggs, Chad Kreuter
08/16/93 Nolan Ryan, Robin Ventura
08/30/93 Don Mattingly
09/20/93 Frank Thomas
10/11/93 John Kruk
10/25/93 Len Dykstra
11/01/93 Jays Celebrate

Sporting News Baseball Guides

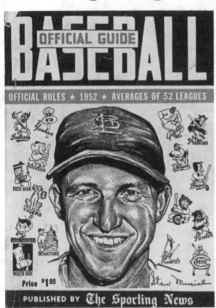

Offer complete team recaps for the previous major league season, plus statistics and lists of the award winners. From 1943-62 the guide was known as *The Sporting News* Baseball Guide & Record Book. It's been called *The Sporting News* Official Baseball Guide from 1963 to present.

1942 Baseball art	$165
1943 Patriotic art	$50-$55
1944 B. Newsom/B. Dahlgren	$35-$40
1945 Marty Marion	$35-$42
1946 Hal Newhouser	$35-$42
1947 Harry Brecheen	$35-$42
1948 Ewell Blackwell	$50-$60
1949 Lou Boudreau	$50-$60
1950 P. Rizzuto/P.W. Reese	$50-$60
1951 Red Schoendienst	$50-$60
1952 Stan Musial	$50-$60
1953 Robin Roberts	$45-$55
1954 Casey Stengel	$45-$55
1955 Baseball action	$45-$55
1956 J. Coleman/B. Martin	$45-$55
1957 Mickey Mantle	$50-$60
1958 Ted Williams	$40-$50
1959 Baseballs	$35-$45
1960 Mullin "Bum" cartoon	$35-$40
1961 Trophy	$25-$35
1962 R. Maris/B. Ruth	$35-$40
1963 Mullin cartoon	$25-$35
1964 Stan Musial	$25-$35
1965 B. Robinson/K. Boyer	$25-$35

1966 W. Mays/S. Koufax	$20-$30
1967 F. Robinson/Koufax/Clemente	$20-$30
1968 Yastrzemski/Cepeda/Lonborg	$15-$25
1969 Rose/Gibson/McLain	$17.50-$27.50
1970 McCovey/Killebrew	$10-$20
1971 Bench/Gibson/Killebrew	$12.50-$17
1972 Jenkins/Blue/Torre	$10-$15
1973 Carlton/Bench/G. Perry	$12.50-$17
1974 Palmer/Jackson/Bonds	$12.50-$17
1975 Brock/Hunter	$10-$15
1976 Morgan/Seaver/Palmer	$13-$18
1977 Munson/Palmer	$8-$12
1978 Carew/Ryan/Carlton	$12.50-$17
1979 Guidry/Rice/Parker	$7-$10
1980 K. Hernandez/Baylor	$6-$10
1981 Steve Carlton	$8-$12
1982 Tom Seaver	$10-$15
1983 Robin Yount	$8-$12
1984 Cal Ripken Jr.	$10-$15
1985 Ryne Sandberg	$9-$13
1986 Willie McGee	$5-$7
1987 Roger Clemens	$8-$12
1988 Andre Dawson	$6-$9
1989 Jose Canseco	$6-$9
1990 Bret Saberhagen	$5-$7
1991 Bob Welch	$5-$7
1992 Will Clark	$5-$7
1993 Kirby Puckett	$5-$7

Sporting News Baseball Register

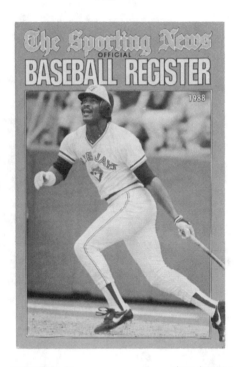

Lists statistics for active major league players from the year before, for every player who appeared in at least one game. Minor league statistics and career accomplishments are also included.

1940 Ty Cobb .... $75-$90
1941 Paul Derringer .... $35-$40
1942 Joe DiMaggio........................ $40-$45
1943 Uncle Sam art .... $25-$30
1944 Rube Waddell art .... $25-$30
1945 Billy Southworth.................. $25-$30
1946 Baseball art .... $35-$40
1947 Walter Johnson .... $40-$45
1948 Baseball art .... $35-$40
1949 Baseball art .... $35-$40
1950 Joe DiMaggio........................ $35-$40
1951 Baseball art .... $25-$30
1952 Baseball art .... $25-$30
1953 Baseball art .... $25-$30
1954 Baseball art .... $22-$25
1955 Baseball art .... $22-$25
1956 Baseball art .... $22-$25
1957 Baseball art .... $22-$25
1958 Baseball art .... $22-$25
1959 Baseball art .... $25-$30
1960 Baseball art .... $17.50-$20
1961 Baseball art .... $22-$25
1962 Baseball art .... $22-$25
1963 Baseball art .... $22-$25
1964 Yankee Stadium .... $22-$25
1965 Ken Boyer.............................. $22-$25
1966 Sandy Koufax........................ $22-$25
1967 Frank & Brooks Robinson ... $22-$25
1968 Boston Red Sox .... $20-$22.50
1969 Willie Horton.................. $20-$22.50

1970 Tom Seaver .... $20-$22.50
1971 Willie Mays........................... $15-$20
1972 Joe Torre .... $15-$20
1973 Wilbur Wood .... $15-$20
1974 Pete Rose .... $15-$20
1975 Catfish Hunter .... $15-$17.50
1976 Jim Palmer .... $15-$17.50
1977 Joe Morgan .... $15-$17.50
1978 Rod Carew .... $12.50-$15
1979 Ron Guidry .... $12.50-$15
1980 Carl Yastrzemski............. $12.50-$15
1981 George Brett .... $12.50-$15
1982 Fernando Valenzuela ...... $12.50-$15
1983 Bruce Sutter .... $10-$12.50
1984 John Denny .... $10-$12.50
1985 Willie Hernandez .... $10-$12.50
1986 Don Mattingly .... $9-$11
1987 Mike Schmidt .... $12.50-$15.00
1988 George Bell .... $9-$11
1989 Frank Viola............................ $9-$11
1990 Kevin Mitchell................. $10-$12.50
1991 Barry Bonds.................... $10-$12.50
1992 Frank Thomas................... $5-$7.50
1993 Gary Sheffield.................... $5-$7.50

American League Red Books

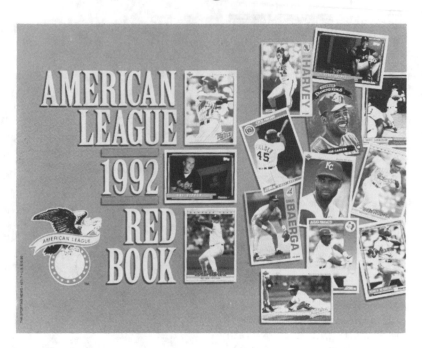

1943 Blue "V," (First Red Book) $100
1944 Blue baseball with red seams $75
1945 Blue baseball with red seams $70
1946 Blue baseball with title $60
1947 Baseball in right corner $50
1948 Title and 1948.. $45
1949 Title and 1949.. $45
1950 Title and 1950 (1st glossy cover) $37.50
1951 A.L. Golden Anniversary $37.50
1952 "Play Ball!", Ted Williams...................... $37.50
1953 Shantz, Fox, Wynn, others.......................... $35
1954 Vernon, Kuenn, Stengel, Rose..................... $35
1955 All-Star Team photo $35
1956 Lemon, Stengel, managers $32.50
1957 Team logos... $32.50
1958 50th Anniversary of BBWAA $32.50
1959 Tiger sliding into home $32.50
1960 Cobb, DiMaggio, Fox, Ruth, Gehrig, others
.... $37.50
1961 Four players with arms linked $30
1962 Mantle, Maris, A.L. HR Leaders.............. $37.50
1963 Team pennants $27.50
1964 Killebrew, Yastrzemski, others..................... $25
1965 D. Chance, Powell, Oliva, others $22.50
1966 McDowell, T. Conigliaro, others.............. $27.50
1967 Frank Robinson "Triple Crown" $27.50
1968 Yastrzemski "MVP/Triple Crown".......... $27.50

1969 Cobb, Ruth, HOF plaques $27.50
1970 Harmon Killebrew.. $20
1971 Boog Powell $20
1972 Team, Major League logos............................ $20
1973 Team hats with Oakland in center $20
1974 Team, Major League logos............................ $20
1975 Team logos.. $15
1976 Carlton Fisk Series homer $17.50
1977 Team logos, with Seattle and Toronto $15
1978 Carew, Nettles, Murray, others $15
1979 Guidry, Rice, Carew, others.......................... $15
1980 Orioles and Eddie Murray $12
1981 Boddicker, Charboneau, Brett $12
1982 1981 Playoffs team pictures $12
1983 Vuckovich, Yount, Ripken............................ $15
1984 L. Hoyt, Ripken, Quisenberry, Kittle $10
1985 Stars and Detroit Tigers Series celebration $8
1986 Newspaper headlines (Boggs, Seaver, others)
.... $8.50
1987 Mattingly, Canseco, Clemens, others $8
1988 Twins World Series celebration................. $7.50
1989 1988 A.L. media guide covers.................... $7.50
1990 1980s Red Book covers $7
1991 League trophies, awards $7
1992 Baseball cards... $7
1993 George Brett, Robin Yount.............................. $7

National League Green Books

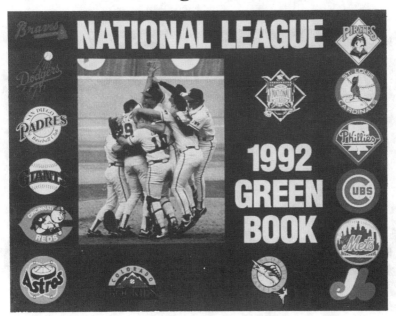

1935 Jan. 30, 1935 (First Green Book) $75
1936 60th Birthday edition, Feb. 2, 1936.............. $60
1937 Title and Feb. 5, 1937 .... $60
1938 Title and 1938.. $60
1939 Centennial edition 1839-1939 .... $55
1940 Title and 1940.. $50
1941 Title and 1941 .... $47.50
1942 Baseball diamond $75
1943 Title and 1943.. $75
1944 Title and 1944.. $70
1945 Title and 1945.. $65
1946 BBWAA logo $60
1947 Title and 1947 in diamond shape.................... $50
1948 Runner thrown out at first base...................... $45
1949 Team logos, pennants $45
1950 Team logos, pennants $40
1951 75th Anniversary, ball in glove $40
1952 National League cities $40
1953 National League cities $40
1954 All-Star Team, 1st glossy cover..................... $40
1955 Eight stars (Mays, Musial, Spahn) $40
1956 Dodgers celebration photos $35
1957 National League $35
1958 N.L. salutes the BBWAA $35
1959 Spahn/Musial clippings $35
1960 Snider, McCovey, Musial, others $37.50
1961 Spahn, Howard, F. Robinson, etc. $30
1962 Map of U.S., team logos.......................... $27.50
1963 1958-62 League Champs' parks............... $27.50
1964 Stan Musial.. $27.50

1965 List of past N.L. Champions $27.50
1966 Stadiums of 1960s, seven $25
1967 1962-66 Attendance figures...................... $27.50
1968 1967 Highlights/news clippings $21
1969 1869 Cincinnati Red Stockings $21
1970 Hodges, Rose, McCovey, Mets $20
1971 Baseball with team names $20
1972 12 bats with team names $15
1973 Roberto Clemente memorial $25
1974 Hank Aaron/Babe Ruth bust........................ $25
1975 Aaron, Brock, Schmidt, others $15
1976 Reds World Series celebration...................... $15
1977 Team logos... $13
1978 12 league stars $13
1979 League helmets, four bats............................ $13
1980 Baseball $12
1981 Schmidt, McGraw, All-Stars, Astros............ $12
1982 Valenzuela, Ryan, Schmidt, Rose................. $13
1983 Sax, D. Murphy, Carlton, others................... $10
1984 Team pennants $10
1985 Garvey, Sandberg, Gooden, Sutcliffe $8.50
1986 Rose, Gooden, Ryan, McGee $9
1987 Worrell, Scott, Mets, Schmidt, Raines $7.50
1988 .... $8
1989 Los Angeles celebration $8
1990 1980s MVPs and Cy Youngs........................... $8
1991 Reds celebration, others $7.50
1992 Braves celebration $7.50
1993 U.S. map with team logos $7.50

Sports Illustrated

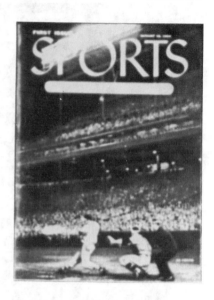

Although the sport ranks second in terms of appearances on the cover, baseball is featured on the granddaddy *Sports Illustrated* issue of them all.

The premiere issue, of what was billed as the nation's first sports weekly, is dated Aug. 16, 1954, with a cover price of just a quarter. That issue, which now among collectors has a value of $250, features the Milwaukee Braves' Eddie Mathews swinging at a pitch in Milwaukee's County Stadium. Catcher Wes Westrum and umpire Augie Donatelli are also included.

The issue's value is also driven up by the three pages of 1954 Topps baseball cards, featuring Willie Mays, Ted Williams and Jackie Robinson, printed on paper stock.

New York Yankees stars, including Mickey Mantle, are featured on 1954 Topps black-and-white and colored cards included in the magazine's second issue, dated Aug. 23, 1954. This magazine, which shows a horde of golf bags on the greens at the Masters, is as rare and as valuable as the first issue.

During *Sports Illustrated's* first 36 years of publication (through 1990), the magazine's cover has featured more than 360 baseball-related pictures. From 1954-1990, football tops the list, with 446 out of approximately 1,900 covers.

Leading the way for baseball players, with 10 appearances, is Reggie Jackson, who also has the distinction of holding the cover record for most different baseball uniforms worn - four, for the A's, Angels, Yankees and Orioles. Dick Groat (Phillies, Pirates and Cardinals) and Billy Martin (Rangers, Yankees, Twins) also each had three appearances. Martin is also one of only three athletes (the others are Gordie Howe and Willie Mays) to have appeared on a cover in four decades of the magazine's existence - the '50s, '60s, '70s and '80s.

The Minnesota Twins are among four teams to have been featured on three consecutive weeks. The team's streak occurred during the team's 1987 World Championship season. The Oct. 19 issue featured Greg Gagne, who was followed by Dan Gladden (Oct. 26) and a team celebration shot on Nov. 2. The team's success in 1991 led to another streak of three, beginning with the Oct. 21 issue with Kirby Puckett, followed by the Oct. 28 issue with Dan Gladden, and the Nov. 4 issue featuring Twins players celebrating a World Series championship.

The same baseball photo was used on two issue covers twice. A photo of Denny McLain was used on the July 29, 1968, issue as he was pursuing 30 wins, and again on Feb. 23, 1970, when he was in trouble for gambling.

George Brett and Mike Schmidt appeared on the April 3, 1981, baseball preview cover and again on Aug. 10, with the billing "HERE WE GO AGAIN," signfying the end of the baseball strike.

In addition to trying to collect an entire run of *SIs*, some topics to pursue include those which feature favorite players, teams, themes (World Series, All-Stars, Previews) or those named as the magazine's Sportsman of the Year. Baseball players named include:

Johnny Podres, 01/02/56; Stan Musial, 12/23/57; Sandy Koufax, 12/20/65; Carl Yastrzemski, 12/25/67; Tom Seaver, 12/22/69; Pete Rose, 12/22-29/75; Willie Stargell, 12/24-31/79; and Orel Hershiser, 12/19/88.

Father/son combinations can also be pursued. During the years they have included Ken Sr. and Ken Griffey Jr., the Ripken clan, Barry and Bobby Bonds, and Bump and Maury Wills.

First cover issues are also especially sought after by those who seek to have them autographed. These issues generally command a higher price than subsequent issues with the same player.

Generally, collectors who seek back issues want them to be in reasonable condition - unripped, uncreased - with the cover attached entirely. But the corners on many issues are often not sharp, especially from the earlier issues.

Old *Sports Illustrateds* can often be purchased at libraries, flea markets, through hobby publications and mail order houses, and card shops and shows.

1954

08/16/54 Eddie Mathews, Braves $250

1955

04/11/55 Mays, Day, Durocher, Giants $100
04/18/55 Al Rosen, Indians $55
05/30/55 Herb Score, Indians $15
06/27/55 Duke Snider, Dodgers $30
07/11/55 Yogi Berra, Yankees $35
08/01/55 Ted Williams, Red Sox .... $50-$75
08/25/55 Don Newcombe, Dodgers $20
09/26/55 Walter Alston, Dodgers $20

1956

01/02/56 Johnny Podres, Dodgers $20
03/05/56 Stan Musial, Cardinals, spring training .. $15
04/09/56 Spring Baseball Preview $25
04/23/56 Billy Martin, Yankees $20
05/14/56 Al Kaline, Harvey Kuenn, Tigers $30
06/18/56 Mickey Mantle, Yankees......................... $55
06/25/56 Warren Spahn, Braves....................... $27.50
07/09/56 Mays, Mantle, All-Stars......................... $35
07/16/56 Kluszewski, Post, Bell, Indians $25
07/30/56 Joe Adcock, Braves............................... $15
08/20/56 Second Anniversary issue $25
09/10/56 Whitey Ford, Yankees............................ $25
10/01/56 World Series, Mickey Mantle $45

1957

03/04/57 Mickey Mantle, Yankees......................... $40
04/15/57 Spring Baseball Preview $20
04/22/57 Wally Moon, Cardinals $12
05/13/57 Billy Pierce, White Sox $15
06/03/57 Clem Labine, Dodgers $15
07/08/57 Stan Musial, Ted Williams..................... $40

07/22/57 Hank Bauer, Yankees $10
09/09/57 Roy McMillan, Reds $9
09/30/57 Whitey Ford, Yankees, World Series $15
12/23/57 Stan Musial, Cardinals, (SOY) $25

1958

03/03/58 Yankees, Spring Training $9
03/17/58 Sal Maglie, Big League Secrets $12
03/31/58 Roy Sievers, Big League Secrets $12
04/14/58 Spring Baseball Preview $20
04/21/58 Del Crandall, Big League Secrets $10
05/19/58 Richie Ashburn, Big League Secrets $15
06/02/58 Eddie Mathews, Braves...................... $17.50
06/23/58 Jackie Jensen, Red Sox $12
07/07/58 Musial/Mantle/Mays $17.50
07/28/58 Frank Thomas, Pirates............................ $10
09/29/58 World Series $15

1959

03/02/59 Fred Haney, Casey Stengel $10
04/13/59 Willie Mays, Giants............................... $27
05/04/59 Bob Turley, Yankees $12
06/15/59 L.A. Coliseum baseball crowd................. $7
08/10/59 Nellie Fox/Luis Aparicio, White Sox $30
09/28/59 Chicago White Sox $16

1960

03/07/60 Spring Training $8
04/11/60 Baseball Preview issue $15
06/06/60 Red Schoendienst, Braves...................... $10
07/04/60 Comiskey Park $8
07/18/60 Candlestick Park $7.50
08/08/60 Dick Groat, Pirates................................. $10
10/10/60 Vernon Law, Pirates $9

Periodicals

1961

03/06/61 Spring Training	$10
04/10/61 Baseball Preview issue	$13
05/15/61 Cookie Lavagetto, Twins	$7
06/26/61 Ernie Broglio, Willie Mays	$10
07/31/61 Baseball umpire	$7
10/02/61 Roger Maris, Yankees	$30
10/09/61 Joey Jay, Reds	$7

1962

03/05/62 Casey Stengel, Mets	$13.50
04/09/62 Frank Lary, Detroit	$7
04/30/62 Luis Aparicio, White Sox	$13
06/04/62 Willie Mays, Giants	$15
07/02/62 Mickey Mantle, Yankees	$27.50
07/30/62 Ken Boyer, Cardinals	$10
08/20/62 Don Drysdale, Dodgers	$12
10/01/62 World Series	$15

1963

03/04/63 Sandy Koufax, Dodgers	$20
04/08/63 Baseball Preview issue	$17.50
04/29/63 Art Mahaffey, Phillies	$6
06/24/63 Roy Face, Pirates	$7.50
07/22/63 Dick Groat, Cardinals	$8.50
09/02/63 Ron Fairly, Dodgers	$7
09/30/63 Whitey Ford, Yankees	$17.50

1964

03/02/64 Casey Stengel, Yogi Berra	$14
04/13/64 Sandy Koufax, Dodgers	$14
05/11/64 Al Kaline, Tigers	$15
05/25/64 Frank Howard, Dodgers	$9
07/06/64 Alvin Dark, Giants	$7.50
08/10/64 Johnny Callison, Phillies	$8
08/31/64 Brooks Robinson, Orioles	$12.50

1965

03/01/65 Jim Bunning, Bo Belinsky, Phillies	$10
04/19/65 Baseball Preview	$17.50
05/17/65 Bill Veeck, White Sox	$6
06/21/65 Mickey Mantle, Yankees	$25
07/12/65 Maury Wills, Dodgers	$8
08/09/65 Juan Marichal, Giants	$12
08/23/65 Tony Oliva, Twins	$10
10/04/65 World Series/Zoilo Versailles, Twins	$12
12/20/65 Sandy Koufax, Dodgers, (SOY)	$15

1966

02/28/66 Leo Durocher, Eddie Stanky, White Sox .	$9
04/18/66 Dick Groat, Phillies	$15
05/23/66 Sam McDowell, Indians	$10
06/06/66 Joe Morgan, Sonny Jackson, Astros	$11
07/11/66 Andy Etchebarren, Orioles	$7
09/05/66 Harry Walker, Pirates	$6
09/26/66 Gaylord Perry, Giants	$12
10/10/66 Brooks and Frank Robinson, Orioles	$15

1967

03/13/67 Jim Nash, A's	$6

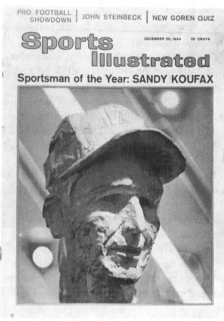

Sportsman of the Year: SANDY KOUFAX

04/17/67 Maury Wills, Pirates	$18
05/08/67 Mickey Mantle, Ken Berry	$25
05/15/67 Sandy Koufax, Don Drysdale, Dodgers..	$10
06/05/67 Al Kaline, Tigers	$20
07/03/67 Roberto Clemente, Pirates, $15	
07/31/67 Spitball	$5
08/21/67 Carl Yastrzemski, Red Sox	$20
09/04/67 Tim McCarver, Cardinals	$8
10/15/67 Lou Brock, Cardinals	$15
12/25/67 Carl Yastrzemski, Red Sox, (SOY)	$20

1968

03/11/68 Johnny Bench, Reds, Baseball rookies	$17
04/15/68 Lou Brock, Cardinals	$20
05/06/68 Ron Swoboda, Mets	$8
05/27/68 Pete Rose, Reds	$22.50
06/17/68 Don Drysdale, Dodgers	$12
07/08/68 Ted Williams, Red Sox	$11
07/29/68 Denny McLain, Tigers	$9
08/19/68 Curt Flood, Cardinals	$8
09/02/68 Ken Harrelson, Red Sox	$8
09/23/68 Denny McLain, Tigers, 30 Wins	$11
10/07/68 St. Louis Cardinals	$15

1969

03/17/69 Ted Williams, Senators	$13
04/14/69 Bill Freehan, Tigers	$10
05/19/69 Walt Alston and Dodgers	$7
06/30/69 Ron Santo, Cubs	$8
07/07/69 Reggie Jackson, A's	$21
07/21/69 Billy Martin, Twins	$6
08/18/69 Hank Aaron, Braves	$15

09/08/69 Pete Rose, Ernie Banks $17.50
10/06/69 Frank Robinson, Orioles $9
10/20/69 Brooks Robinson, Orioles vs. Mets.........$12
12/22/69 Tom Seaver, Mets...................................$20

1970

02/23/70 Denny McLain, Tigers $10
03/23/70 Dick Allen, Cardinals...............................$8
04/13/70 Jerry Koosman, Mets $15
05/25/70 Hank Aaron, Braves, 3,000 Hits $12.50
06/22/70 Tony Conigliaro, Red Sox.....................$10
07/13/70 Johnny Bench, Reds................................$15
07/27/70 Willie Mays, 3,000 Hits $15
09/07/70 Bud Harrelson, Mets $8
09/28/70 Danny Murtaugh, Pirates $8
10/19/70 Reds vs. Orioles $10

1971

03/22/71 Wes Parker, Dodgers $6
04/12/71 Boog Powell, Orioles $12
05/03/71 Dave Duncan, Jim Fregosi $5
05/31/71 Vida Blue, A's..$8
06/21/71 Jerry Grote, Mets......................................$6
07/05/71 Alex Johnson, Angels...............................$6
08/02/71 Willie Stargell, Pirates............................$10
08/30/71 Ferguson Jenkins, Cubs............................$9
09/27/71 Maury Wills, Dodgers $5
10/18/71 Frank Robinson, Orioles $8

1972

03/13/72 Johnny Bench, Reds.................................$15
03/27/72 Vida Blue, A's..$5
04/10/72 Joe Torre, Cardinals................................$10
05/01/72 Willie Davis, Dodgers $5
05/22/72 Willie Mays, Mets $12
06/12/72 Dick Allen, White Sox $8
07/03/72 Steve Blass, Pirates $5
08/21/72 Sparky Lyle, Yankees...........................$5.50
09/25/72 Carlton Fisk, Red Sox $10
10/23/72 Catfish Hunter, A's $10

1973

03/12/73 Bill Melton, White Sox $6
04/09/73 Steve Carlton, Phillies............................$12
04/30/73 Chris Speier, Giants..................................$5
06/04/73 Wilbur Wood, White Sox $8
07/02/73 Bobby Murcer/Ron Blomberg, Yankees ...$8
07/30/73 Carlton Fisk, Red Sox $10
08/20/73 Claude Osteen/Bill Russell, Dodgers........$6
09/24/73 Danny Murtaugh, Pirates $6
10/22/73 Bert Campaneris, A's................................$8

1974

03/18/74 Babe Ruth, Yankees $8
04/08/74 Pete Rose, Reds......................................$15
04/15/74 Hank Aaron, Braves, 715th Homer.........$20
05/27/74 Jim Wynn, Dodgers...................................$5
06/17/74 Reggie Jackson, A's................................$10
07/01/74 Rod Carew, Twins $10

07/22/74 Lou Brock, Cardinals $8
08/12/74 Mike Marshall, Dodgers............................$4
10/07/74 Catfish Hunter, A's $10
10/21/74 Dodgers vs. A's..$7

1975

03/03/75 Reds, Spring Training issue $7
04/07/75 Steve Garvey, Dodgers $9
06/02/75 Billy Martin, Rangers................................$6
06/16/75 Nolan Ryan, Angels $25
07/07/75 Fred Lynn, Red Sox..................................$6
07/21/75 Jim Palmer, Tom Seaver.........................$15
08/11/75 Baseball Boom $4
10/06/75 Reggie Jackson, A's...................................$8
10/20/75 Luis Tiant, Johnny Bench........................$10
11/03/75 Johnny Bench, Reds $10
12/22/75 Pete Rose, Reds......................................$15

1976

03/15/76 Bill Veeck, White Sox $5
04/12/76 Joe Morgan, Reds....................................$10
05/03/76 Mike Schmidt, Phillies $15
05/31/76 Carlton Fisk, Red Sox $7.50
06/21/76 George Brett, Royals................................$12
06/28/76 Bowie Kuhn $4
07/12/76 Randy Jones, Padres..................................$5
08/30/76 Reggie Jackson, Orioles $8
10/11/76 George Foster, Cincinnati.........................$6
11/01/76 Johnny Bench, Reds $12

1977

03/14/77 Tommy Lasorda, Dodgers $5
03/28/77 Bump Wills, Rangers $4

04/11/77 Joe Rudi, Angels $7.50
05/02/77 Reggie Jackson, Yankees $7.50
05/30/77 Dave Parker, Pirates $5
06/27/77 Tom Seaver, Reds $9
07/18/77 Rod Carew, Ted Williams $10
08/15/77 Sadaharu Oh $8
08/29/77 Greg Luzinski, Phillies............................$5
10/24/77 Thurman Munson, Yankees/Dodgers $9

1978

03/20/78 Clint Hurdle, Royals................................$5
04/10/78 George Foster, Rod Carew $8
04/24/78 Mark Fidrych, Tigers............................$4
07/31/78 Billy Martin, Yankees............................$6
08/07/78 Pete Rose, Reds $10
10/23/78 Yankees Best Dodgers.........................$7.50

1979

03/05/79 Spring Training issue, Reds $5
03/19/79 Harry Chappas, White Sox.....................$4
04/09/79 Jim Rice, Dave Parker............................$8
04/30/79 George Bamberger, Brewers $4
05/28/79 Pete Rose, Phillies $9
06/18/79 Earl Weaver, Orioles $4
07/23/79 Nolan Ryan, Angels $20
08/27/79 Yastrzemski/Rose & Golden Oldies.....$5.50
10/22/79 Pirates vs. Orioles..................................$5
12/24/70 Willie Stargell/Terry Bradshaw (SOY) $6.50

1980

03/24/80 Kirk Gibson, Tigers....................................$6
04/07/80 Keith Hernandez, Cardinals $6
06/09/80 Darrell Porter, Royals...............................$4
07/21/80 Steve Carlton, Phillies $9
08/04/80 Reggie Jackson, Yankees $8
08/18/80 J.R. Richard, Astros $4
08/25/80 Orioles vs. Yankees $4
10/06/80 Gary Carter, Expos $5
10/27/80 Mike Schmidt, Phillies $12

1981

01/05/81 Dave Winfield, Yankees $8
03/02/81 J.R. Richard, Astros $4
03/16/81 Rollie Fingers, Brewers.............................$7
04/13/81 Mike Schmidt, George Brett $8
04/27/81 Oakland A's Aces $5
05/18/81 Fernando Valenzuela, Dodgers.................$4
06/08/81 Greg Luzinski, White Sox $4
06/22/81 Baseball Strike $3.50
07/27/81 Tom Seaver, Reds......................................$7
08/10/81 George Brett, Mike Schmidt $10
08/17/81 Gary Carter, Expos $5
10/26/81 Graig Nettles, Yankees $4.50
11/02/81 Yankees vs. Dodgers $5

1982

03/15/82 Reggie Jackson, Angels $6
04/12/82 Steve Garvey, Dodgers..............................$8
05/17/82 Gaylord Perry, Mariners............................$6

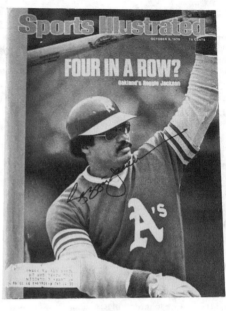

07/05/82 Kent Hrbek, Twins $4
07/19/82 Pete Rose, Carl Yastrzemski $8
08/09/82 Dale Murphy, Braves $7.50
09/06/82 Rickey Henderson, A's $5.50
10/11/82 Robin Yount, Brewers $7
10/25/82 Robin Yount, Brewers $7

1983

03/14/83 Tony Perez, Pete Rose, Joe Morgan $10
04/04/83 Gary Carter, Expos $6
04/18/83 Tom Seaver, Mets......................................$7
04/25/83 Steve Garvey, Padres.................................$6
06/13/83 Rod Carew, Angels....................................$6
07/04/83 Dale Murphy, Braves $7.50
07/18/83 Andre Dawson, Dave Stieb $4
10/03/83 Steve Carlton, Phillies...........................$6.50
10/24/83 Rick Dempsey, Orioles..............................$5

1984

03/12/84 George Brett, Royals $8
04/02/84 Yogi Berra, Yankees.............................$7.50
04/16/84 Rich Gossage/Graig Nettles, Padres $5
04/23/84 Darryl Strawberry, Mets............................$8
05/28/84 Alan Trammell, Tigers $6
06/11/84 Leon Durham, Cubs $4
06/27/84 Pete Rose, Reds...$6
09/24/84 Rick Sutcliffe, Dwight Gooden...........$7.50
10/22/84 Alan Trammell, Tigers $6

1985

03/04/85 Mike Schmidt, Phillies $7
03/18/85 Fred Lynn, Orioles $4
03/25/85 Mays/Mantle/Ueberroth $7
04/15/85 Dwight Gooden, Mets $8
05/06/85 Billy Martin, Yankees................................$5

07/08/85 Fernando Valenzuela, Dodgers..................$4

08/19/85 Pete Rose, Reds..$6

09/02/85 Dwight Gooden, Mets $8

09/23/85 Ozzie Smith, Cardinals...........................$5

10/28/85 Ozzie Smith, Cardinals...........................$6

11/04/85 Royals Win World Series $6

12/09/85 Kirk Gibson, Tigers..................................$5

1986

04/14/86 Wade Boggs, Red Sox.....................$8

05/12/86 Roger Clemens, Red Sox $7

07/14/86 Bo Jackson, Chicks $8

07/28/86 Rickey Henderson, Yankees......................$5

08/04/86 Oil Can Boyd, Red Sox $4

08/25/86 Ron Darling, Mets.................................$5

10/06/86 Darryl Strawberry, Mets.........................$7

10/20/86 Doug DeCinces, Bobby Grich..................$4

10/27/86 Jim Rice, Gary Carter.............................$6

11/03/86 Ray Knight, Mets $5

1987

03/09/87 The Ripkens, Orioles....................$10

04/06/87 Cory Snyder, Joe Carter $5

04/20/87 Baseball Salaries $3

04/27/87 Rob Deer, Brewers $3

05/11/87 Reggie Jackson, A's............................$4.50

05/25/87 Eric Davis, Reds.....................................$5

07/06/87 One Day In Baseball $2.50

07/13/87 Darryl Strawberry, Don Mattingly $7.50

07/20/87 Andre Dawson, Cubs $5

08/17/87 Alan Trammell, Tigers $4

09/28/87 Ozzie Smith, Cardinals............................$5

10/05/87 Lloyd Moseby, Blue Jays $3

10/19/87 Greg Gagne, Twins..................................$3

10/26/87 Dan Gladden, Twins................................$3

11/02/87 Twins Baseball $5

12/14/87 Bo Jackson, Royals $8

1988

03/07/88 Kirk Gibson, Dodgers $5

03/14/88 Umpire Pam Postema..........................$2.50

04/04/88 Will Clark, Mark McGwire $8

05/02/88 Billy Ripken, Orioles $3

05/09/88 Pete Rose, Reds......................................$5

07/11/88 Darryl Strawberry, Mets $4

07/18/88 Casey at Bat.......................................$2.50

09/26/88 Dwight Evans, Red Sox $4

10/17/88 Jose Canseco, A's $8

10/31/88 Orel Hershiser, Dodgers $7

12/09/88 Orel Hershiser, Dodgers, (SOY) $6

1989

03/06/89 Wade Boggs, Red Sox $3.50

04/03/89 Pete Rose, Reds, Baseball Preview $4

05/01/89 Nolan Ryan, Rangers...........................$9.50

05/08/89 Jon Peters $3

06/12/89 Bo Jackson, Royals $6

07/10/89 Rick Reuschel, Giants $2.50

07/24/89 Gregg Jefferies, Mets $3.50

10/16/89 Rickey Henderson, A's $5

10/30/89 Baseball, Earthquake $4

1990

03/12/90 Tony LaRussa, A's................................$3

04/16/90 Ted Williams $4.50

05/07/90 Ken Griffey Jr., Mariners $5.50

05/28/90 Will Clark, Gaints $4

06/04/90 Lenny Dykstra, Phillies..........................$4

07/23/90 Minor League Baseball $3

08/20/90 Jose Canseco, A's $4.50

10/01/90 Bobby Bonilla, Pirates $3.50

10/22/90 Dennis Eckersley, A's...........................$5

10/29/90 Chris Sabo, Reds $4

1991

03/04/91 Darryl Strawberry, Dodgers $2.50

04/15/91 Nolan Ryan, Rangers...............................$4

05/13/91 Roger Clemens, Red Sox $4

05/27/91 Mickey Mantle, Roger Maris $3

07/01/91 Orel Hershiser, Dodgers $2.50

07/29/91 Cal Ripken Jr., Orioles $3

09/30/91 Ramon Martinez, Dodgers $3

10/21/91 Kirby Puckett, Twins...............................$4

10/28/91 Dan Gladden, Twins................................$3

11/04/91 Minnesota Twins Celebrate $3

1992

03/16/92 Ryne Sandberg, Cubs $2.25

04/06/92 Kirby Puckett, Twins...........................$2.25

04/27/92 Deion Sanders, Braves $2.50

05/04/92 Barry Bonds, Pirtes $2.25

05/18/92 Baseball '92..$2.50

06/01/92 Mark McGwire, A's.............................$2.25

07/06/92 Umpire Steve Palermo $2

08/24/92 Deion Sanders, Braves $3

10/05/92 George Brett, Royals $2.25

10/19/92 Dave Winfield, Walt Weiss...................$2.25

10/26/92 John Smoltz, Roberto Alomar.............$2.25

11/02/92 World Series, Toronto Blue Jays $2.00

Fall 1992 *Sports Illustrated* Classic Willie Mays.....$3

1993

03-01-93 George Steinbrenner

03-22-93 Dwight Gooden, Mets

04-05-93 David Cone, Royals

05-03-93 Joe DiMaggio

05-24-93 Barry Bonds, Giants

07-05-93 Mike Piazza, Dodgers

07-12-93 Laurie Crews, Patti Olin

09-27-93 Ron Gant, Braves

11-01-93 Joe Carter, Blue Jays

Dell Sports Publishing
Baseball Annual

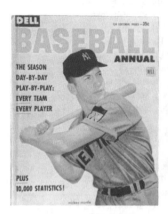  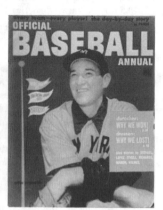

This magazine was issued from 1952-1968, skipping 1969, and then again from 1970-1978. It had several title modifications - Dell Baseball Annual (1953-1957); Dell Sports Baseball (1958-1959 and 1970-1978); Dell Sports Magazine Baseball (1960-1963); and Dell Sports' March issue (1964-1968).

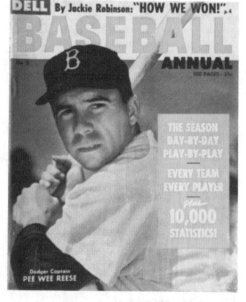

1952 Allie Reynolds ....$25-$30
1953 Mickey Mantle.......................$35-$45
1954 Billy Martin ....$32-$40
1955 Willie Mays...........................$25-$30
1956 Pee Wee Reese......................$22-$27
1957 Mickey Mantle.......................$22-$27
1958 Lew Burdette ....$20-$25
1959 Bob Turley ....$17.50-$22.50
1960 Gil Hodges, Nellie Fox ....$15-$20
1961 Richardson, Mazeroski, Ford..$17.50
1962 Roger Maris $25
1963 Tom Tresh $15
1964 Sandy Koufax $20
1965 Ken Boyer, Brooks Robinson$15-$20
1966 Sandy Koufax ....$15-$20
1967 Frank Robinson...........................$15
1968 Carl Yastrzemski.........................$15
1970 Tom Seaver, Jerry Koosman.......$15
1971 Brooks Robinson $10

1972 Roberto Clemente, Vida Blue $10
1973 Richie Allen $7.50
1974 Hank Aaron.................................$10
1975 Lou Brock $8
1976 Fred Lynn.................................$7.50
1977...$5
1978 Reggie Jackson..............................$8

Dell Sports Publishing

Baseball Stars

This magazine was issued from 1949-1968, known as Dell Sports Baseball Stars. In 1958-1963, and from 1964-1968, it was the May issue of Dell Sports.

1949 Stan Musial $50
1950 Ted Williams, Joe DiMaggio $50
1951 Phil Rizzuto $30
1952 Bobby Thomson........................... $30
1953 Robin Roberts $20
1954 Ted Williams................................ $35
1955 Stan Musial $30
1956 Mickey Mantle............................. $35

1957 Don Larsen................................... $25
1958 Ted Williams $30
1959 Warren Spahn.............................. $20
1960 Kuenn/Aaron/Wynn $15
1961 Vern Law..................................... $17.50
1962 Cepeda/Gentile/Colavito......... $17.50
1963 Maury Wills $15
1964 Sandy Koufax, Mickey Mantle $15
1965 Dean Chance $10
1966 Sandy Koufax............................... $15
1967 Sandy Koufax............................... $15
1968 Lou Brock $12.50

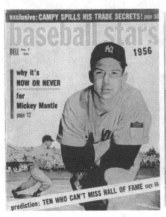  

Dell Sports Publishing
Who's Who in the Big Leagues

This magazine was issued from 1953, and 1955-1958. From 1964-1968 it was issued in the June or July issues of Dell Sports.

1953 Stan Musial $30
1955 Yogi Berra....................................$25
1956 Roy Campanella.....................$22.50
1957 Herb Score $20
1958 Willie Mays..................................$25
1959 Mickey Mantle............................$30
1960 Rocky Colavito $17.50
1961 Chuck Estrada............................$15
1962 Whitey Ford............................$17.50
1963 Harmon Killebrew $17.50
1964 Dick Stuart..................................$15
1965 Willie Mays.............................$17.50
1966 Tony Oliva $15
1967 Boog Powell................................$15
1968 Harmon Killebrew $15

Stan Musial, Willie Mays and Yogi Berra were some of the baseball superstars featured on Dell Publishing's magazine covers from the 1950s.

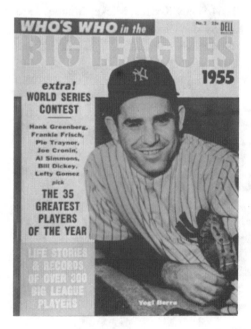

Who's Who In Baseball
by Baseball Magazine

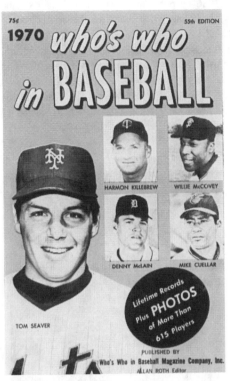

1912 Generic cover	$200

1913-15 not issued

1916 Ty Cobb, A's outfielder	$100
1917 Tris Speaker	$85
1918 George Sisler	$75
1919 Grover Cleveland Alexander	$75
1920 Babe Ruth	$125
1921 Babe Ruth	$125
1922 Rogers Hornsby	$75
1923 George Sisler	$65
1924 Walter Johnson	$70
1925 Dizzy Vance	$60
1926 Max Carey	$60
1927 Frankie Frisch	$60
1928 Hack Wilson	$60
1929 Bob O'Farrell	$50
1930 Burleigh Grimes	$50
1931 Lefty Grove	$50
1932 Al Simmons	$45
1933 Chuck Klein	$45
1934 Bill Terry	$45
1935 Dizzy Dean	$40
1936 Hank Greenberg	$40
1937 Lou Gehrig	$45

1938 Joe Medwick	$37.50
1939 Jimmie Foxx	$40
1940 Bucky Walters	$32
1941 Bob Feller	$32
1942 Joe DiMaggio	$35
1943 Ted Williams	$32.50
1944 Stan Musial	$32
1945 Hal Newhouser, Dizzy Trout	$30
1946 Hal Newhouser	$27.50
1947 Eddie Dyer	$27.50
1948 Ralph Kiner, Johnny Mize	$27.50
1949 Lou Boudreau	$25
1950 Mel Parnell	$22.50
1951 Jim Konstanty	$22.50
1952 Stan Musial	$20
1953 Hank Sauer, Bobby Shantz	$20
1954 Al Rosen	$20
1955 Al Dark	$20
1956 Duke Snider	$20
1957 Mickey Mantle	$25
1958 Warren Spahn	$20
1959 Bob Turley	$20
1960 Don Drysdale	$17
1961 Roger Maris	$18
1962 Whitey Ford	$16
1963 Don Drysdale	$17
1964 Sandy Koufax	$16
1965 Juan Marichal, Ken Boyer	$15.50
1966 Willie Mays, Sandy Koufax	$16
1967 F. Robinson, Koufax, Clemente	$15.50
1968 Carl Yastrzemski	$15
1969 Rose, Gibson, Yaz, McLain	$15.50
1970 Seaver, Killebrew, McCovey	$12
1971 Johnny Bench, Bob Gibson	$11
1972 Vida Blue, Joe Torre	$10
1973 Steve Carlton, Dick Allen	$10
1974 Ryan, Rose, Jackson	$11
1975 Lou Brock, Steve Garvey	$10
1976 Joe Morgan, Fred Lynn	$10
1977 Joe Morgan, Thurman Munson	$10
1978 Rod Carew, George Foster	$10
1979 Guidry, Parker, Rice	$10
1980 Willie Stargell, Keith Hernandez	$8
1981 Mike Schmidt, George Brett	$8
1982 Fernando Valenzuela, Rollie Fingers	$7.50
1983 Dale Murphy, Robin Yount	$7.50
1984 Darryl Strawberry, Cal Ripken	$7.50
1985 Ryne Sandberg	$7
1986 Gooden, Mattingly, McGee	$6
1987 Mike Schmidt, Roger Clemens	$5

1988 to present @ $5.00 each

Sport Magazine

Sport Magazine celebrated its 40th anniversary in 1986 by publishing a special collector's issue which featured stories on the "40 Who Changed Sports," including Ted Williams and Jackie Robinson.

The issue, from December 1986, is worth about $5, had 40 previous covers on its cover. Fourteen of those covers were devoted to baseball, featuring among others Joe DiMaggio, Hank Aaron, Babe Ruth, Ted Williams, Steve Carlton, Pete Rose, Carl Yastrzemski, Whitey Ford, Mickey Mantle and Willie Mays.

The magazine has been published monthly by Macfadden since September of 1946 (featuring Joe DiMaggio and his son), except for one month, January 1952, when no issue was published. Magazines typically have five or six features and lots of color photographs.

Sport Magazine

Sept. 46 Joe DiMaggio .... $400-$450
April 47 Leo Durocher...................... $22.50-$30
June 47 Bob Feller .... $25-$40
July 47 Eddie Dyer, Joe Cronin............ $20-$22
Aug. 47 Ted Williams .... $45-$60
Sept. 47 The DiMaggios................................$75
April 48 Ted Williams .... $40-$50
May 48 Babe Ruth................................ $45-$65
July 48 Ewell Blackwell........................ $20-$22
Aug. 48 Stan Musial.............................. $35-$50
Sept. 48 Joe DiMaggio, Ted Williams...........$95
Oct. 48 Lou Gehrig................................ $45-$65
Feb. 49 Lou Boudreau.......................... $20-$22
April 49 Bob Feller................................ $25-$40
May 49 Enos Slaughter......................... $25-$30
June 49 Hal Newhouser......................... $22-$25
July 49 Lou Boudreau, Joe Gordon.............$25
Aug. 49 Jackie Robinson....................... $35-$45
Sept. 49 Joe DiMaggio .... $55-$75
Oct. 49 Christy Mathewson $22
Feb. 50 Tommy Henrich........................ $16-$22
April 50 Casey Stengel......................... $25-$28
May 50 Ralph Kiner.............................. $28-$30
June 50 Bob Lemon................................ $25-28
July 50 Stan Musial.............................. $30-$45
Aug. 50 Art Houtteman .... $15-$22
Sept. 50 Don Newcombe .... $20-$28
Oct. 50 World Series............................. $25-$28
Nov. 50 Harry Agganis.......................... $15-$22
April 51 Baseball................................... $25-$30
May 51 Baseball Jubilee........................ $25-$30
July 51 Ewell Blackwell................................$15
Aug. 51 Yogi Berra .... $25-$30
Sept. 51 Ted Williams .... $35-$45
Oct. 51 Jackie Robinson........................ $35-$45

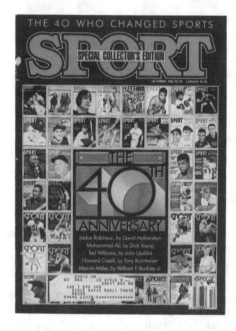

March 52 Gil McDougald...................... $15-$18
April 52 Chico Carrasquel.................... $10-$15
May 52 Alvin Dark $15
June 52 Ralph Kiner............................. $16-$20
July 52 Stan Musial.............................. $25-$40
Aug. 52 Allie Reynolds........................ $12-$15
Sept. 52 Mike Garcia .... $12-$15
Oct. 52 J. Robinson, Pee Wee Reese.............$75
Nov. 52 Jackie Robinson .... $15-$20
April 53 Mickey Mantle..............................$95
May 53 Bob Lemon $14
June 53 Hank Sauer $12
July 53 Ferris Fain .... $10-$12
Aug. 53 Warren Spahn .... $15-$20

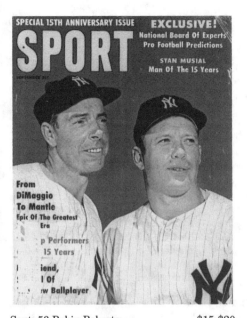

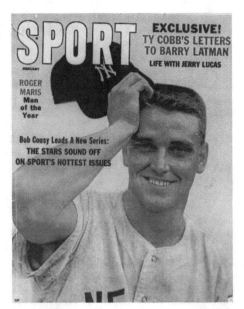

Sept. 53 Robin Roberts........................... $15-$20
Oct. 53 Roy Campanella .... $18-$25
Nov. 53 Phil Rizzuto .... $14-$20
Feb. 54 Eddie Mathews............................$15.50
March 54 Casey Stengel $20
April 54 Don Newcombe $20
May 54 Ted Kluszewski $12.50
July 54 Stan Musial $40
Aug. 54 Minnie Minoso .... $14-$20
Sept. 54 Duke Snider $35
Oct. 54 Al Rosen .... $14-$18
Feb. 55 Alvin Dark .... $12-$14
April 55 Bob Turley $14
May 55 Bobby Thomson..............................$12
June 55 Johnny Antonelli..................... $10-$12
July 55 Ned Garver $10
Aug. 55 Paul Richards $12
Sept. 55 Duke Snider $30
Oct. 55 Yogi Berra $20
March 56 Walt Alston .... $12-$14
April 56 Larry Doby $12
May 56 Bob Lemon............................... $12-$14
June 56 Willie Mays.....................................$25
July 56 Ted Williams............................ $25-$35
Aug. 56 Vinegar Bend Mizell.................. $8-$10
Oct. 56 Mickey Mantle.......................... $30-$60
March 57 Mickey Mantle...................... $30-$50
April 57 Eddie Mathews .... $12-$14
May 57 Roy Campanella...................... $12-$14
June 57 Early Wynn.............................. $10-$14
July 57 Al Kaline.................................. $15-$25
Aug. 57 Joe Adcock................................ $8-$15
Sept. 57 Duke Snider .... $15-$30
Oct. 57 Billy Pierce............................... $10-$12

Jan. 58 Baseball Stars.............................$8-$12
March 58 Lew Burdette........................$10-$12
April 58 Nellie Fox...............................$12-$25
May 58 Yogi Berra $15
June 58 Willie Mays ....$10-$20
July 58 Herb Score................................$10-$15
Aug. 58 Billy Martin..............................$12-$15
Sept. 58 Eddie Mathews.......................$14-$15
Oct. 58 Bob Turley ....$10-$12
Feb. 59 Lew Burdette, R. Johnson..........$8-$10
March 59 Al Kaline................................$15-$25
April 59 Rocky Colavito.........................$12-$25
May 59 Hank Bauer, Gil Hodges $10
June 59 Mickey Mantle, Ted Williams..$30-$40
July 59 Don Newcombe, Jimmy Piersall $8-$12
Aug. 59 Mickey Mantle...............................$25
Sept. 59 Ted Williams, Stan Musial......$25-$35
Oct. 59 Warren Spahn ....$12-$15
March 60 Jackie Robinson, Willie Mays......$15
April 60 Duke Snider............................$12-$15
May 60 Willie McCovey, Harmon Killebrew
....$14-$20
June 60 Don Drysdale ....$10-$12
July 60 Frank Howard, Luis Aparicio ....$8-$10
Aug. 60 Mickey Mantle....................$22.50-$30
Sept. 60 Rocky Colavito................................$12
Oct. 60 Babe Ruth.......................................$10
Nov. 60 Roger Maris...............................$15-$25
Feb. 61 Danny Murtaugh $8
April 61 Frank Howard ....$6-$10
May 61 Dick Groat....................................$6-$8
June 61 Willie Mays $15
July 61 Rocky Colavito $15
Aug. 61 Warren Spahn ....$8-$10

277

Sept. 61 Joe DiMaggio, Mickey Mantle $30-$40

Feb. 62 Roger Maris .... $15-$25

April 62 Norm Cash, Vada Pinson $8

May 62 Baseball Sluggers .... $10-$12

June 62 Hank Aaron .... $12-$14

July 62 Mickey Mantle .... $22-$25

Aug. 62 Rocky Colavito, Harvey Kuenn$10-$18

Sept. 62 Ken Boyer, Stan Musial .... $14-$15

Oct. 62 Willie Mays .... $10-$14

Nov. 62 Tommy Davis, Jim Taylor................. $8

Feb. 63 Maury Wills................................... $8

May 63 Mickey Mantle, Yogi Berra...... $25-$35

June 63 Maury Wills .... $7-$8

July 63 Rocky Colavito, Al Kaline........ $10-$20

Aug. 63 Willie Mays .... $10-$14

Sept. 63 Sandy Koufax.................................. $12

Oct. 63 Mickey Mantle .... $18-$20

Nov. 63 Whitey Ford............................... $10-$15

Dec. 63 Sport Annual $10

Feb. 64 Sandy Koufax .... $10-$12

May 64 Warren Spahn .... $8-$10

June 64 Dick Stuart .... $6-$9

July 64 Carl Yastrzemski...................... $6-$15

Aug. 64 Joe DiMaggio, Willie Mays ..... $25-$30

Sept. 64 Mickey Mantle .... $14-$20

Oct. 64 Willie Mays $12

Nov. 64 Harmon Killebrew .... $11-$12

Feb. 65 Fred Hutchinson .... $6-$7.50

April 65 Dean Chance .... $6-$8

May 65 Sandy Koufax .... $10-$11

June 65 Willie Mays........................ $10-$12.50

July 65 Johnny Callison .... $7.50-$12

Aug. 65 Mickey Mantle $15

Sept. 65 Lou Gehrig .... $10-$15

Oct. 65 Sandy Koufax, Maury Wills........ $9-$11

Feb. 66 Sandy Koufax .... $10-$15

April 66 Willie Mays, Paul Hornung...... $7-$11

May 66 Maury Wills........................... $6-$7.50

July 66 Mickey Mantle .... $15-$20

Aug. 66 Frank Robinson .... $6-$9

Sept. 66 Willie Mays .... $7-$11

Oct. 66 Sandy Koufax $10

Feb. 67 Frank Robinson....................... $6-$8.50

May 67 Mickey Mantle $15

June 67 Willie Mays....................... $8-$12.50

July 67 Dick Allen, Jim Ryan.................. $5-$8

Aug. 67 Roberto Clemente .... $17.50-$25

Sept. 67 Pete Rose........................... $12-$17.50

Oct. 67 Orlando Cepeda, Johnny Unitas . $6-$8

Feb. 68 Carl Yastrzemski....................... $7-$9

May 68 Willie Mays................................ $7-$10

June 68 Carl Yastrzemski...................... $7-$9

July 68 Hank Aaron............................... $7-$10

Aug. 68 Pete Rose.................................. $10-$12

Sept. 68 Don Drysdale .... $7-$8

April 69 Mickey Mantle .... $15-$35

May 69 Hall of Famers .... $6-$10

June 69 Ted Williams .... $8-$15

July 69 Tony Conigliaro........................... $6-$15

Sept. 69 Cubs Stars .... $10-$25

May 70 Tom Seaver................................. $9-$12

June 70 Harmon Killebrew .... $9-$10

Aug. 70 Hank Aaron .... $7-$10

Sept. 70 Johnny Bench .... $11-$12

May 71 Ted Williams .... $10-$12

June 71 Boog Powell .... $5-$8

July 71 Carl Yastrzemski .... $6-$8

Sept. 71 Willie Mays .... $8-$10

Oct. 71 Vida Blue .... $4-$5

June 72 Brooks Robinson $8

Aug. 72 Tom Seaver .... $10-$12

Sept. 72 Frank Robinson .... $7-$8

Aug. 73 Bobby Murcer .... $5-$8

Sept. 73 Gaylord Perry .... $6.50-$7

Oct. 73 Pennant Time................................. $7

May 74 Hank Aaron $10

June 74 Pete Rose $10

Oct. 74 Reggie Jackson .... $10-$12

May 75 Frank Robinson .... $5-$6

July 75 Bobby Bonds .... $5-$8

Aug. 75 Billy Martin .... $5-$9

April 76 Steve Garvey............................... $6-$9

May 76 Tom Seaver............................... $7-$10

Aug. 76 Pete Rose, Joe Morgan..........$7.50-$12

July 77 Mark Fidrych .... $4-$6

Oct. 77 Rod Carew .... $5-$6.50

April 78 Sparky Lyle, Goose Gossage $7

May 78 Craig Nettles................................ $5-$7

July 78 Jim Rice................................. $4.50-$7

Aug. 78 Tom Seaver .... $7-$10

Oct. 78 Carl Yastrzemski.....................$5.50-$7

April 79 Pete Rose .... $6-$10

May 79 Ron Guidry.................................... $5-$6

June 79 Dave Parker $5

July 79 Craig Nettles .... $5-$6

Aug. 79 Rod Carew .... $6-$7

Oct. 79 Reggie Jackson ....$7.50-$9

April 80 Willie Stargell.......................$5.50-$7

May 80 Lou Piniella............................$4.50-$8

July 80 Gorman Thomas ....$4.50-$6

Sept. 80 Tommy John $5.50

April 81 Tug McGraw ....$5.50-$8

May 81 Billy Martin .... $5-$6

June 81 Don Sutton ....$5.50-$6

July 81 Rich Gossage, Bruce Sutter ....$5-$6

April 82 Fernando Valenzuela $5

May 82 Reggie Jackson $7

June 82 Tom Seaver..................................... $6

July 82 Billy Martin $6

March 83 Top 100 Salaries.................$4.50-$6

April 83 Steve Garvey..............................$5-$6

May 83 Steve Carlton ....$6-$7.50

June 83 Schmidt, Dawson, Carter, Yount $6-$7
July 83 Reggie Jackson........................ $7-$8.50
March 84 Top 100 Salaries .... $4-$6
April 84 Cal Ripken Jr. .... $6.50-$10
June 84 Dale Murphy .... $4.50-$6
July 84 Baseball Managers .... $4-$6
March 85 Gary Carter.............................. $5-$6
April 85 Dwight Gooden .... $6.50-$8
May 85 Gary Matthews, Keith Hernandez
.... $4-$6
June 85 George Brett............................ $5-$10
July 85 Kirk Gibson .... $5-$6
March 86 Dwight Gooden .... $4-$8
April 86 Bret Saberhagen.............................$4
May 86 George Brett.................................$4.50
June 86 Top 100 Salaries $3
July 86 P. Rose, R. Jackson, G. Carter...........$5
March 87 Clemens, E. Davis, Schmidt...........$5
April 87 Darryl Strawberry $3.50
June 87 Top 100 Salaries $3.50
July 87 Dave Parker $4
Dec. 87 Andre Dawson, Tim Raines..........$3.50
March 88 Jefferies, J. McDowell, D. Lovell ...$4

April 88 Will Clark, Keith Hernandez...........$4
June 88 Top 100 Salaries..............................$3
March 89 Orel Hershiser...............................$4
April 89 Baseball Preview $4
June 89 Top 100 Salaries $3
July 89 Jose Canseco $4
Oct. 89 Dwight Gooden $4
March 90 Bo Jackson....................................$5
April 90 Joyner, Canseco, Hershiser $4
May 90 Sax, H. Johnson, Burks.................$3.50
July 90 Will Clark..$5
March 91 Ken Griffey Jr., Rickey Henderson$5
April 91 R. Kelly, Reardon, H. Johnson....$3.50
June 91 Darryl Strawberry $4
July 91 Lenny Dykstra.............................$3.50
Oct. 91 Bo Jackson.......................................$4
April 92 Frank Thomas, Bo Jackson $6
May 92 Cal Ripken Jr. $5
Jan. 93 Top 40 dominant names $3
March 93 Steinbrenner, Sheffield, Clemens,
Winfield $3
April 93 Bonds, Bonilla, Clemens, Canseco ..$4

Inside Sports

Inside Sports

Oct. 79 Lemon wearing Yankees hat...........$30
April 80 Nolan Ryan $40
May 80 Mark Fidrych, Johnny Bench, Magic Johnson...$15
July 80 Ken Reitz...$5
Aug. 80 Willie Randolph, Steve Garvey, Roberto Duran $6
April 81 George Brett...............................$7.50
May 81 Outlaw Pitchers $4
June 81 Jim Palmer, Jan Stephenson............$5
Aug. 81 Salary Survey (includes Pete Rose)..$6
April 82 Steve Garvey....................................$5
May 82 Pete Rose $6
March 84 Darryl Strawberry.........................$6
April 84 Cal Ripken Jr., Carlton Fisk, Eddie Murray, Ozzie Smith.....................................$5
May 84 Fernando Valenzuela $5
June 84 Mike Schmidt $5.50
July 84 Steve Garvey, Rich Goosage $5
Aug. 84 Dave Winfield, George Steinbrenner
....$5.75
April 85 Kirk Gibson, Ryne Sandberg, Steve Garvey, Dan Quisenberry $4.50
May 85 Rick Sutcliffe, Gary Carter...............$4
June 85 Rickey Henderson, six Dodgers........$5
July 85 Tom Seaver, Nolan Ryan, Jerry Koosman $8.50
March 86 Baseball's Best Player (Rickey Henderson #1) $5.50
April 86 1986 Baseball Preview $4
May 86 Baseball Ratings and Inside Stuff
....$4.50
March 87 Baseball's Best by Position $4.50
April 87 1987 Baseball Preview $3
May 87 Baseball Ratings and Inside Stuff $3
March 88 Baseball's Best Players $4
April 88 1988 Baseball Preview $3
June 88 Baseball Ratings and Inside Stuff ...$3
March 89 Total Average $3
April 89 Baseball Preview $3.50
Feb. 90 Henderson, Clark, Bo Jackson, G. Carter...$4
April 90 Bo Jackson, Hershiser, McGriff, H. Johnson, Clark, Grace, Boggs..................$4.50
June 90 All-Time greats (Nolan Ryan) $4
Feb. 91 Clemens, Canseco, Stewart, Rijo, Gooden, Fielder $3.50
April 91 Top salaries Canseco Strawberry, Clemens...$3.50
June 91 Bo Jackson...$4
Feb. 92 Larkin, Bonds, Clark, Sandberg, Canseco, Puckett $5
March 92 Lee Smith, Joe Carter, Avery, Henderson...$4
April 93 David Cone, Greg Maddux $3.50

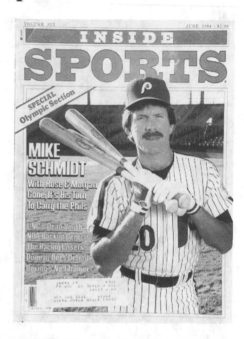

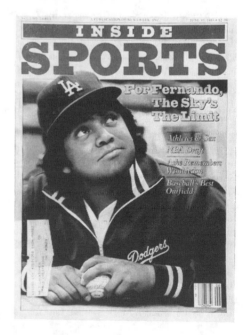

The Mike Schmidt magazine (above) is worth $5.50; the Fernando Valenzuela magazine (below) is worth $5.

Other Magazines

Collecting general circulation news magazines with athletes on the cover, in addition to those related specifically to sports, has become very popular in recent years. Values are determined by who is pictured on the cover and the magazine's condition. Magazines in Excellent condition from the 1960s and 1970s can still be found for less than $20 in antique stores and public libraries.

Time Magazine
1927 Connie Mack $100
1929 Bill Wrigley $75-$100
1930 Wilbert Robinson $75-$100
1932 Col. Jacob Ruppert $50-$75
1934 Lefty Gomez $50-$70
10/07/35 Mickey Cochrane $20-$50
1936 Gehrig/Hubbell $75-$85
12/21/36 Bob Feller $65-$75
07/18/38 Happy Chandler $25-$50
04/21/47 Leo Durocher $45-$50
1947 Jackie Robinson $35-$70
10/04/48 Joe DiMaggio $75-$85
1949 Stan Musial $50-$75
04/10/50 Ted Williams $75
1952 Johnny Pesky $35
04/28/52 Eddie Stanky $40
06/13/53 Mickey Mantle $100
07/26/54 Willie Mays $45
06/13/55 "Damn Yankees" $25
07/11/55 Augie Busch $25
10/03/55 Casey Stengel $30
1955 Roy Campanella $50-$65
05/28/56 Robin Roberts $25-$30
07/08/57 Birdie Tebbetts $20
04/28/58 Walter O'Malley $20
08/24/59 Rocky Colavito $20-$40
1964 Hank Bauer $20
1966 Juan Marichal $15-$20
09/13/68 Denny McLain $15-$20
09/05/69 New York Mets $30
05/24/71 Vida Blue $15
07/10/72 Johnny Bench $20
06/03/74 Reggie Jackson $20
08/18/75 Charley Finley $10-$15
04/26/76 Babe Ruth $10-$20
07/18/77 Rod Carew $20
07/23/79 Earl Weaver $10-$15
05/11/81 Billy Martin $10-$15
07/26/82 Yastrzemski/Rose $15
01/07/85 Peter Ueberroth $8-$15
08/19/85 Pete Rose $10-$20
04/07/86 Dwight Gooden $10-$20
07/10/89 Pete Rose $8-$10

Newsweek Magazine
04/15/33 Play at home $20-$50
04/29/33 Carl Hubbell $30-$125

09/09/33 Connie Mack $25-$75
09/30/33 Clark Griffith $20-$75
12/23/33 Judge Landis $25-$75
02/17/34 Babe Ruth $35-$100
03/17/34 Mel Ott $25-$50
10/06/34 Mickey Cochrane $25-$60
04/20/35 Judge Kenesaw Mountain Landis $25-$50
10/03/36 Carl Hubbell $25-$50
10/11/37 Carl Hubbell $20-$45
04/18/38 Rudy York $15-$30
10/10/38 Yankees/Cubs $30
06/19/39 Abner Doubleday and Cooperstown $30-$75
09/16/46 Ted Williams $30-$50
06/02/47 Bob Feller $20-$40
10/06/47 Dodgers system $12-$30
04/26/48 Southworth, McCarthy $15-$25
08/08/49 Branch Rickey $15-$25
04/17/50 Mel Parnell $10-$15
03/24/52 Dodgers training $10
10/04/54 Feller, Lemon $15-$25
10/03/55 Baseball, tv $8-$10
01/25/56 Mickey Mantle $40
07/01/57 Stan Musial $20-$35
08/03/59 Casey Stengel $15-$25
08/14/60 Home Runs $10-$15
04/26/65 The Astrodome $8-$10

10/11/65 Sandy Koufax $15
10/02/67 Carl Yastrzemski $12-$20
08/13/75 Aaron, Ruth $18-$25
06/16/75 Nolan Ryan $20-$25
07/28/76 Vida Blue $7-$10
08/06/90 George Steinbrenner $4-$7.50

Life Magazines
04/25/38 Brooklyn Dodger $35-$50
05/01/39 Joe DiMaggio $75-$125
04/01/40 New York Giants $20-$50
09/01/41 Ted Williams $65-$125
04/01/46 St. Louis Cardinals $15-$40
08/01/49 Joe DiMaggio $65-$90
05/08/50 Jackie Robinson $50-$60
06/08/53 Roy Campanella $20-$45
09/14/53 Casey Stengel $20-$30
06/25/56 Mickey Mantle $75-$90
04/28/58 Willie Mays $25-$40
07/21/58 Roy Campanella $20-$35
08/18/61 Mantle, Maris $75
09/28/62 Don Drysdale $12-$20
08/02/63 Sandy Koufax $20-$30
07/30/65 Mickey Mantle $40-$50
09/08/67 Carl Yastrzemski $20-$25
09/26/69 Jerry Koosman $15-$20

Street & Smith's Baseball Yearbook

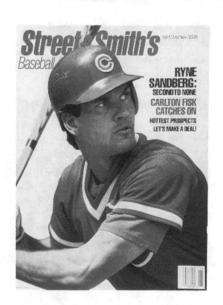

1941	Bob Feller	$200-$250
1942	Howie Pollet	$165-$175
1943	New York Giants	$100-$110
1944	Joe McCarthy	$100-$125
1945	N.Y. Giants Spring Training	$95-$110
1946	Dick Fowler	$85-$110
1947	Leo Durocher	$85-$110
1948	Joe DiMaggio	$100-$135
1949	Lou Boudreau	$80-$100
1950	J. DiMaggio/T. Williams	$100-$125
1951	J. DiMaggio/R.Kiner	$70-$125
1952	Stan Musial	$80-$110
1953	Mickey Mantle	$75-$125
1954	Eddie Matthews	$70-$90
1955	Yogi Berra	$70-$90
1956	M. Mantle/D.Snider	$80-$110
1957	Mantle, D. Larsen, Y. Berra	$75-$110
1958	B. Buhl/L. Burdette	$50-$60
1959	Mantle/Spahn/Burdette	$60-$70
1960	L. Aparicio/N. Fox	$45-$50
1961	Dick Groat	$45-$55
1962	Roger Maris	$55-$70
1963	Tom Tresh	$35-$40
	Stan Musial	$40-$50
	Don Drysdale	$40
1964	Mickey Mantle	$45-$55
	Warren Spahn	$35-$40
	Sandy Koufax	$35-$45
1965	Brooks Robinson	$35-$45
	Ken Boyer	$35-$40
	Dean Chance	$30-$35
1966	Ron Swoboda	$30
	Rocky Colavito	$30

	Sandy Koufax	$35-$40
1967	Andy Etchebarren	$25-$30
	Harmon Killebrew	$30-$30
	Juan Marichal	$25-$30
1968	Jim Lonborg	$25-$30
	Orlando Cepeda	$25-$30
	Jim McGlothlin	$25-$30
1969	B. Gibson/D. McLain	$30
1970	Tom Seaver	$25-$35
	Harmon Killebrew	$25-$30
	Bill Singer	$20-$30
1971	Boog Powell	$20-$25
	Johnny Bench	$20-$25
	Gaylord Perry	$20-$25
1972	Roberto Clemente	$30-$40
	Joe Torre	$20-$25
	Vida Blue	$20-$25
1973	Steve Carlton	$20-$25
	Johnny Bench	$20-$25
	Reggie Jackson	$20-$25
1974	Hank Aaron	$20-$25
	Pete Rose	$20-$25
	Nolan Ryan	$30-$45
1975	Lou Brock	$18-$25
	Catfish Hunter	$18-$25
	Mike Marshall	$18-$25
1976	Fred Lynn	$17-$20
	Joe Morgan	$17-$20
	Davey Lopes	$17-$20
1977	Thurman Munson	$17-$20
	Mark Fidrych	$18-$20
	Randy Jones	$17-$20
1978	Reggie Jackson	$18-$22

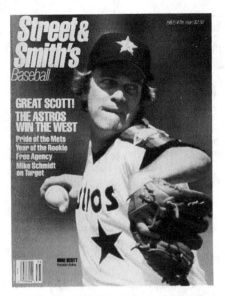

The June 1987 issue is worth $8.

	Rod Carew	$17-$18
	Steve Garvey	$15-$18
1979	Ron Guidry	$15-$18
	J.R. Richard	$15-$18
	Burt Hooten	$15-$18
1980	Mike Flanagan	$12-$18
	Joe Niekro	$10-$18
	Brian Downing	$13-$18
1981	Mike Schmidt	$12-$16
	George Brett	$15
	all other covers	@$13-$15
1982	Nolan Ryan	$25-$45
	R. Gossage/P. Rose	$13-$18
	R. Fingers/T. Seaver	$15-$16
	Valenzuela/Martin	$12-$15
	all other covers	@$12.50-$15
1983	Steve Carlton	$12-$15
	Doug DeCinces	$10-$15
	Robin Yount	$12-$15
	Dale Murphy	$12-$15
	all other covers	@$12-$15
1984	Carlton Fisk	$12-$15
	Pedro Guerrero	$11-$14
	McGregor/Dempsey	$11-$14
	all other covers	@$11-$14
1985	Dwight Gooden	$12-$15
	Detroit Tigers	$11-$14
	Steve Garvey	$11-$14
	all other covers	@$11-$14
1986	Nolan Ryan	$15-$25
	D. Gooden/D. Mattingly	$12-$16
	Kansas City Royals	$10-$14
	Orel Hershiser	$10-$14
	all other covers	@$10-$14

1987	G. Carter/J. Orosco	$10-$12
	Jesse Barfield	$8-$12
	Mike Scott	$8-$12
	Joe Carter	$8-$12
	Wally Joyner	$8-$12
	Roger Clemens	$10-$12
	all other covers	@$8-$12
1988	Don Mattingly	$10-$13
	Dale Murphy	$9-$12.50
	Ozzie Smith	$9-$12
	George Bell	$9-$12
	Jeff Reardon	$8-$12
	McGwire/Santiago	$9-$12
	all other covers	@$8-$12
1989	Jose Canseco	$10-$12
	Mike Greenwell	$8-$10
	Orel Hershiser	$7.50-$11
	M. Grace/C. Sabo	$8-$11
	Kevin McReynolds	$7.50-$11
	Galarraga/McGriff	$9-$10
	all other covers	@$7.50-$10
1990	Anniversary Issue	$7-$8
1991	Lou Piniella	
	Doug Drabek	
	Ryne Sandberg	
	Dave Justice	
	Nolan Ryan	
	Ramon Martinez	
	Kelly Gruber	
	Ken Griffey Jr.	
1992	Roberto Alomar	
	Roger Clemens	
	Bobby Bonilla	
	Terry Pendelton	
	Lee Smith, Jeff Bagwell, Ruben Sierra, Kirby Puckett	
	Frank Thomas, Cecil Fielder, Barry Larkin, Ryne Sanberg	
	Jim Abbott, Will Clark, Brett Butler, Jose Canseco	
1993	Roger Clemens	
	Jim Abbott	
	Tom Glavine	
	Barry Larkin	
	Ryne Sandberg	
	Dennis Eckersley	
	Darryl Strawberry	
	Roberto Alomar	
1994	Aaron Sele	
	Lenny Dykstra	
	Carlos Baerga	
	Paul Molitor	
	Dave Justice	
	Barry Bonds	
	Mike Piazza	

Baseball Digest

Baseball Digest, the oldest surviving baseball monthly in the United States, marked its 50th anniversary in 1992. The first issue, August 1942, was a dream of Editor Herbert F. Simons, who, at the time, was a member of the Baseball Writers Association of America since 1928. The reality, a national baseball magazine, carried a cover price of 15 cents on the newsstands.

The publication, which has survived trucking and paper mill plant strikes, rising printing and publishing-related costs and a bankrupt printing plant, has covered stories on virtually every Hall of Famer, including several first-person stories. Many of the magazine's writers are also enshrined in the Baseball Hall of Fame in Cooperstown, N.Y. Some of their stories have been reprinted in Baseball Digest's 50th Anniversary issue, published in 1992.

Aug. 42	Elmer Valo	$75
Sept. 42		$15
Oct. 42	Pete Reiser	$15
Nov. 42		$15
Dec. 42		$15
Jan. 43		$12.50
Feb. 43		$12.50
March 43		$12.50
April 43		$12.50
May 43		$12.50
July 43	Play at 2nd Base	$12-$15
Aug. 43	Inside Homer	$12
Sept. 43	Stan Musial	$22
Oct. 43	Spud Chandler	$12-$15
Nov. 43	Johnny Lindell	$12
Feb. 44	Bill Johnson	$12-$13
March 44	Joe Sewell, Bill Nicholson	$12-$13
April 44	Dixie Walker	$12-$14
May 44	Lou Boudreau	$15
July 44	Vern Stephens	$12-$15
Aug. 44	Bucky Walters	$12-$15
Sept. 44	Charlie Grimm, G. Barr	$12-$15
Oct. 44	Walker Cooper	$12-$13
Nov. 44	Marty Marion	$12-$14
Feb. 45	Hal Newhouser	$12
March 45	Grover Hartley	$12
April 45	Dixie Walker	$12-$14
May 45	Bill Voiselle	$12-$15
July 45	Hank Borowy	$12-$13
Aug. 45	Tommy Holmes	$12-$14
Sept. 45	Stan Hack	$12-$14
Oct. 45	Hank Greenberg	$15-$25
Nov. 45	Al Lopez	$12-$17.50
Feb. 46	Charlie Keller	$12-$15
March 46	Phil Cavarretta	$12-$15
April 46	Bobby Doerr	$15-$20
May 46	Bob Feller	$15-$20
July 46	Joe DiMaggio, Ted Williams	
		$20-$30
Aug. 46	Joe Cronin	$14-$18
Sept. 46	Hank Wyse	$13.50
Oct. 46	Boo Ferriss	$12-$20
Nov. 46	Johnny Pesky, Red Schoendienst	
		$12-$18
Feb. 47	Bucky Harris	$12-$16
March 47	J. Rigney, P. Knudsen	$12-$15
April 47	Johnny Van Cuyk	$12-$13
May 47	Billy Herman, Hank Greenberg	
		$15-$25
July 47	Lou Boudreau, Joe Gordon	$14-$15
Aug. 47	Buddy Kerr	$12-$15
Sept. 47	Ewell Blackwell	$12
Oct. 47	Joe DiMaggio	$15-$25
Nov. 47	Dodgers/Phillies	$12-$13
Jan. 48	Joe Page	$12-$15
Feb. 48	Leo Durocher, Branch Rickey	
		$14-$17
March 48	Meyer, Ennis, Hubbard	$10-$12
April 48	Joe McCarthy	$12
May 48	Art Houtteman	$12-$13
June 48	Willard Marshall	$10-$13
July 48	Ralph Kiner	$15-$17
Aug. 48	Lou Boudreau	$15-$17
Sept. 48	Stan Musial	$15-$25
Oct. 48	Hank Sauer	$12-$13
Nov. 48	Gene Bearden	$10-$15
Jan. 49	Jim Hegan	$10-$12
Feb. 49	Red Rolfe	$10-$12
March 49	Ted Williams	$20-$25
April 49	Joe DiMaggio	$20-$22
May 49	Play at the plate	$12-$14
June 49	Robin Roberts	$18-$20
July 49	Johnny Groth	$9-$12
Aug. 49	Frankie Frisch	$15-$18
Sept. 49	Vic Raschi	$10-$12
Oct. 49	Mel Parnell, Birdie Tebbetts	
		$10-$12
Nov. 49	Spider Jorgensen	$9-$10
Dec. 49	Tommy Henrich, Allie Reynolds	
		$12-$16
Jan. 50	Roy Smalley, Richie Ashburn	
		$12-$13
Feb. 50	Dave Koslo	$8-$10
March 50	1950 Baseball rules	$9-$11

April 50	1950 Rosters, Bob Feller	$10-$15
May 50	Stanky, Dark, J. Kramer	$10
June 50	Joe DiMaggio	$15
July 50	Phil Rizzuto	$10-$12
Aug. 50	Dick Sisler	$8-$10
Sept. 50	Larry Jansen, Art Houtteman	$8-$15
Oct. 50	Hoot Evers	$8-$12
Nov. 50	Jim Konstanty	$8-$10
Jan. 51	Yogi Berra, Whitey Ford	$12-$15
Feb. 51	Gil Hodges	$12-$15
March 51	Eddie Yost	$8-$10
April 51	Joe DiMaggio	$15-$20
May 51	George Earnshaw, Fogg	$7-$9
June 51	Ted Williams	$15-$20
July 51	Irv Noren	$7-$10
Aug. 51	Nellie Fox, Paul Richards	$12
Sept. 51	Stan Musial	$15
Oct. 51	Gil McDougald	$8-$10
Nov. 51	Charlie Dressen	$7-$12
Jan. 52	Eddie Lopat, Phil Rizzuto ..	$12-$20
Feb. 52	Eddie Stanky	$8-$9
March 52	Sid Gordon	$7-$15
April 52	Mike Garcia	$7-$10
May 52	George Staley	$7-$15
June 52	Pee Wee Reese	$10-$15
July 52	Ted Kluszewski	$10
Aug. 52	Bobby Shantz	$7-$15
Sept. 52	Roy Campanella, Sal Maglie	$8-$15
Oct. 52	Carl Erskine	$8-$10
Nov. 52	Duke Snider	$12-$15
Jan. 53	Robin Roberts	$12-$13
Feb. 53	Eddie Mathews	$9-$20
March 53	Billy Martin	$10-$20
April 53	Mickey Mantle, Stan Musial	$15-$25
May 53	Carl Furillo	$10-$25
June 53	Bob Lemon	$8-$20
July 53	Logan, Kellner, Dorish	$7-$15
Aug. 53	Robin Roberts	$10-$12
Sept. 53	O'Connell, Strickland, Trucks	$7-$10
Oct. 53	Casey Stengel	$10-$11
Jan. 54	Billy Martin	$10
March 54	Jimmy Piersall	$8-$10
April 54	Whitey Ford	$10-$12
May 54	Harvey Kuenn	$8
June 54	Eddie Mathews, Morgan	$9-$10
July 54	Bob Turley	$7.50
Aug. 54	Bob Keegan	$7
Sept. 54	Willie Mays	$12-$15
Oct. 54	World Series issue	$7-$10
N,D. 54	Dusty Rhodes	$7-$10
J,F. 55	Ralph Kiner, Bill Sarni	$9-$10
Mar 55	1955 Rookies	$10
April 55	Alvin Dark	$7.50
May 55	Bob Lemon, Don Mueller	$7.50
June 55	Bobby Avila	$6.50
July 55	Bill Skowron	$7.50-$15
Aug. 55	Roy McMillian, Al Smith	$6.50
Sept. 55	Don Newcombe	$7-$8.50
Oct. 55	Walter Alston, Tommy Byrne	$8
Nov. 55	Johnny Podres	$8-$9
Feb. 56	Al Kaline	$10
March 56	Rookie Report	$9
April 56	Luis Aparicio	$8.50-$10
May 56	Pinky Higgins	$7
June 56	Clem Labine	$7-$7.50
July 56	Mickey Mantle	$15
Aug. 56	Dale Long	$7.50
Sept.	56 Yogi Berra	$9-$10
Oct. 56	World Series	$10-$12
N,D. 56	Don Larsen	$8-$9
J,F. 57	Robin Roberts	$10
March 57	Scouting Reports	$9-$10
April 57	Farrell, Scheffing, Tighe	$8-$9
May 57	Don Blasingame	$6-$7
June 57	Breaking up the D.P./Martin	$7
July 57	Don Hoak	$6-$7
Aug. 57	Stan Musial	$10
Sept. 57	Bobby Shantz	$6-$7.50
O,N. 57	Babe Ruth (World Series) ...	$10-$13
D.57,J.58	Lew Burdette	$6-$7.50
Feb. 58	Von McDaniel	$6-$7
March 58	Scouting Reports	$9
April 58	Willie Mays, Duke Snider ...	$12-$15
May 58	Ted Williams	$15
June 58	Stan Musial	$15
July 58	Warren Spahn	$10
Aug. 58	Bob Turley	$7-$8
Sept. 58	Pete Runnels	$6-$7
O,N. 58	World Series Thrills	$8-$9
D.58,J.59	Turley, Jensen, Roberts	$9
Feb. 59	Baseball's Darling Daughters	$7
March 59	Scouting Reports	$9
April 59	Ernie Banks	$11-$12
May 59	Juan Pizarro	$6-$7
June 59	Antonelli, Pascual, Landis	$6.50
July 59	Vada Pinson	$7
Aug. 59	Hoyt Wilhelm	$8
Sept. 59	Rocky Colavito, Elroy Face	$7-$8
O.N. 59	World Series, H. Wilson ...	$8.50-$10
D.59,J.59	John Roseboro, Larry Sherry..	$6.50
Feb. 60	Harvey Kuenn	$7.50
March 60	Scouting Reports	$8.50
April 60	Willie McCovey	$8-$9
May 60	Early Wynn	$8
June 60	Bunning, Francona, McDaniel	$6.50
July 60	Vern Law	$6.50
Aug. 60	Dick Stuart	$8-$10
Sept. 60	Ron Hansen	$5.50
O,N. 60	Dick Groat	$6

D.60,J.61	Bill Virdon	$7
Feb. 61	Ralph Houk	$6
March 61	Scouting Reports	$8
April 61	Tony Kubek	$7.50
May 61	Glen Hobbie	$5
June 61	Earl Battey	$4.50-$5.50
July 61	Wally Moon	$4.50-$6
Aug. 61	Norm Cash	$6-$8
Sept. 61	Whitey Ford	$8-$9
O.N. 61	Koufax, Robinson, M&M Boys	$12-$15
D.61,J.62	Elston Howard, Ralph Terry	$6-$7
Feb. 62	Joey Jay	$5-$6
March 62	Scouting Reports	$8-$9
April 62	Orlando Cepeda	$7
May 62	Jim Landis	$9-$12
June 62	Mickey Mantle	$14-$15
July 62	Dick Donovan	$5
Aug. 62	20 Dramatic Home Runs	$8-$9
Sept. 62	Rich Rollins	$5
O,N. 62	Frank Howard, Tom Tresh	$6.50-$8
D.62,J.63	Ralph Terry	$6.50
Feb. 63	Ty Cobb, Maury Wills	$8
March 63	Scouting Reports	$8
April 63	1963 Rosters	$7.50
May 63	Dean, Drysdale, Dean	$8
June 63	Al Kaline	$8-$9
July 63	Jim O'Toole	$5-$6
Aug. 63	Jim Bouton	$5-$6
Sept. 63	Denny LeMaster	$5.50
O,N. 63	Al Downing	$5-$6
D.63,J.64	Don Drysdale, Sandy Koufax	$7-$8
Feb. 64	Roger Maris	$12.50-$14
March 64	Scouting Reports	$8-$9
April 64	Sandy Koufax	$10
May 64	Harmon Killebrew	$8
June 64	Tommy Davis, Carl Yastrzemski	$8
July 64	Jim Maloney	$5-$6
Aug. 64	Dave Nicholson	$5
Sept. 64	Dennis Bennett, Willie Smith	$4.50-$6
0,N. 64	Miracle Braves	$7.50
D.64,J.65	Dick Groat	$5-$6
Feb. 65	Winter Trades, Pete Rose	$7-$8
March 65	Scouting Reports	$8
April 65	Which Tag is Phony?	$6
May 65	Bill Freehan	$5
June 65	Tony Conigliaro	$6-$8
July 65	Yankees' Six Mistakes	$4.50-$8
Aug. 65	Don Drysdale	$7-$8
Sept. 65	Joe Morgan, Pete Ward	$6
0,N. 65	Biggest W.S. Mysteries	$5-$6
D.65,J.66	Sandy Koufax	$9
Feb. 66	Willie Mays	$9
March 66	Scouting Reports	$4.50-$8
April 66	1966 Rosters	$7.50

May 66	Sam McDowell	$5-$6
June 66	Should Rules Be Changed?	$4.50-$5.50
July 66	Juan Marichal	$6.50
Aug. 66	Gene Alley, Bill Mazeroski	$4.50-$6
Sept. 66	George Scott	$5-$6
O,N. 66	World Series Special	$5-$6
D.66,J.67	Palmer, Drabowsky, Bunker	$6.50
Feb. 67	Allison, Drysdale, Mathews	$6
March 67	Scouting Reports	$5-$8
April 67	1967 Rosters	$7.50
May 67	Roger Maris	$12-$14
June 67	Juan Marichal, Gaylord Perry	$8-$10
July 67	Denny McLain, Jimmy Wynn	$4
Aug. 67	Joel Horlen	$4.50
Sept. 67	Tim McCarver	$5-$6.50
0,N. 67	World Series Special	$5-$6
D. 67,J.68	Bob Gibson	$6-$7
Feb. 68	Billy Williams	$6-$7
March 68	Scouting Reports	$8-$10
April 68	1968 Rosters	$7.50
May 68	Carew, Johnstone, R. Nye	$6-$7
June 68	Nelson Briles, Cookie Rojas	$4.50-$5.50
July 68	Jerry Koosman	$5.50-$7
Aug. 68	Andy Kosco	$4.50
Sept. 68	Matty Alou, Ken Harrelson	$5-$6
0,N. 68	Bob Gibson, Denny McLain	$6.50-$8
D.68,J.69	World Series	$5.50
Feb. 69	Mickey Mantle	$14-$16
March 69	Scouting Reports	$7.50
April 69	1969 Rosters	$7.50
May 69	Al Lopez	$5.50
June 69	Ernie Banks	$7-$8
July 69	Tony Conigliaro	$6-$9
Aug. 69	Frank Robinson	$6-$8
Sept. 69	Baseball Flirts With Tragedy	$4.50
Oct. 69	World Series Special	$5-$6
Nov. 69	Super Stars of the '70s	$7.50
Dec. 69	Tom Seaver	$7.50-$9
Jan. 70	Harmon Killebrew	$5-$6.50
Feb. 70	Joe Pepitone	$3.50
March 70	Gene Alley	$3.50
April 70	Tony Perez	$5
May 70	Roberto Clemente	$7.50-$9
June 70	Mel Stottlemyre	$4
July 70	Ken Holtzman	$4
Aug. 70	Sal Bando	$4
Sept. 70	Jim Hickman	$4
Oct. 70	Jim Palmer	$5.50-$6.50
Nov. 70	Johnny Bench	$6-$8
Dec. 70	Billy Williams	$5-$6.50
Jan. 71	Brooks Robinson	$5-$6.50
Feb. 71	Sal Bando, Juan Marichal	$5-$6

March 71	Carl Yastrzemski	$6.50-$8
April 71	Bob Gibson	$5.50-$6.50
May 71	Willie Mays	$6.50-$9
June 71	Tony Oliva	$4.50-$6
July 71	Hank Aaron	$6.50-$9
Aug. 71	Vida Blue	$4
Sept. 71	Joe Pepitone	$3.50
Oct. 71	World Series	$5-$6
Nov. 71	Bobby Murcer	$4
Dec. 71	Joe Torre	$4.50
Jan. 72	Steve Blass	$3.50
Feb. 72	Earl Williams	$3.50
March 72	Frank Robinson	$5.50-$7.50
April 72	Bill Melton	$4
May 72	1972 Rosters	$5.50
June 72	Reggie Jackson	$7.50
July 72	Richie Allen	$4.50-$5.50
Aug. 72	Bud Harrelson	$3.50
Sept.72	Roberto Clemente	$7-$8
Oct. 72	Gary Nolan	$3.50
Nov. 72	Carlton Fisk	$5.50-$7.50
Dec. 72	Richie Allen	$4-$5.50
Jan. 73	Pete Rose	$6.50-$8.50
Feb. 73	Cesar Cedeno	$4-$5
March 73	Harmon Killebrew	$5-$6.50
April 73	Don Kessinger	$3.50
May 73	Nolan Ryan	$8-$10
June 73	Tom Seaver	$7
July 73	Pete Rose	$7-$8
Aug. 73	R. Allen, C. May, B. Melton	$4
Sept. 73	Ken Holtzman	$3.50-$4.50
Oct. 73	Bill Russell	$3.50
Nov. 73	Jose Cardenal	$3.50
Dec. 73	Willie Stargell	$5
Jan. 74	Berra, Campaneris (Series)	$5-$6
Feb. 74	Willie Mays	$5.50-$8
March 74	Bobby Grich	$3.50
April 74	Hank Aaron	$6.50-$8
May 74	Ted Sizemore	$3.50
June 74	Felix Milan	$3.50
July 74	Brooks Robinson	$5
Aug. 74	Tony Perez	$4.50
Sept. 74	Tommy John	$4
Oct. 74	Dick Allen	$4
Nov. 74	Bando, Campaneris, Jackson	$6
Dec. 74	Lou Brock	$4.50
Jan. 75	Rollie Fingers	$4
Feb. 75	Steve Garvey	$4
March 75	Jeff Burroughs	$3.50
April 75	Catfish Hunter	$4
May 75	Mike Schmidt	$5.50
June 75	Rod Carew	$4
July 75	Nolan Ryan	$5-$8
Aug. 75	Rick Monday	$3.50
Sept. 75	Johnny Bench	$5
Oct. 75	Vida Blue	$3.50
Nov. 75	Fred Lynn	$3.50
Dec. 75	Joe Morgan	$4.50
Jan. 76	Pete Rose	$6-$7
Feb. 76	Jim Palmer	$3.50
March 76	George Brett	$5-$6
April 76	Carlton Fisk	$4.50-$6
May 76	Frank Tanana	$3.50
June 76	Rick Manning	$3
July 76	Bill Madlock	$3.50
Aug. 76	Randy Jones	$3
Sept. 76	Larry Bowa	$3-$4
Oct. 76	Mickey Rivers	$3-$4
Nov. 76	Mark Fidrych	$4-$5
Dec. 76	Joe Morgan	$5
Jan. 77	World Series highlights	$4-$5
Feb. 77	Thurman Munson	$5
March 77	Amos Otis	$3.50
April 77	Mark Fidrych	$3.50
May 77	John Montefusco	$3
June 77	Steve Carlton	$4-$5
July 77	Dave Parker	$4-$5
Aug. 77	Ivan DeJesus, Manny Trillo	$3
Sept. 77	Carl Yastrzemski	$6-$7
Oct. 77	Steve Garvey	$4
Nov. 77	Bump Wills	$3
Dec. 77	George Foster	$3-$4
Jan. 78	Reggie Jackson	$6-$7
Feb. 78	Willie McCovey	$4.50
March 78	Rod Carew	$5
April 78	Tom Seaver	$5
May 78	Cesar Cedeno	$4.50
June 78	Garry Templeton	$4.50
July 78	Dave Kingman	$3.50
Aug. 78	Jim Rice	$4-$5
Sept. 78	Ron Guidry	$4-$5
Oct. 78	Rich Gale, Clint Hurdle	$3.50
Nov. 78	Reggie Smith	$3.50
Dec. 78	Dave Parker	$4-$5
Jan. 79	World Series highlights	$4.50
Feb. 79	Dave Winfield	$3.50-$5
March 79	Greg Luzinski	$3.50
April 79	Rich Gossage	$3.50
May 79	Jack Clark	$4
June 79	Steve Garvey	$4
July 79	Al Oliver	$4
Aug. 79	Bill Buckner	$3.50
Sept. 79	Tommy John	$3.50
Oct. 79	Mike Schmidt	$5-$6
Nov. 79	Omar Moreno	$3
Dec. 79	George Brett	$5-$6
Jan. 80	Mike Flanagan	$3.50
Feb. 80	Paul Molitor	$4
March 80	Gary Carter	$3-$5
April 80	Willie Stargell	$3.50-$5
May 80	Don Baylor	$3.50
June 80	J.R. Richard, Nolan Ryan	$5-$7

July 80	Baumgarten, Burns, Trout	$3
Aug. 80	Ken Landreaux	$3
Sept. 80	Steve Carlton	$4-$5
Oct. 80	Reggie Jackson	$5-$6
Nov. 80	Joe Charboneau	$3
Dec. 80	George Brett	$4.50
Jan. 81	Tug McGraw	$4
Feb. 81	Eddie Murray	$4
March 81	Rickey Henderson	$5.50
April 81	Mike Schmidt	$5.50
May 81	Gary Carter	$4.50
June 81	Cecil Cooper	$3-$4
July 81	Carlton Fisk	$4.50
Aug. 81	Fernando Valenzuela	$4
Sept. 81	Danny Darwin	$3.50
Oct. 81	Ron Davis	$3.50
Nov. 81	Pete Rose	$6
Dec. 81	Tim Raines	$4
Jan. 82	Steve Garvey	$4
Feb. 82	Carney Lansford	$3.50
March 82	Rollie Fingers	$4
April 82	Dave Winfield	$4.50
May 82	Nolan Ryan	$5.50-$7
June 82	Jerry Reuss	$3.50
July 82	Salome Barojas	$2.50-$3
Aug. 82	Dale Murphy	$4.50
Sept. 82	Rickey Henderson	$4-$5
Oct. 82	Robin Yount	$4.50
Nov. 82	Kent Hrbek	$4
Dec. 82	Ozzie and Lonnie Smith	$4
Jan. 83	Darrell Porter	$3
Feb. 83	Mario Soto	$3
March 83	Doug DeCinces	$3
April 83	Willie McGee	$4
May 83	Pete Vuckovich	$3
June 83	Cal Ripken Jr.	$4.50
July 83	Tony Pena	$4
Aug. 83	Dave Stieb	$4
Sept. 83	Chris Chambliss	$3.50
Oct. 83	Ron Kittle	$3.50
Nov. 83	Steve Carlton	$4.50
Dec. 83	Carlton Fisk	$5
Jan. 84	Rick Dempsey	$3
Feb. 84	Wade Boggs	$4.50
March 84	Dale Murphy	$4.50
April 84	Mike Boddicker	$3.50
May 84	Andre Dawson	$4
June 84	Lance Parrish	$3.50
July 84	Bill Madlock	$3.50
Aug. 84	Leon Durham	$2.50-$3
Sept. 84	Gwynn, C. Martinez, McReynolds	$4
Oct. 84	Ryne Sandberg	$5
Nov. 84	Keith Hernandez	$3.50
Dec. 84	Mark Langston	$4
Jan. 85	Alan Trammell	$3.50

Feb. 85	Don Mattingly	$5
March 85	Frank Viola	$3.50
April 85	Jack Morris	$3.50
May 85	Tony Gwynn	$4
June 85	Dwight Gooden	$5.50
July 85	Bruce Sutter	$3.50
Aug. 85	Pete Rose	$4.50
Sept. 85	Lonnie Smith	$3.50
Oct. 85	Ron Guidry	$3.50
Nov. 85	Pedro Guerrero	$3.50
Dec. 85	Dwight Gooden	$4.50
Jan. 86	Willie McGee	$3.50
Feb. 86	Bret Saberhagen	$3.50
March 86	Tom Browning	$2.50-$3
April 86	Harold Baines	$3
May 86	Darryl Strawberry	$4.50
June 86	Eddie Murray	$4
July 86	Bert Blyleven	$3
Aug. 86	Roger Clemens	$4.50
Sept. 86	Gary Carter	$3.50
Oct. 86	Jose Canseco, Wally Joyner	$4.50
Nov. 86	Bill Doran	$2.50-$3
Dec. 86	Roger Clemens, Ted Higuera	$4
Jan. 87	Wade Boggs, Don Mattingly	$4.50
Feb. 87	Sid Fernandez	$3
March 87	Mike Scott	$2.50-$3
April 87	Chris Brown	$2.50
May 87	Pete O'Brien	$3.50
June 87	Eric Davis, Jody Davis	$3.50
July 87	Mike Witt	$2-$3
Aug. 87	Rickey Henderson	$4
Sept. 87	Jack Clark, Ozzie Smith	$3.50
Oct. 87	Mark McGwire	$4
Nov. 87	George Bell	$3.50
Dec. 87	Kevin Seitzer	$2.50
Jan. 88	Andre Dawson	$3.50
Feb. 88	Frank Viola	$3
March 88	Jimmy Key	$2.50
April 88	Kevin McReynolds, Mike Pagliarulo	$2.50
May 88	Eric Davis	$3-$4
June 88	K.C. Royals pitchers	$3
July 88	Andy Van Slyke	$3.50
Aug. 88	Dave Winfield	$4
Sept. 88	Greg Maddux	$3
Oct. 88	Kirby Puckett	$4
Nov. 88	Jose Canseco	$4
Dec. 88	Danny Jackson	$2
Jan. 89	Jose Canseco	$4
Feb. 89	Orel Hershiser	$3.50
March 89	Gregg Jefferies	$3.50
April 89	Kirk Gibson	$3.50
May 89	Cory Snyder	$2
June 89	Fred McGriff	$3.50
July 89	Will Clark	$3.50
Aug. 89	Nolan Ryan	$5

 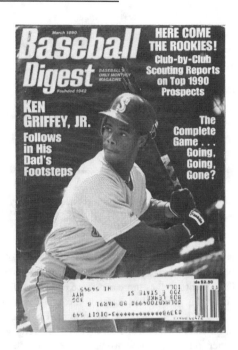

Books

The outlook for baseball books as collectibles is very good; prices of quality used baseball books are relatively low. However, prices have been rising, and, as more and more collectors discover this overlooked area of the memorabilia hobby, prices will escalate accordingly. For lovers of baseball literature and for investors, there is no better time than now to buy quality baseball books.

Four main factors determine the value of a used baseball book: scarcity, desirability, condition, and edition. Generally, scarcity adds to the value of a baseball book, but not significantly unless the book is considered desirable in the first place. In other words, hundreds of fairly hard-to-find baseball books are not particularly valuable because there is no demand for them. However, desirable books that are scarce always command premium prices.

Many older baseball books, especially those published in the 19th century, are the exceptions

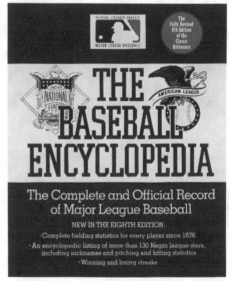

to this rule. These older books, such as Henry Chadwick's The Game of Baseball (1868) and Jacob Morse's Sphere and Ash (1888), are not very entertaining to the average contemporary reader, but they are extremely rare and historically important. Thus, each easily sells for thousands of dollars.

Desirability is ultimately in the eye of the reader/buyer, but the author, the subject, the degree of originality, and the overall quality or "readability" of the book are the main factors that determine a book's standing with collectors. Baseball card collectors should have little trouble understanding that condition greatly affects the value of baseball books. Torn or missing pages, coffee cup rings on the cover, general wear and tear on the spine - such defects definitely reduce any book's value.

Two particularly important aspects of condition to be aware of are: 1) "ex libre" books, i.e. discards from libraries, are considered damaged goods and are shunned by collecting purists; and 2) a lack of a dust jacket (if issued) significantly reduces the value of a book, sometimes up to 50 percent or more. Closely related to condition is the matter of a book's edition. To be worth top dollar a book should be a first printing of a first edition.

Two other influences on value are worth noting. First, although an autograph normally lessens the value of a premier baseball card, it enhances a baseball book, whether the book is signed by the author or the subject(s), or both. Second, a biography is not necessarily valuable because the subject is a superstar.

For example, Mickey Mantle is a magic name in the baseball card market, but there is no scarce (or particularly outstanding) Mantle biography. Thus a much hard-to-find biography of a lesser player, such as Rocky Colavito (Don't Knock the Rock), is considered more valuable than any Mantle biography.

Of course, there is no guarantee that any baseball book will appreciate dramatically, so the average collector would be well advised to collect books he enjoys for his own sake.

Because there are so many baseball books, with a few hundred new ones published annually, most collectors should consider specializing. Four common approaches to specialization are collecting by quality, team, genre (e.g., record books, fiction, picture books, general histories), or topic. Some of the most popular topics for baseball book collectors are ballparks, the Negro Leagues, biographies and the minors.

Finally, there is a wide variety of sources for used baseball books. The top sources, ranging from the least to the most productive, are: garage sales, card shows, library sales, antiquarian book sales, hobby periodicals (such as *Sports Collectors Digest*), used book stores, and used baseball book dealers who issue mail-order catalogs. Remaindered books at cut-rate prices can also be found in new-book book stores, but these offerings will always be recently published books that either didn't sell well or were over-printed.

—

Listed below are some of the best baseball books ever published, books which would form the foundation of any worthy collections. While not truly rare, first editions of many of these titles are becoming quite scarce. Because there is no comprehensive used baseball book price guide, it is difficult to state exact values for these books with any certainty; however, collectors can expect to see these books priced in the following ranges: up to $50; $50-$75; and more than $75.

Babe, The Legend Comes to Live, Robert Creamer, 1974, ($50) — Considered by many as the best sports biography ever written, Babe increases our affection and respect for baseball's foremost hero.

Ball Four, Jim Bouton, 1970, ($50) — Although rather tame by today's standards, Bouton's tell-all shocker of 1970 is still the funniest baseball book in captivity.

The Ballparks, Bill Shannon, 1965, (more than $75) — This photo-history, the first thing on its subject, is tough to find and high on many collectors' want-lists.

Baseball: The Early Years (1960) and Baseball: *The Golden Age (1971)*, Harold Seymour, ($50-$75) — This as-yet-uncompleted triology ranks as baseball literature's most highly regarded general history.

The Baseball Encyclopedia, first edition, ($50 — Now in its eighth edition, the original edition of the most famous baseball record book comes in a neat boxed slip cover.

Baseball I Gave You All The Best Years Of My Life, edited by Richard Grossinger and Kevin Kerrane, ($50 — A mind-bending anthology of eclectic poetry and prose, *Baseball I Gave You* is hard to find but worth the trouble.

The Boys Of Summer, Roger Kahn, 1971, ($50 — The book that immortalized that Brooklyn Dodgers of the early 1950s, *The Boys of Summer* is the quintessential classic baseball book.

Bush League, Robert Obojski, ($50-$75 — Conceived as a companion to *The Baseball Encyclopedia*, *Bush League* was published in 1975 but it is still the best reference book on the minors.

The Celebrant, Eric Rolfe Greenberg, (more than $75 — A novel about Christy Mathewson and his biggest fan, *The Celebrant* is a scarce book with a big following.

The Cincinnati Game, Lonnie Wheeler, 1988, ($50 — This is the most innovative team history ever, but only 3,000 copies of the hardback were published.

Books

The Chrysanthemum and the Bat, Robert Whiting, ($50-$75 — The first major treatment of Japanese baseball, this is also a book about the clash of two cultures.

Eight Men Out, Eliot Asinof, ($50-$75 — This is the best book about baseball's most infamous scandal, the fixed 1919 World Series.

A False Spring, Pat Jordan, ($50 — This beautifully-written coming-of-age autobiography about failure in the minor leagues reads like a novel.

The Fireside Book of Baseball, Vol I, II, & III, edited by Charles Einstein, ($50, $50 and more than $75 — These are the first great (and still unsurpassed) anthologies of baseball literature. Vol. III is especially tough to locate.

The Glory of Their Times, Lawrence Ritter, 1966, ($50 — This collection of first-person accounts by players from the '20s is a favorite with collectors.

The Great American Baseball Card Flipping, Trading and Bubble Gum Book, Brendan C. Boyd and Fred C. Harris, (A — Recently reprinted, this most nostalgic of all baseball books was the first to demonstrate the enormous appeal of baseball cards.

The Long Season, 1960, and *Pennant Race*, Jim Brosnan, ($50 each — Great inside looks at major league baseball, Brosnan's diaries remain the only books to be entirely written by an active major league player.

Only the Ball Was White, Robert Peterson, (more than $75 — This pioneering history of Negro League baseball is a must for anyone interested in its popular topic.

Putnam Sports Series, various authors, (more than $75 — Written by the leading sportswriters of the '50s, these team histories have stood the test of time and fetch increasingly higher prices.

Shoeless Joe, W. P. Kinsella, (more than $75 — The novel that "Field of Dreams" was based on, *Shoeless Joe* is highly sought-after by collectors of American fiction as well as collectors of great baseball books.

Ty Cobb, Charles C. Alexander, (A — This great biography of baseball's fiercest immortal was underestimated and underprinted by its original publisher.

The Ultimate Baseball Book, edited by Dan Okrent, ($50 — Great photos and superb writing by an all-star lineup highlight this coffee-table spectacular.

Veeck As In Wreck, Bill Veeck and Ed Linn, ($50-$75 — Baseball's maverick promoter tells how it's done in a consistently entertaining and seldom-offered-for-sale book.

— Mike Shannon

Mike Shannon is the editor and publisher of *Spitball: the Literary Baseball Magazine*, 6224 Collegevue Place, Cincinnati, Ohio, 45224. *Spitball* magazine annually awards the Casey Award to the best baseball book of the year. Previous winners include:

1983: *The Celebrant*, Eric Rolfe Greenberg

1984: *Bums: An Oral History of the Brooklyn Dodgers*, Peter Golenbock

1985: *Good Enough to Dream*, Roger Kahn

1986: *The Bill James Historical Baseball Abstract*, Bill James

1987: *Diamonds are Forever*, Peter Gordon/Paul Weinman

1988: *Blackball Stars*, John Holway

1989: *The Pitch that Killed*, Mike Sowell

1990: *Baseball: The People's Game*, Harold Seymour

1991: *To Everything a Season: Shibe Park and Urban Philadelphia*, B. Kuklick

1992: *The Negro Baseball Leagues: A Photographic History*, Phil Dixon and Patrick J. Hannigan

1993: *Diamonds: The Evolution of the Ballpark*, Michael Gershman

The following prices are taken from a 1993-94 catalog from A&R Books and Collectibles, a leading used books dealer based in Tiverton, R.I. SC means soft cover, HC means hard cover, PB means paperback.

Classics

Babe: The Legend Comes to Life, by Robert W. Creamer, SC 443 pages, $12.
Ball Four, 20th anniversary issue, by Jim Bouton, SC 427 pages, $13.95; HC autographed, $29.95.
Game Day, by Tom Boswell, SC 394 pages, $10.
How Life Imitates the World Series, by Tom Boswell, SC 296 pages, $9.95.
I *Had a Hammer*, by Hank Aaron with Lonnie Wheeler, PB 333 pages, $5.50; HC 333 pages, $40 autographed.
Late Innings, by Roger Angell, PB 439 pages, $5.99; SC 429 pages, $12.
Once More Around the Park, by Roger Angell, SC 351 pages, $10.
Season Ticket, by Roger Angell, PB 419 pages, $5.99.
The Heart of the Order, by Tom Boswell, SC 363 pages, $9.
The Image of Their Greatness, by Lawrence Ritter and Donald Honig, SC 438 pages, $15.
The Summer Game, by Roger Angell, PB 293 pages, $3.95.
The Ultimate Baseball Book, by Daniel Okrent and Harry Levine, SC 394 pages, $19.95.
Ty Cobb, by Charles C. Alexander, SC 272 pages, $10.95.
Why Time Begins on Opening Day, by Tom Boswell, SC 300 pages, $9.95.

Biographies/Autobiographies

Sparky, by Sparky Anderson with Dan Ewald, SC 264 pages, $9.95.
Lou Boudreau: Covering all the Bases, by Lou Boudreau with Russell Schneider, HC 204 pages, $19.95.
You Can't Hit The Ball With The Bat On Your Shoulder, by Bobby Bragan as told to Jeff Guinn, HC 362 pages, $19.95.
Ty Cobb: My Life in Baseball, by Ty Cobb with Al Stump (reprint of Cobb's autobiography), SC 283 pages, $11.95.
Joe DiMaggio: Baseball's Yankee Clipper, by Jack B. Moore, SC 252 pages, $9.95.
Diz, by Robert Gregory (Dizzy Dean), SC 402 pages, $12.50, HC 402 pages, $22.
Ol' Diz, by Vince Staten (Dizzy Dean), HC 326 pages, $22.50.
Pride Against Prejudice, by Joseph Thomas Moore (Larry Doby), SC 195 pages, $12.95.
The Lip, by Gerald Eskenazi (Leo Durocher), HC 336 pages, $23.
Now Pitching, Bob Feller, by Bob Feller with Bill Gilbert, SC 231 pages, $8.95; HC autographed, $29.95.
Double X: Jimmie Foxx Baseball's Forgotten Slugger, by Bob Gorman, SC 213 pages, $10.
Iron Horse, by Ray Robinson (Lou Gehrig), SC 299 pages, $10.
Bart: A Life of A. Bartlett Giamatti, by Anthony Valerio, SC 123 pages, $10.95.
Calvin: Baseball's Last Dinosaur, by Jon Kerr (Calvin Griffith), SC 206 pages, $12.95.
Gil Hodges: The Quiet Man, by Marino Amoruso, HC 238 pages, $19.95.
Say It Ain't So Joe, by Donald Gropman (Shoeless Joe Jackson), SC 319 pages, $10.95.
Shoeless Joe and Ragtime Baseball, by Harvey Frommer (Shoeless Joe Jackson), SC 225 pages, $10.95; HC 225 pages, $19.95.
Run, Rabbit, Run, by Walter Maranville, SC 96 pages, $9.95.
Roger Maris: A Title To Fame, by Harvey Rosenfeld, HC 287 pages, $19.95.
Maris: Missing from the Hall of Fame, by C.W. Edwards (Roger Maris), SC 96 pages, $9.95.
The Last Yankee, by David Falkner (Billy Martin), SC 349 pages, $12; HC 349 pages, $22.
Matty: An American Hero, by Ray Robinson (Christy Mathewson's career), HC 236 pages, $23.
Willie's Time, by Charles Einstein (Willie Mays), SC 352 pages, $10.
John McGraw, by Charles C. Alexander, SC 358 pages, $8.95.
Joe Morgan: A Life In Baseball, by Joe Morgan with David Falkner, HC 303 pages, $21.95.
A *Tiger In His Time*, by David M. Jordan (Hal Newhouser), HC 289 pages $19.95; HC autographed, $26.
Maybe I'll Pitch Forever, by LeRoy Satchel Paige with David Lipman, (reprint of 1962 autobiography), SC 295 pages, $10.95.
I *Love This Game*, by Kirby Puckett, HC 238 pages, $20.
O *Holy Cow! The Selected Verse of Phil Rizzuto*, by Hart Seely and Tom Peyer, SC 107 pages, $8.95.
Phil Rizzuto: A Yankee Tradition, by Dan Hirshberg, HC 197 pages, $19.95.
Collison at Home Plate, by James Reston Jr. (Pete Rose), SC 328 pages, $10.
Pete Rose: My Story, by Pete Rose with Roger Kahn, HC 300 pages, $18.95.
Hustle: The Myth Life and Lies of Pete Rose, by Michael Y. Sokolove, SC 304 pages, $11.
The Life That Ruth Built, by Marshall Smelser (Babe Ruth), SC 592 pages, $16.95.
Babe Ruth: His Life and Legend, by Karl Wagenheim, SC 274 pages, $12.95.
Miracle Man: Nolan Ryan, by Nolan Ryan with Jerry Jenkins, HC 272 pages, $18.99.

Books

Ron Santo: For Love of Ivy, by Ron Santo with Randy Minkoff, HC 228 pages, $20.
Country Hardball, by Enos Slaughter and Kevin Reid, HC 208 pages, $18.95;autographed, $30.
A.G. Spaulding and the Rise of Baseball, by Peter Levine, SC 184 pages, $9.95.
Stengel: His Life and Times, by Robert W. Creamer, SC 349 pages, $9.95.
Ted Williams: The Season of the Kid, by Richard Ben Cramer, HC 256 pages, $19.95.
The Last .400 Hitter, by John B. Holway (Ted Williams), HC 360 pages, $19.95.
Hitter: The Life and Turmoils of Ted Williams, by Ed Linn, HC 438 pages, $23.95.
My Turn at Bat, by Ted Williams with John Underwood, SC 267 pages, $10.95.

Historical

Our Game, by Charles C. Alexander (history of the game), SC 388 pages, $14.95.
The Red Smith Reader, by Dave Anderson (131 of Red Smith's columns), SC 308 pages, $7.95.
Eight Men Out, by Eliot Asinof (1919 Black Sox scandal), SC 302 pages, $9.95.
1947: When All Hell Broke Loose in Baseball, by Red Barber, SC 367 pages, $10.95.
The Broadcasters, by Red Barber, SC 271 pages, $8.95.
The Minor Leagues, by Mike Blake (history, facts, stats, nostalgia, stories), HC 400 pages, $19.95.
Baseball From A Different Angle, by Bob Broeg and William J. Miller Jr., SC 268 pages, $12.95.
The Milwaukee Braves, by Bob Buege, HC 415 pages, $19.95.
Peanuts and Crackerjacks, by David Cataneo (legends and lore), HC 294 pages, $18.95.
A Magic Summer: The 1969 Mets, by Stanley Cohen, SC 311 pages, $8.95.
Baseball in 1941, by Robert W. Creamer, SC 330 pages, $12.
Lightning In A Bottle, by Herbert F. Crehan with James W. Ryan (1967 Boston Red Sox), HC 260 pages, $19.95.
Big Sticks, by William Curran (1920s home run barrage), SC 288 pages, $8.95.
They Kept Me Loyal to the Yankees, by Victor Debs (tribute to former Yankees), HC 160 pages, $14.95.
Baseball's Greatest Quotations, by Paul Dickson, HC 524 pages, $16.
The New Baseball Reader, by Charles Einstein (baseball anthologies), SC 459 pages, $12.
Play Ball, by John Feinstein (baseball's troubled times), HC 427 pages, $22.50.
The 26th Man, by Steve Fireovid and Mark Winegardner (story of a veteran minor leaguer), HC 229 pages, $18.95.
The Men of Autumn, by Dom Forker (1949-53 New York Yankees), HC 228 pages, $18.95.
Sweet Seasons, by Dom Forker (1955-64 New York Yankees), HC 220 pages, $18.95.
New York City Baseball, by Harvey Frommer (1947-57 baseball in New York), SC 219 pages, $9.95.
Superstars and Screwballs, by Richard Goldstein (baseball in Brooklyn), SC 383 pages, $12.
Baseball's Biggest Bloopers, by Dan Gutman, HC 160 pages, $13.99.
It Ain't Cheatin' if You Don't Get Caught, by Dan Gutman, SC 208 pages, $11.
A Day In The Bleachers, by Arnold Halo (Game 1 of the 1954 World Series), SC 153 pages, $6.95.
When the Cheering Stops, by Lee Helman, Dave Weiner and Bill Gutman (profiles 21 players from the 1950s and 1960s), HC 308 pages, $18.95.
Five O'Clock Lightning, by Tommy Henrich and Bill Gilbert, HC 298 pages, $19.95.
Baseball When the Grass Was Real, by Donald Honig, SC 324 pages, $12.95.
Baseball Between the Lines, by Donald Honig, SC 256 pages, $10.95.
Fridays with Red, by Bob Edwards (Tribute to sportscaster Red Barber), HC 256 pages, $21.
Seasons to Remember, by Curt Gowdy with John Powers, HC 210 pages, $23.
Misfits, J. Thomas Hetrick (1899 Cleveland Spiders), HC 222 pages, $25.95.
Games We Used to Play, by Roger Kahn (Kahn's best sports pieces), HC 269 pages, $21.95.
Baseball for the Hot Stove League, by Robert E. Kelly (15 essays), SC 158 pages, $14.95.
The Worst Team Money Can Buy, by Bob Klapsich and John Harper (1992 New York Mets), HC 228 pages, $21.
Sixty One, by Tony Kubek and Terry Pluto, SC 269 pages, $9.95.
Stolen Season, by David Lamb (portrait of the minor leagues), HC 238 pages, $20.
Baseball's Great Steaks, by Allen Lewis (40 significant streaks in baseball history), HC 272 pages, $29.95.
Two Spectacular Seasons, by William B. Mead (1930 and 1968 seasons recapped), HC 245 pages, $18.95.
Down to the Wire, by Jeff Miller, HC 252 pages, $19.95.
The Man Who Stole First Base, by Eric Nadel and Craig R. Wright (135 off-beat stories), SC 172 pages, $9.95.
Only the Ball Was White, by Robert Peterson (Negro Leagues), SC 406 pages, $10.95.
Lost Summer, by Bill Reynolds, PB 310 pages, $5.50; HC 293 pages, $18.95.
Dandy, Day and the Devil, by James A. Riley (Ray Dandridge, Leon Day and Willie Wells), SC 153 pages, $12.95.
Invisible Men, by Donn Rogosin (Negro Leagues), SC 283 pages, $11.95.
The Great Chase: The Dodgers Giants Pennant Race of 1951, by Harvey Rosenfeld, SC 277 pages, $25.95.

Ball Four has had several editions published, including a Japanese version.

Kings of the Hill, by Nolan Ryan with Mickey Herskowitz (Ryan summarizes pitchers), HC 243 pages, $20.

Streak: Joe DiMaggio and the Summer of 1941, by Michael Seidel, SC 260 pages, $8.95.

Great Moments in Baseball, by Tom Seaver with Marty Appel (Seaver's collection of stories), HC 339 pages, $19.95.

The Curse of the Bambino, by David Shaughnessy (Traces Red Sox history after Babe Ruth was traded), SC 220 pages, $8.95.

Voices of the Game, by Curt Smith (chronicles baseball broadcasting), SC 623 pages, $15.

July 2, 1903, by Mike Sowell, HC 326 pages, $20.

The Pitch That Killed, by Mike Sowell, SC 330 pages, $11.95.

The Year They Called off the World Series, by Benton Stark (details the 1904 season), HC 263 pages, $17.95.

The Minors, by Neil J. Sullivan (historical overview of the minor leagues), SC 307 pages, $12.95.

The Cubs of 69, by Rick Talley (recaps the bittersweet 1969 season), SC 354 pages, $9.95.

The Armchair Book of Baseball, by John Thorn, SC 388 pages, $13.

Men At Work, by George F. Will, SC 353 pages, $9.95.

Diamonds in the Rough, by Joel Zoss and John Bowman (history of baseball), HC 433 pages, $29.95.

Paperbacks

Don Baylor Nothing But The Truth: A Baseball Life, by Don Baylor with Charlie Smith, $4.95.

Dodgers! The First 100 Years, by Stanley Cohen, $4.50.

Real Grass, Real Heroes, by Dom DiMaggio with Bill Gilbert, $4.95.

Once a Bum, Always a Dodger, by Don Drysdale with Bob Verdi, $4.95.

Bums, by Peter Golenbock, $4.95.

Summer of 49, by David Halberstam, $4.95.

Tuned to Baseball, by Ernie Harwell, $3.95.

White Rat, by Whitey Herzog and Kevin Horrigan, $4.95.

T.J.: My 26 Years in Baseball, by Tommy John with Dan Valenti, $5.99.

Shoeless Joe, by W.P. Kinsella (fiction), $5.99.

The Wrong Stuff, by Bill Lee with Dick Lally, $4.95.

Damned Yankees, by Bill Madden and Moss Klein, $5.95.

My Favorite Summer, by Mickey Mantle and Phil Pepe, $5.99.

The Mick, by Mickey Mantle with Herb Gluck, $4.99.

The Babe Ruth Story, by Babe Ruth with Bob Considine, $4.99.

Throwing Heat: The Autobiography of Nolan Ryan, by Nolan Ryan with Harvey Frommer, $4.95.

The Duke of Flatbush, by Duke Snider with Bill Gilbert, $4.95.

Yaz, by Carl Yastzremski and Gerald Eskenazi, $4.95

Commemoratives

Gateway Stamp Co.

Gateway Stamp Co. Inc., of Florissant, Mo., has been producing full-color "silk" commemorative cachets since 1977, when the company produced a set of three cachets commemorating the 50th anniversary of the flight of Charles Lindbergh. Since that time the company has planned more than 540 sports-related cachets, primarily baseball issues. Some of the issue numbers (referred to as GS) are being held or RESERVED for significant events or for signatures of the corresponding athletes.

The limited-edition envelopes are postmarked on the historic dates by the United States Postal Service, which only dates items submitted before midnight. Gateway has employees who track a player's progress toward a milestone accomplishment; they also follow the player, with a determined number of stamped cachets to be postmarked, until the even has occurred. When the event has happened, the employee has the Post Office in that city hand-cancel the envelopes. Whenever possible, Gateway also incorporates philatelic cancellations on the envelopes.

The cachets feature gold borders, biographical information and full-color silk cachets, which are actual event photos, publicity photos, or artists' renditions. A primary attraction of the cachets is that Gateway has designed the envelopes to be autographed, and obtains the signatures of the players represented on them.

Values of the covers are determined by condition (cleanliness, crispness of corners, centering, positioning of copy, clarity of postmarks) and autographs - quality and player represented. In the following checklist, based on Mint condition, A represents autographed; U means unautographed. The prices are the current retail prices on the market.

Gateway Stamp Co.

1977

GS1, GS2 and GS3 are devoted to the 50th anniversary of the flight of Charles Lindbergh.

GS4 LOU BROCK STOLEN BASE 892: Postmarked Aug. 29, 1977, San Diego, Calif., when he tied the all-time stolen base record of Ty Cobb. Artwork by Frank P. Zaso. 5,000 issued, autographed. 4,000 circle and bars used; 1,000 Junipero Serra Museum cancellations used. A $25, U $10.

GS5 LOU BROCK STOLEN BASE 893: Postmarked Aug. 29, 1977, San Diego, Calif., when he broke the all-time stolen base record. 2,500 issued autographed; 2,500 unautographed. 3,000 Junipero Serra Museum cancellations used; 2,000 circle and bars used. A $25, U $10.

GS5a LOU BROCK STOLEN BASE 893: Variation. 50 892 silks attached to 893 envelopes. Autographed. A $250.

GS6 REGGIE JACKSON MR. OCTOBER: 325 envelopes postmarked Oct. 18, 1977, New York, N.Y., from the 1977 World Series Game 6 when Jackson hit three homers. Issued in 1991. A $195.

1978

GS7 BOB FORSCH NO-HITTER: 105 envelopes postmarked April 15, 1978, St. Louis, Mo., after Bob Forsch's no-hitter against Philadelphia. 60 Independence Hall stamps used; 45 Indian Head Penny stamps used. Autographed. A $3,500.

GS8 PETE ROSE 3,000 HITS: Postmarked May 5, 1978, Cincinnati, Ohio, after Rose's 3,000th hit. 5,000 issued, autographed. Round cancellation. $45.

GS9 PETE ROSE PRIDE OF CINCINNATI: Postmarked May 5, 1978, Cincinnati, Ohio, with Fountain Square cancellations. 5,000 issued, unautographed. A $35.

GS10 TOM SEAVER NO-HITTER: 100 #10 size envelopes postmarked June 16, 1978, from Cos Cob, Conn., after Seaver's no-hitter. Autographed. Issued in 1985. A $2,000.

GS10a TOM SEAVER NO-HITTER: 41 regular size envelopes postmarked June 16, 1978, in Cos Cob, Conn., after the no-hitter. Same photo. Autographed. Issued in 1985. A $2,500.

GS11 WILLIE McCOVEY 500 HOME RUNS: Postmarked June 30, 1978, Atlanta, Ga., on Willie McCovey's 500th home run. 2,000 issued, autographed. All cancellations round. $175.

GS12 WILLIE McCOVEY PRIDE OF THE GIANTS: Postmarked June 30, 1978, San Francisco, Calif., commemorating McCovey and San Francisco. Artwork by Marilyn Meystrick. 2,000 issued, unautographed. All cancellations round. A $100.

Pete Rose 44-game hitting streak, set of four

The hitting streak was designed to provide one envelope for each date and place where Pete Rose tied and broke the National League and all-time records up to Joe DiMaggio's 56-game streak. 2,000 envelopes each were postmarked the nights Rose tied and broke the modern National League record and the night he tied the all-time National League record. No plans were made for an envelope for the night the streak would end, but after the dramatics in the game when it ended, Gateway officials realized the ending of the streak was as much a part of the story as the records themselves. At 11:55 p.m. Gateway turned in 1,800 envelopes for cancellation. Thus, the hitting streak is 1,800 complete sets of four and 200 sets of three. The Game 38 variation is found only in complete sets, not as an additional envelope.

GS13 GAME 37: Postmarked July 24, 1978, New York, N.Y., after Rose tied the modern National League consecutive game hitting streak of Tommy Holmes (1945). 2,000 issued, unautographed. With New York philatelic postmark. A $50, U $25.

GS14 GAME 38: Postmarked July 25, 1978, New York, N.Y., when Rose broke the modern National League consecutive game hitting streak record. 1,650 issued, unautographed. With New York philatelic postmark. A $50.

GS14a GAME 38 VARIATION: Postmarked July 25, 1978, New York, N.Y., Bill Perry artwork, with redesigned gold border to accommodate shifted New York postmark. 350 issued, unautographed. A $200, U $175. Not issued by Gateway without a special request from the purchaser.

GS15 GAME 44: Postmarked July 31, 1978, Atlanta, Ga., after Rose tied the all-time National League consecutive game hitting streak record. 2,000 issued, unautographed. With Atlanta philatelic postmark. The opposing pitcher is incorrectly indentified as Joe Niekro; it was Phil Niekro. A $50, U $25.

GS16 THE NIGHT IT ENDED: Postmarked Aug. 1, 1978, Atlanta, Ga., after the streak ended at 44. Artwork by Bill Perry. 1,800 issued, unautographed. With Atlanta philatelic postmark. A $10, U $5.

75th anniversary of the World Series, set of six

Gateway's first World Series issue; 2,000 sets of six envelopes issued. Originally designed for the Reggie Jackson photo on Game 4 and Thurman Munson on Game 5, but the Tommy Lasorda argument in Game 4 altered the Jackson photo on Games 4 and 5. Gateway acquired these autographs: Yogi Berra, Ron Cey, Bucky Dent, Steve Garvey, Ron Guidry, Catfish Hunter, Reggie Jackson, Tommy John, Tom Lasorda, Davy Lopes, Graig Nettles, Reggie Smith and Don Sutton. A by Jackson $60, Garvey $40, Others $30, unautographed $25.

GS17 GAME 1: Postmarked Oct. 10, 1978, Los Angeles, Calif. Stadium artwork by Scott Forst. 2,000 issued with Los Angeles philatelic postmark. Unautographed or autographed (Lasorda, Lopes, Jackson or John). A by Jackson $60, A by Garvey $40, Others $30, unautographed $25.

GS18 GAME 2: Postmarked Oct. 11, 1978, Los Angeles, Calif. Photo of Cey and Lopes. 2,000 issued. With Los Angeles philatelic postmark. Unautographed or autographed (Cey, Garvey or Sutton). A by Garvey $40, Others $30, unautographed $25.

GS19 GAME 3: Postmarked Oct. 13, 1978, Bronx, N.Y. Graig Nettles. 2,000 issued, unautographed or autographed (Guidry or Nettles). Approximately 200 exist where Guidry signed inside the gold frame. Guidry A $25, Guidry A under silk $30, Others $25, unautographed $20.

GS20a GAME 4: Postmarked Oct. 14, 1978, Bronx, N.Y. Lasorda, Cey and Garvey. 1,800 issued, unautographed or autographed (Lasorda, Jackson, Reggie Smith). A by Lasorda $35, Others $25, unautographed $20.

GS20b GAME 4: Reggie Jackson. 200 issued. A $250, U $75.

GS21a GAME 5: Postmarked Oct. 15, 1978, Bronx, N.Y. Thurman Munson. 1,000 issued unautographed. Only one Munson autograph known to exist on Game 5. A $1,500, Others $25, U $20.

GS21b GAME 5: Reggie Jackson. 1,000 issued unautographed. A $60, Others $30, unautographed $25.

GS22 GAME 6: Postmarked Oct. 17, 1978, Los Angeles, Calif. Photo of World Series trophy. 2,000 issued, unautographed or autographed. With Los Angeles philatelic postmark. (Berra, Dent or Hunter). A by Berra $50, A by Hunter $40, A by Dent $30, Others $25, unautographed $20.

40th anniversary of the Hall of Fame, set of three

GS23 MICKEY MANTLE: Postmarked June 12, 1979, Cooperstown, N.Y. Artwork by Phil Daigle. 2,000, autographed. A $150.

GS24 SATCHEL PAIGE: Postmarked June 12, 1979, Cooperstown, N.Y. Artwork by Phil Daigle. 1,000 issued, autographed. A $450.

GS25 WHITEY FORD: Postmarked June 12, 1979, Cooperstown, N.Y. Artwork by Bill Perry. 1,000 issued, autographed. A $80.

50th All-Star Game, set of 16

Set of 16, postmarked July 17, 1979, Seattle, Wash. 2,000 each of four different logo designs and 12 game photos. Issued in sets of three, including National and American League envelopes and a logo envelope. All logo envelopes were printed in the same game information; all N.L. and A.L. envelopes show the players elected as starters and their substitutes. Only the art design and photos are different. 26,000 large round postmarks were used; 4,000 smaller "bullet" postmarks were used, but only on A.L. envelopes. Gateway acquired autographs for Joaquin Andujar, Don Baylor, Bruce Bochte, Larry Bowa, George Brett, Lou Brock, Rod Carew, Steve Carlton, Gary Carter, Ron Cey, George Foster, Steve Garvey, Ron Guidry, Keith Hernandez, Reggie Jackson, Tommy John, Jim Kern, Dave Kingman, Tom Lasorda, Davey Lopes, Fred Lynn, Lee Mazzilli, Graig Nettles, Dave Parker, Gaylord Perry, Darrell Porter, Jim Rice, Pete Rose, Nolan Ryan, Mike Schmidt, Ted Simmons, Ken Singleton, Roy Smalley, Bruce Sutter and Frank White. Any participating player's autograph can be found on a logo envelope. American Leaguers autographed on any of the six A.L. envelopes, and National Leaguers autographed on any of the six N.L. envelopes. Thus, there are available sets of three with three autographs. Very few envelopes were issued without autographs.

GS26 50th ALL-STAR LOGO ON ANIMATED PLAYERS: Artwork by Scott Forst. 2,000 issued, autographed or unautographed. A by stars $35, Others $15, unautographed $7.50.

GS27 ALL-STAR LOGO ON NORTHWEST TREES: Artwork by Scott Forst. 2,000 issued, autographed and unautographed. A by stars $35, Others $15, unautographed $7.50.

GS28 50th ALL-STAR LOGO ON PLAYING FIELD: Artwork by Scott Forst. 2,000 issued, autographed or unautographed. A by stars $35, Others $15, unautographed $7.50.

GS29 59th ALL-STAR LOGO ON KINGDOME: Artwork by Scott Forst. 2,000 issued, autographed or unautographed. A by stars $35, Others $15, unautographed $7.50.

GS30 JOAQUIN ANDUJAR: 2,000 issued, autographed or unautographed. A by stars $25, U $7.50.

GS31 BRUCE BOCHTE: 2,000 issued, autographed or unautographed. A $20, U $7.50.

GS32 STEVE CARLTON & MIKE SCHMIDT: 2,000 issued, autographed or unautographed. A $35, U $10.

GS33 RON CEY: 2,000 issued, autographed or unautographed. A $15, U $7.50.

GS34 RON GUIDRY: 2,000 issued, autographed or unautographed. A $30, U $10.

GS35 REGGIE JACKSON: 2,000 issued, autographed or unautographed. A $50, U $12.50.

GS36 JIM KERN & GRAIG NETTLES: 2,000 issued, autographed or unautographed. A by Kern $12.50, A by Nettles $15.

GS37 FRED LYNN, CARL YASTRZEMSKI, DON BAYLOR: 2,000 issued, autographed or unautographed. A by Lynn $20, A by Yastrzemski $40, A by Baylor, $15, A by Nolan Ryan $50, A by Rod Carew $35, Others $15, unautographed $10.

GS38 DAVE PARKER: 2,000 issued, autographed or unautographed. A $20, Others $15.

GS39 DARRELL PORTER: 2,000 issued, autographed or unautographed. A $12.50, U $5.

GS40 BRUCE SUTTER: 2,000 issued, autographed or unautographed. A $15, U $5.

GS41 DAVE WINFIELD: 2,000 issued, autographed or unautographed. A $30, U $10.

GS42 WILLIE MAYS: Postmarked Aug. 2, 1979, Cooperstown, N.Y. Artwork by Bill Perry. 2,000 issued, autographed. A $175.

GS43 LOU BROCK 3,000th HIT: Postmarked Aug. 14, 1979, St. Louis, Mo. Swinging the bat. 5,000 issued autographed; 1,000 unautographed. A $25, U $10.

GS44 LOU BROCK DAY: Postmarked Sept. 9, 1979, St. Louis, Mo., on the retirement of Brock's uniform #20. 6,000 issued, unautographed. A $25, U $10.

GS45 CARL YASTRZEMSKI: Postmarked Sept. 12, 1979, Boston, Mass., after Yastrzemski's 3,000th base hit. Artwork by Bill Perry. 3,000 issued unautographed. A $100, U $20.

1979 World Series, set of seven

Gateway issued 2,000 sets of 1979 World Series envelopes postmarked in Baltimore and Pittsburgh for each game. The Game 1 logo art was alternated with a Mike Flanagan photo. The Games 2 and 6 silks of Kent Tekulve and Jim Palmer were alternated equally to accommodate a wider distribution of autographs. Standard round cancellations were used in each city. Gateway acquired autographs from Mark Belanger, Al Bumbry, John Candelaria, Rich Dauer, Rick Dempsey, Doug DeCinces, Mike Flanagan, Tim Foli, Kiko Garcia, Phil Garner, Grant Jackson, Scott McGregor, Bill Madlock, Omar Moreno, Eddie Murray, Jim Palmer, Dave Parker, Bill Robinson, Frank Robinson, Ken Singleton, Willie Stargell, Chuck Tanner, Kent Tekulve and Earl Weaver.

GS46a GAME 1: Postmarked Oct. 10, 1979, Baltimore, Md. Stadium artwork by Scott Forst. 1,500 issued, unautographed or autographed (Belanger, Dauer, DeCinces, Flanagan, Garner, Murray, F. Robinson, Singleton or Tanner). A by Robinson $30, A by Murray $20, Others $12.50, unautographed $5.

GS46b GAME 1: Mike Flanagan. 500 issued, unautographed or autographed. A $12.50, U $7.50.

GS47a GAME 2: Postmarked Oct. 11, 1979, Baltimore, Md. Jim Palmer. 1,000 issued, unautographed or autographed. A $25, U $7.50.

GS47b GAME 2: Kent Tekulve. 1,000 issued, unautographed or autographed by Tekulve, Garner or Tanner. A by Tekulve $10, Others $8, unautographed $5.

GS48 GAME 3: Postmarked Oct. 12, 1979, Pittsburgh, Pa. Kiko Garcia. 2,000 issued, unautographed or autographed by Garcia, Belanger, Bumbry, Dauer, McGregor or Singleton. A by Garcia $8, Others $10, unautographed $5.

GS49 GAME 4: Postmarked Oct. 13, 1979, Pittsburgh, Pa. Earl Weaver. 2,000 issued, unautographed or autographed by Weaver, Bumbry, Dauer, Garcia, F. Robinson or Singleton. Double autographs of Weaver and Robinson exist. A by Weaver $20, A by Robinson $30, A by Weaver and Robinson $45, Others $12.50, unautographed $5.

GS50 GAME 5: Postmarked Oct. 14, 1979, Pittsburgh, Pa. Dave Parker and Rick Dempsey. 2,000 issued, unautographed or autographed by Parker, Dempsey, Flanagan, Foli, Garner, Madlock or Tanner. A by Parker $20, A by Dempsey $10, A by Flanagan $10, A by Madlock $15, Others $10, unautographed $5.

GS51a GAME 6: Postmarked Oct. 16, 1979, Baltimore, Md. Kent Tekulve. 1,000 issued, unautographed or autographed by Tekulve, Candelaria, Garner, Moreno or Tanner. Double autographs of Candelaria and Moreno exist. A by Tekulve $10, A by Candelaria and Moreno $15, Others $10.

GS51b GAME 6: Postmarked Oct. 16, 1979, Baltimore, Md. Jim Palmer. 1,000 issued, autographed or unautographed by Palmer, Candelaria or Moreno. Double autographs of Candelaria and Moreno exist. A by Palmer $25, A by Candelaria and Moreno $15, Others $10.

GS52 GAME 7: Postmarked Oct. 17, 1979, Baltimore, Md. Willie Stargell and Bill Robinson. 2,000 issued, unautographed or autographed by Stargell, Robinson, Grant Jackson or Chuck Tanner. A by Stargell $20, A by Robinson $8, Others $10, unautographed $5.

1980

GS53, GS54 and GS55 are related to the 1980 Super Bowl between the Los Angeles Rams and Pittsburgh Steelers.

GS56 NOLAN RYAN 3,000 STRIKEOUTS: Postmarked July 4, 1980, Cincinnati, Ohio, city of Nolan Ryan's 3,000th strikeout. 4,800 issued, autographed. A $300.

GS56a NOLAN RYAN 3,000 STRIKEOUTS: A variation of GS56. Copy rearranged to accommodate room for autographs. 200 issued, autographed. A by Ryan $200.

GS57 NOLAN RYAN 3,000 STRIKEOUTS: Postmarked July 4, 1980, Houston, Texas, Ryan's home city. 5,000 issued, unautographed. A $50, U $10.

GS58 STEVE CARLTON LEFT-HANDED STRIKEOUT RECORD: Postmarked July 6, 1980, St. Louis, Mo., after Carlton passed Mickey Lolich as the all-time left-handed strikeout leader. 1,000 issued, autographed. A $100.

GS59 AL KALINE: Postmarked Aug. 3, 1980, Cooperstown, N.Y., on Kaline's induction into the Hall of Fame. Artwork by Phil Daigle. 3,000 issued, autographed. A $30.

GS60 DUKE SNIDER: Postmarked Aug. 3, 1980, Cooperstown, N.Y. on Snider's induction into the Hall of Fame. Artwork by Scott Forst. 3,000 issued, autographed. A $25.

GS60a DUKE SNIDER: Later issue (1985) of the Snider issue, artwork by Bill Terry. 1,000 issued autographed. A $25.

GS61 REGGIE JACKSON 400 HOME RUNS: Postmarked Aug. 11, 1980, Bronx, N.Y., after Jackson's 400th home run. 2,000 issued autographed. A $75.

GS62 RICK LANGFORD CONSECUTIVE COMPLETED GAMES STREAK, GAME 21: Postmarked Sept. 5, 1980, Baltimore, Md., after Langford's 21st consecutive nine-inning game, started and completed without relief help. 500 issued, unautographed or autographed. A $250, U $125.

GS63 RICK LANGFORD GAME 22: Postmarked Sept. 21, 1980, Oakland, Calif., after Langford's 22nd consecutive complete game. 1,000 issued, unautographed or autographed. A $50, U $25.

GS64 MINNIE MINOSO: Postmarked Oct. 4, 1980, Chicago, Ill., on Minoso's fifth decade of active major league play. White Sox photo. 500 issued autographed. A $650.

1980 World Series, set of six

Set of six, postmarked for each game played in Philadelphia and Kansas City, with standard cancellations. 2,000 sets were issued, with no variations. Gateway acquired autographs from Willie Mays Aikens, Bob Boone, Larry Bowa, Steve Carlton, Larry Christenson, Dallas Green, Larry Gura, Greg Luzinski, Garry Maddox, Bake McBride, Tug McGraw, Hal McRae, Darrell Porter, Amos Otis, Dan Quisenberry, Pete Rose, Mike Schmidt, Manny Trillo, Del Unser, Frank White and Willie Wilson. Each are on the envelopes for the games in which they were a prominent part.

GS5 Lou Brock

GS12 Willie McCovey

GS65 GAME 1: Postmarked Oct. 14, 1980, Philadelphia, Pa. Stadium artwork by Scott Forst. 2,000 issued, unautographed and autographed by Boone, Bowa, Christenson, Green, Luzinski, Maddox, McBride, Otis, Porter, Rose, Trillo, Unser, White or Wilson. A by Rose, Schmidt, Carlton or Brett $35, Others $10, unautographed $5.

GS66 GAME 2: Postmarked Oct. 15, 1980, Philadelphia, Pa. Carlton photo. 2,000 issued, unautographed or autographed by Carlton, Green, Gura, Maddox, Quisenberry, Trillo or Unser. A by Carlton $35, Others $8, unautographed $5.

GS67 GAME 3: Postmarked Oct. 17, 1980, Kansas City, Kan. George Brett. 2,000 issued, unautographed or autographed by Green, McGraw, Otis, Quisenberry, White or Wilson. A by Brett $30, Others $10, unautographed $5.

GS68 GAME 4: Postmarked Oct. 18, 1980, Kansas City, Kan. Willie Mays Aikens. 2,000 issued, unautographed or autographed by Aikens, Christenson, Green, McRae, Otis, White or Wilson. A by Aikens $8, Others $8, unautographed $5.

GS69 GAME 5: Postmarked Oct. 19 1980, Kansas City, Kan. Bob Boone and Darrell Porter. 2,000 issued, unautographed or autographed by Boone, Porter, Green, Luzinski, Maddox, McGraw, Quisenberry, Trillo or Unser. Double autographs of Boone and Porter or Boone and McGraw exist. A by Boone or Porter $10 each, A by Boone and Porter $20, A by Boone and McGraw $20, Others $8, unautographed $5.

GS70 GAME 6: Postmarked Oct. 21, 1980, Philadelphia, Pa. Mike Schmidt. 2,000 issued, unautographed or autographed by Schmidt, Bowa, Green, McGraw and Rose. A by Schmidt $25, Others $8, unautographed $5.

1981

GS71 and GS72 are for the election and inauguration of President Ronald Reagan.

GS73, GS74 and GS75 are for the 1981 Super Bowl between the Philadelphia Eagles and Oakland Raiders.

GS76 TOM SEAVER 3,000 STRIKEOUTS: Postmarked April 18, 1981, Cincinnati, Ohio, city of Seaver's 3,000th strikeout. 5,000 issued autographed. A $25.

GS77 TOM SEAVER 3,000 STRIKEOUTS: Postmarked April 18, 1981. Has Cincinnati philatelic postmark. 5,000 issued unautographed. A $25, U $5.

GS78 STEVE CARLTON'S 3,000 STRIKEOUTS: Postmarked April 29, 1981, Philadelphia, Pa., city of Carlton's 3,000th strikeout. 5,000 issued autographed. A $25.

GS79 STEVE CARLTON 3,000 STRIKEOUTS: Postmarked April 29, 1981, Philadelphia, Pa., Carlton's home city. 3,500 issued unautographed. A $25, U $7.50.

GS80 LEN BARKER PERFECT GAME: Postmarked May 15, 1981, Cleveland, Ohio. 1,000 issued autographed. 100 issued with autographs of Barker and Duane Kuiper. Five different stamps were used - Amber Waves of Grain, Purple Mountains Majesty, Sea to Shining Sea, B Stamp, and Savings & Loan Commemorative. A by Barker $65, A by Barker and Kuiper $75.

GS81 PETE ROSE HIT 3,630: Postmarked June 10, 1981, Philadelphia, Pa., when Rose tied the all-time National League hit record (Stan Musial, 1963). Swinging the bat. 5,000 issued unautographed and autographed. The game was the last Phillies game before the 1981 baseball players strike. 700 issued with 18cts Rose stamp; 4,300 had Amber Waves of Grain stamp. A by Rose $30, A by Rose and Musial $50, envelopes having a "rose" stamp add $20.

GS82 JOE DIMAGGIO: Postmarked July 16, 1981, Cleveland, Ohio, on the 40th anniversary of the 56th game of DiMaggio's all-time record 56-game hitting streak. Artwork by Bill Perry. 2,000 issued autographed. A $175.

GS83 BOB GIBSON: Postmarked Aug. 2, 1981, Cooperstown, N.Y., on Gibson's induction into the Hall of Fame. Artwork by Bill Perry. 3,000 issued autographed. A $20.

GS84 JOHNNY MIZE: Postmarked Aug. 2, 1981, Cooperstown, N.Y., on Johnny Mize's induction into the Hall of Fame. Artwork by Bill Perry. 2,000

issued autographed. A $25.

GS85 PETE ROSE HIT 3,631: Postmarked Aug. 10, 1981, Philadelphia, Pa., on Pete Rose's breaking the all-time National League record. 5,000 issued autographed. The date was the Phillies first game after the 1981 baseball strikeout. 700 issued with 18cts rose stamp; 4,300 with 18cts Amber Waves of Grain stamp. 250 of this issue were signed by Tom Gioiosa. Discovered and recalled by Gateway in 1989. Re-signed by Rose in 1991. A by Rose $45. For double signature add $10. For any combination of signatures on "rose" stamped envelopes add $20.

GS86 ERNIE HARWELL: Set of one postmarked Aug. 2, 1981, Cooperstown, N.Y., on broadcaster Ernie Harwell's receiving the Ford C. Frick Award. Artwork by Bill Perry. 750 issued autographed. Issued in 1992. A $15.

GS87 STAN MUSIAL: Postmarked Aug. 10, 1981, St. Louis, Mo., when Rose broke Musial's all-time National League hit record. Envelope commemorates Musial's leadership through this date. Artwork by Bill Perry. 2,000 issued autographed. A $50.

GS88 NOLAN RYAN FIFTH NO-HITTER: Postmarked Sept. 26, 1981, Houston, Texas, after Ryan's record fifth no-hitter. 1,000 issued autographed. A wide variety of stamps were used. A $300.

GS89 TED WILLIAMS: Postmarked Sept. 28, 1981, Philadelphia, Pa., on the 40th anniversary of Ted Williams' being the last player to bat .400 or more in a season. Artwork by Bill Perry. 2,000 issued autographed. A $80.

1981 World Series Set of Six

Set of six envelopes postmarked each date the Series was played in New York and Los Angeles. Standard hand-cancellations used in New York, while philatelic Terminal Annex postmarks were used in Los Angeles. 2,000 sets were issued with a variation on Game 3. Gateway acquired autographs for Dusty Baker, Ron Cey, Ron Davis, Steve Garvey, Goose Gossage, Pedro Guerrero, Ron Guidry, Steve Howe, Reggie Jackson, Tommy John, Tommy Lasorda, Bob Lemon, Graig Nettles, Lou Piniella, Jerry Reuss, Dave Righetti, Bill Russell, Fernando Valenzuela, Bob Watson, Bob Welch, Dave Winfield and Steve Yeager, each on envelopes where they played a prominent part in the game.

GS90 GAME 1: Postmarked Oct. 20, 1981, Bronx, N.Y. Stadium artwork by B. Scott Forst. 2,000 issued unautographed and autographed by Baker, Guidry, Jackson, John, Lasorda, Lemon, Nettles, Piniella, Russell, Watson or Winfield. A Jackson $30, Winfield or Garvey $20, Lasorda or Lemon $15, Others $10, U $5.

GS91 GAME 2: Postmarked Oct. 21, 1981, Bronx, N.Y. Gossage photo. 2,000 issued signed by Gossage, unsigned, or signed by others. A by Gossage $15, Others $10, U $5.

GS92a GAME 3: Postmarked Oct. 23, 1981, Los Angeles, Calif. Valenzuela photo. 1,500 issued signed or unsigned by Valenzuela, or by Valenzuela and Righetti, or by Valenzuela, Righetti and Ron Davis. A by Valenzuela $20, Valenzuela and Righetti $35, Valenzuela, Righetti and Davis $45, U $7.50.

GS92b GAME 3: Postmarked Oct. 23, 1981, Los Angeles, Calif. Ron Cey photo. 500 issued signed or unsigned by Cey. A $18, U $10.

GS93 GAME 4: Postmarked Oct. 24, 1981, Los Angeles, Calif. Garvey photo. 2,000 issued signed by Garvey, or Garvey and Welch, or by Reggie Jackson, or unsigned. A by Garvey $20, Garvey and Welch $25, Jackson $35, Others $10, U $5.

GS94 GAME 5. Postmarked Oct. 25, 1981, Los Angeles, Calif. Jerry Reuss photo. 2,000 issued signed by Reuss, signed by Reuss and Guidry, or by Guidry, or unsigned. A by Reuss $12, Reuss and Guidry $25, Guidry $15, U $4.

GS95 GAME 6. Postmarked Oct. 28, 1981, Bronx, N.Y. Yeager and Howe photo. 2,000 issued signed by Yeager and Howe, or others, or unsigned. A by Yeager and Howe $16, Others $8, U $4.

GS96 and GS97 are devoted to Bear Bryant, University of Alabama football coach.

GS98 is devoted to hockey star Wayne Gretzky's record 77 goals in a season.

GS99 GAYLORD PERRY 300 WINS: Postmarked May 6, 1982, Seattle Wash., as Perry registered his 300th career win. 3,000 issued, autographed. A $15.

GS100 GAYLORD PERRY 300 CLUB: Postmarked May 6, 1982, Seattle, Wash., as companion envelope to GS99. Photo shows Perry's salute to the crowd. 3,000 issued autographed or unautographed. A $15, U $5.

GS101 WARREN SPAHN 300 CLUB: Postmarked May 6, 1982, Seattle, Wash., the date of Perry's 300th win, tying Hall of Famer Spahn in the 300 win circle. Bill Perry artwork. 1,000 issued, autographed, some with Massachusetts or Wisconsin Bird and Flower stamps (USPS issue). A $75, with Bird and Flower stamps add $10.

GS102 EARLY WYNN 300 CLUB: Postmarked May 6, 1982, Seattle, Wash., the date of Perry's 300th win, tying Hall of Famer Wynn in the 300 win circle. Bill Perry artwork. 1,000 issued autographed, some with Illinois Bird and Flower stamps. A $75, with Bird and Flower stamps add $10.

GS103 FERGUSON JENKINS 3,000 STRIKEOUTS: Set of 2 postmarked May 25, 1982, San Diego, Calif., as Jenkins obtained his 3,000th strikeout. Jenkins photo with scoreboard message in the background. 3,000 issued, autographed, some with California Bird and Flower stamps. A $15, with Bird and Flower stamps add $5.

GS104 FERGUSON JENKINS 3,000 STRIKEOUTS: Second envelope in set of two postmarked May 25, 1982, Chicago, Ill. Photo of Jenkins in home uniform. 3,000 issued autographed or unautographed, some with Illinois Bird and Flower stamps. A $15, U $5, with Bird and Flower stamps add $5.

GS105 STEVE GARVEY IRON MAN: Postmarked June 7, 1982, Los Angeles, Calif., as Garvey played in his 1,000 consecutive game. Garvey photo. 2,000 issued autographed, some with California Bird and Flower stamps. A $20, with Bird and Flower stamps add $2.

GS106 HANK AARON HALL OF FAME INDUCTION: Postmarked Aug. 1, 1982, Cooperstown, N.Y., on Aaron's induction into the Hall of Fame. Artwork by Bill Perry. 4,000 issued, some with Georgia or Wisconsin Bird and Flower stamps. A $25, with Bird and Flower stamps add $2.

GS107 FRANK ROBINSON HALL OF FAME INDUCTION: Postmarked Aug. 1, 1982, Cooperstown, N.Y., on Robinson's induction into the Hall of Fame. Artwork by Bill Perry. 2,250 issued autographed, some with Ohio or Maryland Bird and Flower stamps. A $25, with Bird and Flower stamps add $5.

GS108 HAPPY CHANDLER HALL OF FAME INDUCTION: Postmarked Aug. 1, 1982, Cooperstown, N.Y., on Chandler's induction into the Hall of Fame. Artwork by Bill Perry. 1,000 issued autographed; 500 with Kentucky Bird and Flower stamps. A $80, with Bird and Flower stamps add $5.

GS109 TRAVIS JACKSON HALL OF FAME INDUCTION: Postmarked Aug. 1, 1982, Cooperstown, N.Y., on Jackson's induction into the Hall of Fame. Artwork by Bill Perry. 1,000 issued autographed, some with New York Bird and Flower stamps. A $75, with Bird and Flower stamps add $5.

GS110 JACKIE ROBINSON FIRST DAY OF ISSUE: Postmarked Aug. 2, 1982, Cooperstown, N.Y., "First Day of Issue" upon issuance of the Jackie Robinson postage stamp. Artwork by Bill Perry. 8,000 issued, including 500 hand-cancellations and 7,500 machine cancellations. Unautographed. Hand cancels $5, machine cancels $4.

GS111 RICKEY HENDERSON STOLEN BASES: Set of two. This envelope is postmarked Aug. 28, 1982, Milwaukee, Wis., where Henderson broke Lou Brock's all-time single-season stolen base record of 118. Henderson and Brock photo. 2,250 issued, autographed by Henderson, or Henderson and Brock. A by Henderson $40, A by Henderson and Brock $50.

GS112 RICKEY HENDERSON STOLEN BASES: Second envelope to GS111. Postmarked Oct. 2, 1982, Kansas City, Mo., as Henderson extended his all-time record to 130 bases. 2,250 issued with Kansas City kicking mule philatelic postmark. A by Henderson $40, U $15.

1982 World Series

Set of seven envelopes postmarked each date the Series was played in St. Louis and Milwaukee. Standard cancellations in both cities. Two variations noted below. Gateway acquired autographs for: Joaquin Andujar, Mike Caldwell, Cecil Cooper, Bob Forsch, Jim Gantner, Keith Hernandez, Whitey Herzog, Dane Iorg, Hub Kittle, Harvey Kuenn, Willie McGee, Paul Molitor, Ken Oberkfell, Ben Oglivie, Darrell Porter, Mike Ramsey, Ted Simmons, Lonnie Smith, Ozzie Smith, John Stuper, Bruce Sutter, Don Sutton, Pete Vuckovich and Robin Yount. A scarce autograph in this set would be George Hendrick's.

GS113 GAME 1: Postmarked Oct. 12, 1982, St. Louis, Mo. Stadium artwork by Scott Forst. 2,000 issued, unautographed or autographed by various players. A by Molitor, Hernandez or O. Smith $20, Others $10, U $5.

GS114a GAME 2: Postmarked Oct. 13, 1982, St. Louis, Mo., 1,000 issued with Darrell Porter photo. Issued autographed or unautographed. A $12, U $4.

GS114b GAME 2: Postmarked Oct. 13, 1982, St. Louis, Mo. 1,000 issued with Ted Simmons photo. Issued autographed or unautographed. A $15, U $4.

GS115 GAME 3: Postmarked Oct. 15, 1982, Milwaukee, Wis. 2,000 issued with Andujar photo. Issued autographed or unautographed. A $12, Others $12, U $5.

GS116 GAME 4: Postmarked Oct. 16, 1982, Milwaukee, Wis. 2,000 issued with Cecil Cooper photo. Issued autographed by Cooper, others, or unautographed. A $15, Others $8, U $5.

GS117 GAME 5: Postmarked Oct. 17, 1982, Milwaukee, Wis. 2,000 issued with Robin Yount photo. Approximately 1,000 issued autographed by Yount, or unautographed. A $25, U $5.

GS118a GAME 6: Postmarked Oct. 19, 1982, St. Louis, Mo. 1,000 issued with Keith Hernandez photo. Approximately 750 autographed; 250 unautographed. A $20, U $5.

GS118b GAME 6: Postmarked Oct. 19, 1982, St. Louis, Mo. 1,000 issued with Darrell Porter photo. Approximately 500 autographed, 500 unautographed. A $12, U $4.

GS119 GAME 7: Postmarked Oct. 20, 1982, St. Louis, Mo. 2,000 issued with Bruce Sutter photo. Approximately 1,000 autographed by Sutter. Other autographs appear. 500 unautographed. Includes correction card insert. Envelope incorrectly lists Vuckovich as losing pitcher. (Bob McClure lost Game 7). A by Sutter $18, Others $10, U $4.

GS120 is devoted to Wayne Gretzky's consecutive games points record.

GS121 JIM KAAT 25 YEARS: Postmarked April 5, 1983, St. Louis, Mo., on Kaat's beginning 25 years as a major leaguer, second on the all-time list. Action photo of Kaat. 2,000 issued autographed. A $15.

GS122 STEVE GARVEY 1,118 GAMES: Postmarked April 16, 1983, Los Angeles, as Garvey broke Billy Williams' all-time National League record of 1,117 consecutive games played. Photo of Garvey and Williams. 2,000 issued autographed by Garvey; 500 include Williams. A by Garvey $20, Garvey and Williams $35.

GS123 NOLAN RYAN STRIKEOUT RECORD: Postmarked April 27, 1983, Montreal, as Ryan broke Walter Johnson's all-time strikeout record of 3,508 strikeouts. Action game photo of Ryan. 2,000 issued, autographed by Ryan. A by Ryan $40.

GS124 WALTER JOHNSON: Postmarked April 27, 1983, Montreal, as Nolan Ryan breaks Walter Johnson's all-time strikeout record. Artwork by Bill Perry. 2,000 issued unautographed. Collectors have actively added autographs of pitchers who have passed Walter Johnson. U $15, A by Ryan, Seaver, Perry, Blyleven, Carlton, add autograph fees.

GS125 STEVE CARLTON STRIKEOUT RECORD: Postmarked June 7, 1983, as Steve Carlton passes Nolan Ryan on the all-time strikeout list. Action Carlton photo. 2,000 issued autographed by Carlton. A $25.

GS126 DON SUTTON 3,000 STRIKEOUTS: Postmarked June 24, 1983, Milwaukee, Wis., as a set of two as Sutton obtains his 3,000th strikeout. Action pitching photo. 2,000 issued, autographed by Sutton. A $17.50.

GS127 DON SUTTON 3,000 STRIKEOUTS: Postmarked June 24, 1983, Milwaukee, Wis., as a companion envelope to GS126. 2,000 photo silks of Sutton signing autographs. A variation exists due to two separate printings. Original photo is lighter blue. Second printing is darker and crops part of a fan's helmet. A by Sutton $15, U $5.

GS128 DAVE RIGHETTI NO-HITTER: Postmarked July 4, 1983, New York, N.Y., after Righetti's first career no-hitter. 1,500 postmarked New York. 160 postmarked Bronx. All autographed. Action Righetti photo. New York Postmark $20, Bronx Postmark $250.

1983 All-Star Game

Gateway issued 9,000 envelopes celebrating the 1983 All-Star game played in Chicago and captioned it on each envelope as the "GOLDEN ANNIVERSARY." Three natural sets were created to include three different artworks, three National League action photos of prominent players, including the starting National League pitcher, and three American League action photos of prominent players, including the starting pitcher. Autographs were acquired from each pictured player. Artwork envelopes are considered neutral pieces upon which to acquire autographs of anyone associated with the game in any capacity. Gateway acquired autographs from George Brett, Rod Carew, Gary Carter, Cecil Cooper, Andre Dawson, Atlee Hammaker, Rick Honeycutt, Terry Kennedy, Ron Kittle, Harvey Kuenn, Fred Lynn, Bill Madlock, Willie McGee, Dale Murphy, Ben Oglivie, Al Oliver, Lance Parrish, Pasqual Perez, Tim Raines, Jim Rice, Cal Ripken, Jr., Steve Sax, Mike Schmidt, Ted Simmons, Ozzie Smith, Mario Soto, Dave Stieb, Fernando Valenzuela, Dave Winfield, Carl Yastrzemski, and Robin Yount. The 1983 All-Star game coincided with the issuance of the Babe Ruth 20cts baseball stamp by the United States Postal Service in Chicago, Ill., July 6, 1983. All envelopes pertaining to this issue were postmarked "First Day of Issue" on the Ruth stamp. The game was highlighted by Fred Lynn hitting the first grand slam home run in all-star game history in the same stadium where Ruth had hit the first home run in all-star history 50 years earlier.

GS129 BABE RUTH FIRST DAY COVER: Postmarked July 6, 1983, Chicago, Ill., "First Day of Issue." 5,000 issued, including 50 hand-cancellations and 4,950 machine cancels. Bill Perry artwork. Autographs of various teammates and peers have been acquired on this cover, including Ben Champman, Jimmie Reese, Mel Allen and others. U $5, A add autograph fees.

GS130 BILL DICKEY 50TH ANNIVERSARY ALL-STAR GAME: Postmarked "First Day of Issue" on Babe Ruth stamp July 6, 1983, Chicago, Ill., commemorating Dickey's participation in the first All-Star game (1933). 1,000 issued autographed by Dickey. Bill Perry artwork. A $75.

GS131 BILL TERRY 50TH ANNIVERSARY ALL-STAR GAME: Postmarked "First Day of Issue" on Babe Ruth stamp July 6, 1983, Chicago, Ill., commemorating Terry's participation in the first All-Star game and being the last National League .400 hitter. 800 issued, autographed. Bill Perry artwork. A $100.

GS132 CHARLIE GEHRINGER 50TH ANNIVERSARY ALL-STAR GAME: Postmarked "First Day of Issue" on Babe Ruth stamp July 6, 1983, Chicago, Ill., commemorating Gehringer's participation in the first All-Star game. 500 issued autographed. Bill Perry artwork. A $175.

GS133 LEFTY GOMEZ 50TH ANNIVERSARY ALL-STAR GAME: Postmarked "First Day of Issue" on Babe Ruth stamp July 6, 1983, Chicago, Ill., commemorating Gomez's participation in the 1933 All-Star game and as American League captain in the 1983 All-Star game (50th anniversary). 1,500 issued autographed by Gomez. Bill Perry artwork. A $50.

GS134 ERNIE BANKS 50TH ANNIVERSARY ALL-STAR GAME: Postmarked "First Day of Issue" on Babe Ruth stamp July 6, 1983, Chicago, Ill., commemorating Banks as captain of the National League All-Star team. 1,000 issued autographed by Banks. Bill Perry artwork. A $50.

GS135 COMISKEY PARK 50TH ANNIVERSARY ALL-STAR GAME: Postmarked "First Day of Issue" on Babe Ruth stamp July 6, 1983, Chicago, Ill. Scott Forst artwork. 500 issued, autographed by various 1983 All-Stars or unautographed. A by superstars $12-$20, add autograph fees; A by all-stars $10; add autograph fees; U $10.

GS136 50TH ANNIVERSARY ALL-STAR GAME: Postmarked "First Day of Issue" on Babe Ruth stamp July 6, 1983, Chicago, Ill., depicting a batter in Scott Forst artwork. 1,000 issued autographed by various 1983 All-Stars or unautographed. A by superstars $12-$20, add autographs fees; A by all-stars $10; add autograph fees.

GS137 50TH ANNIVERSARY ALL-STAR GAME: Postmarked "First Day of Issue" on Babe Ruth Stamp July 6, 1983, Chicago, Ill. Scott Forst artpiece depicting bust of old-time player. 1,000 issued autographed by various 1983 all-stars or unautographed. A by superstars $12-$20, add autograph fees; A by all-stars $10, add autograph fees; U $6.

GS138 GARY CARTER 50TH ANNIVERSARY ALL-STAR GAME: Postmarked July 6, 1983, on Babe Ruth stamp, Chicago, Ill. 1,000 issued, autographed by Carter. Action photo. A by Carter $20, A by Carter, Dawson, Raines and Oliver $50.

GS139 DALE MURPHY 50th ANNIVERSARY ALL-STAR GAME: Postmarked "First Day of Issue" July 6, 1983, Chicago, Ill., on Babe Ruth stamp. 1,000 issued picturing Murphy in All-Star action with Ted Simmons catching. Autographed by Murphy or Murphy and Simmons, or Murphy and Perez. A by Murphy $25, A by Murphy and Simmons $30, A by Murphy and Perez $30, U $10.

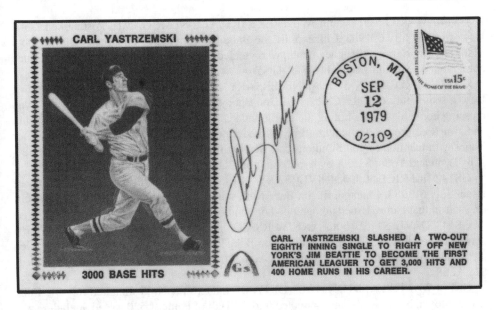

GS45 Carl Yastrzemski

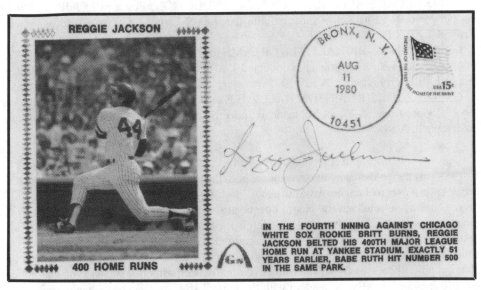

GS61 Reggie Jackson

GS140 MARIO SOTO 50th ANNIVERSARY ALL-STAR GAME: Postmarked "First Day of Issue" July 6, 1983, Chicago, Ill., on Babe Ruth stamp. 1,000 issued picturing Soto as the starting National League pitcher, who yielded Fred Lynn's historic grand slam. Issued autographed or unautographed. A $15, U $5.

GS141 FRED LYNN 50th ANNIVERSARY ALL-STAR GAME: Postmarked "First Day of Issue" July 6, 1983, Chicago, Ill., on Babe Ruth stamp. 1,000 issued picturing Lynn crossing home plate after hitting the first grand slam in All-Star game history. Robin Yount and Jim Rice are shown greeting him. Issued autographed by Lynn, Lynn and Yount, or Yount with teammates Ted Simmons and Ben Oglivie and Harvey Kuenn. A by Lynn $20, A by Lynn and Yount $35, A by Lynn, Simmons, Oglivie, Kuenn, Yount $50, U $15.

GS142 JIM RICE 50th ANNIVERSARY ALL-STAR GAME: Postmarked "First Day of Issue" July 6, 1983, Chicago, Ill., on Babe Ruth stamp. 1,000 issued picturing Rice as a hitting star in that game. Issued autographed or unautographed. A $25, U $10.

GS143 DAVE STIEB 50th ANNIVERSARY ALL-STAR GAME: Postmarked "First Day of Issue" July 6, 1983, Chicago, Ill., on Babe Ruth stamp. 1,000 issued picturing Stieb as the starting pitcher for the American League. Issued autographed or unautographed. A $18, U $8.

GS144 WALTER ALSTON HALL OF FAME INDUCTION: Postmarked July 31, 1983, Cooperstown, N.Y., as Alston is inducted into the Hall of Fame. 1,520 issued, including 500 on Jackie Robinson stamps, 200 on Brooklyn Bridge stamps. Autographed by Alston. Artwork by Bill Perry. A $35, for Jackie Robinson stamps add $5, for Brooklyn Bridge stamps add $2.

GS145 GEORGE KELL HALL OF FAME INDUCTION: Postmarked July 31, 1983, Cooperstown, N.Y., as Kell is inducted into the Hall of Fame. 1,520 issued, autographed. Artwork by Bill Perry. A $17.50.

GS146 JUAN MARICHAL HALL OF FAME INDUCTION: Postmarked July 31, 1983, Cooperstown, N.Y., as Marichal is inducted into the Hall of Fame. 2,000 issued, autographed. Bill Perry artwork. A $17.50.

GS147 BROOKS ROBINSON HALL OF FAME INDUCTION: Postmarked July 31, 1983, Cooperstown, N.Y., as Robinson is inducted into the Hall of Fame. 2,000 issued, autographed. A $18.

50th Anniversary Negro League All-Star Game

1983 was the golden anniversary year for both the major league all-star spectacle and the lesser-known Negro League All-Star game. Both were played at Comiskey Park in Chicago. Gateway selected several Negro League all-stars to commemorate, issuing five envelopes centered on Hall of Famers. Although Buck Leonard had not begun play until 1934, he was included in the set. Gateway had acquired postmarks in 1981 in Cooperstown by which to honor the father of organized Negro League ball, Rube Foster, but the scarcity of photographic likenesses from which to develop artwork postponed issuance of that envelope. Releasing it in 1983 in tandem with the five all-stars has caused its being assigned a GS number within that period.

GS148 RUBE FOSTER HALL OF FAME INDUCTION: Postmarked Aug. 2, 1981, on Foster's induction into the Hall of Fame in Cooperstown, N.Y. 1,000 issued. Artwork by Bill Perry. Various Negro League players have signed this envelope. Gateway released 100 signed by Willie Mays. A by Mays $30, U $10, Others add autograph fees.

GS149 JAMES "COOL PAPA" BELL 50TH ANNIVERSARY: Postmarked Aug. 6, 1983, Chicago, Ill., upon the 50th anniversary of the first Negro League all-star game. Artwork by Bill Perry. 1,000 issued, autographed. A James "Cool Papa" Bell $100, A "Cool Papa" Bell $90.

GS150 JUDY JOHNSON 50TH ANNIVERSARY: Postmarked Aug. 6, 1983, Chicago, Ill., upon the 50th anniversary of the first Negro League all-star game. Bill Perry artwork. 1,000 issued autographed by Judy Johnson. A $75.

GS151 BUCK LEONARD 50TH ANNIVERSARY: Postmarked Aug. 6, 1983, Chicago, Ill., upon the 50th anniversary of the first Negro League all-star game. Bill Perry artwork. 500 issued autographed right-handed. 500 issued autographed left-handed after Buck Leonard's stroke. A right-handed $75, A left-handed $75.

GS152 OSCAR CHARLESTON 50TH ANNIVERSARY: Postmarked Aug. 6, 1983, Chicago, Ill., upon the 50th anniversary of the first Negro League all-star game. Bill Perry artwork. 500 issued unautographed. U $50.

GS153 JOSH GIBSON 50TH ANNIVERSARY: Postmarked Aug. 6, 1983, Chicago, Ill., upon the 50th anniversary of the first Negro League all-star game. Bill Perry artwork. 500 issued unautographed. U $50.

GS154 STEVE CARLTON 300 CLUB: Postmarked Sept. 23, 1983, St. Louis, Mo., as Steve Carlton obtained his 300th career win. Action Carlton photo. 2,000 issued autographed. A $35.

GS155 BOB FORSCH SECOND NO-HITTER: Postmarked Sept. 26, 1983, St. Louis, Mo., as Bob Forsch pitched his second career no-hitter. Action Forsch photo. 950 issued personally autographed. Various stamp combinations used. A $50.

1983 World Series

As in each previous year since 1978, Gateway obtained hand-cancellations for each date the 1983 Series was played in each city. The Postal Service created large pictorial postmarks for the Philadelphia dates, incorporating the Phillies' logo and boxes for collectors to register the outcome of each game. Gateway obtained 2,000 postmarks for each date. The 1983 edition includes variations on Games 3 and 5 as described below. Gateway obtained autographs from Mike Boddicker, Steve Carlton, Storm Davis, Rick Dempsey, John Denny, Mike Flanagan, Al Holland, Scott McGregor, Tippy Martinez, Joe Morgan, Eddie Murray, Paul Owens, Jim Palmer, Tony Perez, Cal Ripken Jr., Pete Rose, and Mike Schmidt.

GS156 GAME 1: Postmarked Oct. 11, 1983, Baltimore, Md., with regular round stamp. 2,000 issued with Scott Forst stadium artwork depicting Veterans Stadium and Memorial Stadium. A neutral location for autographs of non-pictured players, it has been signed by stars and superstars. A by superstars $20-$30, A by stars $8-$10, U $5.

GS157 GAME 2: Postmarked Oct. 12, 1983, Baltimore, Md., with regular round stamp. 2,000 issued with Mike Boddicker action photo. 1,000 autographed by Boddicker. A by Boddicker $10, Others $8-$20, U $5.

GS158a GAME 3: Postmarked Oct. 14, 1983, Philadelphia, Pa., all 2,000 with special World Series philatelic postmarks. 1,000 of this envelope picture Rick Dempsey, World Series MVP, and 500 were issued with his autograph. 100 issued autographed by three Cy Young winners who pitched in that game - Steve Carlton, Jim Palmer and Mike Flanagan. A by Dempsey $10, A by Palmer, Carlton, Flanagan $50, A by Palmer $20, A by Carlton $20, A by Flanagan $10, U $5.

GS158b GAME 3: Postmarked Oct. 14, 1983, Philadelphia, Pa. 1,000 Game 3 envelopes picturing Joe Morgan. 500 autographed by Morgan. The same combination of autographs as on GS158a can appear on this variation. A by Morgan $25, U $5.

GS159 GAME 4: Postmarked Oct. 15, 1983, Philadelphia, Pa., with special World Series philatelic postmarks. 2,000 issued picturing John Denny. 500 autographed by Denny. Some with Denny and Storm Davis, and some by Pete Rose. A by Denny $10, A by Denny and Davis $18, A by Rose $25, U $5.

GS160a GAME 5: Postmarked Oct. 16, 1983, Philadelphia, Pa., with special World Series philatelic postmarks. 1,000 issued picturing Rick Dempsey. 250 autographed by Dempsey. A by Dempsey $10, U $5.

GS160b GAME 5: Postmarked Oct. 16, 1983, Philadelphia, Pa., with special World Series philatelic postmarks. 1,000 issued picturing Eddie Murray. 500 signed by Murray. A by Murray $25, U $5.

GS161 JACK MORRIS NO-HITTER: Postmarked April 7, 1984, Chicago, Ill., as Morris pitched his first career no-hitter. 1,500 issued autographed, picturing Morris. A $18.

GS162a PETE ROSE 4,000 HITS: Postmarked incorrectly April 13, 1984, Ottawa, Quebec, Canada. Error went unnoticed until 1,000 had been circulated, all autographed by Rose. Action photo. A $150.

162b PETE ROSE 4,000 HITS: Postmarked correctly April 13, 1984, Montreal, as replaced by the Canadian Postal Service. All autographed by Pete Rose. Same action photo as GS162a. A $125.

GS163 DAVE PALMER PERFECT GAME: Postmarked April 22, 1984, St. Louis, Mo., as Palmer pitched a five-inning perfect game. Palmer photo. 1,000 issued, autographed. A $15.

GS164 MIKE SCHMIDT 400 HOME RUNS: Postmarked May 15, 1984, Los Angeles, Calif., as Schmidt hits career home run #400. Action silk photo. 1,500 issued, autographed. A $45.

GS165 is devoted to Jim Thorpe.

GS166 PETE ROSE 3,309 GAMES PLAYED: Postmarked June 29, 1984, Cincinnati, Ohio, as Rose broke Carl Yastrzemski's all-time games played record. 1,000 issued with action Rose photo, autographed by Rose. A by Rose $85, A by Rose and Yastrzemski $125.

GS167 PHIL NIEKRO 3,000 STRIKEOUTS: Postmarked July 4, 1984, Arlington, Tex., as Niekro obtained his 3,000th career strikeout. 2,000 issued autographed. Action photo. A $17.50.

GS168 PHIL NIEKRO 3,000 STRIKEOUTS: Postmarked July 4, 1984, Bronx, N.Y., as Niekro obtained his 3,000th strikeout. Companion biographical envelope to GS167. Action photo. 1,000 autographed. A $15, U $5.

GS169 is devoted to racer Richard Petty's 200th win.

GS170 CARL HUBBELL 50TH ANNIVERSARY: Postmarked July 10, 1984, New York, N.Y., to commemorate Hubbell's striking out Babe Ruth, Lou Gehrig, Jimmie Foxx, Al Simmons and Joe Cronin in succession in the 1934 All-Star game. Bill Perry artwork. 1,000 issued, autographed by Hubbell. A $150.

GS171 LUIS APARICIO HALL OF FAME INDUCTION: Postmarked Aug. 12, 1984, Cooperstown, N.Y., on Aparicio's induction into the Hall of Fame. 2,000 issued autographed. Bill Perry artwork. A $25.

GS172 DON DRYSDALE HALL OF FAME INDUCTION: Postmarked Aug. 12, 1984, Cooperstown, N.Y. Bill Perry artwork. 2,000 issued, autographed. A $40.

GS173 RICK FERRELL HALL OF FAME INDUCTION: Postmarked Aug. 12, 1984, Cooperstown, N.Y. Bill Perry artwork. 1,500 issued, autographed. A $20.

GS174 HARMON KILLEBREW HALL OF INDUCTION: Postmarked Aug. 12, 1984, Cooperstown, N.Y. Bill Perry artwork. 2,000 issued, autographed. A $25.

GS175 PEE WEE REESE HALL OF FAME INDUCTION: Postmarked Aug. 12, 1984, Cooperstown. N.Y. Bill Perry artwork. 2,000 issued, autographed. A $50.

GS176a ROBERTO CLEMENTE FIRST DAY OF ISSUE: Postmarked Aug. 17, 1984, Carolina, Puerto Rico, on issuance of Clemente stamp. Bill Perry artwork includes Pirates logo and separate copy from GS176b. 5,000 issued, unautographed. U $5.

GS176b ROBERTO CLEMENTE FIRST DAY OF ISSUE: Postmarked Aug. 17, 1984, Carolina, Puerto Rico, on issuance of Clemente stamp. Bill Perry artwork omits Pirates logo. Separate copy from GS176a. 1,000 issued, unautographed. U $15.

GS177 PETE ROSE MANAGERIAL DEBUT: Postmarked July 10, 1984, Cincinnati, Ohio, by machine cancellation on Rose's debut as manager of the Reds. All envelopes are long #10 size. Action Rose photo. Auction determined prices of issue. 75 also autographed by Ryne Sandberg, pictured in the background. A by Rose by auction $2,400, A by Rose and Sandberg $2,500.

GS178 DWIGHT GOODEN ROOKIE STRIKEOUT RECORD: Postmarked Sept. 12, 1984, New York, N.Y., as Gooden breaks the all-time record for strikeouts by a rookie. Action photo. 1,500 issued autographed by Gooden, including 300 signed by Feller and 200 signed by Herb Score. A by Gooden $75, A by Gooden and Feller $85, A by Gooden, Feller and Score $95.

GS179a REGGIE JACKSON 500 HOME RUNS: Postmarked Sept. 17, 1984, Anaheim, Calif., as Jackson hits career homer #500. 500 issued numbered, including date of each home run and opposing pitcher, written by Reggie Jackson and autographed. A $250.

GS179b REGGIE JACKSON 500 HOME RUNS: Same as above, unnumbered and without dates or opponent pitchers. Action photo. Signed by Jackson or by Jackson and Bud Black. A by Jackson $150, A by Jackson and Black $175.

GS180 SPARKY ANDERSON 100 VICTORIES: Postmarked Sept. 23, 1984, Detroit, Mich., as Anderson became the first manager to win 100 games in each league. 2,000 issued autographed. A $15.

GS181 MIKE WITT PERFECT GAME: Postmarked Sept. 30, 1984, Arlington, Texas, as Witt pitched a perfect game the last day of the regular season. Action photo. 1,500 issued autographed. A $17.

GS182 is devoted to football star Walter Payton's rushing record.

1984 World Series

Gateway issued five envelopes without variation - one for each game the Series was played. The U.S.P.S. prepared philatelic postmarks for each game and city for the first time in history. The San Diego postmark incorporated Jack Murphy Stadium and the Padres' logo, while the Detroit postmark "Bless You Boys" was taken from the title of Sparky Anderson's book. Gateway obtained autographs from Sparky Anderson, Kurt Bevacqua, Darrell Evans, Steve Garvey, Kirk Gibson, Tony Gwynn, Willie Hernandez, Terry Kennedy, Craig Lefferts, Chet Lemon, Kevin McReynolds, Jack Morris, Graig Nettles, Lance Parrish, Dan Petry, Alan Trammell, Garry Templeton, Dick Williams and Milt Wilcox.

GS183 GAME 1: Postmarked Oct. 9, 1984, San Diego, Calif., all with philatelic postmarks. 2,000 issued with Scott Forst stadium artwork. Issued autographed and unautographed. A by superstars $20-$25, Others $ 10, U $5.

GS184 GAME 2: Postmarked Oct. 10, 1984, San Diego, all with philatelic postmarks. Action photo of Bevacqua and Kennedy. Autographed by one or both, or others. A by Bevacqua $8, A by Kennedy $8, Others $8-$12.

GS185 GAME 3: Postmarked Oct. 12, 1984, Detroit, Mich. 1,500 with rebound date and 500 with "Bless You Boys" postmarks. Willie Hernandez photo. 1,000 autographed. A by Hernandez on Bless You Boys $12, A by Hernandez on Round Date $10, U Bless You Boys $6, U Round Date $5.

GS186 GAME 4: Postmarked Oct. 13, 1984, Detroit, Mich. 1,500 with round date and 500 with "Bless You Boys" postmarks. Alan Trammell photo. 1,000 autographed by Trammell. A on Bless You Boys $12, A on Round Date $12, U Bless You Boys $6, U Round Date $5.

GS187 GAME 5: Postmarked Oct. 14, 1984, Detroit, Mich. 1,500 with round date and 500 with "Bless You Boys" postmarks. Kirk Gibson photo. 1,300 autographed by Gibson. A on Bless You Boys $20, A on Round Date $18, U Bless You Boys $6, U Round Date $5.

GS188 is devoted to football star Eric Dickerson's single-season rushing record.

GS189 is devoted to Dan Marino's 5,000 yards passing, a single season record.

GS190 is devoted to President Ronald Reagan's election.

GS191 is devoted to President Ronald Reagan's inauguration day.

GS192 is devoted to President Ronald Reagan's inauguration day.

GS193 is devoted to Super Bowl XIX, between the San Francisco 49ers and Miami Dolphins.

GS194 is devoted to the Miami Dolphins, Super Bowl XIX participants.

GS195 is devoted to the San Fransisco 49ers, Super Bowl XIX participants.

GS196 TOM SEAVER OPENING DAY: Postmarked April 9,1985, Milwaukee, Wis., as Seaver set a new all-time record for opening day starts. Action silk photo. All 1,500 autographed. A $30.

GS197 ROLLIE FINGERS SAVES RECORD: Postmarked April 13, 1985, Arlington, Texas, as Fingers set the new all-time record for saves. 1,500 issued, autographed. Action photo. A $20, A by Fingers and Sparky Lyle $25.

GS198 FERNANDO VALENZUELA ERA RECORD: Postmarked April 28, 1985, Los Angeles, Calif., as Valenzuela went 41 2/3 innings without allowing an earned run at the beginning of the season. 1,000 issued with action photo. All autographed. A $50.

GS199 NOLAN RYAN 4,000 STRIKEOUTS: Postmarked July 11, 1985, Houston, Texas, as Ryan reached 4,000 strikeouts. Action photo. 2,000 issued autographed. A $40.

GS200 LOU BROCK HALL OF FAME INDUCTION: Postmarked July 28, 1985, Cooperstown, N.Y. 2,000 issued autographed. Bill Perry artwork. A $20.

GS201 ENOS SLAUGHTER HALL OF FAME INDUCTION: Postmarked July 28, 1985, Cooperstown, N.Y. 2,000 issued autographed. Bill Perry artwork. A $17.50.

GS202 HOYT WILHELM HALL OF FAME INDUCTION: Postmarked July 28, 1985, Cooperstown, N.Y. 2,000 issued autographed. Bill Perry artwork. A $18.

GS203 ARKY VAUGHAN HALL OF FAME INDUCTION: Postmarked July 28, 1985, Cooperstown, N.Y. 1,000 issued unautographed. Bill Perry artwork. U $4.50.

GS204 VINCE COLEMAN ROOKIE STOLEN BASE RECORD: Postmarked Aug. 1, 1985, Chicago, Ill., as Coleman broke the all-time rookie stolen base record. 3,500 issued autographed. Action photo. A $15.

GS205 ROD CAREW 3,000 HITS: Postmarked Aug. 4, 1985, Anaheim, Calif., as Carew obtained his 3,000th career hit. Action photo with historical copy. 2,000 issued autographed. A $25.

GS206 ROD CAREW 3,000 HITS: Postmarked Aug. 4, 1985, Anaheim, Calif., as Carew reached his 3,000th hit. Action photo with biographical copy. 2,000 issued autographed. A $25.

GS207 TOM SEAVER 300 WINS: Postmarked Aug. 4, 1985, Bronx, N.Y. 1,800 issued, autographed. Action photo. A $30.

GS208 DAVE KINGMAN 400 HOME RUNS: Postmarked Aug. 1, 1985, Seattle, Wash., as Kingman obtained his 400th career home run. 1,500 issued, autographed. Action photo. A $40.

GS209 is devoted to football star Roger Staubach's Hall of Fame induction.

GS210 is devoted to football star O.J. Simpson's Hall of Fame induction.

GS211 is devoted to football star Joe Namath's Hall of Fame induction.

GS212 RESERVED

GS213 RESERVED

GS214 DWIGHT GOODEN 20 GAMES: Postmarked Aug. 25, 1985, New York, N.Y., as Gooden became the youngest 20-game winner in history. 1,000 issued autographed. Action photo. A by Gooden $75, A by Gooden and Feller $95.

GS215 PETE ROSE HIT RECORD: Postmarked Sept. 8, 1985, Chicago, Ill., on Rose's 4,190th hit. Silk features Ty Cobb. Card insert included questioning Cobb's hit total. Postmarks include round dates and "Windy City." Stamps vary with assortment of regular and Illinois Bird and Flowers. Autographs include Rose and Reggie Patterson. A by Rose $30, A by Rose and Patterson $35, Postmarks - no extra charge - no change, U $10.

GS216 PETE ROSE HIT RECORD: Postmarked Sept. 8, 1985, Chicago, Ill., on Rose's 4,191st hit. Silk pictures actual swing of the bat. Postmarks include round dates and Windy City. Stamps vary, matching with GS215. Autographs include Rose, Reggie Patterson and Jody Davis. 2,500 issued. A by Rose $30, A by Rose and Patterson $35, A by Rose, Patterson and Davis $40, Postmarks and stamp varieties - no extra charge - add $2, U $8.

GS217 PETE ROSE HIT RECORD: Postmarked Sept. 11, 1985, Cincinnati, Ohio, as Pete Rose breaks the recognized all-time hit record with 4,192. Action silk photo is swing of the bat. 2,500 issued with round dates. Autographed by Rose or Eric Show, or unautographed. Various stamp combinations used, including Ohio Bird and Flowers. A by Rose $30, A by Rose and Show $40, U $8, Stamp varieties - no extra charge - add $2.

GS218 PETE ROSE HIT RECORD: Postmarked Sept. 11, 1985, Cincinnati, Ohio, as Rose got hit number 4,193 to set and new and yet undetermined all-time hit record. Part of a set of four. Artwork by Bill Perry. 2,500 issued autographed by Rose, Rose and Show, or unautographed. Various stamp varities used, including Ohio Bird and Flowers. A by Rose $30, A by Rose and Show $40, U $8, Stamp varieties - no extra charge - add $2.

GS219 RUSTY STAUB 100 PINCH HITS: Postmarked Sept. 21, 1985, New York, N. Y., on Staub's 100th career pinch hit. 800 issued autographed with action photo. A $75.

GS220 BRET SABERHAGEN: Postmarked Sept. 30, 1985, Kansas City, Mo., as Saberhagen became the second youngest 20-game winner in American League history. 200 issued on action photo. A $350.

GS221 DARRELL EVANS 40 HOMERS: Postmarked Oct. 2, 1985, Detroit, Mich., as Evans became the first player to hit 40 home runs in both leagues and the oldest to hit 40. 650 issued autographed with action silk photo. A $90.

GS222 is devoted to Grambling University football coach Eddie Robinson, winningest coach in college history.

GS223 WILLIE McGEE BATTING RECORD: Postmarked Oct. 6, 1985, St. Louis, Mo., as McGee set a new all-time National League record of .353 as a switch-hitter. 2,000 action silks. Issued autographed. 200 autographed by McGee and Pete Rose. A by McGee $15, A by McGee and Rose $35.

GS224 PHIL NIEKRO 300 WINS: Postmarked Oct. 6,1985, Toronto, Canada, where Niekro obtained his 300th career win the last day of the regular season. 1,500 issued, autographed. Action silk. A $20.

GS225 1920 WORLD SERIES 65TH ANNIVERSARY: Postmarked Oct. 12, 1985, Cleveland, Ohio. 200 #10 size envelopes commemorating JOE SEWELL. Bill Perry artwork with copy describing Sewell's part in the 1920 World Series. A $250.

GS226 1920 WORLD SERIES 65th ANNIVERSARY: Postmarked Oct. 12, 1985, Cleveland, Ohio. 200 #10 size envelopes commemorating ELMER SMITH's place on the 1920 team. Bill Perry artwork. A $200.

GS227 1920 WORLD SERIES 65TH ANNIVERSARY: Postmarked Oct. 12, 1985, Cleveland, Ohio. 200 #10 size envelopes commemorating GEORGE UHLE's part on the 1920 team. Bill Perry artwork. A $200.

GS228 1920 WORLD SERIES 65TH ANNIVERSARY: Postmarked Oct. 12, 1985, Cleveland, Ohio. 200 #10 size envelopes commemorating BILL WAMBSGANSS part on the 1920 team. Bill Perry artwork. A $200.

GS229 1920 WORLD SERIES 65TH ANNIVERSARY: Postmarked Oct. 12, 1985, Cleveland, Ohio. 200 #10 size envelopes commemorating "SMOKEY" JOE WOOD's place on the 1920 team.

1985 World Series

Gateway issued seven envelopes, one for each game the series was played, in 1985. A variation occurs on Game 5 where reprinted Willie Wilson silks were cut to a different size. Otherwise, all postmarks and silks run consistently. Stamp varieties were also used. Autographs acquired by Gateway were Buddy Biancalana, George Brett, Jack Clark, Danny Cox, Tom Herr, Whitey Herzog, Dick Howser, Tito Landrum, Charlie Leibrandt, Terry Pendleton, Dan Quisenberry, Bret Saberhagen, Lonnie Smith, Ozzie Smith, John Tudor, Frank White, Willie Wilson and Todd Worrell.

GS230 GAME 1: Postmarked Oct. 19, 1985, Kansas City, Mo., 2,000 envelopes with Scott Forst stadium artwork. Various autographs were acquired on this neutral envelope. A by superstars $20, Others $8, U $5.

GS231 GAME 2: Postmarked Oct. 20, 1985, Kansas City, Mo., 2,000 envelopes with action Terry Pendleton photo. 500 autographed by Pendleton. A $15, U $7.50.

GS232 GAME 3: Postmarked Oct. 22, 1985, St. Louis, Mo., with special "Show-Me" Series postmarks. 2,000 issued showing Frank White photo after three-run homer. 750 autographed by White. A $10, U $5.

GS233 GAME 4: Postmarked Oct. 23, 1985, St. Louis, Mo., with "Show-Me" Series postmarks. 2,000 issued bearing John Tudor action photo. 500 autographed by Tudor. A $12, U $5.

GS234 GAME 5: Postmarked Oct. 24, 1985, St. Louis, Mo., with "Show-Me" Series postmarks. 2,000 issued bearing Willie Wilson photo. Reprinted photo trims more off Wilson's feet. 500 autographed by Wilson. A $15, U $5.

GS235 GAME 6: Postmarked Oct. 26, 1985, Kansas City, Mo. 2,000 issued bearing Charlie Leibrandt photo. 500 autographed. A $12, U $5.

GS236 GAME 7: Postmarked Oct. 27, 1985, Kansas City, Mo. 2,000 issued bearing Bret Saberhagen and George Brett celebration photo. 1,500 autographed by Bret Saberhagen; 1,000 by Saberhagen and Brett. A by Saberhagen $20, A by Saberhagen and Brett $40, U $10.

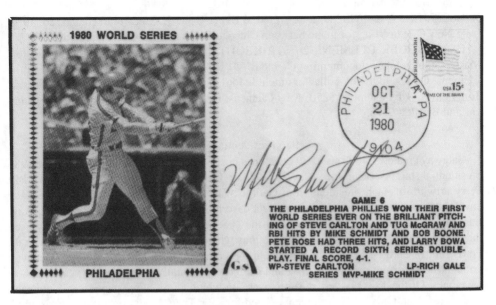

GS70 Mike Schmidt

GS102 Early Wynn

GS237, GS238 and GS239 are devoted to Super Bowl XX, postmarked Jan. 26, 1986, from New Orleans, La., for game between Chicago Bears and New England Patriots.

GS240 ROGER CLEMENS 20 STRIKEOUTS: Postmarked April 29, 1986, Boston, Mass. 750 envelopes documenting Clemens' 20 strikeouts. Action photo. Autographed by Clemens. Others added by collectors include Phil Bradley, Steve Carlton, Nolan Ryan and Tom Seaver. A by Clemens $250, A by Clemens, Ryan, Seaver, Carlton, $325, A by Clemens and Bradley $275.

1986 Presidential Issue

Gateway created 1,400 sets of 39 envelopes postmarked "First Day of Issue" on the 1986 presidential stamp series issued May 22, 1986, in Chicago, Ill. The set of 39 includes a Bill Perry artwork of each president from George Washington through Ronald Reagan. Each envelope bears a biographical and historical description of each president's life and tenure. Each deceased president was honored by the U.S.P.S. with his own stamp. Gateway used the White House stamp to obtain cancellations whereby to include Richard Nixon, Gerald Ford, Jimmy Carter and Ronald Reagan in the complete presidential sequence. Gateway arranged with former presidents Ford and Carter to personally autograph 500 each of their envelopes. Of the 1,400 issued, 400 sets were on white cotton wove paper as gifts to each living president. Only 1,000 sets were offered for sale. Their paper content is regular white consistent with all the other Gateway issues.

GS241-279 are reserved for each former president of the United States from George Washington through Ronald Reagan. A by Gerald Ford and Jimmy Carter $250 per set, Added autographs of Richard Nixon and/or Ronald Reagan $50 each.

GS280 RESERVED

GS281 DON SUTTON 300 WINS: Postmarked June 18, 1986, Anaheim, Calif., as Sutton joined the 300 Wins Club. 1,500 issued with action silk photo and autographed. 250 autographed by Pete Incaviglia. A by Sutton $18, A by Sutton and Incaviglia $25.

GS282 300 GAME WINNERS PITCHING DUEL: Postmarked June 28, 1986, Anaheim, Calif., as Don Sutton and Phil Niekro became the first 300-game winners ever to pitch against each other. 650 issued. Bill Perry artwork. Autographed by Sutton and Niekro. A $80.

GS283 BOB HORNER FOUR HOME RUNS: Postmarked July 6, 1986, Atlanta, Ga., as Horner became only the 11th player in major league history to hit four home runs in a game. 1,500 issued with action silk photo. Autographed by Horner. 100 autographed by Willie Mays. A by Horner $15, A by Horner and Mays $35.

GS284 RUSTY STAUB - REFLECTIONS: Postmarked July 13, 1986, New York, N.Y. 2,000 issued autographed as Mets honor Rusty Staub. Bill Perry artwork. Autographed by Staub. A $15.

GS285 RUSTY STAUB "THANKS RUSTY" DAY: Postmarked July 13, 1986, New York, N.Y., as a companion envelope to GS280. Photo of Mets mimicking Staub's red hair. Copy includes Mets' honors toward Staub. 2,000 issued. A $15.

GS286 WALLY JOYNER: Postmarked July 15, 1986, Houston, Texas, with large pictorial U.S.P.S. postmark commemorating the 1986 All-Star game. 1,200 issued with action photo, autographed, honoring Joyner as the first rookie ever to be elected to the all-star team. A $50.

GS287 BERT BLYLEVEN 3,000 STRIKEOUTS: 1,500 postmarked Aug. 1, 1986, Minneapolis, Minn., as Blyleven got his 3,000th career strikeout. Photo of bearded Blyleven and historical copy. A $15.

GS288 BERT BLYLEVEN 3,000 STRIKEOUTS: 1,500 postmarked Aug. 1, 1986, Minneapolis, Minn., as a companion envelope to GS283. Action photo of non-bearded Blyleven and biographical copy. 500 autographed. A $15. U $7.50.

GS289 RESERVED

GS290 is devoted to football star Paul Hornung's Hall of Fame induction.

GS291 RESERVED

GS292 RESERVED

GS293 RESERVED

GS294 BOBBY DOERR HALL OF FAME INDUCTION: Postmarked Aug. 3, 1986, Cooperstown, N.Y. 1,500 issued, autographed. Bill Perry artwork. A $15.

GS295 WILLIE McCOVEY HALL OF FAME INDUCTION: Postmarked Aug. 3, 1986, Cooperstown, N.Y. 2,000 issued, autographed. Bill Perry artwork. A $25.

GS296 ERNIE LOMBARDI HALL OF FAME INDUCTION: Postmarked Aug. 3, 1985, Cooperstown, N.Y. 1,000 issued, unautographed. U $4.50.

GS297 STEVE CARLTON 4,000 STRIKEOUTS: Postmarked Aug. 5, 1986, San Francisco, Calif., as Carlton became only the second pitcher to reach 4,000 strikeouts and set the all-time National League strikeout record. 2,000 action photo silks (Giants uniform) issued, autographed. A $25.

GS298 TODD WORRELL ROOKIE SAVES RECORD: Postmarked Aug. 10, 1986, St. Louis, as Worrell broke the all-time record for saves by a rookie pitcher. 1,500 issued, autographed. Action photo. A $15.

GS299 BOB FELLER 50th ANNIVERSARY: Postmarked Aug. 23, 1986, Cleveland, Ohio, commemorating Feller's first major league start. 1,800 issued, autographed. Bill Perry artwork. A $15.

GS300 JOE COWLEY NO-HITTER. Postmarked Sept. 19, 1986, Anaheim, Calif., as Cowley obtained his first career no-hitter. 299 issued, autographed. Posed photo. A $150.

GS301 JIM DESHAIES 8 CONSECUTIVE STRIKEOUTS: Postmarked Sept. 23, 1986, Houston, Texas, as Deshaies set a modern major league record of eight consecutive strikeouts at the beginning of a game. 1,000 issued, autographed. Action photo. A $15.

GS302 MIKE SCOTT NO-HITTER: Postmarked Sept. 25, 1986, Houston, Texas, as Mike Scott no-hit the Dodgers to clinch the Western Division title. 1,500 issued, autographed. Action photo. A $15.

GS303 RESERVED

GS304 MANTLE/MARIS: Postmarked Oct. 1, 1986, Bronx, the 25th anniversary of Roger Maris' 61st home run. He and Mickey Mantle set a record for teammates of 115. Bill Perry artwork. 1,500 issued, autographed by Mantle. A by Mantle $75.

GS305 RESERVED

GS306 DON MATTINGLY BATTING RECORD: Postmarked Oct. 5, 1986, Boston, when Don Mattingly set a Yankee hits record and became the sixth player in major league history to combine 230 hits, 30 home runs, and 100 RBI in a season. 1,500 issued, autographed. Action photo. A $45.

GS307 DON LARSEN PERFECT GAME: Postmarked Oct. 8, 1986, to commemorate the 30th anniversary of Larsen's World Series perfect game. 1,000 issued autographed by Larsen. Bill Perry artwork. 300 also autographed by Berra. A by Larsen $15. A by Larsen and Berra $30.

GS308 RESERVED

GS309 RESERVED

1986 World Series

Gateway produced a set of seven envelopes, one for when each game in the 1986 World Series was played, along with two variations for Games 2 and 6. All New York postmarks to this set are regular round dates, whereas all the Boston postmarks are philatelic postmarks bearing the Red Sox logo. Gateway continued following its original format of telling the story of the Series game by game with actual Series photos, historical texts, and acquiring autographs from players on envelopes if they played a prominent part in that game. Game 1 continued to be a neutral location for autographs of non-pictured players. Gateway acquired autographs from: Wade Boggs, Bill Buckner, Gary Carter, Roger Clemens, Ron Darling, Lenny Dykstra, Sid Fernandez, Rich Gedman, Dwight Gooden, Keith Hernandez, Bruce Hurst, Davey Johnson, Howard Johnson, Ray Knight (Series MVP), Bob Ojeda, Jesse Orosco, Jim Rice and Darryl Strawberry.

GS310 GAME 1: Postmarked Oct. 18, 1986, New York, NY. 2,000 issued with Scott Forst artwork and historical copy. A by superstars $18 to $25, Others $8 to $10, U $5.

GS311a GAME 2: Postmarked Oct. 19, 1986, New York, N.Y. 1,000 issued bearing Dwight Gooden action photo. Autographed by Gooden, or Gooden and Clemens, or others. A by Gooden $20, A by Gooden and Clemens $40, A by Others $10, U $8.

GS311b GAME 2: Postmarked Oct. 19, 1986, New York, N.Y. 1,000 issued bearing Roger Clemens' photo. Autographed by Clemens, or Gooden and Clemens, or others, A Clemens $25, A Clemens and Gooden $45, A by Others $10, U $8.

GS312 GAME 3: Postmarked Oct. 21, 1986, Boston, Mass. 2,000 issued bearing Dykstra action silk. Autographed by Dykstra and others. A by Dykstra $15, A by Others $8, U $5.

GS313 GAME 4: Postmarked Oct. 22, 1986, Boston, Mass. 2,000 issued bearing Gary Carter action photo. Autographed by Carter or others. A by Carter $20. A by Others $10, U $5.

GS314 GAME 5: Postmarked Oct. 23, 1986, Boston, Mass. 2,000 issued bearing Bruce Hurst action photo. Autographed by Hurst or others. A by Hurst $15, A by Others $8.

GS315a GAME 6: Postmarked Oct. 25, 1986, New York, N.Y. 1,000 issued bearing Keith Hernandez photo. Autographed by Hernandez and others. A by Hernandez $15, A by Others $8, U $6.

GS315b GAME 6: Postmarked Oct. 25, 1986, New York, N.Y. 1,000 issued bearing action photo of Wade Boggs. Autographed by Boggs, or Boggs and Buckner, or others. A by Boggs $25, A by Boggs and Buckner $35, A by Others $10, U $6.

GS316a GAME 7: Postmarked Oct. 27, 1986, New York, N.Y. 1,500 issued bearing action photo of Ray Knight. Upper caption reads "1986 WORLD SERIES." Autographed by Ray Knight or Knight and others. A by Knight $12, A by Knight and Others $16 to $30, U $5.

GS316b GAME 7: Postmarked Oct. 27, 1986, same as above. 500 issued with upper caption reading "WORLD SERIES." Same autograph arrangement as GS316a. U $10.

GS317 is devoted to Super Bowl XXI in Pasadena, Calif. New York Giants and Denver Broncos participating, postmarked Jan. 25, 1987.

GS318 is devoted to Super Bowl XXI in Pasadena, Calif., for the New York Giants.

GS319 is devoted to Super Bowl XXI in Pasadena, Calif., for the Denver Broncos.

GS320 RESERVED

GS321 RESERVED

GS322 NIEKRO AND CARLTON: Postmarked April 9, 1987, Toronto, Canada, as Phil Niekro and Steve Carlton became the first 300-game winners to pitch together on the same team in the same game. 1,000 issued. Bill Perry artwork. Autographed by both Niekro and Carlton. A by Niekro and Carlton $50.

25th anniversary of Dodger Stadium

Gateway issued a series of seven envelopes in commemoration of Dodger Stadium's 25th anniversary. The U.S.P.S. created a philatelic postmark for each date of the seven-game opening homestand. Each Gateway envelope has a photo of Dodger Stadium and 25th Anniversary logo. Copy is the same on all seven envelopes. About half of the stamps used to obtain postmarks were common 25cts stamps; about half were 25cts Pan American Games commemorative issues. Gateway acquired autographs from various prominent players on each game if they may have played a prominent part.

GS323 APRIL 9, 1987: OPENING DAY. 2,000 issued, autographed, and unautographed. A by Peter O'Malley $15, A by O'Malley and Tommy Lasorda $25, U $8.

GS324 APRIL 10, 1987: Superstar autographs $12 to $25, Others $8, U $8.

GS325 APRIL 11, 1987: Superstar autographs $12 to $25, Others $8, U $8.

GS326 APRIL 12, 1987: Superstar autographs $12 to $25, Others $8, U $8.

GS327 APRIL 13, 1987: Superstar autographs $12 to $25, Others $8, U $8.

GS328 April 14, 1987: Superstar autographs $12 to $25, Others $8, U $8.

GS329 April 15, 1987: Superstar autographs $12 to $25, Others $8, U $8.

40th Anniversary Jackie Robinson

Gateway issued a similar set of Jackie Robinson commemoratives to coincide with the 25th anniversary of Dodger Stadium. Again, the U.S.P.S. granted postmarks with the seven dates of the 1987 season at Dodger Stadium, where the Robinson envelopes were also introduced and sold. The same numbering system applies as with Dodger Stadium.

GS330 April 9, 1987; GS331 April 10, 1987; GS332 April 11, 1987; GS333 April 12, 1987; GS334 April 13, 1987; GS335 April 14, 1987; GS336 April 15, 1987 (2,000 of each envelope issued with Bill Perry artwork). Superstar autographs $12 to $25, Autographed by Joe Black $8, Others $8, Unautographed $8.

GS337 JACKIE ROBINSON 40th ANNIVERSARY: Postmarked April 15, 1987, Brooklyn, N.Y., on the 40th anniversary of Robinson's major league debut. 1,000 issued with the same Bill Perry artwork as with the Los Angeles postmark. Different copy. Unautographed. U $8.

GS338 WYNNE, GWYNN, KRUK: Postmarked April 13, 1987, San Diego, Calif., with philatelic Opening Day postmark as Marvell Wynne, Tony Gwynn and John Kruk led off the game with first-inning home runs, a major league record. 500 issued, autographed. Bill Perry artwork. A by Wynne, Gwynn, Kruk $225.

GS339 JUAN NIEVES NO-HITTER: Postmarked April 15, 1987, Milwaukee, Wis., as Nieves pitched his first career no-hitter. Action photo. 850 issued, autographed. 100 also autographed by Robin Yount. A by Nieves $65, A by Nieves and Yount $100.

GS340 RESERVED

GS341 is devoted to basketball star Julius Erving, postmarked April 27, 1987, when he became the third player in history to score 30,000 career points.

GS342 MIKE SCHMIDT 500 HOME RUNS: Postmarked April 18, 1987, Pittsburgh, Pa., as Schmidt hit his 500th career home run. 3,000 issued with actual swing photo. A $40.

GS343 FENWAY PARK 75th ANNIVERSARY: Postmarked April 20, 1987, Boston, Mass., upon the 75th anniversary of Fenway Park. 1,000 issued with Scott Forst stadium artwork. 500 autographed by Carlton Fisk. A by Fisk $75, Unautographed $75, Others $75 to $150.

GS344 ERIC DAVIS HOME RUN RECORD: Postmarked May 30, 1987, Pittsburgh, Pa., as Davis broke the National League record for grand slam homers in a month and tied the major league record. 1,200 issued with action photo. A $50.

GS345 PERRY BROTHERS WINNINGEST COMBO: Postmarked June 1, 1987, Cleveland, Ohio. 1,000 issued autographed by Jim and Gaylord Perry. Bill Perry artwork. A $50.

GS346 NIEKRO BROTHERS WINNINGEST COMBO: Postmarked June 1, 1987, Cleveland, Ohio, as Phil Niekro wins to combine with brother Joe to set the all-time record for wins by brothers. 1,000 issued, autographed. A $50.

GS347 MARK McGWIRE FIVE HOME RUNS: Postmarked June 28, 1987, Cleveland, Ohio, where McGwire set a rookie record for five home runs in two games. A $75.

GS348 DON MATTINGLY HOME RUN RECORD: Postmarked July 18, 1987, Arlington, Texas, as Mattingly tied Dale Long's all-time record of eight consecutive games in which to hit a home run. 1,000 issued, autographed. Action photo. A $75.

GS349 JIM "CATFISH" HUNTER HALL OF FAME INDUCTION: Postmarked July 26, 1987, Cooperstown, N.Y. 2,000 issued, autographed. Bill Perry silk. 750 issued with "catfish" postage stamps. A $18, with catfish postage stamp add $2.

GS350 BILLY WILLIAMS HALL OF FAME INDUCTION: Postmarked July 26, 1987, Cooperstown, N.Y. 2,000 issued, autographed. Bill Perry silk. A $15.

GS351 RAY DANDRIDGE HALL OF FAME INDUCTION: Postmarked July 26, 1987, in Cooperstown, N.Y. 1,000 issued, autographed. Bill Perry artwork. Autographed. 200 autographed by Willie Mays. A $15, A by Dandridge and Mays $35.

GS352 RESERVED

GS353 RESERVED

GS354 RESERVED

GS355 RESERVED

GS356 RESERVED

GS357 RESERVED

GS358 RESERVED

GS359 MARK McGWIRE ROOKIE HOME RUN RECORD: Postmarked Aug. 14, 1987, Anaheim, Calif., as McGwire broke Wally Berger's all-time rookie home run record of 38. 1,500 issued, autographed. 300 also autographed by Berger. Action photo. A by McGwire $30, A by McGwire and Berger $35.

GS360 PAUL MOLITOR HITTING STREAK: Postmarked Aug. 25, 1987, Milwaukee, Wis., the last date of Molitor's 39-game hitting streak. 1,500 issued, autographed. Action photo. A $25.

GS361 KIRBY PUCKETT 10 HITS: Postmarked Aug. 25, 1987, Milwaukee, Wis., as Puckett set an American League record of 10 consecutive hits in two nine-inning games. 1,500 issued, autographed. Action silk photo. A $25.

GS362 CAL RIPKEN JR. CONSECUTIVE INNINGS RECORD: Postmarked Sept. 14, 1987, Toronto, as Ripken set the new all-time record. 1,000 issued autographed by Ripken Jr., 300 also autographed by Ripken Sr. Action photo. A by Ripken Jr. $50. A by Ripken Jr. and Ripken Sr. $60.

GS363 RESERVED

GS364 BOB BOONE CATCHING RECORD: Postmarked Sept. 16, 1987, Kansas City, Mo., when Boone passed Al Lopez as the all-time leader in games caught. 1,000 issued autographed. Posed photo of Boone and Lopez. A by Boone $18, A by Boone and Lopez $75.

GS365 BENITO SANTIAGO ROOKIE HITTING STREAK: Postmarked Sept. 26, 1987, as Santiago broke the all-time rookie hitting streak record of 27. 1,000 issued. 500 autographed. Action silk photo. A $15, U $5.

GS366 BENITO SANTIAGO ROOKIE HITTING STREAK RECORD: Post marked Oct. 2, 1987, as Santiago set the new rookie hitting streak record at 34 games. Action photo. 1,000 issued with Junipero Serra Museum postmarks. A $15, U $5.

GS367 DON MATTINGLY GRAND SLAM RECORD: Postmarked Sept. 29, 1987, Detroit, Mich., as Mattingly set the all-time record for grand slams in a season. 500 issued autographed. Action photo. A $150.

GS368 ED ROUSH 70th ANNIVERSARY: Postmarked Sept. 30, 1987, Cincinnati, Ohio, to commemorate the 70th anniversary of Roush's National League batting title. Bill Penny artwork. U $5.

GS369 MAURY WILLS 25th ANNIVERSARY: Postmarked Oct. 3, 1987, Los Angeles, Calif., to commemorate the 25th anniversary of Wills' all-time record of 100 stolen bases in a season. 1,000 issued, autographed. Bill Perry artwork. A $15.

1987 World Series

Gateway issued 1,600 sets of seven envelopes without variations to tell the story of the 1987 World Series. A footnote to this series is seen in the postmarks used by the Minneapolis Post Office for Games 1 and 2 compared to 6 and 7. Major League Baseball objected to the use of the Twins' logo within the postmarks, so the Post Office changed the marks in time for the sixth and seventh games. Gateway acquired autographs for Bert Blyleven, Tom Brunansky, Vince Coleman, Dan Gladden, Whitey Herzog, Kent Hrbek, Tom Kelly, Tom Lawless, Steve Lombardozzi, Terry Pendleton, Kirby Puckett, Jeff Reardon, Ozzie Smith and Frank Viola.

GS370 GAME 1: Postmarked Oct. 17, 1987, Minneapolis, Minn. 1,600 issued with Scott Forst Stadium artwork. Various autographs acquired. A by superstars $15, A by Others $8, Unautographed $5.

GS371 GAME 2: Postmarked Oct. 18, 1987, Minneapolis, Minn. 1,600 issued with Blyleven action photo. 1,000 autographed by Blyleven. A by Blyleven $20, A by Others $10, Unautographed $5.

GS372 GAME 3: Postmarked Oct. 20, 1987, St. Louis, Mo., 1,600 issued with Vince Coleman action photo. 750 autographed by Coleman. A by Coleman $10, A by Others $8, Unautographed $5.

GS373 GAME 4: Postmarked Oct. 21, 1987, St. Louis, Mo. 1,600 issued with Tom Lawless action photo. 750 autographed by Lawless. A by Lawless $8, A by Others $8, Unautographed $5.

GS374 GAME 5: Postmarked Oct. 22, 1987, St. Louis, Mo. 1,600 issued with Ozzie Smith photo. 1,000 autographed by Smith. A by Smith $20, A by Others $10, Unautographed $5.

GS375 GAME 6: Postmarked Oct. 24, 1987, Minneapolis, Minn. 1,600 issued with Kent Hrbek action photo. 1,000 autographed by Hrbek. A by Hrbek $15, A by Others $8, Unautographed $5.

GS376 GAME 7: Postmarked Oct. 25, 1987, Minneapolis, Minn. 1,600 issued with Frank Viola action photo. 1,000 autographed Viola, including 250 signed by Jeff Reardon. A by Viola $15, A by Viola and Reardon $25, Unautographed $5.

GS377a FERGUSON JENKINS CANADIAN HALL OF FAME INDUCTION: Postmarked Nov. 11, 1987, Toronto, Ontario, Canada, upon Jenkins' induction. 1,000 issued autographed. Bill Perry artwork. Caption reads "Native Son." A $20.

GS377b FERGUSON JENKINS CANADIAN HALL OF FAME INDUCTION: Postmarked Nov. 11, 1987, Toronto, Ontario, Canada. Same Bill Perry artwork. Caption reads "CANADIAN INDUCTION." 500 created, not yet released, to be autographed by Jenkins.

GS378 GS379 and GS380 are postmarked Jan. 31, 1988, San Diego, Calif., and are devoted to Super Bowl XXII, Washington against Denver.

GS381 SAN DIEGO PADRES 20TH ANNIVERSARY: Postmarked April 12, 1988, San Diego, Calif., with special philatelic "Opening Day" 20th Anniversary postmark. 1,000 issued with Scott Forst stadium artwork. 500 autographed by Randy Jones. A $12, U $8.

GS382 STEVE GARVEY UNIFORM RETIREMENT: Postmarked April 16, 1988, San Diego, Calif., as Padres retired Garvey's uniform number. Platform photo. 1,000 issued, autographed. A $20.

GS383 BALTIMORE STREAK ENDS: Postmarked April 29, 1988, Chicago, Ill., when the Baltimore Orioles ended their record 21-game losing streak. 1,000 issued picturing new manager Frank Robinson. Autographed by Robinson. A $25.

GS384 JOHNNY VANDER MEER 50TH ANNIVERSARY: Postmarked June 11, 1988, Cincinnati, Ohio, commemorating the 50th anniversary of VanderMeer's back-to-back no-hitters. 500 issued, autographed. Bill Perry artwork. A $15, U $3.

GS385 JOHNNY VANDER MEER 50TH ANNIVERSARY: Postmarked June 15, 1988, Brooklyn, N.Y., where Vander Meer pitched the second end of his back-to-back no-hitters. 1,000 issued with the first color photo ever printed in a U.S. newspaper. 1,000 autographed. 250 also autographed by Woody English. A by Vander Meer $15, A by English $10.

GS386 1988 ALL-STAR GAME CINCINNATI: Postmarked July 12, 1988, Cincinnati, Ohio. 635 issued bearing Crosley Field and Riverfront Stadium artwork by Scott Forst. 250 autographed by Will Clark. A $25, U $10.

GS387 1988 ALL-STAR GAME CINCINNATI: 635 issued picturing Terry Steinbach (MVP), autographed. A $20.

GS388 1988 ALL-STAR GAME CINCINNATI: 635 issued picturing Andy Van Slyke, autographed. A $20.

GS389 TOM SEAVER UNIFORM RETIREMENT: Postmarked July 24, 1988, Flushing, N.Y., with large pictorial cancellation designed by Gateway owner Thomas Wiley. Perhaps the first U.S. postal cancellation illustrating a living person; the first U.S. postal cancellation illustrating a living baseball player. 1,200 issued picturing Tom Seaver in ceremonies. Autographed. A $25.

GS390 is devoted to Mike Ditka's induction into the Pro Football Hall of Fame July 30, 1988, in Canton, Ohio.

GS391 is devoted to Fred Biletnikoff's induction into the Hall of Fame July 30, 1988.

GS392 RESERVED

GS393 RESERVED

GS394 WILLIE STARGELL HALL OF FAME INDUCTION: Postmarked July 31, 1988, Cooperstown, N.Y. 2,000 issued, autographed. Bill Perry artwork. A $25.

GS395 RICH GOSSAGE 300 SAVES: Postmarked Aug. 6, 1988, Chicago, Ill., all with "Windy City" postmarks, on Gossage's 300th career save. 1,000 issued autographed. Action photo. Autographed. A $15.

GS396 FIRST NIGHT GAME AT WRIGLEY: Postmarked Aug. 8, 1988, Chicago, Ill., with special "First Night Game at Wrigley Field" postal cancellation. 2,000 issued with

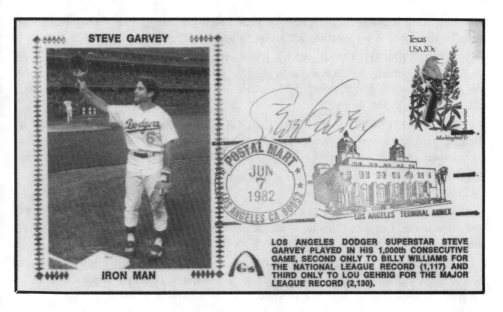

GS105 Steve Garvey

GS107 Frank Robinson

Scott Forst artwork. 500 autographed by Rick Sutcliffe; 100 by Harry Grossman, who turned on the lights. A by Sutcliffe $15, A by Grossman $15, U $6.

GS397 FIRST NIGHT GAME WRIGLEY: Postmarked Aug. 9, 1988, Chicago, Ill., with Windy City postmark due to rainout of Aug. 8 game. Same Scott Forst artpiece as on GS395. 2,000 issued. 500 autographed by Mark Grace; 500 by Mike Bielecki. A by Grace $20, A by Bielecki $15, U $6.

GS398 CARLTON FISK GAMES CAUGHT: Postmarked Aug. 19, 1988, Detroit, Mich., as Fisk set a new American League record of 1,807 games caught. Action photo. 1,000 issued autographed by Fisk, including 500 autographed by Rick Ferrell. A by Fisk $30, A by Fisk and Ferrell $40.

GS399 RESERVED

GS400a CANADIAN FIRST DAY COVER: Postmarked "First Day of Issue" Sept. 14, 1988, Beachville, Ontario, Canada, as Canada issues its first baseball stamp on the 150th anniversary of baseball in Canada. 1,000 issued with Scott Forst artwork. U $6.

GS400b CANADIAN FIRST DAY COVER: Incorrectly issued with postmark of Sept. 28, 1988, on Canadian 150th anniversary stamp. Postmark correctly applies to another event. 500 created unautographed with same Scott Forst artwork. U $10.

GS401 TOM BROWNING PERFECT GAME: Postmarked with 1,200 machine cancellations of Sept. 16, 1988, on Tom Browning's perfect game. Action photo. All autographed. NOTE: Seven exist hand-cancelled Sept. 16, 1988. Not yet offered. A by Tom Browning $15, hand-cancelled and autographed. Auction Valued.

GS402 RESERVED

GS403 DARRELL EVANS 400 HOME RUNS: Postmarked Sept. 20, 1988, Detroit, Mich., as Evans joins the 400 career home run circle. 1,000 issued autographed. Action photo. A $17.

GS404 JOSE CANSECO 40/40: Postmarked Sept. 23, 1988, Milwaukee, Wis., as Canseco became the first player ever to hit 40 home runs and steal 40 bases in a season. 1,250 issued autographed. Action photo. A $100.

GS405A OREL HERSHISER 59 INNINGS: Postmarked Sept. 28, 1988, with San Diego, Calif., Junipero Serra Museum postmark, as Hershiser broke Don Drysdale's all-time consecutive scoreless innings mark. 1,200 issued with museum postmark autographed. 200 autographed by Drysdale. A by Hershiser $125, A by Hershiser and Drysdale $150.

GS405b OREL HERSHISER 59 INNINGS: Postmarked Sept. 28, 1988, San Diego, Calif., with round-dated postmarks. Envelope flaps on back have a pointed flap from a different supplier. 150 issued with same action photo and copy as GS405a. Also autographed by Hershiser and Drysdale. A by Hershiser $125, A by Hershiser and Drysdale $150.

GS406 RESERVED

GS407 JEFF REARDON SAVES RECORD: Postmarked Sept. 30, 1988, Minneapolis, Minn., when Reardon set the all-time record of 41 saves in both leagues. 1,000 issued with action photo and autographed. A $15.

GS408 KIRK GIBSON SERIES TRADITION: Postmarked Oct. 15, 1988, Los Angeles, Calif., with a special U.S.P.S. World Series cancellation. 1,250 issued with action photo capturing Gibson's swing of the bat for the home run that won Game 1 of the 1988 World Series. All autographed. A $25.

1988 World Series

Gateway issued 2,000 sets of five envelopes postmarked each date the Series was played. 1,000 sets have the round dates in Oakland, while another 1,000 sets bear the U.S.P.S. licensed World Series postmarks. All Los Angeles postmarks are the same. Because of the dramatic nature of Gibson's game-winning home run in Game 1, Gateway issued an additional 1,250 envelopes picturing the swing of the bat (GS408). Gateway acquired autographs from Jose Canseco, Kirk Gibson, Mickey Hatcher, Orel Hershiser (MVP), Tommy Lasorda, Mike Marshall, Mark McGwire and Mike Scioscia.

GS409 GAME 1: Postmarked Oct. 15, 1988, Los Angeles, Calif. 2,000 issued with Scott Forst stadium artwork. Autographed by various players. A by Canseco $25, A by Gibson $20, A by Others $10, Unautographed $5.

GS410 GAME 2: Postmarked Oct. 16, 1988, Los Angeles, Calif. 2,000 issued with Orel Hershiser action photo. 1,000 autographed by Hershiser. A by Hershiser $20, A by Others $8, Unautographed $5.

GS411 GAME 3: Postmarked Oct. 18, 1988, Oakland, Calif., with Mark McGwire photo. 1,000 autographed by McGwire. A by McGwire $20, Unautographed $5.

GS412 GAME 4: Postmarked Oct. 19, 1988, Oakland, Calif., with Mike Scioscia photo. 500 autographed by Scioscia. A by Scioscia $8, A by Others $8, Unautographed $5.

GS413 GAME 5: Postmarked Oct. 20, 1988, Oakland, Calif., with Mickey Hatcher photo. 500 autographed by Hatcher. A by Hatcher $8, A by Others $8, Unautographed $5.

GS414 is devoted to President George Bush's election day, Nov. 8, 1988.

GS415 1984 UNITED STATES OLYMPIC TEAM: Postmarked Jan. 7, 1989, Pasadena, Calif., on the reunion of the entire U.S. Olympic baseball team (Silver Medal Winners). 500 issued picturing Mark McGwire, Will Clark and Cory Snyder. Autographs obtained by Gateway are: Sid Akins, Flavio Alfaro, Don August, Scott Bankhead, Bob Caffrey, Will Clark, Mike Dunne, Gary Green, Chris Gwynn, John Hoover, Barry Larkin, Shane Mack, John Marzano, Oddibe McDowell, Mark McGwire, Pat Pacillo, Cory Snyder, B.J. Surhoff, Billy Swift, Bobby Witt and Manager Rod Dedeaux. All on a #10 size envelope. A $225.

GS416a 500 HOME RUNS: Postmarked Jan. 14, 1989, Atlantic City, N.J., on the first ever gathering of all the living 500 home run hitters. 1,000 issued bearing artwork of Mark Lewis and autographed by all 10 500 home run hitters. 250 with Pete Rose. Postmark is correctly dated. A by 500 home run hitters $600; A with Rose, too, $625.

GS416b 500 HOME RUNS: Same as 416a, except that the U.S. Post Office incorrectly dated 233 of 1,000 issued "February 14, 1989," and overstamped the "Feb." portion of the postmark for Jan. 14 issuance. As with GS416a, all are #10 size envelope. A as above, auction value.

GS417 TRIPLE CROWN WINNERS: Postmarked Jan. 14, 1989, Atlantic City, N.J. 700 issued bearing Bill Perry artwork of living Triple Crown winners. Issued autographed by Mickey Mantle, Ted Williams, Carl Yastrzemski and Frank Robinson. A $300.

GS418 MICKEY, WILLIE & THE DUKE: Postmarked Jan. 14, 1989, Atlantic City, N.J. 700 issued bearing Mark Lewis artwork and autographed by Mickey Mantle, Willie Mays and Duke Snider, as three of the greatest center fielders to play in New York. A $250.

GS419 and GS420 are devoted to Super Bowl XXIII in Miami between the San Francisco 49ers and the Cincinnati Bengals, Jan. 22, 1989.

GS421 RESERVED

GS422a KEN GRIFFEY JR.: Postmarked April 3, 1989, Oakland, Calif., on Ken Griffey's debut as the first father/son combination to play simultaneously in the major leagues. Original issue, some silked and perhaps autographed, stolen and never retrieved. This issue is dead unless the stolen articles reappear. Unvalued.

GS422b KEN GRIFFEY JR.: Postmarked April 3, 1989, Oakland, Calif., by business machine cancellation to replace the stolen originals. 1,200 autographed. Gateway applied postage stamps prior to cancellation. Posed Griffey Jr. photo. A $35.

GS423 KEN GRIFFEY SR.: Postmarked April 3, 1989, Cincinnati, Ohio, on the opening day for Griffey Sr. Issued as a set with GS422b. 1,000 issued with action photo and autographed. A by Griffey Sr. A $20.

GS424 RESERVED

GS425 SHEA STADIUM 25th ANNIVERSARY: Postmarked April 17, 1989, New York, N.Y., to observe the 25th anniversary of Shea Stadium. 1,500 issued bearing Scott Forst artwork. 500 autographed by Tom Seaver and Jerry Koosman. A by Seaver and Koosman $40, Unautographed $5.

GS426 HARVEY HADDIX: Postmarked May 26, 1989, Milwaukee, Wis., commemorating the 30th anniversary of Haddix's pitching the only 12-inning perfect game in history. 1,000 issued autographed bearing Bill Perry artwork. A $13.

GS427 LOU GEHRIG FIRST DAY OF ISSUE: Postmarked June 10, 1989, Cooperstown, N.Y., "First Day of Issue" upon issuance of the Lou Gehrig commemorative postage stamp. 3,000 issued bearing Bill Perry artwork. 50 hand-cancellations obtained. Unautographed machine cancellations $5, hand cancellations $8.

GS428 50th ANNIVERSARY HALL OF FAME LANDMARKS: Postmarked June 12, 1989, with pictorial U.S.P.S. 50th anniversary postmark. 4,000 issued bearing Scott Forst landmark artwork. U $5.

GS429a ROY CAMPANELLA 50th ANNIVERSARY: Postmarked June 12, 1989, Cooperstown, N.Y., with pictorial 50th anniversary postmark. 190 issued with correct postmark variety of stamps. 190 issued personally by Campanella on Bill Perry artwork. A $750.

GS429b ROY CAMPANELLA 50th ANNIVERSARY: Same artwork on 67 envelopes incorrectly postmarked "First Day of Issue" on a variety of stamps June 10, 1989. Considered a postal error and scarcity. A by auction $750.

GS430 LUKE APPLING 50th ANNIVERSARY COOPERSTOWN: Postmarked June 12, 1989, Cooperstown, N.Y., with large pictorial postmark. 1,000 issued with Bill Perry artwork. U $5.

GS431 YOGI BERRA 50th ANNIVERSARY COOPERSTOWN: Postmarked June 12, 1989, Cooperstown, N.Y., with large pictorial postmark. 2,000 issued autographed with Bill Perry artwork. A $20.

GS432 LOU BOUDREAU 50th ANNIVERSARY COOPERSTOWN: Postmarked June 12, 1989, Cooperstown, N.Y., with large pictorial postmark. 1,500 issued autographed with Bill Perry artwork. A $15.

GS433 JOCKO CONLON 50th ANNIVERSARY COOPERSTOWN: Postmarked June 12, 1989, Cooperstown, N.Y., with large pictorial postmark. 1,000 issued unautographed with Bill Perry artwork. U $5.

GS434 BILLY HERMAN 50th ANNIVERSARY COOPERSTOWN: Postmarked June 12, 1989, Cooperstown, N.Y., with large pictorial postmark. 1,800 issued autographed with Bill Perry artwork. A $15.

GS435 MONTE IRVIN 50th ANNIVERSARY COOPERSTOWN: Postmarked June 12, 1989, Cooperstown, N.Y., with large pictorial postmark. 1,800 issued autographed with Bill Perry artwork. A $15.

GS436 RALPH KINER 50th ANNIVERSARY COOPERSTOWN: Postmarked June 12, 1989, Cooperstown, N.Y., with large pictorial postmark. 2,000 issued autographed with Bill Perry artwork. A $15.

GS437 SANDY KOUFAX 50th ANNIVERSARY COOPERSTOWN: Postmarked June 12, 1989, Cooperstown, N.Y., with large pictorial postmark. 2,000 issued autographed with Bill Perry artwork. A $35.

GS438 BOB LEMON 50th ANNIVERSARY COOPERSTOWN: Postmarked June 12, 1989, Cooperstown, N.Y., with large pictorial postmark. 2,000 issued autographed with Bill Perry artwork. A $15.

GS439 RESERVED

GS440 RESERVED

GS441 JOE SEWELL 50th ANNIVERSARY COOPERSTOWN: Postmarked June 12, 1989, Cooperstown, N.Y., with large pictorial postmark. 800 issued autographed with Bill Perry artwork, 1,000 issued unautographed. A $40, U $5.

GS442 LOU GEHRIG DAY: Postmarked July 4, 1989, Bronx, N.Y., to observe the 50th anniversary of Lou Gehrig Day in 1939. 1,000 issued with Bill Perry artwork of Babe Ruth and Lou Gehrig. 500 autographed by Don Mattingly. A by Mattingly $60, U $10.

GS443 1989 ALL-STAR GAME ANAHEIM: Postmarked July 11, 1989, Anaheim, Calif., with pictorial All-Star Game postmark. 650 issued bearing Scott Forst artwork. 250 autographed by Will Clark. A by Clark $25, U $5.

GS444 BO JACKSON: Postmarked July 11, 1989, Anaheim, Calif., with pictorial All-Star Game postmark. 650 issued picturing Jackson as MVP and autographed. A $75.

GS445 RESERVED

GS446 AL BARLICK HALL OF FAME INDUCTION: Postmarked July 23, 1989, Cooperstown, N.Y., on Barlick's induction into the Hall of Fame. 1,000 issued bearing Bill Perry artwork and autographed. A $14.

GS447 RED SCHOENDIENST HALL OF FAME INDUCTION: Postmarked July 23, 1989, Cooperstown, N.Y., on Schoendienst's induction into the Hall of Fame. 1,800 issued bearing Bill Perry artwork and autographed. A $18.

GS448 CARL YASTRZEMSKI HALL OF FAME INDUCTION: Postmarked July 23, 1989, Cooperstown, N.Y., on Yastrzemski's induction into the Hall of Fame. 2,000 issued bearing Bill Perry artwork and autographed. A $40.

GS449 JOHNNY BENCH HALL OF FAME INDUCTION: Postmarked July 23, 1989, Cooperstown, N.Y., on Bench's induction into the Hall of Fame. 2,000 issued bearing Bill Perry artwork and autographed. A $50.

GS450 CINCINNATI REDS 14-RUN INNING: Postmarked Aug. 3, 1989, Cincinnati, Ohio, as the Reds set a modem major league record by scoring 14 runs in the first inning against Houston. 800 issued on large #10 sized envelopes and featuring Pete Rose holding his starting lineup card. Autographed by all nine starters. 250 autographed by Jim Clancy and Bob Forsch. Cincinnati autographs include Rose, Tom Browning, Mariano Duncan, Luis Quinones, Eric Davis, Ken Griffey Sr., Rolando Roomes, Todd Benzinger, Jeff Reed and Ron Oester. A by the Reds $145, A by the Reds, Clancy and Forsch $155.

GS451 is devoted to football star Terry Bradshaw's Aug. 5, 1989, induction into the Pro Football Hall of Fame in Canton, Ohio.

GS452 RESERVED

GS453 RESERVED

GS454 RESERVED

GS455 NOLAN RYAN 5,000 STRIKEOUTS: Postmarked Aug. 22, 1989, in Arlington, Texas, as Ryan became the first pitcher to ever amass 5,000 career strikeouts. Action photo. 2,500 issued autographed. 300 autographed by Rickey Henderson, his 5,000th victim. A by Ryan $150, A by Ryan and Henderson $175.

GS456 PETE ROSE BANISHMENT: Postmarked Aug. 24, 1989, New York, N.Y., as Rose is banned from baseball by Commissioner A. Bartlett Giamatti. Photo of Rose and appropriate copy pertaining to the event. 1,500 issued autographed by Rose. A $35.

GS457 RESERVED

1989 World Series

Gateway issued four envelopes commemorating the 1989 World Series between Oakland and San Francisco. An additional envelope was issued for the fateful 1989 earthquake which interrupted the series. No variations exist within the four envelope set. Gateway acquired autographs for Jose Canseco, Will Clark, Rickey Henderson, Carney Lansford, Mark McGwire, Mike Moore and Dave Stewart.

GS458 GAME 1: Postmarked Oct. 14, 1989, Oakland, Calif. 2,000 issued with Scott Forst stadium artwork. All postmarks are philatelic licensed postmarks. Issued autographed by Canseco, Clark, McGwire or Lansford. A by Canseco $30, A by Clark $25, A by McGwire $20, A by Lansford $10, Unautographed $5.

GS459 GAME 2: Postmarked Oct. 15, 1989, Oakland, Calif. 2,000 issued picturing Rickey Henderson and bearing philatelic World Series postmarks. 1,000 issued autographed by Henderson. A $30, U $5.

GS460 EARTHQUAKE: Postmarked Oct. 17, 1989, San Francisco, Calif., with designated Oct. 17 Game 3 philatelic postmark. 3,000 issued bearing Scott Forst earthquake artwork. Initial sales designated to the American Red Cross for earthquake relief. U $5.

GS461 GAME 3: Postmarked Oct. 27, 1989, San Francisco, Calif., upon resumption of Series play. The U.S.P.S. created new Game 3 cancellations for the resumption date. 2,000 envelopes were issued bearing an action photo of Dave Stewart. 1,000 autographed by Stewart. A $20, U $5.

GS462 GAME 4: Postmarked Oct. 28, 1989, San Francisco, Calif. 2,000 issued bearing an action photo of Mike Moore. 1,000 autographed by Moore. A $10, U $5.

GS463 BILLY MARTIN IN MEMORIUM: Postmarked Dec. 29, 1989, New York, N.Y., the date funeral services were held for Martin. 1,000 issued bearing Bill Perry artwork. U $5.

GS464 is devoted to Mario Lemieux, issued Jan. 21, 1990, in Pittsburgh, in conjunction with the National Hockey League's 1990 All-Star Game.

GS465: RESERVED

GS466: RESERVED

GS467 1990 SUPER BOWL SUPERDOME: Issued Jan. 28, 1990, in conjunction with Super Bowl XXIV between the San Francisco 49ers and Denver Broncos.

GS468 1990 SUPER BOWL SUPERDOME: Issued in conjunction with Super Bowl XXIV between the San Francisco 49ers and Denver Broncos.

GS469 1990 SUPER BOWL SUPERDOME: Issued in conjunction with Super Bowl XXIV between the San Francisco 49ers and Denver Broncos.

GS470: RESERVED

GS471: RESERVED

GS472 CANDLESTICK PARK 25th ANNIVERSARY: Postmarked April 12, 1990, San Francisco, Calif., on the 25th anniversary of Candlestick Park. 1,500 issued bearing Scott Forst artwork. U $5.

GS473 HOUSTON ASTRODOME 25th ANNIVERSARY: Postmarked April 12, 1990, Houston, Texas, on the 25th anniversary of the opening of the first dome. 1,500 issued bearing Scott Forst artwork. U $5.

GS474: RESERVED

GS475: RESERVED

GS476 NOLAN RYAN 6th NO-HITTER: Postmarked by machine cancellation June 11, 1990, Oakland, Calif., as Ryan became the first pitcher to toss six no-hitters. 2,000 issued with posed photo of Ryan. All autographed. A $65.

GS477: Is devoted to the 30th anniversary of the fight between Floyd Patterson and Ingomar Johansson, when Patterson became the first fighter to regain the heavyweight title. Postmarked June 20, 1990.

GS478 DAVE STEWART NO-HITTER: Postmarked June 29, 1990, Toronto, Canada, as Stewart pitched his first career no-hitter and first of two no-hitters on this date. 1,000 issued bearing a Stewart action photo and autographed. A $25.

GS479: RESERVED

GS480: RESERVED

GS481: RESERVED

GS482 NOLAN RYAN 300 WINS: Postmarked July 31, 1990, Arlington, Texas, as Ryan gets his 300th career victory. 2,000 issued bearing a Ryan action photo and autographed. A $35.

GS483: Is devoted to Tom Landry's induction into the Pro Football Hall of Fame in Canton, Ohio, on Aug. 8, 1990.

GS484: Is devoted to Bob Griese's induction into the Pro Football Hall of Fame in Canton, Ohio, on Aug. 8,1990.

GS485: RESERVED

GS486: RESERVED

GS487: RESERVED

GS488: RESERVED

GS489: RESERVED

GS490 JIM PALMER HALL OF FAME INDUCTION: Postmarked Aug. 6, 1990, in Cooperstown, N.Y., as Palmer is inducted into the Baseball Hall of Fame. 2,000 issued bearing Bill Perry artwork and autographed. A $25.

GS491 JOE MORGAN HALL OF FAME INDUCTION: Postmarked Aug. 6, 1990, in Cooperstown, N.Y., as Morgan is inducted into the Baseball Hall of Fame. 2,000 issued bearing Bill Perry artwork and autographed. A $30.

GS492: RESERVED

GS493: RESERVED

GS494: RESERVED

GS495 CECIL FIELDER OVER THE ROOF: Postmarked Aug. 25, 1990, Detroit, Mich., as Fielder became only the third player to hit a home run over the left field roof at Tiger Stadium. 500 issued with action Fielder photo and autographed. A $40.

GS496 KEN GRIFFEY JR. AND SR. TEAMMATES: Postmarked Aug. 31, 1990, Seattle, Wash., as father and son play together on the same team simultaneously for the first time in major league history. 1,000 issued bearing Bill Perry artwork and autographed by both Griffeys. A $50.

GS497: RESERVED

GS498: RESERVED

GS499: Is devoted to the 30th anniversary when Muhammad Ali, as Cassius Clay, won an Olympic Gold Medal in boxing.

GS500: RESERVED

GS501 LAST GAME AT COMISKEY PARK: Postmarked Sept. 30, 1990, Chicago, Ill., the date of the last major league game played at old Comiskey Park. 1,500 issued bearing Scott Forst stadium artwork. Issued unautographed. U $5.

GS502 CECIL FIELDER 500 HOME RUNS: Postmarked Oct. 3, 1990, Bronx, N.Y., as Fielder becomes only the 11th player to hit 50 or more home runs in a season. 1,000 issued with action photo and autographed. A $25.

GS503 NEGRO LEAGUE PLAYERS ASSOCIATION ASSISTANCE REUNION: Postmarked Oct. 14, 1990, Baltimore, Md., at the first general meeting of the NLPA. Four envelopes designed and autographed. 1,000 with the design of the Negro League players riding a Model T as illustrated by Bill Perry. Autographed by Armando Vazquez, Garnett Blair, Mahlin Duckett, Stanley Glenn, Gene Benson, Larry Kimbrough, Napoleon Gulley and Double Duty Radcliff. $100.

GS504 NEGRO LEAGUE PLAYERS ASSOCIATION ASSISTANCE REUNION: Postmarked Oct. 14, 1990, Baltimore, Md., at the first general meeting of the NLPA. 1,000 issued with brown background and illustrations of four players in action. Bill Perry artwork. Autographed by Monte Irvin, Leon Day, Colonel Jimmie Crutchfield, Clyde McNeal, Quincy Trouppe, Bill Wright and Max Manning. $100.

GS505 NEGRO LEAGUE PLAYERS ASSOCIATION ASSISTANCE REUNION: Postmarked Oct. 14, 1990, at the first general meeting of the NLPA. 1,000 issued with a red border design with batter and catcher as illustrated by Bill Perry. Autographed by Jake Sanders, Jehosi Head, Frank Evans, Marlin Carter, Lester Lockett, Thomas Sampson, Elmer Knox, Pat Patterson and Buck Leonard. $100.

GS506a NEGRO LEAGUE PLAYERS ASSOCIATION ASSISTANCE REUNION: Postmarked Oct. 14, 1990, Baltimore, Md. 500 issued with "ASSISTANCE REUNION" as top caption. Blue borders with player holding a bat, as illustrated by Bill Perry. Auto-graphed by Wilmer Fields, Verdell Mathis, Bubba Hyde, George Giles, Josh Gibson Jr., John Miles, Bob Thurman, Willie Pope, Josh Johnson and Lou Dials. $110.

GS506b NEGRO LEAGUE PLAYERS ASSOCIATION ASSISTANCE REUNION: Same illustration and autographs as above. 500 issued with ASSISTANCE REUNION cap-tion below the artwork, rather than above. $110.

1990 World Series

Gateway issued a set of four envelopes, one for each game the Series was played in Cin-cinnati and Oakland. As in all previous years, a Scott Forst stadium artwork appears on Game 1, followed by actual game photos for Games 2 through 4. A Game 3 variation exists. Gateway acquired autographs for Eric Davis, Norm Charlton, Rob Dibble, Billy Hatcher, Lou Piniella, Jose Rijo and Chris Sabo.

GS507 GAME 1: Postmarked Oct. 16, 1990, Cincinnati, Ohio. 1,500 issued bearing Scott Forst stadium artwork. Autographed by Lou Piniella or Eric Davis. A by Davis $15, A by Piniella $15, Unautographed $5.

GS508 GAME 2: Postmarked Oct. 17, 1990, Cincinnati, Ohio. 1,500 issued picturing Billy Hatcher and Carney Lansford. 500 autographed by Hatcher. A by Hatcher $8, U $5.

GS106 Hank Aaron

GS110 Jackie Robinson

GS509a GAME 3: Postmarked Oct. 19, 1990, Oakland, Calif. 750 issued picturing Chris Sabo and autographed. A by Sabo $10.

GS509b GAME 3: Postmarked Oct. 19, 1990, Oakland, Calif. 750 issued picturing Rob Dibble. Same copy as GS509a. 500 autographed by Dibble and 200 by Charlton. A by Dibble $8, A by Charlton and Dibble $15.

GS510 GAME 4: Postmarked Oct. 20, 1990, Oakland, Calif. 1,500 issued picturing Jose Rijo and 500 autographed. A by Rijo $10, U $5.

GS511: Is devoted to Otis Anderson, who gained his 10,000th career yard rushing. Postmarked Dec. 9, 1990, New York, N.Y.

GS512: RESERVED

GS513: RESERVED

GS514: RESERVED

GS515: RESERVED

GS516 ATLANTA FULTON COUNTY STADIUM 25th ANNIVERSARY: Postmarked April 12, 1991, Atlanta, Ga. 1,500 issued bearing Scott Forst artwork. U $4.

GS517 NEW COMISKEY FIRST GAME: Postmarked April 18, 1991, Chicago, Ill., upon the first game played in the new park. 1,500 issued bearing Scott Forst stadium artwork. 500 issued autographed by Robin Ventura; 300 by autographed by Ventura and Alan Trammell. A by Ventura $15, A by Ventura and Trammell $25, U $5.

GS518 ANAHEIM STADIUM 25th ANNIVERSARY: Postmarked April 19, 1991, Anaheim, Calif., to commemorate the 25th anniversary of Anaheim Stadium. 1,500 issued bearing large pictorial postal cancellation. Issued unautographed. U $5.

GS519 NOLAN RYAN SEVENTH NO-HITTER: Postmarked by machine cancellation on various postage stamps May 1, 1991, Arlington, Texas, as Ryan became the first pitcher to pitch seven no-hitters. 1,500 issued bearing Ryan action photo and autographed by Ryan. 250 autographed by Roberto Alomar, his last out and strikeout. A by Ryan $75, A by Ryan and Alomar $100.

GS520 RICKEY HENDERSON ALL-TIME STOLEN BASE RECORD: Postmarked May 1, 1991, Oakland, Calif., as Henderson passes Lou Brock on the all-time stolen base list. Photo of Henderson and Brock in ceremonies. 1,000 issued autographed by Henderson. A by Henderson $75, A by Henderson and Brock $100.

GS521 BUSCH STADIUM 25th ANNIVERSARY: Postmarked May 12, 1991, St. Louis, Mo., to commemorate the 25th anniversary of the opening of Busch Stadium. 1,500 issued bearing Scott Forst artwork. 500 autographed by Mike Shannon. A by Shannon $12, U $4.

GS522 RESERVED

GS523 RESERVED

GS524a GEORGE SISLER: Postmarked by hand-cancellation June 29, 1991, Washington, D.C., in commemoration of Sisler's 41-game hitting streak, passed this date in 1941 by Joe DiMaggio. 100 issued bearing Bill Perry artwork. U value by auction, A by DiMaggio add $75.

GS524b GEORGE SISLER: Same design as above. 500 envelopes machine cancelled June 29,1991. U $5, A by DiMaggio add $75.

GS525a "WEE" WILLIE KEELER: Postmarked by hand-cancellation July 2, 1991, Bronx, N.Y., in commemoration of Keeler's 44-game hitting streak, passed this date in 1941 by Joe DiMaggio, thus setting a new record. Issued unautographed. Bill Perry artwork. U value by auction, A by DiMaggio add $75.

GS525b "WEE" WILLIE KEELER: Same design as above. 500 envelope machine-cancelled July 2,1991, Bronx, N.Y. U $5, A by Joe DiMaggio add $75.

GS526 RESERVED

GS527 JOE DIMAGGIO 50th ANNIVERSARY: Postmarked July 16, 1991, Cleveland, Ohio, in commemoration of Joe DiMaggio's record 56-game hitting streak. 500 issued autographed bearing Bill Perry artwork. Another 100 unautographed. A $100.

GS528 KELTNER/BOUDREAU 50th ANNIVERSARY: Postmarked July 17, 1991, Cleveland, Ohio, to commemorate Ken Keltner and Lou Boudreau for their fielding exploits which ended Joe DiMaggio's historic hitting streak at 56 games. 500 issued bearing Bill Perry artwork of Keltner and Boudreau. Autographed by both. A $50.

GS529a GAYLORD PERRY HALL OF FAME INDUCTION: Postmarked July 21, 1991, Cooperstown, N.Y., as Gaylord Perry is inducted into the Hall of Fame. 750 issued bearing Bill Perry artwork of Perry in Cleveland uniform. A by Perry $25.

GS529b GAYLORD PERRY HALL OF FAME INDUCTION: Same design and postmark as above, except Perry is shown in a San Francisco uniform. Artwork by Bill Perry. A $25.

GS530 RESERVED

GS531 RESERVED

GS532 TONY LAZZERI HALL OF FAME INDUCTION: Postmarked July 21, 1991, Cooperstown, N.Y., as Lazzeri is inducted into the Hall of Fame. 1,000 issued unautographed bearing artwork by Bill Perry. U $5.

GS533 RESERVED

GS534 DAVE WINFIELD 400 HOME RUNS: Postmarked Aug. 12, 1991, Minneapolis, Minn., as Winfield hit his 400th home run of his major league career. 1,000 issued autographed. A $30.

GS535 EDDIE GAEDEL 40th ANNIVERSARY: Postmarked Aug. 19, 1991, St. Louis, Mo., to commemorate the 40th anniversary of the St. Louis Browns' hiring a 3'7" midget, Gaedel, to bat against Bob Cain of Detroit. 750 issued autographed by Cain, bearing Bill Perry artwork. A by Cain $15.

GS536 RESERVED

GS537a BRET SABERHAGEN NO-HITTER: 100 envelopes hand-cancelled Aug. 26, 1991, in Kansas City, as Saberhagen no-hit the Chicago White Sox. Of the 100, about 60 were cancelled with purple ink and 40 were cancelled in black ink. Each bears an action photo and is autographed by Saberhagen. A $225.

GS537b BRET SABERHAGEN NO-HITTER: 500 machine-cancelled Aug. 26, 1991, with the same cachet photo, copy and autograph. A $40.

GS538 is devoted to a basketball "First Day of Issue" cachet, postmarked Aug. 28, 1991, in Springfield, Mass.

GS539 is devoted to basketball star Larry Bird and is a "First Day of Issue" postmarked Aug. 28, 1991, Springfield, Mass.

GS540 on - There are various numbers yet to be assigned.

GSxxx When the previous numbers are assigned, the next one is for TED WILLIAMS 50th ANNIVERSARY: Postmarked Sept. 28, 1991, Philadelphia, Pa., in commemoration of Ted Williams being the last player to bat .400 or more in a season. 500 issued bearing Bill Perry artwork and autographed by Williams. A $75.

Z Silk Cachets

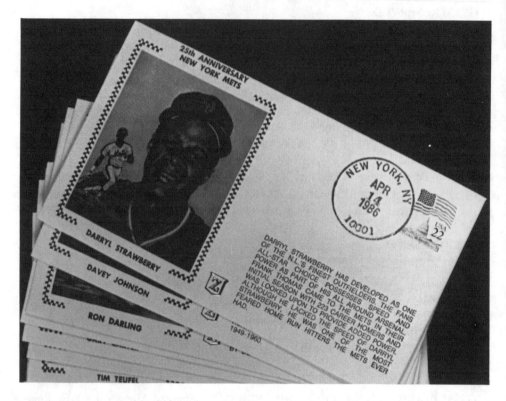

When Don Mattingly tied Dale Long's record of eight homers in eight consecutive games, Historic Limited Editions was there to capture the event on a silk-cacheted philatelic cover.

The process begins with a staff artist who does an original painting of a ballplayer or event. The painting is then reproduced on specially-manufactured silk-like cloth in full color.

These silk cachets are then applied by hand to envelopes which have been stamped and postmarked by the post office in the corresponding city where the event occurred.

In the case of the Mattingly record, company president John Zaso, with a few minutes to spare before a midnight deadline, flew to Arlington, Texas, to secure a postmark with the date of the event - July 18, 1987. Six hundred envelopes were created.

Generally, 200 to 600 covers are produced per event, depending on the player and/or event involved and potential demand by collectors. Mattingly has been one of the more popular players. Several events, including the World Series, playoffs, All-Star games and Hall of Fame inductions, are commemorated annually. Year-end award winners are also recognized.

The covers are suitable for autographing, although the company does offer a limited number already signed by the players. Investment potential varies, but some command far more than the original issue price. For example, the cachet honoring Reggie Jackson's 500th home run had an issue price of $4 but is now up to $65.

Historic Limited Editions is located in Williston Park, N.Y.

REGGIE JACKSON BECAME ONLY THE 13th PLAYER IN MAJOR LEAGUE HISTORY TO REACH 500 CAREER HOMERUNS, WHEN HE CONNECTED IN THE SEVENTH INNING OFF OF ROYALS STARTER BUD BLACK. IT WAS THE 22nd HOMERUN OF THE SEASON FOR THE 38 YEAR OLD SLUGGER. HANK AARON HEADS A LIST OF 11 HALL OF FAMERS WHO HAVE PASSED THE 500 PLATEAU. REGGIE IS SURE TO BE ENSHRINED AND JOIN THE RANKS OF THE HALL OF FAMES ALL-TIME SLUGGERS.

Z Silk Cachets

BASEBALL EVENT COVERS	ISSUE DATE	QNTY	NEW ISSUE PRICE	CURRENT PRICE
60th Anniversary of Yankee Stadium-Ruth Cachet	4/18/83	600	$4.00	$20.00
Billy Martin Returns	4/12/83	600	4.00	20.00
S.F. Giants combo - Marichal, Perry, Cepeda	2&4/05/83	600	4.00	30.00
Dave Righetti No Hitter	7/04/83	600	4.00	15.00
Whitey Herzog Man of the Year	1/20/83	600	4.00	7.50
1983 Yankee Old-Timers Game - DiMaggio	7/16/83	600	4.00	20.00
1983 Yankee Old-Timers Game - Ford	7/16/83	600	4.00	15.00
1983 Yankee Old-Timers Game - Maris	7/16/83	600	4.00	10.00
1983 Yankee Old-Timers Game - Rizzuto	7/16/83	600	4.00	12.00
George Brett Pine Tar Game &	7/24/83			
George Brett Pine Tar Playoff set (2)	8/18/83	600	8.00	40.00
Carl Yastrzemski Retires	9/29/83	600	4.00	35.00
Yogi Berra Named Yankee Manager	12/16/83	600	4.00	10.00
Lou Piniella Retires	6/16/84	600	4.00	8.00
Dwight Gooden 1984 All-Star Game	7/10/84	600	4.00	25.00
Gary Carter 1984 All-Star Game	7/10/84	600	4.00	25.00
1984 Yankee Old-Timers Game - Ford	7/21/84	600	4.00	12.00
1984 Yankee Old-Timers Game - Rizzuto	7/21/84	600	4.00	10.00
1984 Yankee Old-Timers Game - Maris	7/21/84	600	4.00	8.00
1984 Yankee Old-Timers Game - Howard	7/21/84	600	4.00	8.00
Dale Berra Traded to Yankees	12/21/84	600	4.00	5.00
Reggie Jackson 500th Home Run	9/17/84	600	4.00	65.00
Willie Mays Reinstated	2/14/85	600	4.00	8.00
Gene Mauch - Angels Opening Day	4/09/85	600	4.00	5.00
Tommy Lasorda - L.A. Dodgers Opening Day	4/12/86	600	4.00	6.00
Bob Feller Cracker Jacks Classic	7/01/85	600	4.00	7.50
Joe Garagiola Cracker Jacks Classic	7/01/85	600	4.00	7.50
Nolan Ryan 4,000 Strikeouts	7/11/85	600	4.00	25.00
LaMarr Hoyt 1985 All-Star Game	7/26/85	600	4.00	5.00
1985 Baseball Strike	8/06/85	600	4.00	5.00
1985 Baseball Strike Settlement	8/07/85	600	4.00	5.00
Rod Carew Hit #3,024	8/30/85	600	4.00	10.00

Commemoratives

Reggie Jackson 1,000 Extra Base Hits	8/30/85	600	4.00	25.00
Pete Rose Ties &	9/08/85			
Pete Rose Breaks Ty Cobb's Hit Record set	9/11/85	600	4.00	50.00
Hubie Brooks' 100th R.B.I.	10/06/85	600	4.00	6.00
Bret Saberhagen 1985 World Series MVP	10/27/85	600	4.00	7.50
Don Sutton 300 Wins	6/18/86	600	4.00	15.00
Fernando Valenzuela All-Star Game	7/15/86	600	4.00	8.00
Tim Raines All-Star Game	7/14/87	600	4.00	6.00
Paul Molitor 3 Stolen Base Record	7/26/87	600	4.00	6.00
Paul Molitor Hitting Streak	8/25/87	600	4.00	10.00
Bob Boone Record Games Caught	9/16/87	600	4.00	12.00
Wade Boggs 1987 Batting Title	10/04/87	600	4.00	8.00
Frank Viola World Series MVP	10/25/87	600	4.00	7.50
Mike Schmidt Ties Mantle HR Record	6/17/88	600	4.00	15.00
Tom Browning 1st Perfect Game	9/16/88	600	4.00	12.50
Wade Boggs 200 Hits, 6 straight seasons	9/20/88	600	4.00	8.00
Nolan Ryan 5,000 Strikeouts	8/22/89	600	10.00	65.00
Bob Feller 50th Anniversary No Hitter	4/06/90	600	4.00	7.50
Mike Schmidt #20 Retired	5/26/90	600	4.00	15.00
Mike Schmidt #20 Retired, different cachet	5/26/90	600	4.00	15.00
Rickey Henderson Ties Ty Cobb S.B. Record	5/26/90	600	4.00	15.00
Rickey Henderson Breaks Ty Cobb Record	5/29/90	600	4.00	17.50
Nolan Ryan 6th No Hitter	6/11/90	600	10.00	15.00
1990 All-Star Game (logo) Chicago	7/10/90	4000	4.00	5.00
Nolan Ryan 300 Wins	7/31/90	600	10.00	20.00
Cecil Fielder 50 H.R. Club	10/03/90	600	5.00	10.00
Jose Rijo 1990 World Series MVP	10/20/90	600	4.00	5.00
Nolan Ryan 7th No Hitter	5/02/91	600	10.00	25.00
Rickey Henderson Ties Brock's S.B. Record	4/28/91	600	8.00	15.00
Rickey Henderson Breaks Brock's S.B. Record	5/01/91	600	8.00	20.00

BROOKLYN DODGERS EVENTS	DATE	ISSUE QNTY	NEW ISSUE PRICE	CURRENT PRICE
Ebbets Field Opens	4/09/99	600	$4.00	$6.00
Jackie Robinson Signs With The Dodgers	4/11/88	600	4.00	6.00
Jackie Robinson First Game	4/15/88	600	4.00	6.00
Don Drysdale Opening Day 1956	4/17/88	600	4.00	6.00
Red Barber First Dodger Broadcast	4/18/88	600	4.00	6.00
Pee Wee Reese Dodger Shortstop	4/24/88	600	4.00	6.00
Chuck Connors Only Brooklyn Game	5/01/88	600	4.00	6.00
Carl Erskine Second No Hitter	5/12/88	600	4.00	6.00
Cookie Lavagetto Brooklyn Hall of Fame	6/12/88	600	4.00	6.00
Mickey Owen Brooklyn Hall of Fame	6/12/88	600	4.00	6.00
Cal Abrams Brooklyn Hall of Fame	6/12/88	600	4.00	6.00
Gene Hermanski Brooklyn Hall of Fame	6/12/88	600	4.00	6.00
George "Shotgun" Shuba Brooklyn Hall of Fame	6/12/88	600	4.00	6.00
Eddie Miksis Brooklyn Hall of Fame	6/12/88	600	4.00	6.00
1949 All-Star Game Roy Campanella	6/12/88	600	4.00	6.00
Andy Pafko Traded To Dodgers	6/14/88	600	4.00	6.00
Carl Erskine First No Hitter	6/19/88	600	4.00	6.00
Clyde King First Brooklyn Game	6/21/88	600	4.00	6.00
Tom Lasorda First Brooklyn Game	8/05/88	600	4.00	6.00
First T.V. Game	8/26/88	600	4.00	6.00
Clem Labine Pitches First Complete Game	8/28/88	600	4.00	6.00
Dodger Sym-Phoney	9/24/88	600	4.00	6.00
Last Game At Ebbets Field	9/24/88	600	4.00	6.00

RICKEY HENDERSON, THE YANKEES MAN OF STEEL, HAS BROKEN THE YANKEE STOLEN BASE RECORD THAT WAS HELD FOR 71 YEARS BY FRITZ MAISEL. HENDERSON STOLE HIS 75TH BASE IN THE THIRD INNING, WIPING OUT MAISEL'S RECORD OF 74 ACHIEVED IN 1914.

Sal Maglie No-Hitter	9/25/88	600	4.00	6.00
1955 World Series Don Newcombe	9/28/88	600	4.00	6.00
1955 World Series Duke Snider	9/28/88	600	4.00	6.00
1955 World Series Carl Furillo	9/29/88	600	4.00	6.00
1955 World Series Gil Hodges	10/01/88	600	4.00	6.00
1955 World Series Roger Craig	10/02/88	600	4.00	6.00
Leo Durocher 1941 World Series	10/02/88	600	4.00	6.00
Preacher Roe 1949 World Series	10/02/88	600	4.00	6.00
Lavagetto Breaks Up No Hitter	10/03/88	600	4.00	6.00
Ralph Branca Shot Heard Around the World	10/03/88	600	4.00	6.00
1955 World Series Sandy Amoros Catch	10/04/88	600	4.00	6.00
Johnny Podres First World Series Win	10/04/88	600	4.00	6.00
Larry MacPhail 1941 World Series	10/04/88	600	4.00	6.00

BROOKLYN DODGERS SERIES	ISSUE DATE	QNTY	NEW ISSUE PRICE	CURRENCY PRICE
First Night Game At Ebbets Field	xxx	600	$4.00	$6.00
Johnny Vander Meer 2nd No Hitter	6/15/88	600	4.00	6.00
Ed Roebuck - Dodger Series	4/18/89	600	4.00	6.00
Pete Reiser - Dodger Series	5/25/89	600	4.00	6.00
Rex Barney - Dodger Series	6/11/89	600	4.00	6.00
Joe Hattan - Dodger Series	6/11/89	600	4.00	6.00
Eddie Stanky - Dodger Series	6/11/89	600	4.00	6.00
Clyde King - Dodger Series	6/11/89	600	4.00	6.00
Billy Cox - Dodger Series	6/17/89	600	4.00	6.00
Bill Phifer - Dodger Series	6/19/89	600	4.00	6.00
Dixie Walker - Dodger Series	8/07/89	600	4.00	6.00
Dolph Camilli - Dodger Series	8/23/89	600	4.00	6.00
Kirby Higbe - Dodger Series	9/07/89	600	4.00	6.00
Billy Herman - Dodger Series	9/13/89	600	4.00	6.00
Whitlow Wyatt - Dodger Series	9/24/89	600	4.00	6.00
Joe Black - Dodger Series	10/01/89	600	4.00	6.00
Billy Loes - Dodger Series	10/03/89	600	4.00	6.00
Al Gionfriddo - Dodger Series	10/05/89	600	4.00	6.00
Walter Alston - Dodger Series	11/28/89	600	4.00	6.00

Commemoratives

NEW YORK METS EVENTS	ISSUE DATE	QNTY	NEW ISSUE PRICE	CURRENT PRICE
Tom Seaver Returns to Mets	4/15/83	600	$4.00	$10.00
Dwight Gooden Rookie Strikeout Record	9/07/84	600	4.00	8.00
Gooden All-Time Rookie S.O. Record	9/12/84	600	4.00	15.00
Gooden - Strawberry back-to-back R.O.Y.	11/20/84	600	4.00	8.00
Gooden 1984 Rookie of the Year	11/20/84	600	4.00	20.00
Gary Carter Traded to Mets	12/10/84	600	4.00	7.50
Carter Opening Day	4/09/85	600	4.00	6.00
Seaver 15th Start Opener (White Sox)	4/09/85	600	4.00	7.50
Gooden K Day	4/14/85	600	4.00	8.00
Gooden Receives Rookie of Year Award	4/28/85	600	4.00	8.00
Keith Hernandez Gold Glove Award	4/28/85	600	4.00	6.00
Keith Hernandez Silver Slugger Award	4/28/85	600	4.00	6.00
Strawberry All-Star Game 1985	7/16/85	600	4.00	6.00
Seaver 300th Win	8/04/85	600	4.00	10.00
Gooden Youngest 20-Game Winner	8/25/85	600	4.00	8.00
Gooden Cy Young Award	11/13/85	600	4.00	10.00
25th Anniversary of Mets set of 25 covers	4/14/86	600	75.00	125.00
Gooden Opening Day	4/24/86	600	4.00	6.00
Sid Fernandez All-Star Game	7/15/86	600	4.00	7.50
Strawberry All-Star Game 1986	7/15/86	600	4.00	7.50
Gooden - Mets Clinch N.L. East	9/17/87	600	4.00	8.00
Tom Seaver Returns	6/06/87	600	4.00	6.00
Tom Seaver Retires	6/22/87	600	4.00	7.00
Keith Hernandez 2,000 Hits	9/15/87	600	4.00	7.00
Gooden All-Star Game 1988	7/22/88	600	4.00	6.00
Strawberry All-Star Game 1988	7/12/88	600	4.00	6.00
Gooden 1,000 Strikeouts	7/22/88	600	4.00	7.00
Mookie Wilson 1,000 Career Hits	7/22/88	600	4.00	7.00
Seaver #41 Retired	7/24/88	600	4.00	8.00
Gary Carter 300th Home Run	8/11/88	600	4.00	9.00
Ray Knight World Series MVP	10/27/86	600	4.00	6.00

YANKEE SERIES NO. 1	ISSUE DATE	QNTY	NEW ISSUE PRICE	CURRENT PRICE
Mantle Throws First Ball	4/16/85	600	$4.00	$10.00
Billy's Back IV	4/28/85	600	4.00	10.00
Dale & Yogi Berra	4/16/85	600	4.00	6.00
Mickey Mantle Reinstated	2/14/85	600	4.00	10.00
Roger Maris Honored	4/15/85	600	4.00	6.00
Don Baylor - Roberto Clemente Award	2/14/85	600	4.00	7.50
Butch Wynegar - Opening Day	4/16/85	600	4.00	5.00
Dave Winfield - All-Star Game	7/16/85	600	4.00	12.00
Enos Slaughter - Elected to H.O.F.	3/06/85	600	4.00	6.00
Don Mattingly - 145 RBI	10/06/85	600	4.00	25.00
Phil Niekro - 300 Wins	10/06/85	600	4.00	15.00
Rickey Henderson - All-Star Game	7/16/85	600	4.00	15.00
Phil Rizzuto Day	8/04/85	600	4.00	8.00
Rickey Henderson - Stolen Base Record	9/25/85	600	4.00	20.00
Mattingly Breaks Maris RBI record	10/03/85	600	4.00	20.00
Lefty Gomez - Pocono Memorabilia Show	9/21/85	600	4.00	7.00
Bill Virdon - 4th Cracker Jack Classic	7/01/85	600	4.00	5.00
Bobby Richardson - 4th Cracker Jack Classic	7/01/85	600	4.00	6.00
Hank Bauer - Old-Timers Day	7/13/85	600	4.00	6.00

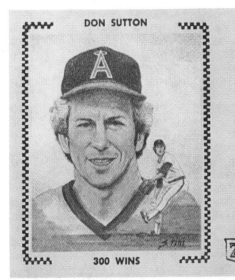

DON SUTTON BECAME THE 19TH PITCHER IN MAJOR LEAGUE HISTORY TO WIN 300 GAMES BY BEATING THE TEXAS RANGERS 5-1 BEFORE AN ANAHEIM STADIUM CROWD OF 37,004. THE 41 YEAR OLD SUTTON, WHO IS PITCHING IN HIS 21ST YEAR IN THE MAJORS PITCHED HIS FINEST GAME OF THE YEAR EVENING HIS RECORD AT 5-5 WITH HIS "NIFTY" 3-HITTER.

Eddie Lopat - Old-Timers Day	7/13/85	600	4.00	6.00
Gene Woodling - Old-Timers Day	7/13/85	600	4.00	6.00
Tommy Byrne - Old-Timers Day	7/13/85	600	4.00	6.00
Don Mattingly - 200 Hits	xxx	600	4.00	30.00
Joe DiMaggio Day	7/13/85	600	4.00	15.00
Baylor Breaks Minoso Record	8/28/85	600	4.00	8.00
Rickey Henderson Scores 138th Run	9/25/85	600	4.00	15.00
Mattingly Ties Gehrig Doubles	9/25/85	600	4.00	20.00
Thurman Munson - Memorial Park	7/13/85	600	4.00	25.00
Miller Huggins - Memorial Park	7/13/85	600	4.00	5.00
Lou Gehrig - Memorial Park	7/13/85	600	4.00	6.00
Babe Ruth - Memorial Park	7/13/85	600	4.00	6.00
Yogi Berra Dismissed	4/28/85	600	4.00	5.00
Rickey Henderson - Yankee Debut	4/23/85	600	4.00	8.00
Mike Pagliarulo - Sports Show	10/20/85	600	4.00	5.00
Baseball Strike	8/06/85	600	4.00	5.00
Baseball Strike Settlement	8/07/85	600	4.00	5.00

YANKEE SERIES NO. 2	ISSUE DATE	QNTY	NEW ISSUE PRICE	CURRENT PRICE
Don Mattingly - 1985 A.L. M.V.P.	11/20/85	600	$4.00	$40.00
Lou Piniella Named Manager	10/27/85	600	4.00	5.00
Ron Guidry - Gold Glove Award	11/20/85	600	4.00	6.00
Dave Righetti - All-Star Game	7/15/86	600	4.00	12.50
Rodger Maris Dies	12/14/85	600	4.00	6.00
Dave Winfield - Gold Glove Award	11/20/85	600	4.00	7.50
Final Tribute to Roger Maris	12/23/85	600	4.00	6.00
Mickey Mantle - 7th National	7/25/86	600	4.00	8.00
Whitey Ford - 7th National	7/26/86	600	4.00	7.00
Dave Righetti - Opening Day	4/08/86	600	4.00	7.00
Ralph Houk - Nat'l. Old-Timers Day	6/23/86	600	4.00	6.00
Bill Skowron - Nat'l. Old-Timers Day	6/23/86	600	4.00	6.00
Whitey Ford Honored	4/17/86	600	4.00	6.00
Lou Piniella - Opening Day	4/08/86	600	4.00	6.00
Mickey Mantle - Memorial Park	7/19/86	600	4.00	35.00

Commemoratives

Mickey Mantle - Diamond Legends Show	10/05/86	600	4.00	10.00
Casey Stengel - Memorial Park	7/19/86	600	4.00	6.00
Joe McCarthy - Memorial Park	7/19/86	600	4.00	5.00
Don Mattingly - Gold Glove	11/20/85	600	4.00	15.00
Ed Barrow - Memorial Park	7/19/86	600	4.00	6.00
Tony Kubek - Old-Timers Day	7/19/86	600	4.00	6.00
Luis Arroyo - Old-Timers Day	7/19/86	600	4.00	6.00
Dave Winfield - 300th Home Run	8/20/86	600	4.00	10.00
John Blanchard - Old-Timers Day	7/19/86	600	4.00	6.00
"Catfish" Hunter - Nat'l. Old-Timers Day	6/23/86	600	4.00	7.50
Ron Guidry - Career Milestones	4/24/86	600	4.00	7.00
25th Anniversary - Maris 61st Home Run	10/01/86	600	4.00	8.00
Billy Martin Day	8/10/86	600	4.00	7.00
Dave Winfield - 100 RBI	9/29/86	600	4.00	10.00
30th Anniversary Larsen Perfect Game	10/08/86	600	4.00	10.00
Mattingly Breaks Doubles Record	10/05/86	600	4.00	20.00
Dave Winfield - All-Star Game	7/15/86	600	4.00	8.00
Don Mattingly 200 Hits	11/09/86	600	4.00	20.00
Clete Boyer - Old-Timers Day	7/19/86	600	4.00	6.00
Bill Monbouquette - National Classic	6/23/86	600	4.00	6.00
Virgil Trucks - Arlington National	7/26/86	600	4.00	6.00
35th Anniversary Reynolds' No-Hitter	9/28/86	600	4.00	7.00

YANKEE SERIES NO. 3	ISSUE DATE	QNTY	NEW ISSUE PRICE	CURRENT PRICE
Rick Rhoden - Yankee Debut	4/15/87	600	$4.00	$5.00
Willie Randolph - Opening Day	4/13/87	600	4.00	6.00
Dave Winfield - Opening Day	4/13/87	600	4.00	7.50
"Catfish" Hunter - Old-Timers Day	7/11/87	600	4.00	6.00
Don Mattingly - 100 Career Home Runs	6/27/87	600	4.00	15.00
Tommy Henrich - Pride of the Yankees	4/16/87	600	4.00	6.00
Elston Howard - Memorial Park	7/11/87	600	4.00	6.00
Joe DiMaggio - Memorial Park	7/11/87	600	4.00	15.00
Tommy John - All-Time Win List	6/15/87	600	4.00	7.00
Bob Lemon - Old-Timers Day	7/11/87	600	4.00	6.00
Billy Martin - Old-Timers Day	7/11/87	600	4.00	7.00
Bobby Murcer - Old-Timers Day	7/11/87	600	4.00	6.00
Mattingly - Breaks Ruth's Record	7/19/87	600	4.00	15.00
Niekro Brothers - 530 Victories	6/01/87	600	4.00	8.00
Phil Rizzuto - Memorial Park	7/11/87	600	4.00	8.00
Charles Hudson - Opening Day	4/13/87	600	4.00	5.00
Jacob Ruppert - Memorial Park	7/11/87	600	4.00	6.00
Mattingly Ties Consecutive Home Run Record	7/18/87	600	4.00	15.00
Joe DiMaggio - 8th National	7/08/87	600	4.00	25.00
Special Ruth/Mantle Limited Edition	7/06/83	600	4.00	8.00
Mattingly - 6th Grand Slam Home Run	9/29/87	600	4.00	15.00
Whitey Ford - Memorial Park	8/02/87	600	4.00	8.00
Rick Cerone - Opening Day	4/13/87	600	4.00	5.00
Wayne Tolleson - Opening Day	4/13/87	600	4.00	5.00
Dave Righetti - Rolaids Relief Man	10/05/87	600	4.00	6.00
Al Leiter Debut	9/15/87	600	4.00	5.00
Dick Howser - Memorial Tribute	6/17/87	600	4.00	6.00
Billy's Back V	10/19/87	600	4.00	7.00
Lefty Gomez - Pride of Yankees	4/16/87	600	4.00	7.00
Don Mattingly - Gold Glove	7/10/87	600	4.00	15.00
Dave Winfield - All-Star Game	7/14/87	600	4.00	7.50

BALLPARK SERIES

BUSCH STADIUM COMPLETED THE 1990 SEASON ON SEPTEMBER 30, 1990. HOME OF THE ST. LOUIS CARDINALS SINCE MAY 12, 1966. A STATUE OF STAN "THE MAN" MUSIAL ALONG WITH THE GATEWAY ARCH ARE AMONG THE LANDMARKS AT THE HOTBED OF BASEBALL. HOME OF LOU BROCK AND BOB GIBSON BOTH HALL OF FAMERS.

BUSCH STADIUM

"Catfish" Hunter Day	8/02/87	600	4.00	6.00
Ron Guidry - Gold Glove	7/10/87	600	4.00	6.00
Dennis Rasmussen - 1st Home Game	4/18/87	600	4.00	5.00
Ernie Lombardi - 1st Stadium Home Game	9/17/87	600	4.00	5.00
"Catfish" Hunter - Induction to H.O.F.	7/26/87	600	4.00	6.00
Reggie Jackson - Last Stadium Game	9/02/87	600	4.00	10.00

YANKEE SERIES NO. 4	ISSUE DATE	QNTY	NEW ISSUE PRICE	CURRENT PRICE
Rickey Henderson - All-Star Game	7/12/88	600	$4.00	$6.00
Don Mattingly - Gold Glove Award	12/02/87	600	4.00	6.00
Dave Winfield - Gold Glove Award	12/02/87	600	4.00	6.00
Jack Clark - New Designated Hitter	1/06/88	600	4.00	5.00
Thurman Munson - Opening Day	4/05/88	600	4.00	6.00
Elston Howard - Opening Day	4/05/88	600	4.00	5.00
Mike Pagliarulo - Opening Day	4/05/88	600	4.00	5.00
Gary Ward - Opening Day	4/05/88	600	4.00	5.00
Rickey Henderson - Opening Day	4/05/88	600	4.00	6.00
Dallas Green - New Manager	10/07/88	600	4.00	5.00
Dave Winfield - All-Star Game	7/12/88	600	4.00	7.50
Pope Paul VI - Memorial Park	10/04/88	600	4.00	7.50
Rickey Henderson - Stolen Base Record	9/25/88	600	4.00	5.00
Claudell Washington - Longest Season Game	9/11/88	600	4.00	5.00
Phil Rizzuto - Announcer	6/11/88	600	4.00	5.00
Bill Dickey - Memorial Park	7/16/88	600	4.00	5.00
Lefty Gomez - Memorial Park	7/16/88	600	4.00	6.00
Yogi Berra - Memorial Park	7/16/88	600	4.00	6.00
Lou Piniella - New York Manager	6/23/88	600	4.00	5.00
Bucky Dent - Old-Timers Day	7/16/88	600	4.00	5.00
Sparky Lyle - Old-Timers Day	7/16/88	600	4.00	5.00
Don Mattingly - Gold Glove	12/07/88	600	4.00	6.00
Al Leiter - First Season Win	4/09/88	600	4.00	5.00
Mantle - Second East Coast National	8/18/89	600	4.00	6.00
Dave Winfield - 200th Home Run	8/17/88	600	4.00	6.00

Commemoratives

Chambers - Old-Timers Day	7/16/88	600	4.00	6.00
Joe DiMaggio - Second East Coast Nat'l.	8/18/89	600	4.00	10.00
Bill White - Announcer	7/16/88	600	4.00	5.00
Roger Maris - Monument Park	7/16/88	600	4.00	6.00
Pope John Paul II - Memorial Park	10/02/88	600	4.00	8.00
Elston Howard - Pride of Yankees	4/04/88	600	4.00	5.00
Don Mattingly - Opening Day	4/05/88	600	4.00	6.00
Dave Winfield - RBI Mark	4/30/88	600	4.00	6.00
Mickey Rivers - Old-Timers Day	7/16/88	600	4.00	5.00
Rick Rhoden - Last Season Game	9/25/88	600	4.00	5.00
Thurman Munson - Pride of Yankees	4/04/88	600	4.00	5.00

YANKEE SERIES NO. 5	ISSUE DATE	QNTY	NEW ISSUE PRICE	CURRENT PRICE
Joe Pepitone Old-Timers Day	7/15/89	600	$4.00	$5.00
Rickey Henderson Lead-Off H.R. Record	4/28/89	600	4.00	5.00
Don Mattingly - All-Star Game	7/11/89	600	4.00	6.00
Mike Pagliarulo - Exhibition Game	4/01/89	600	4.00	5.00

BALLPARK SERIES COVERS	ISSUE DATE	QNTY	NEW ISSUE PRICE	CURRENT PRICE
Ebbets Field	4/09/88	600	$4.00	$7.00
Ebbets Field	4/09/90	600	4.00	6.00
Wrigley Field 1st Official Night Game	8/08/88	600	4.00	12.50
Wrigley Field 1st night game played	8/09/88	600	4.00	12.50
Seals Stadium	8/15/88	600	4.00	10.00
Yankee Stadium	4/18/88	600	4.00	7.00
Los Angeles Coliseum	4/18/88	600	4.00	8.00
Fenway Park 75th Anniversary Postmark	4/20/87	550	4.00	15.00
Candlestick Park	4/12/88	600	4.00	6.00
Forbes Field	6/30/89	600	4.00	6.00
Shea Stadium	4/03/89	600	4.00	6.00
Polo Grounds	10/03/89	600	4.00	6.00
Baltimore Memorial Stadium	4/15/89	600	4.00	6.00
Shibe Park	7/13/90	600	4.00	6.00
Arlington Stadium	4/21/90	600	4.00	6.00
Wrigley Field	4/23/90	600	4.00	6.00
Griffith Stadium	9/21/89	600	4.00	6.00
Busch Stadium	9/30/90	600	4.00	6.00
Los Angeles Coliseum	9/30/90	600	4.00	6.00
Comiskey Park	9/30/90	600	4.00	6.00
Wrigley Field - Los Angeles	10/01/90	600	4.00	6.00
Sportsmans Park	10/15/90	600	4.00	6.00
Braves Field	9/21/90	600	4.00	6.00
Houston Astrodome	9/30/90	600	4.00	6.00
Crosley Field	4/08/91	600	4.00	6.00
Royals Stadium	7/01/91	600	4.00	6.00
Anaheim Stadium	7/01/91	600	4.00	6.00
Veteran's Stadium	7/01/91	600	4.00	6.00

MAJOR LEAGUE PLAYOFFS	ISSUE DATE	QNTY	NEW ISSUE PRICE	CURRENT PRICE
N.L. Phillies - Steve Carlton	10/08/83	600	$4.00	$12.50
A.L. Orioles - Jim Palmer	10/08/83	600	4.00	12.50
N.L. Padres - Steve Garvey	10/07/84	600	4.00	10.00
A.L. Tigers - Kirk Gibson	10/05/84	600	4.00	12.50

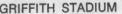

BALLPARK SERIES

GRIFFITH STADIUM

GRIFFITH STADIUM WAS THE HOME OF THE WASHINGTON SENATORS. IT WAS NAMED AFTER CLARK GRIFFITH THE OWNER OF THE SENATORS AND WAS THE SITE OF MICKEY MANTLE'S FAMOUS 565 FT. HOME RUN, ONE OF THE LONGEST EVER MEASURED. THE STADIUM CLOSED ON SEPTEMBER 21, 1961.

N.L. Cardinals - Ozzie Smith	10/16/85	600	4.00	10.00
A.L. Royals - George Brett	10/16/85	600	4.00	12.50
N.L. Houston - Mike Scott	10/15/86	600	4.00	6.00
A.L. Red Sox - Marty Barrett	10/15/86	600	4.00	6.00
N.L. Cardinals - Jeffrey Leonard	10/14/87	600	4.00	6.00
A.L. Twins - Gary Gaetti	10/12/87	600	4.00	5.00
N.L. Dodgers - Orel Hershiser	10/12/88	600	4.00	7.50
A.L. Oakland - Jose Canseco	10/09/88	600	4.00	8.00
N.L. Giants - Will Clark	10/09/89	600	4.00	8.00
A.L. Oakland - Rickey Henderson	10/08/89	600	4.00	8.00
N.L. Reds - Randy Myers	10/12/90	300	7.00	7.50
N.L. Reds - Rob Dibble	10/12/90	300	7.00	7.50
A.L. Oakland - Dennis Eckersley	10/10/90	600	4.00	5.00

WORLD SERIES COVERS	ISSUE DATE	QNTY	NEW ISSUE PRICE	CURRENT PRICE
1983 World Series set of 5 covers	1983	600	$20.00	$50.00
1984 World Series set of 5 covers	1984	600	20.00	45.00
1985 World Series set of 7 covers	1985	600	28.00	45.00
1986 World Series set of 7 covers	1986	600	28.00	45.00
1987 World Series set of 7 covers	1987	600	25.00	40.00
1988 World Series set of 5 covers	1988	600	20.00	35.00
1989 World Series set of 4 covers	1989	600	16.00	30.00
1989 Game 3 Earthquake Cover - Red Cross	1989	600	5.00	25.00
1989 Game 3 Earthquake Cover	1989	600	5.00	15.00
1990 World Series set of 4 covers	1990	600	16.00	20.00

HALL OF FAME ELECTIONS	ISSUE DATE	QNTY	NEW ISSUE PRICE	CURRENT PRICE
1985 - Lou Brock	1985	600	$4.00	$8.00
1985 - Hoyt Wilhelm	1985	600	4.00	6.00
1985 - Floyd Vaughan	1985	600	4.00	5.00
1985 - Enos Slaughter	1985	600	4.00	7.00
1986 - Willie McCovey	1986	600	4.00	8.00

Commemoratives

1986 - Bobby Doerr	1986	600	4.00	7.00
1986 - Ernie Lombardi	1986	600	4.00	5.00
1987 - Catfish Hunter	1987	600	4.00	7.00
1987 - Billy Williams	1987	600	4.00	7.00
1987 - Ray Dandridge	1987	600	4.00	7.00
1988 - Willie Stargell	1988	600	4.00	6.00
1989 - Johnny Bench	1989	600	4.00	7.00
1989 - Al Barlick	1989	600	4.00	6.00
1989 - Red Schoendienst	1989	600	4.00	6.00
1989 - Carl Yastrzemski	1989	600	4.00	7.00

HALL OF FAME INDUCTIONS	ISSUE DATE	QNTY	NEW ISSUE PRICE	CURRENT PRICE
1983 - Juan Marichal	1983	600	$4.00	$12.50
1983 - Walter Alston	1983	600	4.00	6.00
1983 - Brooks Robinson	1983	600	4.00	12.50
1983 - George Kell	1983	600	4.00	9.00
1984 - Pee Wee Reese	1984	600	4.00	12.50
1984 - Harmon Killebrew	1984	600	4.00	8.00
1984 - Luis Aparicio	1984	600	4.00	9.00
1984 - Don Drysdale	1984	600	4.00	10.00
1984 - Rick Ferrell	1984	600	4.00	9.00
1985 - Lou Brock	1985	600	4.00	9.00
1985 - Hoyt Wilhelm	1985	600	4.00	6.00
1985 - Floyd Vaughan	1985	600	4.00	6.00
1985 - Enos Slaughter	1985	600	4.00	7.00
1986 - Willie McCovey	1986	600	4.00	9.00
1986 - Bobby Doerr	1986	600	4.00	7.00
1986 - Ernie Lombardi	1986	600	4.00	5.00
1987 - Catfish Hunter	1987	600	4.00	9.00
1987 - Billy Williams	1987	600	4.00	7.00
1987 - Ray Dandridge	1987	600	4.00	7.00
1988 - Willie Stargell	1988	600	4.00	7.00
1989 - Johnny Bench	1989	600	4.00	10.00
1989 - Al Barlick	1989	600	4.00	6.00
1989 - Red Schoendienst	1989	600	4.00	6.00
1989 - Carl Yastrzemski	1989	600	4.00	8.00
1990 - Joe Morgan	1990	600	4.00	6.00
1990 - Jim Palmer	1990	600	4.00	7.00
1990 - Combo: Morgan and Palmer	1990	600	4.00	8.00
1991 - Rod Carew	1991	400	4.00	7.00
1991 - Ferguson Jenkins	1991	400	4.00	7.00
1991 - Gaylord Perry	1991	400	4.00	7.00

ROTHSTEIN SHOW COVERS	ISSUE DATE	QNTY	NEW ISSUE PRICE	CURRENT PRICE
First East Coast National - Grote-Snider	8/20/88	300	$3.00	$12.50
First East Coast National	8/20/88	300	3.00	12.50
Second East Coast National - Seaver	8/18/89	300	3.00	12.50
Second East Coast National - Mantle	8/18/89	400	3.00	15.00
Second East Coast National - DiMaggio	8/18/89	400	3.00	15.00
Third East Coast National - Killebrew	8/17/90	400	3.00	7.50
Third East Coast National - Hunter	8/17/90	300	3.00	10.00
Third East Coast National - Seaver	8/17/90	400	3.00	10.00
Third East Coast National - Mantle	8/17/90	300	3.00	10.00
Fourth East Coast National - Mantle	8/17/91	400	3.00	12.50

Fourth E.C.N. - Aaron, Mantle, Musial, Robinson	8/16/91	400	3.00	10.00
N.Y. Spectacular - Salute to 1969 Mets (5)	3/17/89	300	10.00	35.00
N.Y. Spectacular II - Kranepool	2/17/90	400	3.00	5.00
N.Y. Spectacular III - Thomson, Vander Meer	2/09/91	250	3.00	20.00
N.Y. Spectacular III - Throneberry-Podres	2/09/91	250	3.00	20.00
Hall of Fame Show: 19 players on six covers	5/26/91	146	15.00	250.00
Raritan Center II - Irvin, Roberts, Kiner	10/27/90	250	3.00	20.00
Raritan Center II - Kaline, Robinson, Ford	10/27/90	250	3.00	20.00
Raritan Center II - Mantle	10/27/90	350	3.00	25.00
Raritan Center IV - Mays, Gravey, McGraw	10/26/91	300	3.00	5.00

CY YOUNG AWARD WINNERS	ISSUE DATE	ISSUE QNTY	NEW CURRENT PRICE	PRICE
A.L. 1984 Willie Hernandez	10/30/84	600	$4.00	$6.00
N.L. 1984 Rick Sutcliffe	10/23/84	600	4.00	10.00
A.L. 1985 Bret Saberhagen	11/11/85	600	4.00	7.50
N.L. 1985 Dwight Gooden	11/13/85	600	4.00	12.50
A.L. 1986 Roger Clemens	11/12/86	600	4.00	10.00
N.L. 1986 Mike Scott	11/11/86	600	4.00	6.00
A.L. 1987 Roger Clemens	11/11/87	600	4.00	8.00
N.L. 1987 Steve Bedrosian	11/09/87	600	4.00	7.00
A.L. 1988 Frank Viola	11/09/88	600	4.00	6.00
N.L. 1988 Orel Hershiser	11/10/88	600	4.00	7.00
A.L. 1989 Bret Saberhagen	11/15/89	600	4.00	6.00
N.L. 1989 Mark Davis	11/13/89	600	4.00	5.00

ROOKIE OF THE YEAR	ISSUE DATE	ISSUE QNTY	NEW CURRENT PRICE	PRICE
A.L. 1984 Alvin Davus	11/23/84	600	$4.00	5.00
N.L. 1984 Dwight Gooden	11/20/84	600	4.00	17.50
A.L. 1985 Ozzie Guillen	11/25/85	600	4.00	7.50
N.L. 1985 Vince Coleman	11/27/85	600	4.00	10.00
N.L. 1986 Todd Worrell	11/24/86	600	4.00	5.00
N.L. 1987 Benito Santiago	11/04/87	600	4.00	6.00
A.L. 1988 Walt Weiss	11/02/88	600	4.00	6.00
N.L. 1988 Chris Sabo	11/01/88	600	4.00	6.00
A.L. 1989 Gregg Olson	11/07/89	600	4.00	6.00

M.V.P. COVERS	ISSUE DATE	ISSUE QNTY	NEW CURRENT PRICE	PRICE
A.L. 1983 Cal Ripken Jr.	1/29/84	600	$4.00	45.00
N.L. 1983 Dale Murphy	1/29/84	600	4.00	45.00
A.L. 1984 Willie Hernandez	11/06/85	600	4.00	7.00
A.L. 1985 Don Mattingly	11/20/85	600	4.00	40.00
N.L. 1985 Willie McGee	11/18/85	600	4.00	7.00
A.L. 1986 Roger Clemens	11/18/86	600	4.00	15.00
N.L. 1986 Mike Schmidt	11/19/86	600	4.00	35.00
N.L. 1987 Andre Dawson	11/02/87	600	4.00	8.00
N.L. 1988 Kirk Gibson	11/15/88	600	4.00	7.00
A.L. 1989 Robin Yount	11/20/89	600	4.00	10.00
N.L. 1989 Kevin Mitchell	11/22/89	600	4.00	6.001

Perez-Steele postcards

Perez-Steele
Hall of Fame art postcards

In its first postcard set issued in 1980, Perez-Steele Galleries of Ft. Washington, Pa., produced the first of four limited-edition sets. The first set is devoted to members of the Hall of Fame and is updated every two years to add the new inductees. 10,000 numbered sets are produced each time. The postcards are generally collected autographed; the prices below are for autographed postcards. "I" means it's impossible that the player could have signed the postcard. Generally, unsigned postcards range from $5-$20, with the following exceptions: Satchel Paige and Jackie Robinson are $35 each; Roberto Clemente and Willie Mays are $40 each; Ty Cobb and Lou Gehrig are $50 each; Babe Ruth is $75; Joe DiMaggio and Ted Williams are $100; and Mickey Mantle and Stan Musial are $150 each.

First Series (Brown, 1980)

1 Ty Cobb I
2 Walter Johnson I
3 Christy Mathewson I
4 Babe Ruth I
5 Honus Wagner I
6 Morgan Bulkeley I
7 Ban Johnson I
8 Nap Lajoie I
9 Connie Mack I
10 John McGraw I
11 Tris Speaker I
12 George Wright I
13 Cy Young I
14 Grover Alexander I
15 Alexander Cartwright I
16 Henry Chadwick I
17 Cap Anson I
18 Eddie Collins I
19 Candy Cummings I
20 Charles Comiskey I
21 Buck Ewing I

Connie Mack

22 Lou Gehrig I
23 Willie Keeler I
24 Hoss Radbourne I
25 George Sisler I
26 A.G. Spalding I
27 Rogers Hornsby I
28 Kenesaw Landis I
29 Roger Bresnahan I
30 Dan Brouthers I

Second Series (Green, 1980)

31 Fred Clarke I
32 Jimmy Collins I
33 Ed Delahanty I
34 Hugh Duffy I
35 Hughie Jennings I
36 King Kelly I
37 Jim O'Rourke I
38 Wilbert Robinson I
39 Jesse Burkett I
40 Frank Chance I
41 Jack Chesbro I
42 Johnny Evers I
43 Clark Griffith I
44 Thomas McCarthy I
45 Joe McGinnity I
46 Eddie Plank I
47 Joe Tinker I
48 Rube Waddell I
49 Ed Walsh I
50 Mickey Cochrane I
51 Frankie Frisch I
52 Lefty Grove I
53 Carl Hubbell .... $75-$125
54 Herb Pennock I
55 Pie Traynor I
56 Mordecai Brown I
57 Charlie Gehringer .... $60-$85
58 Kid Nichols I
59 Jimmy Foxx I
60 Mel Ott I

Third Series (Blue, 1980)

61 Harry Heilmann I
62 Paul Waner I
63 Edward Barrow I
64 Chief Bender I
65 Tom Connolly I
66 Dizzy Dean I
67 Bill Klem I
68 Al Simmons I
69 Bobby Wallace I

70 Harry Wright I
71 Bill Dickey .... $75-$100
72 Rabbit Maranville I
73 Bill Terry .... $65-$100
74 Frank Baker I
75 Joe DiMaggio .... $250-$300
76 Gabby Hartnett I
77 Ted Lyons $300
78 Ray Schalk I
79 Dazzy Vance I
80 Joe Cronin .... $900-$1,100
81 Hank Greenberg .... $400-$450
82 Sam Crawford I
83 Joe McCarthy I
84 Zack Wheat I
85 Max Carey I
86 Billy Hamilton I
87 Bob Feller .... $25-$35
88 Bill McKechnie I
89 Jackie Robinson I
90 Edd Roush .... $100-$150

Fourth Series (1981, Red)

91 John Clarkson I
92 Elmer Flick I
93 Sam Rice I
94 Eppa Rixey I
95 Luke Appling .... $40-$65
96 Red Faber I
97 Burleigh Grimes .... $275-$350
98 Miller Huggins I
99 Tim Keefe I
100 Heinie Manush I
101 John Ward I
102 Pud Galvin I
103 Casey Stengel I
104 Ted Williams $235
105 Branch Rickey I
106 Red Ruffing .... $650-$800
107 Lloyd Waner .... $3,200-$3,500
108 Kiki Cuyler I
109 Goose Goslin I
110 Joe Medwick I
111 Roy Campanella .... $275-$350
112 Stan Coveleski .... $650-$700
113 Waite Hoyt .... $550-$650
114 Stan Musial .... $50-$75
115 Lou Boudreau .... $15-$25
116 Earl Combs I
117 Ford Frick I
118 Jesse Haines I

119 David Bancroft I
120 Jake Beckley...I

Fifth Series (1981, Yellow)

121 Chick Hafey..I
122 Harry Hooper...I
123 Joe Kelley..I
124 Rube Marquard..I
125 Satchel Paige ....$3,200-$3,500
126 George Weiss...I
127 Yogi Berra $35
128 Josh Gibson I
129 Lefty Gomez....................................$70-$100
130 William Harridge.......................................I
131 Sandy Koufax ....$40-$60
132 Buck Leonard ....$25-$35
133 Early Wynn.....................................$25-$35
134 Ross Youngs I
135 Roberto Clemente.......................................I
136 Billy Evans I
137 Monte Irvin..$25
138 George Kelly ....$650-$700
139 Warren Spahn $30
140 Mickey Welch I
141 Cool Papa Bell...............................$65-$85
142 Jim Bottomley I
143 Jocko Conlan ....$70-$90
144 Whitey Ford....................................$30
145 Mickey Mantle ....$250-$275
146 Sam Thompson...I
147 Earl Averill ....$800-$900
148 Bucky Harris I
149 Billy Herman..................................$40-$50
150 Judy Johnson ....$80-$100

Sixth Series (1981, Orange)

151 Ralph Kiner $25
152 Oscar Charleston I
153 Roger Connor I
154 Cal Hubbard I
155 Bob Lemon $25
156 Freddie Lindstrom I
157 Robin Roberts...$25
158 Ernie Banks $40
159 Martin Dihigo..I
160 John Lloyd..I
161 Al Lopez...$80-$90
162 Amos Rusie I
163 Joe Sewell...$75
164 Addie Joss I
165 Larry MacPhail...I
166 Eddie Mathews....................................$25

167 Warren Giles I
168 Willie Mays..$65
169 Hack Wilson..I
170 Al Kaline...$25-$30
171 Chuck Klein I
172 Duke Snider ....$25-$30
173 Tom Yawkey I
174 Rube Foster I
175 Bob Gibson $25
176 Johnny Mize..$40
A. Abner Doubleday I
B. Stephen C. Clark I
C. Paul S. Kerr I
D. Edward W. Stack......................................$15

Seventh Series (1983, Brown)

177 Hank Aaron...$40
178 Happy Chandler ....$40-$55
179 Travis Jackson............................$80-$125
180 Frank Robinson $25
181 Walter Alston ....$1,000-$1,250
182 George Kell $20
183 Juan Marichal..$25
184 Brooks Robinson..................................$25

Eighth Series (1985, Green)

185 Luis Aparicio $25

186 Don Drysdale...$50
187 Rick Ferrell...$25
188 Harmon Killebrew..............................$25
189 Pee Wee Reese $35
190 Lou Brock..$25
191 Enos Slaughter......................................$20
192 Arky Vaughan..I
193 Hoyt Wilhelm $20

Ninth Series (1987, Blue)
194 Bobby Doerr..$20
195 Ernie Lombardi I
196 Willie McCovey $25
197 Ray Dandridge.......................................$20
198 Catfish Hunter $20
199 Billy Williams $20
E. Perez-Steele Galleries

Tenth Series (1989, Red)
200 Willie Stargell $20
201 Al Barlick..$20
202 Johnny Bench............................... $30-$40
203 Red Schoendienst....................................$20
204 Carl Yastrzemski.....................................$35
F. George Bush/Edward D. Stack

Eleventh Series (1991)
205 Joe Morgan $30
206 Jim Palmer $25
207 Rod Carew $30
208 Ferguson Jenkins $20
209 Tony Lazzeri I
210 Gaylord Perry..$20
211 Bill Veeck.. I

Perez-Steele Great Moments Checklist

In 1985, Perez-Steele Galleries offered 5,000 numbered sets of Great Moments postcards, with periodical updates. These cards are generally purchased for the autograph, or to be autographed; these prices listed are for signed postcards. "I" means it's impossible that the player could have signed the card. Generally, unsigned cards sell for about $5-$15 each, except for higher priced cards for players such as Babe Ruth, Lou Gehrig, Ted Williams, Mickey Mantle, Stan Musial and Charlie Gehringer.

First Series (1985)
1 Babe Ruth...I
2 Al Kaline $25
3 Jackie Robinson...............................I
4 Lou Gehrig I
5 Whitey Ford.........................$25-$30
6 Christy Mathewson I
7 Roy Campanella ....$225-$300
8 Walter Johnson I
9 Hank Aaron $35
10 Cy Young.......................................I
11 Stan Musial...................................$60
12 Ty Cobb I

Second Series (1987)
13 Ted Williams ....$100-$135
14 Warren Spahn $20
15 The Waner Brothers I
16 Sandy Koufax.....................$45-$60
17 Robin Roberts..............................$20
18 Dizzy Dean.....................................I
19 Mickey Mantle $135
20 Satchel Paige I
21 Ernie Banks $35
22 Willie McCovey $20

CARL YASTRZEMSKI

23 Johnny Mize.................................$30
24 Honus Wagner...............................I

Third Series (1988)

25 Willie Keeler I
26 Pee Wee Reese $35
27 Monte Irvin...$20
28 Eddie Mathews...$20
29 Enos Slaughter..$18
30 Rube Marquard...I
31 Charlie Gehringer.......................................$80
32 Roberto Clemente..I
33 Duke Snider...$25
34 Ray Dandridge...$20
35 Carl Hubbell.......................................$50-$80
36 Bobby Doerr...$15

Fourth Series (1988)

37 Bill Dickey ....$50-$80
38 Willie Stargell...$18
39 Brooks Robinson $20
40 Tinker-Evers-Chance.....................................I
41 Billy Herman......................................$30-$40
42 Grover Alexander..I
43 Luis Aparicio......................................$20-$30
44 Lefty Gomez......................................$50-$75
45 Eddie Collins I
46 Judy Johnson I
47 Harry Heilmann...I
48 Harmon Killebrew......................................$25

Fifth Series (1990)

49 Johnny Bench $30
50 Max Carey I
51 Cool Papa Bell.................................$70-$100
52 Rube Waddell I
53 Yogi Berra $25
54 Herb Pennock I
55 Red Schoendienst $20
56 Juan Marichal $20
57 Frankie Frisch..I
58 Buck Leonard $25
59 George Kell $20
60 Chuck Klein...I

Sixth Series (1990)

61 King Kelly..I
62 Jim Hunter..$20
63 Lou Boudreau...$20
64 Al Lopez..$65-$100
65 Willie Mays.......................................$30-$50
66 Lou Brock...$20
67 Bob Lemon..$15
68 Joe Sewell, Improbable $50
69 Billy Williams $15

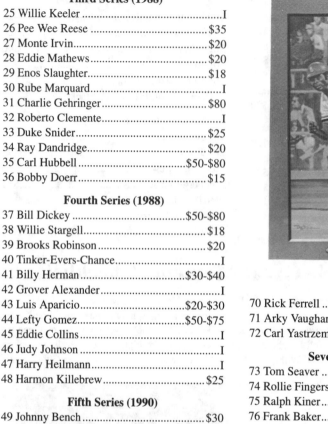

LOU BROCK

70 Rick Ferrell $20
71 Arky Vaughan I
72 Carl Yastrzemski $30

Seventh Series (1991)

73 Tom Seaver $30
74 Rollie Fingers...$20
75 Ralph Kiner...$25
76 Frank Baker..I
77 Rod Carew $30
78 Goose Goslin..I
79 Gaylord Perry..$20
80 Hack Wilson...I
81 Hal Newhouser...$20
82 Early Wynn $20
83 Bob Feller...$20
84 Branch Rickey...I

Eighth Series (1992)

85 Jim Palmer $25
86 Al Barlick...$20
87 Willie, Mickey & Duke.........................$150
88 Hank Greenberg..I
89 Joe Morgan..$20
90 Chief Bender...I
91 Reese, Robinson...$30
92 Jim Bottomley..I
93 Ferguson Jenkins.......................................$20
94 Frank Robinson..$25
95 Hoyt Wilhelm...$20
96 Cap Anson..I

Perez-Steele Celebration checklist

This 45-card set was issued in 1989 to commemorate the 50th anniversary of the Baseball Hall of Fame and the Galleries' 10th anniversary. There were 10,000 sets made. The set will not be updated; a complete set has 44 Hall of Famers and one checklist. Cards are 3 1/2-by-5 1/4 inches in size. The prices below are for signed cards. "I" means it is impossible that the player could have signed the card. Unsigned cards are generally about $8-$10 each, but are generally more for players such as Mickey Mantle, Stan Musial and Ted Williams.

1 Hank Aaron... $30
2 Luis Aparicio $20
3 Ernie Banks................................$25-$40
4 Cool Papa Bell ....$50-$100
5 Johnny Bench.................................... $30
6 Yogi Berra.. $20
7 Lou Boudreau $15
8 Roy Campanella....................$275-$350
9 Happy Chandler............................... $40
10 Jocko Conlan ....$300-$700
11 Ray Dandridge $15
12 Bill Dickey..............................$50-$75
13 Bobby Doerr $15
14 Rick Ferrell $18
15 Charlie Gehringer ....$50-$80
16 Lefty Gomez I
17 Billy Herman $30
18 Catfish Hunter................................ $15
19 Monte Irvin $18
20 Judy Johnson......................................I
21 Al Kaline... $18
22 George Kell...................................... $15
23 Harmon Killebrew $18
24 Ralph Kiner..................................... $18
25 Bob Lemon $15
26 Buck Leonard..........................$20-$30
27 Al Lopez ....$50-$100
28 Mickey Mantle............................ $125
29 Juan Marichal.................................. $15
30 Eddie Mathews $15
31 Willie McCovey.............................. $15
32 Johnny Mize............................$20-$35
33 Stan Musial ....$40-$65
34 Pee Wee Reese........................$30-$40
35 Brooks Robinson $18
36 Joe Sewell ....$50-$60
37 Enos Slaughter $15
38 Duke Snider ....$20-$30
39 Warren Spahn................................. $20

40 Willie Stargell $15
41 Bill Terry...I
42 Billy Williams................................. $12
43 Ted Williams ....$100-$125
44 Carl Yastrzemski $25

STAN MUSIAL

Collectors usually pursue Perez-Steele Celebration cards to have the players autograph them.

Perez-Steele Master Works checklist

This 50-card set was produced in two 25-card series beginning in 1990 and features 10 players on five different postcard styles. The players are Charlie Gehringer, Mickey Mantle, Willie Mays, Duke Snider, Warren Spahn, Yogi Berra, Johnny Mize, Willie Stargell, Ted Williams and Carl Yastrzemski. Four designs are modeled after the the 1888 Goodwin Champions baseball card set, the 1908 Rose Cards, the Ramly 1909 set, the 1911 gold-bordered T205 set. The last design was created by the artist, Dick Perez. There were 10,000 sets produced. Prices are for individual cards.

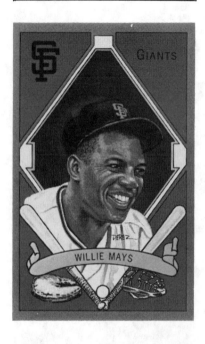

Charlie Gehringer
($7 unsigned, $60 signed)
1 Ramly
2 Goodwin
3 Rose
4 Gold Border
5 Perez-Steele

Mickey Mantle
($15 unsigned, $100 signed)
6 Ramly
7 Goodwin
8 Rose
9 Gold Border
10 Perez-Steele

Willie Mays
($8 unsigned, $40 signed)
11 Ramly
12 Goodwin
13 Rose
14 Gold Border
15 Perez-Steele

Duke Snider
($8 unsigned, $25 signed)
16 Ramly
17 Goodwin
18 Rose
19 Gold Border
20 Perez-Steele

Warren Spahn
($7 unsigned, $20 signed)
21 Ramly
22 Goodwin
23 Rose
24 Gold Border
25 Perez-Steele

Yogi Berra
($8 unsigned, $25 signed)
26 Ramly
27 Goodwin
28 Rose
29 Gold Border
30 Perez-Steele

Johnny Mize
($7 unsigned, $40 signed)
31 Ramly
32 Goodwin
33 Rose
34 Gold Border
35 Perez-Steele

Willie Stargell
($8 unsigned, $20 signed)
36 Ramly
37 Goodwin
38 Rose
39 Gold Border
40 Perez-Steele

Ted Williams
($15 unsigned, $100 signed)
41 Ramly
42 Goodwin
43 Rose
44 Gold Border
45 Perez-Steele

Carl Yastrzemski
($11 unsigned, $30 signed)
46 Ramly
47 Goodwin
48 Rose
49 Gold Border
50 Perez-Steele

Pins

Press Pins

Press pins, which have been issued since 1911, are distributed to members of the media by the host teams for World Series and All-Star games. The lapel pins provide the reporters legitimate access to cover the game.

Enamel pins have replaced the fairly ornate pins, with ribbons and medals, of the early years. Many are quite simple in their designs, which is a factor in the value of the pin; generally, the better-looking, better-conditioned pins are more valuable. Also, pins for the teams which lost usually cost less than those of the winners. But rarity and the reputation of the team are the main factors. Each team, except the 1918 Chicago Cubs, has issued a pin.

Phantom pins are those which are created by teams which might end up in post-season play, but don't, by failing to make the World Series; teams must decide to produce pins before the season is over. Several major league teams already have unused, undated pins available for future use.

All-Star pins first appeared in 1938, skipping 1939, 1940, 1942, 1944 and 1945, and then running consecutively since 1946. There are usually fewer All-Star pins available for collectors, because not as many have been made; fewer reporters cover this game compared to the number who cover the World Series.

Hall of Fame pins were first produced in 1982 by L.B. Balfour Co. to honor Hall of Fame induct-ees. Those players have their names featured on the pins, which are given to the media and dignitaries who attend the induction ceremonies.

The following pin listings show the year, the manufacturer, type of fastener, color and value.

In general, here's a price range for World Series pins for each decade:

1910s	$2,500-$18,000
1920s	$600-$4,000
1930s	$300-$5,000
1940s	$250-$2,400
1950s	$125-$1,800
1960s	$75-$450
1970s	$65-$400
1980s	$20-$150
1990s	$25-$150

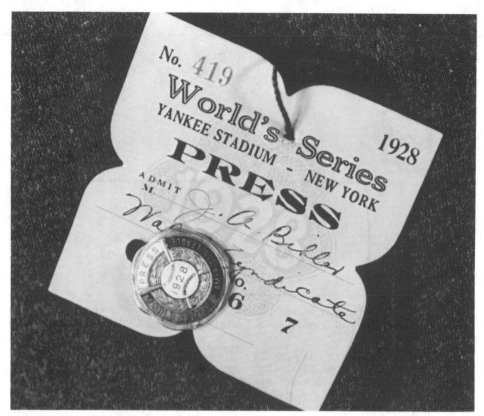

This 1928 pin, with its original card, is worth up to $2,400.

World Series

1911 Philadelphia Athletics: Allen A. Kerr; brooch; blue .... $13,850-$18,000
1912 New York Giants: Whitehead & Hoag; brooch; blue .... $6,500-$12,500
1912 Boston Red Sox: Unknown; threaded post; red .... $5,000-$6,000
1913 New York Giants: Whitehead & Hoag; threaded post; blue............................... $5,000-$10,000
1913 Philadelphia Athletics: J.E. Caldwell; brooch; blue/green .... $6,500-$6,800
1914 Boston Braves: Bent & Bush; threaded post; blue... $5,000-$5,500
1914 Philadelphia Athletics: J.E. Caldwell; brooch; blue/white/green .... $6,500-$11,000
1915 Philadelphia Phillies: J.E. Caldwell; brooch; red.. $6,000-$11,000
1915 Boston Red Sox: Bent & Bush; threaded post; gold .... $4,000-$5,500
1916 Brooklyn Dodgers: Dieges & Clust; threaded post; blue/white .... $4,000-$4,400
1916 Boston Red Sox: Bent & Bush; threaded post; red/blue.. $4,000-$5,000
1917 New York Giants: Unknown; brooch; gold... $4,000-$7,000
1917 Chicago White Sox, with banner: Greenduck; threaded post; blue .... $4,000-$9,500
1918 Boston Red Sox: Bent & Bush; threaded post; gold .... $3,000-$5,500
1919 Cincinnati Reds: Gustave Fox; threaded post; gold .... $2,500-$4,750
1919 Chicago White Sox, with banner: Greenduck; threaded post; gold................... $5,000-$12,000
1920 Brooklyn Dodgers: Unknown; threaded post; red... $2,500-$3,000
1920 Cleveland Indians enamel: Unknown; threaded post; green/white..................... $1,500-$3,000
1920 Cleveland Indians celluloid button: Unknown; safety brooch; black/white .... $2,500-$3,500
1921 New York Yankees/Giants: Whitehead & Hoag; brooches; blue/white .... $1,500-$2,500
1922 New York Yankees/Giants: Whitehead & Hoag; brooches; blue/white .... $1,500-$4,000
1923 New York Yankees: Dieges & Clust; threaded post; red/white/blue .... $1,500-$3,800
1924 New York Giants: Dieges & Clust; threaded post; blue .... $1,300-$2,600

This collection of World Series pins is from New York Yankees series.

1924 Washington Senators: Dieges & Clust; threaded post; red/white/blue .... $1,000-$1,500
1925 Pittsburgh Pirates: Whitehead & Hoag; threaded post; black/white .... $1,500-$2,500
1925 Washington Senators: Dieges & Clust; threaded post; blue .... $1,500-$2,200
1926 St. Louis Cardinals: Unknown; threaded post; red .... $1,300-$2,400
1926 New York Yankees: Dieges & Clust; threaded bost; red/white/blue .... $1,500-$2,800
1927 Pittsburgh Pirates: Whitehead & Hoag; threaded post; black/white .... $1,500-$2,400
1927 New York Yankees: Dieges & Clust; threaded post; red/white/blue .... $2,000-$3,500
1928 St. Louis Cardinals: St. Louis Button; threaded post; red/white/blue .... $650-$1,200
1928 New York Yankees: Dieges & Clust; threaded post; red/white/blue .... $1,500-$2,400
1929 Chicago Cubs: Hipp & Coburn; threaded post; red/white/blue .... $1,500-$2,200
1929 Philadelphia Athletics: Unknown; threaded post; blue/white............................... $600-$1,750
1930 St. Louis Cardinals: St. Louis Button; threaded post; red/white/blue .... $500-$1,000
1930 Philadelphia Athletics: Unknown; threaded post; blue/white............................. $2,000-$5,000
1931 St. Louis Cardinals: St.Louis Button; threaded post; red/white/blue .... $500-$900
1931 Philadelphia Athletics: Unknown; threaded post; blue/white............................. $1,300-$1,500
1932 Chicago Cubs: Dieges & Clust; threaded post; black/white................................. $1,500-$2,200
1932 New York Yankees: Dieges & Clust; threaded post; gold .... $750-$1,200
1933 New York Giants: Dieges & Clust; threaded post; red/green/blue............................. $450-$850
1933 Washington Senators: Dieges & Clust; threaded post; gold..................................... $700-$950
1934 St. Louis Cardinals: St. Louis Button; threaded post; red/white .... $600-$800
1934 Detroit Tigers: Dieges & Clust; threaded post; black/white..................................... $750-$850

World Series Pins

1912 Red Sox
$6,000

1930 Cardinals
$1,000

1936 Yankees
$800

1935 Chicago Cubs: S.D. Childs; brooch; red/white/blue .... $1,750-$2,200
1935 Detroit Tigers: Unknown; threaded post; black .... $300-$800
1936 New York Giants: Dieges & Clust; threaded post; black/white/orange .... $300-$400
1936 New York Yankees: Dieges & Clust; threaded post; red/white/blue .... $400-$800
1937 New York Giants: Dieges & Clust; threaded post; black/orange .... $400-$800
1937 New York Yankees: Dieges & Clust; threaded post; red/white/blue .... $450-$800
1938 Chicago Cubs: Lambert Bros.; brooch; red/white/blue .... $1,500-$2,250
1938 New York Yankees: Dieges & Clust; threaded post; red/white/blue .... $300-$750
1939 Cincinnati Reds: Bastian Bros.; threaded post, brooch; red/white/blue.................... $300-$450
1939 New York Yankees: Dieges & Clust; threaded post; red/white/blue .... $300-$750
1940 Cincinnati Reds: Bastian Bros.; threaded post, brooch; red/white/blue.................... $300-$475
1940 Detroit Tigers: Unknown; threaded post; gold .... $300-$650
1941 Brooklyn Dodgers: Dieges & Clust; threaded post; red/white/blue .... $450-$725
1941 New York Yankees: Dieges & Clust; threaded post; red/white/blue .... $300-$475
1942 St. Louis Cardinals: St. Louis Button; safety brooch; red/white/black .... $1,500-$2,400
1942 New York Yankees: Dieges & Clust; threaded post, brooch; silver .... $400-$500
1943 St. Louis: St. Louis Button; safety brooch; red/black/white .... $950-$1,100
1943 New York Yankees: Dieges & Clust; threaded post, brooch; silver .... $300-$500
1944 St. Louis Cardinals: St. Louis Button; threaded post; copper................................. $300-$575
1944 St. Louis Browns: St. Louis Button; threaded post; copper .... $400-$575
1945 Chicago Cubs: Unknown; threaded post; red/white/blue .... $450-$550
1945 Detroit Tigers: Unknown; threaded post; red/blue .... $300-$575
1946 St. Louis Cardinals: St. Louis Button; threaded post; red/white/silver .... $350-$500
1946 Boston Red Sox: Balfour; threaded post; red/white... $300-$600
1947 Brooklyn Dodgers: Dieges & Clust; threaded post, brooch; blue .... $400-$800
1947 New York Yankees: Dieges & Clust; threaded post; red/white/blue .... $300-$775
1948 Boston Braves: Balfour; threaded post; red/white/copper .... $325-$500
1948 Cleveland Indians: Balfour; threaded post; red/white/black...................................... $250-$450
1949 Brooklyn Dodgers: Dieges & Clust; threaded post, brooch; blue .... $375-$575
1949 New York Yankees: Dieges & Clust; threaded post, brooch red/white/blue .... $300-$550
1950 Philadelphia Phillies: Martin; needle post; red/silver .... $250-$350
1950 New York Yankees: Dieges and Clust; threaded post, brooch red/white/blue .... $300-$375

World Series Pins

1937 Giants
$800

1941 Yankees
$475

1945 Cubs
$550

1951 New York Giants: Dieges & Clust; threaded post; black/white .... $175-$300
1951 New York Yankees: Dieges & Clust; threaded post, brooch; red/white/blue .... $150-$300
1952 Brooklyn Dodgers: Dieges & Clust; threaded post, brooch; red/blue .... $400-$600
1952 New York Yankees: Balfour; threaded post, brooch; red/white/blue .... $225-$300
1953 Brooklyn Dodgers: Dieges & Clust; threaded post, brooch; white/blue .... $300-$400
1953 New York Yankees: Balfour; threaded post and brooch; red/white/blue.................... $250-$325
1954 New York Giants: Dieges and Clust; threaded post; black/white............................... $125-$200
1954 Cleveland Indians: Balfour; threaded post; red/white/blue/black............................. $200-$250
1955 Brooklyn Dodgers: Dieges & Clust; threaded post, brooch; silver/white/blue .... $350-$500
1955 New York Yankees: Balfour; threaded post, brooch; red/white/blue .... $150-$250
1956 Brooklyn Dodgers: Dieges & Clust; clasps; silver/white/blue............................. $1,400-$1,800
1956 New York Yankees: Balfour; threaded post, brooch; red/white/blue .... $150-$250
1957 Milwaukee Braves: Balfour; threaded post; copper/red... $150-$200
1957 New York Yankees: Balfour; threaded post, brooch; red/white/blue .... $150-$200
1958 Milwaukee Braves: Balfour; threaded post; black/white .... $150-$250
1958 New York Yankees: Balfour; threaded post, brooch white/blue.................................. $150-$200
1959 Los Angeles Dodgers: Balfour; threaded post, charm, brooch; white/blue................. $175-$200
1959 Chicago White Sox: Balfour; threaded post, brooch; blue/green............................... $175-$300
1960 Pittsburgh Pirates: Josten; threaded post; black/white.. $200-$375
1960 New York Yankees: Balfour; threaded post, brooch white/blue.................................. $150-$225
1961 Cincinnati Reds: Balfour; threaded post, charm; red/white/blue .... $100-$200
1961 New York Yankees: Balfour; threaded post, brooch; red/white/blue .... $150-$275
1962 San Francisco Giants: Balfour; threaded post; white .... $200-$350
1962 New York Yankees: Balfour; threaded post, brooch; red/white/blue .... $150-$200
1963 Los Angeles Dodgers: Balfour; threaded post; blue... $150-$250
1963 New York Yankees: Balfour; needle post, brooch; red/white/blue............................. $150-$200
1964 St. Louis Cardinals: Josten; threaded post, brooch; red... $125-$200
1964 New York Yankees: Balfour; needle post; red/white/blue.. $150-$200
1965 Los Angeles Dodgers: Balfour; needle post, charm; blue .... $100-$200
1965 Minnesota Twins: Balfour; needle post; red/white/blue... $75-$100
1966 Los Angeles Dodgers: Balfour; needle post, charm; blue .... $75-$100
1966 Baltimore Orioles: Balfour; needle post, clasp, charm, brooch; black/white/orange . $150-$200
1967 St. Louis Cardinals: Balfour; needle post, charms; red/white/black.......................... $75-$100
1967 Boston Red Sox: Balfour; needle post, charm; red/white/blue .... $75-$175
1968 St. Louis Cardinals: Balfour; needle post, charms; red/white/black.......................... $65-$100
1968 Detroit Tigers: Balfour; needle post, charms; blue.. $100-$175

World Series Pins

1947 Yankees
$775

1948 Indians
$450

1952 Yankees
$300

1969 New York Mets: Balfour; needle post, charm; blue/orange .... $200-$450
1969 Baltimore Orioles: Balfour; needle post, charms, clasp, brooch; black/white/orange $125-$175
1970 Cincinnati Reds: G.B. Miller; needle post, charms; red/white/black .... $100-$150
1970 Baltimore Orioles: Jenkins; needle post, clasp, charm, brooch; black/white/orange .. $100-$125
1971 Pittsburgh Pirates: Balfour; needle post; black .... $100-$125
1971 Baltimore Orioles: Balfour; needle post, clasp, brooch; black/white/orange .... $100-$150
1972 Cincinnati Reds: Balfour; needle post, charm; red/white .... $65-$125
1972 Oakland A's: Balfour; needle post, charm; green/white .... $175-$275
1973 New York Mets: Balfour; needle post, charm; orange/blue .... $100-$175
1973 Oakland A's: Josten; needle post, charms; green/white .... $200-$325
1974 Los Angeles Dodgers: Balfour; needle post, charms; blue .... $75-$150
1974 Oakland A's: Josten; needle post; green/white .... $300-$400
1975 Cincinnati Reds: Balfour; needle post, charms; red .... $100-$150
1975 Boston Red Sox: Balfour; needle post, charms; red/white .... $200-$300
1976 Cincinnati Reds: Balfour; needle post, charms; red .... $125-$150
1976 New York Yankees: Balfour; needle post; red/white/blue .... $100-$125
1977 Los Angeles Dodgers: Balfour; needle post, charms; red/white/blue .... $75-$100
1977 New York Yankees: Balfour; needle post, charms; blue .... $50-$125
1978 Los Angeles Dodgers: Balfour; needle post, charms; blue/white .... $75-$100
1978 New York Yankees: Balfour; needle post, charms; red/white/blue .... $50-$100
1979 Pittsburgh Pirates: Balfour; needle post; gold .... $45-$75
1979 Baltimore Orioles: Balfour; needle post, clasp, charm, brooch; white/black/orange ..... $45-$75
1980 Philadelphia Phillies: Balfour; needle post; gold .... $35-$50
1980 Kansas City Royals: Green Co.; needle post, charms; blue/white .... $50-$100
1981 Los Angeles Dodgers: Balfour; needle post, charms; red/white/blue .... $50-$75
1981 New York Yankees: Balfour; needle post; blue .... $45-$60
1982 St. Louis Cardinals: Balfour; needle post, charms; red .... $20-$50
1982 Milwaukee Brewers: Balfour; needle post, charms; blue .... $50-$75
1983 Philadelphia Phillies: Balfour; needle post, charms; red/white/green .... $35-$40
1983 Baltimore Orioles: Balfour; needle post, charm, brooch; orange/white/black .... $30-$50
1984 San Diego Padres: Balfour; needle post, charms; brown/white .... $40-$50
1984 Detroit Tigers: Balfour; needle post, charms; blue .... $45-$75
1985 Kansas City Royals: Green Co.; needle post, charms; blue/white .... $75-$100
1985 St. Louis Cardinals: Balfour; needle post, charms; red/black .... $75-$90

World Series Pins

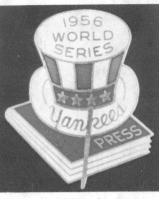

1955 Yankees
$250

1956 Yankees
$250

1960 Yankees
$225

1986 New York Mets: Balfour; needle post, charms; blue/orange .... $100-$150
1986 Boston Red Sox: Balfour; needle post, charms; red/white/blue .... $40-$75
1987 St. Louis Cardinals: Balfour; needle post, charms; red/white/gold .... $30-$65
1987 Minnesota Twins: Josten; needle post, charms; gold .... $40-$60
1988 Oakland A's: .... $40-$65
1988 Los Angeles Dodgers: .... $30-$50
1989 San Francisco Giants: .... $95-$125
1989 Oakland A's: .... $95-$125
1990 Cincinnati Reds: .... $125-$150
1990 Oakland A's: .... $50-$125
1991 Atlanta Braves: .... $30-$60
1991 Minnesota Twins: .... $30-$60
1992 Atlanta Braves: $30
1992 Toronto Blue Jays: $25
1993 Philadelphia Phillies: $30
1993 Toronto Blue Jays: $25

1963 Yankees
$200

1965 Giants
Phantom $150

1976 Reds
$150

1985 Royals
$100

1986 Red Sox
$75

1985 Cardinals
$90

1983 Orioles
$50

Phantoms

1938 Pittsburgh Pirates: Whitehead & Hoag; threaded post; red/white/black .... $500-$1,000
1944 Detroit Tigers: Unknown; threaded post; red/white/blue .... $350-$500
1945 St. Louis Cardinals: St. Louis Button; threaded post; red/white .... $400-$600
1946 Brooklyn Dodgers: Dieges & Clust; threaded post, brooch .... $100-$300
1948 Boston Red Sox: Balfour; threaded post; red/white/blue.. $1,200-$1,800
1948 New York Yankees: Dieges & Clust, threaded post; red/white/blue .... $1,600-$1,800
1949 St. Louis Cardinals: Unknown; threaded post; red/white/black .... $500-$725
1949 Boston Red Sox: Balfour; threaded post; red/white/blue.. $1,400-$1,800
1950 Brooklyn Dodgers: Balfour; threaded post; red/white/blue .... $1,600-$2,400
1951 Cleveland Indians: Balfour; threaded post; red/white/black.. $1,200-$1,750

Phantom Pins

1951 Brooklyn Dodgers: Dieges & Clust; threaded post, brooch; red/white/blue .... $125-$400
1952 New York Giants: Dieges & Clust; threaded post, brooch; white/black .... $250-$500
1955 Chicago White Sox: Unknown; threaded post; red/white/blue .... $800-$1,400
1955 Cleveland Indians: Balfour; threaded post; red/white/blue/black .... $600-$800
1956 Milwaukee Braves: Balfour; threaded post; red/copper...................................... $50-$85
1959 San Francisco Giants: Balfour; threaded post; white/black................................ $500-$800
1959 Milwaukee Braves: Balfour; threaded post, charm; red/copper............................... $475-$800
1960 Chicago White Sox: Balfour; threaded post; red/white...................................... $1,200-$1,600
1960 Baltimore Orioles: Balfour; threaded post; red/green/black .... $800-$1,250
1963 St. Louis Cardinals: Josten; threaded post; red... $75-$150
1964 Philadelphia Phillies: Martin; needle post; red/blue .... $15-$30
1964 Chicago White Sox: Balfour; needle post; red/white/blue .... $800-$1,100
1964 Baltimore Orioles: Balfour; needle post; orange/white/black................................ $625-$850
1964 Cincinnati Reds: Balfour; needle post, brooch; red/white/black............................ $100-$125
1965 San Francisco Giants: Balfour; threaded post; white/black................................. $95-$150
1966 Pittsburgh Pirates: Balfour; needle post; black .... $375-$450
1966 San Francisco Giants: Balfour; threaded post; white/black................................ $1,200-$1,400
1967 Minnesota Twins: Balfour; needle post; red/white/blue..................................... $25-$50
1967 Chicago White Sox: Balfour; needle post; red/white/blue .... $50-$75
1969 San Francisco Giants: Balfour; needle post; white/black................................... $100-$150
1969 Atlanta Braves: Josten; needle post and charm; blue .... $45-$75
1969 Minnesota Twins: Balfour; needle post; red/white/blue..................................... $15-$35
1970 California Angels: Balfour; needle post; red/white/blue.................................... $450-$500
1970 Chicago Cubs: Balfour; needle post; blue/white .... $450-$500
1971 San Francisco Giants: Balfour; needle post; black... $125-$150
1971 Oakland A's (smaller pin): Unknown; needle post; green/white .... $100-$150
1971 Oakland A's (larger pin): Balfour; needle post, charm; green/white .... $650-$750
1972 Chicago White Sox: Balfour; needle post; red/white/blue .... $900-$1100
1972 Pittsburgh Pirates: Balfour; needle post; no color.. $900-$1,000
1974 Texas Rangers: Balfour; needle post; red/white/blue/gold.................................. $400-$550
1975 Oakland A's: Josten; needle post; green/white .... $300-$450
1976 Philadelphia Phillies: Balfour; needle post; no color..................................... $35-$75
1977 Boston Red Sox: Balfour; needle post, charm; red/blue..................................... $50-$75
1978 San Francisco Giants: Balfour; needle post; black/orange.................................. $35-$50
1978 Cincinnati Reds: Balfour; needle post, charm; red .... $50-$75
1978 Milwaukee Brewers: .... $50-$75
1979 Montreal Expos: Balfour; needle post; no color .... $45-$65
1979 California Angels: Balfour; needle post; red/white/blue.................................... $200-$300
1979 Houston Astros: Balfour; needle post; white/blue.. $850-$900
1980 Houston Astros: Balfour; needle post, charm; blue/orange.................................. $85-$125
1981 Oakland A's: Balfour; needle post, charm; green... $85-$125
1981 Chicago Cubs: Balfour; needle post; red/white/blue .... $175-$200
1981 Philadelphia Phillies: Balfour; needle post; red/white.................................... $45-$75
1982 Los Angeles Dodgers: Balfour; needle post, charm; red/white/blue .... $125-$150
1983 Milwaukee Brewers: Balfour; needle post; white/black...................................... $200-$250
1983 Chicago White Sox: Balfour; needle post; red/blue .... $35-$50
1983 Pittsburgh Pirates: Balfour; needle post; black .... $200-$275
1984 Chicago Cubs: Balfour; needle post, charm; red/black .... $200-$250
1985 Toronto Blue Jays: Balfour; needle post, charm; red/white/blue .... $200-$250

Phantom Pins

1986 California Angels: Gem Peddler; needle post, charm; no color .... $175-$200
1986 Houston Astros: Balfour; needle post, charm; red/blue .... $150-$175
1987 Detroit Tigers: Balfour; needle post; blue/white/gold .... $100-$175
1987 New York Yankees: Balfour; threaded post; blue/white/gold .... $175-$200
1987 New York Mets: Balfour; needle post; orange/black/white/gold .... $200-$225
1987 San Francisco Giants: Balfour; needle post; black/white/gold .... $60-$75
1987 Boston Red Sox: .... $150-$175
1988 Boston Red Sox: .... $75-$100
1990 Pittsburgh Pirates: .... $300-$350
1990 Boston Red Sox: .... $60-$75

All-Star Pins

1938 Cincinnati: Bastian Brothers; safety pin; red/white/blue .... $7,000-$8,000
1941 Detroit: Dodge; threaded post; blue .... $2,200-$2,500
1943 Philadelphia: Unknown; threaded post; silver .... $1,200-$1,500
1946 Boston: Balfour; threaded post; red .... $600-$1,000
1947 Chicago: Unknown; threaded post; red/white/blue .... $500-$1,750
1948 St. Louis: St. Louis Button; threaded post; brown/white .... $1,000-$2,000
1949 Brooklyn: Balfour; threaded post, brooch; blue .... $300-$500
1950 Chicago: Balfour; threaded post, brooch; red/white .... $200-$400
1951 Detroit: Unknown; threaded post, brooch; red/white/blue .... $275-$400
1952 Philadelphia: Martin; needle post; red/white/blue .... $300-$400
1953 Cincinnati: Robbins; threaded post; red/white/black .... $200-$425
1954 Cleveland: Balfour; threaded post; red/white/black .... $200-$300
1955 Milwaukee: Balfour; brooch; gold .... $200-$350
1956 Washington: Balfour; threaded post, clasp; red/white/blue .... $200-$450
1957 St. Louis: Balfour; threaded post, brooch; black/red .... $450-$550
1958 Baltimore: Balfour; threaded post, charm; black/white/orange .... $375-$550
1959 Los Angeles: Balfour; threaded post, brooch; blue/white .... $75-$200
1959 Pittsburgh: Balfour; threaded post; red/white/black .... $200-$400
1960 Kansas City: Balfour; threaded post; red .... $300-$350
1960 New York Yankees: Balfour; threaded post; red/white/blue .... $200-$400
1961 Boston: Balfour; needle post; red/white/blue .... $500-$600
1961 San Francisco: Balfour; threaded post; white .... $500-$700
1962 Chicago: Balfour; needle post; red/white/blue .... $300-$400
1962 Washington: Balfour; threaded post, clasp; white/blue .... $200-$300
1963 Cleveland: Balfour; threaded post; red/white/blue/black .... $75-$125
1964 New York (Shea Stadium): Balfour; needle post, charm; blue/orange .... $200-$250
1965 Minnesota: Balfour; needle post; red/white/blue .... $125-$200
1966 St. Louis: Balfour; needle post; red .... $40-$50
1967 California: Balfour; needle post, charm; blue/white .... $100-$150
1968 Houston: Balfour; needle post, charm; blue/white .... $100-$125
1969 Washington: Balfour; needle post, clasp; blue .... $75-$100
1970 Cincinnati: Balfour; needle post, charm; red/white/black .... $50-$100
1971 Detroit: Balfour; needle post, charms; red/white/blue .... $100-$175
1972 Atlanta: Balfour; needle post, charm; red/blue .... $50-$150
1973 Kansas City: Balfour; needle post, charm; blue .... $75-$200
1974 Pittsburgh: Balfour; needle post; gold .... $75-$250
1975 Milwaukee: Unknown; brooch; gold .... $50-$100

All-Star Pins

1976 Philadelphia: Balfour; needle post; gold .... $50-$75
1977 New York Yankees: Balfour; (pin) .... $75-$125
1977 New York: Balfour; (charm); gold .... $25-$50
1978 San Diego: Balfour; needle post, charm, brooch; brown/blue .... $45-$75
1979 Seattle: Balfour; needle post, charm, brooch; blue/white .... $40-$60
1980 Los Angeles: Balfour; needle post, charm; gold .... $30-$50
1981 Cleveland: Balfour; needle post, charm; red/white/blue.. $15-$25
1982 Montreal: Balfour; needle post, straight pin; gold... $30-$50
1983 Chicago: Balfour; needle post, charms; red/blue .... $25-$50
1984 San Francisco: Balfour; needle post, charm; orange/black/white .... $25-$40
1985 Minnesota: Peter David; needle post, charms; red/white/blue................................ $40-$75
1986 Houston: Balfour; needle post, charms; red/white/blue/silver................................ $30-$65
1987 Oakland: Josten; needle post; copper .... $40-$80
1988 Cincinnati: Josten; needle post; red/white/blue/silver .... $75-$100
1989 California: .... $60-$85
1990 Chicago:.. $100-$150
1991 Toronto:.. $125-$150
1992 San Diego: .... $20-$100
1993 Baltimore: $150

Hall of Fame

1982: Balfour; charms and standard needle post: Hank Aaron, Happy Chandler, Travis Jackson, Frank Robinson .... $400-$700
1983: Balfour; charms and standard needle post: Walter Alston, George Kell, Juan Marichal, Brooks Robinson: .... $525-$675
1984: Balfour; charms and standard needle post: Luis Aparicio, Don Drysdale, Harmon Killebrew, Rick Ferrell, Pee Wee Reese .... $375-$450
1985: Balfour; charms and standard needle post: Lou Brock, Enos Slaughter, Arky Vaughan, Hoyt Wilhelm.. $350-$425
1986: Balfour; charms and standard needle post: Bobby Doerr, Ernie Lombardi, Willie McCovey
.... $350-$425
1987: Balfour; charms and standard needle post: Ray Dandridge, Jim Hunter,
Billy Williams .... $550-$650
1988: Balfour; charms and standard needle post: Willie Stargell..$650
1989: Al Barlick, Johnny Bench, Red Schoendienst, Carl Yastrzemski............................ $550-$650
1990: Joe Morgan, Jim Palmer .... $550-$650
1991: Rod Carew, Fergie Jenkins, Gaylord Perry, Tony Lazzeri, Bill Veeck .... $575-$625
1992: (1992 inductees) Rollie Fingers, Bill McGowan, Hal Newhouser, Tom Seaver
1992: (1955 inductees) Frank Baker, Joe DiMaggio, Gabby Hartnett, Ted Lyons, Ray Schalk, Dazzy Vance
1993: (1993 inductees) Reggie Jackson
1993: (1939 inductees) Charles Comiskey, Buck Ewing, Cap Anson, Candy Cummings, Eddie Collins
1993: (1939 inductees) Charles Radbourne, George Sisler, Al Spalding, Lou Gehrig, Wee Willie Keeler

1910 P2
Sweet Caporal Pins

Expanding its premiums to include more than just trading cards, the American Tobacco Co. issued a series of baseball pins between 1910 and 1912. The sepia-colored pins, each measuring 7/8" in diameter, were distributed under the Sweet Caporal brand name. The set includes 152 different major league players, but because of numerous "large letter" variations, collectors generally consider the set complete at 204 different pins. Fifty of the players are pictured on a second pin that usually displays the same photo but has the player's name and team designation printed in larger letters. Two players (Roger Bresnahan and Bobby Wallace) have three pins each. It is now generally accepted that there are 153 pins with "small letters" and another 51 "large letter" variations in a complete set. Research among advanced collectors has shown that 19 of the pins, including six of the "large letter" variations, are considered more difficult to find. The back of each pin has either a black or a red paper insert advertising Sweet Caporal Cigarettes. The red backings, issued only with the "large letter" pins, are generally less common. The Sweet Caporal pins are closely related to the popular T205 Gold Border tobacco cards, also issued by the American Tobacco Co. about the same time. All but nine of the players featured in the pin set were also pictured on T205 cards, and in nearly all cases the photos are identical. The Sweet Caporal pins are designated as P2 in the American Card Catalog. The complete set price includes all variations.

		NR MT	EX	VG
Complete Set:		5250.	2625.	1575.
Common Player:		15.00	7.50	4.50
(1)	Ed Abbaticchio	15.00	7.50	4.50
(2)	Red Ames	15.00	7.50	4.50
(3a)	Jimmy Archer (small letters)			
		15.00	7.50	4.50
(3b)	Jimmy Archer (large letters)			
		20.00	10.00	6.00
(4a)	Jimmy Austin (small letters)			
		15.00	7.50	4.50
(4b)	Jimmy Austin (large letters)			
		20.00	10.00	6.00
(5)	Home Run Baker	30.00	15.00	9.00
(6)	Neal Ball	15.00	7.50	4.50

(7)	Cy Barger	15.00	7.50	4.50
(8)	Jack Barry	15.00	7.50	4.50
(9)	Johnny Bates	15.00	7.50	4.50
(10)	Beals Becker	15.00	7.50	4.50
(11)	Fred Beebe	15.00	7.50	4.50
(12a)	George Bell (small letters)			
		15.00	7.50	4.50
(12b)	George Bell (large letters)			
		20.00	10.00	6.00
(13a)	Chief Bender (small letters)			
		30.00	15.00	9.00
(13b)	Chief Bender (large letters)			
		50.00	25.00	15.00
(14)	Bill Bergen	15.00	7.50	4.50
(15)	Bob Bescher	15.00	7.50	4.50
(16)	Joe Birmingham	15.00	7.50	4.50
(17)	Kitty Bransfield	35.00	17.50	10.50
(18a)	Roger Bresnahan (mouth closed, small letters)			
		30.00	15.00	9.00
(18b)	Roger Bresnahan (mouth closed, large letters)			
		90.00	45.00	27.00
(19)	Roger Bresnahan (mouth open)			
		30.00	15.00	9.00
(20)	Al Bridwell	15.00	7.50	4.50
(21a)	Mordecai Brown (small letters)			
		30.00	15.00	9.00
(21b)	Mordecai Brown (large letters)			
		50.00	25.00	15.00
(22)	Bobby Byrne	15.00	7.50	4.50
(23)	Nixey Callahan	15.00	7.50	4.50
(24a)	Howie Camnitz (small letters)			
		15.00	7.50	4.50
(24b)	Howie Camnitz (large letters)			
		20.00	10.00	6.00
(25a)	Bill Carrigan (small letters)			
		15.00	7.50	4.50
(25b)	Bill Carrigan (large letters)			
		20.00	10.00	6.00
(26a)	Frank Chance (small letters)			
		35.00	17.50	10.50
(26b)	Frank Chance (large letters)			
		50.00	25.00	15.00
(27)	Hal Chase (different photo, small letters)			
		15.00	7.50	4.50
(28)	Hal Chase (different photo, large letters)			
		25.00	12.50	7.50
(29)	Ed Cicotte	15.00	7.50	4.50
(30a)	Fred Clarke (small letters)			
		30.00	15.00	9.00
(30b)	Fred Clarke (large letters)			
		50.00	25.00	15.00
(31a)	Ty Cobb (small letters)	250.00	125.00	75.00
(31b)	Ty Cobb (large letters)	375.00	187.00	112.00
(32a)	Eddie Collins (small letters)			
		30.00	15.00	9.00
(32b)	Eddie Collins (large letters)			
		70.00	35.00	21.00
(33)	Doc Crandall	15.00	7.50	4.50
(34)	Birdie Cree	35.00	17.50	10.50
(35)	Bill Dahlen	15.00	7.50	4.50
(36)	Jim Delahanty	15.00	7.50	4.50

(37)	Art Devlin	15.00	7.50	4.50
(38)	Josh Devore	15.00	7.50	4.50
(39)	Wild Bill Donovan	35.00	17.50	10.50
(40a)	Red Dooin (small letters)	15.00	7.50	4.50
(40b)	Red Dooin (large letters)	20.00	10.00	6.00
(41a)	Mickey Doolan (small letters)	15.00	7.50	4.50
(41b)	Mickey Doolan (large letters)	20.00	10.00	6.00
(42)	Patsy Dougherty	15.00	7.50	4.50
(43a)	Tom Downey (small letters)	15.00	7.50	4.50
(43b)	Tom Downey (large letters)	20.00	10.00	6.00
(44a)	Larry Doyle (small letters)	15.00	7.50	4.50
(44b)	Larry Doyle (large letters)	20.00	10.00	6.00
(45)	Louis Drucke	15.00	7.50	4.50
(46a)	Hugh Duffy (small letters)	30.00	15.00	9.00
(46b)	Hugh Duffy (large letters)	50.00	25.00	15.00
(47)	Jimmy Dygert	15.00	7.50	4.50
(48a)	Kid Elberfeld (small letters)	15.00	7.50	4.50
(48b)	Kid Elberfeld (large letters)	20.00	10.00	6.00
(49a)	Clyde Engle (small letters)	15.00	7.50	4.50
(49b)	Clyde Engle (large letters)	20.00	10.00	6.00
(50)	Tex Erwin	15.00	7.50	4.50
(51)	Steve Evans	15.00	7.50	4.50
(52)	Johnny Evers	30.00	15.00	9.00
(53)	Cecil Ferguson	15.00	7.50	4.50
(54)	John Flynn	15.00	7.50	4.50
(55a)	Russ Ford (small letters)	15.00	7.50	4.50
(55b)	Russ Ford (large letters)	20.00	10.00	6.00
(56)	Art Fromme	15.00	7.50	4.50
(57)	Harry Gaspar	15.00	7.50	4.50
(58a)	George Gibson (small letters)	15.00	7.50	4.50
(58b)	George Gibson (large letters)	20.00	10.00	6.00
(59)	Eddie Grant	35.00	17.50	10.50
(60)	Dolly Gray	15.00	7.50	4.50
(61a)	Clark Griffith (small letters)	30.00	15.00	9.00
(61b)	Clark Griffith (large letters)	50.00	25.00	15.00
(62)	Bob Groom	15.00	7.50	4.50
(63)	Bob Harmon	15.00	7.50	4.50
(64)	Topsy Hartsel	15.00	7.50	4.50
(65)	Arnold Hauser	35.00	17.50	10.50
(66)	Ira Hemphill	15.00	7.50	4.50
(67a)	Buck Herzog (small letters)	15.00	7.50	4.50
(67b)	Buck Herzog (large letters)	20.00	10.00	6.00
(68)	Dick Hoblitzell	15.00	7.50	4.50
(69)	Danny Hoffman	15.00	7.50	4.50
(70)	Harry Hooper	15.00	7.50	4.50
(71a)	Miller Huggins (small letters)	30.00	15.00	9.00
(71b)	Miller Huggins (large letters)	50.00	25.00	15.00
(72)	John Hummel	15.00	7.50	4.50
(73)	Hugh Jennings (different photo, small letters)	30.00	15.00	9.00
(74)	Hugh Jennings (different photo, large letters)	50.00	25.00	15.00
(75a)	Walter Johnson (small letters)	90.00	45.00	27.00
(75b)	Walter Johnson (large letters)	125.00	62.00	37.00
(76)	Tom Jones	35.00	17.50	10.50
(77)	Ed Karger	15.00	7.50	4.50
(78)	Ed Killian	35.00	17.50	10.50
(79a)	Jack Knight (small letters)	15.00	7.50	4.50
(79b)	Jack Knight (large letters)	20.00	10.00	6.00
(80)	Ed Konetchy	15.00	7.50	4.50
(81)	Harry Krause	15.00	7.50	4.50
(82)	Rube Kroh	15.00	7.50	4.50
(83)	Nap Lajoie	60.00	30.00	18.00
(84a)	Frank LaPorte (small letters)	15.00	7.50	4.50
(84b)	Frank LaPorte (large letters)	20.00	10.00	6.00
(85)	Arlie Latham	15.00	7.50	4.50
(86a)	Tommy Leach (small letters)	15.00	7.50	4.50
(86b)	Tommy Leach (large letters)	20.00	10.00	6.00
(87)	Sam Leever	15.00	7.50	4.50
(88)	Lefty Leifield	15.00	7.50	4.50
(89)	Hans Lobert	15.00	7.50	4.50
(90a)	Harry Lord (small letters)	15.00	7.50	4.50
(90b)	Harry Lord (large letters)	20.00	10.00	6.00
(91)	Paddy Livingston	15.00	7.50	4.50
(92)	Nick Maddox	15.00	7.50	4.50
(93)	Sherry Magee	15.00	7.50	4.50
(94)	Rube Marquard	30.00	15.00	9.00
(95a)	Christy Mathewson (small letters)	90.00	45.00	27.00
(95b)	Christy Mathewson (large letters)	110.00	55.00	33.00
(96a)	Al Mattern (small letters)	15.00	7.50	4.50
(96b)	Al Mattern (large letters)	20.00	10.00	6.00
(97)	George McBride	15.00	7.50	4.50
(98a)	John McGraw (small letters)	40.00	20.00	12.00
(98b)	John McGraw (large letters)	60.00	30.00	18.00
(99a)	Larry McLean (small letters)	15.00	7.50	4.50
(99b)	Larry McLean (large letters)	20.00	10.00	6.00
(100)	Harry McIntyre (Cubs)	15.00	7.50	4.50
(101a)	Matty McIntyre (White Sox, small letters)	15.00	7.50	4.50
(101b)	Matty McIntyre (White Sox, large letters)	20.00	10.00	6.00
(102)	Fred Merkle	15.00	7.50	4.50
(103)	Chief Meyers	15.00	7.50	4.50
(104)	Clyde Milan	15.00	7.50	4.50
(105)	Dots Miller	15.00	7.50	4.50
(106)	Mike Mitchell	15.00	7.50	4.50
(107)	Pat Moran	15.00	7.50	4.50
(108a)	George Mullen (Mullin) (small letters)	15.00	7.50	4.50
(108b)	George Mullen (Mullin) (large letters)	20.00	10.00	6.00
(109)	Danny Murphy	15.00	7.50	4.50
(110a)	Red Murray (small letters)	20.00	10.00	6.00
(110b)	Red Murray (large letters)	15.00	7.50	4.50
(111)	Tom Needham	35.00	17.50	10.50
(112a)	Rebel Oakes (small letters)	15.00	7.50	4.50
(112b)	Rebel Oakes (large letters)	20.00	10.00	6.00
(113)	Rube Oldring	15.00	7.50	4.50
(114)	Charley O'Leary	15.00	7.50	4.50
(115)	Orval Overall	35.00	17.50	10.50
(116)	Fred Parent	15.00	7.50	4.50
(117a)	Dode Paskert (small letters)	15.00	7.50	4.50
(117b)	Dode Paskert (large letters)	20.00	10.00	6.00
(118)	Barney Pelty	15.00	7.50	4.50
(119)	Jake Pfeister	15.00	7.50	4.50
(120)	Eddie Phelps	15.00	7.50	4.50
(121)	Deacon Phillippe	15.00	7.50	4.50
(122)	Jack Quinn	15.00	7.50	4.50
(123)	Ed Reulbach	15.00	7.50	4.50
124	Lew Richie	15.00	7.50	4.50
(125)	Jack Rowan	15.00	7.50	4.50
(126a)	Nap Rucker (small letters)	15.00	7.50	4.50
(126b)	Nap Rucker (large letters)	20.00	10.00	6.00
(127)	Doc Scanlon (Scanlan)	35.00	17.50	10.50
(128)	Germany Schaefer	15.00	7.50	4.50
(129)	Jimmy Scheckard (Sheckard)	15.00	7.50	4.50
(130a)	Boss Schmidt (small letters)	15.00	7.50	4.50
(130b)	Boss Schmidt (large letters)	20.00	10.00	6.00
(131)	Wildfire Schulte	15.00	7.50	4.50
(132)	Hap Smith	15.00	7.50	4.50
(133a)	Tris Speaker (small letters)	50.00	25.00	15.00
(133b)	Tris Speaker (large letters)	70.00	35.00	21.00
(134)	Oscar Stanage	15.00	7.50	4.50
(135)	Harry Steinfeldt	15.00	7.50	4.50
(136)	George Stone	15.00	7.50	4.50
(137a)	George Stoval (Stovall) (small letters)	15.00	7.50	4.50
(137b)	George Stoval (Stovall) (large letters)	20.00	10.00	6.00

(138a)	Gabby Street (small letters)		
		15.00	7.50	4.50
(138b)	Gabby Street (large letters)		
		20.00	10.00	6.00
(139)	George Suggs	15.00	7.50	4.50
(140a)	Ira Thomas (small letters)		
		15.00	7.50	4.50
(140b)	Ira Thomas (large letters)		
		20.00	10.00	6.00
(141a)	Joe Tinker (small letters)	30.00	15.00	9.00
(141b)	Joe Tinker (large letters)	50.00	25.00	15.00
(142a)	John Titus (small letters)	15.00	7.50	4.50
(142b)	John Titus (large letters)	20.00	10.00	6.00
(143)	Terry Turner	20.00	10.00	6.00
(144)	Heinie Wagner	15.00	7.50	4.50
(145a)	Bobby Wallace (with cap, small letters)		
		30.00	15.00	9.00
(145b)	Bobby Wallace (with cap, large letters)		
		50.00	25.00	15.00
(146)	Bobby Wallace (without cap)		
		30.00	15.00	9.00
(147)	Ed Walsh	30.00	15.00	9.00
(148)	Jack Warhop	35.00	17.50	10.50
(149a)	Zach Wheat (small letters)		
		30.00	15.00	9.00
(149b)	Zach Wheat (large letters)		
		50.00	25.00	15.00
(150)	Doc White	15.00	7.50	4.50
(151)	Art Wilson (Giants)	35.00	17.50	10.50
(152)	Owen Wilson (Pirates)	15.00	7.50	4.50
(153)	Hooks Wiltse	15.00	7.50	4.50
(154)	Harry Wolter	15.00	7.50	4.50
(155a)	Cy Young (small letters)	55.00	27.00	16.50
(155b)	Cy Young (large letters)	75.00	37.00	22.00

1930 PM8
Our National Game Pins

This unnumbered 30-pin set issued in the 1930s carries the American Card Catalog designation of PM8 and is known as "Our National Game." The pins, which measure 7/8" in diameter, have a "tab" rather than a pin back. The black-and-white player photo is tinted blue, and the player's name and team are printed in a band near the bottom.

		NR MT	EX	VG
Complete Set:		525.00	262.00	157.00
Common Player:		6.00	3.00	1.75
(1)	Wally Berger	6.00	3.00	1.75
(2)	Lou Chiozza	6.00	3.00	1.75
(3)	Joe Cronin	15.00	7.50	4.50
(4)	Frank Crosetti	8.00	4.00	2.50
(5)	Jerome (Dizzy) Dean	25.00	12.50	7.50
(6)	Frank DeMaree	6.00	3.00	1.75
(7)	Joe DiMaggio	90.00	45.00	27.00
(8)	Bob Feller	20.00	10.00	6.00
(9)	Jimmy Foxx	20.00	10.00	6.00
(10)	Charles Gehringer	15.00	7.50	4.50
(11)	Lou Gehrig	90.00	45.00	27.00
(12)	Lefty Gomez	15.00	7.50	4.50
(13)	Hank Greenberg	15.00	7.50	4.50
(14)	Irving (Bump) Hadley	6.00	3.00	1.75
(15)	Leo Hartnett	15.00	7.50	4.50
(16)	Carl Hubbell	15.00	7.50	4.50

(17)	John (Buddy) Lewis	6.00	3.00	1.75
(18)	Gus Mancuso	6.00	3.00	1.75
(19)	Joe McCarthy	15.00	7.50	4.50
(20)	Joe Medwick	15.00	7.50	4.50
(21)	Joe Moore	6.00	3.00	1.75
(22)	Mel Ott	15.00	7.50	4.50
(23)	Jake Powell	6.00	3.00	1.75
(24)	Jimmy Ripple	6.00	3.00	1.75
(25)	Red Ruffing	15.00	7.50	4.50
(26)	Hal Schumacher	6.00	3.00	1.75
(27)	George Selkirk	6.00	3.00	1.75
(28)	"Al" Simmons	15.00	7.50	4.50
(29)	Bill Terry	15.00	7.50	4.50
(30)	Harold Trosky	6.00	3.00	1.75

1956 PM15
Yellow Basepath Pins

These pins were issued circa 1956; the sponsor of this 32-pin set is not indicated. The set, which has been assigned the American Card Catalog designation PM15, is commonly called "Yellow Basepaths" because of the design of the pin, which features a black-and-white player photo set inside a green infield with yellow basepaths. The unnumbered pins measure 7/8" in diameter. The names of Kluszewski and Mathews are misspelled.

		NR MT	EX	VG
Complete Set:		2200.	1100.	660.00
Common Player:		25.00	12.50	7.50
(1)	Hank Aaron	175.00	87.00	52.00
(2)	Joe Adcock	40.00	20.00	12.00
(3)	Luis Aparicio	60.00	30.00	18.00
(4)	Richie Ashburn	60.00	30.00	18.00
(5)	Gene Baker	25.00	12.50	7.50
(6)	Ernie Banks	90.00	45.00	27.00
(7)	Yogi Berra	90.00	45.00	27.00
(8)	Bill Bruton	25.00	12.50	7.50
(9)	Larry Doby	35.00	17.50	10.50
(10)	Bob Friend	25.00	12.50	7.50
(11)	Nellie Fox	45.00	22.00	13.50
(12)	Jim Greengrass	25.00	12.50	7.50
(13)	Steve Gromek	25.00	12.50	7.50
(14)	Johnny Groth	25.00	12.50	7.50
(15)	Gil Hodges	75.00	37.00	22.00
(16)	Al Kaline	90.00	45.00	27.00
(17)	Ted Kluzewski (Kluszewski)		
		50.00	25.00	15.00
(18)	Johnny Logan	25.00	12.50	7.50
(19)	Dale Long	25.00	12.50	7.50
(20)	Mickey Mantle	450.00	225.00	135.00
(21)	Ed Mathews	80.00	40.00	24.00
(22)	Minnie Minoso	35.00	17.50	10.50
(23)	Stan Musial	175.00	87.00	52.00
(24)	Don Newcombe	40.00	20.00	12.00
(25)	Bob Porterfield	25.00	12.50	7.50
(26)	Pee Wee Reese	75.00	37.00	22.00
(27)	Robin Roberts	50.00	25.00	15.00
(28)	Red Schoendienst	40.00	20.00	12.00
(29)	Duke Snider	100.00	50.00	30.00
(30)	Vern Stephens	25.00	12.50	7.50
(31)	Gene Woodling	25.00	12.50	7.50
(32)	Gus Zernial	25.00	12.50	7.50

1932 PR2
Orbit Gum Pins
Numbered

Issued circa 1932, this skip-numbered set of small (13/16" in diameter) pins was produced by Orbit Gum and carries the Amerian Card Catalog designation of PR2. A player lithograph is set against a green background with the player's name and team printed on a strip of yellow below. The pin number is at the very bottom.

		NR MT	EX	VG
Complete Set:		1200.	500.00	300.00
Common Player:		15.00	7.50	4.50
1	Ivy Andrews	15.00	7.50	4.50
2	Carl Reynolds	15.00	7.50	4.50
3	Riggs Stephenson	18.00	9.00	5.50
4	Lon Warneke	15.00	7.50	4.50
5	Frank Grube	15.00	7.50	4.50
6	Kiki Cuyler	30.00	15.00	9.00
7	Marty McManus	15.00	7.50	4.50
8	Lefty Clark	15.00	7.50	4.50
9	George Blaeholder	15.00	7.50	4.50
10	Willie Kamm	15.00	7.50	4.50
11	Jimmy Dykes	18.00	9.00	5.50
12	Earl Averill	30.00	15.00	9.00
13	Pat Malone	15.00	7.50	4.50
14	Dizzy Dean	95.00	47.00	28.00
15	Dick Bartell	15.00	7.50	4.50
16	Guy Bush	15.00	7.50	4.50
17	Bud Tinning	15.00	7.50	4.50
18	Jimmy Foxx	50.00	25.00	15.00
19	Mule Haas	15.00	7.50	4.50
20	Lew Fonseca	15.00	7.50	4.50
21	Pepper Martin	25.00	12.50	7.50
22	Phil Collins	15.00	7.50	4.50
23	Bill Cissell	15.00	7.50	4.50
24	Bump Hadley	15.00	7.50	4.50
25	Smead Jolley	15.00	7.50	4.50
26	Burleigh Grimes	30.00	15.00	9.00
27	Dale Alexander	15.00	7.50	4.50
28	Mickey Cochrane	35.00	17.50	10.50
29	Mel Harder	15.00	7.50	4.50
30	Mark Koenig	15.00	7.50	4.50
31a	Lefty O'Doul (Dodgers)	45.00	22.00	13.50
31b	Lefty O'Doul (Giants)	25.00	12.50	7.50
32a	Woody English (with bat)	15.00	7.50	4.50
32b	Woody English (without bat)	45.00	22.00	13.50
33a	Billy Jurges (with bat)	15.00	7.50	4.50
33b	Billy Jurges (without bat)	45.00	22.00	13.50
34	Bruce Campbell	15.00	7.50	4.50
35	Joe Vosmik	15.00	7.50	4.50
36	Dick Porter	15.00	7.50	4.50
37	Charlie Grimm	18.00	9.00	5.50
38	George Earnshaw	15.00	7.50	4.50
39	Al Simmons	30.00	15.00	9.00
40	Red Lucas	15.00	7.50	4.50

51	Wally Berger	15.00	7.50	4.50
52	Jim Levey	15.00	7.50	4.50
58	Ernie Lombardi	30.00	15.00	9.00
64	Jack Burns	15.00	7.50	4.50
67	Billy Herman	30.00	15.00	9.00
72	Bill Hallahan	15.00	7.50	4.50
92	Don Brennan	15.00	7.50	4.50
96	Sam Byrd	15.00	7.50	4.50
99	Ben Chapman	15.00	7.50	4.50
103	John Allen	15.00	7.50	4.50
107	Tony Lazzeri	30.00	15.00	9.00
111	Earl Combs (Earle)	30.00	15.00	9.00
116	Joe Sewell	30.00	15.00	9.00
120	Vernon Gomez	35.00	17.50	10.50

1932 PR3
Orbit Gum Pins
Unnumbered

This set, issued by Orbit Gum circa 1932, has the American Card Catalog designation PR3. The pins are identical to the PR2 set, except they are unnumbered.

		NR MT	EX	VG
Complete Set:		2400.	900.00	540.00
Common Player:		30.00	15.00	9.00
(1)	Dale Alexander	30.00	15.00	9.00
(2)	Ivy Andrews	30.00	15.00	9.00
(3)	Earl Averill	60.00	30.00	18.00
(4)	Dick Bartell	30.00	15.00	9.00
(5)	Wally Berger	30.00	15.00	9.00
(6)	George Blaeholder	30.00	15.00	9.00
(7)	Jack Burns	30.00	15.00	9.00
(8)	Guy Bush	30.00	15.00	9.00
(9)	Bruce Campbell	30.00	15.00	9.00
(10)	Bill Cissell	30.00	15.00	9.00
(11)	Lefty Clark	30.00	15.00	9.00
(12)	Mickey Cochrane	75.00	37.00	22.00
(13)	Phil Collins	30.00	15.00	9.00
(14)	Kiki Cuyler	60.00	30.00	18.00
(15)	Dizzy Dean	150.00	75.00	45.00
(16)	Jimmy Dykes	40.00	20.00	12.00
(17)	George Earnshaw	30.00	15.00	9.00
(18)	Woody English	30.00	15.00	9.00
(19)	Lew Fonseca	30.00	15.00	9.00
(20)	Jimmy Foxx	90.00	45.00	27.00
(21)	Burleigh Grimes	60.00	30.00	18.00
(22)	Charlie Grimm	40.00	20.00	12.00
(23)	Lefty Grove	90.00	45.00	27.00
(24)	Frank Grube	30.00	15.00	9.00
(25)	Mule Haas	30.00	15.00	9.00
(26)	Bump Hadley	30.00	15.00	9.00
(27)	Chick Hafey	60.00	30.00	18.00
(28)	Jesse Haines	60.00	30.00	18.00
(29)	Bill Hallahan	30.00	15.00	9.00
(30)	Mel Harder	30.00	15.00	9.00
(31)	Gabby Hartnett	60.00	30.00	18.00
(32)	Babe Herman	40.00	20.00	12.00
(33)	Billy Herman	60.00	30.00	18.00
(34)	Rogers Hornsby	100.00	50.00	30.00
(35)	Roy Johnson	30.00	15.00	9.00
(36)	Smead Jolley	30.00	15.00	9.00
(37)	Billy Jurges	30.00	15.00	9.00
(38)	Willie Kamm	30.00	15.00	9.00

(39)	Mark Koenig	30.00	15.00	9.00
(40)	Jim Levey	30.00	15.00	9.00
(41)	Ernie Lombardi	60.00	30.00	18.00
(42)	Red Lucas	30.00	15.00	9.00
(43)	Ted Lyons	60.00	30.00	18.00
(44)	Connie Mack	80.00	40.00	24.00
(45)	Pat Malone	30.00	15.00	9.00
(46)	Pepper Martin	40.00	20.00	12.00
(47)	Marty McManus	30.00	15.00	9.00
(48)	Lefty O'Doul	40.00	20.00	12.00
(49)	Dick Porter	30.00	15.00	9.00
(50)	Carl Reynolds	30.00	15.00	9.00
(51)	Charlie Root	30.00	15.00	9.00
(52)	Bob Seeds	30.00	15.00	9.00
(53)	Al Simmons	60.00	30.00	18.00
(54)	Riggs Stephenson	35.00	17.50	10.50
(55)	Bud Tinning	30.00	15.00	9.00
(56)	Joe Vosmik	30.00	15.00	9.00
(57)	Rube Walberg	30.00	15.00	9.00
(58)	Paul Waner	60.00	30.00	18.00
(59)	Lon Warneke	30.00	15.00	9.00
(60)	Pinky Whitney	30.00	15.00	9.00

1930 PR4 Cracker Jack Pins

Although no manufacturer is indicated on the pins themselves, this 25-player set was apparently issued by Cracker Jack in the early 1930s. Each pin measures 13/16" in diameter and features a line drawing of a player portrait. The unnumbered pins are printed in blue and gray with a background of yellow. The player's name appears below.

		NR MT	EX	VG
Complete Set:		700.00	350.00	210.00
Common Player:		15.00	7.50	4.50
(1)	Charles Berry	15.00	7.50	4.50
(2)	Bill Cissell	15.00	7.50	4.50
(3)	KiKi Cuyler	25.00	12.50	7.50
(4)	Dizzy Dean	40.00	20.00	12.00
(5)	Wesley Ferrell	15.00	7.50	4.50
(6)	Frank Frisch	25.00	12.50	7.50
(7)	Lou Gehrig	100.00	50.00	30.00
(8)	Vernon Gomez	25.00	12.50	7.50
(9)	Goose Goslin	25.00	12.50	7.50
(10)	George Grantham	15.00	7.50	4.50
(11)	Charley Grimm	15.00	7.50	4.50
(12)	Lefty Grove	30.00	15.00	9.00
(13)	Gabby Hartnett	25.00	12.50	7.50
(14)	Travis Jackson	25.00	12.50	7.50
(15)	Tony Lazzeri	25.00	12.50	7.50
(16)	Ted Lyons	25.00	12.50	7.50
(17)	Rabbit Maranville	25.00	12.50	7.50
(18)	Carl Reynolds	15.00	7.50	4.50
(19)	Charles Ruffing	25.00	12.50	7.50
(20)	Al Simmons	25.00	12.50	7.50
(21)	Gus Suhr	15.00	7.50	4.50
(22)	Bill Terry	25.00	12.50	7.50
(23)	Dazzy Vance	25.00	12.50	7.50
(24)	Paul Waner	25.00	12.50	7.50
(25)	Lon Warneke	15.00	7.50	4.50

1933 PX3 Double Header Pins

Issued by Gum Inc. circa 1933, this unnumbered set consists of 43 metal discs approximately 1-1/4" in diameter. The front of the pin lists the player's name and team beneath his picture. The numbers "1" or "2" also appear inside a small circle at the bottom of the disc, and the wrapper advised collectors to "put 1 and 2 together and make a double header." The set is designated as PX3 in the American Card Catalog.

		NR MT	EX	VG
Complete Set:		900.00	450.00	270.00
Common Player:		25.00	12.50	7.50
(1)	Sparky Adams	25.00	12.50	7.50
(2)	Dale Alexander	25.00	12.50	7.50
(3)	Earl Averill	45.00	22.00	13.50
(4)	Dick Bartell	25.00	12.50	7.50
(5)	Walter Berger	25.00	12.50	7.50
(6)	Jim Bottomley	45.00	22.00	13.50
(7)	Lefty Brandt	25.00	12.50	7.50
(8)	Owen Carroll	25.00	12.50	7.50
(9)	Lefty Clark	25.00	12.50	7.50
(10)	Mickey Cochrane	50.00	25.00	15.00
(11)	Joe Cronin	45.00	22.00	13.50
(12)	Jimmy Dykes	25.00	12.50	7.50
(13)	George Earnshaw	25.00	12.50	7.50
(14)	Wes Ferrell	25.00	12.50	7.50
(15)	Neal Finn	25.00	12.50	7.50
(16)	Lew Fonseca	25.00	12.50	7.50
(17)	Jimmy Foxx	90.00	45.00	27.00
(18)	Frankie Frisch	50.00	25.00	15.00
(19)	Chick Fullis	25.00	12.50	7.50
(20)	Charley Gehringer	45.00	22.00	13.50
(21)	Goose Goslin	45.00	22.00	13.50
(22)	Johnny Hodapp	25.00	12.50	7.50
(23)	Frank Hogan	25.00	12.50	7.50
(24)	Si Johnson	25.00	12.50	7.50
(25)	Joe Judge	25.00	12.50	7.50
(26)	Chuck Klein	45.00	22.00	13.50
(27)	Al Lopez	45.00	22.00	13.50
(28)	Ray Lucas	25.00	12.50	7.50
(29)	Red Lucas	25.00	12.50	7.50
(30)	Ted Lyons	45.00	22.00	13.50
(31)	Firpo Marberry	25.00	12.50	7.50
(32)	Oscar Melillo	25.00	12.50	7.50
(33)	Lefty O'Doul	30.00	15.00	9.00
(34)	George Pipgras	25.00	12.50	7.50
(35)	Flint Rhem	25.00	12.50	7.50
(36)	Sam Rice	45.00	22.00	13.50
(37)	Muddy Ruel	25.00	12.50	7.50
(38)	Harry Seibold	25.00	12.50	7.50
(39)	Al Simmons	45.00	22.00	13.50
(40)	Joe Vosmik	25.00	12.50	7.50
(41)	Gerald Walker	25.00	12.50	7.50
(42)	Pinky Whitney	25.00	12.50	7.50
(43)	Hack Wilson	45.00	22.00	13.50

1909 PX7 Domino Discs

Domino Discs, distributed by Sweet Caporal Cigarettes from 1909 to 1912, are among the more obscure 20th-century tobacco issues. Although the disc set contains many of the same players - some even pictured in the same poses - as the Sweet Caporal P2 pin set, the discs have always lagged behind the pins in collector appeal. The Domino Discs, so called because each disc has a large, white domino printed on the back, measure approximately 1-1/8" in diameter and are made of thin card cardboard surrounded by a metal rim. The fronts of the discs contain a player portrait set against a background of either red, green or blue. The words "Sweet Caporal Cigarettes" appear on the front along with the player's last name and team. There are 135 different major leaguers featured in the set, each pictured in two different poses for a total of 270 different subjects. Also known to exist as part of the set is a "game disc" which pictures a "generic" player and contains the words "Home Team" against a red background on one side and "Visiting Team" with a green background on the reverse. Because each of the 135 players in the set can theoretically be found with three different background colors and with varying numbers of dots on the dominoes, there is almost an impossible number of variations available. Collectors, however, generally collect the discs without regard to background color or domino arrangement. The Domino Disc set was assigned the designation PX7 in the American Card Catalog.

	NR MT	EX	VG
Complete Set:	5500.	2700.	1650.
Common Player:	25.00	12.50	7.50
(1) Red Ames	25.00	12.50	7.50
(2) Jimmy Archer	25.00	12.50	7.50
(3) Jimmy Austin	25.00	12.50	7.50
(4) Home Run Baker	60.00	30.00	18.00
(5) Neal Ball	25.00	12.50	7.50
(6) Cy Barger	25.00	12.50	7.50
(7) Jack Barry	25.00	12.50	7.50
(8) Johnny Bates	25.00	12.50	7.50
(9) Beals Becker	25.00	12.50	7.50
(10) George Bell	25.00	12.50	7.50
(11) Chief Bender	60.00	30.00	18.00
(12) Bill Bergen	25.00	12.50	7.50
(13) Bob Bescher	25.00	12.50	7.50
(14) Joe Birmingham	25.00	12.50	7.50
(15) Roger Bresnahan	60.00	30.00	18.00
(16) Al Bridwell	25.00	12.50	7.50
(17) Mordecai Brown	60.00	30.00	18.00
(18) Bobby Byrne	25.00	12.50	7.50
(19) Nixey Callahan	25.00	12.50	7.50
(20) Howie Camnitz	25.00	12.50	7.50
(21) Bill Carrigan	25.00	12.50	7.50
(22) Frank Chance	60.00	30.00	18.00
(23) Hal Chase	40.00	20.00	12.00
(24) Ed Cicotte	40.00	20.00	12.00
(25) Fred Clarke	60.00	30.00	18.00
(26a) Ty Cobb ("D" on cap)	600.00	300.00	180.00
26b Ty Cobb (no "D" on cap)	600.00	300.00	180.00
(27) Eddie Collins	60.00	30.00	18.00
(28) Doc Crandall	25.00	12.50	7.50
(29) Birdie Cree	25.00	12.50	7.50
(30) Bill Dahlen	25.00	12.50	7.50
(31) Jim Delahanty	25.00	12.50	7.50
(32) Art Devlin	25.00	12.50	7.50
(33) Josh Devore	25.00	12.50	7.50
(34) Red Dooin	25.00	12.50	7.50
(35) Mickey Doolan	25.00	12.50	7.50
(36) Patsy Dougherty	25.00	12.50	7.50
(37) Tom Downey	25.00	12.50	7.50
(38) Larry Doyle	25.00	12.50	7.50
(39) Louis Drucke	25.00	12.50	7.50
(40) Clyde Engle	25.00	12.50	7.50
(41) Tex Erwin	25.00	12.50	7.50
(42) Steve Evans	25.00	12.50	7.50
(43) Johnny Evers	60.00	30.00	18.00
(44) Cecil Ferguson	25.00	12.50	7.50
(45) Russ Ford	25.00	12.50	7.50
(46) Art Fromme	25.00	12.50	7.50
(47) Harry Gaspar	25.00	12.50	7.50
(48) George Gibson	25.00	12.50	7.50
(49) Eddie Grant	35.00	17.50	10.50
(50) Clark Griffith	60.00	30.00	18.00
(51) Bob Groom	25.00	12.50	7.50
(52) Bob Harmon	25.00	12.50	7.50
(53) Topsy Hartsel	25.00	12.50	7.50
(54) Arnold Hauser	25.00	12.50	7.50
(55) Dick Hoblitzell	25.00	12.50	7.50
(56) Danny Hoffman	25.00	12.50	7.50
(57) Miller Huggins	60.00	30.00	18.00
(58) John Hummel	25.00	12.50	7.50
(59) Hugh Jennings	60.00	30.00	18.00
(60) Walter Johnson	300.00	150.00	90.00
(61) Ed Karger	25.00	12.50	7.50
(62a) Jack Knight (Yankees)	25.00	12.50	7.50
(62b) Jack Knight (Senators)	25.00	12.50	7.50
(63) Ed Konetchy	25.00	12.50	7.50
(64) Harry Krause	25.00	12.50	7.50
(65) Frank LaPorte	25.00	12.50	7.50
(66) Nap Lajoie	150.00	75.00	45.00
(67) Tommy Leach	25.00	12.50	7.50
(68) Sam Leever	25.00	12.50	7.50
(69) Lefty Leifield	25.00	12.50	7.50
(70) Paddy Livingston	25.00	12.50	7.50
(71) Hans Lobert	25.00	12.50	7.50
(72) Harry Lord	25.00	12.50	7.50
(73) Nick Maddox	25.00	12.50	7.50
(74) Sherry Magee	25.00	12.50	7.50
(75) Rube Marquard	60.00	30.00	18.00
(76) Christy Mathewson	300.00	150.00	90.00
(77) Al Mattern	25.00	12.50	7.50
(78) George McBride	25.00	12.50	7.50
(79) John McGraw	60.00	30.00	18.00
(80) Harry McIntire (McIntyre)	25.00	12.50	7.50
(81) Matty McIntyre	25.00	12.50	7.50
(82) Larry McLean	25.00	12.50	7.50
(83) Fred Merkle	25.00	12.50	7.50
(84) Chief Meyers	25.00	12.50	7.50
(85) Clyde Milan	25.00	12.50	7.50
(86) Dots Miller	25.00	12.50	7.50
(87) Mike Mitchell	25.00	12.50	7.50
(88a) Pat Moran (Cubs)	25.00	12.50	7.50
(88b) Pat Moran (Phillies)	25.00	12.50	7.50
(89) George Mullen (Mullin)	25.00	12.50	7.50
(90) Danny Murphy	25.00	12.50	7.50
(91) Red Murray	25.00	12.50	7.50
(92) Tom Needham	25.00	12.50	7.50
(93) Rebel Oakes	25.00	12.50	7.50
(94) Rube Oldring	25.00	12.50	7.50
(95) Fred Parent	25.00	12.50	7.50
(96) Dode Paskert	25.00	12.50	7.50
(97) Barney Pelty	25.00	12.50	7.50
(98) Eddie Phelps	25.00	12.50	7.50
(99) Deacon Phillippe	25.00	12.50	7.50
(100) Jack Quinn	25.00	12.50	7.50
(101) Ed Reulbach	25.00	12.50	7.50
(102) Lew Richie	25.00	12.50	7.50
(103) Jack Rowan	25.00	12.50	7.50

(104)	Nap Rucker	25.00	12.50	7.50
(105a)	Doc Scanlon (Scanlan) (Superbas)			
		25.00	12.50	7.50
(105b)	Doc Scanlon (Scanlan) (Phillies)			
		25.00	12.50	7.50
(106)	Germany Schaefer	25.00	12.50	7.50
(107)	Boss Schmidt	25.00	12.50	7.50
(108)	Wildfire Schulte	25.00	12.50	7.50
(109)	Jimmy Sheckard	25.00	12.50	7.50
(110)	Hap Smith	25.00	12.50	7.50
(111)	Tris Speaker	100.00	50.00	30.00
(112)	Harry Stovall	25.00	12.50	7.50
(113a)	Gabby Street (Senators)	25.00	12.50	7.50
(113b)	Gabby Street (Yankees)	25.00	12.50	7.50
(114)	George Suggs	25.00	12.50	7.50
(115)	Ira Thomas	25.00	12.50	7.50
(116)	Joe Tinker	60.00	30.00	18.00
(117)	John Titus	25.00	12.50	7.50

(118)	Terry Turner	25.00	12.50	7.50
(119)	Heinie Wagner	25.00	12.50	7.50
(120)	Bobby Wallace	60.00	30.00	18.00
(121)	Ed Walsh	60.00	30.00	18.00
(122)	Jack Warhop	25.00	12.50	7.50
(123)	Zach Wheat	60.00	30.00	18.00
(124)	Doc White	25.00	12.50	7.50
(125a)	Art Wilson (dark cap, Pirates)			
		25.00	12.50	7.50
(125b)	Art Wilson (dark cap, Giants)			
		25.00	12.50	7.50
(126a)	Owen Wilson (white cap, Giants)			
		25.00	12.50	7.50
(126b)	Owen Wilson (white cap, Pirates)			
		25.00	12.50	7.50
(127)	Hooks Wiltse	25.00	12.50	7.50
(128)	Harry Wolter	25.00	12.50	7.50
(129)	Cy Young	250.00	125.00	75.00

1969 MLBPA Pins

Issued by the Major League Baseball Players Association in 1969, this unnumbered set consists of 60 pins - 30 players from the N.L. and 30 from the A.L. Each pin measures approximately 7/8" in diameter and features a black-and-white player photo. A.L. players are surrounded by a red border, while N.L. players are framed in blue. The player's name and team appear at the top and bottom. Also along the bottom is a line reading "1969 MLBPA MFG. R.R. Winona, MINN."

		NR MT	EX	VG
Complete Set:		175.00	87.00	52.00
Common Player:		.75	.40	.25
(1)	Hank Aaron	15.00	7.50	4.50
(2)	Richie Allen	3.00	1.50	.90
(3)	Felipe Alou	1.50	.70	.45
(4)	Max Alvis	.75	.40	.25
(5)	Luis Aparicio	4.00	2.00	1.25
(6)	Ernie Banks	8.00	4.00	2.50
(7)	Johnny Bench	8.00	4.00	2.50
(8)	Lou Brock	4.00	2.00	1.25
(9)	George Brunet	.75	.40	.25
(10)	Johnny Callison	1.00	.50	.30
(11)	Rod Carew	7.00	3.50	2.00
(12)	Orlando Cepeda	3.00	1.50	.90
(13)	Dean Chance	.75	.40	.25
(14)	Roberto Clemente	15.00	7.50	4.50
(15)	Willie Davis	1.00	.50	.30
(16)	Don Drysdale	7.00	3.50	2.00
(17)	Ron Fairly	1.00	.50	.30
(18)	Curt Flood	2.50	1.25	.70
(19)	Bill Freehan	1.00	.50	.30
(20)	Jim Fregosi	1.00	.50	.30
(21)	Bob Gibson	7.00	3.50	2.00
(22)	Ken Harrelson	.75	.40	.25
(23)	Bud Harrelson	.75	.40	.25
(24)	Jim Ray Hart	.75	.40	.25
(25)	Tommy Helms	.75	.40	.25
(26)	Joe Horlen	.75	.40	.25
(27)	Willie Horton	1.00	.50	.30
(28)	Frank Howard	2.50	1.25	.70
(29)	Tony Horton	1.00	.50	.30
(30)	Al Kaline	8.00	4.00	2.50
(31)	Don Kessinger	1.00	.50	.30
(32)	Harmon Killebrew	8.00	4.00	2.50
(33)	Jerry Koosman	1.00	.50	.30
(34)	Mickey Lolich	2.00	1.00	.60
(35)	Jim Lonborg	1.00	.50	.30
(36)	Jim Maloney	.75	.40	.25
(37)	Juan Marichal	7.00	3.50	2.00
(38)	Willie Mays	15.00	7.50	4.50
(39)	Tim McCarver	2.00	1.00	.60
(40)	Willie McCovey	7.00	3.50	2.00
(41)	Sam McDowell	1.00	.50	.30
(42)	Denny McLain	2.00	1.00	.60
(43)	Rick Monday	1.00	.50	.30
(44)	Tony Oliva	2.00	1.00	.60
(45)	Joe Pepitone	1.00	.50	.30
(46)	Boog Powell	2.50	1.25	.70
(47)	Rick Reichardt	.75	.40	.25
(48)	Pete Richert	.75	.40	.25
(49)	Brooks Robinson	8.00	4.00	2.50
(50)	Frank Robinson	8.00	4.00	2.50
(51)	Pete Rose	15.00	7.50	4.50
(52)	Ron Santo	2.00	1.00	.60
(53)	Mel Stottlemyre	1.00	.50	.30
(54)	Ron Swoboda	.75	.40	.25
(55)	Luis Tiant	1.00	.50	.30
(56)	Joe Torre	1.50	.70	.45
(57)	Pete Ward	.75	.40	.25
(58)	Billy Williams	5.00	2.50	1.50
(59)	Jim Wynn	1.00	.50	.30
(60)	Carl Yastrzemski	15.00	7.50	4.50

1983 MLBPA pins

This pin set of 36, commonly mistaken for the 1969 Major League Baseball Player's Association version which is patterned after, has 18 unnumbered pins for each league; American Leaguers have red borders, National Leaguers have blue borders. Each pin is 7/8" in diameter and contains a black-and-white player mug shot.

Hank Aaron, blue .... $5-$6
Bob Allison, red $1
Yogi Berra, red $3
Roy Campanella, blue .... $5-$6
Norm Cash, red................................ $1-$3
Orlando Cepeda, blue $3
Roberto Clemente, blue..................... $5-$7
Joe DiMaggio, red .... $8-$15
Bobby Doerr, red............................. $2-$4
Don Drysdale, blue........................... $4-$5
Bob Feller, red .... $3-$6
Whitey Ford, red................................... $3
Nelson Fox, red .... $3-$5
Frank Howard, red............................ $1-$3
Jim Hunter, red .... $3-$4
Al Kaline, red .... $3-$5
Sandy Koufax, blue .... $3-$5
Mickey Mantle, red .... $10-$15
Juan Marichal, blue .... $3-$4
Eddie Mathews, blue .... $3-$4
Willie Mays, blue .... $5-$6
Willie McCovey, blue............................ $3
Stan Musial, blue .... $3-$5
Tony Oliva, red .... $2-$3
Satchel Paige, red .... $3-$10
Phil Rizzuto, red $3
Robin Roberts, blue .... $3-$4
Brooks Robinson, red $3
Jackie Robinson, blue .... $6-$7
Ron Santo, blue $3
Bill Skowron, red .... $2-$3
Duke Snider, blue .... $3-$5
Warren Spahn, blue $3
Billy Williams, blue........................... $3-$4
Ted Williams, red .... $6-$10
Maury Wills, blue.............................. $2-$4

PM10 Stadium Photo issues

These pins were issued in various sizes and were sold at ball parks around the country; the most popular pin size is 1 3/4". All of the pins have black-and-white photos on various color backgrounds, as noted after the players' names.

1. Hank Aaron, blue $275
2. Sandy Amoros, blue $50
3. Harry Anderson, black $75
4. Johnny Antonelli, white/N.Y. $45
   Johnny Antonelli, black, white/S.F....... $25
5. Richie Ashburn, gray....................... $135
6. Dick Bartell, photo in circle $15
7. Gus Bell, white................................ $85
8. Yogi Berra, blue................................ $50

Yogi Berra, white................................. $75
Yogi Berra, gray more expensive $95
9. Joe Black, white/profile..................... $95
Joe Black, white/portrait...................... $50
Joe Black, black/white......................... $25
10. Don Bollweg, gray $20
11. Lou Boudreau, white $15
Lou Boudreau, cap is red/blue.............. $250
12. Eric Bressoud, gray........................ $20
13. Billy Bruton, white......................... $25
14. Dolph Camilli, white $15
15. Roy Campanella, white $75
Roy Campanella, blue $95
Roy Campanella, ivory......................... $75
16. Chico Carrasquel, White Sox $125
17. Phil Cavaretta, stars in border $150
18. Orlando Cepeda, dirty white $45
Orlando Cepeda, railing $50
19. Roberto Clemente, We remember $30
20. Gerry Coleman, gray $15
21. Tony Conigliaro, gray...................... $50
Tony Conigliaro, gray/teeth showing $50
22. Morton Cooper, white/black............. $15
23. Billy Cox, white............................. $15
Billy Cox, ivory................................. $45
24. Al Dark, white $15
25. Jim Davenport, grey $95
Jim Davenport, white $95
26. Jerome (Dizzy) Dean, black $50
27. Bill Dickey, Yankees $145
28. Dom DiMaggio, black...................... $50
Dom DiMaggio, ivory $15
29. Joe DiMaggio, green $275
Joe DiMaggio, black.......................... $275
Joe DiMaggio, white $275
Joe DiMaggio, light blue $65
Joe DiMaggio, white circle $300
Joe DiMaggio, autograph $275
30. Larry Doby, white........................... $15
Larry Doby, black................................ $65
Larry Doby, Congratulations $85
31. Luke Easter, Indians $65
32. Del Ennis, dirty gray $95
Del Ennis, brown................................ $95
33. Carl Erskine, white......................... $35
34. Bob Feller, white............................ $15
Bob Feller, autograph $175
35. Whitey Ford, white......................... $70
36. Nelson Fox, foxes......................... $250
37. Carl Furillo, black/white, facing right $125
Carl Furillo, black/white, facing left $95
Carl Furillo, ivory.............................. $125
Carl Furillo, blue $145
38. Len Gabrielson, SF......................... $75
39. Ned Garver, white......................... $125
40. Lou Gehrig, photo in circle $300
41. Junior Gilliam, small print............... $95
Junior Gilliam, large print $95
42. Lefty Gomez, Yankees $125
43. Ruben Gomez, black/white, photo in circle $15
44. Billy Goodman, white $65
45. Granny Hamner, gray $125
46. Jim Hart, ear missing...................... $125
47. Gabby Hartnett, black..................... $50
48. Grady Hatton, Reds $75
49. Jim Hegan, name in red................... $250

Pins

50. Tom Henrich, light gray $50
Tom Henrich, white...$20
51. Mike Higgins, black $15
52. Gil Hodges, white/eyes left $75
Gil Hodges, white/eyes front.................................$125
Gil Hodges, black/white.......................................$75
Gil Hodges, orange...$75
53. Elston Howard, white.......................................$25
54. Carl Hubbell, photo in circle $125
Carl Hubbell, white circle $25
55. Monte Irvin, black $40
Monte Irvin, white circle $125
Monte Irvin, white..$125
56. Forrest "Spook" Jacobs, black/white...............$20
57. Jackie Jensen, black..$25
 Jackie Jensen, natural $50
Jackie Jensen, white..$95
58. Walter Johnson, Senators.................................$250
59. Willie Jones, gray..$85
60. Harmon Killebrew, natural $175
61. Ralph Kiner, white circle.................................$175
62. Ted Kluszewski, white......................................$75
63. Jim Konstanty, gray...$145
64. Ed Kranepool, white..$20
65. Hal Lanier, black circle $125
66. Big Bill Lee, black/gray...................................$15
67. Bob Lemon, white..$15
Bob Lemon, white circle $145
68. Jim Lemon, white circle $125
69. Whitey Lockman, black/white $15
70. Stan Lopata, gray...$125
71. Sal Maglie, black/white $45
72. Frank Malzone, ivory $45
Frank Malzone, natural..$15
73. Mickey Mantle, blue/ear missing $250
Mickey Mantle, ivory, baseball style.....................$175
Mickey Mantle, blue, name at wrist $135
Mickey Mantle, white/name at elbow.....................$125
Mickey Mantle, white/both hands visible $40
Mickey Mantle, white/eyes closed $300
Mickey Mantle, with Teresa Brewer $50
74. Juan Marichal, black..$135
75. Marty Marion, white circle...............................$135
76. Roger Maris, yellow $25
Roger Maris, pink..$50
Roger Maris, orange...$25
Roger Maris, white...$125
77. Willie Mays, gray/S.F.......................................$175
Willie Mays, white/N.Y..$45
Willie Mays, gray/N.Y..$195
Willie Mays, natural/S.F...$145
Willie Mays, S.F./stands...$275
Willie Mays, white circle..$175
Willie Mays, turquoise..$250
78. Willie McCovey, gray.......................................$50
79. Gil McDougald, dirty gray $15
80. Clift Melton, photo in circle $15
81. Bill Meyer, white circle $125
82. Orestes Minoso, white circle $145
83. Bill Monbouquette, gray...................................$15
84. Don Mueller, white...$15
85. Bobby Murcer, white...$15
86. Danny Murtaugh, white circle..........................$150
87. Stan Musial, yellow $45
Stan Musial, white..$250
Stan Musial, white/ear noticeable $225

88. Don Newcombe, ivory $25
Don Newcombe, blue..$75
Don Newcombe, white/mouth open.......................$30
89. Dan O'Connell, photo in a white border $15
90. Andy Pafko, black...$145
91. Joe Page, ivory $35
92. Leroy Paige, ivory $175
93. Mel Parnell, white...$15
94. Joe Pepitone, white...$20
95. Gaylord Perry, white...$50
96. Johnny Pesky, white..$65
97. Rico Petrocelli, gray...$50
98. Jimmy Piersall, ivory..$30
99. Johnny Podres, white...$45
100. Johnny Pramesa, dirty gray $75
101. Dick Radatz, gray..$30
102. Vic Raschi, white...$45
103. Pee Wee Reese, white......................................$75
Pee Wee Reese, gray/B on cap $45
Pee Wee Reese, gray/ear missing $125
Pee Wee Reese, light gray $75
104. Pete Reiser, photo in circle $15
105. Bill Rigney, black/white..................................$15
106. Phil Rizzuto, ivory..$50
107. Robin Roberts, black/white.............................$20
Robin Roberts, brown..$125
108. Jackie Robinson, yellow $50
Jackie Robinson, red...$250
Jackie Robinson, ROY $125
Jackie Robinson, blue..$125
Jackie Robinson, gray/white....................................$275
Jackie Robinson, white..$275
Jackie Robinson, white/ear missing $300
Jackie Robinson, natural..$125
109. Preacher Roe, white...$125
110. Saul Rogovin, photo in circle $15
111. Stan Rojek, white circle..................................$125
112. Al Rosen, white..$15
113. Charles Herbert Ruffing, gray $25
114. Babe Ruth, black...$400
115. Chuck Schilling, white $65
Chuck Schilling, white $65
116. George Scott, white...$15
117. Andy Seminick, gray.......................................$125
118. Bobby Shantz, white..$20
Bobby Shantz, gray $125
119. Frank Shea, black/white $15
120. Curt Simmons, brown......................................$125
121. Enos Slaughter, black $85
122. Roy Smalley, white circle................................$125
123. Duke Snider, dirty gray $45
Duke Snider, blue $175
Duke Snider, black $95
124. Dick Stuart, gray...$50
125. Hank Thompson, white circle..........................$45
126. Bobby Thomson, ivory....................................$40
127. Gus Triandos, light gray $70
128. Robert Lee Trice, natural................................$75
129. Eddie Waitkus, gray...$125
130. Dixie Walker, white circle...............................$45
131. Bill Werle, white circle...................................$145
132. Sam White, white $15
133. Ted Williams, black/white, name on bottom..$75
Ted Williams, black/white, name on top $175
Ted Williams, black $175
Ted Williams, white..$175

Ted Williams, white..$175
Ted Williams, natural, name at bottom...................$75
134. Gene Woodling, natural................................$145
135. Whitlow Wyatt, photo in circle $15
136. Carl Yastrzemski, gray $150
Carl Yastrzemski, white.......................................$150
137. Gus Zernial, gray $125

1956 Topps Pins

One of Topps first specialty issues, the 60-pin set of ballplayers issued in 1956 contains a high percentage of big-name stars which, combined with the scarcity of the pins, makes collecting a complete set extremely challenging. Compounding the situation is the fact that some pins are seen far less often than others, though the reason is unknown. Chuck Stobbs, Hector Lopez and Chuck Diering are unaccountably scarce. Measuring 1-1/8" in diameter, the pins utilize the same portraits found on 1956 Topps baseball cards. The photos are set against a solid color background.

		NR MT	EX	VG
Complete Set:		2750.	1350.	825.00
Common Player:		17.50	8.75	5.25
(1)	Hank Aaron	120.00	60.00	35.00
(2)	Sandy Amoros	17.50	8.75	5.25
(3)	Luis Arroyo	17.50	8.75	5.25
(4)	Ernie Banks	60.00	30.00	18.00
(5)	Yogi Berra	75.00	37.00	22.00
(6)	Joe Black	17.50	8.75	5.25
(7)	Ray Boone	17.50	8.75	5.25
(8)	Ken Boyer	20.00	10.00	6.00
(9)	Joe Collins	17.50	8.75	5.25
(10)	Gene Conley	17.50	8.75	5.25
(11)	Chuck Diering	225.00	112.00	67.00
(12)	Dick Donovan	17.50	8.75	5.25
(13)	Jim Finigan	17.50	8.75	5.25
(14)	Art Fowler	17.50	8.75	5.25
(15)	Ruben Gomez	17.50	8.75	5.25
(16)	Dick Groat	20.00	10.00	6.00
(17)	Harvey Haddix	17.50	8.75	5.25
(18)	Jack Harshman	17.50	8.75	5.25
(19)	Grady Hatton	17.50	8.75	5.25
(20)	Jim Hegan	17.50	8.75	5.25
(21)	Gil Hodges	40.00	20.00	12.00
(22)	Bobby Hofman	17.50	8.75	5.25
(23)	Frank House	17.50	8.75	5.25
(24)	Jackie Jensen	20.00	10.00	6.00
(25)	Al Kaline	65.00	32.00	19.50
(26)	Bob Kennedy	17.50	8.75	5.25
(27)	Ted Kluszewski	25.00	12.50	7.50
(28)	Dale Long	17.50	8.75	5.25
(29)	Hector Lopez	200.00	100.00	60.00
(30)	Ed Mathews	50.00	25.00	15.00
(31)	Willie Mays	120.00	60.00	35.00
(32)	Roy McMillan	17.50	8.75	5.25
(33)	Willie Miranda	17.50	8.75	5.25
(34)	Wally Moon	17.50	8.75	5.25
(35)	Don Mossi	17.50	8.75	5.25
(36)	Ron Negray	17.50	8.75	5.25
(37)	Johnny O'Brien	17.50	8.75	5.25
(38)	Carlos Paula	17.50	8.75	5.25
(39)	Vic Power	17.50	8.75	5.25
(40)	Jim Rivera	17.50	8.75	5.25
(41)	Phil Rizzuto	40.00	20.00	12.00
(42)	Jackie Robinson	100.00	50.00	30.00
(43)	Al Rosen	25.00	12.50	7.50
(44)	Hank Sauer	17.50	8.75	5.25
(45)	Roy Sievers	17.50	8.75	5.25
(46)	Bill Skowron	20.00	10.00	6.00
(47)	Al Smith	17.50	8.75	5.25
(48)	Hal Smith	17.50	8.75	5.25
(49)	Mayo Smith	17.50	8.75	5.25
(50)	Duke Snider	75.00	37.00	22.00
(51)	Warren Spahn	60.00	30.00	18.00
(52)	Karl Spooner	17.50	8.75	5.25
(53)	Chuck Stobbs	175.00	87.00	52.00
(54)	Frank Sullivan	17.50	8.75	5.25
(55)	Bill Tremel	17.50	8.75	5.25
(56)	Gus Triandos	17.50	8.75	5.25
(57)	Bob Turley	20.00	10.00	6.00
(58)	Herman Wehmeier	17.50	8.75	5.25
(59)	Ted Williams	125.00	62.50	37.50
(60)	Gus Zernial	17.50	8.75	5.25

Crane Potato Chips team pins

Crane Potato Chips issued 7/8" team pins during the 1960s. Generally, the pins can be purchased for about $10 each, with the Yankees, Mets and Dodgers selling for $15 each. In 1961 the company issued two versions - dated (red, black and white) and undated (red, white and blue) for all 18 major league teams. In 1963 the company issued dated, red, black and yellow pins for all 20 teams. Variations exist for the Braves (red stripe, $10, or no stripe, $12) and Red Sox (black background, $10, or yellow background, $12). The 1964 dated pins are gold, red and light blue and range from $5-$15 each. The 1965 pins, which are also dated, are silver, red and dark blue. The 1967 pins, which are not dated, have red, white and light blue borders. Pins from 1968 are red, yellow and black and are dated. The undated pins from 1969 are dark blue, white and orange, while those from 1984, which are dated, have two styles - a base path for National League teams and a baseball style for American League teams.

Guy's Potato Chips

This company issued pins from 1964-66. Generally, pins sell for about $10 each. The 1964 pins, which are undated, are red, white and light blue. Variations exist for the Braves (red stripe or no stripe) and Red Sox (white background or blue background). The 1965 pins are dated and are red, yellow and light blue. Once again, variations exist for the Braves (red stripe or no stripe) and Red Sox (blue background or yellow background). The 1966 pins are also dated and are yellow, brown and green.

1969 Kelly's Potato Chips Pins

Consisting of 20 pins, each measuring approximately 1-3/16" in diameter, this set was issued by Kelly's Potato Chips in 1969 and has a heavy emphasis on St. Louis Cardinals. The pin has a black and white player photo in the center surrounded by either a red border (for A.L. players) or a blue border (for N.L. players) that displays the player's team and name at the top and bottom. "Kelly's" appears to the left while the word "Zip!" is printed to the right. The pins are unnumbered.

	NR MT	EX	VG
Complete Set:	150.00	75.00	45.00
Common Player:	1.50	.70	.45

		NR MT	EX	VG
(1)	Luis Aparicio	7.00	3.50	2.00
(2)	Ernie Banks	15.00	7.50	4.50
(3)	Glenn Beckert	1.50	.70	.45
(4)	Lou Brock	10.00	5.00	3.00
(5)	Curt Flood	2.00	1.00	.60
(6)	Bob Gibson	10.00	5.00	3.00
(7)	Joel Horlen	1.50	.70	.45
(8)	Al Kaline	10.00	5.00	3.00
(9)	Don Kessinger	1.50	.70	.45
(10)	Mickey Lolich	2.50	1.25	.70
(11)	Juan Marichal	8.00	4.00	2.50
(12)	Willie Mays	22.00	11.00	6.50
(13)	Tim McCarver	2.50	1.25	.70
(14)	Denny McLain	2.50	1.25	.70
(15)	Pete Rose	20.00	10.00	6.00
(16)	Ron Santo	2.50	1.25	.70
(17)	Joe Torre	2.50	1.25	.70
(18)	Pete Ward	1.50	.70	.45
(19)	Billy Williams	7.00	3.50	2.00
(20)	Carl Yastrzemski	15.00	7.50	4.50

1985 Fun Food Buttons

Fun Foods of Little Silver, N.J. issued a set of 133 full-color metal pins in 1985. The buttons, which are 1-1/4" in diameter and have a "safety pin" back, have bright borders which correspond to the player's team colors. The button backs are numbered and contain the player's 1984 batting or earned run average. The buttons were available as complete sets through hobby dealers and were also distributed in packs (three buttons per pack) through retail stores.

	MT	NR MT	EX
Complete Set:	25.00	20.00	10.00
Common Player:	.10	.08	.04

		MT	NR MT	EX
1	Dave Winfield	.40	.30	.15
2	Lance Parrish	.25	.20	.10
3	Gary Carter	.35	.25	.14
4	Pete Rose	.80	.60	.30
5	Jim Rice	.35	.25	.14
6	George Brett	.60	.45	.25
7	Fernando Valenzuela	.30	.25	.12
8	Darryl Strawberry	.70	.50	.30
9	Steve Garvey	.35	.25	.14
10	Rollie Fingers	.20	.15	.08
11	Mike Schmidt	1.25	.90	.50
12	Kent Tekulve	.10	.08	.04
13	Ryne Sandberg	.40	.30	.15
14	Bruce Sutter	.15	.11	.06
15	Tom Seaver	.30	.25	.12
16	Reggie Jackson	.70	.50	.30
17	Rickey Henderson	.70	.50	.30
18	Mark Langston	.35	.25	.14
19	Jack Clark	.20	.15	.08
20	Willie Randolph	.15	.11	.06
21	Kirk Gibson	.30	.25	.12
22	Andre Dawson	.30	.25	.12
23	Dave Concepcion	.15	.11	.06
24	Tony Armas	.10	.08	.04
25	Dan Quisenberry	.10	.08	.04
26	Pedro Guerrero	.25	.20	.10
27	Dwight Gooden	1.00	.70	.40
28	Tony Gwynn	.40	.30	.15
29	Robin Yount	.70	.50	.30
30	Steve Carlton	1.00	.70	.40
31	Bill Madlock	.15	.11	.06
32	Rick Sutcliffe	.15	.11	.06
33	Willie McGee	.20	.15	.08
34	Greg Luzinski	.15	.11	.06
35	Rod Carew	.40	.30	.15
36	Dave Kingman	.15	.11	.06
37	Alvin Davis	.40	.30	.15
38	Chili Davis	.15	.11	.06
39	Don Baylor	.15	.11	.06

40	Alan Trammell	.30	.25	.12
41	Tim Raines	.35	.25	.14
42	Cesar Cedeno	.15	.11	.06
43	Wade Boggs	1.00	.70	.40
44	Frank White	.15	.11	.06
45	Steve Sax	.25	.20	.10
46	George Foster	.15	.11	.06
47	Terry Kennedy	.10	.08	.04
48	Cecil Cooper	.15	.11	.06
49	John Denny	.10	.08	.04
50	John Candelaria	.10	.08	.04
51	Jody Davis	.10	.08	.04
52	George Hendrick	.10	.08	.04
53	Ron Kittle	.15	.11	.06
54	Fred Lynn	.20	.15	.08
55	Carney Lansford	.10	.08	.04
56	Gorman Thomas	.10	.08	.04
57	Manny Trillo	.10	.08	.04
58	Steve Kemp	.10	.08	.04
59	Jack Morris	.20	.15	.08
60	Dan Petry	.10	.08	.04
61	Mario Soto	.10	.08	.04
62	Dwight Evans	.20	.15	.08
63	Hal McRae	.10	.08	.04
64	Mike Marshall	.15	.11	.06
65	Mookie Wilson	.15	.11	.06
66	Graig Nettles	.15	.11	.06
67	Ben Oglivie	.10	.08	.04
68	Juan Samuel	.20	.15	.08
69	Johnny Ray	.15	.11	.06
70	Gary Matthews	.15	.11	.06
71	Ozzie Smith	.20	.15	.08
72	Carlton Fisk	.40	.30	.15
73	Doug DeCinces	.10	.08	.04
74	Joe Morgan	.60	.45	.25
75	Dave Stieb	.15	.11	.06
76	Buddy Bell	.15	.11	.06
77	Don Mattingly	1.75	1.25	.70
78	Lou Whitaker	.25	.20	.10
79	Willie Hernandez	.10	.08	.04
80	Dave Parker	.20	.15	.08
81	Bob Stanley	.10	.08	.04
82	Willie Wilson	.15	.11	.06
83	Orel Hershiser	.30	.25	.12
84	Rusty Staub	.15	.11	.06
85	Goose Gossage	.20	.15	.08
86	Don Sutton	.25	.20	.10
87	Al Holland	.10	.08	.04
88	Tony Pena	.15	.11	.06
89	Ron Cey	.15	.11	.06
90	Joaquin Andujar	.10	.08	.04
91	LaMarr Hoyt	.10	.08	.04
92	Tommy John	.20	.15	.08
93	Dwayne Murphy	.10	.08	.04
94	Willie Upshaw	.10	.08	.04
95	Gary Ward	.10	.08	.04
96	Ron Guidry	.20	.15	.08
97	Chet Lemon	.10	.08	.04
98	Aurelio Lopez	.10	.08	.04
99	Tony Perez	.20	.15	.08
100	Bill Buckner	.15	.11	.06
101	Mike Hargrove	.10	.08	.04
102	Scott McGregor	.10	.08	.04
103	Dale Murphy	.60	.45	.25
104	Keith Hernandez	.35	.25	.14
105	Paul Molitor	.20	.15	.08
106	Bert Blyleven	.15	.11	.06
107	Leon Durham	.10	.08	.04
108	Lee Smith	.15	.11	.06
109	Nolan Ryan	2.00	1.50	.80
110	Harold Baines	.15	.11	.06
111	Kent Hrbek	.25	.20	.10
112	Ron Davis	.10	.08	.04
113	George Bell	.30	.25	.12
114	Charlie Hough	.10	.08	.04
115	Phil Niekro	.25	.20	.10
116	Dave Righetti	.20	.15	.08
117	Darrell Evans	.15	.11	.06
118	Cal Ripken, Jr.	1.75	1.25	.60
119	Eddie Murray	.45	.35	.20
120	Storm Davis	.10	.08	.04
121	Mike Boddicker	.10	.08	.04
122	Bob Horner	.15	.11	.06
123	Chris Chambliss	.10	.08	.04
124	Ted Simmons	.15	.11	.06
125	Andre Thornton	.15	.11	.06
126	Larry Bowa	.15	.11	.06
127	Bob Dernier	.10	.08	.04
128	Joe Niekro	.15	.11	.06
129	Jose Cruz	.15	.11	.06
130	Tom Brunansky	.20	.15	.08
131	Gary Gaetti	.25	.20	.10
132	Lloyd Moseby	.15	.11	.06
133	Frank Tanana	.10	.08	.04

Ticket Stubs, Schedules

Ticket stubs do not command high prices unless they are from World Series, All-Star or playoff games, or from a game in which a significant achievement or record occurred. Generally, the stubs are in either Poor or Fair condition, because they have been bent and are worn, or Very Good to Excellent because they have been preserved. Full, unused tickets are worth more money than stubs, and are generally for seats which went unsold for a playoff or World Series game, or one in which a baseball milestone occurred. Shortly after Nolan Ryan won his 300th game in 1990, unused tickets were being offered for $60; an unused ticket and program were priced at $75. Special commemorative certificates, printed by the respective teams, also add to the value and make for an attractive display.

Other tickets which would command premium prices would be those for games such as when Reggie Jackson hit his three homers in the sixth game of the 1977 World Series, and the 1956 World Series game when Don Larsen pitched a perfect game against the Brooklyn Dodgers. One ticket stub from that game sold for $532 in a 1992 auction. It was autographed, framed and matted and included a photo of the final pitch and a copy of the box score.

Other examples from auction results have shown prices realized from games from the 1922 and 1923 World Series (at the Polo Grounds and Yankee Stadium) were between $177-$296, while a 1920 Cleveland Indians full ticket from Game 4 sold for $967. A full ticket from Stan Musial's last game, Sept. 29, 1963, at St. Louis, sold for $242, while a full ticket from Catfish Hunter's perfect game on May 8, 1968, at Oakland, sold for $370. A 1978 All-Star Game full ticket from San Diego sold for $77. But in general, ticket stubs shouldn't set you back more than $30.

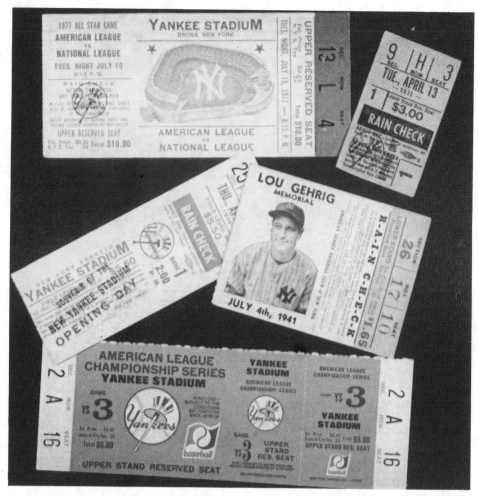

Alan Rosen, in his book **Mr. Mint's Insider's Guide to Investing in Baseball Cards and Collectibles,** advises collectors to not buy old tickets unless they have seat numbers, which are generally printed in a different ink color in a separate press run. Those without, generally from the 1940s and 1950s, and sold in large blocks, are usually worthless because they aren't artist's proofs.

If you search through the scrapbooks, wallets and shoe boxes of memorabilia long enough, inevitably you'll find an annual schedule or two for a favorite team of yesteryear.

Schedules

Schedules, or skeds for short, offer collectors an inexpensive alternative to the big-ticket items which anchor any fan's collection. The limits are endless.

Although the most common form is a pocket schedule, skeds come in all shapes, sizes and for all sports. Collegiate sports such as baseball, football and hockey often utilize sked-cards, which are usually a single piece of paper or tagboard stock with artwork on one side and a game schedule on the back. Professional sports teams generally use folded skeds, similar to sked-cards, but with multiple panels separated by folds. These types of schedules are commonly provided by the major league teams' ticket offices. Other schedule varieties include matchbook covers, schedule cups, ticket brochures, decals, magnets, rulers, napkins, place mats, stickers, key chains, plastic coin purses and poster skeds.

The easiest way to begin or add to a schedule collection is to contact professional teams for ticket information. You'll usually get a response, especially if you send a self-addressed stamped envelope, which means the team isn't paying postage and already has a pre-addressed envelope to send back. When mailing to Canada, remember that any SASEs sent to the Montreal Expos or Toronto Blue Jays require Canadian postage.

Because schedules are primarily advertising pieces through which the sponsors can reach a wide, varying target audience, the sponsors themselves can be a source for schedules. Other possible sources can be found by determining who advertises in the team's yearbook and programs. Radio and television sponsors, and stations which carry the broadcasts, also often produce skeds, as may those who advertise on the television and radio broadcasts.

Off-the-wall skeds can be found in a variety of locations, such as restaurants, which often offer matchbook schedules, liquor stores, sporting goods stores, museums, banks and credit unions, motels and hotels, and ticket offices. When traveling, remember to check gas stations, convenience stores, and kiosks which are located along interstate rest stops.

Another way to obtain schedules is by trading, searching for prospective partners in classified ads in hobby publications such as *Sports Collectors Digest* and sked newsletters.

If the conventional shoe box or scrapbook is not used for displaying schedules, many pocket schedules will fit into eight- or nine-pocket baseball card plastic sheets which are held together in an album. These sheets protect the skeds from getting dinged and folded. Oversized schedules may fit into 5-by-7 inch, dollar bill-sized, or postcard-sized plastic sheets.

Condition is not a critical factor in determining a schedule's value, but it is important. It's more valuable if it isn't damaged, ripped or torn, or marked on. Schedules for defunct teams carry a slight premium value compared to other schedules of the same year, as do localized, scarcer schedules and those featuring team or player photos.

Schedules and their general values: 1901-1909 ($150); 1910-19 ($100); 1920-29 ($75); 1930-39 ($35); 1940-49 ($30); 1950-59 ($25); 1960-69 ($15); 1970-79 ($10); 1980-85 ($2); 1986-on ($1).

Tickets

Note: The first ticket price is for a full ticket, the second is a stub. A means All-Star, P means play-off game, WS means World Series.

Boston Braves tickets: 1936 A ($400/$200); 1914 WS ($1,600/$800); 1948 WS ($200/$100).

Brooklyn Dodgers tickets: 1949 A ($170/$85); 1916 WS ($1,200/$600); 1920 WS ($800/$400); 1941-47-49 WS ($200/$100); 1952-53-56 WS ($150/$75); 1955 WS ($250/$125).

Colorado Rockies tickets: None.

Florida Marlins tickets: None.

Houston Colt 45s tickets: None.

Kansas City A's tickets: 1960 A ($70/$35).

Milwaukee Braves tickets: 1955 A ($150/$75); 1957-58 WS ($150/$75).

New York Giants tickets: 1934 A ($400/$200); 1942 A ($200/$100); 1905 WS ($2,500/$1,200); 1911-12-13 WS ($1,600/$800); 1917 WS (1,200/$600); 1921-22-23-24 WS ($800/$400); 1933-36-37 WS ($400/$200); 1951 WS ($150/$75).

Philadelphia A's tickets: 1943 A ($200/$100); 1905 WS ($2,500/$1,200); 1910-11-13-14 WS ($1,600/$800); 1915 WS ($1,200-$600); 1930-31 WS ($400/$200).

St. Louis Browns tickets; 1948 A ($200/$100); 1944 WS ($200/$100).

Seatle Pilots tickets: 1979 A ($40/$20).

Washington Senators tickets: 1937 A ($400/$200); 1956 A ($150/$75); 1962 A ($75/$35); 1969 A ($75/$35); 1924-25 WS ($800-$400); 1933 ($400/$200).

Atlanta Braves tickets: 1972 A ($55/$15); 1969 P ($30/$15); 1982 P ($15/$5); 1991-92 P ($10/$5); 1991-92 WS ($20/$10).

Cincinnati Reds tickets: 1938 A ($400/$200); 1953 A ($150/$75); 1970 A ($40/$20); 1988 A ($30/$15); 1970-72-73-75-76-79 P ($35/$18); 1990 P ($18/$10); 1919 WS ($2,000/$1,000); 1939 WS ($400/$200); 1940 WS ($200/$100); 1961 WS ($70/$35); 1970-75-76 WS ($40/$20); 1990 WS ($20/$10).

Houston Astros tickets: 1868 A ($70/$35); 1986 A ($30/$15); 1981-86 P ($28/$15).

Los Angeles Dodgers tickets: 1959 A ($150/$75); 1980 ($30/$15); 1974-77-78 P ($38/$18); 1981-83-85-88 P ($28/$15); 1959 WS ($150/$75); 1963-65-66 WS ($70/$35); 1974-77-78 WS ($40/$20); 1981-88 WS ($30/$15).

San Diego Padres tickets: 1978 A ($40/$20); 1992 A ($20/$10); 1984 P ($28/$15); 1984 WS ($30/$15).

San Francisco Giants tickets: 1961 A ($70/$35); 1984 A ($30/$15); 1971 P ($38/$15); 1987-89 P ($28/$15); 1962 WS ($70/$35); 1989 WS ($30/$15).

Chicago Cubs tickets: 1947 A ($200/$100); 1962 A ($70/$35); 1990 A ($20/$10); 1984 P ($35/$15); 1989 P ($30/$15); 1906-07-08 WS ($2,000/$1,000); 1910 WS ($1,600/$800); 1918 WS ($1,200/$600); 1929 WS ($600/$300); 1932-35-38 WS ($400/$200); 1945 WS ($200/$100).

Montreal Expos tickets: 1982 A ($30/$15); 1981 P ($28/$15).

New York Mets tickets: 1964 A ($70/$35); 1969 P ($65/$30); 1973 P ($35/$15); 1986-88 P ($28/$15); 1969 WS ($70/$35); 1973 WS ($40/$20); 1986 WS ($30/$15).

Philadelphia Phillies tickets: 1952 A ($150/$75); 1976 A ($40/$20); 1976-77-78 P ($38-$20); 1980-83 P ($28/$15); 1915 WS ($1,200/$600); 1950 WS ($250/$125); 1980-83 WS ($30/$15).

Pittsburgh Pirates tickets: 1944 A ($200/$100); 1959 A ($150/$75); 1974 A ($45/$20); 1970-71-72-74-75-79 ($38/$20), 1990-91-92 P ($18/$10); 1903 WS ($6,000/$3,000); 1909 WS ($2,000/$1,000); 1925 WS ($800/$400); 1927 WS ($600/$300); 1960 WS ($70/$35); 1971-79 WS ($40/$20).

St. Louis Cardinals tickets: 1940 A ($200/$100); 1957 A ($150/$75); 1966 A ($70/$35); 1982-85-87 P ($28/$15); 1926-28 WS ($600/$300); 1930-31-34 WS ($400/$200); 1942-43-44-46 WS ($200/$100); 1964-67-68 WS ($70/$35); 1982-85-87 WS ($30/$15).

Baltimore Orioles tickets: 1958 A ($200/$100); 1993 A ($40); 1969 P ($50/$25); 1970-71 P ($30/$15); 1973-74 P ($20/$10); 1979 P ($20/$7); 1983 P ($15/$5); 1966 WS ($100/$40); 1969-70 WS ($70/$25); 1971 WS ($50/$20); 1979 WS ($30/$10); 1983 WS ($20/$10).

Boston Red Sox tickets: 1946 A ($200/$100); 1961 A ($75/$35); 1975 P ($45/$20); 1986-88 P ($30/$15); 1990 P ($20/$10); 1903 WS ($6,000/$3,000); 1915-16-18 WS ($1,200/$600); 1946 WS ($100/$70); 1967 WS ($70/$36); 1975 WS ($40/$20); 1986 WS ($30/$15).

Cleveland Indians tickets: 1935 A ($400/$200); 1954 A ($150/$75); 1963 A ($70/$35); 1981 A ($30/$15); 1920 WS ($800/$400); 1948 WS ($200/$100); 1954 WS ($150/$75).

Detroit Tigers tickets: 1941 A ($200/$100); 1951 A ($150/$75); 1971 A ($40/$20); 1972 P ($38/$18); 1984-87 P ($28/$15); 1908-09 WS ($2,000/$1,000); 1934-35 WS ($400/$200); 1940-45 WS ($200/$100); 1968 WS ($70/$35); 1984 WS ($30/$15).

Milwaukee Brewers tickets: 1975 A ($45/$20); 1982 P ($28/$15); 1982 WS ($30/$15).

New York Yankees tickets: 1939 A ($400/$200); 1960 A ($70/$35); 1977 A ($40/$20); 1976-77-78 P ($38/$15); 1980-81 P ($28/$15); 1921-22-23 WS ($800/$400); 1926-27-28 WS ($600/$300); 1932-36-37-38-39 WS ($400/$200); 1941-42-43-47-49 WS ($200/$100); 1950-51-52-53-55-56-57-58 WS ($150/$75); 1960-61-62-63-64 WS ($70-$35); 1976-77-78 WS ($40/$20); 1981 WS ($30/$15).

Toronto Blue Jays tickets: 1991 A ($20/$10); 1985-89 P ($28/$15); 1991-92 P ($18/$10); 1992 WS ($30/$15).

California Angels tickets: 1967 A ($70/$30); 1989 A ($30/$15); 1979-82 P ($30/$15); 1986 ($25/$10).

Chicago White Sox tickets: 1933 A ($400/$200); 1950 A ($150/$75); 1983 A ($30/$15); 1986 P ($15/$5); 1906 WS ($2,000/$1,000); 1917 WS ($1,200/$600); 1919 WS ($3,000/$1,500); 1959 WS ($150/$75).

Kansas City Royals tickets: 1973 A ($40/$20); 1976-77-78 P ($38/$18); 1980-81-84-85 P ($28/$15); 1980-85 WS ($30-$15).

Minnesota Twins tickets: 1965 A ($70/$35); 1985 A ($30/$15); 1969 P ($65/$30); 1970-87 P ($35/$15); 1991 P ($18/$10); 1965 WS ($100/$50); 1987 WS ($30/$15); 1991 WS $20/$10).

Oakland A's tickets: 1987 A ($30/$15); 1971-72-73-74-75 P ($38/$20); 1988-89 P ($28/$15); 1990-92 P ($18/$10); 1972-73-74 WS ($40-$20); 1988-89 WS ($30/$15); 1990 WS ($20/$10).

Seattle Mariners tickets: 1979 A ($40/$20).

Texas Rangers tickets: None.

Medallions

1964 Topps Coins

The 164 metal coins in this set were issued by Topps as inserts in the company's baseball card wax packs. The series is divided into two principal types, 120 "regular" coins and 44 All-Star coins. The 1 1/2" diameter coins feature a full-color background for the player photos in the "regular" series, while the players in the All-Star series are featured against plain red or blue backgrounds. There are two variations each of the Mantle, Causey and Hinton coins among the All-Star subset.

		NR MT	EX	VG
Complete Set:		700.00	350.00	210.00
Common Player:		2.00	1.00	.60
1	Don Zimmer	3.00	1.50	.90
2	Jim Wynn	2.00	1.00	.60
3	Johnny Orsino	2.00	1.00	.60
4	Jim Bouton	3.00	1.50	.90
5	Dick Groat	3.00	1.50	.90
6	Leon Wagner	2.00	1.00	.60
7	Frank Malzone	2.00	1.00	.60
8	Steve Barber	2.00	1.00	.60
9	Johnny Romano	2.00	1.00	.60
10	Tom Tresh	3.00	1.50	.90
11	Felipe Alou	3.00	1.50	.90
12	Dick Stuart	2.00	1.00	.60
13	Claude Osteen	2.00	1.00	.60
14	Juan Pizarro	2.00	1.00	.60
15	Donn Clendenon	2.00	1.00	.60
16	Jimmie Hall	2.00	1.00	.60
17	Larry Jackson	2.00	1.00	.60
18	Brooks Robinson	12.50	6.25	3.75
19	Bob Allison	2.00	1.00	.60
20	Ed Roebuck	2.00	1.00	.60
21	Pete Ward	2.00	1.00	.60
22	Willie McCovey	8.00	4.00	2.50
23	Elston Howard	3.00	1.50	.90
24	Diego Segui	2.00	1.00	.60
25	Ken Boyer	3.00	1.50	.90
26	Carl Yastrzemski	15.00	7.50	4.50
27	Bill Mazeroski	4.00	2.00	1.25

28	Jerry Lumpe	2.00	1.00	.60
29	Woody Held	2.00	1.00	.60
30	Dick Radatz	2.00	1.00	.60
31	Luis Aparicio	8.00	4.00	2.50
32	Dave Nicholson	2.00	1.00	.60
33	Ed Mathews	12.00	6.00	3.50
34	Don Drysdale	15.00	7.50	4.50
35	Ray Culp	2.00	1.00	.60
36	Juan Marichal	8.00	4.00	2.50
37	Frank Robinson	12.50	6.25	3.75
38	Chuck Hinton	2.00	1.00	.60
39	Floyd Robinson	2.00	1.00	.60
40	Tommy Harper	2.00	1.00	.60
41	Ron Hansen	2.00	1.00	.60
42	Ernie Banks	15.00	7.50	4.50
43	Jesse Gonder	2.00	1.00	.60
44	Billy Williams	8.00	4.00	2.50
45	Vada Pinson	3.00	1.50	.90
46	Rocky Colavito	4.00	2.00	1.25
47	Bill Monbouquette	2.00	1.00	.60
48	Max Alvis	2.00	1.00	.60
49	Norm Siebern	2.00	1.00	.60
50	John Callison	2.00	1.00	.60
51	Rich Rollins	2.00	1.00	.60
52	Ken McBride	2.00	1.00	.60
53	Don Lock	2.00	1.00	.60
54	Ron Fairly	2.00	1.00	.60
55	Roberto Clemente	25.00	12.50	7.50
56	Dick Ellsworth	2.00	1.00	.60
57	Tommy Davis	2.00	1.00	.60
58	Tony Gonzalez	2.00	1.00	.60
59	Bob Gibson	12.00	6.00	3.50
60	Jim Maloney	2.00	1.00	.60
61	Frank Howard	3.00	1.50	.90
62	Jim Pagliaroni	2.00	1.00	.60
63	Orlando Cepeda	4.00	2.00	1.25
64	Ron Perranoski	2.00	1.00	.60
65	Curt Flood	2.50	1.25	.70
66	Al McBean	2.00	1.00	.60
67	Dean Chance	2.00	1.00	.60
68	Ron Santo	2.50	1.25	.70
69	Jack Baldschun	2.00	1.00	.60
70	Milt Pappas	2.00	1.00	.60
71	Gary Peters	2.00	1.00	.60
72	Bobby Richardson	2.50	1.25	.70
73	Lee Thomas	2.00	1.00	.60
74	Hank Aguirre	2.00	1.00	.60
75	Carl Willey	2.00	1.00	.60
76	Camilo Pascual	2.00	1.00	.60
77	Bob Friend	2.00	1.00	.60
78	Bill White	2.50	1.25	.70
79	Norm Cash	3.00	1.50	.90
80	Willie Mays	25.00	12.50	7.50
81	Duke Carmel	2.00	1.00	.60
82	Pete Rose	20.00	10.00	6.00
83	Hank Aaron	25.00	12.50	7.50
84	Bob Aspromonte	2.00	1.00	.60
85	Jim O'Toole	2.00	1.00	.60
86	Vic Davalillo	2.00	1.00	.60
87	Bill Freehan	2.00	1.00	.60
88	Warren Spahn	12.00	6.00	3.50
89	Ron Hunt	2.00	1.00	.60
90	Denis Menke	2.00	1.00	.60
91	Turk Farrell	2.00	1.00	.60
92	Jim Hickman	2.00	1.00	.60
93	Jim Bunning	3.00	1.50	.90
94	Bob Hendley	2.00	1.00	.60
95	Ernie Broglio	2.00	1.00	.60
96	Rusty Staub	3.00	1.50	.90
97	Lou Brock	8.00	4.00	2.50
98	Jim Fregosi	2.50	1.25	.70
99	Jim Grant	2.00	1.00	.60
100	Al Kaline	15.00	7.50	4.50
101	Earl Battey	2.00	1.00	.60
102	Wayne Causey	2.00	1.00	.60
103	Chuck Schilling	2.00	1.00	.60
104	Boog Powell	3.50	1.75	1.00
105	Dave Wickersham	2.00	1.00	.60
106	Sandy Koufax	18.00	9.00	5.50
107	John Bateman	2.00	1.00	.60
108	Ed Brinkman	2.00	1.00	.60
109	Al Downing	2.00	1.00	.60
110	Joe Azcue	2.00	1.00	.60
111	Albie Pearson	2.00	1.00	.60
112	Harmon Killebrew	12.00	6.00	3.50
113	Tony Taylor	2.00	1.00	.60
114	Alvin Jackson	2.00	1.00	.60
115	Billy O'Dell	2.00	1.00	.60
116	Don Demeter	2.00	1.00	.60
117	Ed Charles	2.00	1.00	.60
118	Joe Torre	2.50	1.25	.70
119	Don Nottebart	2.00	1.00	.60
120	Mickey Mantle	45.00	22.00	13.50

121	Joe Pepitone (All-Star)	2.00	1.00	.60
122	Dick Stuart (All-Star)	3.00	1.50	.90
123	Bobby Richardson (All-Star)			
		2.50	1.25	.70
124	Jerry Lumpe (All-Star)	2.00	1.00	.60
125	Brooks Robinson (All-Star)			
		12.50	6.25	3.75
126	Frank Malzone (All-Star)	2.00	1.00	.60
127	Luis Aparicio (All-Star)	8.00	4.00	2.50
128	Jim Fregosi (All-Star)	2.50	1.25	.70
129	Al Kaline (All-Star)	15.00	7.50	4.50
130	Leon Wagner (All-Star)	2.00	1.00	.60
131a	Mickey Mantle (All-Star, lefthanded)			
		45.00	22.00	13.50
131b	Mickey Mantle (All-Star, righthanded)			
		45.00	22.00	13.50
132	Albie Pearson (All-Star)	2.00	1.00	.60
133	Harmon Killebrew (All-Star)			
		12.00	6.00	3.50
134	Carl Yastrzemski (All-Star)			
		15.00	7.50	4.50
135	Elston Howard (All-Star)	3.00	1.50	.90
136	Earl Battey (All-Star)	2.00	1.00	.60
137	Camilo Pascual (All-Star)	2.00	1.00	.60
138	Jim Bouton (All-Star)	3.00	1.50	.90
139	Whitey Ford (All-Star)	12.00	6.00	3.50
140	Gary Peters (All-Star)	2.00	1.00	.60
141	Bill White (All-Star)	2.50	1.25	.70
142	Orlando Cepeda (All-Star)	3.00	1.50	.90
143	Bill Mazeroski (All-Star)	4.00	2.00	1.25
144	Tony Taylor (All-Star)	2.00	1.00	.60
145	Ken Boyer (All-Star)	3.00	1.50	.90
146	Ron Santo (All-Star)	2.50	1.25	.70
147	Dick Groat (All-Star)	2.00	1.00	.60
148	Roy McMillan (All-Star)	2.00	1.00	.60
149	Hank Aaron (All-Star)	25.00	12.50	7.50
150	Roberto Clemente (All-Star)			
		25.00	12.50	7.50
151	Willie Mays (All-Star)	25.00	12.50	7.50
152	Vada Pinson (All-Star)	3.00	1.50	.90
153	Tommy Davis (All-Star)	2.00	1.00	.60
154	Frank Robinson (All-Star)	12.50	6.25	3.75
155	Joe Torre (All-Star)	2.50	1.25	.70
156	Tim McCarver (All-Star)	2.50	1.25	.70
157	Juan Marichal (All-Star)	8.00	4.00	2.50
158	Jim Maloney (All-Star)	2.00	1.00	.60
159	Sandy Koufax (All-Star)	18.00	9.00	5.50
160	Warren Spahn (All-Star)	12.00	6.00	3.50
161a	Wayne Causey (All-Star, A.L. on back)			
		15.00	7.50	4.50
161b	Wayne Causey (All-Star, A.L. on back)			
		2.00	1.00	.60
162a	Chuck Hinton (All-Star, N.L. on back)			
		15.00	7.50	4.50
162b	Chuck Hinton (All-Star, A.L. on back)			
		2.00	1.00	.60
163	Bob Aspromonte (All-Star)	2.00	1.00	.60
164	Ron Hunt (All-Star)	2.00	1.00	.60

1971 Topps Coins

Measuring 1 1/2" in diameter, the latest edition of the Topps coins was a 153-piece set. The coins feature a color photograph surrounded by a colored band on the front. The band carries the player's name, team, position and several stars. Backs have a short biography, the coin number and encouragement to collect the entire set. Back colors differ, with #s 1-51 having a brass back, #s 52-102 chrome backs, and the rest have blue backs. Most of the stars of the period are included in the set.

		NR MT	EX	VG
Complete Set:		400.00	200.00	120.00
Common Player:		.90	.45	.25
1	Cito Gaston	1.50	.70	.45
2	Dave Johnson	1.25	.60	.40
3	Jim Bunning	2.00	1.00	.60
4	Jim Spencer	.90	.45	.25
5	Felix Millan	.90	.45	.25
6	Gerry Moses	.90	.45	.25
7	Fergie Jenkins	5.00	2.50	1.50
8	Felipe Alou	1.50	.70	.45
9	Jim McGlothlin	.90	.45	.25
10	Dick McAuliffe	.90	.45	.25
11	Joe Torre	1.50	.70	.45

12	Jim Perry	1.25	.60	.40
13	Bobby Bonds	1.50	.70	.45
14	Danny Cater	.90	.45	.25
15	Bill Mazeroski	3.00	1.50	.90
16	Luis Aparicio	5.00	2.50	1.50
17	Doug Rader	.90	.45	.25
18	Vada Pinson	1.50	.70	.45
19	John Bateman	.90	.45	.25
20	Lew Krausse	.90	.45	.25
21	Billy Grabarkewitz	.90	.45	.25
22	Frank Howard	1.50	.70	.45
23	Jerry Koosman	1.25	.60	.40
24	Rod Carew	8.00	4.00	2.50
25	Al Ferrara	.90	.45	.25
26	Dave McNally	.90	.45	.25
27	Jim Hickman	.90	.45	.25
28	Sandy Alomar	.90	.45	.25
29	Lee May	.90	.45	.25
30	Rico Petrocelli	1.25	.60	.40
31	Don Money	.90	.45	.25
32	Jim Rooker	.90	.45	.25
33	Dick Dietz	.90	.45	.25
34	Roy White	1.25	.60	.40
35	Carl Morton	.90	.45	.25
36	Walt Williams	.90	.45	.25
37	Phil Niekro	3.25	1.75	1.00
38	Bill Freehan	1.25	.60	.40
39	Julian Javier	.90	.45	.25
40	Rick Monday	.90	.45	.25
41	Don Wilson	.90	.45	.25
42	Ray Fosse	.90	.45	.25
43	Art Shamsky	.90	.45	.25
44	Ted Savage	.90	.45	.25
45	Claude Osteen	.90	.45	.25
46	Ed Brinkman	.90	.45	.25
47	Matty Alou	.90	.45	.25
48	Bob Oliver	.90	.45	.25
49	Danny Coombs	.90	.45	.25
50	Frank Robinson	7.00	3.50	2.00
51	Randy Hundley	.90	.45	.25
52	Cesar Tovar	.90	.45	.25
53	Wayne Simpson	.90	.45	.25
54	Bobby Murcer	1.25	.60	.40
55	Tony Taylor	.90	.45	.25
56	Tommy John	1.50	.70	.45
57	Willie McCovey	7.00	3.50	2.00
58	Carl Yastrzemski	12.00	6.00	3.50
59	Bob Bailey	.90	.45	.25
60	Clyde Wright	.90	.45	.25
61	Orlando Cepeda	2.00	1.00	.60
62	Al Kaline	7.00	3.50	2.00
63	Bob Gibson	7.00	3.50	2.00
64	Bert Campaneris	1.25	.60	.40
65	Ted Sizemore	.90	.45	.25
66	Duke Sims	.90	.45	.25
67	Bud Harrelson	.90	.45	.25
68	Jerry McNertney	.90	.45	.25
69	Jim Wynn	.90	.45	.25
70	Dick Bosman	.90	.45	.25
71	Roberto Clemente	15.00	7.50	4.50
72	Rich Reese	.90	.45	.25
73	Gaylord Perry	5.00	2.50	1.50
74	Boog Powell	1.50	.70	.45
75	Billy Williams	5.00	2.50	1.50
76	Bill Melton	.90	.45	.25
77	Nate Colbert	.90	.45	.25
78	Reggie Smith	1.25	.60	.40
79	Deron Johnson	.90	.45	.25
80	Catfish Hunter	5.00	2.50	1.50
81	Bob Tolan	.90	.45	.25
82	Jim Northrup	.90	.45	.25
83	Ron Fairly	.90	.45	.25
84	Alex Johnson	.90	.45	.25
85	Pat Jarvis	.90	.45	.25
86	Sam McDowell	.90	.45	.25
87	Lou Brock	6.00	3.00	1.75
88	Danny Walton	.90	.45	.25
89	Denis Menke	.90	.45	.25
90	Jim Palmer	7.00	3.50	2.00
91	Tommie Agee	.90	.45	.25
92	Duane Josephson	.90	.45	.25
93	Willie Davis	1.25	.60	.40
94	Mel Stottlemyre	1.25	.60	.40
95	Ron Santo	1.25	.60	.40
96	Amos Otis	.90	.45	.25
97	Ken Henderson	.90	.45	.25
98	George Scott	.90	.45	.25
99	Dock Ellis	.90	.45	.25
100	Harmon Killebrew	7.00	3.50	2.00
101	Pete Rose	25.00	12.50	7.50
102	Rick Reichardt	.90	.45	.25
103	Cleon Jones	.90	.45	.25
104	Ron Perranoski	.90	.45	.25

105	Tony Perez	2.50	1.25	.70
106	Mickey Lolich	1.25	.60	.40
107	Tim McCarver	1.25	.60	.40
108	Reggie Jackson	12.00	6.00	3.50
109	Chris Cannizzaro	.90	.45	.25
110	Steve Hargan	.90	.45	.25
111	Rusty Staub	1.50	.70	.45
112	Andy Messersmith	.90	.45	.25
113	Rico Carty	.90	.45	.25
114	Brooks Robinson	7.00	3.50	2.00
115	Steve Carlton	7.00	3.50	2.00
116	Mike Hegan	.90	.45	.25
117	Joe Morgan	5.00	2.50	1.50
118	Thurman Munson	4.00	2.00	1.25
119	Don Kessinger	.90	.45	.25
120	Joe Horlen	.90	.45	.25
121	Wes Parker	.90	.45	.25
122	Sonny Siebert	.90	.45	.25
123	Willie Stargell	5.00	2.50	1.50
124	Ellie Rodriguez	.90	.45	.25
125	Juan Marichal	5.00	2.50	1.50
126	Mike Epstein	.90	.45	.25
127	Tom Seaver	7.00	3.50	2.00
128	Tony Oliva	2.50	1.25	.70
129	Jim Merritt	.90	.45	.25
130	Willie Horton	.90	.45	.25
131	Rick Wise	.90	.45	.25
132	Sal Bando	.90	.45	.25
133	Ollie Brown	.90	.45	.25
134	Ken Harrelson	.90	.45	.25
135	Mack Jones	.90	.45	.25
136	Jim Fregosi	1.25	.60	.40
137	Hank Aaron	15.00	7.50	4.50
138	Fritz Peterson	.90	.45	.25
139	Joe Hague	.90	.45	.25
140	Tommy Harper	.90	.45	.25
141	Larry Dierker	.90	.45	.25
142	Tony Conigliaro	1.50	.70	.45
143	Glenn Beckert	.90	.45	.25
144	Carlos May	.90	.45	.25
145	Don Sutton	2.50	1.25	.70
146	Paul Casanova	.90	.45	.25
147	Bob Moose	.90	.45	.25
148	Leo Cardenas	.90	.45	.25
149	Johnny Bench	9.00	4.50	2.75
150	Mike Cuellar	1.25	.60	.40
151	Donn Clendenon	.90	.45	.25
152	Lou Piniella	1.25	.60	.40
153	Willie Mays	15.00	7.50	4.50

1987 Topps Coins

For the first time since 1971, Topps issued a set of baseball "coins." Similar in design to the 1964 edition of Topps coins, the metal discs measure 1 1/2" in diameter. The aluminum coins were sold on a limited basis in retail outlets. Three coins and three sticks of gum were found in a pack. The coin fronts feature a full-color photo along with the player's name, team and position in a white band at the bottom of the coin. Gold-colored rims are found for American League players; National League players have silver-colored rims. Backs are silver in color and carry the coin number, player's name and personal and statistical information.

		MT	NR MT	EX
Complete Set:		10.00	7.50	4.00
Common Player:		.15	.11	.06
1	Harold Baines	.15	.11	.06
2	Jesse Barfield	.15	.11	.06
3	George Bell	.15	.11	.06
4	Wade Boggs	.70	.50	.30
5	George Brett	.75	.60	.30
6	Jose Canseco	.60	.45	.25
7	Joe Carter	.25	.20	.10
8	Roger Clemens	.40	.30	.15
9	Alvin Davis	.15	.11	.06
10	Rob Deer	.15	.11	.06
11	Kirk Gibson	.20	.15	.08
12	Rickey Henderson	.60	.45	.25
13	Kent Hrbek	.20	.15	.08
14	Pete Incaviglia	.15	.11	.06
15	Reggie Jackson	.50	.40	.20

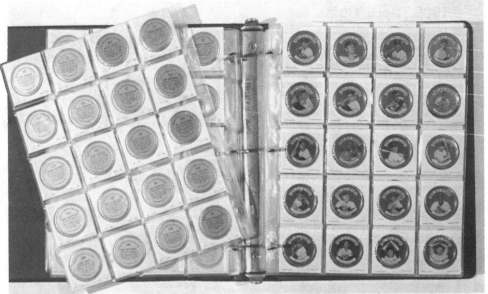

		MT	NR MT	EX
16	Wally Joyner	.25	.20	.10
17	Don Mattingly	.75	.60	.30
18	Jack Morris	.15	.11	.06
19	Eddie Murray	.25	.20	.10
20	Kirby Puckett	.45	.35	.20
21	Jim Rice	.25	.20	.10
22	Dave Righetti	.15	.11	.06
23	Cal Ripken, Jr.	1.50	1.25	.60
24	Cory Snyder	.15	.11	.06
25	Danny Tartabull	.20	.15	.08
26	Dave Winfield	.45	.35	.20
27	Hubie Brooks	.15	.11	.06
28	Gary Carter	.25	.20	.10
29	Vince Coleman	.20	.15	.08
30	Eric Davis	.50	.40	.20
31	Glenn Davis	.15	.11	.06
32	Steve Garvey	.25	.20	.10
33	Dwight Gooden	.40	.30	.15
34	Tony Gwynn	.30	.25	.12
35	Von Hayes	.15	.11	.06
36	Keith Hernandez	.15	.11	.06
37	Dale Murphy	.30	.25	.12
38	Dave Parker	.30	.25	.12
39	Tony Pena	.15	.11	.06
40	Nolan Ryan	2.00	1.50	.80
41	Ryne Sandberg	1.50	1.25	.60
42	Steve Sax	.15	.11	.06
43	Mike Schmidt	.60	.45	.25
44	Mike Scott	.15	.11	.06
45	Ozzie Smith	.25	.20	.10
46	Darryl Strawberry	.20	.15	.08
47	Fernando Valenzuela	.15	.11	.06
48	Todd Worrell	.15	.11	.06

1988 Topps Coins

This edition of 60 lightweight metal coins is similar in design to Topps' 1964 set. The 1988 coins are 1 1/2" in diameter and feature full-color player closeups under crimped edges in silver, gold and pink. Curved under the photo is a red and white player name banner pinned by two gold stars. Coin backs list the coin number, player name, personal information and career summary in black letters on a silver background.

		MT	NR MT	EX
Complete Set:		10.00	7.50	4.50
Common Player:		.10	.08	.04
1	George Bell	.10	.08	.04
2	Roger Clemens	.40	.30	.15
3	Mark McGwire	.40	.30	.15
4	Wade Boggs	.70	.50	.30
5	Harold Baines	.10	.08	.04
6	Ivan Calderon	.10	.08	.04
7	Jose Canseco	.50	.40	.20
8	Joe Carter	.20	.15	.08
9	Jack Clark	.10	.08	.04
10	Alvin Davis	.10	.08	.04
11	Dwight Evans	.10	.08	.04
12	Tony Fernandez	.10	.08	.04
13	Gary Gaetti	.10	.08	.04
14	Mike Greenwell	.20	.15	.08
15	Charlie Hough	.10	.08	.04
16	Wally Joyner	.20	.15	.08
17	Jimmy Key	.10	.08	.04
18	Mark Langston	.10	.08	.04
19	Don Mattingly	1.00	.70	.40
20	Paul Molitor	.25	.20	.10
21	Jack Morris	.10	.08	.04
22	Eddie Murray	.20	.15	.08
23	Kirby Puckett	.35	.25	.14
24	Cal Ripken, Jr.	1.25	.90	.50
25	Bret Saberhagen	.10	.08	.04
26	Ruben Sierra	.15	.11	.06
27	Cory Snyder	.10	.08	.04
28	Terry Steinbach	.10	.08	.04
29	Danny Tartabull	.15	.11	.06
30	Alan Trammell	.20	.15	.08
31	Devon White	.15	.11	.06
32	Robin Yount	.50	.40	.20
33	Andre Dawson	.15	.11	.06
34	Steve Bedrosian	.10	.08	.04
35	Benny Santiago	.10	.08	.04
36	Tony Gwynn	.25	.20	.10
37	Bobby Bonilla	.15	.11	.06
38	Will Clark	.30	.25	.12
39	Eric Davis	.25	.20	.10
40	Mike Dunne	.10	.08	.04
41	John Franco	.10	.08	.04
42	Dwight Gooden	.30	.25	.12
43	Pedro Guerrero	.10	.08	.04
44	Dion James	.10	.08	.04
45	John Kruk	.15	.11	.06
46	Jeffrey Leonard	.10	.08	.04
47	Carmelo Martinez	.10	.08	.04
48	Dale Murphy	.30	.25	.12
49	Tim Raines	.20	.15	.08
50	Nolan Ryan	1.50	1.25	.60
51	Juan Samuel	.10	.08	.04
52	Ryne Sandberg	1.25	.90	.50
53	Mike Schmidt	.60	.45	.25
54	Mike Scott	.10	.08	.04
55	Ozzie Smith	.25	.20	.10
56	Darryl Strawberry	.20	.15	.08
57	Rick Sutcliffe	.10	.08	.04
58	Fernando Valenzuela	.10	.08	.04
59	Tim Wallach	.10	.08	.04
60	Todd Worrell	.10	.08	.04

1989 Topps Coins

Similar in format to previous Topps coins, this 60-piece set features 1-1/2" diameter coins with rolled colored edges. A shooting star device printed over the player photo gives his name, team and position. Backs have a few biographical details and a summary of the player's previous season performance printed in black on silver. The coins were sold three per pack, with each pack including an offer card for an album to house the pieces.

		MT	NR MT	EX
Complete set (60):		9.00	6.75	3.50
Common player:		.10	.08	.04
1	Kirk Gibson	.15	.11	.06
2	Orel Herhiser	.15	.11	.06
3	Chris Sabo	.10	.08	.04
4	Tony Gwynn	.20	.15	.08
5	Brett Butler, Bobby Bonilla	.15	.11	.06
7	Jack Clark, Will Clark	.35	.25	.14
9	Eric Davis	.15	.11	.06
10	Glenn Davis	.10	.08	.04
11	Andre Dawson	.20	.15	.08
12	John Franco	.10	.08	.04
13	Andres Galarraga	.15	.11	.06
14	Dwight Gooden	.20	.15	.08
15	Mark Grace	.15	.11	.06
16	Pedro Guerrero	.10	.08	.04
17	Ricky Jordan	.10	.08	.04
18	Mike Marshall	.10	.08	.04
19	Dale Murphy	.25	.20	.10
20	Eddie Murray	.20	.15	.08
21	Gerald Perry	.10	.08	.04
22	Tim Raines	.15	.11	.06
23	Juan Samuel	.10	.08	.04
24	Benito Santiago	.15	.11	.06
25	Ozzie Smith	.20	.15	.08
26	Darryl Strawberry	.15	.11	.06
27	Andy Van Slyke	.15	.11	.06
28	Gerald Young	.10	.08	.04
29	Jose Canseco	.25	.20	.10
30	Frank Viola	.10	.08	.04
31	Walt Weiss	.15	.11	.06
32	Wade Boggs	.35	.25	.14
33	Harold Baines	.10	.08	.04
34	George Brett	.45	.35	.20
35	Jay Buhner	.15	.11	.06
36	Joe Carter	.20	.15	.08
37	Roger Clemens	.35	.25	.14
38	Alvin Davis	.10	.08	.04
39	Tony Fernandez	.10	.08	.04
40	Carlton Fisk	.20	.15	.08
41	Mike Greenwell	.15	.11	.06
42	Kent Hrbek	.15	.11	.06
43	Don Mattingly	.50	.40	.20
44	Fred McGriff	.25	.20	.10
45	Mark McGwire	.25	.20	.10
46	Paul Molitor	.25	.20	.10
47	Rafael Palmeiro	.20	.15	.08
48	Kirby Puckett	.25	.20	.10
49	Johnny Ray	.10	.08	.04
50	Cal Ripken, Jr.	.50	.40	.20
51	Ruben Sierra	.15	.11	.06
52	Pete Stanicek	.10	.08	.04
53	Dave Stewart	.15	.11	.06
54	Greg Swindell	.10	.08	.04
55	Danny Tartabull	.15	.11	.06
56	Alan Trammell	.20	.15	.08
57	Lou Whitaker	.15	.11	.06
58	Dave Winfield	.45	.35	.20
59	Mike Witt	.10	.08	.04
60	Robin Yount	.45	.35	.20

The player's name and team appear below. Most coins feature natural aluminum coloring on the rolled edges and on the back. Special coins of major award winners have different colors in the background and edges. Backs feature a coin number, minimal biographical data and a previous season career summary. Coins were sold three per pack which included an offer card for a coin holder and Topps magazine subscription offer.

		MT	NR MT	EX
Complete set (60):		8.00	6.00	3.25
Common player:		.10	.08	.04
1	Robin Yount	.40	.30	.15
2	Bret Saberhagen	.10	.08	.04
3	Gregg Olson	.10	.08	.04
4	Kirby Puckett	.20	.15	.08
5	George Bell	.10	.08	.04
6	Wade Boggs	.35	.25	.14
7	Jerry Browne	.10	.08	.04
8	Ellis Burks	.10	.08	.04
9	Ivan Calderon	.10	.08	.04
10	Tom Candiotti	.10	.08	.04
11	Alvin Davis	.10	.08	.04
12	Chil Davis	.15	.11	.06
13	Chuck Finley	.10	.08	.04
14	Gary Gaetti	.10	.08	.04
15	Tom Gordon	.10	.08	.04
16	Ken Griffey, Jr.	.60	.45	.25
17	Rickey Henderson	.20	.15	.08
18	Kent Hrbek	.15	.11	.06
19	Bo Jackson	.25	.20	.10
20	Carlos Martinez	.10	.08	.04
21	Don Mattingly	.35	.25	.14
22	Fred McGriff	.20	.15	.08
23	Paul Molitor	.20	.15	.08
24	Cal Ripken, Jr.	.35	.25	.14
25	Nolan Ryan	.60	.45	.25
26	Steve Sax	.10	.08	.04
27	Gary Sheffield	.15	.11	.06
28	Ruben Sierra	.15	.11	.06
29	Dave Stewart	.10	.08	.04
30	Mickey Tettleton	.10	.08	.04
31	Alan Trammell	.20	.15	.08
32	Lou Whitaker	.15	.11	.06
33	Kevin Mitchell	.10	.08	.04
34	Mark Davis	.10	.08	.04
35	Jerome Walton	.10	.08	.04
36	Tony Gwynn	.20	.15	.08
37	Roberto Alomar	.20	.15	.08
38	Tim Belcher	.10	.08	.04
39	Craig Biggio	.10	.08	.04
40	Barry Bonds	.25	.20	.10
41	Bobby Bonilla	.15	.11	.06
42	Joe Carter	.15	.11	.06
43	Will Clark	.25	.20	.10
44	Eric Davis	.15	.11	.06
45	Glenn Davis	.10	.08	.04
46	Sid Fernandez	.10	.08	.04
47	Pedro Guerrero	.10	.08	.04
48	Von Hayes	.10	.08	.04
49	Tom Herr	.10	.08	.04
50	Howard Johnson	.15	.11	.06
51	Barry Larkin	.15	.11	.06
52	Joe Magrane	.10	.08	.04
53	Dale Murphy	.20	.15	.08
54	Tim Raines	.15	.11	.06
55	Willie Randolph	.10	.08	.04
56	Ryne Sandberg	.35	.25	.14
57	Dwight Smith	.10	.08	.04
58	Lonnie Smith	.10	.08	.04
59	Robby Thompson	.15	.11	.06
60	Tim Wallach	.10	.08	.04

1990 Topps Coins

Sixty of the game's top stars and promising rookies are featured in this fourth annual coin set. Fronts of the 1-1/2" diameter coins feature a player photo with a symbolic infield in front of and behind the photo.

Armour Franks Medallions

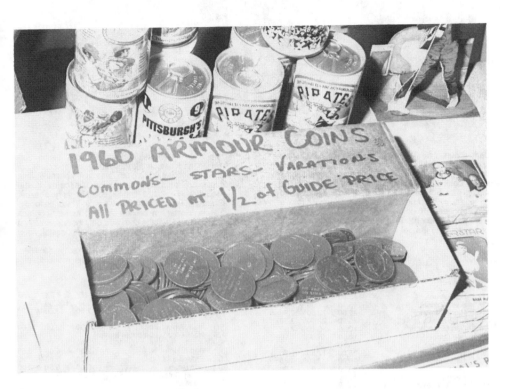

1955 Armour Coins

In 1955, Armour inserted a plastic "coin" in its packages of hot dogs. A raised profile of a ballplayer is on the front of each coin along with the player's name, position, birthplace and date, batting and throwing preference, and 1954 hitting or pitching record. The coins, which measure 1 1/2" in diameter and are un-numbered, came in a variety of colors, including the more common ones in aqua, dark blue, light green, orange, red and yellow. Scarcer colors are black, pale blue, lime green, very dark green, gold, pale orange, pink, silver, and tan. Scarce colors are double the value of the coins listed in the checklist that follows. Twenty-four different players are included in the set. Variations exist for Harvey Kuenn (letters in his name are condensed or spaced) and Mickey Mantle (name is spelled Mantle or incorrectly as Mantel). The complete set price includes the two variations.

		NR MT	EX	VG
Complete Set:		1000.	500.00	300.00
Common Player:		12.00	6.00	3.50
(1)	John "Johnny" Antonelli	15.00	7.50	4.50
(2)	Larry "Yogi" Berra	60.00	30.00	18.00
(3)	Delmar "Del" Crandall	15.00	7.50	4.50
(4)	Lawrence "Larry" Doby	18.00	9.00	5.50
(5)	James "Jim" Finigan	12.00	6.00	3.50
(6)	Edward "Whitey" Ford	60.00	30.00	18.00
(7)	James "Junior" Gilliam	20.00	10.00	6.00
(8)	Harvey "Kitten" Haddix	12.00	6.00	3.50
(9)	Ranson "Randy" Jackson (name actually Ransom)	20.00	10.00	6.00
(10)	Jack "Jackie" Jensen	18.00	9.00	5.50
(11)	Theodore "Ted" Kluszewski	24.00	12.00	7.25
(12a)	Harvey E. Kuenn (spaced letters in name)	25.00	12.50	7.50
(12b)	Harvey E. Kuenn (condensed letters in name)	40.00	20.00	12.00
(13a)	Charles "Mickey" Mantel (incorrect spelling)	150.00	75.00	45.00
(13b)	Charles "Mickey" Mantle (correct spelling)	400.00	200.00	125.00
(14)	Donald "Don" Mueller	20.00	10.00	6.00
(15)	Harold "Pee Wee" Reese	40.00	20.00	12.00
(16)	Allie P. Reynolds	18.00	9.00	5.50
(17)	Albert "Flip" Rosen	18.00	9.00	5.50
(18)	Curtis "Curt" Simmons	12.00	6.00	3.50
(19)	Edwin "Duke" Snider	60.00	30.00	18.00
(20)	Warren Spahn	40.00	20.00	12.00
(21)	Frank J. Thomas	35.00	17.50	10.50
(22)	Virgil "Fire" Trucks	12.00	6.00	3.50
(23)	Robert "Bob" Turley	18.00	9.00	5.50
(24)	James "Mickey" Vernon	12.00	6.00	3.50

1959 Armour Coins

After a three-year layoff, Armour again inserted plastic baseball "coins" into its hot dog packages. The coins retained their 1 1/2" size but did not include as much detailed information as in 1955. Missing from the coins' backs is information such as birthplace and date, team, and batting and throwing preference. The fronts contain the player's name and, unlike 1955, only the team nickname is given. The set consists of 20 coins which come in a myriad of colors. Common colors are navy blue, royal blue,

dark green, orange, red, and pale yellow. Scarce colors are pale blue, cream, grey-green, pale green, dark or light pink, pale red, tan, and translucent coins of any color with or without multi-colored flecks in the plastic mix. Scarce colors are double the value listed for coins in the checklist. In 1959, Armour had a write-in offer of 10 coins for $1. The same 10 players were part of the write-in offer, accounting for why half of the coins in the set are much more plentiful than the other.

		NR MT	EX	VG
	Complete Set:	400.00	200.00	120.00
	Common Player:	10.00	5.00	3.00
(1)	Hank Aaron	45.00	22.00	13.50
(2)	John Antonelli	15.00	7.50	4.50
(3)	Richie Ashburn	25.00	12.50	7.50
(4)	Ernie Banks	45.00	22.00	13.50
(5)	Don Blasingame	10.00	5.00	3.00
(6)	Bob Cerv	10.00	5.00	3.00
(7)	Del Crandall	15.00	7.50	4.50
(8)	Whitey Ford	35.00	17.50	10.50
(9)	Nellie Fox	15.00	7.50	4.50
(10)	Jackie Jensen	30.00	15.00	9.00
(11)	Harvey Kuenn	15.00	7.50	4.50
(12)	Frank Malzone	10.00	5.00	3.00
(13)	Johnny Podres	15.00	7.50	4.50
(14)	Frank Robinson	25.00	12.50	7.50
(15)	Roy Sievers	10.00	5.00	3.00
(16)	Bob Skinner	10.00	5.00	3.00
(17)	Frank J. Thomas	15.00	7.50	4.50
(18)	Gus Triandos	10.00	5.00	3.00
(19)	Bob Turley	18.00	9.00	5.50
(20)	Mickey Vernon	15.00	7.50	4.50

1960 Armour Coins

The 1960 Armour coin issue is identical in number and style to the 1959 set. The unnumbered coins, which measure 1 1/2" in diameter, once again came in a variety of colors. Common colors for 1960 are

dark blue, light blue, dark green, light green, red-orange, dark red, and light yellow. Scarce colors are aqua, grey-blue, cream, tan, and dark yellow. Scarce colors are double the value of the coins in the checklist. The Bud Daley coin is very scarce, although it is not exactly known why. Theories for the scarcity center on broken printing molds, contract disputes, and that the coin was only inserted in a test product that quickly proved to be unsuccessful. As in 1959, a mail-in offer for 10 free coins was made available by Armour. The set price for the 1960 Armour set does not include the three more difficult variations.

		NR MT	EX	VG
	Complete Set:	1200.	600.00	360.00
	Common Player:	7.00	3.50	2.00
(1a)	Hank Aaron (Braves)	45.00	22.00	13.50
(1b)	Hank Aaron (Milwaukee Braves)			
		75.00	37.00	22.00
(2)	Bob Allison	12.00	6.00	3.50
(3)	Ernie Banks	18.00	9.00	5.50
(4)	Ken Boyer	10.00	5.00	3.00
(5)	Rocky Colavito	15.00	7.50	4.50
(6)	Gene Conley	10.00	5.00	3.00
(7)	Del Crandall	10.00	5.00	3.00
(8)	Bud Daley	750.00	375.00	225.00
(9a)	Don Drysdale (L.A condensed)			
		20.00	10.00	6.00
(9b)	Don Drysdale (space between L. and A.)			
		25.00	12.50	7.50
(10)	Whitey Ford	20.00	10.00	6.00
(11)	Nellie Fox	15.00	7.50	4.50
(12)	Al Kaline	30.00	15.00	9.00
(13a)	Frank Malzone (Red Sox)	7.00	3.50	2.00
(13b)	Frank Malzone (Boston Red Sox)			
		25.00	12.50	7.50
(14)	Mickey Mantle	100.00	50.00	30.00
(15)	Ed Mathews	25.00	12.50	7.50
(16)	Willie Mays	45.00	22.00	13.50
(17)	Vada Pinson	10.00	5.00	3.00
(18)	Dick Stuart	10.00	5.00	3.00
(19)	Gus Triandos	7.00	3.50	2.00
(20)	Early Wynn	20.00	10.00	6.00

1969 Citgo Medallions

1969 Citgo Coins

This 20-player set of small (about 1" in diameter) metal coins was issued by Citgo in 1969 to commemorate professional baseball's 100th anniversary. The brass-coated coins, susceptible to oxidation, display the player in a crude portrait with his name across the top. The backs honor the 100th anniversary of pro ball. The coins are unnumbered but are generally checklisted according to numbers that ap-

pear on a display card which was available from Citgo by mail.

		NR MT	EX	VG
	Complete Set:	60.00	30.00	18.00
	Common Player:	1.00	.50	.30
1	Denny McLain	1.25	.60	.40
2	Dave McNally	1.00	.50	.30
3	Jim Lonborg	1.00	.50	.30
4	Harmon Killebrew	5.00	2.50	1.50
5	Mel Stottlemyre	1.00	.50	.30
6	Willie Horton	1.00	.50	.30

7	Jim Fregosi	1.25	.60	.40
8	Rico Petrocelli	1.00	.50	.30
9	Stan Bahnsen	1.00	.50	.30
10	Frank Howard	1.25	.60	.40
11	Joe Torre	1.25	.60	.40
12	Jerry Koosman	1.00	.50	.30
13	Ron Santo	1.25	.60	.40
14	Pete Rose	15.00	7.50	4.50
15	Rusty Staub	1.25	.60	.40
16	Henry Aaron	18.00	9.00	5.50
17	Richie Allen	1.25	.60	.40
18	Ron Swoboda	1.00	.50	.30
19	Willie McCovey	5.00	2.50	1.50
20	Jim Bunning	2.00	1.00	.60

1965 Old London Medallions

1965 Old London Coins

These 1 1/2" diameter metal coins were included in Old London snack food packages. The 40 coins in this set feature two players from each of the major leagues' 20 teams, except St. Louis (3) and the New York Mets (1). Coin fronts have color photos and player names, while the silver-colored coin backs give brief biographies of each player. An Old London logo is also displayed on each coin back. Space Magic Ltd. produced the coins. This is the same company which produced similar sets for Topps in 1964 and 1971.

		NR MT	EX	VG
Complete Set:		700.00	350.00	210.00
Common Player:		5.00	2.50	1.50
(1)	Henry Aaron	75.00	37.00	22.00
(2)	Richie Allen	8.00	4.00	2.50
(3)	Bob Allison	6.50	3.25	2.00
(4)	Ernie Banks	35.00	17.50	10.50
(5)	Ken Boyer	8.00	4.00	2.50
(6)	Jim Bunning	11.00	5.50	3.25
(7)	Orlando Cepeda	9.00	4.50	2.75
(8)	Dean Chance	5.00	2.50	1.50
(9)	Rocky Colavito	11.00	5.50	3.25

(10)	Vic Davalillo	5.00	2.50	1.50
(11)	Tommy Davis	8.00	4.00	2.50
(12)	Ron Fairly	6.50	3.25	2.00
(13)	Dick Farrell	5.00	2.50	1.50
(14)	Jim Fregosi	6.50	3.25	2.00
(15)	Bob Friend	6.50	3.25	2.00
(16)	Dick Groat	8.00	4.00	2.50
(17)	Ron Hunt	5.00	2.50	1.50
(18)	Chuck Hinton	5.00	2.50	1.50
(19)	Ken Johnson	5.00	2.50	1.50
(20)	Al Kaline	35.00	17.50	10.50
(21)	Harmon Killebrew	27.50	13.50	8.25
(22)	Don Lock	5.00	2.50	1.50
(23)	Mickey Mantle	175.00	87.00	52.00
(24)	Roger Maris	35.00	17.50	10.50
(25)	Willie Mays	75.00	37.00	22.00
(26)	Bill Mazeroski	11.00	5.50	3.25
(27)	Gary Peters	5.00	2.50	1.50
(28)	Vada Pinson	8.00	4.00	2.50
(29)	Boog Powell	8.00	4.00	2.50
(30)	Dick Radatz	5.00	2.50	1.50
(31)	Brooks Robinson	35.00	17.50	10.50
(32)	Frank Robinson	35.00	17.50	10.50
(33)	Tracy Stallard	5.00	2.50	1.50
(34)	Joe Torre	8.00	4.00	2.50
(35)	Leon Wagner	5.00	2.50	1.50
(36)	Pete Ward	5.00	2.50	1.50
(37)	Dave Wickersham	5.00	2.50	1.50
(38)	Billy Williams	25.00	12.50	7.50
(39)	John Wyatt	5.00	2.50	1.50
(40)	Carl Yastrzemski	75.00	37.00	22.00

Salada Tea Coins

1962 Salada-Junket Dessert Coins

These 1 3/8" diameter plastic coins were issued in packages of Salada Tea and Junket Pudding mix. There are 221 different players available, with variations bringing the total of different coins to 261. Each coin has a paper color photo inserted in the front which contains the player's name and position plus the coin number. The plastic rims come in six different colors, all color coded per team. (For example, the New York Yankees are found with light blue rims). Production began with 180 coins, but the addition of the New York Mets and Houston Colt .45's to the National League allowed the company to expand the set's size. Twenty expansion players were added along with 21 other players. Several players' coins were dropped after the initial 180 run, causing some scarcities. A Gary Geiger coin with a "BO" instead of a "B" on his cap is sometimes found on collectors' want lists. However, most Salada experts do not consider this coin to be a legitimate variation. The mark, which somewhat resembles an "O", is merely a printing smear and not an intended cap emblem. It has also been determined by Salada experts that a Jim Lemon coin with red shirt buttons does not exist.

		NR MT	EX	VG
Complete set: (without variations)		3250.	1600.	975.00
Complete set: (with variations)		8000.	4000.	2400.
Common player 1-180:		4.00	2.00	1.25
Common player 181-221:		8.00	4.00	2.50
1	Jim Gentile	5.50	2.75	1.75
2	Bill Pierce	125.00	62.00	37.00
3	Chico Fernandez	4.00	2.00	1.25
4	Tom Brewer	35.00	17.50	10.50
5	Woody Held	4.00	2.00	1.25
6	Ray Herbert	35.00	17.50	10.50
7a	Ken Aspromonte (Angels)	16.50	8.25	5.00
7b	Ken Aspromonte (Indians)	5.50	2.75	1.75
8	Whitey Ford	29.00	14.50	8.75
9	Jim Lemon	5.00	2.50	1.50
10	Billy Klaus	4.00	2.00	1.25
11	Steve Barber	35.00	17.50	10.50
12	Nellie Fox	15.00	7.50	4.50
13	Jim Bunning	11.00	5.50	3.25
14	Frank Malzone	5.00	2.50	1.50

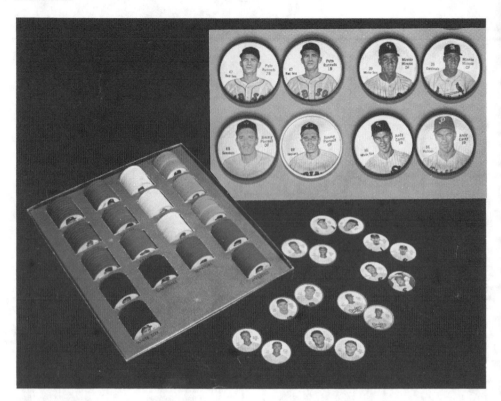

15	Tito Francona	4.00	2.00	1.25
16	Bobby Del Greco	4.00	2.00	1.25
17a	Steve Bilko (red shirt buttons)			
		8.25	4.25	2.50
17b	Steve Bilko (white shirt buttons)			
		5.50	2.75	1.75
18	Tony Kubek	60.00	30.00	18.00
19	Earl Battey	5.00	2.50	1.50
20	Chuck Cottier	4.00	2.00	1.25
21	Willie Tasby	4.00	2.00	1.25
22	Bob Allison	5.50	2.75	1.75
23	Roger Maris	35.00	17.50	10.50
24a	Earl Averill (red shirt buttons)			
		8.25	4.25	2.50
24b	Earl Averill (white shirt buttons)			
		5.50	2.75	1.75
25	Jerry Lumpe	4.00	2.00	1.25
26	Jim Grant	35.00	17.50	10.50
27	Carl Yastrzemski	75.00	37.00	22.00
28	Rocky Colavito	12.00	6.00	3.50
29	Al Smith	4.00	2.00	1.25
30	Jim Busby	35.00	17.50	10.50
31	Dick Howser	4.00	2.00	1.25
32	Jim Perry	4.00	2.00	1.25
33	Yogi Berra	35.00	17.50	10.50
34a	Ken Hamlin (red shirt buttons)			
		9.00	4.50	2.75
34b	Ken Hamlin (white shirt buttons)			
		5.50	2.75	1.75
35	Dale Long	4.00	2.00	1.25
36	Harmon Killebrew	25.00	12.50	7.50
37	Dick Brown	4.00	2.00	1.25
38	Gary Geiger	4.00	2.00	1.25
39a	Minnie Minoso (White Sox)			
		35.00	17.50	10.50
39b	Minnie Minoso (Cardinals)			
		20.00	10.00	6.00
40	Brooks Robinson	42.50	21.00	12.50
41	Mickey Mantle	130.00	65.00	39.00
42	Bennie Daniels	4.00	2.00	1.25
43	Billy Martin	12.50	6.25	3.75
44	Vic Power	5.00	2.50	1.50
45	Joe Pignatano	4.00	2.00	1.25
46a	Ryne Duren (red shirt buttons)			
		8.25	4.25	2.50

46b	Ryne Duren (white shirt buttons)			
		5.50	2.75	1.75
47a	Pete Runnels (2B)	12.50	6.25	3.75
47b	Pete Runnels (1B)	6.00	3.00	1.75
48a	Dick Williams (name on right)			
		1000.	500.00	300.00
48b	Dick Williams (name on left)			
		6.00	3.00	1.75
49	Jim Landis	4.00	2.00	1.25
50	Steve Boros	4.00	2.00	1.25
51a	Zoilo Versalles (red shirt buttons)			
		8.25	4.25	2.50
51b	Zoilo Versalles (white shirt buttons)			
		5.50	2.75	1.75
52a	Johnny Temple (Indians)	20.00	10.00	6.00
52b	Johnny Temple (Orioles)	5.50	2.75	1.75
53a	Jackie Brandt (Oriole)	6.00	3.00	1.75
53b	Jackie Brandt (Orioles)	850.00	425.00	255.00
54	Joe McClain	4.00	2.00	1.25
55	Sherm Lollar	5.00	2.50	1.50
56	Gene Stephens	4.00	2.00	1.25
57a	Leon Wagner (red shirt buttons)			
		8.25	4.25	2.50
57b	Leon Wagner (white shirt buttons)			
		5.50	2.75	1.75
58	Frank Lary	4.00	2.00	1.25
59	Bill Skowron	8.50	4.25	2.50
60	Vic Wertz	4.00	2.00	1.25
61	Willie Kirkland	4.00	2.00	1.25
62	Leo Posada	4.00	2.00	1.25
63a	Albie Pearson (red shirt buttons)			
		11.00	5.50	3.25
63b	Albie Pearson (white shirt buttons)			
		5.50	2.75	1.75
64	Bobby Richardson	11.00	5.50	3.25
65a	Marv Breeding (SS)	22.00	11.00	6.50
65b	Marv Breeding (2B)	5.50	2.75	1.75
66	Roy Sievers	85.00	42.00	25.00
67	Al Kaline	37.50	18.50	11.00
68a	Don Buddin (Red Sox)	20.00	10.00	6.00
68b	Don Buddin (Colts)	10.00	5.00	3.00
69a	Lenny Green (red shirt buttons)			
		8.25	4.25	2.50
69B	Lenny Green (white shirt buttons)			
		5.50	2.75	1.75
70	Gene Green	40.00	20.00	12.00

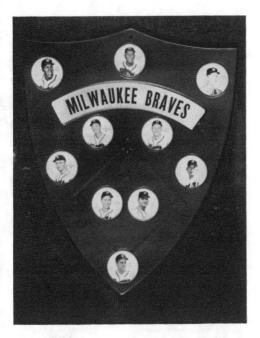

71	Luis Aparicio	19.00	9.50	5.75
72	Norm Cash	9.00	4.50	2.75
73	Jackie Jensen	45.00	22.00	13.50
74	Bubba Phillips	4.00	2.00	1.25
75	Jim Archer	4.00	2.00	1.25
76a	Ken Hunt (red shirt buttons)	11.00	5.50	3.25
76b	Ken Hunt (white shirt buttons)	5.50	2.75	1.75
77	Ralph Terry	6.00	3.00	1.75
78	Camilo Pascual	4.00	2.00	1.25
79	Marty Keough	40.00	20.00	12.00
80	Cletis Boyer	5.50	2.75	1.75
81	Jim Pagliaroni	4.00	2.00	1.25
82a	Gene Leek (red shirt buttons)	8.25	4.25	2.50
82b	Gene Leek (white shirt buttons)	5.50	2.75	1.75
83	Jake Wood	4.00	2.00	1.25
84	Coot Veal	35.00	17.50	10.50
85	Norm Siebern	5.00	2.50	1.50
86a	Andy Carey (White Sox)	50.00	25.00	15.00
86b	Andy Carey (Phillies)	9.00	4.50	2.75
87a	Bill Tuttle (red shirt buttons)	8.25	4.25	2.50
87b	Bill Tuttle (white shirt buttons)	5.50	2.75	1.75
88a	Jimmy Piersall (Indians)	17.50	8.75	5.25
88b	Jimmy Piersall (Senators)	9.00	4.50	2.75
89	Ron Hansen	45.00	22.00	13.50
90a	Chuck Stobbs (red shirt buttons)	9.50	4.75	2.75
90b	Chuck Stobbs (white shirt buttons)	5.50	2.75	1.75
91a	Ken McBride (red shirt buttons)	8.25	4.25	2.50
91b	Ken McBride (white shirt buttons)	5.50	2.75	1.75
92	Bill Bruton	4.00	2.00	1.25
93	Gus Triandos	4.00	2.00	1.25
94	John Romano	4.00	2.00	1.25
95	Elston Howard	11.00	5.50	3.25
96	Gene Woodling	6.00	3.00	1.75
97a	Early Wynn (pitching pose)	75.00	37.00	22.00
97b	Early Wynn (portrait)	30.00	15.00	9.00
98	Milt Pappas	5.00	2.50	1.50
99	Bill Monbouquette	4.00	2.00	1.25
100	Wayne Causey	4.00	2.00	1.25
101	Don Elston	4.00	2.00	1.25
102a	Charlie Neal (Dodgers)	16.50	8.25	5.00
102b	Charlie Neal (Mets)	7.00	3.50	2.00
103	Don Blasingame	4.00	2.00	1.25
104	Frank Thomas	40.00	20.00	12.00
105	Wes Covington	5.00	2.50	1.50
106	Chuck Hiller	4.00	2.00	1.25
107	Don Hoak	5.00	2.50	1.50
108a	Bob Lillis (Cardinals)	35.00	17.50	10.50
108b	Bob Lillis (Colts)	7.00	3.50	2.00
109	Sandy Koufax	45.00	22.00	13.50
110	Gordy Coleman	4.00	2.00	1.25
111	Ed Matthews (Mathews)	25.00	12.50	7.50
112	Art Mahaffey	4.00	2.00	1.25
113a	Ed Bailey (red period above "i" in Giants)	11.00	5.50	3.25
113b	Ed Bailey (white period)	4.00	2.00	1.25
114	Smoky Burgess	5.50	2.75	1.75
115	Bill White	5.00	2.50	1.50
116	Ed Bouchee	35.00	17.50	10.50
117	Bob Buhl	4.00	2.00	1.25
118	Vada Pinson	6.00	3.00	1.75
119	Carl Sawatski	4.00	2.00	1.25
120	Dick Stuart	4.00	2.00	1.25
121	Harvey Kuenn	65.00	32.00	19.50
122	Pancho Herrera	4.00	2.00	1.25
123a	Don Zimmer (Cubs)	15.00	7.50	4.50
123b	Don Zimmer (Mets)	7.00	3.50	2.00
124	Wally Moon	5.00	2.50	1.50
125	Joe Adcock	5.50	2.75	1.75
126	Joey Jay	4.00	2.00	1.25
127a	Maury Wills (blue "3" on shirt)	20.00	10.00	6.00
127b	Maury Wills (red "3" on shirt)	7.00	3.50	2.00
128	George Altman	4.00	2.00	1.25
129a	John Buzhardt (Phillies)	20.00	10.00	6.00
129b	John Buzhardt (White Sox)	7.00	3.50	2.00
130	Felipe Alou	6.00	3.00	1.75
131	Bill Mazeroski	10.00	5.00	3.00
132	Ernie Broglio	4.00	2.00	1.25
133	John Roseboro	5.00	2.50	1.50
134	Mike McCormick	4.00	2.00	1.25
135a	Chuck Smith (Phillies)	20.00	10.00	6.00
135b	Chuck Smith (White Sox)	7.00	3.50	2.00
136	Ron Santo	7.00	3.50	2.00
137	Gene Freese	4.00	2.00	1.25
138	Dick Groat	6.00	3.00	1.75
139	Curt Flood	7.00	3.50	2.00
140	Frank Bolling	4.00	2.00	1.25
141	Clay Dalrymple	4.00	2.00	1.25
142	Willie McCovey	42.50	21.00	12.50
143	Bob Skinner	5.00	2.50	1.50
144	Lindy McDaniel	4.00	2.00	1.25
145	Glen Hobbie	4.00	2.00	1.25
146a	Gil Hodges (Dodgers)	55.00	27.00	16.50
146b	Gil Hodges (Mets)	35.00	17.50	10.50
147	Eddie Kasko	4.00	2.00	1.25
148	Gino Cimoli	45.00	22.00	13.50
149	Willie Mays	90.00	45.00	27.00
150	Roberto Clemente	90.00	45.00	27.00
151	Red Schoendienst	7.50	3.75	2.25
152	Joe Torre	5.50	2.75	1.75
153	Bob Purkey	4.00	2.00	1.25
154a	Tommy Davis (3B)	12.50	6.25	3.75
154b	Tommy Davis (OF)	6.00	3.00	1.75
155a	Andre Rogers (incorrect spelling)	13.50	6.75	4.00
155b	Andre Rodgers (correct spelling)	5.50	2.75	1.75
156	Tony Taylor	4.00	2.00	1.25
157	Bob Friend	4.00	2.00	1.25
158a	Gus Bell (Redlegs)	13.50	6.75	4.00
158b	Gus Bell (Mets)	7.00	3.50	2.00
159	Roy McMillan	4.00	2.00	1.25
160	Carl Warwick	4.00	2.00	1.25
161	Willie Davis	5.50	2.75	1.75
162	Sam Jones	65.00	32.00	19.50
163	Ruben Amaro	4.00	2.00	1.25
164	Sam Taylor	4.00	2.00	1.25
165	Frank Robinson	35.00	17.50	10.50
166	Lou Burdette	5.00	2.50	1.50
167	Ken Boyer	7.00	3.50	2.00
168	Bill Virdon	6.00	3.00	1.75
169	Jim Davenport	4.00	2.00	1.25
170	Don Demeter	4.00	2.00	1.25
171	Richie Ashburn	55.00	27.00	16.50
172	John Podres	5.50	2.75	1.75
173a	Joe Cunningham (Cardinals)	55.00	27.00	16.50
173b	Joe Cunningham (White Sox)	25.00	12.50	7.50
174	ElRoy Face	7.00	3.50	2.00
175	Orlando Cepeda	9.00	4.50	2.75
176a	Bobby Gene Smith (Phillies)	20.00	10.00	6.00
176b	Bobby Gene Smith (Mets)	7.00	3.50	2.00

177a	Ernie Banks (OF)	60.00	30.00	18.00
177b	Ernie Banks (SS)	30.00	15.00	9.00
178a	Daryl Spencer (3B)	17.50	8.75	5.25
178b	Daryl Spencer (1B)	7.00	3.50	2.00
179	Bob Schmidt	35.00	17.50	10.50
180	Hank Aaron	90.00	45.00	27.00
181	Hobie Landrith	10.00	5.00	3.00
182a	Ed Broussard	400.00	200.00	120.00
182b	Ed Bressoud	35.00	17.50	10.50
183	Felix Mantilla	10.00	5.00	3.00
184	Dick Farrell	10.00	5.00	3.00
185	Bob Miller	10.00	5.00	3.00
186	Don Taussig	10.00	5.00	3.00
187	Pumpsie Green	11.00	5.50	3.25
188	Bobby Shantz	12.00	6.00	3.50
189	Roger Craig	12.00	6.00	3.50
190	Hal Smith	10.00	5.00	3.00
191	John Edwards	8.00	4.00	2.50
192	John DeMerit	10.00	5.00	3.00
193	Joe Amalfitano	10.00	5.00	3.00
194	Norm Larker	10.00	5.00	3.00
195	Al Heist	10.00	5.00	3.00
196	Al Spangler	10.00	5.00	3.00
197	Alex Grammas	8.00	4.00	2.50
198	Gerry Lynch	8.00	4.00	2.50
199	Jim McKnight	8.00	4.00	2.50
200	Jose Pagen (Pagan)	8.00	4.00	2.50
201	Junior Gilliam	24.00	12.00	7.25
202	Art Ditmar	8.00	4.00	2.50
203	Pete Daley	8.00	4.00	2.50
204	Johnny Callison	24.00	12.00	7.25
205	Stu Miller	8.00	4.00	2.50
206	Russ Snyder	8.00	4.00	2.50
207	Billy Williams	35.00	17.50	10.50
208	Walter Bond	8.00	4.00	2.50
209	Joe Koppe	8.00	4.00	2.50
210	Don Schwall	30.00	15.00	9.00
211	Billy Gardner	15.00	7.50	4.50
212	Chuck Estrada	8.00	4.00	2.50
213	Gary Bell	8.00	4.00	2.50
214	Floyd Robinson	8.00	4.00	2.50
215	Duke Snider	60.00	30.00	18.00
216	Lee Maye	8.00	4.00	2.50
217	Howie Bedell	8.00	4.00	2.50
218	Bob Will	8.00	4.00	2.50
219	Dallas Green	11.00	5.50	3.25
220	Carroll Hardy	16.00	8.00	4.75
221	Danny O'Connell	11.00	5.50	3.25

1963 Salada-Junket Dessert Coins

A much smaller set of baseball coins was issued by Salada/Junket in 1963. The 63 coins issued were called "All-Star Baseball Coins" and included most the top players of the day. Unlike 1962, the coins were made of metal and measured a slightly larger 1 1/2" diameter. American League players have blue rims on their coins, while National Leaguers are rimmed in red. Coin fronts contain no printing on the full-color player photos, while backs list coin number, player name, team and position, along with brief statistics and the sponsors' logos.

		NR MT	EX	VG
	Complete Set:	950.00	475.00	275.00
	Common Player:	5.00	2.50	1.50
1	Don Drysdale	18.00	9.00	5.50
2	Dick Farrell	5.00	2.50	1.50
3	Bob Gibson	18.00	9.00	5.50
4	Sandy Koufax	30.00	15.00	9.00
5	Juan Marichal	18.00	9.00	5.50
6	Bob Purkey	5.00	2.50	1.50
7	Bob Shaw	5.00	2.50	1.50
8	Warren Spahn	18.00	9.00	5.50
9	Johnny Podres	5.00	2.50	1.50
10	Art Mahaffey	5.00	2.50	1.50
11	Del Crandall	6.50	3.25	2.00
12	John Roseboro	6.50	3.25	2.00
13	Orlando Cepeda	7.00	3.50	2.00
14	Bill Mazeroski	11.00	5.50	3.25
15	Ken Boyer	8.00	4.00	2.50
16	Dick Groat	7.00	3.50	2.00
17	Ernie Banks	25.00	12.50	7.50
18	Frank Bolling	5.00	2.50	1.50
19	Jim Davenport	5.00	2.50	1.50
20	Maury Wills	7.00	3.50	2.00
21	Tommy Davis	6.50	3.25	2.00
22	Willie Mays	65.00	32.00	19.50
23	Roberto Clemente	65.00	32.00	19.50
24	Henry Aaron	65.00	32.00	19.50
25	Felipe Alou	6.50	3.25	2.00
26	Johnny Callison	6.50	3.25	2.00
27	Richie Ashburn	9.00	4.50	2.75
28	Eddie Mathews	20.00	10.00	6.00
29	Frank Robinson	22.50	11.00	6.75
30	Billy Williams	18.00	9.00	5.50
31	George Altman	5.00	2.50	1.50
32	Hank Aguirre	5.00	2.50	1.50
33	Jim Bunning	9.00	4.50	2.75
34	Dick Donovan	5.00	2.50	1.50
35	Bill Monbouquette	5.00	2.50	1.50
36	Camilo Pascual	6.50	3.25	2.00
37	David Stenhouse	5.00	2.50	1.50
38	Ralph Terry	6.50	3.25	2.00
39	Hoyt Wilhelm	18.00	9.00	5.50
40	Jim Kaat	11.00	5.50	3.25
41	Ken McBride	5.00	2.50	1.50
42	Ray Herbert	5.00	2.50	1.50
43	Milt Pappas	6.50	3.25	2.00
44	Earl Battey	5.00	2.50	1.50
45	Elston Howard	9.00	4.50	2.75
46	John Romano	5.00	2.50	1.50
47	Jim Gentile	5.00	2.50	1.50
48	Billy Moran	5.00	2.50	1.50
49	Rich Rollins	5.00	2.50	1.50
50	Luis Aparicio	18.00	9.00	5.50
51	Norm Siebern	5.00	2.50	1.50
52	Bobby Richardson	15.00	7.50	4.50
53	Brooks Robinson	30.00	15.00	9.00
54	Tom Tresh	11.00	5.50	3.25
55	Leon Wagner	5.00	2.50	1.50
56	Mickey Mantle	140.00	70.00	42.00
57	Roger Maris	40.00	20.00	12.00
58	Rocky Colavito	11.00	5.50	3.25
59	Lee Thomas	5.00	2.50	1.50
60	Jim Landis	5.00	2.50	1.50
61	Pete Runnels	6.50	3.25	2.00
62	Yogi Berra	30.00	15.00	9.00
63	Al Kaline	30.00	15.00	9.00

Chicagoland Processing Enviromint Corp.

Nolan Ryan liked one particular medallion commemorating his 300th win so much that he gave one to each of his Texas Rangers teammates. The medallion, created by Chicagoland Processing Enviromint Corp., remains one of the company's most popular.

The company's silver medallions, dating back to 1985, are officially licensed by Major League Baseball. The one-troy ounce medallions are made from silver extracted from recycled film; the company annually keeps an estimated 12 million pounds of scrap out of landfills.

Chicagoland does not produce coins from any non-precious metal material. Limited-edition medallions are created only to commemorate events or special occasions, thus limiting the variety of coins produced and making them more valuable.

Regarding mintage, the company follows the same format for all events. Mintage on Division Champions is 5,000, Conference Champions or American League/National League Champions is 10,000 and the Super Bowl and World Series Champions is 25,000. Individual player mintages is limited to 15,000 each. Each medallion is individually numbered.

After a medallion has been sold out, the company destroys the dies to ensure there is never a second mintage; the company vows it has never duplicated a second edition and never will.

In addition to baseball, Chicagoland has minted medallions licensed by the National Hockey League, the National Football League, the National Basketball Association, the National Collegiate Athletic Association, Paramount Pictures, Warner Bros., Winterland Productions, Carolco Licensing, Curtis Licensing, Determined Productions, MCA Records and Apple Records. Non-sport events commemorated by the company have included Batman's 50th anniversary, Star Trek's 25th anniversary, and the history of the Beatles.

The company is located in Mt. Prospect, Ill. The initial release price for the company's medallions has usually been $29.95. S/O means the medallion is sold out.

Major League Baseball medallions

	Mintage		Issue	Value
* Colorado Rockies record-breaking attendance	5,000		1993	$30
* 1993 Rockies/Andres Galarraga two-piece set	1,000		1993	$30
* Indians final game at Municipal Stadium	10,000		1993	$30
* Indians final game at Municipal Stadium, gold	61		1993	$30
* Arlington Stadium Old and New	1,000	S/O	1993	$75
* Kansas City Royals 25th Anniversary	5,000		1993	$30

* Montreal Expos 25th Anniversary	5,000		1993	$30
* San Diego Padres 25th Anniversary	5,000		1993	$30
* Toronto Blue Jays Back-to-Back two-piece set	400	S/O	1993	N/A
(note: issue price was $82.95)				
* 1993 three-piece World Series Champs set	500	S/O	1993	N/A
(note: issue price was $125)				
* 1993 seven-piece World Series Champs set	500		1993	$250
(note: issue price was $250)				
* 1993 Toronto Blue Jays World Series Champs	25,000		1993	$30
* 1993 Toronto Blue Jays World Series Champs, gold	193		1993	$850
(note: issue price was $850)				
* 1993 Philadelphia Phillies N.L. Champs	10,000		1993	$30
* 1993 Toronto Blue Jays A.L. Champs	10,000		1993	$30
* 1993 Division Winners				
Toronto Blue Jays	5,000		1993	$30
Atlanta Braves	5,000		1993	$30
Chicago White Sox	5,000		1993	$30
Philadelphia Phillies	5,000		1993	$30
* Miami Marlins inaugural	10,000		1993	$30
* Colorado Rockies inaugural	10,000		1993	$30
* Inaugural two-piece set	1,000		1993	$82.50
(note: issue price was $82.50)				
* 1992 three-piece World Series Champs set	500	S/O	1992	$290
(note: issue price was $125)				
* 1992 seven-piece World Series Champs set	500		1992	$440
(note: issue price was $250)				
* 1992 Toronto Blue Jays World Series Champions	25,000	S/O	1992	$60
* 1992 Toronto Blue Jays World Series Champions, gold	192		1992	$850
(note: issue price was $850)				
* 1992 Toronto Blue Jays A.L. Champions	10,000	S/O	1992	$55
* 1992 Atlanta Braves N.L. Champions	10,000		1992	$30
* 1992 Atlanta Braves N.L. Champions, gold	unknown		1992	$850
(note: issue price was $850)				
* 1992 Division Winners				
Toronto Blue Jays	5,000	S/O	1992	$58
Atlanta Braves	5,000		1992	$30
Oakland A's	5,000	S/O	1992	$30

Pittsburgh Pirates	5,000		1992	$30
* St. Louis Cardinals 100th Anniversary	5,000		1992	$30
* Baltimore Memorial Stadium	48,000		1992	$30
* Oakland A's 25th Anniversary	5,000		1991	$30
* 1991 Minnesota Twins World Series Champions	25,000		1991	$30
* 1991 Minnesota Twins A.L. Champions	10,000		1991	$30
* 1991 Atlanta Braves N.L. Champions	10,000	S/O	1991	$49.50
* 1991 Division Winners				
Minnesota Twins	5,000		1991	$30
Atlanta Braves	5,000		1991	$35
Toronto Blue Jays	5,000	S/O	1991	$75
Pittsburgh Pirates	1,300		1991	$40
* Miami Marlins franchise	10,000		1991	$30
* Colorado Rockies franchise	10,000		1991	$30
* New York Giants Cooperstown Collection	10,000		1991	$35
* 1990 Cincinnati World Series Champions	25,000		1990	$30
* 1990 Cincinnati N.L. Champions	10,000		1990	$30
* 1990 Oakland A's A.L. Champions	10,000	S/O	1990	$30
* 1990 Division Winners				
Cincinnati Reds	1,050	S/O	1990	$55
Oakland A's	150	S/O	1990	$75
Boston Red Sox	450	S/O	1990	$50
Pittsburgh Pirates	450	S/O	1990	$50
* Comiskey Park Commemorative Old & New	43,931		1990	$30
* Wrigley Field 75th Anniversary	10,000		1990	$30
* Dodgers 100th Anniversary	5,000		1990	$30
* 1955 Brooklyn Dodgers Cooperstown Collection	10,000		1990	$35
* Chicago Cubs 1989 Division Championship	10,000		1989	$30
* 1989 Oakland A's World Series Champions	6,550	S/O	1989	$35
* 1989 Oakland A's A.L. Champions	6,550	S/O	1989	$32.50
* 1989 San Francisco Giants N.L. Champions	8,100	S/O	1989	$35
* 1989 Division Winners				
San Francisco Giants	600	S/O	1989	$35
Oakland A's	900	S/O	1989	$35
Chicago Cubs	6,200	S/O	1989	$34.50
Toronto Blue Jays	2,300	S/O	1989	$75
* Wrigley Field First Night Game	39,012	S/O	1988	$42.50
* 1988 L.A. Dodgers World Series Champions	25,000		1988	$30
* 1988 Los Angeles Dodgers N.L. Champions	4,050	S/O	1988	$32.50
* 1988 Oakland A's A.L. Champions	4,250	S/O	1988	$32.50
* 1988 Division Winners				
Oakland A's	800	S/O	1988	$35
Boston Red Sox	500	S/O	1988	$45
New York Mets	1,100	S/O	1988	$35
Los Angeles Dodgers	800	S/O	1988	$35
* 1987 Minnesota Twins World Series Champions	25,000	S/O	1987	$45
* 1987 Minnesota Twins A.L. Champions	5,000		1987	$35
* 1987 St. Louis Cardinals N.L. Champions	5,000		1987	$30
* 1987 Division Winners				
Minnesota Twins	3,000	S/O	1987	$35
San Francisco Giants	1,000	S/O	1987	$35
Detroit Tigers	1,800	S/O	1987	$35
St. Louis Cardinals	1,500	S/O	1987	$35
* 1986 N.Y. Mets World Series Champions	25,000		1987	$30
* Comiskey Park 75th Anniversary	680	S/O	1985	$125
* Team Commemorative - All teams (logos/names)	1,000 each			$30
* Pittsburgh Pirates All-Star 1994	5,000		1994	$30

Medallions

* 1993 All-Star Team, 10-piece set	1,000		1993	$450
(note: issue price was $450)				
* Baltimore Orioles All-Star 1993	5,000		1993	$30
* San Diego Padres All-Star 1992	5,000		1992	$30
* Toronto Blue Jays All-Star 1991	5,000	S/O	1991	$60
* Chicago Cubs All-Star 1990	5,000		1990	$30
* California Angels All-Star 1989	5,000	S/O	1989	$45
* All-Star 1991 for Commissioner's Office	500	S/O	1991	N/A
* All-Star 1990	10,000		1990	$30
* All-Star 1990 for Commissioner's Office	400	S/O	1990	N/A
* All-Star 1989	2,000	S/O	1989	$45
* All-Star 1989 for Commissioner's Office	350	S/O	1989	N/A
* All-Star 1988	2,000	S/O	1988	$75
* All-Star 1988 for Commissioner's Office	300	S/O	1988	N/A
* All-Star 1987 for Commissioner's Office	300	S/O	1987	N/A
* Johnny Bench - 1989 Hall of Fame	15,000		1989	$30
* Blue Jay Bashers - Alomar, Carter & White	15,000		1992	$30
* Blue Jay Bashers - Olerud, Alomar & Molitor	15,000		1993	$30
* Wade Boggs - 1987 A.L. Batting Champ	1,249	S/O	1988	$30
* Wade Boggs - New York Yankees	13,751		1993	$30
* Barry Bonds - 1993 N.L. MVP	15,000		1993	$30
* Barry Bonds/San Francisco Giants generic, two-piece set	500		1993	$30
* George Brett - 3 Decades of Batting Titles	15,000		1991	$30
* George Brett - 3,000th career hit	15,000		1992	$30
* George Brett/Robin Yount 3,000th hit, two-piece set	$1,000		1992	$82.95
(note: issue price was $82.95)				
* Jose Canseco - 40/40 Oakland A's	6,000	S/O	1990	$40
* Jose Canseco - 40/40 Texas Rangers	9,000		1992	$30
* Steve Carlton - 4-Time Cy Young Winner	15,000		1990	$30
* Will Clark	15,000		1990	$30
* Roger Clemens - 1986-87 Cy Young Winner	740		1990	$75
* Roberto Clemente - 1973 Hall of Fame	15,000	S/O	1988	$45
* Ty Cobb	15,000		1988	$30
* Mark Davis - 1989 Cy Young Winner	270	S/O	1989	$65
* Andre Dawson - 1987 N. L. MVP	10,900		1990	$35
* Andre Dawson - Boston Red Sox	4,100		1993	$30
* Dennis Eckersley - 40 Saves/3 straight years	400	S/O	1992	$50
* Dennis Eckersley	14,600		1992	$30
* Cecil Fielder - A.L. Home Run/RBI Leader	15,000		1991	$30
* Carlton Fisk - Most Career Hits by a Catcher	15,000		1990	$30
* Andres Galarraga - 1993 N.L. Batting Champion	15,000		1993	$30
* Steve Garvey - 1,207 Consecutive Games Played	15,000		1989	$30
* Lou Gehrig - 2,130 Consecutive Games Played	15,000		1987	$30
* Kirk Gibson - 1988 N.L. MVP	600 S/O		1988	$45
* Tom Glavine - Atlanta Braves	15,000		1992	$30
* Dwight Gooden - 1985 Cy Young Winner	15,000		1989	$30
* Ken Griffey Jr. & Sr. - Mariners/Reds	3,300	S/O	1990	$85
* Ken Griffey Jr. & Sr. - Mariners	3,700	S/O	1990	$65
* Tony Gwynn - 1987, '88, '89 Batting Champion	1,075	S/O	1990	$50
* Rickey Henderson - All-Time Stolen Bases	7,109	S/O	1990	$45
* Rickey Henderson - Toronto Blue Jays	7,891		1993	$30
* Orel Hershiser - 1988 Cy Young Winner	600	S/O	1989	$45
* Bo Jackson - L.A. Raiders/K.C. Royals	4,400	S/O	1990	$45
* Bo Jackson - White Sox/White Sox error	NA		1990	$75
* Bo Jackson - L.A. Raiders/White Sox	10,900		1991	$30
* Bo Jackson - Chicago White Sox	15,000		1992	$30
* Reggie Jackson - 1993 Hall of Fame	15,000		1993	$30
* Reggie Jackson - 1993 Hall of Fame, gold	44		1993	$850

(note: issue price was $850).

Item		S/O	Year	Price
* Reggie Jackson - Hall of Fame, two piece set	100	S/O	1993	$125
(note: issue price was $82.95)				
* Ferguson Jenkins - 1991 Hall of Fame	15,000		1991	$30
* Howard Johnson - N.L. Home Run/RBI Leader	15,000		1991	$30
* Dave Justice - 1990 Rookie of the Year	15,000		1991	$30
* Harmon Killebrew - 1984 Hall of Fame	15,000		1991	$30
* Chuck Knoblauch - Minnesota Twins	1993		15,000	$30
* Greg Maddux - 1992 N.L. Cy Young Winner	309	S/O	1992	$45
* Greg Maddux - Atlanta Braves	14,691		1993	$30
* Greg Maddux - 1993 N.L. Cy Young Winner	14,600		1993	$30
* Greg Maddux - 1993 N.L. Division, two-piece set	500		1993	$82.95
(note: issue price was $82.95)				
* Don Mattingly - Most Grand Slams, season	15,000		1988	$30
* Jack McDowell - 1993 A.L. Cy Young Winner	15,000		1993	$30
* Jack McDowell/Frank Thomas, two-piece set	1,000		1993	$30
* Mark McGwire - 30 Homers 1st Four Seasons	15,000		1991	$30
* Kevin Mitchell - 1989 N.L. MVP	1,200	S/O	1990	$35
* Kevin Mitchell - Seattle Mariners	108	S/O	1992	$75
* Kevin Mitchell - Cincinnati Reds	13,692		1993	$30
* Paul Molitor - 39-Game Hitting Streak	11,001	S/O	1990	$30
* Paul Molitor - Toronto Blue Jays	3,999		1992	$30
* Joe Morgan - 1990 Hall of Fame	15,000		1990	$30
* John Olerud - 1993 A.L. Batting Champion	15,000		1993	$30
* Greg Olson - 1989 A.L. Rookie of the Year	15,000		1990	$30
* Terry Pendleton - 1991 N.L. Batting Champion	900 S/O		1991	$45
* Terry Pendleton - 1991 N.L. MVP	14,100		1991	$30
* Kirby Puckett - 1989 A.L. Batting Champion	15,000		1990	$30
* Cal Ripken - 1991 A.L. MVP	15,000		1992	$30
* Brooks Robinson - 1983 Hall of Fame	15,000		1991	$30
* A's Rookies (McGwire, Weiss, Canseco)	15,000		1990	$30
* Pete Rose - All-Time Hit Leader	25,000	S/O	1985	$65
* Babe Ruth	15,000		1987	$49.95
* Nolan Ryan - 300th Victory	15,000	S/O	1990	$75
* Nolan Ryan - 5,000th Strikeout	15,000	S/O	1989	$75
* Nolan Ryan - 7th No-Hitter	15,000	S/O	1991	$65
* Nolan Ryan - Retirement, matched two-piece set	500	S/O	1993	$145
(note: issue price was $125)				
* Nolan Ryan - Retirement, gold	100		1993	$850
(note: issue price was $850)				
* Bret Saberhagen - 1988 A.L. Cy Young Winner	300		1990	$65
* Bret Saberhagen - New York Mets	14,700		unknown	$30
* Chris Sabo - 1988 N.L. Rookie of the Year	15,000		1989	$30
* Ryne Sandberg - All-Time Errorless Streak	15,000		1990	$30
* Deion Sanders - Atlanta Braves	15,000		1992	$30
* Mike Schmidt - Player of the Decade	10,000	S/O	1990	$45
* Tom Seaver - 300th Win	377	S/O	1987	$750
* Tom Seaver - 1992 Hall of Fame	15,000		1992	$30
* Darryl Strawberry - New York Mets	1,200	S/O	1990	$45
* Darryl Strawberry - Los Angeles Dodgers	13,800		1991	$30
* Frank Thomas - 1993 A.L. MVP	15,000		1993	$30
* Frank Viola - 1988 N.L. Cy Young Winner	15,000		1988	$30
* Jerome Walton - 1989 N.L. Rookie of the Year	900 S/O		1990	$55
* Billy Williams - 1987 Hall of Fame	15,000		1991	$30
* Dave Winfield - Toronto Blue Jays	389	S/O	1992	$60
* Dave Winfield - Minnesota Twins	14,611		1993	$30
* Robin Yount - 1989 A.L. MVP	15,000		1990	$30
* Robin Yount - 3,000th career hit	15,000		1992	$30

Stamps

There have been six general issue baseball postage stamps issued by the United States. They are listed with prices according to the **Official 1994 Blackbook Price Guide of United States Postage Stamps:**

1) 1939 3-cent Baseball Centennial, violet - block of 4 for $7-$8.50; unused stamp, 60 cents to $1.90; used stamp, 16-18 cents.

2) 1969 6-cent Professional Baseball Centenary, multicolored - a Mint sheet for $39; block of 4 for $4; an unused stamp, 95 cents; a used stamp, 14 cents.

3) 1982 20-cent Jackie Robinson, multicolored - Mint sheet, $28; block, $6; unused, $1.25; used, 14 cents.

4) 1983 20-cent Babe Ruth, blue - sheet, $58; block, $6.50; unused, $1.25; used, 14 cents.

5) 1984 20-cent Roberto Clemente, multicolored - sheet, $50; block, $6; unused, $1.50; used, 13 cents.

6) 1988 25-cent Lou Gehrig, multicolored - sheet, $24; block, $3.90; unused, 55 cents; used, 13 cents.

Two post offices in the Caribbean, Grenada and St. Vincent, have issued multi-player sheets of stamps. In 1988, Grenada, licensed by Major League Baseball, issued nine sheets portraying 79 past and present baseball stars. Sheets of nine stamps (each stamp is 30 cents in East Caribbean currency) have reached the $35-$40 range. Three players from each team were depicted, except the Yankees.

The groups of nine are: A) Johnny Bench, Dave Stieb, Reggie Jackson, Harold Baines, Wade Boggs, Pete O'Brien, Stan Musial, Wally Joyner and Grover Cleveland Alexander.

B) Jose Cruz, American League logo, Al Kaline, Chuck Klein, Don Mattingly, Mike Witt, Mark Langston, Hubie Brooks and Harmon Killebrew.

C) Jackie Robinson, Dwight Gooden, Brooks Robinson, Nolan Ryan, Mike Schmidt, Gary Gaetti, Nellie Fox, Tony Gwynn and Dizzy Dean.

D) Luis Aparicio, Paul Molitor, Lou Gehrig, Jeffrey Leonard, Eric Davis, Pete Incaviglia, Steve Rogers, Ozzie Smith and Randy Jones.

E) Gary Carter, Hank Aaron, Gaylord Perry, Ty Cobb, Andre Dawson, Charlie Hough, Kirby Puckett, Robin Yount and Don Drysdale.

F) Mickey Mantle, Roger Clemens, Rod Carew, Ryne Sandberg, Mike Scott, Tim Raines, Willie Mays, Bret Saberhagen and Honus Wagner.

G) George Brett, Joe Carter, Frank Robinson, Mel Ott, Benito Santiago, Teddy Higuera, Lloyd Moseby, Bobby Bonilla and Warren Spahn.

H) Ernie Banks, National League logo, Julio Franco, Jack Morris, Fernando Valenzuela, Lefty Grove, Ted Williams, Darryl Strawberry and Dale Murphy.

I) Roberto Clemente, Cal Ripken Jr., Bob Feller, George Bell, Mark McGwire, Alvin Davis, Pete Rose, Dan Quisenberry and Babe Ruth.

St. Vincent's stamps, issued July 23, 1989, commemorate the 1988 All-Star Game, great rookies, Hall of Famers and award winners. Major League Baseball and the Major League Baseball Players Association gave approval for the stamps.

One set of 12 $2 stamps features Hall of Famers Bob Feller, Ernie Banks, Al Kaline, Stan Musial, Ty Cobb, Jackie Robinson, Ted Williams, Willie Mays, Lou Gehrig, Red Schoendienst, Carl Yastrzemski and Johnny Bench.

Another set features three sheetlets of nine each. Two sheets feature rookies, mainly from 1989. The first sheet shows Tom McCarthy, Jerome Walton, Dante Bichette, Gaylord Perry, Ramon Martinez, Carl Yastrzemski, John Smoltz, Ken Hill and Randy Johnson. The second has Bob Milacki, Babe Ruth, Jim Abbott, Gary Sheffield, Gregg Jefferies, Kevin Brown, Cris Carpenter, Johnny Bench and Ken Griffey Jr. The third sheet has nine award winners - Chris Sabo, Walt Weiss and Willie Mays (Rookie of the Year winners); Kirk Gibson, Ted Williams and Jose Canseco (MVP winners); and Gaylord Perry, Orel Hershiser and Frank Viola (Cy Young Award winners).

The final sheet was a $5 souvenir sheet showing the starting lineups from the 1989 All-Star Game. Another sheet of two $2 stamps features the 1988 World Series participants - the Oakland A's and Los Angeles Dodgers.

Blankets, pennants leathers, silks

1914 B18 Blankets

These 5 1/4" flannels were issued in 1914 with several popular brands of tobacco. The flannels, whose American Card Catalog designation is B18, picked up the nickname blankets because many of the square pieces of cloth were sewn together to form pillow covers or bed spreads. Different color combinations on the flannels exist for all 10 teams included in the set. The complete set price in the checklist that follows does not include higher-priced variations.

		NR MT	EX	VG
Complete Set:		4500.	2200.	1350.
Common Player:		24.00	12.00	7.25
(1a)	Babe Adams (purple pennants)			
		48.00	24.00	14.50
(1b)	Babe Adams (red pennants)			
		55.00	27.00	16.50
(2a)	Sam Agnew (purple basepaths)			
		48.00	24.00	14.50
(2b)	Sam Agnew (red basepaths)			
		55.00	27.00	16.50
(3a)	Eddie Ainsmith (green pennants)			
		24.00	12.00	7.25
(3b)	Eddie Ainsmith (brown pennants)			
		24.00	12.00	7.25
(4a)	Jimmy Austin (purple basepaths)			
		48.00	24.00	14.50
(4b)	Jimmy Austin (red basepaths)			
		55.00	27.00	16.50
(5a)	Del Baker (white infield)	24.00	12.00	7.25
(5b)	Del Baker (brown infield)	90.00	45.00	27.00
(5c)	Del Baker (red infield)	275.00	137.00	82.00
(6a)	Johnny Bassler (purple pennants)			
		48.00	24.00	14.50
(6b)	Johnny Bassler (yellow pennants)			
		90.00	45.00	27.00
(7a)	Paddy Bauman (Baumann) (white infield)			
		24.00	12.00	7.25
(7b)	Paddy Bauman (Baumann) (brown infield)			
		90.00	45.00	27.00
(7c)	Paddy Bauman (Baumann) (red infield)			
		275.00	137.00	82.00
(8a)	Luke Boone (blue infield)	24.00	12.00	7.25
(8b)	Luke Boone (green infield)			
		24.00	12.00	7.25
(9a)	George Burns (brown basepaths)			
		24.00	12.00	7.25
(9b)	George Burns (green basepaths)			
		24.00	12.00	7.25
(10a)	Tioga George Burns (white infield)			
		24.00	12.00	7.25
(10b)	Tioga George Burns (brown infield)			
		90.00	45.00	27.00
(11a)	Max Carey (purple pennants)			
		90.00	45.00	27.00

(11b)	Max Carey (red pennants)		
	100.00	50.00	30.00
(12a)	Marty Cavanaugh (Kavanagh) (white infield)		
	24.00	12.00	7.25
(12b)	Marty Cavanaugh (Kavanagh) (brown infield)		
	125.00	62.00	37.00
(12c)	Marty Cavanaugh (Kavanagh) (red infield)		
	275.00	137.00	82.00
(12d)	Marty Kavanaugh (Kavanagh)		
	24.00	12.00	7.25
(13a)	Frank Chance (green infield)		
	48.00	24.00	14.50
(13b)	Frank Chance (brown pennants, blue infield)		
	48.00	24.00	14.50
(13c)	Frank Chance (yellow pennants, blue infield)		
	275.00	137.00	82.00
(14a)	Ray Chapman (purple pennants)		
	48.00	24.00	14.50
(14b)	Ray Chapman (yellow pennants)		
	90.00	45.00	27.00
(15a)	Ty Cobb (white infield)	275.00	137.00	82.00
(15b)	Ty Cobb (brown infield)	600.00	300.00	180.00
(15c)	Ty Cobb (red infield)	2500.	1250.	750.00
(16a)	King Cole (blue infield)	24.00	12.00	7.25
(16b)	King Cole (green infield)	24.00	12.00	7.25
(17a)	Joe Connolly (white infield)		
	24.00	12.00	7.25
(17b)	Joe Connolly (brown infield)		
	90.00	45.00	27.00
(18a)	Harry Coveleski (white infield)		
	24.00	12.00	7.25
(18b)	Harry Coveleski (brown infield)		
	90.00	45.00	27.00
(19a)	George Cutshaw (blue infield)		
	24.00	12.00	7.25
(19b)	George Cutshaw (green infield)		
	24.00	12.00	7.25
(20a)	Jake Daubert (blue infield)		
	30.00	15.00	9.00
(20b)	Jake Daubert (green infield)		
	30.00	15.00	9.00
(21a)	Ray Demmitt (white infield)		
	24.00	12.00	7.25
(21b)	Ray Demmitt (brown infield)		
	90.00	45.00	27.00
(22a)	Bill Doak (purple pennants)		
	48.00	24.00	14.50
(22b)	Bill Doak (yellow pennants)		
	90.00	45.00	27.00
(23a)	Cozy Dolan (purple pennants)		
	48.00	24.00	14.50
(23b)	Cozy Dolan (yellow pennants)		
	90.00	45.00	27.00
(24a)	Larry Doyle (brown basepaths)		
	30.00	15.00	9.00
(24b)	Larry Doyle (green basepaths)		
	30.00	15.00	9.00
(25a)	Art Fletcher (brown basepaths)		
	24.00	12.00	7.25
(25b)	Art Fletcher (green basepaths)		
	24.00	12.00	7.25
(26a)	Eddie Foster (brown pennants)		
	24.00	12.00	7.25
(26b)	Eddie Foster (green pennants)		
	24.00	12.00	7.25
(27a)	Del Gainor (white infield)	24.00	12.00	7.25
(27b)	Del Gainor (brown infield)		
	90.00	45.00	27.00
(28a)	Chick Gandil (brown pennants)		
	40.00	20.00	12.00
(28b)	Chick Gandil (green pennants)		
	40.00	20.00	12.00
(29a)	George Gibson (purple pennants)		
	48.00	24.00	14.50
(29b)	George Gibson (red pennants)		
	55.00	27.00	16.50
(30a)	Hank Gowdy (white infield)		
	24.00	12.00	7.25
(30b)	Hank Gowdy (brown infield)		
	90.00	45.00	27.00
(30c)	Hank Gowdy (red infield)		
	275.00	137.00	82.00
(31a)	Jack Graney (purple pennants)		
	48.00	24.00	14.50
(31b)	Jack Graney (yellow pennants)		
	90.00	45.00	27.00
(32a)	Eddie Grant (brown basepaths)		
	24.00	12.00	7.25
(32b)	Eddie Grant (green basepaths)		
	24.00	12.00	7.25
(33a)	Tommy Griffith (white infield, green pennants)		
	24.00	12.00	7.25
(33b)	Tommy Griffith (white infield, red pennants)		
	275.00	137.00	82.00

(33c)	Tommy Griffith (brown infield)		
	90.00	45.00	27.00
33d	Tommy Griffith (red infield)		
	275.00	137.00	82.00
(34a)	Earl Hamilton (purple basepaths)		
	48.00	24.00	14.50
(34b)	Earl Hamilton (red basepaths)		
	55.00	27.00	16.50
(35a)	Roy Hartzell (blue infield)	24.00	12.00	7.25
(35b)	Roy Hartzell (green infield)		
	24.00	12.00	7.25
(36a)	Miller Huggins (purple pennants)		
	90.00	45.00	27.00
(36b)	Miller Huggins (yellow pennants)		
	150.00	75.00	45.00
(37a)	John Hummel (brown infield)		
	24.00	12.00	7.25
(37b)	John Hummel (green infield)		
	24.00	12.00	7.25
(38a)	Ham Hyatt (purple pennants)		
	48.00	24.00	14.50
(38b)	Ham Hyatt (red pennants)		
	55.00	27.00	16.50
(39a)	Shoeless Joe Jackson (purple pennants)		
	1200.	600.00	350.00
(39b)	Shoeless Joe Jackson (yellow pennants)		
	1500.	750.00	450.00
(40a)	Bill James (white infield)	24.00	12.00	7.25
(40b)	Bill James (brown infield)	90.00	45.00	27.00
(41a)	Walter Johnson (brown pennants)		
	275.00	137.00	82.00
(41b)	Walter Johnson (green pennants)		
	275.00	137.00	82.00
(42a)	Ray Keating (blue infield)	24.00	12.00	7.25
(42b)	Ray Keating (green infield)		
	24.00	12.00	7.25
(43a)	Joe Kelley (Kelly) (purple pennants)		
	90.00	45.00	27.00
(43b)	Joe Kelley (Kelly) (red pennants)		
	100.00	50.00	30.00
(44a)	Ed Konetchy (purple pennants)		
	48.00	24.00	14.50
(44b)	Ed Konetchy (red pennants)		
	55.00	27.00	16.50
(45a)	Nemo Leibold (purple pennants)		
	48.00	24.00	14.50
(45b)	Nemo Leibold (yellow pennants)		
	90.00	45.00	27.00
(46a)	Fritz Maisel (blue infield)	24.00	12.00	7.25
(46b)	Fritz Maisel (green infield)		
	24.00	12.00	7.25
(47a)	Les Mann (white infield)	24.00	12.00	7.25
(47b)	Les Mann (brown infield)	90.00	45.00	27.00
(48a)	Rabbit Maranville (white infield)		
	55.00	27.00	16.50
(48b)	Rabbit Maranville (brown infield)		
	150.00	75.00	45.00
(48c)	Rabbit Maranville (red infield)		
	350.00	175.00	105.00
(49a)	Bill McAllister (McAllester) (purple pennants)		
	48.00	24.00	14.50
(49b)	Bill McAllister (McAllester) (red pennants)		
	55.00	27.00	16.50
(50a)	George McBride (brown pennants)		
	24.00	12.00	7.25
(50b)	George McBride (green pennants)		
	24.00	12.00	7.25
(51a)	Chief Meyers (brown basepaths)		
	24.00	12.00	7.25
(51b)	Chief Meyers (green basepaths)		
	24.00	12.00	7.25
(52a)	Clyde Milan (brown pennants)		
	24.00	12.00	7.25
(52b)	Clyde Milan (green pennants)		
	24.00	12.00	7.25
(53a)	Dots Miller (purple pennants)		
	48.00	24.00	14.50
(53b)	Dots Miller (yellow pennants)		
	90.00	45.00	27.00
(54a)	Otto Miller (blue infield)	24.00	12.00	7.25
(54b)	Otto Miller (green infield)	24.00	12.00	7.25
(55a)	Willie Mitchell (purple pennants)		
	48.00	24.00	14.50
(55b)	Willie Mitchell (yellow pennants)		
	90.00	45.00	27.00
(56a)	Danny Moeller (brown pennants)		
	24.00	12.00	7.25
(56b)	Danny Moeller (green pennants)		
	24.00	12.00	7.25
(57a)	Ray Morgan (brown pennants)		
	24.00	12.00	7.25
(57b)	Ray Morgan (green pennants)		
	24.00	12.00	7.25

		NR MT	EX	VG
(58a)	George Moriarty (white infield)	24.00	12.00	7.25
(58b)	George Moriarty (brown infield)	90.00	45.00	27.00
(58c)	George Moriarty (red infield)	275.00	137.00	82.00
(59a)	Mike Mowrey (purple pennants)	48.00	24.00	14.50
(59b)	Mike Mowrey (red pennants)	55.00	27.00	16.50
(60a)	Red Murray (brown basepaths)	24.00	12.00	7.25
(60b)	Red Murray (green basepaths)	24.00	12.00	7.25
(61a)	Ivy Olson (purple pennants)	48.00	24.00	14.50
(61b)	Ivy Olson (yellow pennants)	90.00	45.00	27.00
(62a)	Steve O'Neill (purple pennants)	48.00	24.00	14.50
(62b)	Steve O'Neill (red pennants)	90.00	45.00	27.00
(63a)	Marty O'Toole (purple pennants)	48.00	24.00	14.50
(63b)	Marty O'Toole (red pennants)	55.00	27.00	16.50
(64a)	Roger Peckinpaugh (blue infield)	30.00	15.00	9.00
(64b)	Roger Peckinpaugh (green infield)	30.00	15.00	9.00
(65a)	Hub Perdue (white infield)	24.00	12.00	7.25
(65b)	Hub Perdue (brown infield)	90.00	45.00	27.00
(65c)	Hub Purdue (red infield)	275.00	137.00	82.00
(66a)	Del Pratt (purple pennants)	48.00	24.00	14.50
(66b)	Del Pratt (yellow pennants)	55.00	27.00	16.50
(67a)	Hank Robinson (purple pennants)	48.00	24.00	14.50
(67b)	Hank Robinson (yellow pennants)	90.00	45.00	27.00
(68a)	Nap Rucker (blue infield)	24.00	12.00	7.25
(68b)	Nap Rucker (green infield)	24.00	12.00	7.25
(69a)	Slim Sallee (purple pennants)	48.00	24.00	14.50
(69b)	Slim Sallee (yellow pennants)	90.00	45.00	27.00
(70a)	Howard Shanks (brown pennants)	24.00	12.00	7.25
(70b)	Howard Shanks (green pennants)	24.00	12.00	7.25
(71a)	Burt Shotton (purple basepaths)	48.00	24.00	14.50
(71b)	Burt Shotton (red basepaths)	55.00	27.00	16.50
(72a)	Red Smith (blue infield)	24.00	12.00	7.25
(72b)	Red Smith (green infield)	24.00	12.00	7.25
(73a)	Fred Snodgrass (brown basepaths)	30.00	15.00	9.00
(73b)	Fred Snodgrass (green basepaths)	30.00	15.00	9.00
(74a)	Bill Steele (purple pennants)	48.00	24.00	14.50
74b	Bill Steele (yellow pennants)	90.00	45.00	27.00
(75a)	Casey Stengel (blue infield)	150.00	75.00	45.00
(75b)	Casey Stengel (green infield)	165.00	85.00	48.00
(76a)	Jeff Sweeney (blue infield)	24.00	12.00	7.25
(76b)	Jeff Sweeney (green infield)	24.00	12.00	7.25
(77a)	Jeff Tesreau (brown basepaths)	24.00	12.00	7.25
(77b)	Jeff Tesreau (green basepaths)	24.00	12.00	7.25
(78a)	Terry Turner (purple pennants)	48.00	24.00	14.50
(78b)	Terry Turner (yellow pennants)	90.00	45.00	27.00
(79a)	Lefty Tyler (white infield)	24.00	12.00	7.25
(79b)	Lefty Tyler (brown infield)	90.00	45.00	27.00
(79c)	Lefty Tyler (red infield)	275.00	137.00	82.00
(80a)	Jim Viox (purple pennants)	48.00	24.00	14.50
(80b)	Jim Viox (red pennants)	55.00	27.00	16.50
(81a)	Bull Wagner (blue infield)	24.00	12.00	7.25
(81b)	Bull Wagner (green infield)	24.00	12.00	7.25
(82a)	Bobby Wallace (purple basepaths)	90.00	45.00	27.00
(82b)	Bobby Wallace (red basepaths)	90.00	45.00	27.00
(83a)	Dee Walsh (purple basepaths)	48.00	24.00	14.50
(83b)	Dee Walsh (red basepaths)	55.00	27.00	16.50
(84a)	Jimmy Walsh (blue infield)	24.00	12.00	7.25
(84b)	Jimmy Walsh (green infield)	24.00	12.00	7.25
(85a)	Bert Whaling (white infield)	24.00	12.00	7.25
(85b)	Bert Whaling (brown infield)	90.00	45.00	27.00
(85c)	Bert Whaling (red infield)	275.00	137.00	82.00
(86a)	Zach Wheat (blue infield)	90.00	45.00	27.00
(86b)	Zach Wheat (green infield)	90.00	45.00	27.00
(87a)	Possum Whitted (purple pennants)	48.00	24.00	14.50
(87b)	Possum Whitted (yellow pennants)	90.00	45.00	27.00
(88a)	Gus Williams (purple basepaths)	48.00	24.00	14.50
(88b)	Gus Williams (red basepaths)	55.00	27.00	16.50
(89a)	Owen Wilson (purple pennants)	48.00	24.00	14.50
(89b)	Owen Wilson (yellow pennants)	90.00	45.00	27.00
(90a)	Hooks Wiltse (brown basepaths)	24.00	12.00	7.25
(90b)	Hooks Wiltse (green basepaths)	24.00	12.00	7.25

1916 BF2
Felt Pennants

Issued circa 1916, this unnumbered set consists of 97 felt pennants with a small black-and-white player photo glued to each one. The triangular pennants measure approximately 8 1/4" long, while the photos are 1 3/4" by 1 1/4" and appear to be identical to photos used for The Sporting News issues of the same period. The pennants list the player's name and team.

		NR MT	EX	VG
Complete Set:		7750.	3875.	2325.
Common Player:		45.00	22.00	13.50
(1)	Grover Alexander	125.00	62.00	37.00
(2)	Jimmy Archer	45.00	22.00	13.50

(3)	Home Run Baker	75.00	37.00	22.00
(4)	Dave Bancroft	75.00	37.00	22.00
(5)	Jack Barry	45.00	22.00	13.50
(6)	Chief Bender	75.00	37.00	22.00
(7)	Joe Benz	45.00	22.00	13.50
(8)	Mordecai Brown	75.00	37.00	22.00
(9)	George J. Burns	45.00	22.00	13.50
(10)	Donie Bush	45.00	22.00	13.50
(11)	Hick Cady	45.00	22.00	13.50
(12)	Max Carey	75.00	37.00	22.00
(13)	Ray Chapman	75.00	37.00	22.00
(14)	Ty Cobb	550.00	275.00	165.00
(15)	Eddie Collins	75.00	37.00	22.00
(16)	Shano Collins	45.00	22.00	13.50
(17)	Commy Comiskey	100.00	50.00	30.00
(18)	Harry Coveleskie (Coveleski)			
		45.00	22.00	13.50
(19)	Gavvy Cravath	45.00	22.00	13.50
(20)	Sam Crawford	75.00	37.00	22.00
(21)	Jake Daubert	45.00	22.00	13.50
(22)	Josh Devore	45.00	22.00	13.50
(23)	Red Dooin	45.00	22.00	13.50
(24)	Larry Doyle	45.00	22.00	13.50
(25)	Jean Dubuc	45.00	22.00	13.50
(26)	Johnny Evers	75.00	37.00	22.00
(27)	Red Faber	75.00	37.00	22.00
(28)	Eddie Foster	45.00	22.00	13.50
(29)	Del Gainer (Gainor)	45.00	22.00	13.50
(30)	Chick Gandil	75.00	37.00	22.00
(31)	Joe Gedeon	45.00	22.00	13.50
(32)	Hank Gowdy	45.00	22.00	13.50
(33)	Earl Hamilton	45.00	22.00	13.50
(34)	Claude Hendrix	45.00	22.00	13.50
(35)	Buck Herzog	45.00	22.00	13.50
(36)	Harry Hooper	75.00	37.00	22.00
(37)	Miller Huggins	75.00	37.00	22.00
(38)	Shoeless Joe Jackson	750.00	375.00	225.00
(39)	Seattle Bill James	45.00	22.00	13.50
(40)	Hugh Jennings	75.00	37.00	22.00
(41)	Walter Johnson	350.00	175.00	105.00
(42)	Fielder Jones	45.00	22.00	13.50
(43)	Joe Judge	45.00	22.00	13.50
(44)	Benny Kauff	45.00	22.00	13.50
(45)	Bill Killefer	45.00	22.00	13.50
(46)	Nap Lajoie	125.00	62.00	37.00
(47)	Jack Lapp	45.00	22.00	13.50
(48)	Doc Lavan	45.00	22.00	13.50
(49)	Jimmy Lavender	45.00	22.00	13.50
(50)	Dutch Leonard	45.00	22.00	13.50
(51)	Duffy Lewis	45.00	22.00	13.50
(52)	Hans Lobert	45.00	22.00	13.50
(53)	Fred Luderus	45.00	22.00	13.50
(54)	Connie Mack	100.00	50.00	30.00
(55)	Sherry Magee	45.00	22.00	13.50
(56)	Al Mamaux	45.00	22.00	13.50
(57)	Rabbit Maranville	75.00	37.00	22.00
(58)	Rube Marquard	75.00	37.00	22.00
(59)	George McBride	45.00	22.00	13.50
(60)	John McGraw	75.00	37.00	22.00
(61)	Stuffy McInnes (McInnis)	45.00	22.00	13.50
(62)	Fred Merkle	45.00	22.00	13.50
(63)	Chief Meyers	45.00	22.00	13.50
(64)	Clyde Milan	45.00	22.00	13.50
(65)	Otto Miller	45.00	22.00	13.50
(66)	Pat Moran	45.00	22.00	13.50
(67)	Ray Morgan	45.00	22.00	13.50
(68)	Guy Morton	45.00	22.00	13.50
(69)	Eddie Murphy	45.00	22.00	13.50
(70)	Rube Oldring	45.00	22.00	13.50
(71)	Dode Paskert	45.00	22.00	13.50
(72)	Wally Pipp	50.00	25.00	15.00
(73)	Pants Rowland	45.00	22.00	13.50
(74)	Nap Rucker	45.00	22.00	13.50
(75)	Dick Rudolph	45.00	22.00	13.50
(76)	Reb Russell	45.00	22.00	13.50
(77)	Vic Saier	45.00	22.00	13.50
(78)	Slim Sallee	45.00	22.00	13.50
(79)	Ray Schalk	75.00	37.00	22.00
(80)	Wally Schang	45.00	22.00	13.50
(81)	Wildfire Schulte	45.00	22.00	13.50
(82)	Jim Scott	45.00	22.00	13.50
(83)	George Sisler	75.00	37.00	22.00
(84)	George Stallings	45.00	22.00	13.50
(85)	Oscar Stanage	45.00	22.00	13.50
(86)	Jeff Tesreau	45.00	22.00	13.50
(87)	Joe Tinker	75.00	37.00	22.00
(88)	Lefty Tyler	45.00	22.00	13.50
(89)	Hippo Vaughn	45.00	22.00	13.50
(90)	Bobby Veach	45.00	22.00	13.50
(91)	Honus Wagner	325.00	162.00	97.00
(92)	Ed Walsh	75.00	37.00	22.00
(93)	Buck Weaver	80.00	40.00	24.00
(94)	Ivy Wingo	45.00	22.00	13.50
(95)	Joe Wood	45.00	22.00	13.50
(96)	Ralph Young	45.00	22.00	13.50
(97)	Heinie Zimmerman	45.00	22.00	13.50

1936 - 37 BF3
Felt Pennants

The checklist for this obscure set of felt pennants issued circa 1936-1937 is not complete, and new examples are still being reported. The pennants do not carry any manufacturer's name and their method of distribution is not certain, although it is believed they were issued as a premium with candy or gum. The pennants vary in size slightly but generally measure approximately 2 1/2" by 4 1/2" and were issued in various styles and colors, including red, yellow, white, blue, green, purple, black and brown. Most of the printing is white, although some pennants have been found with red or black printing, and the same pennant is often found in more than one color combination. The pennants feature both individual players and teams, including some minor league clubs. Advanced collectors have categorized the BF3 pennants into the following 11 design types, depending on what elements are included on the pennant: Type I: Player's name and figure. Type II: Player's name, team nickname and figure. Type III: Player's name and team nickname. Type IV: Team nickname and figure. Type V: Team nickname with emblem. Type VI: Team nickname only. Type VII: Player's name and team nickname on two-tailed pennant displayed inside the BF3 pennant. Type VIII: Player's name, year, and team nickname on ball. Type IX: Player's name, year on ball and team nickname. Type X: Team nickname and year. Type XI: Minor league and team.

		NR MT	EX	VG
Complete Set:		4000.	2000.	1250.
Common Pennant:		15.00	7.50	4.50
(1)	Luke Appling (batting)	25.00	12.50	7.50
(2)	Wally Berger (fielding)	15.00	7.50	4.50
(3)	Zeke Bonura (fielding ground ball)			
		15.00	7.50	4.50
(4)	Dolph Camilli (fielding)	15.00	7.50	4.50
(5)	Ben Chapman (batting)	15.00	7.50	4.50
(6)	Mickey Cochrane (catching)			
		25.00	12.50	7.50
(7)	Rip Collins (batting)	15.00	7.50	4.50
(8)	Joe Cronin (batting)	25.00	12.50	7.50
(9)	Kiki Cuyler (running)	25.00	12.50	7.50
(10)	Dizzy Dean (pitching)	40.00	20.00	12.50
(11)	Frank Demaree (batting)	15.00	7.50	4.50
(12)	Paul Derringer (pitching)	15.00	7.50	4.50
(13)	Bill Dickey (catching)	35.00	17.50	10.50
(14)	Jimmy Dykes (fielding)	15.00	7.50	4.50
(15)	Bob Feller (pitching)	35.00	17.50	10.50
(16)	Wes Ferrell (running)	15.00	7.50	4.50
(17)	Jimmy Foxx (batting)	35.00	17.50	10.50
(18)	Larry French (pitching)	15.00	7.50	4.50
(19)	Franky Frisch (running)	25.00	12.50	7.50
(20)	Lou Gehrig (fielding at 1st base)			
		150.00	75.00	45.00
(21)	Charles Gehringer (running)			
		25.00	12.50	7.50
(22)	Lefty Gomez (pitching)	25.00	12.50	7.50
(23)	Goose Goslin (batting)	25.00	12.50	7.50
(24)	Hank Greenberg (fielding)			
		25.00	12.50	7.50
(25)	Charlie Grimm (running)	18.00	9.00	5.50
(26)	Lefty Grove (pitching)	25.00	12.50	7.50
(27)	Gabby Hartnett (catching)			
		25.00	12.50	7.50
(28)	Rollie Hemsley (catching)			
		15.00	7.50	4.50
(29)	Billy Herman (fielding at 1st base)			
		25.00	12.50	7.50
(30)	Frank Higgins (fielding)	15.00	7.50	4.50
(31)	Rogers Hornsby (batting)	25.00	12.50	7.50
(32)	Carl Hubbell (pitching)	25.00	12.50	7.50

(33)	Chuck Klein (throwing)	25.00	12.50	7.50
(34)	Tony Lazzeri (batting)	25.00	12.50	7.50
(35)	Hank Leiber (fielding ground ball)			
		15.00	7.50	4.50
(36)	Ernie Lombardi (catching)			
		25.00	12.50	7.50
(37)	Al Lopez (throwing)	25.00	12.50	7.50
(38)	Gus Mancuso (running)	15.00	7.50	4.50
(39)	Heinie Manush (batting)	25.00	12.50	7.50
(40)	Pepper Martin (batting)	18.00	9.00	5.50
(41)	Joe McCarthy (kneeling)	25.00	12.50	7.50
(42)	Wally Moses (running)	15.00	7.50	4.50
(43)	Van Mungo (standing)	15.00	7.50	4.50
(44)	Mel Ott (throwing)	35.00	17.50	10.50
(45)	Schoolboy Rowe (pitching)			
		18.00	9.00	5.50
(46)	Babe Ruth (batting)	250.00	125.00	75.00
(47)	George Selkirk (batting)	15.00	7.50	4.50
(48)	Luke Sewell (sliding)	15.00	7.50	4.50
(49)	Joe Stripp (batting)	15.00	7.50	4.50
(50)	Hal Trosky (fielding)	15.00	7.50	4.50
(51)	Floyd Vaughan (running, script signature)			
		25.00	12.50	7.50
(52)	Floyd Vaughan (running, not script signature)			
		25.00	12.50	7.50
(53)	Paul Waner (batting)	25.00	12.50	7.50
(54)	Lon Warneke (pitching)	15.00	7.50	4.50
(55)	Jimmy Wilson (fielding ground ball)			
		15.00	7.50	4.50
(56)	Joe Vosmik (running)	15.00	7.50	4.50

Type II

(1)	Luke Appling (batting)	25.00	12.50	7.50
(2)	Zeke Bonura (batting)	15.00	7.50	4.50
(3)	Dolph Camilli (batting)	15.00	7.50	4.50
(4)	Dizzy Dean (batting)	40.00	20.00	12.50
(5)	Frank Demaree (batting)	15.00	7.50	4.50
(6)	Bob Feller (pitching)	40.00	20.00	12.50
(7)	Wes Ferrell (throwing)	15.00	7.50	4.50
(8)	Frank Frisch (fielding)	25.00	12.50	7.50
(9)	Lou Gehrig (batting)	90.00	45.00	27.50
(10)	Lou Gehrig (fielding)	90.00	45.00	27.50
(11)	Hank Greenberg (throwing)			
		25.00	12.50	7.50
(12)	Charlie Grimm (fielding)	18.00	9.00	5.50
(13)	Charlie Grimm (throwing)			
		18.00	9.00	5.50
(14)	Lefty Grove (pitching)	25.00	12.50	7.50
(15)	Gabby Hartnett (batting)	25.00	12.50	7.50
(16)	Billy Herman (batting)	25.00	12.50	7.50
(17)	Tony Lazzeri (running)	25.00	12.50	7.50
(18)	Tony Lazzeri (throwing)	25.00	12.50	7.50
(19)	Hank Leiber (batting)	15.00	7.50	4.50
(20)	Ernie Lombardi (batting)	25.00	12.50	7.50
(21)	Ducky Medwick (batting)	25.00	12.50	7.50
(22)	Joe Stripp (batting)	15.00	7.50	4.50
(23)	Floyd Vaughan (batting)	25.00	12.50	7.50
(24)	Joe Vosmik (throwing)	15.00	7.50	4.50
(25)	Paul Waner (batting)	25.00	12.50	7.50
(26)	Lon Warneke (batting)	15.00	7.50	4.50
(27)	Lon Warneke (pitching)	15.00	7.50	4.50

Type III

(1)	Zeke Bonura	15.00	7.50	4.50
(2)	Dolph Camilli	15.00	7.50	4.50
(3)	Ben Chapman	15.00	7.50	4.50
(4)	Dizzy Dean	40.00	20.00	12.50
(5)	Bill Dickey	35.00	17.50	10.50
(6)	Joe DiMaggio (name in script)			
		150.00	75.00	45.00
(7)	Bob Feller (name in script)			
		35.00	17.50	10.50
(8)	Wes Ferrell	15.00	7.50	4.50
(9)	Lou Gehrig (name in script)			
		150.00	75.00	45.00
(10)	Charles Gehringer	25.00	12.50	7.50
(11)	Lefty Grove	25.00	12.50	7.50
(12)	Billy Herman (name in script)			
		25.00	12.50	7.50

(13)	Carl Hubbell	25.00	12.50	7.50
(14)	Chuck Klein	25.00	12.50	7.50
(15)	Tony Lazzeri	25.00	12.50	7.50
(16)	Al Lopez	25.00	12.50	7.50
(17)	Johnny Marcum	15.00	7.50	4.50
(18)	Pepper Martin	18.00	9.00	5.50
(19)	Van Lingo Mungo	15.00	7.50	4.50
(20)	Schoolboy Rowe	18.00	9.00	5.50
(21)	George Selkirk	15.00	7.50	4.50
(22)	Bill Terry	25.00	12.50	7.50
(23)	Hal Trosky	15.00	7.50	4.50
(24)	Floyd Vaughan	25.00	12.50	7.50
(25)	Lon Warneke	15.00	7.50	4.50

Type IV

(1)	Athletics (fielder)	15.00	7.50	4.50
(2)	Browns (catcher)	15.00	7.50	4.50
(3)	Cubs (batter)	15.00	7.50	4.50
(4)	Dodgers (batter)	15.00	7.50	4.50
(5)	Dodgers (fielder)	15.00	7.50	4.50
(6)	Giants (standing by base)			
		15.00	7.50	4.50
(7)	Giants (two players)	15.00	7.50	4.50
(8)	Phillies (pitcher)	15.00	7.50	4.50
(9)	Reds (batter)	15.00	7.50	4.50
(10)	Reds (pitcher)	15.00	7.50	4.50
(11)	White Sox (batter)	15.00	7.50	4.50
(12)	White Sox (catcher)	15.00	7.50	4.50
(13)	White Sox (pitcher)	15.00	7.50	4.50
(14)	Yankees (batter)	25.00	12.50	7.50
(15)	Yankees (fielding ball, from waist up)			
		25.00	12.50	7.50

Type V

(1)	Athletics (bat)	15.00	7.50	4.50
(2)	Athletics (elephant)	15.00	7.50	4.50
(3)	Bees (bee)	15.00	7.50	4.50
(4)	Browns (bat)	15.00	7.50	4.50
(5)	Cardinals (bat)	15.00	7.50	4.50
(6)	Cardinals (cardinal)	15.00	7.50	4.50
(7)	Cardinals (four birds flying)			
		15.00	7.50	4.50
(8)	Cubs (cub)	15.00	7.50	4.50
(9)	Cubs (cub's head)	15.00	7.50	4.50
(10)	Dodgers (ball, bat and glove)			
		15.00	7.50	4.50
(11)	Dodgers (ball)	15.00	7.50	4.50
(12)	Indians (Indian)	15.00	7.50	4.50
(13)	Indians (Indian's head)			
		15.00	7.50	4.50
(14)	Indians (Indian's head with hat)			
		15.00	7.50	4.50
(15)	Phillies (Liberty Bell)			
		15.00	7.50	4.50
(16)	Pirates (skull and crossbones)			
		15.00	7.50	4.50
(17)	Red Sox (ball and bat)			
		15.00	7.50	4.50
(18)	Red Sox (bat)	15.00	7.50	4.50
(19)	Reds (ball)	15.00	7.50	4.50
(20)	Senators (bat)	15.00	7.50	4.50
(21)	Senators (Capitol building)			
		15.00	7.50	4.50
(22)	Tigers (cap)	15.00	7.50	4.50
(23)	Tigers (tiger)	15.00	7.50	4.50

Type VI

(1)	Cardinals	15.00	7.50	4.50
(2)	Cubs	15.00	7.50	4.50
(3)	Dodgers	15.00	7.50	4.50
(4)	Giants	15.00	7.50	4.50
(5)	Indians	15.00	7.50	4.50
(6)	Phillies (Phillies on spine)			
		15.00	7.50	4.50
(7)	Pirates (Pirates on spine)			
		15.00	7.50	4.50
(8)	Pirates (no Pirates on spine)			
		15.00	7.50	4.50
(9)	Yankees	25.00	12.50	7.50

Type VII

(1)	Earl Grace	15.00	7.50	4.50
(2)	Al Lopez	25.00	12.50	7.50

Type VIII

(1)	Larry French	15.00	7.50	4.50
(1)	Type IX, Clay Bryant	15.00	7.50	4.50
(2)	Tex Carleton	15.00	7.50	4.50
(3)	Phil Cavaretta (Cavarretta)			
		15.00	7.50	4.50
(4)	Irving Cherry	15.00	7.50	4.50
(5)	Ripper Collins	15.00	7.50	4.50

(6)	Curt Davis	15.00	7.50	4.50
(7)	Vince DiMaggio	20.00	10.00	6.00
(8)	Frank Demaree	15.00	7.50	4.50
(9)	Wes Flowers	15.00	7.50	4.50
(10)	Larry French	15.00	7.50	4.50
(11)	Linus Frey	15.00	7.50	4.50
(12)	Augie Galan	15.00	7.50	4.50
(13)	Charlie Grimm	18.00	9.00	5.50
(14)	Stan Hack	15.00	7.50	4.50
(15)	Gabby Hartnett	25.00	12.50	7.50
(16)	Billy Herman	25.00	12.50	7.50
(17)	Walt Higbee	15.00	7.50	4.50
(18)	Billy Jurges	15.00	7.50	4.50
(19)	Andy Lotshaw	15.00	7.50	4.50
(20)	Henry Majeski	15.00	7.50	4.50
(21)	Joe Marty	15.00	7.50	4.50
(22)	Tony Piet	15.00	7.50	4.50
(23)	Chas. Root	15.00	7.50	4.50
(24)	Tuck Stainback	15.00	7.50	4.50

Type X
(1)	Yankees (1936 Champions)			
		25.00	12.50	7.50
(1)	Barons (Type XI,) (Southern Association)			
		15.00	7.50	4.50
(2)	Bears (International League)			
		15.00	7.50	4.50
(3)	Blues (American Association)			
		15.00	7.50	4.50
(4)	Brewers (American Association)			
		15.00	7.50	4.50
(5)	Chicks (Southern Association)			
		15.00	7.50	4.50
(6)	Colonels (American Association)			
		15.00	7.50	4.50
(7)	Giants (International League)			
		15.00	7.50	4.50
(8)	Maple Leafs (International League)			
		15.00	7.50	4.50
(9)	Millers (American Association)			
		15.00	7.50	4.50
(10)	Mud Hens (American Association)			
		15.00	7.50	4.50
(11)	Orioles (International League)			
		15.00	7.50	4.50
(12)	Red Birds (American Association)			
		15.00	7.50	4.50
(13)	Saints (American Association)			
		15.00	7.50	4.50
(14)	Smokies (Southern Association)			
		15.00	7.50	4.50
(15)	Travelers (Southern Association)			
		15.00	7.50	4.50

1912 L1 Leathers

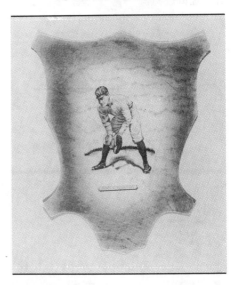

1913 Cravats
Felt Pennants

Little is known about this felt pennant issue, including the complete checklist. The name "Cravats" in the baseball above the player picture may represent the issuer, or describe the issue; the word "cravat" is an arcane term for a triangular piece of cloth. The pennants measure 4-1/8" across the top and are 9" long. Background colors are dark, with all printing in white. At center is a line art represntation of the player, with his name horizontally beneath and his team nickname vertically at bottom. At top is a bat and ball logo with the "Cravats" name. Most specimens are seen with a metal ring reinforcing the hole punched at top center. The known checklist points to 1913 as the most probably year of issue.

		NR MT	EX	VG
Common player:		75.00	37.00	22.00
(1)	Eddie Ainsmith	75.00	37.00	22.00
(2)	Jack Coombs	75.00	37.00	22.00
(3)	Ed Konethy (Konetchy)	75.00	37.00	22.00
(4)	Stuffy McInnes (McInnis)	75.00	37.00	22.00
(5)	J.T. (Chief) Meyer (Meyers)			
		75.00	37.00	22.00
(6)	Jeff Tesreau	75.00	37.00	22.00

One of the more unusual baseball collectibles of the tobacco era, the L1 "Leathers" were issued by Helmar Tobacco Co. in 1912 as a premium with its "Turkish Trophies" brand of cigarettes. The set featured 25 of the top baseball players and shared a checklist with the closely-related S81 "Silks," which were another part of the same promotion. The "Leathers," advertised as being 10" by 12", featured drawings of baseball players on horsehide-shaped pieces of leather. The drawings were based on the pictures used for the popular T3 Turkey Red series issued a year earlier. Twenty of the 25 players

405

in the "Leathers" set are from the T3 set. Five pitchers (Rube Marquard, Rube Benton, Marty O'Toole, Grover Alexander and Russ Ford) not pictured in T3 were added to the "Leathers" set, and the Frank Baker error was corrected. According to the promotion, each "Leather" was available in exchange for 50 Helmar coupons. In addition to the 25 baseball stars, the "Leathers" set also included more than 100 other subjects, including female athletes and bathing beauties, famous generals, Indian chiefs, actresses, national flags, college mascots and others.

		NR MT	EX	VG
Complete Set:		90000.	47500.	28500.
Common Player:		2250.	1125.	675.00
86	Rube Marquard	4500.	2250.	1350.
87	Marty O'Toole	2250.	1125.	675.00
88	Rube Benton	2250.	1125.	675.00
89	Grover Alexander	6000.	3000.	1800.
90	Russ Ford	2250.	1125.	675.00
91	John McGraw	4500.	2250.	1350.
92	Nap Rucker	2250.	1125.	675.00
93	Mike Mitchell	2250.	1125.	675.00
94	Chief Bender	4500.	2250.	1350.
95	Home Run Baker	4500.	2250.	1350.
96	Nap Lajoie	6000.	3000.	1800.
97	Joe Tinker	4500.	2250.	1350.
98	Sherry Magee	2250.	1125.	675.00
99	Howie Camnitz	2250.	1125.	675.00
100	Eddie Collins	4500.	2250.	1350.
101	Red Dooin	2250.	1125.	675.00
102	Ty Cobb	15000.	7500.	4500.
103	Hugh Jennings	4500.	2250.	1350.
104	Roger Bresnahan	4500.	2250.	1350.
105	Jake Stahl	2250.	1125.	675.00
106	Tris Speaker	5500.	2750.	1650.
107	Ed Walsh	4500.	2250.	1350.
108	Christy Mathewson	7500.	3750.	2250.
109	Johnny Evers	4500.	2250.	1350.
110	Walter Johnson	7500.	3750.	2250.

1909 S74 Silks - White

Designated as S74 in Jefferson Burdick's American Card Catalog, these small, delicate fabric collectibles are growing in popularity among advanced collectors. Another tobacco issue from the 1910-1911

period, the silks were issued as premiums with three different brands of cigarettes: Turkey Red, Old Mill and Helmar. The satin-like silks can be found in two different styles, either "white" or "colored." The white silks measure 1 7/8" by 3" and were originally issued with a brown paper backing that carried an advertisement for one of the three cigarette brands mentioned above. The backing also advised that the silks were "useful in making pillow covers and other fancy articles for home decoration." Many undoubtedly were used for such purposes, making silks with the paper backing still intact more difficult to find. White silks must, however, have the backing intact to command top value. Although similar, the S74 "colored" silks, as their name indicates, were issued in a variety of colors. They are also slightly larger, measuring 1 7/8" by 3 1/2", and were issued without a paper backing. The colored silks, therefore, contained the cigarette brand name on the lower front of the fabric, either "Old Mill Cigarettes" or "Turkey Red Cigarettes." (No colored silks advertising the Helmar brand are known to exist.) There are 121 different players reported: six have been found in two poses, resulting in 127 different subjects. Ninety-two subjects are known in the "white" silk, while 120 have been found in the "colored." The silks feature the same players pictured in the popular T205 Gold Border tobacco card set.

		NR MT	EX	VG
Complete Set:		22500.	11000.	6500.
Common Player:		135.00	67.00	40.00
(1)	Home Run Baker	300.00	150.00	90.00
(2)	Cy Barger	135.00	67.00	40.00
(3)	Jack Barry	135.00	67.00	40.00
(4)	Johnny Bates	135.00	67.00	40.00
(5)	Fred Beck	135.00	67.00	40.00
(6)	Beals Becker	135.00	67.00	40.00
(7)	George Bell	135.00	67.00	40.00
(8)	Chief Bender	300.00	150.00	90.00
(9)	Roger Bresnahan	300.00	150.00	90.00
(10)	Al Bridwell	135.00	67.00	40.00
(11)	Mordecai Brown	300.00	150.00	90.00
(12)	Bobby Byrne	135.00	67.00	40.00
(13)	Howie Camnitz	135.00	67.00	40.00
(14)	Bill Carrigan	135.00	67.00	40.00
(15)	Frank Chance	375.00	187.00	112.00
(16)	Hal Chase	190.00	95.00	57.00
(17)	Fred Clarke	300.00	150.00	90.00
(18)	Ty Cobb	2100.	1000.	600.00
(19)	Eddie Collins	300.00	150.00	90.00
(20)	Doc Crandall	135.00	67.00	40.00
(21)	Lou Criger	135.00	67.00	40.00
(22)	Jim Delahanty	135.00	67.00	40.00
(23)	Art Devlin	135.00	67.00	40.00
(24)	Red Dooin	135.00	67.00	40.00
(25)	Mickey Doolan	135.00	67.00	40.00
(26)	Larry Doyle	135.00	67.00	40.00
(27)	Jimmy Dygert	135.00	67.00	40.00
(28)	Kid Elberfield (Elberfeld)	135.00	67.00	40.00
(29)	Steve Evans	135.00	67.00	40.00
(30)	Johnny Evers	300.00	150.00	90.00
(31)	Bob Ewing	135.00	67.00	40.00
(32)	Art Fletcher	135.00	67.00	40.00
(33)	John Flynn	135.00	67.00	40.00
(34)	Bill Foxen	135.00	67.00	40.00
(35)	George Gibson	135.00	67.00	40.00
(36)	Peaches Graham (Cubs)	135.00	67.00	40.00
(37)	Peaches Graham (Rustlers)	135.00	67.00	40.00
(38)	Clark Griffith	300.00	150.00	90.00
(39)	Topsy Hartsel	135.00	67.00	40.00
(40)	Arnold Hauser	135.00	67.00	40.00
(41)	Charlie Hemphill	135.00	67.00	40.00
(42)	Tom Jones	135.00	67.00	40.00
(43)	Jack Knight	135.00	67.00	40.00
(44)	Ed Konetchy	135.00	67.00	40.00
(45)	Harry Krause	135.00	67.00	40.00
(46)	Tommy Leach	135.00	67.00	40.00
(47)	Rube Marquard	300.00	150.00	90.00
(48)	Christy Mathewson	675.00	337.00	202.00
(49)	Al Mattern	135.00	67.00	40.00
(50)	Amby McConnell	135.00	67.00	40.00
(51)	John McGraw	375.00	187.00	112.00
(52)	Harry McIntire (McIntyre)	135.00	67.00	40.00

		NR MT	EX	VG
(53)	Fred Merkle	150.00	75.00	45.00
(54)	Chief Meyers	135.00	67.00	40.00
(55)	Dots Miller	135.00	67.00	40.00
(56)	Danny Murphy	135.00	67.00	40.00
(57)	Red Murray	135.00	67.00	40.00
(58)	Tom Needham	135.00	67.00	40.00
(59)	Rebel Oakes	135.00	67.00	40.00
(60)	Rube Oldring	135.00	67.00	40.00
(61)	Orval Overall	135.00	67.00	40.00
(62)	Fred Parent	135.00	67.00	40.00
(63)	Fred Payne	135.00	67.00	40.00
(64)	Barney Pelty	135.00	67.00	40.00
(65)	Deacon Phillippe	135.00	67.00	40.00
(66)	Jack Quinn	135.00	67.00	40.00
(67)	Bugs Raymond	135.00	67.00	40.00
(68)	Ed Reulbach	135.00	67.00	40.00
(69)	Doc Scanlon (Scanlan)	135.00	67.00	40.00
(70)	Germany Schaefer	135.00	67.00	40.00
(71)	Admiral Schlei	135.00	67.00	40.00
(72)	Wildfire Schulte	135.00	67.00	40.00
(73)	Dave Shean	135.00	67.00	40.00
(74)	Jimmy Sheckard	135.00	67.00	40.00
(75)	Hap Smith (Superbas)	135.00	67.00	40.00
(76)	Harry Smith (Rustlers)	525.00	262.00	157.00
(77)	Fred Snodgrass	135.00	67.00	40.00
(78)	Tris Speaker	450.00	225.00	135.00
(79)	Harry Steinfeldt (Cubs)	150.00	75.00	45.00
(80)	Harry Steinfeldt (Rustlers)	150.00	75.00	45.00
(81)	George Stone	135.00	67.00	40.00
(82)	Gabby Street	135.00	67.00	40.00
(83)	Ed Summers	135.00	67.00	40.00
(84)	Lee Tannehill	135.00	67.00	40.00
(85)	Joe Tinker	300.00	150.00	90.00
(86)	John Titus	135.00	67.00	40.00
(87)	Terry Turner	135.00	67.00	40.00
(88)	Bobby Wallace	300.00	150.00	90.00
(89)	Doc White	135.00	67.00	40.00
(90)	Ed Willett	135.00	67.00	40.00
(91)	Art Wilson	135.00	67.00	40.00
(92)	Harry Wolter	135.00	67.00	40.00

1910 S74 Silks - Colored

		NR MT	EX	VG
Complete Set:		22000.	11000.	6750.
Common Player:		125.00	62.00	37.00
(1)	Red Ames	125.00	62.00	37.00
(2)	Jimmy Archer	125.00	62.00	37.00
(3)	Home Run Baker	250.00	125.00	75.00
(4)	Cy Barger	125.00	62.00	37.00
(5)	Jack Barry	125.00	62.00	37.00
(6)	Johnny Bates	125.00	62.00	37.00
(7)	Beals Becker	125.00	62.00	37.00
(8)	George Bell	125.00	62.00	37.00
(9)	Chief Bender	250.00	125.00	75.00
(10)	Bill Bergen	125.00	62.00	37.00
(11)	Bob Bescher	125.00	62.00	37.00
(12)	Roger Bresnahan (mouth closed)	335.00	167.00	100.00
(13)	Roger Bresnahan (mouth open)	335.00	167.00	100.00
(14)	Al Bridwell	125.00	62.00	37.00
(15)	Mordecai Brown	250.00	125.00	75.00
(16)	Bobby Byrne	125.00	62.00	37.00
(17)	Howie Camnitz	125.00	62.00	37.00
(18)	Bill Carrigan	125.00	62.00	37.00
(19)	Frank Chance	335.00	167.00	100.00
(20)	Hal Chase	200.00	100.00	60.00
(21)	Ed Cicotte	175.00	87.00	52.00
(22)	Fred Clarke	250.00	125.00	75.00
(23)	Ty Cobb	1600.	800.00	480.00
(24)	Eddie Collins	250.00	125.00	75.00
(25)	Doc Crandall	125.00	62.00	37.00
(26)	Bill Dahlen	125.00	62.00	37.00
(27)	Jake Daubert	175.00	87.00	52.00
(28)	Jim Delahanty	125.00	62.00	37.00
(29)	Art Devlin	125.00	62.00	37.00
(30)	Josh Devore	125.00	62.00	37.00
(31)	Red Dooin	125.00	62.00	37.00
(32)	Mickey Doolan	125.00	62.00	37.00
(33)	Tom Downey	125.00	62.00	37.00
(34)	Larry Doyle	125.00	62.00	37.00
(35)	Hugh Duffy	250.00	125.00	75.00
(36)	Jimmy Dygert	125.00	62.00	37.00
(37)	Kid Elberfield (Elberfeld)	125.00	62.00	37.00
(38)	Steve Evans	125.00	62.00	37.00
(39)	Johnny Evers	250.00	125.00	75.00
(40)	Bob Ewing	125.00	62.00	37.00
(41)	Art Fletcher	125.00	62.00	37.00
(42)	John Flynn	125.00	62.00	37.00
(43)	Russ Ford	125.00	62.00	37.00
(44)	Bill Foxen	125.00	62.00	37.00
(45)	Art Fromme	125.00	62.00	37.00
(46)	George Gibson	125.00	62.00	37.00
(47)	Peaches Graham	125.00	62.00	37.00
(48)	Eddie Grant	125.00	62.00	37.00
(49)	Clark Griffith	250.00	125.00	75.00
(50)	Topsy Hartsel	125.00	62.00	37.00
(51)	Arnold Hauser	125.00	62.00	37.00
(52)	Charlie Hemphill	125.00	62.00	37.00
(53)	Dick Hoblitzell	125.00	62.00	37.00
(54)	Miller Huggins	250.00	125.00	75.00
(55)	John Hummel	125.00	62.00	37.00
(56)	Walter Johnson	675.00	337.00	202.00
(57)	Davy Jones	125.00	62.00	37.00
(58)	Johnny Kling	125.00	62.00	37.00
(59)	Jack Knight	125.00	62.00	37.00
(60)	Ed Konetchy	125.00	62.00	37.00
(61)	Harry Krause	125.00	62.00	37.00
(62)	Tommy Leach	125.00	62.00	37.00
(63)	Lefty Leifield	125.00	62.00	37.00
(64)	Hans Lobert	125.00	62.00	37.00
(65)	Rube Marquard	250.00	125.00	75.00
(66)	Christy Mathewson	675.00	337.00	202.00
(67)	Al Mattern	125.00	62.00	37.00
(68)	Amby McConnell	125.00	62.00	37.00
(69)	John McGraw	335.00	167.00	100.00
(70)	Harry McIntire (McIntyre)	125.00	62.00	37.00
(71)	Fred Merkle	175.00	87.00	52.00
(72)	Chief Meyers	125.00	62.00	37.00
(73)	Dots Miller	125.00	62.00	37.00
(74)	Mike Mitchell	125.00	62.00	37.00
(75)	Pat Moran	125.00	62.00	37.00
(76)	George Moriarty	125.00	62.00	37.00
(77)	George Mullin	125.00	62.00	37.00
(78)	Danny Murphy	125.00	62.00	37.00
(79)	Red Murray	125.00	62.00	37.00
(80)	Tom Needham	125.00	62.00	37.00
(81)	Rebel Oakes	125.00	62.00	37.00
(82)	Rube Oldring	125.00	62.00	37.00
(83)	Orval Overall	125.00	62.00	37.00
(84)	Fred Parent	125.00	62.00	37.00
(85)	Dode Paskert	125.00	62.00	37.00
(86)	Billy Payne	125.00	62.00	37.00
(87)	Barney Pelty	125.00	62.00	37.00
(88)	Deacon Phillippe	125.00	62.00	37.00
(89)	Jack Quinn	125.00	62.00	37.00
(90)	Bugs Raymond	125.00	62.00	37.00
(91)	Ed Reulbach	125.00	62.00	37.00
(92)	Jack Rowan	125.00	62.00	37.00
(93)	Nap Rucker	125.00	62.00	37.00

(94)	Doc Scanlon (Scanlan)	125.00	62.00	37.00
(95)	Germany Schaefer	125.00	62.00	37.00
(96)	Admiral Schlei	125.00	62.00	37.00
(97)	Wildfire Schulte	125.00	62.00	37.00
(98)	Dave Shean	125.00	62.00	37.00
(99)	Jimmy Sheckard	125.00	62.00	37.00
(100)	Happy Smith	125.00	62.00	37.00
(101)	Fred Snodgrass	125.00	62.00	37.00
(102)	Tris Speaker	500.00	250.00	150.00
(103)	Jake Stahl	125.00	62.00	37.00
(104)	Harry Steinfeldt	175.00	87.00	52.00
(105)	George Stone	125.00	62.00	37.00
(106)	Gabby Street	125.00	62.00	37.00
(107)	Ed Summers	125.00	62.00	37.00
(108)	Lee Tannehill	125.00	62.00	37.00
(109)	Joe Tinker	250.00	125.00	75.00
(110)	John Titus	125.00	62.00	37.00
(111)	Terry Turner	125.00	62.00	37.00
(112)	Bobby Wallace	250.00	125.00	75.00
(113)	Zack Wheat	250.00	125.00	75.00
(114)	Doc White (White Sox)	125.00	62.00	37.00
(115)	Kirby White (Pirates)	125.00	62.00	37.00
(116)	Ed Willett	125.00	62.00	37.00
(117)	Owen Wilson	125.00	62.00	37.00
(118)	Hooks Wiltse	125.00	62.00	37.00
(119)	Harry Wolter	125.00	62.00	37.00
(120)	Cy Young	675.00	337.00	202.00

1912 S81 Silks

1912 S81 Silks

The 1912 S81 "Silks," so-called because they featured pictures of baseball players on a satin-like fabric rather than paper or cardboard, are closely related to the better-known T3 Turkey Red cabinet cards of the same era. The silks, which featured 25 of the day's top baseball players among its other various subjects, were available as a premium with Helmar "Turkey Trophies" cigarettes. According to an advertising sheet, one silk could be obtained for 25 Helmar coupons. The silks measure 7" by 9" and, with a few exceptions, used the same pictures featured on the popular Turkey Red cards. Five players (Rube Marquard, Rube Benton, Marty O'Toole, Grover Alexander and Russ Ford) appear in the "Silks" set that were not included in the T3 set. In addition, an error involving the Frank Baker card was corrected for the "Silks" set. (In the T3 set, Baker's card actually pictured Jack Barry.) Several years ago a pair of New England collectors found a small stack of Christy Mathewson "Silks," making his, by far, the most common. Otherwise, the "Silks" are generally so rare that it is difficult to determine the relative scarcity of the others. Baseball enthusiasts are usually only attracted to the 25 baseball players in the "Silks" premium set, but it is interesting to note that the promotion also offered dozens of other subjects, including "beautiful women in bathing and athletic costumes, charming dancers in gorgeous attire, natiional flags and generals on horseback."

		NR MT	EX	VG
Complete Set:		47500.	24000.	14000.
Common Player:		975.00	487.00	292.00
90	Russ Ford	1100.	550.00	330.00
91	John McGraw	3250.	1625.	975.00
92	Nap Rucker	975.00	487.00	292.00
93	Mike Mitchell	975.00	487.00	292.00
94	Chief Bender	2600.	1300.	780.00
95	Home Run Baker	2600.	1300.	780.00
96	Nap Lajoie	3500.	1750.	1000.
97	Joe Tinker	2600.	1300.	780.00
98	Sherry Magee	975.00	487.00	292.00
99	Howie Camnitz	975.00	487.00	292.00
100	Eddie Collins	2600.	1300.	780.00
101	Red Dooin	975.00	487.00	292.00
102	Ty Cobb	8000.	4000.	2400.
103	Hugh Jennings	2600.	1300.	780.00
104	Roger Bresnahan	2600.	1300.	780.00
105	Jake Stahl	1100.	550.00	330.00
106	Tris Speaker	4200.	2100.	1250.
107	Ed Walsh	2600.	1300.	780.00
108	Christy Mathewson	2800.	1400.	800.00
109	Johnny Evers	2750.	1375.	825.00
110	Walter Johnson	4500.	2250.	1350.
111	Rube Marquard	2600.	1300.	780.00
112	Marty O'Toole	975.00	487.00	292.00
113	Rube Benton	975.00	487.00	292.00
114	Grover Alexander	2750.	1375.	825.00

408

Auctions

How to buy through the mail

Sports Collectors Digest, as do all Krause Publications hobby publications, screens its advertisers to weed out dishonesty, but these guidelines are helpful when buying collectibles through the mail:

1) Read the entire ad carefully before you order.

2) Condition and authenticity of the merchandise should be guaranteed.

3) For quicker service, send a money order or certified check instead of a personal check.

4) Pack and unpack the items carefully; damaged or broken items can't always be blamed on the post office. If damaged product should arrive, take the entire contents to the post office and file a claim.

How to buy at auctions and through auction houses

1) Learn the bidding process; rules for buying vary from state to state.

2) Listen to the auctioneer for a while to determine nuances and his acknowledgements of bids; a scratch of your nose might mean you just bid.

3) Bidding may be done by voice or by hand raising.

4) Many auction houses do not take responsibility for the correctness of description, authenticity, genuineness or condition of the item. So, go early and look at the items in person. Check out the con-

dition, size and whether the item has been repaired or restored.

5) Items are often sold "as is" and the house, in issuing catalogs, does not take responsibility or issue warranties regarding the description or physical condition, size, quality, rarity, importance or historical relevance, or errors.

6) The highest bid accepted is usually the buyer's, but disputes may result. If so, bidding is often reopened, but only between the two, with the highest bidder becoming the owner. Then it's his responsibility and risk for relocating the item. Sometimes the house will send the purchased property to a public warehouse for the account, risk and expense of the purchaser.

7) At unrestricted sales, or those without a reserve, the consigners of the items being sold are not supposed to bid. If they do bid back their own items, they still pay the full sales commission.

8) Most auctioneers reserve the right to refuse a bid if it does not match the item's value or is a nominal advance over the previous bid. He's looking to make the most on a bid. If the auctioneer decides an opening bid is below the reserve value for the article offered, he may reject the same and withdraw the article from the sale. A buyers premium, often 10 percent, is generally added on to the successful bid, and is payable by the purchaser as part of the total purchase price.

9) Get there early to browse, pick up a bidder's number, and get a good seat.

10) Local auctions will probably accept personal checks, but traveler's checks are wise for out-of-town auctions.

11) When dealing as a consigner, read the contract in its entirety before signing it and understand what you've just signed.

Telephone auctions

Convey the lot you wish to bid on and your absolute top bid. Normal bidding progresses with bids being raised by the regular 10 percent. When someone tops your current bid, the auctioneer automatically increases your bid by the mandatory 10 percent. This process continues until your absolute top bid is reached.

Often the times are designated and the bidding ends promptly, with no exceptions.

Pre-registration by potential bidders is usually required a few days in advance. A bidding number is obtained at that time and is later given when the auction occurs. Then the lots and absolute top bids for each are given and the process continues.

Bidders are generally discouraged from calling immediately after the auction to check on results. Winners are contacted within the next day; those wishing results may generally do so after the auction's deadline by sending an SASE for a prices realized list.

Absentee bids are encouraged, too, but require top limits on the bids for each lot. Lots are purchased for the absentee bidders at the lowest possible price under their top limit. For example: If you write in with an absentee top limit bid of $500 and the highest bid received by other phone bidders is $300, you win the lot for $330 - ($300 plus 10 percent) plus the 10 percent buyer's fee.

Mr. Mint's 24th Major Telephone Auction

New York Yankee memorabilia was the center of attention during Alan "Mr. Mint" Rosen's 24th major telephone auction Dec. 6, 1993, in Montvale, N.J. But there were plenty of unusual items for non-Yankee fans, too.

Honus Wagner's personal shaving kit sold for $970, against a minimum bid of $500. The gold-plated Gillette safety razor box is engraved with the letters "J.H.W." Inside the purple velvet-lined box is a razor-blade holder and a very ornate initialed two-piece razor. It came from the Wagner estate and included a letter of authenticity from Leslie Wagner Blair, the granddaughter of Honus Wagner.

• A 1902 Pittsburgh Pirates spring training tour book sold for its minimum bid of $300. The 5x9 booklet, tied together in silk string, has a photo on the cover of the National League Championship trophy from 1901 and a team photo inside. It also included a letter of authenticity.

• An autographed copy of Christy Mathewson's autobiography, "Pitching in a Pinch," sold for the minimum bid of $1,750. The book, copyrighted in 1912, is signed on the inside picture sleeve "To Joseph, Christy Mathewson 1919."

• A 1923 World Series unscored/ unfolded program, from the first ever to be played at the new Yankee Stadium, sold for $970, against a minimum bid of $800, while a lot of three scored programs from the 1951 World Series sold for $445 against a $300 minimum. Two programs are from Yankee Stadium; one is from the Polo Grounds.

• A 1908 Chicago Cubs World Championship award sold for the minimum bid of $3,800. The 14-karat gold piece has the appearance of an oak leaf cluster which surrounds a baseball diamond housing a 3/4 karat diamond. Around the stone are the words "World Champions 1908." The award was issued to A.B. Semmons, a team executive.

• A Lou Gehrig "Never Forgotten" black-and-white pin, with a ribbon, ball and glove attached, sold for $325, $100 more than the minimum.

• Food-related pieces were also sold. A complete set of six unfolded 1951 Wheaties boxes sold for $850, against a minimum of $700. The boxes featured Ted Williams, Stan Musial, Bob Feller, Johnny Lujack, Sam Snead and George Mikan.

• A Mickey Mantle Shirriff Potato Chip advertising piece sold for the minimum bid of $250. The 4x12 piece depicts three plastic coins - two say "free Major League baseball coins, now in Shirriff 10 cent potato chips." The other coin shows the Mickey Mantle coin.

• The spikes former New York Yankee Rookie of the Year Dave Righetti wore when he pitched a no-hitter on George Steinbrenner's birthday sold for the minimum $350 bid. The Adidas spikes, dated 7-4-83, were signed in black Sharpie.

• A Ty Cobb Near Mint single-signed baseball sold for $1,135, against a minimum bid of $700. The ball, signed on the wide panel in blue ink, reads "To Jerome from Ty Cobb 2/6/60", and is a Professional League ball.

• A single-signed Walter Alston ball, signed on the sweet spot of an official National League ball, sold for $750, against a minimum bid of $150, while a Joe DiMaggio ball brought $335, against a minimum bid of $200. DiMaggio signed the official American League ball on the sweet spot.

• A hand-painted ball featuring DiMaggio's likeness sold for the minimum bid of $450. DiMaggio signed the official American League ball on the sweet spot; artist

Erwin Sadler's artwork is on the wide panel below the signature. A hand-painted Mickey Mantle ball, bearing the likeness of Mantle on his 1953 Topps baseball card, sold for $270, against a minimum bid of $200.

• A Mickey Mantle/Roger Maris autographed game-used New York Yankees hat brought the minimum bid of $750. The player who actually wore the hat is undetermined, but it is a New Era size 7 1/4 and shows game use. Mantle and Maris each signed it on the bill. A limited-edition Mantle/Maris bat, commemorating the teammates' record of 115 home runs in a season, sold for the minimum bid of $2,500. The bat was #8 of 115 produced.

• A single-signed Roger Maris Louisville Slugger model bat sold for $1,480, against a minimum bid of $1,000, while a Roger Maris bobbing head doll, including the box, sold for $570, against a minimum bid of $350.

• Twenty-six members of the 1956 World Champion New York Yankees signed a ball which sold for $825, against a minimum bid of $750. Key signatures include Billy Martin, Mickey McDermott, Elston Howard and Mickey Mantle.

• A Louisville Slugger Mickey Mantle model bat signed by 38 Yankee greats sold for $750, against a minimum of $500. Signatures included those of Mickey Mantle, Ron Guidry, Yogi Berra, Phil Rizzuto, Ron Blomberg, Steve Sax, Graig Nettles, Rich Gossage and Joe Pepitone.

• Babe Ruth items included a prototype 34-inch "Hillerich & Bradsby Company" bat, which sold for $750, the minimum bid. The bat, having the exact specifications of Babe Ruth's bat, is stenciled 4-22-37 and included a letter of authenticity.

• A Babe Ruth cancelled check, drawn on a Chemical Bank & Trust Co. check dated March 16, 1940, sold for $1,320, against a minimum bid of $1,200. The check, signed "G.H. Ruth," is made out to "Cash" for $2 and is endorsed by the Second National Bank in Cooperstown, N.Y.

• A framed, matted 8x10 autographed Babe Ruth photo sold for $1,475, against an $800 minimum bid. Ruth signed his name in red ink across the chest.

• Seven oversized 33 1/3 LPs containing excerpts of an interview with Ruth sold for the minimum bid of $400. The phonographic records are titled "The Adventures of Babe Ruth."

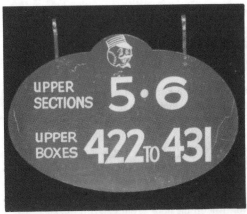

Crosley Field Stadium sign, 36x24: $750-$1,000.

(209)

Bill Buckner's 1986 World Series ring: $33,000.

Dizzy Dean "Jolly Boy Kite," 1930s cereal premium: $600-$800

Robin Roberts' retired number, wooden sign hung at the Vet, autographed:$500-$800.

(780)   *(781)*

(612)

Left to right: 1980 Phillies World Series Trophy, from front office ($3,000-$4,000); 1957 Braves National League Championship trophy, given to manager Fred Haney ($2,200-$2,500); Denny McLain's 1968 Cy Young Award ($15,000-$20,000)

Leland's Nov. 20-21, 1993, Doubleheader auction

Boston Red Sox first baseman Bill Buckner has kept his sense of humor regarding the 1986 World Series, when he made a costly error in Game 6 to allow the winning run to score for the New York Mets.

The 10k-gold diamond-studded ring Buckner was awarded after the Mets ultimately went on to win the World Series was up for bids in Leland's Nov. 20-21, 1993, Doubleheader auction. The ring sold for $33,000, against a presale estimate of $6,500-$7,500 made by the New York City auction house.

In a letter which accompanied the ring, Buckner wrote: "Hope you enjoy my 1986 World Series ring (Losers reward). The nightmare of 1986 is over! I'm off the hook. Your pal, Bill Buckner."

The ring has a diamond-studded "B" on a maroon stone, framed by the words "American League Champions." "Buckner 6" (his uniform number) and a Red Sox logo are on one side, while an image of Fenway Park and the date, 1986, are on the other.

Ted Williams' jersey from the year he hit .406 sold for $71,500. The #9 flannel with cut-down sleeves was a 1941 Boston Red Sox road uniform. Ernie Banks' 1970 Chicago Cubs jersey sold for $13,200, as did a sleeveless 1967 Roberto Clemente Pittsburgh Pirates road jersey. Pete Rose's 1981 Philadelphia Phillies road jersey went for $3,025, as did a Carl Yastrzemski 1975 Red Sox road jersey.

But the most expensive jersey sold was Babe Ruth's 1929-30 New York Yankees grey road flannel, which had had the #3 removed from the back for use by a semi pro team in the Bahamas, but included Ruth's name stitched inside the collar.

The jersey, which sold for $132,000, was one of a complete team set the Yankees sent to the organizer of the Bahamas team; the rest of the jerseys were eventually returned to the Yankees, but the owner kept Ruth's.

A double-breasted overcoat Ruth referred to as his "white mink" sold for $16,500. Ruth wore the coat, made of a soft white vicuna, after his playing days were over. Made during the early 1940s, the custom-made coat, from Dobbs of Manhattan, had an original price tag of $800.

Four postseason rings collectively sold for $29,975, with Pete Rose's 1975 World Series MVP 10k ring bringing $16,500, as did Denny McClain's 1968 Cy Young Award from the year he won 31 games. Bob Welch's 1981 Los Angeles Dodgers World Series ring sold for $4,950, while Dale Berra's 1979 Pittsburgh Pirates Wold Series ring went for $3,850. Steve Carlton's 1983 Philadelphia Phillies National League Championship ring went for $4,675.

Leland's Aug. 21, 1993, Pastimes auction

Classic sports cartoons and signature artwork were among the featured items during Leland's Aug. 21, 1993, Pastimes auction.

Bill Gallo, a cartoonist from the New York Daily News, created a 12x16 tribute to Roberto Clemente after the Pirate outfielder's tragic death in 1972. The piece sold for $1,760.

Gallo also created a double-paneled cartoon of Pete Rose "The Ballplayer" and Pete Rose "The Convicted Felon," in light of Rose's gambling problems. Entitled "It's Your Call, Kids," the piece, which sold for $220, had a ballot for readers to decide if Rose's name should be on the Hall of Fame ballot.

At left, from top to bottom: Babe Ruth Pathes Freres 78 rpm record premium ($1,500-$2,000); Babe Ruth candy wrapper from the 1920s, 5x7.5 ($900-$1,200); "Bambino" pinball machine front, 19x17, reverse painting on glass, 1930s ($1,000-$1,500). Above: Babe Ruth's 1929-30 Yankee grey road flannel ($132,000).

At left, Babe Ruth "Quaker Oats" cardboard sign, framed 26x35, shows premiums issued for Ruth's radio show ($3,000-$4,000). At right, 1933 Feen-A-Mint Babe Ruth mask, 7x10, says "If Babe Ruth hits a homer today, wear this mask to show your appreciation" ($1,500-$2,000).

A 19x24 cartoon of Joe DiMaggio in his Yankee pinstripes sold for $1,320. The piece, created in the early 1960s by Bruce Stark of the New York Daily News, shows the Yankee Clipper following through on a swing.

Stark's 18x21 cartoon of Jackie Robinson in the dugout bending down to pick up a bat went for $770, while a 1970 piece honoring Yankee catcher Thurman Munson for being named Rookie of the Year sold for $550.

A 1960s Stellar electric Mickey Mantle/Roger Maris clock radio sold for $770. The radio had a plastic baseball player on the speaker, with a dial using a bat for the hands and baseballs for the numbers.

Don Mattingly's 1983 minor league Columbus Clippers jersey brought $3,025. The royal blue and red pinstriped Triple A shirt, a home uniform #19, had the team logo on the front and Mattingly's signature in the tail. A letter of authenticity from a club official was also included.

A sterling black, red and white Cleveland Indians logo sold for $1,320. The 24x32-inch wooden logo had hung in former club owner Bill Veeck's office.

Leland's Feb. 20, 1993, Souvenirs auction

The contract which sent Babe Ruth from the Boston Red Sox to the New York Yankees was one of several big-ticket items sold during Leland's Feb. 20, 1993, Souvenirs auction.

The New York city auction house had a phone bidder who paid $99,000 for the 1919 contract, which detailed the conditions and sale of Ruth from the Red Sox to the Yankees, including a stipulation that if Ruth demanded a raise over his $10,000 salary, the Red Sox would help the Yankees pay the increase. The six-page typed document, dated Dec. 26, 1919, was notarized by Yankees' owner Jacob Ruppert and Red Sox President Harry Frazee.

An autographed bat used by Ruth during his first year with the Yankees, 1920, when he hit 54 home runs, sold for $38,500, while a lot of more than 100 documents pertaining to Ruth's funeral, including 31 acceptance telegrams from pallbearers, sold for $3,850.

A red, white and blue pinstriped jersey of another Yankee legend, Lou Gehrig, sold for $110,000. Gehrig wore the shirt during a first-ever tour of Japan by American ballplayers in 1931. Three photographs of Gehrig wearing the uniform were also included.

A 43-pound bronze commemorative slab identical to one given to Mickey Mantle on his day at Yankee Stadium in 1969 sold for $33,000. The 24x18-inch slab, which lists Mantle's accomplishments, is one of only three known to exist; one is at Mantle's New York restaurant, while another is in Yankee Stadium's Yankee Park.

Pete Rose's 1978 Silver Wraith Rolls Royce, with "PETE" Ohio license plates, sold for $44,000, while his 1975 World Series Most Valuable Player ring sold for $12,000. His 3,000th hit baseball, as noted by Rose on the ball, sold for $13,750.

Ty Cobb's 14k-gold pocket watch, given to him after he won his first of 12 batting titles in 1907, sold for $55,000. The engraved watch has a Pierre Droit & Co. porcelain face and says "Presented to Tyrus Raymond Cobb Through The Atlanta Journal, By the Georgia Fans for His Brilliant Career on the Diamond 1907." The reverse is engraved with a detailed tiger, two baseballs and two crossed bats, plus a pennant with Cobb's average - .352.

A Joe Jackson payment voucher for $500 sold for $27,500. The voucher, dated Feb. 28, 1916, was used as a down payment by Jackson on his new home. Because Jackson was illiterate, few of his signatures exist, but this item included a letter of authenticity from his family.

Roberto Clemente's game-used Pittsburgh Pirates batting helmet, black with a yellow "P", sold for $3,025, while Steve Carlton's 1968 St. Louis Cardinals World Series ring sold for $8,250.

Ted Williams "Drink Moxie" cardboard standup, 15x12: $1,500-$2,000.

Top: 1927 Lucky Strike cigarette trolley sign, framed 26x16 ($1,000-$1,200); Bottom: Mickey Mantle/Yogi Berra Yoo-Hoo drink sign, framed 32x26 ($2,000-$2,500).

Pee Wee Reese Wheaties cardboard sign, framed 28x18: $1,000-$1,200.

1927 Frankie Frisch Spalding baseball glove cardboard sign, framed 29x21: $1,200-$1,500.

Casey Stengel Gillette sign, framed 40x48: $900-$1,000.

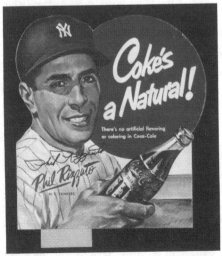

Phil Rizzuto Coca-Cola advertising piece, 10x12, autographed: $800-$1,000.

417

Leland's Aug. 4, 1992,
Hall of Fame auction

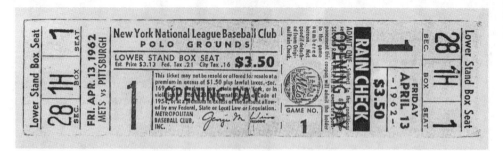

This unused ticket ($300-$400) is from the Mets' first-ever home game.

What would you pay for the ball Mookie Wilson hit through Bill Buckner's legs to give the New York Mets a victory over the Boston Red Sox in Game 6 of the 1986 World Series?

One ex "Major Leaguer" was willing to pay the highest price ever paid for one baseball, according to Joshua Evans, the owner of Leland's, the New York city auction house which put the ball up for bids in its Hall of Fame auction Aug. 4, 1992.

Evans had estimated the ball would sell for between $8,000-$10,000. But a telephone bidder, actor Charlie Sheen, he of "Eight Men Out" and "Major League" movie fame, paid $93,500 for the ball.

Memorabilia from another popular Mets player, Tom Seaver, generated quite a bit of interest, too. Seaver's 1969 autographed home jersey sold for $55,000, while a 1974 autographed Rawlings road version went for $7,700 and included a letter of authenticity from Seaver written on Yankees stationery; Seaver is a Yankees broadcaster.

An autographed Mets warmup jacket Seaver wore between 1967-69 sold for $11,000, but contained an item inside its pocket which Evans deemed priceless; he gave the item - a toothpick - a presale estimate of "?".

The toothpick, which eventually sold for $440, included a letter of authenticity from Seaver, which stated, in part, "This is a toothpick left in my Mets warm-up jacket worn by me in the late 60's (sic). I had given this to my good friend Arthur Richman. It is 100% authentic, original and unrestored."

The two-page document Babe Ruth sent to Yankees owner Jacob Ruppert announcing his retirement sold for $25,300, against an estimate of $8,000-$10,000. The typed letter, dated Oct. 11, 1934, was on Ruth's personal "Babe Ruth, New York" stationery, with his address and telephone number.

"I have explained to you why I think it would be an imposition on your ball club and on the public, for me to attempt to play as a regular next year. As I take too much pride in my baseball record for the past twenty-one years to sit on the bench as a utility-player, I will never again sign a player's contract with any club," the letter said.

Other Yankee items sold included a 1930s Lou Gehrig cap with his name embroidered in it, which sold for $14,300, and 1960-61 batting helmets for Mickey Mantle ($7,700), Roger Maris ($4,675) and Yogi Berra ($1,320).

Mets items sold included Keith Hernandez's 1987 Gold Glove Award ($7,150) and a "Miracle Mets" official National League ball from 1969, signed by 28 players from that World Championship team ($2,310).

Oddball items included a 1930s Crosley Field usher's uniform which sold for $2,310, a wine chest (a gift to Ty Cobb in the 1940s), which sold for $1,980, and a turnstile from old Yankee Stadium, which sold for $3,575.

The most expensive item sold during the auction was a Ty Cobb jersey. The 1924 Detroit Tigers road shirt, which included a letter of authenticity from Cobb, went for $176,000.

Photos courtesy Wolffers Auction House

Lou Gehrig's 1935-37 New York Yankees grey flannel road jersey, "L. Gehrig" chain stitched in tail, game used: $198,000.

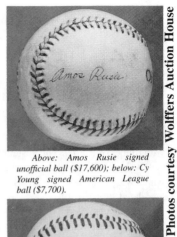

Above: Amos Rusie signed unofficial ball ($17,600); below: Cy Young signed American League ball ($7,700).

1914 Boston Garter, #9 "Home Run Baker" well-centered, rare baseball card: ($8,000-$10,000).

Roy Campanella game-used Spalding catcher's mitt, obtained from Dodgers batboy betweem 1947-51, letter of authenticity: $7,000-$8,000.

1913 Philadelphia A's World Series press pin, elephant medal, Ex-Nr Mt: $5,500-$6,000.

Richard Wolffers auction,
Sept. 8, 1993

The first patented baseball and patented bat, contributed by the U.S. Patent Office, were among the items which were sold during a Richard Wolffers auction Sept. 8, 1993.

The 14-inch model bat, which sold for $41,250, included a handwritten tag dated Oct. 30, 1886, and was issued to George W. Hill. The bat was slit at the top of the barrel, allowing it to be packed with rubber or leather. The designer claimed this would send the ball further when it was hit.

The baseball, which had patent number 79719 handwritten on its tag, sold for $14,300. The ball, which was cut in half to show its construction and stuffing, was issued to inventor Henry A. Alden and was dated July 7, 1868.

A baseball signed by Joe DiMaggio and his wife Norma Jean (Marilyn Monroe) sold for $9,350.

Several Hall of Famers' uniforms were also sold by the San Francisco auction house, including Joe DiMaggio's 1939 #5 New York Yankees jersey, which went for $132,000 against a presale estimate of $225,000-$275,000. The DiMaggio jersey, obtained from Yankee scout Dan Crowley, had the NY logo on the front, a 1939 centennial patch on the sleeve, and DiMaggio's name stitched in the collar.

Honus Wagner's flannel Pittsburgh road shirt went for $115,500. The jersey, which had Wagner's name stitched inside the Spalding label in the collar, had a three-button front with a breast pocket.

John McGraw's 1913-14 New York Giants flannel road jersey and pants sold for $15,950, while Casey Stengel's 1924 Boston Braves shirt sold for $7,700.

An autographed Ted Williams 1955 Boston Red Sox #9 jersey went for $93,500. The jersey included a black arm band for his teammate, Harry Agganis. Stan Musial's autographed 1956 St. Louis Cardinals shirt, #6, sold for $14,300, while Willie Mays' 1965 San Francisco Giants jersey, #24, went for $12,650.

Several pieces of hardware were sold during the auction, too. A 1917 gold pocket watch, presented to Honus Wagner by the Pirates, sold for $10,450, but Dutch Reuther's 1927 New York Yankees World Series 14k ring topped that mark, bringing in $19,800. Junior Gilliam's 1965 Los Angeles Dodgers world championship ring sold for $6,000, while Harmon Killebrew's 1969 Babe Ruth crown trophy, given to him for leading the majors in home runs (49) and RBI (140) that year, went for $7,975.

Richard Wolffers auction,
June 2, 1993

Nearly $200,000 was paid for a 1937-39 Lou Gehrig New York Yankees jersey sold during a Richard Wolffers auction in San Francisco June 3, 1993.

The grey flannel road jersey, one of the several Hall of Famers' jerseys which were up for bids, sold for $198,000, compared to Gehrig's 1927 Yankee home pinstripe, which Wolffers sold for $363,000 in September of 1992.

Gehrig's game-used road jersey had "L. Gehrig" stitched in the shirt tail, and a centennial patch, featuring a red, white and blue baseball, on the left sleeve. NEW YORK was written in block letters across the chest, while Gehrig's #4 was on the back.

Although they didn't garner six-figure bids, there were several other Hall of Famers' jerseys which were sold. Sandy Koufax's autographed 1966 Los Angeles Dodgers #32 jersey, which he wore during his final season in the big leagues, sold for $24,200, as did Eddie Mathews' autographed 1965 Milwaukee Braves #41 home jersey.

His teammate's jersey, an autographed 1962 Milwaukee Braves #21 home jersey belonging to

Left: Nolan Ryan's autographed, game-used, seventh no-hitter ball, dated 5-1-91 ($3,800). Right: Tom Seaver's autographed, game-used, 300th-win ball, dated 8-4-85 ($3,500-$4,000).

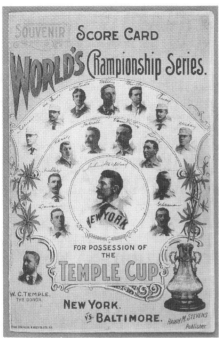

1894 "Temple Cup" World's Championship program, New York Giants vs. Baltimore Orioles, scored in pencil from Oct. 12, 1984, game, a 4-1 New York win: $26,400.

Frankie Frisch's 1922 New York Giants World Championship ring: $20,900.

Marilyn Monroe autographed 7 1/2x9 1/2 black-and-white photo, taken after her wedding to Joe DiMaggio: $4,500-$5,000.

pitcher Warren Spahn, sold for $16,500. Willie Mays' 1965 San Francisco Giants #24 road jersey and pants sold for $13,200.

Oakland A's uniforms for Rickey Henderson - a 1991 #24 home jersey and pants - and Jose Canseco - a 1989 jersey - sold for $4,125 and $1,320, while Cecil Fielder's size 52 1990 Detroit Tigers road jersey and pants went for $1,155.

Nolan Ryan's 1991 Texas Rangers home jersey and pants sold for $7,425, while his 1988 Houston Astros warm-up jacket went for $3,850. A Ryan-autographed Texas Rangers cap sold for $557, while an autographed and dated game ball used during Ryan's sixth no-hitter, thrown on June 11, 1990, sold for $3,080.

Baseballs autographed by Hall of Famers Amos Rusie and Cy Young fetched $17,600 and $7,700, while a baseball signed by 24 members of the 1927 New York Yankees, including Gehrig, Babe Ruth and three other Hall of Famers, sold for $12,100.

A bat Ted Williams used one at bat before he hit a home run in his final major league at bat sold for $7,975.

All prices include a 10 percent buyer's premium.

Richard Wolffers auction,
Feb. 18, 1993

A 1922 World Series ring worn by the "Fordham Flash" sold for $20,900 during a Richard Wolffers auction Feb. 18, 1993.

The 14k-gold world championship ring was presented to Frankie Frisch after the New York Giants defeated the New York Yankees for the title. He and his teammates became the first players to receive commemorative rings; prior to 1922, players were given commemorative watch fobs.

Frisch's well-worn diamond ring says "Giants World Champions, 1922" in block letters. The ring is engraved with a ball, infielder's glove and two crossed bats.

Hall of Famers' uniforms generated big money during the 1,200-lot auction. Jackie Robinson's 1950 Brooklyn Dodgers home flannel sold for $55,000. The jersey, #42, had Robinson's name and year stitched into the shirt tail. It included two letters of authenticity and a notarized letter from a Dodger minor leaguer who was assigned the jersey after the season was completed.

Ted Williams' autographed 1954 #9 Red Sox uniform, including pants, sold for $52,250. Willie Mays' 1954 #24 New York Giants flannel road jersey sold for $31,900. Mays wore the jersey, which had his name stitched in the tail, during the year he hit 51 home runs.

Stan Musial's and Roger Maris' game-used uniforms from 1962 sold for $25,300 each. Musial's autographed jersey, #6, was a St. Louis Cardinals road jersey; Maris' #9 was a Yankee road flannel. Nolan Ryan's 1973 home California Angels jersey sold for $7,150, while a 1980s Houston Astros shirt sold for $3,300.

An autographed ball from Nolan Ryan's seventh no-hitter, dated 5-1-91, sold for $3,850. The ball, signed by Ryan, included a letter of authenticity from the second base umpire in that game. A similar ball, used by Tom Seaver during his only no-hitter as a Cincinnati Red, also sold for $3,850. The ball is dated "6/16/78" and has the notation "0" on it.

A "first pitch" ball signed by President Lyndon Johnson sold for $4,125. The ball, which included a letter of authenticity from the man who caught it, was used on Opening Day in 1965 for the game between the Washington Senators and the Boston Red Sox.

An autographed Louisville Slugger bat used by Joe DiMaggio during his last trip through Boston's Fenway Park sold for $11,500. DiMaggio dated the bat "Sept. 22/51" and had given it to an usher at Fenway.

A scorecard from the 1894 Temple Cup world championship game between the New York Giants and the Baltimore Orioles, indicating a 4-1 New York win, sold for $26,400.

Prices listed include a 10 percent commission.

Nolan Ryan's 1973 Angels home knit, game used, name on back, tags: $7,150.

Nolan Ryan's early 1980s Astros home knit, game used, name on back, tags: $3,300.

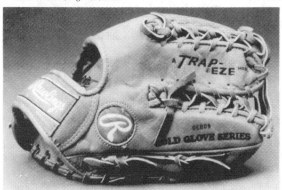

Ozzie Smith's game-used Rawlings "Gold Glove Series" glove, custom number OEB09: $1,000-$1,250.

President Lyndon B. Johnson autographed "first pitch" ball for 1965 season, opener pitted Washington and Boston: $4,125.

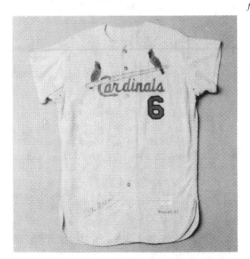

Stan Musial's 1962 Cardinals flannel road jersey, name on back, tags, "Musial 62" in tail, autographed: $25,300.

Leland's IX May 21, 1993, telephone auction

- Seals Stadium seat: $708.
- Crosley Field figural stadium seat: $2,750.
- Polo Grounds stadium seat with figural design: $2,750.
- Boston Braves Stadium seat figural side: $391.
- Ebbets Field stadium seat: $1,560.
- Crosley Field stadium seat: $750.
- Wrigley Field stadium seat: $484.
- Briggs Stadium seat: $726.
- Exchange Booth sign (52x20): $304.
- Detroit Tigers stretcher (1920s): $133.
- Tiger Stadium third base (circa 1977): $183.
- Yankee Stadium scoreboard letters, three 19x22 hard plastic Ws with cast-iron frames: $198.
- 1950s Crosley Field celluloid usher's badge: $110.
- 1950s Mickey Mantle Zippo Lighter, with box: $330.
- 1910 tin lithograph baseball game: $204.
- 1935 Dizzy Dean cardboard advertising sign for Saturday Evening Post, 10 1/2x13: $220.
- Leo Durocher Chesterfield Cigarettes color cardboard advertisement: $198.
- 1930s Carl Hubbell "Strike 3" baseball board game: $333.
- "Home Run by Babe Ruth" flip book: $229.
- Rogers Hornsby sheet music with 1926 St. Louis Cardinals team photo in the center: $160.
- 1950s Ted Williams' Root Beer soda bottle: $165.
- Jackie Robinson check, dated Jan. 10, 1957, made out to American Airlines: $303.
- Jackie Robinson check, dated Aug. 28, 1960, made out to Sea Breeze Motel: $275.
- 1870s baseball bat: $320.
- D&M mushroom bat from the early 1900s: $273.
- Johnny Bench game-used Louisville 125 bat: $466.
- Vida Blue game-used 1977 All-Star Game Louisville Slugger: $399.
- Will Clark autographed game-used Rawlings Adirondack bat: $385.
- Willie Davis game-used 1971 All-Star Game Louisville Slugger: $399.
- Carlton Fisk game-used Worth bat: $317.
- Tony Gwynn game-used Louisville 125 C263 model bat: $215.
- Joe Morgan game-used Louisville Slugger: $336.
- Sadaharu Oh game-used bat: $1,650.
- Ryne Sandberg game-used brown Louisville 125 bat: $583.
- Ozzie Smith game-used H238 model Louisville Slugger: $327.
- Robin Yount game-used Louisville Slugger model P72: $514.
- 1950s Portland Beavers uniform: $586.
- 1992 Philadelphia Phillies Turn-Back-the-Clock uniform, John Kruk: $545.
- Film-worn spikes from the movie "The Natural": $121.
- Pete Rose/Johnny Bench autographed caps: $330.
- St. Louis Browns 1950s uniform patch: $167.
- Puerto Rican baseball jersey collection of 19, Caguas team: $645.
- Orlando Cepeda 1967 game-used St. Louis Cardinals flannel pants: $167.
- Luis Aparicio 1971 game-used Boston Red Sox home flannel pants: $88.
- Dennis Eckersley game-worn spring training jersey: $212.
- Dave Winfield game-used batting gloves: $152.
- Clark Griffith typed letter on Washington Senators stationery, 1934: $266.
- Connie Mack handwritten letter on A's stationery, 1939: $300.
- Rogers Hornsby 1952 typed letter on Cincinnati Reds stationery: $363.
- Six Bowie Kuhn letters from 1970-74 on "Office of the Commissioner" stationery: $182.
- Stan Coveleski handwritten letter, 1970: $99.
- Frankie Frisch typed letter, 1967: $220.
- Sports Illustrated issue #1, signed in silver by Eddie Mathews: $516.
- 1937 Jackie Robinson yearbook, Pasadena Junior College varsity baseball team: $439.
- 1948 Negro League All-Star Game unused ticket: $484.
- Tom Browning perfect game autographed ticket (9/16/88): $121.
- 1880s baseball program: $363.
- 1914 Federal League unused ticket: $152.
- 1930 World Series Game 3 unused phantom ticket: $99.
- Don Larsen 1956 World Series Game 5 perfect game ticket stub: $495.
- Ticket from Major League Baseball's 100,000th game, Sept. 6, 1963, Tigers vs. Yankees, Whitey Ford wins #21: $121.
- Pete Rose unused 3,000th hit ticket: $216.
- 1935 Negro League game ticket: $278.
- 1964 New York Mets tour Mexico program, all in Spanish: $110.
- 1945 Detroit Tigers World Series Banquet ticket, for the day after the series ended: $121.
- 1982 Los Angeles Dodgers phantom World Series press pin: $66.
- Joe DiMaggio letter, 1974 request from collector for him to authenticate a pair of spikes, includes letter from collector, plus photo of the spikes and a handwritten response on the bottom: $147.

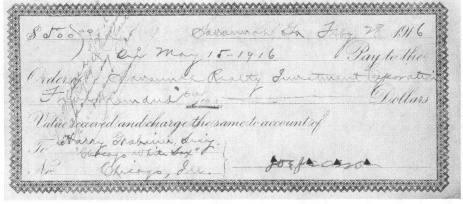

Photos courtesy Leland's Inc.

This Feb. 28, 1916, payment voucher, ink-signed "Joe Jackson," is a direct payment of his Chicago White Sox salary towards a new home: $27,500.

Left to right: Rod Carew's 1974 game-used Twins road jersey ($2,000-$2,500); Tom Seaver's autographed 1978 Reds road jersey ($2,500-$3,000); Willie Stargell's game-used 1979 Pirates road jersey ($1,800-$2,200); Bob Gibson's 1972-73 game-used Cardinals road jersey ($2,000-$2,500).

Pete Rose purchased this $86,000 1978 Silver Wraith Rolls Royce during the height of his popularity with the Reds: $44,000.

Leland's Hobby IV (Feb. 21, 1992) and Hobby V (April 24, 1992) results

• 1870s baseball bat, square headed, in original green paint, rounded knob handle: $319.

• Reach Mushroom bat, patented Aug. 1, 1905, with keystone and baseball logo in the center, shaped as a mushroom, used only in the early 1900s for a few years: $666.

• Boston Bees jacket, circa 1939, player jacket with a real wool body and white piping with stylized "B", snap front, in white paint: $990.

• 1987 Roberto Alomar Wichita Pilots jersey, Rawlings, "Pilots" across the chest, with #15 on the front and back: $358.

• 1950s Cleveland Indian uniform patch, in full color: $133.

• 1912 Reach Official American League baseball, "The Official Ball of the World's Series," with Ban Johnson facsimile, box: $1,033.

• Official Dizzy and Daffy Dean Nok-Out Baseball Game, large tube with label picturing the Deans, contains giant game board: $303.

• 1950s Ted Williams bottle, original, once held "Ted's Delicious Creamy Root Beer," logo had facsimile signature: $248.

• 1949 Detroit Tigers pennant, scroll of names includes Newhouser, Kell, Keller, Hutchinson: $110.

• 1940s Chicago Cubs pennant, shows batter in front of crossed bats, baseball: $163.

• Collection of 1930s eight-inch pennants, for Browns, Athletics, Phillies, Reds, and three colleges: $95.

• 1948 Cleveland Indians book mark, with tassel in original log folder and envelope with stadium, three pieces: $66.

• 1950s Brooklyn Dodger window scraper, Bum in plastic on original card (1952): $77.

• 1950s Brooklyn Bum, "Ho-Jo the Bo," in rubber by Rempel, with box: $550.

• 1947 Babe Ruth sheet music, entitled "Babe" and "Dedicated to Babe Ruth," posed in Yankee duds against a green field: $196.

• Sports Collectors Digest #1 issue, dated Oct. 12, 1973: $290.

• 1923 World Series Opening Game ticket stub for the first ever World Series game at Yankee Stadium: $296.

• Yankee Stadium seat, original seat, repainted to a dark blue: $1,198.

• 1901 Comiskey Park stadium chair, a fire engine red folding chair, used in 1947 by a minor league affiliate, includes a letter of authenticity: $585.

• Crosley Field seat, wood and cast metal, installed in the 1930s, restored to the original barn red color: $1,352.

• Boston Braves stadium seat, folding chair from the box seat section in the original green paint: $1,464.

• Ty Cobb signed check, a First National Bank check dated Feb. 5, 1959, made out to Clifford Pharmacy for $17.79: $484.

• Babe Ruth signed St. Mary's Yearbook, from the Diamond Jubilee (1866-1941) of the Babe's famous reform school, he attended this occasion and signed the cover to a classmate "To My Friend Al Sincerely Babe" in ink; includes a pin saying "Saint Mary's Industrial School" with a hanging ribbon "Campaign Worker": $714.

• Autographed 1984 Olympic Games Team U.S.A. bat, featuring signatures of 21 players, including Will Clark, Cory Snyder, Barry Larkin, Billy Swift, B.J. Surhoff: $466.

• Autographed 500 Home Run Club bat, a Rawlings black Adirondack bat signed by Williams, Frank Robinson, Aaron, Killebrew, McCovey, Mathews, Mays, Schmidt, Jackson, Mantle: $1,185.

• Baltimore Orioles usher's uniform, orange blazer with celluloid usher's pin, "641," Orioles tie, pants in black with red stripe, visored cap with Orioles patch on the front: $266.

• Kansas City Athletics green windbreaker from the early 1960s, gold and white lettering with "Athletics" across the back: $147.

• 19th-century baseball belt, circa 1880s, a white cloth belt with heavy brass-colored buckle and Victorian pattern of crossed bats and elegant shield, engraved "B.B. Club": $485.

• Vida Blue 200th-win game ball, signed "Vida Blue #200": $347.

• Johnny Bench's 378th home run ball, inscribed "Home Run Ball 4-16-83 at San Francisco off Breining #378": $506.

• Autographed Dave Collins 1978 Reds St. Patrick's Day jersey, from spring training, with green logo, name and letters on off-white uniform, with green shamrock on sleeve: $308.

• Orlando Cepeda's equipment bag, used during the year he won Comeback Player of the Year Award as a Red Sox: $207.

• Frank Frisch 1971 cancelled check, made out to New England Telephone: $143.

• Roberto Clemente unlined autographed 3x5 index card: $440.

• Thurman Munson autographed photo, closeup, signed "To Ed Best Regards Thurman Munson," framed and matted: $220.

• Babe Ruth signed 1938 no-hitter scorecard, unscored,

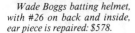

Wade Boggs batting helmet, with #26 on back and inside, ear piece is repaired: $578.

Rod Carew Twins batting helmet, uncracked, signed: $683.

Dave Winfield Padres batting helmet, broken side, signed: $414.

signed by Ruth (Brooklyn Dodgers' coach) and Johnny Vander Meer, from the first ever Ebbets Field night game, when Vander Meer pitched the first of his two consecutive no-hitters: $650.

• Sadaharu Oh autographed baseball, on a Yomiuri Giants ball: $146.

• Ralph Kiner 1952 Red Man advertising poster, shows his 1952 Red Man baseball card and a pack of Red Man tobacco: $275.

• 1948 Cleveland Indians World Series banner (33x108) says "WELCOME CLEVELAND INDIANS" and shows two Indian heads: $596.

• Seven baseball printing blocks, used in the actual printing of 1920s-1950s newspapers, show baseball scenes in metal on wood, including a catcher's mask, early equipment: $88.

• Tom Seaver Action Baseball Game, tin litho board in wood frame with Seaver facsimile signature, plus mechanical wood bat: $94.

• Babe Ruth watch from the mid-1930s, "Shock Proof...U.S.A.", has a facsimile signature, still runs: $765.

• Catfish Hunter perfect game full ticket, Minnesota at Oakland May 8, 1969: $370.

• Stan Musial's last game full ticket, dated Sept. 29, 1963, at St. Louis: $242.

• Don Larsen perfect game ticket stub, signed, famed and matted, with a photo of the final pitch and a box score: $532.

• Don Larsen perfect game program, from Game 5 of the 1956 World Series at Yankee Stadium, scored: $484.

• The Earthquake Series full tickets, uncut, unused strip of tickets for the 1989 World Series at San Francisco, games 3 (the earthquake game), 4 and 5 (unplayed; the A's swept the Giants in four): $212.

• Rube Waddell funeral program, eight-page pamphlet entitled "Rube," was handed out at his funeral in 1914: $110.

• 1927 Babe Ruth Police Gazette, March 26 issue shows Ruth swinging for a home run: $298.

• Satchel Paige "1876" autographed photograph, black-and-white, shows him in an "1876" uniform during the Bicentennial, inscribed "Best Wishes From Satchel Paige": $133.

1934 Tour of Japan baseball, signed by Babe Ruth, Lou Gehrig and Charlie Gehringer: $1,452.

1974 Oakland Athletics World Series ring/box: $3,461.

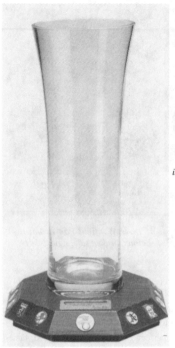

1907 Ty Cobb pocket watch, given to him after he won his first batting title, engraving mentions his feat and .352 batting average: $55,000.

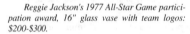

Reggie Jackson's 1977 All-Star Game participation award, 16" glass vase with team logos: $200-$300.

Steve Carlton's 1968 World Series ring, 14k Balfour, original box: $8,250.

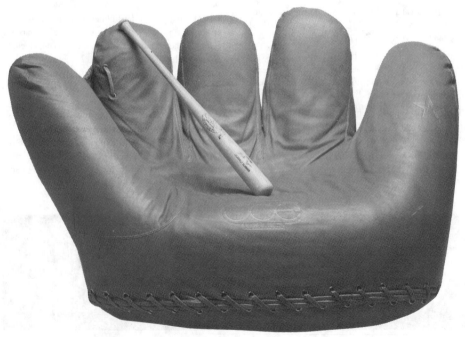

Joe DiMaggio baseball chair, 63x31x51, tan leather, laced and webbed, made in Italy during the 1970s, imprinted "Joe [Dimaggio]:" $7,000-$8,000.

Leland's Heavy Hitters/Glory Days auctions prices realized

The first New York Yankees home pinstripe worn by Babe Ruth to be put up for public auction sold for $82,500.

The jersey, worn by Ruth during the 1926 World Series against the St. Louis Cardinals, was one of the nearly 300 pieces offered by Leland's as part of the New York auction house's "Heavy Hitters" live auction Jan. 15, 1992.

But Mickey Mantle reigns. His 1960 New York Yankees home jersey brought a record price for a jersey - $111,100, topping the $71,500 paid for Mantle's 1967 road top during Leland's "Glory Days" auction in July 1991.

The 1960 Mantle jersey was a promotional piece in the window of Whitehouse and Hardy, a clothing store in New York's Rockefeller Center. The store obtained it through a contact inside the ball club, but the Yankees never asked for its return. Until the auction, the jersey remained in the store owner's family.

The Ruth jersey surprisingly sold for $82,500, considering it isn't as appealing as Mantle's. Ruth's Yankee jersey shows the name of a semi-pro team which used it after the Yankees were finished with it (a common practice in the late 1920s). The jersey also lacks a number on the back and the intertwined "NY" logo on the front, and the tail was trimmed.

The following is a list of prices realized from items sold in the Heavy Hitters auction (Jan. 2, 1992) and the Glory Days auction (July 24, 1991). All prices quoted in this article include a 10 percent buyer's premium.

Heavy Hitters results

• Roger Maris' 1960 home jersey, from the same source as Mantle's, sold for $66,000, against an estimate of $15,000-$20,000. Gil Hodges' last uniform, a 1971 New York Mets road jersey, went for $24,200 (est. $10,000-$12,000).

• 'Zoilo Versalles' 1965 American League MVP award - the first actual MVP award ever publicly offered - went for $11,000.

• Many important Joe DiMaggio pieces were offered. A bat, used in 1951, his last season, went for $22,000. A 1936 (pre-rookie) telegram, requesting DiMaggio's minor league contracts, sold for $358; a 1937 telegram stating "our last offer to DiMaggio will be withdrawn and cancelled if the player does not sign and report at training camp..." sold for $825.

• A ticket stub from the 1903 World Series, one of three examples known, exceeded the estimate with a final price of $10,450. A ticket stub from Don Larsen's perfect game, signed by Larsen, sold for $440.

• A Tom Seaver no-hitter baseball, signed and dated by the Hall of Famer, sold for $3,520. A Mint baseball, autographed by Babe Ruth to his duck hunting partner, with the original box, sold for $6,050, against a $1,000-$1,500 estimate.

• Ted Williams' last spikes from 1960 sold for $4,400.

Glory Days results

• Mickey Mantle's unrestored 1967 road jersey sold for a then-record $71,500, besting the previous high of $24,750 paid for a 1948 Stan Musial jersey. Mantle had presented his jersey to a close friend on Sept. 1, 1968, straight from his locker, along with his New York Yankees cap. During the auction, the cap sold directly after the matching shirt for $6,600. An anonymous bidder won both the cap and the jersey.

• A game bat from the "Babe Ruth of Japan," Sadaharu Oh, sold for $4,125.

• A pair of Fenway Park seats, circa 1934, in a faded shade (the catalogue says it's the "Original Monster Green Paint," sold for $2,970.

• A package of Ted Williams prophylactics sold for $165.

Sotheby's March 1991 — prices realized

The first time the prestigious Sotheby's Auction House devoted an entire sale to sports memorabilia it was a success — a record breaker.

On March 22-23, 1991, the New York auction house, founded in London in 1744, offered the entire collection, worth more than $5 million, of noted collector Jim Copeland, a California sporting goods retailer. His collection, mainly baseball cards, is one of the most impressive ever offered for sale at one time.

Nearly 900 lots, with an emphasis on baseball memorabilia, were auctioned off. Values ranged from as little as $500 a lot to several lots worth more than $100,000. The total pre-sale value of the collection was estimated at between $5 and $7 million. Total sales reached $4.6 million at the auction's conclusion.

Some staggering prices were seen, including a record $451,000 for the famous T206 Honus Wagner baseball card, a record $49,500 for a 1952 Topps Mickey Mantle card, and $82,500 for an 1886 St. Louis pendant.

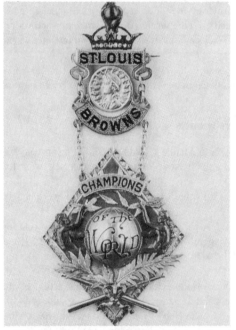

This pendant commemorates the St. Louis Browns' victory over the Chicago White Stockings in the 1886 World Series. Each Browns player received a pendant; A.J. Bushmond was given the one pictured here. But his identity is a mystery. The pendant sold for $82,500 during Sotheby's reccord-breaking auction March 22-23, 1991, in New York.

The pendant was crafted to commemorate the St. Louis Browns' victory over the Chicago White Stockings in the 1886 World Series. First baseman Charles A. Comiskey managed the Browns, representing the American Association over the White Stockings, managed by first baseman Adrian C. "Cap" Anson. The Browns were dubbed as "World Beaters" after winning this Series.

According to Sotheby's, "each player on the team was given an individual pendant and the example to be offered in the sale is inscribed on the back to the player A.J. Bushmond. It is the only such pendant which is still known to exist." Sotheby's estimated the pendant at $50,000-$75,000.

Bushmond's identity is a mystery; his name is not in any of the standard baseball encyclopedias, which list every major league player (even those who appeared in a single game) since 1876.

Another top offering was a World Series press pins collection, the finest of its type ever assembled. A complete run of more than 150 press pins, given to journalists covering World Series games from 1911 to present, was expected to generate $300,000. But the lot failed to attract a buyer.

Nearly 1,000 people attended the auction, held at Sotheby's Galleries on Manhattan's East Side. Hundreds were prepared to bid by phone, and hundreds had also mailed in bids. The following is a list of the many prices realized at the Sotheby's auction. All prices include the additional 10 percent buyer's premium. Nearly every item in the auction was in Near Mint to Mint condition:

- Honus Wagner for Sheriff pin .... $1,210.
- 1938-88 Collection of 57 phantom World Series press pins............................ $17,900.
- 1938-89 Collection of 51 All-Star Game press pins .... $30,800.
- 1912 Who's Who in Baseball, 1st edition..$990.
- 1888-1941 Spalding Guides, 54 total...$9,900.
- Cy Young Day Program Aug. 13, 1908 ....$2,200.
- 1935-88 All-Star Game tickets, 33 different.. $2,530.
- 1916 World Series ticket stub .... $2,200.
- 1919 World Series ticket stub .... $2,750.
- 1929-88 World Series ticket collection, 98 different ....$3,300.
- 1869 Cincinnati Red Stocking sheet music....................................$11,000.
- 1933 Feen-A-Mint Babe Ruth mask .... $2,750.
- 1933 Lou Gehrig Knot Hole League membership packet .... $990.
- 1930 Babe Ruth underwear.. $880.
- 1950 Babe Ruth wristwatch .... $3,025.
- Hartland Statues set, complete set of 19 ....$6,600.

Goober's Memorabilia Auction, May 2, 1992

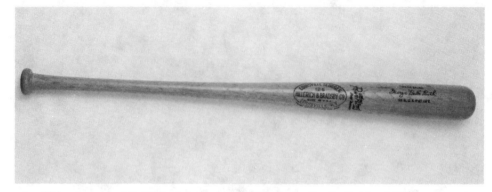

This game-used Babe Ruth bat sold for $30,000 in Goober's May 1992 auction.

How much would the ball Babe Ruth hit for his 60th home run in 1927 be worth?

Perhaps as much as $200,000, if it's the real thing. That's the winning bid placed on the alleged ball during Goober's memorabilia auction, designated as a tribute to baseball's greatest home run hitters, held May 2, 1992, in San Francisco.

But the ball, owned by George Siegel, of Ellenwood, Ga., remains surrounded in controversy.

According to a story in the May 22, 1992, issue of *Sports Collectors Digest*, Tom O'Rourke, from Alpharetta, Ga., withdrew his bid after he became aware that the National Baseball Hall of Fame in Cooperstown, N.Y., claims to have the ball Ruth hit off Washington pitcher Tom Zachery for home run #60, a then single-season record. Peter Clark, a Hall of Fame spokesman, told *Sports Collectors Digest* that he's researched the ball at the museum and is confident it's the real thing. An Oct. 1, 1927, New York Times story seems to substantiate Clark's claim. Douglas Warner gave the ball to the Hall in 1964. His father, Truly, had purchased the ball from Joe Forner, the man who said he caught the ball off Ruth's bat. Forner is referred to in the newspaper article.

But Siegel claims his father, then 14, caught the real Reach ball when he was sitting in the bleachers at Yankee Stadium, and later turned down Ruth's offer of $5, another ball, a glove and a bat for the home run ball. The ball has been autographed by Ruth, Zachery, Lou Gehrig and 10 other Yankee teammates. The #60 is also written on the ball, above Ruth's signature.

The ball also has stamped the signature of Ernest S. Barnard as president of the American League. However, he did not become president until Oct. 17, 1927, after Ban Johnson resigned for health reasons. The man who authenticated the Siegel ball for Goober's, Roger Pavey, says Barnard could have stamped the Reach baseball while he was acting as president for the ailing Johnson during the 1927 season. He also says the ball the Hall of Fame has is too beat up to be the one Ruth hit.

The Siegel ball has been returned to his possession because O'Rourke withdrew his bid and the next highest bid did not meet the reserve, which was set at $200,000. Siegel said his mother told him his father turned down an offer of $50,000 for the ball in 1961, when Ruth's record was being pursued by Mickey Mantle and Roger Maris, who wound up breaking the record by hitting 61.

Sotheby's Feb. 29, 1992, auction prices realized

Sotheby's second annual sale of baseball cards and memorabilia included a wide selection featuring autographed bats and players' uniforms - including a 1961 Roger Maris New York Yankees uniform which sold for $132,000.

The auction, held Feb. 29, 1992, in New York, generated sales of between the pre-sale estimate of $1.8 to $2.4 million for the 569-item lot. In addition to the Maris jersey, a T206 Honus Wagner baseball card brought $220,000, while a 1941 Joe DiMaggio New York Yankees uniform sold for $99,000 and a 1921-22 Ty Cobb Detroit Tigers jersey brought $82,500.

The Maris uniform was a white wool flannel pinstripe he wore during the 1961 season when he broke Babe Ruth's single season home run record by hitting 61. The uniform included his size 41 Spalding #9 jersey, with #61 stitched into the fabric, his matching pants with labels, cap, socks and cleats.

The DiMaggio uniform was a grey wool flannel jersey with its Wilson label in the collar and "DiMaggio" stitched into it. It features a black arm band sewn onto the left sleeve in memory of teammate Lou Gehrig, but the number on the back side was removed. Matching pants with labels were included.

The Ty Cobb game-used jersey was a Tigers home navy pinstripe shirt by Spalding. It shows wear and looks somewhat soiled. "Cobb" is stitched in the tail.

A Ted Williams uniform.

A Roger Maris uniform.

Other results from the auction, including a 10 percent buyer's premium, included:

• Joe DiMaggio game-worn spikes: From 1941; acquired by a friend of DiMaggio, saved by the friend's daughter; to keep the toes from collapsing, newspapers from 1941 were stuffed inside ....$7,150.

• Robin Yount game jersey, helmet, shoes and bat: 1985 Milwaukee Brewers #19 Medalist home shirt; ABC helmet;

Adidas shoes; Louisville Slugger bat, cracked and repaired .... $4,175.

• Ty Cobb sweater: Heavy Detroit Tigers grey black warm-up by Bradley; includes a June 1924 Baseball Magazine advertisement showing Cobb wearing one of these sweaters; has tobacco stains down the front .... $13,200.

• Ty Cobb mausoleum check: for $6,289, made out by a terminally ill Cobb on Feb.

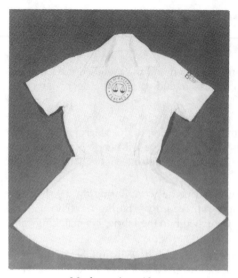

Madonna's uniform.

Roberto Clemente memorabilia.

15, 1961, to Coggins Granite Industries Inc., for payment of the family mausoleum; five months later he died and now rests in the structure ....$1,320.

• Carl Yastrzemski contract: Player's contract for the Boston Red Sox for 1977; signed twice by Yastrzemski and once by Lee MacPhail ....$770.

• Lou Brock game-worn jersey: 1977 St. Louis Cardinals #20 road shirt; Rawlings; name on back; 1976 National League commemorative patch........................... $1,980.

• Cal Ripken Jr. game-worn jersey: 1986 Baltimore Orioles road; #22; Rawlings; name on back $2,200.

• Don Drysdale jersey: 1958 Los Angeles Dodgers flannel; Wilson; with tags, autographed.....................................$3,300.

• Madonna baseball uniform: Pink jumper worn by singer Madonna in the baseball movie "League of Their Own;" Rockford Peaches emblem; GPBL patch; #5 .... $7,150.

• Group of All-Star press pins: 14 total (1954, 1955, 1956, 1957, 1959, 1964, 1966, 1968, 1969, 1970, 1971, 1972, 1973, 1974); Near Mint condition ....$1,760.

• Cap Anson hand-written letter: two pages from early August 1912 in response to an autograph request from a friend in his home town of Marshalltown, Iowa; personal letterhead has "A Better Actor than any Ball Player, A Better Ball Player than any Actor" and shows Anson in a tuxedo on each page; signed manuscript . $11,000.

• Billy Martin Topps Baseball Card contract and check: 1960, signed by Martin, granting Topps permission to produce his cards for two more seasons; $75 check; some staple holes .... $550.

• Roberto Clemente autographed Exhibit card and memorial patch: 1963 black-and-white Exhibit card, autographed "Best Wishes Roberto Clemente"; patch worn by the Pirates in 1973, honoring the Hall of Famer after his death, removed from a jersey .... $990.

• A piece of Joe DiMaggio's wedding cake: Nov. 19, 1939; DiMaggio weds actress Dorothy Arnold in San Francisco; guests were given cake wrapped in cellophane to take home; two bisque columns and a rose; includes wedding and reception invitations and a picture of the newlyweds cutting the cake .... $1,210.

Miscellaneous

The following is a potpourri of collectibles. Some items are priced from ads or auction results published in *Sports Collectors Digest*; others are unpriced and contain just general information.

Hall of Fame items

• Since 1936, the National Baseball Hall of Fame and Museum, in Cooperstown, N.Y., has offered several plaque postcards honoring those enshrined.

The companies producing the postcards have been the Albertype Co., of Brooklyn, N.Y., (1936-52, black-and-white); Artvue Post Card Co., of New York, (1953-63, black-and-white); and since 1964, in brown-and-yellow, by Curteichcolor - 3D Natural Color Reproduction and "Mike Roberts Color Productions" of Oakland, Calif. These are generally collected to be autographed, and generally cost about $25, depending on who's pictured. A complete Artvue set of 50, unsigned, is worth about $500.

• Twenty players enshrined in Cooperstown have also been depicted on 6 3/4-inch statuettes, produced by Sports Hall of Fame, Long Island, N.Y., in 1963. The statuettes were issued in two 10-player series, with the second series statues being more scarce. Jimmie Foxx is considered the scarcest, and usually brings the highest price.

The other players are Ty Cobb, Mickey Cochrane, Joe Cronin ($500), Bill Dickey ($95), Joe DiMaggio (slightly yellow, EX, no box, $35), Bob Feller ($95), Lou Gehrig ($150-$200), Hank Greenberg, Rogers Hornsby ($60), Walter Johnson ($95), Christy Mathewson ($50), John McGraw (EX+, no box, $300), Jackie Robinson (Nr. Mt., no box, $160), Babe Ruth (bent, otherwise Mint in box, $45), George Sisler ($200), Tris Speaker ($200), Pie Traynor ($50), Honus Wagner ($60) and Paul Waner (Mint, rewrapped box, $300). The given prices are advertised or auction prices realized; the statues are in Mint condition with box, unless noted.

Bats

• A Famous Slugger plastic bat rack and miniature player bats; circa late 1950s, offered by Famous Slugger Yearbooks $75
• Hillerich & Bradsby Honus Wagner mini bat, circa 1921.. $95
• Hillerich & Bradsby Cy Young mini bat, circa 1921... $95
• Babe Ruth mini black bat, circa 1965 .... $30

• Jimmie Foxx mini black bat, circa 1965 ...$30
• Mini Louisville Slugger bat, autographed by American League President Bobby Brown..$75

Baseballs

• Baseball signed by 11 living members of the 500 Home Run Club (Mickey Mantle, Ted Williams, Willie Mays, Hank Aaron, Frank Robinson, Mike Schmidt, Willie McCovey, Reggie Jackson, Harmon Killebrew, Ernie Banks, Eddie Mathews) $440
• Baseball signed by eight members of the 300 Wins Club (Nolan Ryan, Tom Seaver, Steve Carlton, Warren Spahn, Don Sutton, Early Wynn, Gaylord Perry, Phil Niekro)............$198
• Baseball signed by four players with 100 or more stolen bases in a season (Maury Wills, Rickey Henderson, Lou Brock, Vince Coleman) $97.75
• Baseball signed by nine pitchers with 3,000 or more strikeouts (Nolan Ryan, Steve Carlton, Tom Seaver, Bert Blyleven, Don Sutton, Gaylord Perry, Phil Niekro, Fergie Jenkins, Bob Gibson)...$310
• Baseball signed by the "Magnificent Seven" outfielders (Joe DiMaggio, Mickey Mantle, Ted Williams, Hank Aaron, Willie Mays, Duke Snider, Frank Robinson).....................$4,312.50
• A Ted Williams, Whitey Ford, Eddie Mathews wiffle ball from the late 1950s, showing Williams and Ford on one side of the cardboard plastic pouch, and Williams/Mathews on the back $80

Advertising/promotional

• Jim Beam 100th Anniversary of Baseball decanter $60
• Ezra Brooks old-time baseball player decanter $60
• 1958 Philadelphia Phillies Cigar Counter Box, top stands in box to display a large picture of a Phillies player sliding in safely at home, attached 3D baseball says "Major League Baseball TV-Radio" $100
• Ted Williams Blue Diamond matchbook, with a small crease $35
• 1940s Joe DiMaggio bat-shaped pencil from his San Francisco restaurant.......................$200
• 1956 Toots Shore menu, pictures Ty Cobb, Tris Speaker, Charlie Gehringer, more.........$85

• Mickey Mantle Holiday Inn matchbook ... $85
• Tom Seaver matchbook, issued in 1988 upon the retiring of his uniform #41 ....$40
• 1950s Joe DiMaggio Fisherman's Wharf Restaurant matchbook..$50
• 1982 Slurpee cups 8 1/2x11 advertising broadside picturing all 20 stars in the set, including Pete Rose, Mike Schmidt, Nolan Ryan, George Brett...$7.50
• 1961 Duke Snider cardboard advertising display for Cooper tires, 17x20, with easel back, Near Mint...$395
• A framed, 51x14 red Louisville Slugger advertising poster proclaiming "Ask for the Bats They Use!" with photos of Lou Gehrig, Joe DiMaggio, Joe Cronin and others, circa 1939 ....$3,850
• 1954 Ballantine Beer advertising sign featuring a color team photo of the New York Yankees, 17x15 ....$225
• 1950 Ted Williams 10x13 Haveline Motor Oil color ad, with Williams in full uniform swinging a bat...$40
• 1984 Reggie Jackson Pony 18x24 poster of his 500th home run $15

Baseball card cartoons

• These original drawings for the reverse side of Topps baseball cards were purchased at the historic 1989 Topps auction. Each is stamped on the reverse with an official Topps stamp to indicate the source. These are advertised selling prices; * means the card is included with the artwork.

1962 Topps - #346 Jack Kralick, Minnesota Twins * ($50); #391 Bill Mazeroski, Pittsburgh Pirates ($95); #448 Joe Gibbon, Pittsburgh Pirates ($50) #451 Jose Tartabull, Kansas City A's ($50); #479 Joel Horlen, Chicago White Sox ($50).

1969 Topps - #110 Mike Shannon, St. Louis Cardinals ($35); #117 Jim Fairey, Montreal Expos * ($25); #160 Vada Pinson, St. Louis Cardinals ($50); #204 Jack Hiatt, San Francisco Giants ($25); #276 Gary Wagner, Philadelphia Phillies * ($30); #279 Roger Nelson, Kansas City Royals ($25); #293 Dick Dietz, San Francisco Giants ($25); #571 Cap Peterson, Cleveland Indians ($25).

1970 Topps - #311 Dick Green, Oakland A's * ($25); #318 Willie Smith, Chicago Cubs *

($25); #321 Lou Piniella, Kansas City Royals * ($40); #331 Charles Dobson, Oakland A's * ($25); #338 Paul Schaal, Kansas City Royals * ($25); #510 Tony Oliva, Minnesota Twins * ($50); #531 Ron Clark, Oakland A's * ($25); #594 Jake Gibbs, New York Yankees * ($30); #597 Sonny Siebert, Boston Red Sox * ($30); #627 Gary Wagner, Boston Red Sox * ($30).

1973 Topps - #274 Darold Knowles, Oakland A's * ($25); #284 Glenn Borgmann, Minnesota Twins * ($25); #286 Frank Linzy, Milwaukee Brewers * ($25); #358 Jim Nettles, Minnesota Twins * ($25); #366 Brock Davis, Milwaukee Brewers * ($25); #371 Mike Kekich, New York Yankees * ($30); #382 Mike Hegan, Oakland A's * ($25); #385 Jim Perry, Minnesota Twins * ($40).

1974 Topps - #415 Gary Gentry, Atlanta Braves ($25); #569 Rick Dempsey, New York Yankees ($30); #613 Dan Monzon, Minnesota Twins ($25).

1980 Topps - #109 Bill Travers, Milwaukee Brewers ($25); #239 Don Aase, California Angels * ($25); #246 Tim Foli, Pittsburgh Pirates * ($25); #367 Billy Smith, Baltimore Orioles * ($25); #383 Ed Ott, Pittsburgh Pirates * ($25); #388 Mike Paxton, Cleveland Indians ($25); #427 Tommy Hutton, Montreal Expos * ($25); #624 Lerrin LaGrow, Los Angeles Dodgers * ($25).

1982 Topps - the artwork in 1982 is not related to the player on the front of the card. The subject matter of the artwork is listed, not the player on the front of the card: Glenn Adams, Minnesota Twins * ($20); Glenn Adams, Minnesota Twins * ($20); Jim Bibby, Cleveland Indians ($20); Brian Doyle, New York Yankees ($20); Tommy Hutton, Montreal Expos ($25); Don Money, Milwaukee Brewers ($20); Ben Oglivie, Milwaukee Brewers ($25); Willie Randolph, New York Yankees * ($25); Mike Schmidt/Greg Luzinski ($150); Willie Stargell, Pittsburgh Pirates ($75); Garry Templeton, St. Louis Cardinals ($20).

Movie memorabilia

• A variety of means are used to advertise newly-released movies including posters, lobby cards, inserts, half-sheets, press kits, video posters and stand-ups. Original full-size movie posters generally measure 27x41 and have a five-digit National Screen Service code printed at the bottom; the first two numbers indicate the year the film was released. "Advance" posters are also sometimes made to promote coming attractions; because they are printed in smaller quantities, these posters are generally more valuable than regular posters. Most older movie posters will be folded into eighths; they were folded so they could be mailed easier.

Lobby cards generally are 11x14 and contain eight separate photos. Inserts are 14x36, and oftentimes have the same design as their larger movie poster counterparts. Half-sheets generally look the same as a full-size poster, but are 22x28. Video posters are used by stores to publicize the release of a movie on home video; generally they have the movie company's video logo on them. Stand-ups are cardboard fold-outs, usually found in a theater lobby. Press kits contain production information, cast lists, black-and-white photos and data used by movie reviewers. The price of a kit is usually determined by the number of photos it includes.

When looking for originals, look for the NSS code, and look for those without pin holes or fading or creases, which lessen the value. Posters can be found at movie memorabilia shops and sports card shops, too. Mail order businesses are also a source, as are video stores and movie theaters themselves.

For new movies, full-size poster prices begin at around $10-$15. Bull Durham posters featuring Kevin Costner by himself are around $35, while those with Costner and Susan Sarandon are about $25. Other movies posters from the 1980s which range from $20-$30 include Field of Dreams (1989), Eight Men Out (1988) and The Natural (1984). 1970s movie posters in the $35-$50 range include The Bad News Bears (1976), Bad News Bears in Breaking Training (1977), The Bad News Bears Go To Japan (1978), Bang the Drum Slowly (1973) and Bingo Long Traveling All-Stars and Motor Kings (1976).

1940s-1950s examples include: The Stratton Story (1949) poster $325, inserts/half sheets $250; The Jackie Robinson Story (1950) poster $350, lobby card $250; The Pride Of St. Louis (1952) poster $225-$400, lobby card $50; Fear Strikes Out (1957) poster $250; The Babe Ruth Story (1948) poster $425; The Winning Team (1952) poster $325; Pride of the Yankees (1942) poster $3,000; It Happens Every Spring (1949) poster $325; Take Me Out To The Ballgame (1949) poster $330-$525, inserts/half-sheets $425; Damn Yankees (1958) poster $285, lobby cards $65; Angels in the Outfield (1951) poster $275; Safe at Home! poster $300-$450.

Wire photos

• 8x10 non-glossy wire photo of Nolan Ryan delivering the pitch that made Rickey Henderson his 5,000th K.....................................$15.75

• 6 1/2x8 1/2 Chicago Cubs celebrate victory over Detroit in Game 1 in the 1945 World Series (Andy Pafko, Phil Cavaretta, Hank Borowy, Bill Nicholson) $20

• 7x9 Joe DiMaggio slides home on a double steal in 1948 ....$25

• 7x9 Jackie Jensen (Yankees) slides home avoiding Roy Campanella's tag in a 1951 World Series game $20

The reproduction featuring a George Loh drawing of Jerry Koosman is from an ad of The Equitable Life Assurance Society of the United States.

Equitable Life Sports prints

• The 1960s Equitable Life Assurance Sports Hall of Fame Portraits print set of at least 95 athletes includes 21 different baseball players. Since there were two artists, Robert Riger (1964-67) and George Loh (1961-69), who created the black-and-white prints, it is believed that at least two series were released. The prints were advertised in magazines. Equitable Life offered a 26-print set through the mail, and included a 4x7, 32-page booklet featuring all the subjects and short bios. The set, recently priced at $100, includes Babe Ruth, Carl Hubbell, Lefty Grove, Bob Feller and Allie Reynolds. Later players featured were: Ernie Banks, Roy Campanella, Johnny Evers, Lou Gehrig, Tommy Henrich, Al Kaline, Jerry Koosman, Mickey Mantle, Eddie Mathews, Willie Mays, Stan Musial, Pee Wee Reese, Robin Roberts, Brooks Robinson, Red Ruffing and Warren Spahn.

Books

• Jackie Robinson autographed comic book, famous plays of Jackie Robinson, Baseball Hero #6, copyright 1952, back cover has full-length autographed photo of Robinson.................$300

• Sandy Koufax University of Cincinnati yearbook, autographed $475

• Babe Ruth Quaker Oats "How To" premium booklets, 1935, complete set of four $225

Toys

• Babe Ruth Aurora model, unassembled, with box $375

• Roger Maris Bat-A-Round, with box, which shows Maris, Willie Mays and Jimmy Piersall using the device, includes an 8x10 photo of Maris with a facsimile autograph $150

• Yogi Berra inflatable catcher/pitch kit, in original box picturing Yogi, with 36" inflatable Yogi $250

• 1978 Johnny Bench Batting Trainer in original box, which pictures Bench, never opened.... $75

• Mickey Mantle's 1950s isometric exercise machine $150

• Mickey Mantle-Willie Mays wiffle bat, ball and helmet (1963), original cardboard pictures both $185

• Mickey Mantle "On-Deck Cards" batting trainer, a plastic bat to be filled with sand, cardboard pictures Mantle and his son (1962) .. $175

• 1969 Globe Import playing cards, 1 5/8x2 1/4, with black-and-white photos and blank backs. Hearts - A Willie Mays, 2 Chris Short, 3 Tony Conigliaro, 4 Bill Freehan, 5 Willie McCovey, 6 Joel Horlen, 7 Ernie Banks, 8 Jim Wynn, 9 Brooks Robinson, 10 Orlando Cepeda, J Al Kaline, Q Gene Alley, K Rusty Staub.

Clubs - A Richie Allen, 2 Reggie Smith, 3 Jerry Koosman, 4 Tony Oliva, 5 Bud Harrelson, 6 Rick Reichardt, 7 Billy Williams, 8 Pete Rose, 9 Jim Maloney, 10 Tim McCarver, J Max Alvis, Q Ron Swoboda, K Johnny Callison.

Diamonds - A Bob Gibson, 2 Paul Casanova, 3 Juan Marichal, 4 Jim Fregosi, 5 Earl Wilson, 6 Tony Horton, 7 Harmon Killebrew, 8 Tom Seaver, 9 Curt Flood, 10 Frank Robinson, J Bob Aspromonte, Q Lou Brock, K Jim Lonborg.

Spades - A Ken Harrelson, 2 Denny McLain, 3 Rick Monday, 4 Richie Allen, 5 Mel Stottlemyre, 6 Tommy John, 7 Don Mincher, 8 Chico Cardenas, 9 Willie Davis, 10 Campy Campaneris, J Ron Santo, Q Al Ferrara, K Clete Boyer.

Viewmaster's 1953 Baseball Stars

• Bright, sharp Kodachrome images of Baseball Hall of Famers spring to life in this 21-player set of three reels issued by Viewmaster in 1953. All of the photos were shot in spring training in Florida, which accounts for the lack of some teams being represented in the set. Each reel, featuring seven players, was in its own blue-and-cream colored envelope and included a 3 1/2x13 8-page fold-out brochure giving biographical details, stats and a facsimile autograph of the seven players. A yellow-and-green envelope was made to hold all three reels, too. Reel 725 players are: Al Rosen, Phil Rizzuto, Jackie Jensen, Preacher Roe, Whitey Lockman, Minnie Minoso and Yogi Berra. Reel 726 players are Johnny Mize, Bob Lemon, Al Schoendienst, Ferris Fain, Monte Irvin, Bob Shantz and Sid Gordon. Reel 727 players are Bob Thomson, Grady Hatton, Vic Wertz, Mel Parnell, Gene Woodling, Sal Maglie and Roy Campanella.

Music

• More than 500 records in the form of baseabll recording have been made. The first actual baseball record - "Casey at the Bat" - was released in 1907 as performed by T. Wolfe Hopper, a prominent actor of that era. This piece is one of the most prolific pieces of baseball literature, as is "Take Me Out to the Ballgame," whose lyrics are sung the third most frequently in the United States (behind "Happy Birthday" and the National Anthem). The song has been done by more than 30 different artists since it was first released in 1910. Historical broadcasts and significant events such as Carlton Fisk's dramatic home run in the 1975 World Series have also been captured on record. The best place to find records are at garage sales, flea markets and used record stores and thrift shops.

Some of the players who have been featured on records include Joe DiMaggio (Little Johnny Strikeout); Jackie Robinson and Pee Wee Reese (Slugger at the Bat); Babe Ruth (Babe Ruth, Babe Ruth, We Love You); Mickey Mantle (I Love Mickey, sung by Theresa Brewer); Willie Mays (Say Hey, Willie Mays); Mays, Mantle and Duke Snider (Willie, Mickey and the Duke); Tony Oliva (My Favorite Music); and Waite Hoyt (The Best of Waite Hoyt In The Rain).

• Stan the Man Musial's Hit Record, by Phillips 66, includes booklet with Musial demonstrating hitting techniques $60
• St. Louis Cardinals World Champions 1964, highlights narrated by Harry Caray, Jack Buck $45
• "Yes We Can," highlights of the California Angels' first 19 years, from 1961-79 .... $50
• "Move Over Babe, Here Comes Henry Aaron" 45 rpm record $15
• "Hank Aaron, A Night To Remember" 45 rpm record $15
• "Tony Conigliaro, Limited Man" 45 rpm record $20
• "1969 Mickey Mantle, A Day To Remember" 45 rpm record $40
• 1966 "Sandy Koufax Talks With Vin Scully" Union 76 record in original sleeve $50
• "That Holler Guy" by Joe Garagiola, 45 rpm with original sleeve, pictures Stan Musial, Joe Garagiola, Ken Boyer, Yogi Berra $40
• "Ralph Kiner Talks to the Amazin' Mets" - Gil Hodges, Tom Seaver, Tommie Agee, etc. 7" 33 1/3 rpm record $75
• 1980 45 rpm record in jacket, Teamwork plus "Ernie's Song" by Ernie Banks, pictured on cover $7.95
• 1971 Frank Robinson Mattel mini record . $15
• 1971 Willie Stargell Mattel mini record.... $15
• Joe DiMaggio album "Little Johnny Strike-out" $175
• Mickey Mantle album, his favorite hits... $150
• Carl Yastrzemski album $25
• Ernie Banks album $30

• Ted Williams 78 rpm photo record (1946), includes original envelope, 8 1/2x8 1/2, glossy color photo on one side, other side shows Williams and ballpark $225
• 1962 record, "Baseball Tips from the Stars," by Willie Mays, #1, How to Bat $25
• 1962 record, "Baseball Tips from the Stars," by Willie Mays, #3, How to Field................ $25
• 1964 Auravision: 33 1/3 rpm sports records, set of 16: Rocky Colavito, Bill Mazeroski, Warren Spahn, Jim Gentile, Mickey Mantle, Ken Boyer, Willie Mays, Roger Maris, Whitey Ford, Sandy Koufax, Don Drysdale, Ernie Banks, Al Kaline, Bob Allison, Frank Robinson, Pete Ward, each with 1963 stats, plus story of player's career. A set of 15, without Mays, sells for about $500. There were 50,000 copies made of each player, with an estimated 1,000 complete sets in existence, due to a fire which destroyed the bulk of them.
• "Oh! You Babe Ruth" sheet music....... $1,141
• Safe at Home sheet music $60

Baseball videos

• Several teams have put out season-highlights tapes over the years, and several players have done instructional tapes, too, such as Steve Garvey, Charlie Lau and Maury Wills. A Greatest Sports Legends series features among others Hank Aaron, Roberto Clemente, Lou Gehrig, Stan Musial and Ted Williams. World Series moments and the lighter side of baseball have also been captured on video.

Among the top baseball-related videos, as selected by David Craft, *Sports Collectors Digest*'s Tale of the Tape columnist:

1) An Amazin' Era - The New York Mets 1962-1986; 2) The Boys of Summer; 3) The Chicago White Sox: A Visual History; 4) Detroit Tigers: The Movie; 5) Forever Fenway: 75 Years of Red Sox Baseball; 6) The Glory of Their Times; 7) The History of the Game; 8) New York Yankees: The Movie; 9) St. Louis Cardinals: The Movie; 10) Chicago and the Cubs: A Lifelong Love Affair; 11) Pinstripe Power: The Story of the 1961 New York Yankees; 12) Reds: The Official History of the Cincinnati Reds; 13) Centennial: 100 Years of Phillies Baseball.

Among the most memorable baseball movies, as selected by Craft: 1) Pride of St. Louis; 2)

Pride of the Yankees; 3) A Love Affair: The Eleanor and Lou Gehrig Story; 4) The Babe Ruth Story; 5) The Jackie Robinson Story; 6) The Bingo Long Traveling All-Stars And Motor Kings; 7) Don't Look Back: The Story Of Leroy "Satchel" Paige; 8) One In A Million: The Ron LeFlore Story; 9) Fear Strikes Out; 10) The Stratton Story; 11) Damn Yankees; 12) Take Me Out To The Ball Game; 13) Angels In The Outfield; 14) Elmer the Great; 15) Bang The Drum Slowly; 16) The Natural; 17) Bull Durham and 18) Eight Men Out.

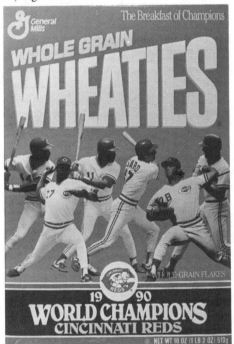

Food/drink

- Ted's Root Beer bottle cap $5
- 1982 Johnny Bench Cheerios box $10
- 1983 Fernando Valenzuela Corn Flakes box $50
- 1987 Minnesota Twins Wheaties box........ $35
- 1990 Cincinnati Reds Wheaties box $30
- 1991 Johnny Bench Wheaties box $25
- 1991 Rod Carew Wheaties box $80
- 1991 Joe Morgan Wheaties box $25
- 1991 Jim Palmer Wheaties box $25
- 1991 Minnesota Twins Wheaties box........ $30
- 1991 Minnesota Twins Frosted Flakes box $20

- 1992 Lou Gehrig 60 Years of Sports Heritage (Wheaties)... $5
- 1992 Willie Mays 60 Years of Sports Heritage (Wheaties)... $5
- 1992 Babe Ruth 60 Years of Sports Heritage (Wheaties)... $5
- 1993 Nolan Ryan Corn Flakes box $20
- 1993 Reggie Jackson Mini-Wheats box.... $20
- 1993 Ken Griffey Jr. Frosted Flakes box .. $20
- 1993 Nolan Ryan Corn Flakes box $20

Other Wheaties boxes have pictured on the cover: Hank Aaron ($75), Sparky Anderson ($15), Johnny Bench ($15), Yogi Berra ($75), Lou Boudreau ($50), Roy Campanella ($75), Ron Cey ($25), Joe DiMaggio ($100), Bob Feller ($75), Jimmie Foxx ($100), Lou Gehrig ($150), Hank Greenberg ($100), Lefty Grove ($85), Carl Hubbell ($65), Ralph Kiner ($60), Ernie Lombardi ($75), Willie Mays ($80), Stan Musial ($85), Hal Newhouser ($75), Mel Ott ($100), Pee Wee Reese ($60), Phil Rizzuto ($60), Brooks Robinson ($50), Jackie Robinson ($125), Pete Rose ($20), Al Rosen ($50), Babe Ruth ($150), Eddie Stanky ($60) and Ted Williams ($100).

- Yoo Hoo chocolate can, 6", featuring 1961 New York Yankees caps of Mantle, Berra, Ford, Richardson, Skowron $100
- Reggie candy bar wrapper from 1978 .... $25
- Ted Williams Root Beer wooden crate, refinished $145

Beer cans

- More than 50 commemorative baseball-related beer cans have been produced featuring major league players, minor league teams and six major league teams (Pirates, Twins, Cubs,

White Sox, Reds and Orioles). Many have team/player photos, drawings, schedules or stats incorporated into the design and were sold for a limited time in a limited area. Beer can trade shows are the best places to find older cans not sold in stores any longer. Most collectors prefer cans which have been opened from the bottom.

Anheuser-Busch, St. Louis, Mo., issued a Red Schoendienst commemorative bank can in 1977, honoring the dedication of Schoendienst Field, Feb. 20, 1977, in Germantown, Ill.

C. Schmidt & Sons Inc., Philadelphia, Pa. issued four Casey's Lager Beer cans in 1980 featuring Duke Snider, Richie Ashburn, Whitey Ford and Monte Irvin.

National Brewing Co., Baltimore, Md., issued a National Bohemian Beer can with a 1970 Baltimore Orioles schedule and a can in 1992 commemorating Baltimore's Memorial Stadium from 1954-91. Adolph Coors Co., Golden, Colo., issued a can in 1992 commemorating the Baltimore Orioles' 1991 season.

G. Heileman Brewing Co., La Crosse, Wis., has done several cans. Old Style 16 oz. brands in 1990 featured Comiskey Park, Ron Santo, Billy Williams, Fergie Jenkins and the 1990 Divisional Championship. A 1991 Old Style Light can featured Billy Williams, while 1992 Special Export 16-oz. green cans honor the 1961-91 Minnesota Twins and 1992 Special Export Light 16-oz. blue cans honor the 1961-91 Minnesota Twins.

Hudepohl Brewing Co., Cincinnati, Ohio, issued cans in 1976 and 1977 commemorating the 1975 and 1976 World Champion Cincinnati Reds. There are two varieties in 1976 - with either a cream or grey box score background.

Pittsburgh Brewing Co., Pittsburgh, Pa., issued Iron City Beer & Draft cans, focusing on the Pittsburgh Pirates. The 1973 cans featured Three Rivers Stadium. Ten 1974 cans featured the Pirates' team record from 1887-1973; participation in the World Series; 1974 home schedule; 1974 TV schedule; 1974 roster of pitchers, catchers; 1974 roster of infielders, outfielders; 1960 World Series; 1971 World Series; World Championships from 1950-73; and a letter from the brewery's president. Two 1980 cans featured the 1979 World Champions and a salute to the 1979 champs. A 1988 can featured "Hardball 88," while a 1990 can honored the Pittsburgh

Tradition. Two 1991 cans were issued featuring the Eastern Division Championship and ticket stubs.

Team souvenirs, items

• 1950s Chicago White Sox popcorn/megaphone......................$35
• 1987 plastic cup from Yankee Stadium, features Willie Randolph $5
• 1987 plastic cup from Yankee Stadium, features Dave Righetti $5
• 1989 Oakland A's ticket brochure..............$2
• 1967 Boston Red Sox hospitality room pass $25
• 1904 Baltimore Orioles 2 1/2x7 1/2 policeman's ribbon, red, white and blue ribbon with black and gold overlapping ribbon, worn by patrolman at the ballpark, says "Baltimore Base Ball Club 1904 Police" $400
• New York Yankees beach towel autographed by Joe DiMaggio......................$200
• 1911 Philadelphia Athletics china plate, elephant with player's face in the body and Connie Mack sitting on top of the elephant, 10" diameter $1,100
• 1930s Pittsburgh Pirates figural ashtray, features bowl with a 7" Pirate wielding a knife atop of the baseball which says "Pittsburgh Pirates" $250
• 1965 World Series "Go-Go Twins" souvenir styrofoam hat, convention-style with a red-white-blue streamer depicting two Twins cartoon figures on the front and four different baseball scenes winding around the side............$50
• 1980s Fenway Park picture glass from Citgo $20
• 1966 St. Louis Cardinals team coin set.....$20
• 1980s California Angels uniform sleeve patch $8
• 1968 St. Louis Cardinals World Champs matchbook....................$12

Pennants

• Pre-1920 Detroit Tigers, Detroit stitched into blue and orange pennant $200
• 1930s New York Yankees, right-handed batter ready to swing............................$200
• 1940s Boston Braves, black and white $85
• 1940s Boston Red Sox, red socks on white $60
• 1940s Cincinnati Reds, player sliding.....$100

- 1940s Cleveland Indians, blue and white..$65
- 1940s Detroit Tigers, tiger leaping at you.$95
- 1940s Detroit Tigers, orange and black...$125
- 1940s Philadelphia Athletics, elephant with players' names, numbers............................$160
- 1940s Phillies logo features "Quaker" carrying large bat with "Philadelphia" on barrel......$140
- 1940s St. Louis Cardinals..........................$95
- 1950 Philadelphia Phillies N.L. Champs, red and white $95
- Early 1950s Fightin' Phillies, players and uniform numbers scattered throughout the pennant $50
- 1950s Baltimore Orioles, bird on baseball $100
- 1950s Boston Red Sox, lefty batter swinging atop stadium, red $50
- 1950s Chicago Cubs, has two cubs playing on small plot of grass, blue...............................$65
- 1950s Chicago Cubs, multi-colored bear cubs $40
- 1950s Cincinnati Redlegs, batting swinging inside letter C, black....................................$25
- 1950s Cleveland Indians, multi-colored Chief Wahoo head $65
- 1950s Cleveland Indians, Chief Wahoo, red $35
- 1950s Detroit Tigers, multi-colored with a Tiger stepping out of Briggs Stadium $65
- 1950s Detroit Tigers, Tiger over Briggs Stadium...$95
- 1950s Milwaukee Braves mid-size, Indian with single feather $55
- 1950s Milwaukee Braves, Chief head, blue $65
- 1950s Milwaukee Braves, Indian head, dark blue..$100
- 1950s Milwaukee Braves, Brave batting atop stadium, blue $60
- 1950s New York Giants, orange on black$125
- 1950s New York Yankees, red-white-blue "American League Champions"...................$45

- 1950s New York Yankees $150
- 1950s New York Yankees, Uncle Sam batting atop Yankee Stadium $35
- 1950s Philadelphia A's, elephant holding ball $125
- 1950s Philadelphia Phillies, National League Champions $145
- 1950s Pittsburgh Pirates, Pirate with knife in mouth $100
- 1950s St. Louis Cardinals, bird on bat $85
- 1951 All-Star Game pennant with player names such as DiMaggio, Williams, Robinson, Campanella, Snider, etc. $275
- 1955 Brooklyn Dodgers National League Champions $525
- 1960s Baltimore Orioles, bird on ball/crossed bats, black $65
- 1960s Minnesota Twins 5" felt pennant....$35
- 1960s Cincinnati Reds, Mr. Redlegs over Crosley $75
- 1961 Cincinnati Reds mid-size, features Mr. Red mascot and "National League Champions" $65
- 1964 Baltimore Orioles, picture pennant with button $125
- 1965 Minnesota Twins 12" felt pennant, American League Champs, red...................$12
- 1968 Baltimore Orioles American League Champs $125
- 1969-71 Washington Senators, red and white $75
- 1970s Cleveland Indians, Wahoo on stadium $35
- 1972 Oakland A's World Champions, white $35
- 1973 Oakland A's World Champions, yellow $25
- 1979 Pittsburgh Pirates World Champs, yellow...$5
- 1983 Philadelphia Phillies N.L. Champs $5

Tickets/skeds

- 1981 Cincinnati Reds used ticket from Tom Seaver's 3,000th strikeout game $75
- Nolan Ryan 300th win full ticket, autographed $150
- Nolan Ryan 6th no-hitter full ticket, 06/11/90 ....$125
- Nolan Ryan 6th no hitter full ticket, autographed, plus photo from the game, framed and matted...$225

Miscellaneous

- 1975 NLCS ticket stub from Game 1, signed by Pete Rose $60
- Pete Rose record-breaking 4,192nd hit, full ticket, 09/11/85, autographed $275
- Chicago Cubs first night game ticket stub, 08/08/88 .... $75
- George Brett 3,000th hit full ticket, autographed $150
- Robin Yount 3,000th hit full ticket, autographed $125
- Colorado Rockies Opening Day full tickets, 04/09/93 .... $50
- Ticket from Ryan's last game, 09/22/93, at Seattle, autographed $60
- Nolan Ryan's 4th no-hitter ticket stub, 06/01/75 .... $225
- Nolan Ryan's 5th no-hitter, 09/26/81, unused ticket $225
- Nolan Ryan's 5th no-hitter, 09/26/81, ticket stub $100
- Steve Carlton 300th win, 09/23/83 ticket stub $40
- Lou Brock plays his last game, 09/30/79 ticket stub $30
- Dave Winfield 3,000th hit, 09/16/93, unused ticket $20
- Rickey Henderson ties Ty Cobb's stolen base mark, 05/26/90, large stub $35
- Rod Carew 3,000th hit, 08/04/85, unused ticket $75
- 1926 "Everything at a Glance" pocket schedule, calendar, shows Ty Cobb $85
- 1941 Boston Red Sox Fenway Park matchbook schedule $20
- 1954 Pittsburgh Pirates matchbook schedule $15
- 1963 Minnesota Twins metal ruler schedule $24
- 1969 Oakland A's matchbook schedule $10
- 1970 Seattle Pilots schedule, team issued . $25
- 1983 Chicago White Sox pennant, AL West Champs, team photo $8
- 1988 Minnesota Twins poster schedule 1987 World Series Celebration $7

Programs

- Nolan Ryan 300th win program, autographed $75
- Robin Yount 3,000th hit program $22
- George Brett 3,000th hit program $22
- Johnny Bench Night program, Sept. 19, 1983 .... $20
- Pete Rose 4,000th hit certificate, "I Was There," signed $25
- Nolan Ryan 7th no-hitter program, signed $90
- Pete Rose 4,192 hit program with box score enclosed, signed $40
- Nolan Ryan Day program from Arlington Stadium, 09/12/93, autographed $60

Game-used lineup cards

- 04/16/74 Red Sox vs. Angels, with Yastrzemski, Fisk $75
- 04/16/74 Angels vs. Red Sox, with Yastrzemski, Fisk $65
- 05/26/74 A's vs. Angels, with Jackson, Bando, Rudi $85
- 05/29/74 Angels vs. Brewers, with Yount, Tanana, Alomar $75
- 09/08/74 Angels vs. White Sox, with Downing, Dent, Santo $45
- 07/25/75 Twins vs. Angels, with Oliva, Blyleven, Rivers $50
- 07/29/75 White Sox vs. Angels, with Gossage, Dent, Stanton $45
- 04/04/76 Angels vs. Dodgers, with Garvey, Ryan, Lopes, Cey $70
- 04/11/76 Oakland vs. Angels, with Fingers, Bando, Tenace $60
- 05/13/76 Rangers vs. Angels, with Fregosi, Tanana, Bonds $45
- 06/26/77 Rangers vs. Angels dugout lineup card, with Perry, Blyleven, Bonds, signed by Nolan Ryan, Don Drysdale $225
- 05/19/79 Angels vs. White Sox, with Carew, Baylor, Grich $50
- 1970-73 Gillette All-Star Game ballots, unused .... $20 each
- 1976-79 Gillette All-Star Game ballots, unused .... $15 each
- 1980-87 Gillette All-Star Game ballots, unused .... $10 each
- 1988-93 Gillette All-Star Game ballots, unused .... $5 each

Jewelry/trophies

- Babe Ruth wristwatch, with original case, box, still works $1,000
- Johnny Bench's 1975 50th Anniversary All-Star watch $1,250

• Babe Ruth Quaker Oats premium ring (1935), Bakelite plastic with Ruth's image............. $180

• 1906 Chicago Cubs stickpin, brass-colored pin with front of a hand fan with enamel ball in center, border says "Chicago Cubs - World's Record Breakers." $600

• Willie Mays 1967 Rawlings Gold Glove award, his 11th, and one of only four not in his collection $16,675

• 1965 Minnesota Twins World Series ring $1,650

• 1974 Oakland A's World Series ring $2,200

• 1981 Los Angeles Dodgers World Series ring $2,200

• 1968 Harmon Killebrew watch, Swiss-made with black imitation leather wristband, face features Killebrew with facsimile signature against a green baseball diamond background $350

• 1982 World Series trophy, of the type distributed to players $2,200

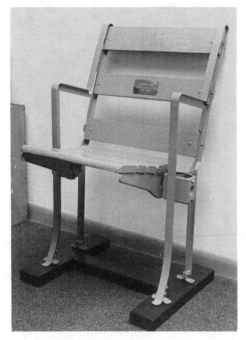

Stadium seats

• Although many of the stadium seats offered in auctions have been restored, they are commanding the same amounts of dollars as those in their natural state. Generally, it's a matter of preference on how collectors want their seats - "lived in" or restored to their original, "pristine" state -

and if they are going to display them or actually use them.

Before buying a seat, research the ballpark, especially the paint color of the seat, to aid in determining authenticity. Auction houses and newsletters are also available to offer historical information and price structures.

Advertised and auction-result values for various styles of seats from five of the eight original National League ballparks debuting in the 1800s-early 1900s include: Wrigley Field (1930s, $100); Crosley Field (non-aisle, $200-$500); Ebbets Field: (blue, straight-backed, free-standing, $2,000-$5,000); Polo Ground (figural seats, $2,500) and Braves Field (aisle seats; $5,000).

Values for various styles of seats from five of the eight original American League ballparks include: Comiskey Park (folding chairs, $280; round-back or straight back, $250); Yankee Stadium (straight-back, $500-$800); Tiger Stadium (single seat, $150-$200); Griffith Stadium (three-seater, $1,650-$2,000); and Fenway Park (straight-back, single-seater, $1,500-$1,800).

Miscellaneous

• Pete Rose Way street sign, autographed by Rose... $150

• Section 1 wooden sign from Metropolitan Stadium, 2x2 white sign with red lettering hung behind home plate during the team's entire stay at the stadium $495

• Mid-60s Houston Colt 45s 29x60 banner hanging in Wrigley Field $225

• 1975 Pittsburgh Pirates National League Championship Series portfolio with more than 40 sheets of media information................... $25

• 1961 All-Star Game press pass, at Boston, tie-on pass for sidelines $85

• Bill Dickey Hall of Fame lifetime admission pass... $330

• 1965 All-Star Game commemorative plate by Red Wing Pottery, green "home" plate inscribed "1965 All-Star Game, Metropolitan Stadium, Bloomington, Minn. Make Your Home Plate Minnesota," given to dignitaries, sports figures who attended the All-Star Game luncheon the day before the game $250

• 1944 World Series fountain pen and pencil set, Browns vs. Cardinals, in original box, bat barrels read "St. Louis - Browns vs. Cardinals -

1944 World Series" $150
• Mid-1930s Lou Gehrig wooden pencil and bat, barrel features a famous image of Gehrig batting pose from his Goudey baseball card $125
• Babe Ruth mechanical pencil, late 1920s/early 1930s, plastic pen features baseball on top of cap with Ruth's facsimile autograph on pen clasp...$275
• Chicago Cubs cancelled check, 6/15/23, signed by William L. Veeck $225
• 1973 Cincinnati Reds contract to Johnny Bench offering him $85,000 per year, refused by Bench..$1,500
• Typed letter from Warren C. Giles on National League letterhead, signed...........................$195
• Typed letter from Charles S. Feeney on New York Giants stationery, signed, 3/16/57 .....$195
• Phillip K. Wrigley typed letter, 3/26/48, signed by Wrigley...$195
• Babe Ruth label shorts, size 36, from the 1920s, never worn, still has the Babe Ruth Reg. U.S. patent office label $450
• Babe Ruth 1970s Sultan of Swat pocketknife $60
• 1976 Nolan Ryan Mr. Softee Ice Cream premium iron-on transfer...................................$40
• 1974 Cleveland Indians bat boy transistor radio, 9" with carry strap, works..................$40
• 1960s Los Angeles Angels "Crazy Curve" inflatable cylindrical-shaped baseball $10
• Willie Mays sunglasses, 1960s plastic, white frames says "Say Hey Willie Mays" and has an embossed, smiling face of Willie at the nose bridge $275
• In the 1970s and 1980s the Franklin Mint has issued several sterling-silver medals featuring baseball players on them, including Babe Ruth, Lou Gehrig, Connie Mack, Roberto Clemente, Hank Aaron and Jackie Robinson. Among numismatists, most of these medallions do not command much more than issue price, which is usually less than $20.
• In 1991, Starshots Sports Collectibles, Palm Desert, Calif., issued a series of sports celebrity badges which each fold into a display easel. There were 54 baseball players represented, 27 from each league. American Leaguers are Jim Abbott, Sandy Alomar Jr., Wade Boggs, George Brett, Jose Canseco, Roger Clemens, Cecil Fielder, Carlton Fisk, Ken Griffey Jr., Kelly Gruber, Rickey Henderson, Wally Joyner, Don Mattingly, Mark McGwire, Paul Molitor, Dave Parker, Kirby Puckett, Billy Ripken, Cal Ripken Jr., Nolan Ryan, Bret Saberhagen, Steve Sax, Ruben Sierra, Dave Stieb, Alan Trammell, Bob Welch and Dave Winfield.

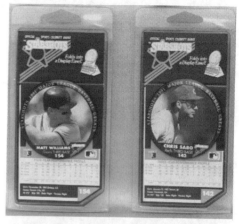

National Leaguers are Barry Bonds, Bobby Bonilla, Will Clark, Eric Davis, Glenn Davis, Andre Dawson, Delino DeShields, Doug Drabek, Shawon Dunston, Lenny Dykstra, Ron Gant, Dwight Gooden, Tony Gwynn, Orel Hershiser, Dave Justice, Barry Larkin, Kevin McReynolds, Kevin Mitchell, Eddie Murray, Chris Sabo, Ryne Sandberg, Benito Santiago, Mike Scioscia, Ozzie Smith, Darryl Strawberry, Tim Wallach and Matt Williams.
• In 1990, Ace Novelty Inc., Bellevue, Wash., issued MVP Major League Players col-

Sr., Pedro Guerrero, Tony Gwynn, Billy Hatcher, Von Hayes, Tom Herr, Orel Hershiser, Danny Jackson, Howard Johnson, Dennis Martinez, Roger McDowell, Kevin Mitchell, Dale Murphy, Tim Raines, Dennis Rasmussen, Chris Sabo, Ryne Sandberg, Benito Santiago, Mike Scioscia, Mike Scott, Lonnie Smith, Ozzie Smith, John Smoltz, Darryl Strawberry, Fernando Valenzuela, Andy Van Slyke, Frank Viola, Tim Wallach, Jerome Walton, Matt Williams, Mitch Williams and Todd Worrell.

• In 1988, the Sheaffer Eaton Co., Pittsfield, Mass., produced 9 1/2x11 3/4 two-pocket portfolios of 130 1988 Topps baseball cards; five players from each major league team were selected. Each folder showed the front and back of the player's card. They were originally offered at several retail outlets for between 99 cents to $1.49 each. Dealers had to by team boxes containing 10 folders of each of the five players.

The players are Harold Baines, Jesse Barfield, Marty Barrett, Steve Bedrosian, Buddy Bell, George Bell, Mike Boddicker, Wade Boggs, Barry Bonds, Bobby Bonilla, Phil Bradley, George Brett, Hubie Brooks, DeWayne Buice, Brett Butler, Ivan Calderon, Jose Canseco, Gary Carter, Joe Carter, Jack Clark, Will Clark, Roger Clemens, Vince Coleman, Ron Darling, Alvin Davis, Chili Davis, Eric Davis, Glenn Davis, Jody Davis, Andre Dawson, Bo Diaz, Bill Doran, Brian Downing, Mike Dunne, Dwight Evans, Brian Fisher, Carlton Fisk, John Franco, Gary Gaetti, Greg Gagne, Andres Galarraga, Kirk Gibson, Dwight Gooden, Rich Gossage, Pedro Guerrero, Tony Gwynn, Billy Hatcher, Von Hayes, Keith Hernandez, Rickey Henderson, Orel Hershiser, Teddy Higuera, Charlie Hough, Kent Hrbek, Pete Incaviglia, Bo Jackson, Brook Jacoby, Dion James, Wally Joyner, Terry Kennedy, Jimmy Key, John Kruk, Mark Langston, Barry Larkin, Jeffrey Leonard, Don Mattingly, Lance McCullers, Mark McGwire, Kevin Mitchell,

Paul Molitor, Jack Morris, Lloyd Moseby, Dale Murphy, Dwayne Murphy, Eddie Murray, Matt Nokes, Pete O'Brien, Lance Parrish, Larry Parrish, Tony Pena, Gerald Perry, Dan Plesac, Luis Polonia, Jim Presley, Kirby Puckett, Dan Quisenberry, Tim Raines, Willie Randolph, Rick Reuschel, Harold Reynolds, Jim Rice,

lectors lapel pins which feature current players and include a 1990 Score baseball card. American League players are: Jim Abbott, Harold Baines, George Bell, Bert Blyleven, Wade Boggs, George Brett, Jose Canseco, Roger Clemens, Alvin Davis, Brian Downing, Dennis Eckersley, Tony Fernandez, Carlton Fisk, Julio Franco, Gary Gaetti, Dan Gladden, Tom Gordon, Mike Greenwell, Ken Griffey Jr., Ozzie Guillen, Rickey Henderson, Teddy Higuera, Kent Hrbek, Bo Jackson, Brook Jacoby, Doug Jones, Wally Joyner, Chet Lemon, Jeffrey Leonard, Don Mattingly, Fred McGriff, Mark McGwire, Paul Molitor, Jack Morris, Gregg Olson, Kirby Puckett, Harold Reynolds, Dave Righetti, Bill Ripken, Cal Ripken Jr., Nolan Ryan, Bret Saberhagen, Steve Sax, Ruben Sierra, Lee Smith, Cory Sndyer, Dave Stewart, Dave Stieb, B.J. Surhoff, Greg Swindell, Mickey Tettleton, Bobby Thigpen, Alan Trammell, Greg Walker, Lou Whitaker, Dave Winfield and Robin Yount.

National Leaguers are: Barry Bonds, Bobby Bonilla, Tom Brunansky, Brett Butler, Jack Clark, Will Clark, Eric Davis, Glenn Davis, Andre Dawson, Billy Doran, Doug Drabek, Shawon Dunston, Lenny Dykstra, Sid Fernandez, Andres Galarraga, Kirk Gibson, Tom Glavine, Doc Gooden, Mark Grace, Ken Griffey

Dave Righetti, Cal Ripken Jr., Nolan Ryan, Bret Saberhagen, Juan Samuel, Ryne Sandberg, Benito Santiago, Steve Sax, Mike Schmidt, Mike Scott, Larry Sheets, Ruben Sierra, Lee Smith, Ozzie Smith, Zane Smith, Cory Snyder, Dave Stewart, Dave Stieb, Darryl Strawberry, B.J. Surhoff, Rick Sutcliffe, Pat Tabler, Bobby Thigpen, Alan Trammell, Fernando Valenzuela, Andy Van Slyke, Frank Viola, Ozzie Virgil, Greg Walker, Tim Wallach, Mitch Webster, Bob Welch, Lou Whitaker, Devon White, Willie Wilson, Dave Winfield, Mike Witt, Todd Worrell and Robin Yount.

Miscellaneous issues from the 1990s include:

• Bandai America, Cerritos, Calif.: Sport stars collectors coins of major league baseball players, minted in brass (including Mike Scioscia, Alan Trammell, Jim Abbott, Dale Murphy, Andy Van Slyke, Nolan Ryan, Darryl Strawberry).

• Starline Inc., East Elmhurst, N.Y.: Individual and team collage posters, paper bookcovers featuring player photos, door posters, posters featuring team collages, jigsaw puzzles, greeting cards.

• Costacos Brothers Sports, Seattle, Wash.: Several fantasy posters picturing modern baseball players.

• Football USA Inc., San Diego, Calif.: Synthetic baseballs with retired and current baseball players' likenesses, and baseballs featuring team rosters and logos.

• Sports Puzzles Inc., Palatine, Ill.: "Signa" Chip puzzles, suitable for autographing, featuring major league players.

• TV Sports Mailbag/Photo File, Elmsford, N.Y.: Glossy photographs and lithographs of current and retired players, and several 8x10 card sets, featuring Nolan Ryan, baseball's 300-game winners and Hall of Fame inductees.

Newspapers

Chances are, every Major League baseball team has had its name splashed across the front page of a newspaper. And sometimes, even players make the front page, too. These papers not only offer a glimpse of baseball's storied past, but they offer affordable alternatives for today's ambitious collectors.

Historical sports moments, such as Hank Aaron's 715th home run or Babe Ruth's death, which are captured in the headlines make the best collectibles, and most valuable ones, too, oftentimes ranging from $100-$500. But some papers have hit four-figures, too, including those covering the 1919 Chicago Black Sox scandal and Babe Ruth's 60th home run. Great events are often easier newspapers to find, too, compared to the average daily story of your favorite player or team.

Value is determined by several factors, including what section features the story. Was the story on the front page of the entire newspaper, or just the sports page? Are the photos game shots, or posed? Who's pictured? Is it a photo taken the day before, or is it a stock shot which has had repeated use?

Condition plays a role in the value of a newspaper, too. Because of the high acidic content in the paper, and the fact newspapers were not made to be saved, they deteriorate over time. Papers should be stored flat (unfolded) in Mylar and other acid-free materials. Vinyl holders should be avoided. A spray called Wei-T'O claims it will protect prints, books, paper and works of art from brittleness and yellowing, and extends the life of the item two to four times.

Two sources for newspapers catalogs include: Jim Lyons Historical Newspapers, Dept. 4, 970 Terra Bella Ave., Suite 3, Mountain View, Calif. 94043; or Box Seat Collectibles, P.O. 2013, Halesite, N.Y. 11743.

- 1923 Los Angeles Times: "Babe Ruth Is Awarded Top Honors" - wins MVP Award, VG+..$90
- 1926 Des Moines Register: "Scandal Hits Stars! Speaker, Cobb Wood Accused of Tossing Game in 1919 Season!" (Cobb, Speaker, Wood,
- Landis, Leonard) $175
1939 New York Times: "Gehrig Is Forced To Quit Baseball! Mayo Clinic Bars Lou From Playing!" (Gehrig, Dickey, Gomez, Gordon,

McCarthy)..$125
- 1941 Des Moines Register: "It's Over! Brooklyn Wins To Clinch Pennant As Cardinals Bow" (pictures Reese, Wyatt, Reiser, Durocher)... $75
1941 New York Times: "DiMaggio Sets All-Time Record As Yankees Win! DiMaggio's Wallop Stretches Hitting Streak to 45 Games!" (DiMaggio, Rolfe, Henrich).....................$150
- 1943 New York Times: "Yankee Clipper Inducted Into Army!" Nr. Mt. (DiMaggio)
....$50
- 1945 New York Daily News: "Dodgers Sign Negro Player! 1st in 70 Baseball Years" (J. Robinson)..$200
- 1947 New York Times: "Gionfriddo's Great Catch of DiMaggio's Drive Prevents Losers From Tying Score" (Gionfriddo, Robinson, Rizzuto, Stirnweiss, Stanky, Reese) $65
- 1948 Des Moines Register: "Praise Campanella! Durocher Not Fooling When He Raves About Negro Catcher" - Dodgers call up Campy, (Campanella, J. Robinson).............$50
- 1951 Des Moines Register: "Mantle Looks To Joe's Job" (Mantle, Stanky, Schoendienst).. $75
- 1951 New York Times: "DiMaggio Retires As Player" (DiMaggio, Weiss, Stengel, Webb, Topping) $125
- 1954 Des Moines Register: "Musial Hits 5 Homers To Set Mark!" (Musial, Fox, Feller)
....$75
- 1956 Des Moines Register: "Yanks' Larsen Hurls Perfect No-Hitter! 1st in Series History" (Larsen, Berra, Labine, Snider, Robinson) $200
- 1957 Des Moines Register: "Dodgers Gone, New York To Seek New N.L. Team"........ $100
- 1957 Des Moines Register: "2 A.M. Trouble Benches Ford and Berra" - Copacabana incident (Berra, Thomas, Kluszewski, Turley, Bragan)
....$150
- 1958 Des Moines Register: "Musial Makes It 3,000 With Pinch Double!" (Musial, Campanella)..$100
- 1960 Des Moines Register: "Ted Slams 500th-He's 4th To Do It!" (Ted Williams, Clemente)
....$150
- 1961 Des Moines Register: "4 By Mays as Giants Hit 8 Homers! (Mays, Dykes) $75
- 1961 Des Moines Register: "Maris Wins MVP Again!" - 61-Homer Star (Maris) $75
- 1963 Des Moines Register: "Mantle Jolts 500-Footer To Win In 11th! Hits Facade 117 Ft.

Above Ground!" (Mantle, Hodges, Kaat) ..$125

1966 Des Moines Register: "Koufax Quits Baseball At Peak of Career" - Koufax fears permanent elbow harm, pitched in agony (Koufax) $75

• 1966 Des Moines Register: Roberto Clemente N.L. MVP....................$40

1966 Des Moines Register: Frank Robinson Most Valuable 1st in 2 Leagues! (Robinson) $40

• 1969 Des Moines Register: "Mays Cracks 600th Homer! (Mays, Killebrew, Oliva, Seaver) $60

• 1969 New York Daily News: "We Win It! Mets East Champs!" (Hodges caricature) $50

• 1970 Des Moines Register: "Say Hey! 3,000th Mays Hits!" (Mays, Killebrew)....................$75

• 1973 Des Moines Register: "Ryan Tosses 2nd No Hitter! Fans 17, Stuns Tigers, 6-0" (Ryan) $75

• 1975 Des Moines Register: "Red Sox Win In 12 On Fisk Homer! Carbo's Pinch Blast, Evan's Catch Help Take 7-6 Thriller!" (Fisk, Carbo, Petrocelli, Lynn, Doyle, Bench, Anderson) .$75

• 1980 Des Moines Register: "George Brett 'Player of the Year!' Batted 390!" $40

• 1989 Dallas News: "5,000 K's For Ryan! Stadium Erupts As He Gets Historic Strikeout!" (Ryan, R. Henderson)....................$25

1972-73 7-Eleven cups

• In 1972-73, 7-Eleven convenience stores gave away, with the purchase of a soda or 14-ounce Slurpee crushed-ice drink, cups which feature portraits of Major League baseball players.

The 5 5/16" tall plastic cups are 3 1/4" in diameter at the top and 2 1/8" inches at the bottom. The player's full-color sketched picture is on one side of the cup above his name and the team name; on the opposite side in between his team's logo and the 7-Eleven logo is a brief biography.

The 1972 60-cup set includes 18 Hall of Famers. Twenty-one of the players were carried over to the 1973 set; all but seven (Dick Allen, Lou Brock, Cesar Cedeno, Ralph Garr, Willie Mays, Vada Pinson and Tom Seaver) were the same portraits. The 1973 cups differed little from the 1972 cups; the major change in format was that in 1972 the player's name and team

name are flush left above his biography, while in 1973 they were centered.

The 80-cup 1973 series includes 20 old-time Hall of Famers, whose cups were the same format and styles as the current players' cups, except the portraits were done in gold rather than in color.

7-Eleven later produced full-color cups using reproduced photos. These, and the earlier cups, have not survived in quantity or quality, in part because too much dishwashing took its toll on them. Also, the cups are very susceptible to cracking, so don't put too much pressure on them.

1972 7-Eleven cups	Joe Pepitone
Hank Aaron	Jim Perry
Tommie Agee	Lou Piniella
Rich Allen	Vada Pinson
Sal Bando	Dave Roberts
Johnny Bench	Brooks Robinson
Steve Blass	Frank Robinson
Vida Blue	Pete Rose
Lou Brock	George Scott
Norm Cash	Tom Seaver
Cesar Cedeno	Sonny Siebert
Orlando Cepeda	Reggie Smith
Roberto Clemente	Willie Stargell
Nate Colbert	Bill Stoneman
Willie Davis	Mel Stottlemyre
Ray Fosse	Joe Torre
Ralph Garr	Maury Wills
Bob Gibson	Don Wilson
Bud Harrelson	Rick Wise
Frank Howard	Wilbur Wood
Ron Hunt	Carl Yastrzemski
Reggie Jackson	
Ferguson Jenkins	**1973 7-Eleven cups**
Alex Johnson	Hank Aaron
Deron Johnson	Dick Allen
Al Kaline	Dusty Baker
Harmon Killebrew	Johnny Bench
Mickey Lolich	Yogi Berra
Jim Lonborg	Larry Biittner
Juan Marichal	Bill Blass
Willie Mays	Lou Boudreau *
Willie McCovey	Lou Brock
Denny McLain	Roy Campanella *
Dave McNally	Bert Campaneris
Bill Melton	Rod Carew
Andy Messersmith	Steve Carlton
Bobby Murcer	Cesar Cedeno
Tony Oliva	Ty Cobb *
Amos Otis	Nate Colbert
Jim Palmer	Willie Davis

Bill Dickey *	Reggie Jackson	Thurman Munson	Nolan Ryan
Carlton Fisk	Walter Johnson *	Bobby Murcer	Manny Sanguillen
Bob Feller *	Don Kessinger	Stan Musial *	Ron Santo
Bill Freehan	Leron Lee	Gary Nolan	Richie Scheinblum
Ralph Garr	Mickey Lolich	Tony Oliva	Tom Seaver
Lou Gehrig *	Sparky Lyle	Al Oliver	Ted Simmons
Charlie Gehringer *	Greg Luzinski	Claude Osteen	Reggie Smith
Bob Gibson	Mike Marshall	Jim Palmer	Chris Speier
Hank Greenberg *	Mickey Mantle *	Gaylord Perry	Don Sutton
Bobby Grich	Carlos May	Lou Piniella	Luis Tiant
Lefty Grove *	Lee May	Vada Pinson	Pie Traynor *
Toby Harrah	John Mayberry	Brooks Robinson	Honus Wagner *
Richie Hebner	Willie Mays *	Ellie Rodriguez	Billy Williams
Ken Henderson	John McGraw *	Joe Rudi	Wilbur Wood
Carl Hubbell *	Joe Medwick *	Red Ruffing *	Carl Yastrzemski
Jim "Catfish" Hunter	Joe Morgan	Babe Ruth *	* Old-time Hall of Famer

1977-1978 Royal Crown Cola cans

They don't fit into plastic sheets, they rust and they may leak, and all they do is collect dust. But if you have the room to display or store them, Royal Crown cans featuring baseball players on them pose a fairly inexpensive challenge to collectors.

The cans, issued in 1977-78, feature 16 Hall of Famers, even though the team insignias are blacked out on the players' caps. The cans, produced prior to the introduction of today's one-piece aluminum pop cans, are constructed in three parts - a top, center and bottom which are crimped and soldered together. Rust may appear at the seams if the cans are in storage for a while; if the can still has soda inside it, you can expect it to spring a leak, due to the acidity of the cola. Cans are more valuable when they appear to be full, so they should be opened from the bottom.

There were 70 cans produced in 1977; in 1978 100 cans were made. Many of the players appeared in both sets, some with the same black-and-white pictures, some with different ones. The photos were set in a plain, white circle; 1978 cans have a red border around the circle. No insignias appeared on the players' caps, indicating RC didn't pay the teams for the rights to reproduce their logos.

Both years used the same basic blue color scheme, with red and white trim. Cans from 1977 had player biographical data in a square, while those produced in 1978 had a career-highlights summary inside a baseball. At the bottom of the ball was the can number, designated as "No. x of 100."

The biggest problem with buying RC cans is not the cost, but rather finding the cans. Many dealers do not take them to card shows because they are too bulky and take up valuable table space. Nor are the cans generally advertised for sale in hobby papers because it usually costs more to mail them than they are worth.

1977 Royal Crown cans

Sal Bando	Jose Cardenal	Bobby Grich	Gary Matthews
Mark Belanger	Rod Carew	Ken Griffey	Bake McBride
Johnny Bench	Dave Cash	Don Gullett	Hal McRae
Vida Blue	Cesar Cedeno	Mike Hargrove	Andy Messersmith
Bobby Bonds	Ron Cey	Catfish Hunter	Rick Monday
Bob Boone	Chris Chambliss	Randy Jones	John Montefusco
Larry Bowa	Dave Concepcion	Dave Kingman	Joe Morgan
Steve Braun	Mark Fidrych	Dave LaRoche	Thurman Munson
George Brett	Rollie Fingers	Ron LeFlore	Al Oliver
Lou Brock	George Foster	Greg Luzinski	Amos Otis
Bert Campaneris	Wayne Garland	Fred Lynn	Jim Palmer
Bill Campbell	Ralph Garr	Bill Madlock	Dave Parker
	Steve Garvey	Jon Matlack	Fred Patek

Miscellaneous

Gaylord Perry	11. Ken Griffey	42. Greg Luzinski *	73. Andre Dawson
Marty Perez	12. Ron LeFlore	43. Vida Blue *	74. Al Cowens
Tony Perez	13. George Foster	44. Bobby Bonds	75. Eddie Murray
J.R. Richard	14. Tony Perez	45. Jim Palmer	76. Dan Driessen
Pete Rose	15. Thurman Munson	46. Claudell Washington	77. Jim Rice
Joe Rudi	16. Bill Campbell	47. Dave Concepcion	78. Garry Maddox
Mike Schmidt	17. Andy Messersmith	48. Rod Carew	79. Larry Hisle
Tom Seaver	18. Mike Schmidt	49. J.R. Richard	80. Al Hrabosky
Bill Singer	19. Ron Cey	50. Rich Gossage	81. Reggie Jackson
Rusty Staub	20. Chris Chambliss	51. Cesar Cedeno	82. Tommy John
Don Sutton	21. Ralph Garr	52. Bert Campaneris	83. Willie McCovey
Gene Tenace	22. Dave LaRoche	53. Marty Perez	84. Sparky Lyle
Luis Tiant	23. George Brett	54. Bill Madlock	85. Tug McGraw
Ellis Valentine	24. Bob Boone	55. Amos Otis	86. Paul Splittorff
Claudell Washington	25. Jeff Burroughs	56. Robin Yount	87. Bobby Murcer
Butch Wynegar	26. Bake McBride	57. Bobby Grich	88. Graig Nettles
Carl Yastzremski	27. Gary Matthews	58. Catfish Hunter	89. Phil Niekro
Robin Yount	28. Don Gullett	59. Butch Hobson	90. Lou Piniella
Richie Zisk	29. Rick Monday	60. Larry Bowa	91. Rick Reuschel
	30. Al Oliver	61. Randy Jones *	92. Frank Tanana
1978 Royal Crown cans	31. Ellis Valentine	62. Richie Hebner	93. Nolan Ryan
1. Don Sutton	32. Mike Hargrove	63. Fred Patek	94. Garry Templeton
2. Bill Singer	33. Hal McRae	64. John Denny	95. Reggie Smith
3. Pete Rose	34. Rollie Fingers	65. Johnny Bench	96. Bruce Sutter
4. Gene Tenace	35. Dave Parker	66. Doyle Alexander	97. Jason Thompson
5. Dave Kingman	36. Tom Seaver	67. Dusty Baker	98. Mike Torrez
6. Dave Cash	37. Wayne Garland	68. Bert Blyleven	99. Rick Wise
7. Joe Morgan	38. Jon Matlack	69. Lyman Bostock	100. Bump Wills
8. Mark Belanger	39. Richie Zisk	70. Bill Buckner	* indicates the player
9. Steve Braun	40. Joe Rudi	71. Steve Carlton	photo is different from
10. Butch Wynegar	41. Sal Bando	72. John Candelaria	that used on the 1977 can.

Marbles

In 1968 Creative Creations Inc. produced a series of Official Major League Baseball Player Marbles which were sold in packages of 20 for a suggested retail of $1.49. Twenty Hall of Famers are in the set.

Each marble was two pieces of clear, hard plastic with a round 3/4" disc inserted into it. The front featured the player's face against a pastel background. His team's logo was airbrushed from his cap. The back had a facsimile autograph and the word JAPAN.

The 20 marbles were packaged in a 12"-square colorful cardboard store hanger display which featured larger photos of the players in the pack, plus facsimile autographs of many of the 120 players.

Although the blister-packed display piece encourages buyers to "Collect All 24 Series," apparently only 120 marbles were released, not 240 as promised.

Original packages of 20 marbles, even without major superstars, can sell for between $35-$50, while common players range from $3-$5. Superstars such as Pete Rose have been sold for as much as $150.

1968 Baseball Player	Bob Allison	Bob Aspromonte	Ken Berry
Marbles	Felipe Alou	Stan Bahnsen	Paul Blair
Hank Aaron	Jesus Alou	Bob Bailey	Bob Bolin
Tommie Aaron	Matty Alou	Ernie Banks	Dave Boswell
Tommie Agee	Max Alvis	Glenn Beckert	Nelson Briles
Richie Allen	Mike Andrews	Gary Bell	Lou Brock
Gene Alley	Luis Aparicio	Johnny Bench	Wally Bunker

452

Johnny Callison	Frank Howard	Tim McCarver	Pete Reichardt
Norm Cash	Dick Hughes	Willie McCovey	Brooks Robinson
Orlando Cepeda	Randy Hundley	Sam McDowell	Frank Robinson
Dean Chance	Ron Hunt	Denny McLain	Pete Rose
Roberto Clemente	Jim "Catfish" Hunter	Dave McNally	Chico Salmon
Donn Clendenon	Pat Jarvis	Dennis Menke	Ron Santo
Tony Cloninger	Julian Javier	Jim Merritt	George Scott
Tommy Davis	Tommy John	Bob Miller	Tom Seaver
Al Downing	Deron Johnson	Rick Monday	Dick Selma
Curt Flood	Mack Jones	Joe Morgan	Mike Shannon
Bill Freehan	Jim Kaat	Gary Nolan	Joe Sparma
Jim Fregosi	Al Kaline	Jim Northrup	Willie Stargell
Bob Gibson	Don Kessinger	Rich Nye	Mel Stottlemyre
Jim "Mudcat" Grant	Harmon Killebrew	Tony Oliva	Luis Tiant
Jerry Grote	Jerry Koosman	Milt Pappas	Cesar Tovar
Jimmie Hall	Jim Lefebvre	Camilo Pascual	Tom Tresh
Tom Haller	Mickey Lolich	Joe Pepitone	Pete Ward
Ron Hansen	Jim Lonborg	Tony Perez	Billy Williams
Steve Hargan	Juan Marichal	Jim Perry	Maury Wills
Ken Harrelson	Roger Maris	Gary Peters	Earl Wilson
Jim Hart	Eddie Mathews	Fritz Peterson	Dooley Womack
Jim Holt	Jerry May	Rico Petrocelli	
Joe Horlen	Willie Mays	Vada Pinson	
Willie Horton	Dick McAuliffe	Boog Powell	

In 1991, Spectra Star, a Pacoima, Calif.-based marketer of toys and sporting goods, produced a series of 20 SuperStar marbles featuring baseball players inside. The full-color, one-inch diameter "Rad Rollers" were offered in four sets of five players, based on the division in which the players compete. American League East players are Robin Yount, Cecil Fielder, Cory Sndyer, Fred McGriff and Cal Ripken Jr.; American League West players are Ken Griffey Jr., Jose Canseco, Nolan Ryan, Kirby Puckett and Jim Abbott. National League East players are Tim Raines, Darryl Strawberry, Barry Bonds, Len Dykstra and Ryne Sandberg; National League West players are Ron Gant, Chris Sabo, Craig Biggio, Fernando Valenzuela and Benito Santiago. The packages of five originally sold for $4-$5.

Sports Illustrated posters

During the late 1960s and early 1970s, Sports Illustrated produced several posters featuring hockey, basketball, football and baseball players. The posters, made available through ads in the magazine beginning in 1969, originally sold for $1.50 each. Today, some have reached $200, including Mickey Mantle and Roberto Clemente.

The year listed behind a player's name is the year the poster was released. The year of release of some posters is not known, so those posters are indicated by 1968-70.

Sports Illustrated posters

Hank Aaron, 1968 ....$35-$45	Gary Bell, 1968 (Pilots)................................$10-$20
Tommie Agee, 1968-70.................................$8-$15	Bobby Bonds, 1970......................................$10-$18
Richie Allen, 1968..$10-$15	Clete Boyer, 1968...$8-$12
Gene Alley, 1968...$8-$15	Lou Brock, 1968...$18-$25
Felipe Alou, 1968..$8-$15	Johnny Callison, 1968 ....$10-$15
Max Alvis, 1968...$8-$15	Bert Campaneris, 1968 ....$10-$15
Mike Andrews, 1969 ....$8-$12	Leo Cardenas, 1968.....................................$10-$15
Bob Aspromonte, 1968-70 ....$10-$15	Rod Carew, 1970 ....$25-$45
Ernie Banks, 1968 ....$20-$30	Paul Casanova, 1968 ....$10-$15
Glenn Beckert, 1968-70 ....$8-$20	Orlando Cepeda, 1968..................................$10-$18
Gary Bell, 1968 (Indians)............................$10-$15	Roberto Clemente, 1968............................$125-$200
	Tony Conigliaro, 1968..................................$12-$20

Mike Cuellar, 1970	$8-$15	Willie McCovey, 1968	$75-$150
Tommy Davis, 1968	$10-$20	Sam McDowell, 1970	$8-$15
Willie Davis, 1968	$10-$15	Denny McLain, 1968	$12-$18
Don Drysdale, 1968	$18-$30	Don Mincher, 1968 (Angels)	$8-$15
Mike Epstein, 1970	$8-$15	Don Mincher, 1968 (Pilots)	$8-$20
Al Ferrara, 1968	$8-$12	Rick Monday, 1968	$10-$15
Curt Flood, 1968	$10-$15	Bobby Murcer, 1968-70	$10-$18
Bill Freehan, 1968	$10-$15	Phil Niekro, 1970	$12-$20
Jim Fregosi, 1968	$8-$15	John Odom, 1968-70	$10-$15
Bob Gibson, 1968	$18-$25	Tony Oliva, 1968	$12-$18
Bud Harrelson, 1968	$8-$15	Wes Parker, 1970	$8-$12
Ken Holtzman, 1970	$8-$15	Tony Perez, 1970	$12-$20
Joe Horlen, 1968	$8-$15	Rico Petrocelli, 1968	$8-$15
Tony Horton, 1968	$8-$12	Boog Powell, 1968-70	$10-$18
Frank Howard, 1968	$12-$20	Rick Reichart, 1968	$8-$15
Reggie Jackson, 1969	$90-$120	Brooks Robinson, 1968	$50-$100
Ferguson Jenkins, 1968-70	$25-$50	Frank Robinson, 1968	$30-$50
Tommy John, 1968	$10-$18	Pete Rose, 1968	$25-$50
Cleon Jones, 1970	$8-$15	Ron Santo, 1968	$10-$15
Al Kaline, 1968	$18-$25	Tom Seaver, 1968	$50-$85
Harmon Killebrew, 1968	$25-$35	Chris Short, 1968	$8-$15
Jerry Koosman, 1968	$10-$18	Bill Singer, 1970	$8-$15
Let's Go Mets, 1969	$25-$45	Reggie Smith, 1968	$8-$15
Mickey Lolich, 1970	$10-$18	Rusty Staub, 1968	$10-$18
Jim Lonborg, 1968	$8-$15	Mel Stottlemyre, 1968	$10-$15
Jim Maloney, 1968	$8-$15	Ron Swoboda, 1968	$8-$15
Mickey Mantle, 1968	$150-$225	Cesar Tovar, 1968	$10-$15
Juan Marichal, 1968	$20-$35	Roy White, 1968-70	$8-$12
Willie Mays, 1968	$125-$200	Walt Williams, 1970	$8-$12
Bill Mazeroski, 1968	$12-$18	Earl Wilson, 1968	$8-$15
Tim McCarver, 1968	$10-$15	Jimmy Wynn, 1968	$8-$15
Mike McCormick, 1968	$8-$15	Carl Yastrzemski, 1968	$25-$40

Matches

Collecting matchcovers has been an organized hobby since the 1939 New York World's Fair. Today, there are at least 24 clubs, with at least 4,000 members. Amongst the gamut of subjects, ranging from beer, to politics to transportation, sports covers remain the most popular, with an estimated 1,000 people having sports covers in their collections. The easiest types to find are those from motels, banks and restaurants, with 50 out of every 100 coming from restaurants. Sports VIPs - players such as Mickey Mantle, Joe DiMaggio and Lefty O'Doul who have lent their names and likenesses for advertising purposes - remain quite popular among those who collect the restaurants/hotel covers.

In the late 1870s, approximately 100 small companies joined to form the Diamond Match Co. in Barberton, Ohio. The company's first baseball set, which appeared in 1934, is the largest. The set, called the silver border (because of the silver line framing the player's photo) or U-1 (Sports Collectors Bible designation) set, has 200 different players featured, each with four different background colors - red, green, blue and orange. Thus, there are 800 covers to be collected.

Hall of Famers in the set include Jim Bottomley, Kiki Cuyler, Dizzy Dean, Leo Durocher, Rick Ferrell, Frankie Frisch, Charlie Gehringer, Chick Hafey, Jesse Haines, Gabby Hartnett, Billy Herman, Waite Hoyt, Carl Hubbell, Chuck Klein, Bill Klem, Ernie Lombardi, Al Lopez, Ted Lyons, Rabbit Maranaville, Bill McKechnie, Joe Medwick, Met Ott, Casey Stengel, Dazzy Vance, Lloyd Waner, Paul Waner and Hack Wilson. Prices for the non-Hall of Famers range from $5-$20, while HOFers are about $75 each in Mint condition, with matches that haven't been struck.

The second set, U-2, was produced in 1935 and is the most difficult to assemble. Each of the 24 covers has a black border entirely around the picture on the front and history on the back. There are eight each of three colors - red, green and blue. Eleven Hall of Famers are represented.

The third set, U-3, was produced in 1935 and 1936 with green, red and blue colors. Two smaller sets were also produced through 1938. Those designated as U-4 and U-5 consist of a combined 23 players, each having three different colors (green, blue and red), making the set complete at 69. However, the set is available in two styles - with brown ink or black ink. The final set, U-6, has 14 covers in it.

Sports Collectors Digest memorabilia covers

*Mickey Mantle
Nov. 29, 1991*

*Steve Carlton
Oct. 16, 1992*

*Harmon Killebrew
Oct. 19, 1990*

*Warren Spahn
Feb. 28, 1992*

Games

Baseball-related games are the most popular of all sports games; more than 300 board and card games exist. The game recognized as the first professional baseball game, The New Parlor Game of Baseball, was produced in 1869. Published by M.B. Sumner, the game included team rosters and lineup cards.

The first data-enhanced game based on player statistics appeared in 1950, when APBA Game Co. of Lancaster, Pa., created a dice and card game. The company produces new player game cards annually. The first game to be endorsed by a player - the Rube Walker & Harry Davis Baseball Game - was produced in 1905 by Champion Athletics. Since that time several athletes have loaned their names to games - Hank Aaron, Bob Feller, Lou Gehrig, Walter Johnson, Mickey Mantle, Christy Mathewson, Willie Mays, Babe Ruth and Carl Yastrzemski, to name a few.

Generally, player or team-related games are in greater demand than generic games, while board games are more valuable than card games. Game values are also determined in part by age (older is more valuable); company (McLoughlin Bros., Bliss, Singer, Selchow and Righter, Parker Bros., Cadaco-Ellis and Milton Bradley are tops); graphics/illustrations (those with higher quality of lithography and highly-detailed, colorful illustrations, especially on the box, are more valuable); box and board style (wooden boxes are more valuable, then heavy cardboard; metal games are more valuable than cardboard ones); theme; the region in which the item is being sold; rarity; implements (game parts); and completeness (missing game cards or integral parts may drop a value by 50 percent). The American Game Collectors Association has archives of game instructions and can supply copies by contacting AGCA, 49 Brooks Ave., Lewiston, Maine, 04240.

Condition is also a big factor in determining game values. Look for games which are in Very Good or Excellent condition - those which are not faded, water stained, covered with soot or mildew, and have all the parts and instructions.

The best places to find board games are at game conventions, collectibles shows, antique shops, flea markets, and through auction houses and hobby publications, such as Krause Publications' Toy Shop and Today's Collector publications. When buying sight-unseen through the mail, however, get as detailed of a description about condition beforehand, and inquire if the seller has return policy if material is not satisfactory.

Many games are repairable, but that's best left to an archivist or other professional who can clean your game using special materials such as acid-free glue and paper. Rubber cement thinner can be used to remove price stickers or tape on the outside box cover on games which are taped shut. Mildew can be cleaned with a bathroom mildew remover and a damp sponge, but test a small area first.

Games should be kept out of extremely cold or hot temperatures and places with wide temperature fluctuations. Direct sunlight, spotlights and other bright lights should be avoided, too, to prevent fading. Damp areas can cause mildew buildup, so a dehumidifier is recommended. Also, although stacking is not suggested, if you are going to stack your games, do so by cross-stacking them, alternating them vertically and horizontally, so that the weight of the games on top do not crush those underneath.

Note: Because so few exist in that condition, games from 1844-1945 are not priced in Mint condition. Prices fluctuate, too, oftentimes based on auction fever, which tends to drive prices up. Remember, value is what someone is willing to pay, not necessarily the selling price.